Guide

London for Children

timeout.com

Published by
Time Out Guides Limited
Universal House
251 Tottenham Court Road
London W1T 7AB
Tel + 44 (0) 20 7813 3000
Fax + 44 (0) 20 7813 6001
email guides@timeout.com
www.timeout.com

Editorial

Editor Ronnie Haydon
Consultant Editor Melanie Dakin
Deputy Editor Lesley McCave
Listings Editor Cathy Limb
Proofreader Tamsin Shelton
Indexer Selena Cox

Editorial Director Peter Fiennes
Series Editor Sarah Guy
Guides Co-ordinator Jenny Noden

Design

Group Art Director John Oakey
Art Director Mandy Martin
Art Editor Scott Moore
Designers Benjamin de Lotz, Lucy Grant
Scanning & Imaging Dan Conway
Ad make-up Glen Impey
Picture Editor Kerri Miles
Deputy Picture Editor Olivia Duncan-Jones
Picture Librarian Sarah Roberts

Advertising

Group Commercial Director Lesley Gill
Sales Director/Sponsorship Mark Phillips
Sales Manager Alison Gray
Advertisement Sales James Coulbault,
Jason Trotman, Terina Rickit
Copy Controller Angela Davis
Advertising Assistant Sabrina Ancilleri

Administration

Publisher Tony Elliott
Managing Director Mike Hardwick
Group Financial Director Kevin Ellis
Group General Manager Nichola Coulthard
Circulation Director Jim Heinemann
Production Manager Mark Lamond
Production Controller Samantha Furniss
Marketing Director Christine Cort
Marketing Manager Mandy Martinez
Marketing Executives Sandie Tozer, Sammie Squire
Marketing Assistant Claire Hojem
Accountant Georgina Way

Features in this guide were written and researched by: Introduction Ronnie Haydon. **The Story of London** Ronnie Haydon. **New London** David Littlefield. **By Season** Nana Ocran. **Sightseeing** *Central London* Rick Jones (*Marylebone, Kensington & Chelsea* Ronnie Haydon); *North London* Dorothy Boswell; *East London* Sam McEvoy; *South-east London* Ronnie Haydon, Nikki Spencer; *South-west London* Lisa Osborne; *West London* Mary Dohnal. **Eating** Lily Dunn. **Shopping** Vanessa Raison, Ronnie Haydon. **Arts & Entertainment** Sarah Jacobs, Ronnie Haydon. **Parties** Nana Ocran, Sarah Jacobs, Emma Paterson. **Sport & Leisure** Andrew Shields (*Hoof dreams* Ronnie Haydon). **Days Out** *Activities* Joanna Souter; *Castles* Karen Wolman; *Farms & Zoos* Lisa Osborne; *Gardens* Janice Fuscoe; *Seaside* Jane Bartlett, Ronnie Haydon; *Steam Trains* Peter Fiennes, Janice Fuscoe; *Theme Parks* Melanie Dakin. **Directory** Ronnie Haydon.

The editor would like to thank the following: John Trafford, Rachel Sawyer, Becky Wootton, James Mitchell, the Museum of London, Teresa Trafford, Will Fulford-Jones, Ruth Jarvis and Rick, John, Bruce and Jane Jones.

Maps by JS Graphics, 17 Beadles Lane, Old Oxted, Surrey RH8 9JG.

Illustrations in The Story of London Chris Joselyn.

Cover photography Jon Perugia.

Photography Nicola Levinsky, Nigel Bennerr, Victoria Gomez, Matt Carr, Jon Perugia, Georgie Scott, James Winspear, Paul Salmon, Paul Avis, Michael Franke, Barry J Holmes, Dominic Dibbs, Sarah Blee, Alys Tomlinson, Ulla Nyeman, Tony Gibson except: pages 11, 12, 18 AKG; pages 14, 15, 17, 19 Hulton Archive; page 20 Associated Press; page 270 National Trust Photographic Library.

The following images were supplied by the featured establishments/artists 26, 94 top, 97, 110, 122, 132, 136, 165, 215, 216, 217, 218, 223, 225, 226, 228, 233, 234, 235, 236, 237, 239, 240, 243, 244, 246, 249, 250, 251, 252, 254, 255, 257, 258, 260, 265, 273, 278, 279, 287, 289, 290.

Repro by Icon Reproduction, Crowne House, 56-58 Southwark Street, London SE1 1UN.

Printed and bound by Southernprint, Factory Road, Upton Industrial Estate, Poole, Dorset BH16 5SN.

ISBN 0 903446 66 9

Distribution by Seymour Ltd (020 7396 8000)

Kids go free

Top days out in London

With this brand new *Time Out London for Children Guide* we aim to make the capital as entertaining as possible. We'd also like to make it a little cheaper for you, too, so we've teamed up with some great London venues to offer free tickets for children. Just cut out the vouchers at the back of this guide and let the kids enjoy a day out on us. Opening times and details can be found in the guide under each listing.

THE TOWER OF LONDON
Tower Hill, EC3
Admire the breathtaking Crown Jewels, hear tales aplenty on a free Yeoman Warder 'Beefeater' tour and see history come to life with events throughout the year.
Entry (at time of going press) £11.30 adults, £7.50 children. For more information call 020 7709 0765 or visit www.hrp.org.uk

THE LONDON DUNGEON
28/34 Tooley Street, SE1
Journey back to 1666 as you relive the Great Fire of London, take a trip to a Torture Chamber, a tour through Jack the Ripper's Victorian

Whitechapel or a boat ride to Traitors Gate to face your doom! But watch out for the gruesome actors. With Deadly Dungeon events running throughout the year, you'd be a scaredy cat to miss out! Not recommended for the very young or those with a nervous disposition. Children under 15 must be accompanied by an adult.
Entry (at time of going press) £10.95 adults, £6.95 children. For more information call 0870 846 0666 (calls charged at national rate) or visit www.thedungeons.com

HAMPTON COURT
Surrey
Take a magical history tour back through 500 years of royal history and discover the famous maze, costumed guides and many special events. With so much to see and do, you'll be spellbound.
Entry (at time of going press) £10.80 adults, £7.20 children. For more information call 020 8781 9500 or visit www.hrp.org.uk

THE HUMAN BODY at the Science Museum's IMAX© Cinema
Exhibition Road, SW7
Fancy travelling into the biological blender of the stomach, journeying into the depths of the inner ear and accompanying a red blood cell into the pumping chamber of the

body's engine room – the heart? Well, you can at the awe-inspiring, large-format film 'The Human Body' at the IMAX Cinema in the Science Museum. The museum exhibits the most important scientific advances of the last 300 years and has 2,000 hands-on exhibits.
IMAX entry (at time of going press £6.75 adults, £5.75 children). For more information call 0870 870 4771 or visit www.sciencemuseum.org.uk/imax

To save £££s, simply cut out the vouchers on the card at the back of this guide.

LEGOLAND®
W I N D S O R

Call 08705 04 04 04 or visit www.legoland.co.uk

Fireworks & Fantasy 26th, 27th & 28th October and 3rd & 4th November.

LEGOLAND® Windsor 2001 season, closed every Tuesday & Wednesday, excluding Half Term (23rd & 24th October) 2001 season ends 4th November 2001.

Contents

Introduction

Noisy, grubby and exasperating... is London a fit place to bring a child? Ask the average noisy, grubby and exasperating kid and the answer is a resounding 'yes'. For the young, this vast adventure playground of a city has the best of everything.

As far as little ones are concerned, the best comes cheap, or even free: riding the buses, tubes and the DLR, playing in parks and fountains and watching the Queen's Guard stomping about all bring a twinkle to a toddler's eye. As they get older, and their tastes change, the glorious museums and galleries, busy shops and restaurants, state-of-the-art sports facilities, cinemas and theatres hold a lasting fascination.

In this Guide we present a wider map of the city for children of all ages, listing the places we love best beyond the picture-postcard sights. We suggest short walks that will help give children a taste of local London. Anyway, as any Londoner will tell you, the benighted transport system makes Shanks's pony the most efficient option for getting around.

Lastly, a thought for those parents formerly known as Londoners, who moved away from the smoke 'for the sake of the children'. Rest assured that those children, once they're old enough to travel in on their own, will be making a beeline for this buzzing city, because the young love London, and London loves the young.

THE TIME OUT LONDON FOR CHILDREN GUIDE
This is the first edition of the *Time Out London for Children Guide*, produced by the people behind the successful listings magazines, and travel guide series. It is written by resident experts to provide you with all the information you'll need to explore the city or read up on its background, whether you're a local or a first-time visitor.

We hope you enjoy this Guide, and we'd like to know what you think. There's a reader's reply card at the back of the book for feedback.

THE LOWDOWN ON THE LISTINGS
Addresses, phone numbers, websites, transport information, opening times, admission prices and credit card details are included in the listings.

Details of facilities, services and events were all checked and correct as we went to press. Before you go out of your way, however, we'd advise you to phone and check opening times, ticket prices and other particulars. While every effort has been made to ensure the accuracy of the information contained in this Guide, the publishers cannot accept any responsibility for any errors it may contain.

FAMILY-FRIENDLY INFORMATION
Having visited all the places with our own children, we've added what we consider essential information for family groups. In chapters where we think it's particularly important, we've stated whether a building can accommodate pushchairs ('buggy access'), or if there's anywhere you can change a nappy ('nappy-changing facilities'). We've also listed a spot nearby where you can eat your packed lunch ('nearest picnic place'). This is not listed if the sight is a park or garden, an ideal picnic place in itself.

Visitor attractions are required to provide reasonable provision for disabled visitors, although it's always best to ring for details. By October 2002, places open to the public will be obliged by law to provide disabled access (ramps etc). Disabled visitors requiring more information can call GLAD (Greater London Action for Disability) on 7346 5808.

PRICES AND PAYMENT
We have noted where venues accept the following credit cards: American Express (**AmEx**), Diners Club (**DC**), MasterCard (**MC**) and Visa (**V**).

THE LIE OF THE LAND
We've included map references for each venue that falls on our maps (starting on page 312). However, we recommend that you follow the example of the locals and invest in a standard *A-Z* map of the city.

PHONE NUMBERS
The area code for London is 020. All phone numbers given in this Guide take this code unless otherwise stated, so add 020 if calling from outside London; otherwise, simply dial the number as written. The international dialling code for the UK is 44.

Sponsors and advertisers
We would like to thank our sponsor Nickelodeon for its involvement in this Guide. However, we would like to stress that no establishment has been included because it has advertised in any of our publications and no payment of any kind has influenced any review. The opinions given in this book are those of *Time Out* writers and editors and are entirely independent.

In Context

The Story of London

A history lesson without the tears.

ROMAN LONDON

Was there a London before the Romans? There's no evidence remaining of a settlement on the Thames until Claudius and his legions invaded in AD 43. Once he arrived, though, trade became brisk. Roman historian Tacitus describes swinging London as 'a celebrated centre of commerce'.

It was the resourceful Romans who built the first bridge – of wood – across the Thames, near the site of today's London Bridge. Their progress, however, was held up by warlike Boudicca, rebelling against the soldiers who had seized her lands and raped her daughters. After she had sacked London in AD 61, there was little left to rebuild, but rebuild they did, and around AD 200 a strong defensive wall was erected around London, chunks of which still survive today (*see p50*).

Continued rebellions over the years forced the Roman outpost into decline. In 410, the last troops were withdrawn and London became a ghost town. Only the roads and the wall were left, along with the beginnings of Christianity.

SAXON & VIKING LONDON

Historians believe that during the fifth and sixth centuries Saxons crossed the North Sea to settle in eastern and southern England. Little is known about this period, except it seems that the Saxon settlers eschewed the rubble that was London. They preferred life in the country, and built up farmsteads and trading posts outside the city.

The city that became known as 'Lundenwic' stood west of the Roman city, where Covent Garden is today. The name Aldwych comes from the Saxon 'the old wic' (town or port), and the Strand from 'strand', meaning a beach for grounding ships. Gradually, London's status as trading post came to the fore. The Venerable Bede referred to Lundenwic as 'the mart of many nations resorting to it by land and sea'.

London's first bishop was called Mellitus. He was one of Augustine's missionaries and, like his boss, converted a king (King Sebert). Mellitus founded a cathedral, built of wood and dedicated to St Paul. Although his people turned back to paganism after Sebert's death, later generations of Christians rebuilt St Paul's.

In the ninth century, successive waves of Vikings attacked London. In 888 Alfred the Great ordered the reoccupation of the Roman town as its stone walls were still standing and could be defended by his soldiers. While Alfred reigned, churches were built and markets thrived in London, though Winchester was still the capital of England.

As the Saxon city prospered, however, harassment from the Vikings continued, until in the 11th century, the English had to bow to a Danish king. King Cnut (Canute), who reigned from 1016 to 1040, saw London take over from Winchester as the capital.

A child in time: Sextus

Sextus is a nine-year-old boy living in Londinium at the time of the Roman occupation. He considers himself lucky, as he works in a grand, warm house for an important general in the army. His master rarely stays long in his London quarters, but his kind and beautiful wife is there, with her chubby baby boys. Sextus has many jobs to do in this big house and garden. He collects charcoal for the kitchens, helps with the laundry and goes on errands for the mistress. Her brother, a poet, is fond of Sextus and gives him lessons in Latin and arithmetic. Sextus hopes one day to be a charioteer: he adores horses.

News flash, Saxon-style: the Bayeux Tapestry commemorates the **Battle of Hastings** in 1066.

Edward the Confessor, an English king, gained the throne in 1042. He devoted almost all his life to building a church. Westminster Abbey, which replaced an old wooden church called St Peter's, took 15 years to build. Edward, who had moved into the new Palace of Westminster, died one week after his Abbey was consecrated. At least it was ready in time for his burial.

The death caused strife. Edward's cousin William, Duke of Normandy, swore that his kinsman had promised him the crown. Edward's brother-in-law Harold was favourite with the English people. The two prepared their armies to slug it out at Hastings. On 14 October 1066, William defeated Harold and marched to London. He was crowned in Westminster Abbey on Christmas Day.

MEDIEVAL LONDON

William knew he had to keep the merchants in the City of London sweet. He decided to give them independent trading rights in return for taxes. The charter that he drew up to state this is kept at the Guildhall. He was worried about the large, possibly rebellious, population of the city, however, and ordered strongholds to be built alongside its wall. One of these is the White Tower, the tallest building in the Tower of London.

The earliest surviving account of what life was like in Norman London was written in 1106 by a monk called William Fitz Stephen. In it, he describes the busy walled city, and the woods and pastures beyond, where all kinds of country sports took place.

A child in time: Esica

Esica is a clever young Saxon boy. When he was just three years old he left his parents and went to live in a monastery to learn Greek and Latin, ecclesiastical poetry and arithmetic. He's nine years old now, and his greatest wish is to be able to create the kind of beautiful illuminated manuscripts that the older brothers work on so patiently. He sometimes wishes he could run around and play with mini-axes and spears, like the other boys do outside the monastery walls, but he gets plenty of exercise digging the garden and growing vegetables for the pot, and herbs for medicines.

The moment of death: **Wat Tyler** in 1381.

From the late 12th to the late 15th centuries, London became a hotbed of political struggle. Fighting for supremacy were three powerful bodies: the king and aristocracy; the Church; and the Lord Mayor and city guilds.

In the early Middle Ages, the king was responsible for making all the laws in the country, and had powerful lords and bishops to help him do so. During the 14th and 15th centuries, the Palace of Westminster became the seat of law and government, and the king's meetings with the noblemen and clergy – called Parliaments – became increasingly important. As the number of advisors to the king kept growing, Parliament divided into two groups, called the House of Lords (populated by nobles and members of the clergy chosen by the king) and the House of Commons (full of powerful people elected by wealthy merchants and landowners).

The city merchants had plenty of power as trade with Europe grew. As more imports of spices, cloth, furs, precious metals and wine crowded the wharves by London Bridge, people travelled to the city's markets to do business. Foreign traders and craftsmen settled around the port of London. The population grew from about 18,000 in 1100 to more than 50,000 in the 1340s.

With crowds come hygiene problems: London was incredibly dirty and smelly. Houndsditch in the east gained its name because people threw dead dogs into the boundary ditch there. At Smithfield, the meat market, butchers dumped animal guts wherever they wanted. Filthy conditions let the Black Death, a plague brought over by rats on ships from Europe, run riot. Around 30 per cent of England's population died during the Black Death's blackest moments (1348-9). The epidemic reoccurred on several occasions over the next three centuries.

With plague killing many of the workers, London was left with a labour shortage, and the working populace found itself greatly overstretched. When the poll tax was introduced, the peasants revolted. In 1381 thousands of them, led by Wat Tyler and Jack Straw, marched on London and rioted. When the young king, Richard II, aged just 14, rode out to face the angry workers, Lord Mayor William Walworth stabbed Wat Tyler. This put a stop to the rioting, and the ringleaders were rounded up and hanged.

The poor sought comfort from the Church. London was full of churches, from the vast, awe-inspiring St Paul's, to little local parish churches where working folk were baptised, married and buried.

Monasteries and convents were founded within and without the city walls. Poor people looked to the men and women who inhabited them for help; indeed, the friars were like early social workers for the dispossessed. Different orders were known by the colour of their habits: Dominicans were the Blackfriars, Carmelites Whitefriars, Franciscans Greyfriars; such names linger in the city today (Blackfriars Bridge; Greyfriars Passage; Whitefriars Street).

A child in time: Eleanor

Eleanor thanks God she has made it to the age of nine. Her mother, little sister and big brother all died of the plague. She and her baby brother live with their father above their bakery near the Greyfriars monastery. Women come from all over with bread dough to be baked in their wood-fired oven. When she is not helping her father, Eleanor washes clothes, prepares meals, goes out to buy meat and ale, and looks after her brother and the chickens they keep – in the house! Eleanor and her brother love the chickens, and cry when their father wrings a bird's neck for a special meal.

Bob the Builder

Little Bill

Thomas the Tank Engine & Friends

Blue's Clues

Face

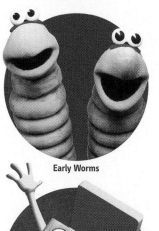
Early Worms

Sesame Street

Cubeez

Whose adventures will your child get into today?

Nick Jr. is the digital TV channel created specially for children under 7.

It's an entertaining, stimulating and safe environment in which your child can play, laugh and learn.

From 6am to 7pm every day, we have a variety of programmes for your child to enjoy.

You can also visit us online at nickjr.co.uk. You'll find more adventures as well as games, printables and ideas for lots of exciting things you and your child can do together.

So come and join the Nick Jr. characters for adventures from breakfast to bedtime.

A Nickelodeon UK Channel

Play, Laugh & Learn

For more details on programme times, visit nickjr.co.uk

WATCH THE NICK JR. CHANNEL ON DIGITAL CABLE AND SATELLITE, EVERY DAY, 6AM – 7PM.

AVAILABLE ON **skydigital**, **Telewest** AND **ntl:home**.

The unstoppable, much-married **Henry VIII**.

The land he kept for hunting purposes became the Royal Parks (Hyde, Regent's, Greenwich and Richmond).

His daughter Queen Mary's five-year reign saw a brief Catholic revival. She was nicknamed 'Bloody Mary' following her order that 300 Protestants be burned at the stake in Smithfield.

Mary's half-sister Elizabeth I oversaw a huge upsurge in commerce: the Royal Exchange was founded by Sir Thomas Gresham in 1566 and London became Europe's leading commercial centre. With Drake, Raleigh and Hawkins sailing to America and beyond, new trading enterprises were developing all the time. By 1600, there were 200,000 people living in London, many in overcrowded, rat-infested conditions. Plague was a constant threat.

It was during the Elizabethan era that London became an important cultural centre, particularly for drama. Two famous theatres, the Rose (1587) and the Globe (1599), were built on the south bank of the Thames, and the plays of William Shakespeare and Christopher Marlowe performed. More earthy drama often took place on the street. Bankside was considered a 'naughty place' where people visited taverns and engaged in popular pursuits of bear-baiting, cock-fighting and brothel visiting.

Elizabeth's successor, the Stuart James I, narrowly escaped being blown up. The Gunpowder Plot, remembered every 5 November, was instigated by a group of Catholics led by Guy Fawkes, who planned to protest at their persecution by dynamiting the Palace of Westminster. They were rounded up, and hanged, drawn and quartered.

TUDOR & STUART LONDON

In Tudor times, new lands were discovered and new trade brought to London. The city became one of the largest in Europe. Henry VII, who brought an end to the Wars of the Roses, left his mark on London by commissioning the building of the Henry VII Chapel in Westminster Abbey, where he and his queen are buried.

His successor was Henry VIII, whose insistence that he was the Supreme Head of the Church of England (he defied the Pope by insisting his marriage to Catherine of Aragon be annulled) started the move to Protestantism. The dissolution of its monasteries changed the face of medieval London: the land sold off as a result was given over to streets and houses. Henry VIII also founded the Royal Dockyards at Woolwich.

A child in time: Robert

Robert is proud to be a chorister of the Chapel Royal at St James's Palace. It all happened so quickly. Having been encouraged by his God-fearing parents to sing in their local church choir, he is now, at the age of nine, singing and acting in plays for King Henry. His delicate treble voice was heard by the English Cathedral Musician Richard Farrant, who asked Robert's parents if their son could join his distinguished team of choristers. Robert loves to perform, and when his voice breaks, he intends to become an actor and take manly roles in the dramatic tragedies the king loves so much.

The **Fire of London**, one of many tribulations suffered in the 1660s.

The City of London's tax-free status was threatened by Charles I, James's son, who stirred up trouble both in the City and in Parliament. Eventually, the supporters of Parliament (later led by Oliver Cromwell) could tolerate the king's interference no longer and a civil war ensued, in which Charles and his Royalists were eventually the losers. Charles was tried for treason and beheaded outside the Banqueting House in Whitehall in 1649. Once the Puritans had declared Britain a Commonwealth, London became a very dull place. The theatres were closed down and the drinking and gambling dens of Bankside went with them. When the exiled Charles II was restored to the throne in 1660, the English in general and Londoners in particular were relieved.

The 1660s were a bad time for London, however. In 1665 the bubonic plague killed nearly 100,000 Londoners before cold weather brought an end to its spread. The following year, a baker's oven in Pudding Lane started a fire that lasted for three days and destroyed four-fifths of the city.

London was rebuilt after the disaster in brick and stone. One of the busiest people at this time was Christopher Wren, who as well as completing his greatest work, the new St Paul's Cathedral, also oversaw the rebuilding of 51 city churches. The Royal Exchange was also rebuilt in the City, but by this time many merchants preferred to conduct their business in coffee houses.

Charles's brother James II took the throne in 1685, but his Catholicism proved unpopular; he fled the country in 1688. His daughter Mary and her Dutch husband William of Orange were invited to rule in his place. The Bank of England was founded during their reign, in 1694.

GEORGIAN LONDON

When the throne passed to George, the great-grandson of James I, the country had to settle for a German-speaking king who had been brought up in Hanover. In Parliament, the Whig party, led by Sir Robert Walpole, was in power. The opposition were Tories who supported the Stuarts and had never approved of James II's ejection from the throne. Walpole was the first prime minister and was given 10 Downing Street as an official home. This famous address has been occupied by the serving PM ever since.

Streets and squares of attractive Georgian houses around central London are testament to how the city boomed during the Georgian period. It was at this time, too, that crossings over the river were built to increase accessibility. Westminster Bridge (built 1750) and Blackfriars Bridge (1763) joined London Bridge, until then the only bridge to span the river.

While the well-to-do enjoyed their Georgian homes, life for the poor was squalid. Living in slum conditions and grinding poverty, ruined by the

A child in time:
George

As a baby, George had been left on the church steps near the slums of Seven Dials in Covent Garden. Luckily, it was a warm night in June when he was abandoned, so he suffered no ill effects. The priest had heard of Captain Coram's new Foundling Hospital, so took the bundle there, to be brought up by the nurses. George sleeps in a big dormitory with 16 other boys. He's nine now, and will soon be leaving to be a gardener's boy in a big, smart house up in Hertfordshire. His love of plants, trees and flowers has stood him in good stead; ever since he was tiny he has enjoyed growing plants from any seeds and pips he could get his hands on, and now he has a chance to make a living from this interest.

cheap and plentiful gin that they drank to escape ghastly reality, it's little wonder people turned to street crime. The writer Henry Fielding and his brother John established a volunteer force of 'thief takers' in 1751 to help the parish constables and watchmen catch the criminals. This force, known as the Bow Street Runners, eventually became the Metropolitan Police (established 1829).

If it hadn't been for the work of enlightened people like Fielding and other philanthropists, life for the poor in London would have been far worse. Attempts to alleviate their suffering include the founding of five major new hospitals. St Bartholomew's and St Thomas's had been established by monks many years before but they were joined by Westminster, Guy's, St George's, London and the Middlesex Hospitals from 1720

to 1745, all of which went on to become world-famous teaching hospitals. Big-hearted sea captain Thomas Coram built his Foundling Hospital for abandoned children during this time (part of the gate of this hospital, demolished in 1926, still remains at the top of Lamb's Conduit Street, in front of Coram's Fields park).

Swelling the ranks of Londoners in the 18th century were thousands of country folk who had lost their land due to the laws of enclosures, which meant that a few farmers had exclusive control of the land. Poor immigrant workers flocked to the East End via the docks. By 1801, London's population had grown to almost a million, the largest in Europe.

VICTORIAN LONDON

By the time Victoria came to the throne in 1837, five more bridges spanned the Thames and the city's first railway line (London Bridge to Greenwich) had been laid. London, the administrative and financial capital of the British empire, was a huge, grimy industrial town. Fine buildings, posh shops and grand houses made rich living easy, but a few streets away, slums continued to breed misery. Down by the river, life became increasingly malodorous. A less than modern sewerage system meant that city dwellers' waste products flowed into the Thames. As there were now millions of Londoners, this resulted in filthy, disease-ridden water. No fish could survive in the polluted water, but many poor people still washed in it and drank it. Cholera was rife and killed thousands. The year of 1858 was famous for its smell: the Great Stink meant that politicians in the Houses of Parliament could not work with their windows open during the hot summer. Bad smells continued until 1860, when Joseph Bazalgette's new drainage system was up and running.

Novelist Charles Dickens wrote prolifically about the social problems of this huge metropolis, but as the years rolled by, many improvements were made to ease the lot of Londoners. The new sewerage system made a great difference, and some slum housing was replaced by social housing funded by philanthropists, such as George Peabody.

Building continued apace: streets and streets of houses were constructed for workers, miles upon miles of railway line laid to service the industries. By the end of the 19th century, London's population stood at over six million. Workers travelling to and from their jobs were transported in horse-drawn buses until 1829; trains came about seven years later and the first underground steam train (which ran between Paddington and Farringdon Road) opened in 1863. Travellers had to wait till 1890 for the first electric tube to operate; it ran between the City and Stockwell.

In 1851, the Queen's consort Prince Albert helped to organise the Great Exhibition to celebrate the achievements of the empire. Exhibits from all over the world – jewels, textiles, glass, engines – were proudly displayed in the iron and glass Crystal Palace erected in Hyde Park. The Palace was a terrific success; Queen Victoria liked it so much she visited almost every day for three months. When it closed in October six million people had passed through its doors.

20TH-CENTURY LONDON

The last few years of Victoria's reign had been somewhat gloomy, so when Edward VII came to the throne in 1901, a new, fun-filled era began. The luxurious Ritz Hotel was opened and the Café Royal was the favourite haunt of fashionable, cultured people. More humble souls took their refreshments at the huge Lyons Corner Houses. Department stores, an American idea, made it across to England – the first to open was Selfridges, in 1909, followed two years later by Whiteley's in Bayswater. Horse-drawn buses were finally put out to grass in 1911 – now buses were motorised and electric trams clanked around outer London areas.

World War I saw the first bomb to be dropped on London. It came from a Zeppelin and landed near Guildhall. Nightly raids continued throughout the Great War, killing 650 people. When it was finally over, and those soldiers who had survived were promised 'homes for heroes' on their return, political change was set in motion. Few such new homes ever materialised and the mood of the nation was black. In 1924 Lloyd George's Liberal Party was deposed in favour of a promised fresh start with the Labour Party, under Ramsay MacDonald.

While the upper classes partied their way through the 'Roaring Twenties', the working classes were in the grip of mass unemployment caused by the post-war slump. Dissatisfaction was eventually expressed when all the workers downed tools to

Without **Guy Fawkes**, there wouldn't be fireworks and bonfires on 5 November. *See p14.*

support the striking miners. The General Strike of 1926 lasted for nine days: the army was called in to help distribute food and students drove the buses. After the strike, unemployment continued to rise. The New York Stock Exchange crash of 1929 had a devastating knock-on effect; the British economic situation was grim. Nevertheless, the London County Council worked to improve conditions for its people. As the city's population grew (8.7 million in 1939), so did its sprawl. Suburbia expanded, and so did the tube lines. The main entertainment for people was the radio,

A child in time: Annie

Annie is one of nine children. She lives with her family in a little four-room cottage in Rotherhithe. As one of the eldest, she has to do what she can to bring money into the household. Her father's wage as a stevedore on the docks is not enough to feed them all. She and her brother go scavenging for likely pieces of wood, discarded beads, scraps of cloth, anything that she can make into little dolls and trinkets to sell. She makes the toys during the week, then on Saturday and Sunday walks with her brother and sister to Greenwich or Blackheath, to sell her wares to the rich folk taking the air. She has a pretty smile, and a polite manner, so often does quite well.

but the first television broadcast went out live from the British Broadcasting Corporation (BBC) at Alexandra Palace studios in 1936.

On 3 September 1939 Britain declared war on Germany and Londoners began digging their air raid shelters and sending children and pregnant women to the countryside. In fact, the air raids did not begin until almost a year later. In September 1940 hundreds of German bombers devastated east London and the docks. The raid continued for 57 nights in a row. Londoners under siege became known for their resilience during this time. In 1942

there was a new type of bomb flattening Londoner's homes – the V1 or doodlebug. These caused widespread destruction, as did their successor, the more powerful V2 rocket, 500 of which were dropped on east London. By the end of the war about a third of the city and the East End was in ruins. Even when the war ended the country was suffering. In the General Election that took place soon after VE Day, Churchill was defeated by the Labour Party under Clement Attlee. Swift changes went ahead to improve the life of the nation. The National Health Service was founded in 1948; public transport and

The devastation caused by the *Luftwaffe* in September 1940, known as the **Blitz**.

A child in time: Johnny

Johnny loves planes and wishes he was ten years older, so that he could fly a bomber like his uncle Walter. Instead, his mother has told him he and his little brother must go on a train to Cornwall tomorrow, in case the *Luftwaffe* drop their bombs on his street in south-east London. He must carry his gas mask in a special box around his neck, and have his name on a label on his coat. He has to pack all his favourite possessions in the suitcase his mother has put out for him. He only hopes there's room for his model plane collection.

communications services were overhauled. For Londoners facing a terrible housing shortage, ambitious initiatives put a roof over their heads. Some of the buildings whisked up for them – prefabricated bungalows – were supposed to be temporary, but many were still inhabited 50 years later. High-rise estates, a new idea put up in too much of a hurry, were consequently rather shoddy.

It was not all doom and gloom for Londoners, though. The city hosted the Olympic Games of 1948, and in 1951 the Festival of Britain, which celebrated all that was great about British technology and design. It took place on derelict land on the south bank of the river and when it ended, the land became the site of the South Bank Centre arts complex.

During the 1950s, Britain enjoyed a gradual return to relative prosperity. London, however, was facing a problem: people were moving out of the city, resulting in a labour shortage. Workers from the country's former colonies, particularly in the West Indies, were recruited to work in the city, notably for London Transport and in the hospitals. Many of these emigrants faced an unfriendly reception from indigenous Londoners: matters came to a head in the Notting Hill race riots of 1958. Some parts of London were more tolerant than others: Soho became known as an enlightened place, with its arty, bohemian clubs and jazz joints.

The 1960s belonged to swinging London. It became the fashion capital of the world, and Carnaby Street the hippest street. To find out where the gigs were, young people bought a fold-out weekly guide to London called *Time Out*; the first issue came out in August 1968. People from around the world started flocking to Abbey Road, NW8, because it adorned the cover of the Beatles album of the same name. Hyde Park was the hottest place to be in the summer of '69: the Rolling Stones played a free gig there for half a million fans.

During the 1970s, the lights went out, often quite literally, on London's glamour. Inflation, unemployment, strikes, IRA bombing campaigns and an increasingly fractured Labour government all contributed to an air of gloom. The punk explosion and the Vivienne Westwood gear it inspired made a few sparks fly, but that fire was shortlived.

Margaret Thatcher came to power in 1979, and the 1980s are generally regarded as her decade. Her Conservative government made sweeping changes, and stood up for 'market forces'. This was the era of the yuppie (Young Urban Professionals), who benefited from the Conservatives' monetarist policies and the arrival of the global economy. Meanwhile, the gap between these lucky yuppies and less fortunate people in low-paid jobs was only too apparent. It did not take long for the

The Sex Pistols, the most publicity hungry of the punk bands.

underdogs to start snarling, giving rise to the inner city riots, first in Brixton in 1981, and four years later in Tottenham.

One of the lasting legacies of the Thatcher era is the Docklands redevelopment. This scheme, set up in 1981 to create a new business centre in the docks to the east of the City, was slow to take shape, but that shape, dominated by the amazing Canary Wharf tower, is extraordinary.

In 1986 the Greater London Council (GLC) with its anti-Thatcher outlook (despite being Conservative back in the 1960s) was abolished. (Its leader, Ken Livingstone, 'Red Ken', bided his time, and in 2000 was voted mayor with authority over all the city.)

When a city's economy booms, however, a bust is often just around the corner, and that is precisely what happened to London in the early 1990s. There was a spectacular slump in house prices and the reign of the yuppies came to an end. The last straw for Londoners was the introduction of a poll tax to replace the rates (whereby people pay a flat fee for water, according to the size of their property). Demonstrations against it led to riots in Trafalgar Square. It marked the loosening of Mrs Thatcher's grip on the nation, and she was replaced by John Major in 1990.

The recession continued and its effects were only too evident in London. The numbers of rough sleepers rose as people continued to lose their homes through unemployment and mortgage rate rises. The IRA stepped up their campaign against the mainland, bombing the City in 1992 and Docklands

Politician kisses baby –
Tony Blair and his youngest son, Leo.

content and the massive sums of money the enterprise swallowed up. In 2001 no one can decide what to do about the empty Dome.

But despite this fiasco, along with doomy predictions about education, health and traffic chaos in London, there are plenty of reasons to be cheerful about being in the capital in the new millennium. You only have to look to the city's skyline to see them – the bold and beautiful London Eye, a new landmark, has been an unqualified success, and the gloriously revamped Tate Modern has turned everyone into art lovers. The North Greenwich tube station, built for the Dome, makes that once-inaccessible peninsula a hot London property, where new developments and tourist attractions are planned. There has never been a more energetic proponent of quality public transport than Mayor Ken Livingstone. Londoners can look forward to a brave new city with trams, reliable tubes, shiny new buses and pedestrian-friendly housing developments. Schools will be beacons of learning and salmon will leap in the Thames.

Well, we may have to wait a while for the salmon, even longer for the schools, but London does look like an exciting place to be in the 21st century. And at least we have an extra bank holiday to look forward to in June, when the Queen celebrates 50 years on the throne with a spot of pageantry in the Mall, and Londoners must decide on the best vantage point for the inevitable fireworks display.

in 1996. Most of the capital cheered up when Tony Blair's fresh New Labour ousted the tired Tories in May 1997, but went into shock when, later in the year, Princess Diana was killed in Paris. The gates of Kensington Palace became the focus for the nation's tears and bouquets, which flooded the streets for days afterwards.

INTO THE 21ST CENTURY
New Labour continued with Conservative plans to celebrate the new millennium with the Millennium Dome, to house another Great Exhibition to celebrate the nation's achievements. The spectacular tent shape on the once-derelict Greenwich peninsula didn't manage to capture the spirit of the nation, however. Its opposers complained loudly about the

A child in time: Nina

Four years ago, when she was only five, Nina went with her parents and big sister to see all the flowers left outside the gates of Kensington Palace. She can remember how the whole of the city seemed to stand still for a while, after Princess Diana died. The most recent time that they had a big outing that involved going into town on the tube was to visit the Millennium Dome, just before it closed. Nina thought the Dome was wonderful, especially the shop. Nina likes living in London, but wishes she could convince her mother that a) she can walk to the tube station on her own and b) living near Clapham Common is a brilliant reason for the family to buy a puppy.

No wobbles.
The **Millennium Bridge**. *See p23.*

New London

Building up to a better city.

If Ken Livingstone is to be believed, London is one of three 'world cities' – New York and Tokyo being the other two. What he means is that the capital is a city for everybody, children included. This is a bold claim. London is, by and large, an imperial and commercial city built by men for men. Consequently, public spaces, such as the museums and art galleries, were originally designed for quiet study and contemplation. Even the parks were set out for fresh air and exercise rather than fun.

Fortunately, a ten-year building boom fuelled by a multi-billion-pound lottery bonus has transformed London into a genuinely interesting and family-oriented centre. Large museums have begun to cater specifically for children, and buildings generally have become brighter and more welcoming to people of all ages. The winner of the Stirling Prize, British architecture's most prestigious award, went in 2000 to the new **Peckham Library** (*see p136*), a colourful and playful building that attracts far more children than its decrepid predecessors – proof, if any was needed, that good design actually can make a difference.

For families new to London (or those who haven't visited a museum here for, say, three years) a trip to one of the city's major institutions will come as a revelation. All the big galleries (and some of the smaller ones) have been in receipt of large amounts of lottery money, money that has generally been well spent. Compared to the Dome, all the new building projects are already hugely successful, while plenty more are in the pipeline.

Just a quick word on the **Dome**. Whatever the merits or otherwise of this £750-million project, this story is not finished yet. It's worth bearing in mind that the Greenwich Peninsula now has a stunning new tube station on the Jubilee Line extension and what was once contaminated land is now ripe for redevelopment. Watch that space.

Developers are queuing up to have a go at the place (in a positive sense, that is), and it's estimated that around 100 schemes have been placed in front of ministers. The most interesting idea has been proposed by Marks Barfield, the architects responsible for the **British Airways London Eye** (*see p33*), which has become a much-loved part of the capital's skyline, visible all over London. They have suggested turning the Dome into an ecological centre. The firm has already recruited one of the managers of Cornwall's Eden Project (the hugely successful indoor botanical gardens) to advise on the scheme. The rumour is that the government has been impressed by early drawings of an east London version. So if you live on the wrong side of town for Kew Gardens, a modern equivalent may well be opening near you within a few years.

British Airways London Eye. *See p21.*

EASTERN PROMISE

In fact, the regeneration of east London is likely to prove more exciting than developments elsewhere in the capital – especially if Mayor Livingstone enters London as a host for the 2012 Olympics, as he plans to. Building land is cheap and there is plenty to be done. Just take the DLR to Heron Quays and you will see a vision of the London of the future. Building sites are certain to capture the imagination of even the smallest children, but unfortunately they tend to be disguised by hoardings and scaffolding covers.

Not so the site adjacent to Heron Quays, an elevated transport link looking down on one of the largest building projects in Europe. In a few years, the entire Docklands area will be twice its current size and will boast another half-dozen skyscrapers to go with the current three. Families are already stopping just to stand and stare at what's going on. For the price of a railcard, this is budget entertainment indeed.

But in terms of completed projects, the East End's **Mile End Park** (*see p120*) is the best this part of town has to offer. The result of war bombing, this is not strictly a new space but a £23-million restoration job. Adjacent to the Grand Union Canal and straddling the five lanes of Mile End Road, the two sides of the park have now been united through the construction of a tree-covered bridge (now part of the

National Cycle Network), while the remainder has been the subject of a serious building, landscaping and tree-planting programme.

The bridge is an eye-catching addition to the bleak urban landscape surrounding Mile End tube station. Clad in a yellow/green case, this bosky structure is a delight for children. You stand among birch trees and wild flowers while the noise and grime of passing traffic disappear underneath you. Although the bridge is the centrepiece of the park's regeneration, it is just one piece of the jigsaw. New landscaping, ponds and fountains have created a place that is worth exploring, with winding paths and hidden outposts that give views over the borough. A new ecology centre recently opened in the park, powered by solar and wind power and fronted by a new lake and sculpture garden, and facilities for Rollerblading and 'extreme sports' were due to open as this guide was going to press.

WILD AND WET

An equally successful open space, but one far more centrally placed, can be found in what was once a civil servants' car park in the courtyard of **Somerset House** (*see p62*), just off the Strand. The Edmond J Safra Fountain Court is an enormous expanse of cobblestones, enlivened by 55 water fountains and lights set within the ground. And because the water drains away into the ground, the space remains clear for walkers who don't mind getting their shoes a little wet. Be warned: these fountains are computer controlled and spring into life for a choreographed display every half hour. The Mexican waves and mesmerising changes of tempo are enough to stop anyone in their tracks and make Trafalgar Square fountains look suddenly very dull. During the harshest winter months the courtyard is converted into an equally popular skating rink.

Most family excursions, however, will centre on the internal experience of one of London's major museums or arts venues. Just around the corner from Somerset House is the **National Portrait Gallery** (*see p87*), redesigned by the same architects responsible for the fountains described above. A new £15.9-million extension has not only increased the building's size by 50 per cent but has also incorporated a child-friendly IT gallery, where touchscreen PCs allow you to explore painting techniques and the histories of 10,000 images.

Of course, it is **Tate Modern** (*see p41*) that, of all the millennial openings, stole the architectural and artistic limelight – understandably so. Prompted by the fact that the original Tate Gallery up the river at Millbank was suffering serious overcrowding both in terms of visitors and paintings, managers took the decision to buy a giant redundant power station to convert into an extraordinary interior space.

Slotted into the cavernous spaces of a building designed by the same man who designed Battersea Power Station and the traditional telephone box (Sir Giles Gilbert Scott), Tate Modern looks set to do for London what the new Guggenheim has done for Bilbao; that is, create a distinctive new building offering a world-class venue for large-scale exhibitions and art events. The £134-million conversion has been a hit with the public, but on a recent inspection this success appeared to have come at a considerable cost. Around twice the number of expected visitors have flocked to see what all the fuss is about, and there is no sign that numbers are abating. It is a sad irony, therefore, that such a large space has become so crowded. When curators first showed Swiss architects Herzog and de Meuron around the empty building, all agreed that it would be a shame to lose sight of just how big this building is; the solution was to build in just half of it, stacking galleries along one side of the 100-foot-(30-metre) high former turbine hall, leaving the other half empty to accommodate truly giant art pieces.

Now home to international artworks completed since 1900, the early architectural decisions have left the building seriously deficient in some respects. Firstly, it is frustrating to look out over the clear vistas of empty space in what is left of the turbine hall when you are hemmed in by crowds of other visitors flocking through a set of relatively small galleries. Secondly, the location of the main entrance is not clear; if you approach the gallery from the wrong (London Bridge) end, you could walk the length of this giant building in order to find the door. There is access under the chimney on the river side, but the main entrance is actually down a hidden ramp at the west end.

MILLENNIUM WOBBLES

The **Millennium Bridge** (*see p21*), which caused its designers such embarrassment when it opened in 2000, is set to reopen by the end of 2001. Designed by Sir Norman Foster and engineers Arup, the innovative design is being modified by the addition of 'dampers' – essentially large weights – which should prevent the wobble. This new pedestrian bridge, linking Tate Modern with St Paul's Cathedral to the north of the river, will be the first cross-Thames link in London since Tower Bridge was completed in 1894. The engineers have told us that the opening fiasco will be no more than a minor historical footnote in the long run – which is probably true. Whatever happens, we'll have a smart new footbridge soon: another one is being built, to replace the **Hungerford Bridge** (*see p63*) that currently links the Embankment with the **South Bank** (*see p35*).

The Millennium Bridge is not the only public relations disaster to befall Norman Foster, who was the subject of much unwanted press coverage when

Factfile: Tate Galleries

● The Tate Art Gallery was founded by Sir Henry Tate, the sugar magnate who made his fortune through the invention of the sugar lump.

● Known as the National Gallery of British Art when it first opened to the public in 1897, it didn't begin acquiring international pieces until well into World War I.

● The area now occupied by Tate Britain was once the site of a notorious prison, where convicts were held until they were deported to Australia.

● Bankside Power Station, now accommodating Tate Modern, did not generate power for very long. Designed in 1947 by Sir Giles Gilbert Scott, the building was completed 16 years later, only to be decommissioned in 1981. It stood empty until its grand reopening as a cutting-edge art space in May 2000.

it emerged that the 'wrong type of stone' has been used in the reconstruction of part of the **British Museum** (*see p57*). The £100-million Great Court project is, however, a tremendous success and is a model of how a formal and largely academic institution can reach out to families and children. What was once a space reserved for the literary and cultural elite is now open for inspection and genuine use by everyone.

The museum was originally designed to wrap around a large public square, but only seven years after it was completed in 1850 the now-celebrated round Reading Room of the British Library took over

Truly a Great Court. The **British Museum**.

the space, along with book stacks, offices and a warren of corridors. The British Library was moved to the new premises in 1997, and all the books went with it. Museum chiefs took the decision to return the original Reading Room to the public by stripping away everything but the reading space, and roofing it over to form the largest covered square in Europe. It now houses reference books relating to exhibits at the museum, so it's broadly arts/history based. Moreover, this scheme makes the museum half as big again, allowing extra facilities to be accommodated, such as new exhibition spaces, an education centre, a young visitors' centre and a children's shop. The museum recognises the importance of its young visitors – after all, more than 250,000 visit the BM every year (and that's just as part of organised school parties).

In a sense, however, it doesn't matter what facilities are on offer because the roof itself is the main attraction. Protecting the court from the elements by a structure that bends, twists and warps over the space in a way that would have been impossible without computer-aided design, the roof consists of more than 3,300 glass triangles, no two of which are alike. It is a triumph, and neck-ache is virtually guaranteed. Your child is sure to be wowed – and so will you.

The book service has received a further boost with Compass, an online multimedia tool that allows visitors to discover more about items on display – and watch video reconstructions of archeological sites or demonstrations of ancient technology. Also available on the Internet, Compass can be used to locate specific objects within the museum and plan a tour of the building in advance; it also has links with the national curriculum. The computer terminals on hand in the Reading Room are in stark contrast to the room itself, essentially a gilded papier-mâché dome pinned to a cast iron frame (and a wonder of Victorian technology).

LOOK TO THE FUTURE NOW
Now that the millennium boom is over it would be easy to think that the building bonanza was at an end. Actually, it has only just begun. During 2002 both **Tate Britain** (the original Tate, housing just British art; see p88) and the **Natural History Museum** (see p71) are set to open giant new galleries. The Tate's centenary development will make a series of new galleries available and open up another entrance to reduce the crush at the revolving doors of its main entrance and create vastly superior access for disabled people.

Around March time the Natural History Museum is due to unveil its £27-million Darwin Centre, a new concept in museum design where the public will be able to look directly into the laboratories and see the scientists and curators at work. Now in the final stages

of construction, the centre promises to complement the original Victorian building nicely, with the structural metalwork being sculpted to resemble biological forms and dinosaur bones.

But what the architectural world is really holding its breath for is a decision on the 'spiral' development for the **V&A** (see p73). Designed by Daniel Libeskind, the building would be quite unlike anything Londoners have seen before. In contrast to the Victorian lines of the current building, the spiral looks like a semi-collapsed house of cards. Astonishingly, the building has received planning permission but museum managers are busy negotiating with the Berlin-based architect in order to reduce costs. We could see something within five years.

TRANSPORTS OF DELIGHT
Transport is also to be improved, with rail links into Victoria and another footbridge (by the same engineers who designed the wobbly one – but they promise they've done their research this time). Not that we'd advise driving into London anyway, but car users are in for an even tougher time in the next year or two as Ken Livingstone introduces £5 fixed fees to drive through the centre of the capital. Hand in hand with this initiative is a move for further pedestrianisation, including the north side of Trafalgar Square. For the first time visitors to the National Gallery will be able to walk into the square without having to negotiate one of the busiest roads in Westminster – which is good news for anyone with kids in tow. Ken has, in fact, staked his career on improving the city's transport for families – among the proposals of his Transport Strategy are plans for more buggy-friendly buses and tubes and free public transport in London for the under-11s. Meanwhile, if you want to see a model of success, look no further than Croydon. The Tramlink here is one of the most child-friendly services in London, and if Mayor Ken wants to extend it and add a few more around the city, that's fine by us.

This chapter is too short to list all the modern, spruced-up spaces and places London now has to offer. Here are some others that, if space allowed, would easily qualify for inclusion: the **Wallace Collection** (see p96), the **National Maritime Museum** (see p128), the **Dulwich Picture Gallery** (see p139), the **British Airways London Eye** (see p33) and the **Imperial War Museum** (see p134).

And if you can't decide where to start, here's a tip. In summer 2002, the egg-shaped **Greater London Authority** building next to Tower Bridge will open. As usual, it will have a rooftop café and restaurant allowing people both to look down into Ken Livingstone's debating chamber and out across the capital. There won't be a more modern, new and exciting vantage point in the whole of the city.

By Season

Dates for your diary.

For military parading about and general pomposity you can't beat London. Royalty and government both make sure their ancient traditions are marked with due ceremony. Yet for every smart and uniformed official event, there's a wackier, anarchic occasion to mark. We've listed our favourite annual events, ones that are bound to hit the spot with children. Some may need booking ahead, but you should phone in advance of all of them, to check they're still happening. Also look in local listings magazines, in particular *Time Out*. All the dates in this chapter were correct at the time of going to press.

As well as the events and parades we've listed below, many parks, such as **Brockwell Park** (*see p137*), museums, such as the **Science Museum** (*see p72*), and galleries, such as the **Wallace Collection** (*see p96*), hold their own festivals and open days. Phone the individual institution for details.

June 2002 is a very important month for royalists, being the Queen's Golden Jubilee. We have an extra bank holiday to put us in celebratory mood (for a list of public holidays in the UK, *see p30*).The Department of Culture, Media and Sport is in charge of all national Golden Jubilee information. If you want to see what's going on in London and elsewhere to mark the occasion, and even make a suggestion about the celebrations, log on to its website (www.goldenjubilee.gov.uk).

Spring

London Harness Horse Parade
Battersea Park, Albert Bridge Road, SW11 (01733 234451). Battersea Park rail. **Date** 1 Apr 2002.
A parade of splendidly groomed horses and commercial work carts of yesteryear tour Battersea Park in this popular traditional event, which has been taking place every Easter Monday – bar the 2001 foot and mouth crisis – since the idea was first put forward by Sir Walter Gibley and Baroness Burdett-Coutts in 1886.

London Marathon
Greenwich to Westminster Bridge via the Isle of Dogs, Victoria Embankment and St James's Park (7620 4117/ www.london-marathon.co.uk). Start Blackheath rail; finish Charing Cross tube/rail. **Date** 14 Apr 2002.
Spectators of this 23-year-old sporting event can choose from which point of the course they want to watch the hundreds and thousands of elite and novice runners. As well as the main race, there's a wheelchair race and a mini-London Marathon for youngsters. Those with the intention of putting their best foot forward for the occasion should apply by the October before the race.

Museums & Galleries Month
various venues (7233 9796/www.may2002.org.uk). **Date** 1 May-4 June 2002.
An annual, national event organised by museums and galleries across the country. Participating museums run creative events and activities for all ages. Classroom projects, open days, special exhibitions and interactive activities are all laid on for kids.

Covent Garden Festival
Covent Garden, WC2 (7379 0870/0845 601 3600/ www.cgf.co.uk). Covent Garden or Embankment tube/Charing Cross tube/rail. **Map** p317 L6.
Date 12 May-2 June 2002.
The festival's programme usually holds plenty to interest family groups. The events, most of which are free, take place (as you'd expect) at venues around the Covent Garden area. It has become traditional for the oak-panelled law courts at Bow Street to open to the public during the festival for performances of Gilbert & Sullivan's satirical operetta *Trial by Jury*.

May Fayre & Puppet Festival
St Paul's Church Garden, WC2 (7375 0441). Covent Garden or Embankment tube/Charing Cross tube/rail. **Map** p319 L7. **Date** 12 May 2002.

A pearly white smile from his majesty – **Pearly Kings & Queens Harvest Festival**. *See p29*.

You don't have to be mad to run the **London Marathon**, but it helps. *See p25.*

An annual celebration of the art of puppetry. Fans of Punch & Judy from all over the country converge on St Paul's Church in memory of the first sighting in England of Mr Punch by Samuel Pepys in 1662.

Chelsea Flower Show
Grounds of Royal Hospital, Royal Hospital Road, SW3 (recorded info 7649 1885/tickets 08700 906 3781/ www.rhs.org.uk). Sloane Square tube. **Map** p315 F12. **Date** 21-24 May 2002.
The world-famous gardening extravaganza by the river. The first two days are specifically for members of the Royal Horticultural Society, with the other two days open to everyone else. There are usually some activities for children.

Victoria Embankment Gardens Summer Events
Victoria Embankment Gardens, WC2 (7375 0441). Embankment tube/Charing Cross tube/rail. **Map** p319 L7. **Date** 26 May-21 July 2002.
These free outdoor events are organised by Alternative Arts. Highlights include the Open Dance Festival (1, 2 June), the Westminster Youth Slam (16 June), the Midsummer Poetry Festival (23 June) and the Summer Season of Street Theatre (open-air, lunchtime performances throughout July).

Summer

Biggin Hill International Air Fair
Biggin Hill, Kent (01959 578101). Bromley South rail. **Date** 1, 2 June 2002; 8am start.
Keep your eyes to the sky to catch a glimpse of spectacular aeronautic displays featuring aircraft such as the B17 Flying Fortress, Tigercat and the show-stopping Red Arrows.

Golden Jubilee Celebrations
Various locations around London (www.goldenjubilee.gov.uk). Carriage parade starts at Buckingham Palace mid-morning. **Date** 1-4 June 2002.
The weekend of the Golden Jubilee celebrations sees events going on all over the city. The Monday is a bank holiday taking the place of the usual Whitsun holiday. The big day is an extra bank holiday on 4 June, when the Queen will take part in a grand carriage parade, starting at Buckingham Palace in the morning, then travelling to St Paul's Cathedral for a special service (by invitation only).

Derby Day
Epsom Downs Racecourse, Epsom Downs, Surrey (01372 470047/www.epsomderby.co.uk). Epsom Town Centre/Tattenham Corner rail, then shuttle bus. **Date** 8 June 2002.
A carnival atmosphere fills the Downs on the day of this prestigious flat race. Stands and spectator enclosures are open to all, and there's plenty to see apart from the racing, with a funfair on hand in which to spend even more of your money.

Young Pavement Artists Competition
Colonnade Walk, 123 Buckingham Palace Road, SW1 (7732 1651). Victoria tube/rail. **Map** p318 H10. **Date** 8 June 2002.
Part of a national event, this fun day out (though it's £1 for a pitch and chalk) includes chalking competitions, music, entertainers, Punch & Judy shows, puppet making, refreshments and stalls. Celebrity visitors such as Rolf Harris have made an appearance in the past. The fun starts at noon and lasts till 5pm, with judging at 4pm.

Beating Retreat
Horse Guards Parade, Whitehall, SW1 (7414 2271). Westminster tube/Charing Cross tube/rail. **Map** p319 K8. **Date** 11, 12 June 2002.
Ceremonial revels with the Mounted Bands of the Household Cavalry and the Massed Bands of the Guards Division, who beat a 'Retreat' on drums as part of this colourful musical ceremony. Things kick off at 7pm.

Trooping the Colour
Horse Guards Parade, Whitehall, SW1 (7414 2271). Westminster tube. **Date** 15 June 2002.
A celebration of the Queen's official birthday (her real one is actually 21 April). The regal fun starts with Liz leaving Buckingham Palace at 10.45am and arriving at Horse Guards Parade at 11am, before returning to the Palace at around noon when the Royal Air Force flies past and a 41-Gun Royal Salute takes place in her honour at Green Park. Spectator vantage points are at either side of the Mall. At 1pm there's a 62-Gun Royal Salute at the Tower of London.

Wimbledon Lawn Tennis Championships
Church Road, SW19 (8944 1066/recorded info 8946 2244/www.wimbledon.org). Southfields tube/Wimbledon tube/rail. **Date** 24 June-7 July 2002.
Netting a ticket to this all-important tournament is an onerous task. For the most exciting seats (those for Centre and Number One), you must write into the All England Lawn Tennis Club (PO Box 98, Church Road, Wimbledon, SW19) for an application form between 1 September and 31 December. The only other way to secure a ticket is by dint of queuing for hours on the day of the match. Once you're in, you can wander the outside courts. Later in the day, you can buy returned show-court tickets cheaply.

IT'S TAKEN 900 YEARS
TO MAKE A DAY OUT THIS GOOD

If you thought history was stuck in the past, you are in for a few surprises at Hampton Court Palace and the Tower of London. There's so much going on throughout the year, especially for families. At Hampton Court Palace, hear tales of myth and legend from costumed guides, discover what life was like in the time of Henry VIII and lose yourself in the famous maze. Visit the Tower and see the legendary ravens, admire the breathtaking Crown Jewels and learn exciting secrets on a free 'Beefeater' tour. With events and children's trails, you're guaranteed the best fun in history. See our special offers at the front of this guide. For details of family events, children's trails, opening hours and admission prices, please visit our website.

www.hrp.org.uk

Best: Events

For seeing stars
Christmas Lights. *See p30.*

For patting pooches
Discover Dogs. *See p29.*

For puppet pageantry
May Fayre & Puppet Festival. *See p25.*

For pony lovers
International Showjumping Championships. *See p30.*

For top guns
Trooping the Colour. *See p26.*

Henley Royal Regatta
Henley Reach, Henley-on-Thames, Oxon (01491 572153/ www.hrr.co.uk). Henley-on-Thames rail. **Date** 3-7 July 2002.
A well-heeled affair where stylish hats and blazers are given an outing, while muscular types mess about on the river. Spectators can watch from the Henley enclosures and there is no admittance charge for children under 14.

City of London Festival
various venues (7377 0540/www.colf.org). **Date** 25 June-11 July 2002.
Three weeks of musical events take place at venues around the City, from hidden churches to the majestic spaces of St Paul's Cathedral or the Guildhall Great Hall. Free lunchtime concerts encompass music from classical works to jazz.

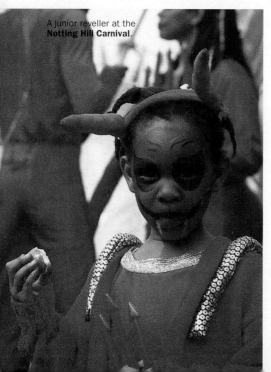

A junior reveller at the **Notting Hill Carnival.**

London Heathrow Youth Games
Crystal Palace National Sports Centre, Ledrington Road, SE19 (8778 0131). Crystal Palace rail. **Date** 13, 14 July 2002.
An annual London youth sporting event in which over 20,000 young people from London's 33 boroughs show what they're made of in about 50 sporting events, which include athletics, canoeing and volleyball.

Greenwich & Docklands International Festival
various venues near the Thames (8305 1818/ www.festival.org). **Date** 5-13 July 2002.
The Greenwich & Docklands International Festival traditionally features a huge range of indoor and outdoor events taking place across east London. Popular locations for the activities include Cutty Sark Gardens, the Old Royal Naval College in Greenwich, and Canary Wharf. Many of the events are free. The opening night celebrations include a firework display.

Swan Upping on the Thames
various points along the Thames (7236 1863). **Date** 15-19 July 2002.
An archaic ceremony in which groups of herdsmen, under the eyes of the Queen's Keeper of the Swans, round up, divide and mark all the cygnets on the Thames belonging to either the Queen, or the Vintners or Dyers livery companies. All this can be seen from the towpaths along the Thames. The route and departure times are changeable so phone for details.

Notting Hill Carnival
Notting Hill, W10, W11 (8964 0544/www.thecarnival.tv). Ladbroke Grove, Notting Hill or Westbourne Park tube. **Map** p312 A7. **Date** 25, 26 Aug 2002.
Staged on the Sunday and Monday of August bank holiday weekend, the Notting Hill Carnival is Europe's biggest street party, attracting more than a million revellers over the two days. A massive costume parade, live music and plenty of sound systems are among the attractions. The Children's Day takes place on the Sunday and is usually slightly quieter, although there'll be no avoiding the massive crowds whichever day you choose to visit. In recent years, plans to move the carnival to a less residential route have been put forward, so keep an eye out in the local press.

Autumn

CBBC Proms in the Park
Hyde Park (7765 3021/booking line 0870 0100222/ www.bbc.co.uk/proms). Hyde Park Corner tube. **Map** p313 F7. **Date** Sept.
Hosted by well-known children's TV presenters, this alternative Prom is a light-hearted afternoon for all the family, featuring accessible classical music and fluffy pop tunes performed by a number of big-name pop stars and the BBC Philharmonic.

London Open House
various venues in London (0900 160 0061/ www.londonopenhouse.org). **Date** Sept.
To promote an awareness of architecture among Londoners, the organisers of this event arrange for free access to buildings of architectural and cultural interest that are normally closed to the public. About 500 buildings participate each year, with anything from the hulking Bank of England

building to individual rooms in private homes on show. Check the website for a list of buildings open for examination, and to find out how to claim your free Architecture Pack if you're aged between eight and 11 years old.

Regent Street Festival
Regent Street, W1 (info 7491 4429). Oxford Circus or Piccadilly Circus tube. **Map** p318 J7. **Date** Sun in early Sept.
In only its second year, 2001, this festival was already attracting lots of attention for its fairground (complete with rollercoaster, big wheel and carousel) and activities such as ice hockey and cricket. The normally car-clogged street is closed to traffic, and nearby Carnaby Street also gets involved in the fun. A great day out.

Great River Race
on the Thames, from Richmond, Surrey, to Island Gardens, E14 (8398 9057/www.greatriverrace.co.uk). **Date** 7 Sept 2002.
More than 250 boats compete in this 22-mile (35km) marathon, aiming to scoop the UK Traditional Boat Championship. The race sets off from Ham House in Richmond and ends at Island Gardens near Greenwich.

Thames Festival
on the Thames, between Waterloo Bridge and Blackfriars Bridge (7928 8998/www.thamesfestival.org). **Date** 13-15 Sept 2002.
A celebration of the river with a funfair, a food village, live entertainment and an atmospheric river procession with lanterns (lantern-making workshops for children are held during the day: ring for details) and a splendid firework display. Ring this number for details of free weekend and bank holiday events taking place during the Coin Street festival (May-Aug).

Horseman's Sunday
Church of St John & St Michael, Hyde Park Crescent, W2 (7262 1732). Edgware Road tube/Paddington tube/rail. **Map** p313 E6. **Date** 22 Sept 2002.
Dating back to 1969, when local riding stables feared closure and held an open-air service to protest, this ceremony sees a vicar on horseback ride out to bless more than 100 horses before the animals trot through Hyde Park.

Horse of the Year Show
Wembley Arena, Empire Way, Wembley, Middlesex (8900 9282/www.hoys.co.uk). Wembley Park tube/Wembley Central tube/rail. **Date** 1-6 Oct 2002.
This international showjumping event attracts top riders and horses from around the world and is a must for pony lovers. The Pony Club Mounted Games Championships are staged here: nippy little ponies and their lanky riders tear round the bending poles, lob potatoes in buckets and generally do silly things at breakneck speed. The big draw in the showjumping is the Puissance (when the wall jump gets ever higher), which takes place on the Saturday evening. Scurry driving competitions can be seen on the Sunday.

Pearly Kings & Queens Harvest Festival
St Martin-in-the-Fields, Trafalgar Square, WC2 (7766 1100/www.pearlies.co.uk). Leicester Square or Embankment tube/Charing Cross tube/rail. **Map** p319 L7. **Date** 6 Oct 2002.
Dressed in their traditional button-strewn costumes, pearly kings and queens of London gather at 3pm for a thanksgiving service.

Fabulous fireworks at the **Thames Festival.**

Punch & Judy Festival
Covent Garden Piazza, WC2 (7836 9136). Covent Garden tube. **Map** p319 L7. **Date** 6 Oct 2002.
Gather in Covent Garden from 10.30am to watch Punch & Judy engage in their traditional skirmish; pay no attention to the man behind the curtain.

Trafalgar Day Parade
Trafalgar Square, WC2 (7928 8978/www.sea-cadets.org). Charing Cross tube/rail. **Map** p319 K7. **Date** 20 Oct 2002.
A parade of over 500 sea cadets with marching bands and musical performances commemorating Nelson's victory at the Battle of Trafalgar (21 October 1805). It all ends with the laying of a wreath at the foot of Nelson's Column.

State Opening of Parliament
House of Lords, Palace of Westminster, SW1 (7219 4272). Westminster tube. **Map** p319 L9. **Date** early/mid Nov.
The Queen officially reopens Parliament after the summer recess in a ceremony that has changed little since the 16th century. It's a private (though televised) affair, but the public gets a glimpse of Her Royal Highness as she arrives and departs in her Irish or Australian State Coach, attended by the Household Cavalry. As she enters the House of Lords, a gun salute is fired.

Discover Dogs
Earls Court 2, Lillie Road, SW6 (7518 1012). West Brompton tube. **Date** usually 1st weekend in Nov.
Every kind of pedigree dog is proudly represented with stands for breeders from all over the country. If you're thinking of buying a dog, all the contacts you need are here. It's a great day out for children, with police dogs' agility and obedience displays, working dog trials and Scruffts (like Crufts, but for mongrels) classes like 'the dog with the waggiest tail' providing just some of the fun to be had. In 2000 this prestigious event was judged by Ricky Tomlinson (aka Jim Royle).

Public holidays

New Year's Day Tue 1 Jan 2002

Good Friday Fri 29 Mar 2002

Easter Monday Mon 1 Apr 2002

May Day holiday Mon 6 May 2002

Queen's Jubilee holiday Mon 3, Tue 4 June 2002

Summer bank holiday Mon 26 Aug 2002

Christmas Day Tue 25 Dec 2001; Wed 25 Dec 2002

Boxing Day Wed 26 Dec 2001; Thur 26 Dec 2002

London to Brighton Veteran Car Run

starting at Serpentine Road, Hyde Park, W2 (01753 681736/www.msauk.org). Hyde Park Corner tube. **Map** p313 E8. **Date** 4 Nov 2001; 3 Nov 2002.
Limited to an average speed of 20mph (32kph), a procession of vintage motorcars aims to reach Brighton before 4pm. The start (7.30am) at Hyde Park has a great sense of occasion, but if you can't get there, join the crowds lining the rest of the route (via Westminster Bridge).

Bonfire Night

Date 5 Nov 2001; 5 Nov 2002.
Every year Britain celebrates the failure of the Gunpowder Plot of 1605, when Guy Fawkes attempted to blow up James I and his Parliament. People across the country get together to burn a 'guy' on a giant bonfire and set off loads of fireworks. Most public displays are held on the weekend nearest to 5 November; among the best in London are those at Primrose Hill, Alexandra Palace and Crystal Palace. It's probably best to phone your local council nearer the time for specific details of individual firework displays, as events have been known to face cancellation (usually due to bad weather) at the 11th hour.

Lord Mayor's Show

various streets in the City (7606 3030). **Date** 10 Nov 2001; 9 Nov 2002.
This ceremony dates back to the signing of the Magna Carta in 1215, which stated that the newly elected Mayor must be presented to the monarch or their justices for approval. Leaving at 11am, the Lord Mayor, accompanied by a procession of 140 floats, travels from Mansion House through the City to the Royal Courts of Justice on the Strand. Once there the new Lord Mayor is sworn in before returning to Mansion House by 2.20pm. The day's merriment ends with fireworks launched from a barge moored between Waterloo and Blackfriars bridges. Anywhere along the river around these bridges offers a great vantage point for what's always a good display.

Remembrance Sunday Ceremony

Cenotaph, Whitehall, SW1. Embankment or Westminster tube/Charing Cross tube/rail. **Date** 11 Nov 2001; 10 Nov 2002.
A ceremony during which the Queen, the Prime Minister and other dignitaries lay wreaths at the Cenotaph, Britain's national memorial to 'the Glorious Dead', and observe a minute's silence at 11am in honour of those who gave their lives in both World Wars. Afterwards, the Bishop of London leads a service of remembrance.

International Showjumping Championships

Olympia, Hammersmith Road, W14 (7370 8202/www.olympiashowjumping.com). Olympia tube. **Date** 19-23 Nov 2001; 18-22 Dec 2002.
Top-class international showjumping action is interspersed with more light-hearted displays of dog agility and the Shetland Pony Grand National.

Christmas Lights & Tree

Covent Garden, WC2 (7836 9136). Covent Garden tube. **Map** p317 L6.
Oxford Street, W1 (7629 2738). Oxford Circus tube. **Map** p316 G6.
Regent Street, W1 (7491 4429). Oxford Circus tube. **Map** p316 J6.
Bond Street, W1 (7821 5230). Oxford Circus tube. **Map** p316 H6.
Trafalgar Square, SW1 (7983 4234). Leicester Square tube. **Map** p319 K7.
Date *all* mid Nov-early Dec.
Each year a giant fir tree from Norway takes up residence in Trafalgar Square. The main shopping streets boast impressive festive displays; the lights on Regent Street and Oxford Street are invariably switched on by some jobbing celebrity, but those on St Christopher's Place, Bond Street, and Kensington High Street are often more charming.

Winter

London International Boat Show

Earl's Court Exhibition Centre, Warwick Road, SW5 (info 01784 223600). Earl's Court tube. **Date** 3-13 Jan 2002; 9-19 Jan 2003.
The latest in boats, equipment and holidays create one of London's most popular events. All types of sea-going craft are buffed up for display. Prices range from £300 to more than £1 million. Alternatively, leave the credit card at home and have a day out enjoying the entertainment and impressive vessels.

London International Mime Festival

various venues (7637 5661/www.mimefest.co.uk). **Date** 12-27 Jan 2002; 11-26 Jan 2003.
If you still think mime is all about a clown stuck in an invisible box, think again. This visual treat of alternative theatre and performance art encompasses animation, puppetry, circus performance and more.

Chinese New Year Festival

around Gerrard Street, W1 (7439 3822). Leicester Square or Piccadilly Circus tube. **Date** 17 Feb 2002.
The high point of the Chinese calendar sees Chinatown buzzing with stalls selling crafts and delicacies, and dragons snaking their way through the streets, gathering gifts of money and food.

Great Spitalfields Pancake Day Race

Spitalfields Market, entrance on Commercial Street or Brushfield Street, E1 (7375 0441). Liverpool Street tube/rail. **Map** p321 R5. **Date** 12 Feb 2002.
On the day before Ash Wednesday and the subsequent 40 days of Lenten fasting comes Shrove Tuesday, aka Pancake Day. Teams start racing at 12.30pm. Would-be competitors should phone a few days in advance.

Sightseeing

Introduction

Big sights for little eyes.

There has never been a better time to take the family around London's vast stock of museums and galleries. Not only have many of them received generous wodges of lottery dosh to improve their buildings and facilities for visitors of all ages, they've also done away with the entrance fee.

All national museums, which means those funded by the department of Culture, Media & Sport, became free for children in April 1999. Pensioners enjoyed free access from April 2000. In December 2001, adults will join their elders and juniors by getting into some popular museums, and most of their provincial outposts, for absolutely nothing. The government department has increased its grant for museums, and made a change to the VAT levied on museums. The upshot is that the following London sights will be able to open their doors free to all:

Imperial War Museum (*see p134*).
Museum of London (*see p48*).
National Maritime Museum (*see p128*).
Natural History Museum (*see p71*).
Royal Air Force Museum Hendon (*see p111*).
Science Museum (*see p72*).
Victoria & Albert Museum (*see p73*).

USEFUL INFORMATION

Round-ups of notable places to eat and shop are included in the relevant sections of each sightseeing chapter. Some of these places have their own review in the Eating (pages 170-189) and Shopping (pages 191-211) chapters, but note that in such cases reviews may be of a different branch. At any rate, it's always a good idea to ring to check that a listed place – whether it's a museum, gallery, restaurant or shop – is open before you visit, as many may not be open every day.

To help you plan your activities, we've included a short, child-friendly walk for each area, as well as great places to spend a whole day in. Nor has it escaped our attention that all of London's major sights (and many of the minor ones) now have an education department, whose staff are dedicated to entertaining and informing children, whether they are in a school group or are visiting with their families. Workshops, play days, special exhibitions and activity sessions are laid on by the tireless folk working in these education departments. Our 'Meet the teacher' boxes, one in every sightseeing chapter, shed some light on the work of these enthusiastic education officers.

LONDON PASS

If you intend a gruelling schedule of sightseeing, it may be worth investing in a **London Pass**. The card, which costs from £19 for one day (£14 for children aged 5-15) without a travelcard included, rising to £89 for six days (£45 children) with a travelcard thrown in, lets you in free to more than 60 attractions. It also gives discounts in certain restaurants and theatres. To receive a leaflet about the London Pass, with a full list of prices, ring 0870 2429988 or log on to www.londonpass.com.

On the buses

You can learn an awful lot about this old city from the top of a double-decker bus (the best ones are **Routemasters**, the open-backed buses that you can hop on and off). Try the excellent and frequent number 12, which trundles all the way from Notting Hill Gate, via Oxford Circus, Marble Arch, Trafalgar Square, over Westminster Bridge and down south to Dulwich. For a dedicated sightseeing bus ride, try the following two companies (phone for further details).

Big Bus Company
(7233 9533/0800 169 1365/www.bigbus.co.uk).
Open-top bus tours three routes. **Departures** every 10-30 minutes from Green Park, Victoria and Marble Arch. *Summer* 8.30am-7pm daily. *Winter* 8.30am-4.30pm daily. **Pick-up** Green Park (near the Ritz); Marble Arch (Speakers' Corner); Victoria (outside Royal Westminster Hotel, 48 Buckingham Palace Road, SW1). **Fares** £15; £6 5-15s; free under-5s. **Credit** AmEx, DC, MC, V.
Hop on and off at over 50 stops. Each route has live commentaries in English, and there are also 'Audio Reality Tours', available in 12 different languages.

Original London Sightseeing Tour
(8877 1722/www.londonpride.co.uk).
Open-top bus tours six routes. **Departures** *Summer* 9am-7pm daily. *Winter* 9.30am-5pm daily. **Pick-up** Victoria Street, SW1; Marble Arch (Speakers' Corner); Baker Street tube (forecourt); Haymarket (at bus stop L); Embankment tube station; Coventry Street, WC2; Trafalgar Square (north side). **Fares** £14; £7.50 5-15s; free under-5s. **Credit** MC, V.
Hop on and off at more than 80 locations. The main English-speaking tour includes a live commentary, and there are also specialised tours based around sights and shopping areas.

Southwark & Bankside

Down by the river.

For centuries, London existed only on the north bank of the Thames. All roads from the south converged on London Bridge, which from Roman times until 1750 was the sole dry crossing into the city. The community that grew up around the southern end of the bridge, Southwark, in time came to be embraced as part of the capital and from there south London grew.

In Elizabeth I's day, Shakespeare lived and worked in the area. The tradition continues today not only with the replica **Shakespeare's Globe** theatre, but also with the post-war establishment of the **South Bank Centre**, including the Royal Festival Hall and the Royal National Theatre, which lie on either side of the southern end of Waterloo Bridge.

The entire area experienced great revitalisation during the 1990s. Warehouses and railway arches became museums and exhibition centres. The Tate Gallery (now Tate Britain) opened its spectacular sister gallery **Tate Modern** in a huge, redundant Victorian power station. **County Hall**, the former home of London's local government, became an expensive hotel and the birth of a new age was celebrated in style with the erection of the Millennium Wheel (officially the **British Airways London Eye**), which has quickly become a familiar silhouette on the capital's famous skyline.

The South Bank has always been a perfect place for a walk with the children (the only traffic to worry about being skateboarders and inliners). Thanks to its millennial makeover, it is now the number one choice for a Sunday afternoon stroll among discerning families.

British Airways London Eye

Riverside Building, next to County Hall, Westminster Bridge Road, SE1 (0870 500 0600/customer services 7654 0828/www.ba-londoneye.com). Westminster tube/ Waterloo tube/rail. **Open** *Jan-Mar* 10am-7pm daily. *Apr-June, Oct-Dec* 10am-8pm daily. *July-Sept* 9am-10pm daily. Closed 25 Dec. **Admission** *Jan-Mar* £8.50; £6.50 concessions. *Apr-June, Oct-Dec* £9; £7 concessions. *July-Sept* £9.50; £7.50 concessions. All year £5 5-15s; free under-5s. **Credit** AmEx, MC, V. **Map** p319 M8.
Within just a few weeks of its opening, following months of hassle trying to get the thing upright, the London Eye became one of the city's best-loved attractions. It affords stunning views in most weather conditions. A 'flight' on the Eye is one revolution and lasts half an hour, which means you travel at

Trails of the riverbank.

Factfile: London Eye

● The concept of the British Airways London Eye first appeared in 1992, as an entry in a competition for a structure to celebrate the millennium. The Eye came second and nobody can now recall what the winning entry was.

● The Eye weighs 1,700 tons and took a week to haul upright.

● The London Eye is the largest observation wheel in the world, allowing passengers to see 25 miles (40 kilometres) in every direction on a clear day – Windsor Castle, the Dartford Bridge and St Albans can be seen in a single panorama.

● At 450 feet (135 metres) high, the Eye is London's tallest tourist attraction. At the top you can not only look down on Big Ben and St Paul's Cathedral, but your view is entirely unobstructed because the glass passenger capsules are located on the outside of the wheel rim.

only twice the speed of Big Ben's minute hand. This stately bearing, and the holiday atmosphere inside the all-window pod, makes it a completely non-scary experience for small children. A night ride, a feast of twinkly lights, offers fewer sightseeing opportunities on the wider nap, but landmarks in central London are still easy to distinguish, and the bridges of the Thames, all lit up, are inspirational.

When you're on the Eye, the Thames shrinks to a long, thin, meandering snake, St Paul's is no more than a tin helmet and you can see right into the Queen's enormous back garden at Buckingham Palace. Traffic moves in impatient queues and the railways look like the greatest children's train set ever created. The trees in the north are Hampstead Heath, in the south Forest Hill. If anyone says they can see France, they're lying. Stewards offer a reassuring presence in each pod, and are usually able to let you know where all the important buildings are, though the one we met, being Australian, wasn't too knowledgeable about outerlying bits of London. The capsules take 25 people, although the central seat is big enough only for a dozen elbow-to-elbow. All passengers are photographed before the ride and tempted with the Polaroid at the end. Advance booking is advised; those who turn up on

a whim take pot luck, especially on a clear, sunny day, when the queues are offputting. Note that you can take a buggy on board though it must be folded first.

The new playground in Jubilee Gardens, which opened in September as a joint venture between the South Bank Centre and the London Eye, should come as a welcome distraction to small people whose parents have arrived too early for pod-boarding.

Buggy access. Café. Nappy-changing facilities. Nearest picnic place: Jubilee Gardens.

Clink Prison Museum

1 Clink Street, SE1 (7378 1558/www.clink.co.uk). London Bridge tube/rail. **Open** 10am-6pm daily. Closed 25 Dec. **Admission** £4; £3 5-15s, concessions; £9 family (2+2); free under-5s. *Tours* £1 extra; hourly. **No credit cards**. **Map** p320 P8.

The skeleton in the cage above the entrance and the sounds of monkish plainchant from below promise more than this subterranean exhibition delivers. The few re-creations of prison scenes from the 12th to 15th centuries have seen better days, while the explanatory notes and displays are less than illuminating and shabbily maintained. The axe marks in the chopping block are the wrong way round. The Clink, from which we get the phrase 'in the clink' meaning 'in jail', has a long and interesting history as the Bishop of Winchester's private prison, but little is made of this. This is Bankside's feeblest attraction.

Nearest picnic place: Southwark Cathedral Gardens. Shop.

Dalí Universe

County Hall, Riverside Building, Queen's Walk, SE1 (7620 2720/www.daliuniverse.com). Waterloo tube/rail. **Open** 10am-5.30pm daily. Closed 25 Dec. **Tours** phone for details. **Admission** £8.50; £6 concessions; £5 5-16s, £22 family (2+3); free under-5s. **Credit** AmEx, DC, MC, V. **Map** p319 M9.

By now, all the school and youth groups in the country know about Dali Universe, the world's largest permanent exhibition of the works of the Spanish surrealist painter Salvador Dali. The sales reps have been out on the road plugging the long-legged elephants and molten clocks to fascinated teenagers and now have several thousand schools booked for visits. Groups generally combine the Dali Universe with river trips and visits to other art galleries such as Tate Britain, Tate Modern or the National Gallery.

The gallery is housed in County Hall right beside the London Eye. It runs no youth programme as such but it has a strong appeal to young thinkers and intellectuals. Curated by longtime Dali friend and collector Benjamin Levi, the exhibition features more than 500 works by the artist, including *Spellbound*, the enormous oil painting he created for the set of the 1945 Alfred Hitchcock film of the same name, along with dozens of sculptures (including *Persistence of Memory*). There are also graphics, watercolours, etchings and lithographs, plus jewellery, gold and glass objects and a few pieces of furniture such as his Mae West Lips sofa.

Buggy access. Lift. Nearest picnic place: Jubilee Gardens.

Design Museum

28 Shad Thames, SE1 (7403 6933/www.designmuseum.org). Bermondsey or Tower Hill tube/London Bridge tube/rail/15, 78, 100 bus. **Open** 10am-5.45pm daily. Last entry 5.15pm. **Admission** £5.50; £4 5-15s, concessions; £15 family (2+2); free under-5s. **Credit** AmEx, MC, V. **Map** p321 S9.

Occasional family days notwithstanding, this is not the sort of museum to entertain children under 12 for long. After Chair Alley, where visitors enjoy sitting and wondering whether a

Bauhaus is more comfortable than an Eames or Rennie Mackintosh, there is too little to touch or play with. Older children, however, find the content, colour and style of the museum exciting. Keen school groups attend two-hour workshops where lecturers introduce the principles and theories of design and technology. Practical exercises include a 'mystery objects' game in which students handle and examine certain exhibits while trying to identify them.

The Collection Gallery features early televisions, washing machines, telephones, tableware and other consumer durables. The Review Gallery displays design innovations from around the world and the Temporary Gallery takes transitory exhibitions – coming up are the work of fashion designer John Galliano (30 Nov 2001-31 Mar 2002) and the Italian architect and designer Gio Ponti (3 May-6 Oct 2002). Note that the revamp of the second-floor galleries was due to finish as this guide went to press.

Buggy access. Café. Nappy-changing facilities. Nearest picnic place: Butler's Wharf riverside benches. Restaurant. Shop.

Florence Nightingale Museum

St Thomas's Hospital, 2 Lambeth Palace Road, SE1 (7620 0374/www.florence-nightingale.co.uk). Westminster tube/Waterloo tube/rail. **Open** 10am-5pm Mon-Fri; 11.30am-4.30pm Sat, Sun. Last entry 1hr before closing. **Admission** £4.80; £3.60 5-18s, concessions; £10 family (2+2); free under-5s. **Credit** AmEx, MC, V. **Map** p319 M9.

This exhibition commemorating 'the Lady of the Lamp' is of interest to primary schoolchildren, who come across Florence Nightingale frequently in national curriculum Key Stages 1 and 2. She is the most common subject of study under the heading Victorian Projects. It is also worth visiting by GCSE students taking courses in the History of Medicine. Worksheets encourage children to study pictures of hospitalisation in peace and war before and after Nightingale's career. Objects to handle include examples of soldier food before and after her arrival in the Crimea in the 1850s. The museum contains many of Nightingale's personal effects, including her medicine chest and the lamp that gave rise to her nickname. The Crimea Ward Scene is rather bloody, which will be of interest to small children when they're colouring in worksheets. The exhibition naturally focuses mostly on the army hospital at Scutari, but it also draws attention to Nightingale's unparalleled achievements in peace-time health care. She improved living conditions in the army and raised public funds by subscription to set up the Nightingale School for Nurses at St Thomas's – the first of its kind anywhere in the world. The shop sells Florence Nightingale shopping bags, tea towels, teddy bears and stacks of books about nursing.

Buggy access. Café. Nearest picnic place: benches by entrance of St Thomas's hospital/Archbishop's Park. Restaurant (in hospital). Shop.

Golden Hinde

St Mary Overie Dock, Cathedral Street, SE1 (0870 011 8700/www.goldenhinde.co.uk). Monument tube/London Bridge tube/rail. **Open** daily, times vary; phone for details. Closed 25 Dec. **Admission** £2.50; £2.10 concessions; £1.75 4-13s; £6.50 family (2+3); free under-4s. **Credit** MC, V. **Map** p321 P8.

This actual-size reconstruction of Admiral Sir Francis Drake's 16th-century flagship is open to the public and available for hire. Children's 'pirate parties', aimed at 5- to 12-year-olds,

Walk: between two bridges

▶ Start at London Bridge station. Look for the clock tower of **Southwark Cathedral** (*see p40*) and head towards it. Walk through the cathedral's newly landscaped garden. Sniff the air around **Borough Market** (*see p43*), which has been selling vegetables for a millennium and more and carry on along cobbled **Cathedral Street** towards the tubby life-size replica of the *Golden Hinde*, in which Sir Francis Drake pursued the Spanish and confiscated their gold. In Clink Street, pause briefly at the ancient ruins of the Bishop of Winchester's palace. Almost all of England south of the Thames belonged to him at one point. You might want to avert sensitive eyes from the caged skeleton hanging above the entrance to the **Clink Prison** (*see p34*), which is now a museum. Shiver at the eerie chants emanating from the underground jail. Dodge the tourist coaches outside the Anchor Tavern, where Samuel Johnson drank and thought up new definitions. 'Drudge: writing dictionaries is a drudge,' he wrote. Peer through the wrought-iron gates at the authentically reconstructed **Shakespeare's Globe** Theatre (*see p40*) and admire the resilience of the late Sam Wanamaker, who held to his dream when others scoffed.

▶ Join paved **Queen's Walk**, which continues beside the river for a mile or more. Outside **Tate Modern** (*see p41*) you can mingle with culture vultures; from here you might be able to hear the violinist who often busks under Blackfriars Bridge. Carrying on past the bridge, where you can browse in the outlets beneath the **Oxo Tower** (*see p43*) and the arty establishments at **Gabriel's Wharf** (*see p43*). Modern architecture lovers can admire the play of intersecting planes and the 'petrified wood' concrete of Denys Lasdun's National Theatre. Buy a second-hand book at the stalls under Waterloo Bridge. Applaud the impassive skateboarders clattering beneath the Royal Festival Hall. Read William Wordsworth's short poem, 'Remembrance of Collins', etched into a paving stone. Contemplate the Jubilee Oracle (1980) by the sculptor Alexander. Wonder at the half-hour queues for the half-hour ride on the **London Eye** (*see p33*). Here, you won't be able to miss the pungent smells from the hot dog stalls or the din emanating from the **Namco Station** amusement arcade (*see p39*).

▶ Pass under the stone lions on **Westminster Bridge** and think how the gaudy tents spoil the beauty of the Houses of Parliament on the opposite bank. Pay 20p to peer through the telescope at them. Stroll past **Lambeth Palace**, the home of the Archbishop of Canterbury. He owned the rest of England south of the Thames. Round things off with a picnic in **Archbishop's Park**.

are popular (*see p237* and *p246*). Otherwise, school groups and pre-arranged bookings may take part in workshops, including Living History Days and Overnights, in which participants learn the story of the ship and how men lived on board. The 'Overnight' affords children the experience of sleeping on the gun-deck – not in hammocks, alas, but in sleeping bags on mattresses. Both groups learn to give signals with the bell and how to run the cannons through the portholes.

The ship is open to the public only in the absence of party or workshop groups, so call first to check (note that tickets are sold in the gift shop nearby). Explanatory leaflets direct visitors on self-guided tours of the main-, fore-, half- and gun-decks. The ship is surprisingly small, yet it spent two decades circumnavigating the globe as a floating museum earlier in its career. Drake spent as long plundering Spanish settlements in the New World in the original – all with the positive approval of Queen Elizabeth I. The present 'crew' are students and actors who dress up and do a lot of shouting.
Nearest picnic place: Southwark Cathedral churchyard/riverside benches. Shop (7403 0123).

Hayward Gallery

Belvedere Road, SE1 (box office 7960 424/ www.hayward-gallery.org.uk). Embankment tube/ Waterloo tube/rail. **Open** *during exhibitions* 10am-6pm Mon, Thur-Sun; 10am-8pm Tue, Wed. **Admission** varies; phone for details. **Credit** AmEx, DC, MC, V. **Map** p320 M8.

The South Bank's gallery space is rightly feted for the flexibility of its space and the diversity of its programme. The temporary exhibitions, including retrospectives and themed shows, such as last year's amazing Spectacular Bodies, attract a great deal of interest, which is nurtured among the under-16s, who are given free access to exhibitions during school holidays. We love it for its energetic education programme. Every temporary exhibition has its element: bookable and drop-in workshops for children and young people take place during half-terms, school holidays and weekends. They are free, popular and a must for any child who loves making models, collages, sketching and painting. *See also p217.* *Buggy access. Café. Lifts. Nappy-changing facilities. Nearest picnic place: Jubilee Gardens/riverside benches. Shop.*

HMS Belfast

Morgan's Lane, Tooley Street, SE1 (7940 6328/ www.iwm.org.uk). London Bridge tube/rail. **Open** *Mar-Oct* 10am-6pm daily. *Nov-Feb* 10am-5pm daily. Last entry 45min before closing. **Admission** £5.40; £4 concessions; free under-16s (must be accompanied by an adult). **Credit** MC, V. **Map** p321 R8.

Daily school holidays programmes aimed at 7- to 14-year-olds study the history of this 11,500-ton World War II battlecruiser, which floats peacefully on the Thames just upstream from Tower Bridge. Children use film, photos, documents and quiz sheets to find out more about the ship. Term-time schools' events involve tailor-made workshops and talks using both video and live presentations. Two-hour conducted tours explore the nine decks from the quarter-deck to the captain's bridge visiting the boiler room, engine room, galley, sick bay, dentist, NAAFI canteen, mess deck and the permanent exhibition entitled HMS *Belfast* in War and Peace. But what children really want to see are the three sets of guns that destroyed the German battleship *Scharnhorst* in the Arctic Ocean in 1943. There is usually a queue to climb into the port deck Bofors gun, which young enthusiasts can swivel, elevate, aim, but not, of course, fire.
Café. Children's parties. Nappy-changing facilities. Nearest picnic place: William Curtis Park. Shop.

All ship-shape: the **Golden Hinde**. *See p35.*

IMAX Cinema

1 Charlie Chaplin Walk, SE1 (7902 1234/ www.bfi.org.uk/imax). Waterloo tube/rail. **Open** 12.30-8pm Mon-Thur; 12.30-9.15pm Fri; 11.45am-9.15pm Sat; noon-8pm Sun. **Admission** £6.95; £4.95 5-16s; £5.95 concessions; film costs an extra £4.20 per adult or child (no concessions); free under-5s. **Credit** AmEx, MC, V. **Map** p320 M8.

Though it's impressive even from the outside, looming over the roundabout at the southern end of Waterloo Bridge, the circular IMAX nonetheless seems much bigger inside than from the outside. The screen is flat and the 2,000 seats are very steeply banked, so no one, not even tots, has to look over anyone's head to see the screen. The bar sells soft drinks and popcorn (it's pricey at £2 a bag – buy one to share).

Most of the specially made films shown here are aimed at children. The most popular is *Cyberworld*, a 3-D fantasy animation with a brief appearance by the Simpsons (Homer gets sucked into a black hole). The necessary glasses are provided. Leaders of school groups prefer the 2-D documentary *Mysteries of Egypt* as it touches on topics covered by the national curriculum. The most recent addition is *Dolphins*, an Oscar-nominated 3-D documentary with a tongue-in-cheek voice-over by James Bond (Pierce Brosnan). All shows last an hour including a 15-minute Pearl and Dean trailer projected at normal cinema size, which emphasises the vastness of the subsequent IMAX experience – the screen is the largest in the UK, the projector is the size of a car and the celluloid itself (70mm as opposed to the normal 35mm) is the width of a five-pound note. Sound is delivered through no fewer than 44 speakers placed all over the hall, which really give the audience the feeling of being within the film. Five different films

Nasty business at the **London Dungeon**.

are scheduled at different times daily – phone to see what's running, or check the website for details.

The cinema is approached by underground walkways from Waterloo Station. Take time to read the fine poem etched on to the tunnel walls. It's called 'I dream of a Garden', and is written by *Time Out* contributor Sue Hubbard.
Café. Nappy-changing facilities. Nearest picnic place: Jubilee Gardens. Shop.

London Aquarium

County Hall, Riverside Building, Westminster Bridge Road, SE1 (7967 8000/tours 7967 8007/ www.londonaquarium.co.uk). Westminster tube/ Waterloo tube/rail. **Open** 10am-6pm daily. Last entry 5pm. Phone for opening times during holidays. Closed 25 Dec. **Tours** (groups of 10 or more) phone for details. **Admission** £8.75; £5.25 3-14s, £6.50 concessions; £3.50 disabled; £25 family (2+2); free under-3s. **Credit** MC, V. **Map** p319 M9.
'Most fish show no parental care', reads the caption under the Tanganyikan cichlid's tank. 'But the Cichlid devotes a great deal of energy to protecting its young…' Still for all the cichlid's praiseworthy attitude to family life, it is the sleek man-eating sharks in the Pacific tank that children really want to see. The sharks are fed on Tuesdays and Thursdays at 2.30pm, piranhas on Mondays, Wednesdays, Fridays and either Saturday or Sunday at 1pm. Divers descend into the Atlantic tank every weekday at noon to feed the rays, skates, dogfish and eels that dwell at the bottom. Children are keen on the two touch-pools where they can stroke the skates and rays as they rise to the surface or pat the crabs if they're careful.

An extensive schools' programme attracts noisy but enthusiastic groups. Educational tours last an hour and can be designed to focus on any one aspect of marine life such as habitats, the coral reef, the rain forest or defence strategies. A talk aimed at art students looks at the reasons why nature paints her sea creatures the way she does. A constant sound-track of crashing waves and eerie whale music accompanies visitors as they shuffle from tank to tank. The graceful jellyfish, the nodding seahorses (it's the daddy of this species that does all the childcare), the crustacea scuttering about the rockpools and the black and green hopping mangrove frog are all of more than passing interest but nothing quite attracts children (or their parents) like the languid, grinning sharks.
Buggy access. Café. Lifts. Nappy-changing facilities. Nearest picnic place: Jubilee Gardens. Shop.

London Dungeon

28-34 Tooley Street, SE1, SE1 (7403 7221/ www.thedungeons.com). London Bridge tube/rail. **Open** Oct-Mar 10.30am-6pm daily. Sept, Oct, Apr-mid July 10am-5.30pm daily. Nov-Mar 10.30am-5pm daily. Mid July-early Sept 10am-8pm daily. Closed 25 Dec. **Admission** £10.95; £9.50 students; £6.95 5-14s, concessions; £2 reduction wheelchair users, carers free; free under-5s. **Credit** AmEx, MC, V. **Map** p321 Q8.
This is an excellent place to take children over eight but who enjoy the delicious frisson of being spooked. Set under the Victorian railway arches of London Bridge, the dank, dark and gloomy atmosphere is a perfect background for the horrors on display. Even waiting in the ticket queue is part of the experience as hooded figures lurk to startle adults and children alike. Once inside, the different exhibits, scenes and cameos emphasise the true horror of crime and punishment throughout the ages. Highlights of the visit include a court scene where punters engage in interactive theatre with an utterly unreasonable 'judge' who sends them to Traitor's Gate. The boat journey transports the guilty to fresh heights of terror until they are faced with a firing squad and loud gun-fire followed by complete darkness. The Jack the Ripper experience is also pretty spooky and suitably bloodthirsty, a subtle mixture of gruesome facts and horrors conjured by individual imaginations.

Do not inflict this on anyone of a nervous or highly sensitive disposition. The dark, grimy air, the haunting sounds and the disorientation evoked by weaving your way around different areas all provide the thrill of fear and horror that is a vital part of the dungeon's addictive attraction. Allow at least two hours for your visit, more if it is busy. The shop is raved about by the sort of children who love the fake blood, cap cigarette lighters, stick-on warts and edible eyeballs.
Café. Nearest picnic place: Hay's Galleria. Shop.

London Fire Brigade Museum

94A Southwark Bridge Road, SE1 (7587 2894/ www.london-fire.gov.uk). Borough tube. **Tours** 10.30am, 2pm Mon-Fri by appointment only. Closed bank hols, 25 Dec. **Admission** £3; £2 7-14s, concessions; free under-7s. **Credit** MC, V. **Map** p320 O9
Visitors must book in advance for this museum of firefighting in London. Tours last roughly an hour. Small children are given colouring pencils and invited to draw the fire engines. This should keep them busy as there are 20 of them, ranging from a hand-drawn, hand-pumped model of the 1750s to the streamlined monsters of today. Older children try on the uniforms. There is no pole to slide down but there is a training yard next door where visitors may see recruits learning to rescue people from upper-storey windows. Exhibits in the eight small rooms detail the history of firefighting since the Great Fire in 1666 and include uniforms, equipment and paintings, especially those done by war artists during the Blitz. Plastic fireman's helmets are on sale in the shop.
Buggy access. Nappy-changing facilities. Nearest picnic place: public park & playground in Marshalsea Road. Shop.

Museum of Garden History

Church of St Mary-at-Lambeth, Lambeth Palace Road, SE1 (7401 8865/www.museumgardenhistory.org). Waterloo tube/rail/C10, 507 bus. **Open** Feb-mid Dec 10.30am-5pm daily. **Admission** free; suggested donations of £2.50 adults, £2 concessions appreciated. **Credit** AmEx, MC, V. **Map** p319 L10.
A new 'Garden of the World' mural depicting the plant-hunting and gathering expeditions of such horticultural explorers as the Tradescant family, gardeners to James I and

Charles I, and Captain William Bligh of the *Bounty*, whose remains are interred here, form the basis for this fascinating museum's programme of children's lectures, talks and activities geared towards national curriculum subjects. The museum building is a former church that was rescued from demolition. Exhibits include antique horticultural tools and photographic panels on famous garden designers and plant hunters illustrating the development of the English passion for gardening. The old graveyard has been redesigned as a Jacobean knot garden with restored 17th-century topiary.
Buggy access. Café. Nearest picnic place: Archbishop's Park. Shop.

Namco Station

County Hall (riverfront entrance), Westminster Bridge Road, SE1 (7967 1066/www.namcostation.co.uk). Westminster tube/Waterloo tube/rail. **Open** 10am-midnight daily. Closed 25 Dec. **Admission** free. **Map** p319 M9.
Children clamour to be let into this noisy amusement arcade within County Hall and only the most hard-hearted guardian would refuse them even a look. Especially if they need to shelter from the rain. The new generation of video game includes a cliff-top race sequence that the player operates from behind the steering wheel in a bright red, stationary sports car with a space for a passenger.

Beyond the high-tech video games lies a 12-lane bowling alley including 'children's bowling facilities', dodgem arena with the latest 'drift' system, and seven-table pool hall with licensed bar. Next door is McDonald's and next to that the London Aquarium. You could waste hours, and much pocket money, here.
Bar. Nappy-changing facilities. Nearest picnic place: Jubilee Gardens.

Old Operating Theatre, Museum & Herb Garret

9A St Thomas's Street, SE1 (79554791/ www.thegarret.org.uk). London Bridge tube/rail. **Open** 10.30am-5pm daily. Last entry 4.45pm. Closed 15 Dec-4 Jan. **Admission** £3.50; £2.50 concessions; £1.75 6-16s; £8 family (2+4); free under-6s. **No credit cards. Map** p321 Q8.
This genuine Victorian operating theatre attached to St Thomas's Hospital offers talks and demonstrations to young people. 'Pills and Potions', aimed at 7- to 11-year-olds, shows the manufacture of medicines from herbs into tablets, infusions, poultices and creams. 'Victorian Surgery', suitable for less squeamish older students, especially those taking GCSE in the History of Medicine, includes the gruesome enactment of an amputation c1850 using a volunteer from the audience and real antique surgical equipment, which sounds appalling but guinea pigs retain all their limbs and no blood is spilled. Students, then as now, watch in nauseated wonder from the tiered observation gallery as the patient is laid on a wooden operating table resembling an old ironing board. The theatre was installed in this ancient church bell-tower in 1821 and closed 40 years later. No one thought to look behind its locked doors again until the 1950s. Exhibits in the herb garret illustrate the history of medicine and nursing at Guy's and St Thomas's hospitals. Jars filled with formaldehyde preserve fascinating specimens. Horrifyingly large bladder stones lurk in one; in another a polluted lung shows the debilitating effects of London's famous 'pea-soupers', the thick yellow fogs that caused so much respiratory failure at the beginning of the last century. A spiral staircase of 32 steps leads up to the museum and there are no lifts.
Nearest picnic place: Southwark Cathedral Gardens.

Rose Theatre

56 Park Street, SE1 (7593 0026/www.rosetheatre.org.uk). Cannon Street or London Bridge tube/rail. **Open** 11am-5pm daily. Last entry 4.30pm. Closed 25 Dec, 31 Dec, 1 Jan. **Tours** free; by arrangement. **Admission** £4; £2 5-15s; £3 concessions; £10 family (2+4); free under-5s. **Credit** DC, MC, V. **Map** p320 P8.
The Rose Theatre was built in 1587 and pulled down in 1606 when the owner Philip Henslowe's lease expired. It was gone and all but forgotten until its foundations were discovered and excavated during the 1980s. They lie beneath a shiny grey office block just near the rebuilt Globe and are visible to the curious for the above prices. There's nothing else in the exhibition, although you do get a reasonably worthwhile video presentation of the history of the theatre that staged Christopher Marlowe's plays just as the Globe staged Shakespeare's. You can see the ancient cobbles that encircled the original Globe for nothing across the way. The video presentation ends with a plea for more money with which the Rose Theatre Trust hopes to continue the excavations.
Buggy access. Nearest picnic place: Southwark Cathedral Gardens. Shop.

Royal National Theatre

South Bank, SE1 (info 7452 3400/box office 7452 3400/ www.nt-online.org). Waterloo tube/rail. **Open** Box office 10am-8pm Mon-Sat; 4-8pm bank hols. Closed 24, 25 Dec, Good Friday. **Tickets** *Olivier & Lyttelton* £10-£32. *Cottesloe* £13-£24. Standby £8, £15. *Backstage tours* £5; £4.25 concessions; not suitable for under-7s. **Credit** AmEx, DC, MC, V. **Map** p320 M8.

Sharks in the dark at the **London Aquarium**. *See p38.*

Taking a break at **Gabriel's Wharf**. *See p43*.

Children's activities take place in all school holidays. These usually involve bookable workshops or foyer theatre, although the summer months are given over to the ten-week annual festival of outdoor theatre. *See also p225.*

Backstage tours occur three times a day throughout the year, last an hour and may be booked at the information desk by phone or in person. Tours take in the rehearsal rooms, workshops where costumes and props are made, dressing rooms, and the stage, where the guide demonstrates some of the more exciting items of stage machinery like the flying harnesses. Free informal foyer concerts take place daily at 6pm.

The National Film Theatre, nearby, has its own film club for young people (Movie Magic; *see p221* for details). The NFT and the currently defunct Museum of the Moving Image, which was so beloved of screen-addict children, will be given a brand spanking new premises in the Jubilee Gardens. Quite when, nobody really knows – it may be 2004 before the MOMI comes back for its fans.
Buggy access. Cafés. Lifts. Nappy-changing facilities. Nearest picnic place: Bernie Spain Gardens by Gabriel's Wharf. Restaurants. Shop.

Shakespeare's Globe

21 New Globe Walk, Bankside, SE1 (7902 1500/ www.shakespeares-globe.org). Mansion House or Southwark tube/London Bridge tube/rail. **Open** *Tours & exhibitions* May-Sept 9am-12.30pm daily. *Oct-Apr* 10am-5pm daily. Closed 24, 25 Dec. **Tours** *late Sept-mid May* half-hourly; 10am-5pm daily. **Virtual tours** *mid May-late Sept* 12.30-5pm Tue-Sun. **Admission** *Tours only late Sept-mid May* £7.50; £5 5-15s; £6 concessions; £23 family (2+3); free under-5s. *Mid May-late Sept* £5; £4 concessions £3.50 5-16s; under-5s free. **Credit** MC, V. **Map** p320 O7.
School students of Shakespeare enhance their researches with organised excursions to this amazing reconstruction of the

Bard's own theatre, the 'wooden O' referred to in *Henry V*, built only 100 yards from where the original stood. The project was masterminded and paid for by the American actor Sam Wanamaker, who was astounded that no memorial to Shakespeare existed in the area where he lived and worked. The construction is entirely authentic. The beams are oak, the walls are wattle and daub, the nails holding it all together are wooden pegs, and the roof is thatched – the only one in London. Actor-led tours and workshops happen throughout the year and include attendance at staged performances from April to September. The weather precludes winter acting as it did in Shakespeare's day. Tours include backstage visits.

The theatre lies behind iron gates and beyond the administration buildings housing the box office, café, shop and museum on two floors. Exhibits here include few period artefacts but plenty of costumes, props, touch-screen information posts and models of the theatres in Southwark at the end of the 16th century. Sadly, Sam Wanamaker did not live to see his undertaking completed but his name lives on in the Globe. So do those of the benefactors, which have been etched into the stone paving slabs surrounding the theatre and include many leading thespians of the post-war era.
Buggy access. Café. Nappy-changing facilities. Nearest picnic place: Southwark Cathedral Gardens. Restaurant. Shop.

South Bank Centre

Belvedere Road, SE1 (box office 7960 4242/Gamelan workshops 7921 0848/poetry workshop info 7921 0953). Waterloo tube/rail. **Open** 10am-10pm daily. Closed 25 Dec. **Admission** free to foyers. **Map** p319 M8.
This great concrete haven of art and learning goes out of its way to encourage visits from the young. School groups, youth clubs and play-schemes choose between four activities. The most popular is the Gamelan Workshop (*see p215*). Ring for details of the poetry workshop.

The Maths Trail is aimed at 5- to 11-year-olds or candidates for Key Stages 1 and 2 and involves touring the centre while filling in a worksheet available from the information desk on Level 2. Anyone may do this without official supervision, although parents may need to be on hand to explain what several of the terms mean. Or if that all sounds too educational, children can spend the day surfing the concrete in the skateboarding pit beneath the Queen Elizabeth Hall. *See also p215.*
Buggy access. Cafés. Lifts. Nappy-changing facilities. Nearest picnic place: Jubilee Gardens. Restaurants. Shops.

Southwark Cathedral

Montague Close, SE1 (7367 6700/tours 7367 6734/ www.dswark.org). London Bridge tube/rail. **Open** 8am-6pm daily (closing times vary; depending on religious holidays). **Tours** by arrangement; phone for details. **Services** 8am, 8.15am, 12.30pm, 12.45pm, 5.30pm Mon-Fri; 9am, 9.15am, 4pm Sat; 9am, 9.15am, 11am, 3pm Sun. **Choral Evensong** 5.30pm Tue, Fri, Sun (boys), 5.30pm Thur (girls). **Admission** *Exhibition* £3; £2.50 concessions; £1.50 5-16s; £12.50 family (5 people, minimum 2 children); free under-5s. **Credit** AmEx, MC, V. **Map** p321 8P.
The ancient cathedral at the heart of Southwark is the beneficiary of a large millennium grant, which it has spent on beautiful new family-friendly buildings and gardens. The newly landscaped churchyard is a pleasant place to picnic. Inside, the cathedral shows the work of many centuries. There are Roman mosaics in the south aisle and medieval stonework in the transepts, while the nave is Victorian. The

contemporary millennium grant buildings include a library, refectory and museum, which displays relics of the centuries found during excavations.

The cathedral commemorates many historic figures and events. The Harvard Chapel recalls John Harvard's baptism in the cathedral. His family owned a pub in Borough High Street (a plaque now recalls its existence). Harvard sold the pub and left for America with a pile of books, which became the basis of his university library. Immortalised in stained glass are Chaucer, who set off for Canterbury from a pub in Borough High Street; John Bunyan who preached in the vicinity; and John Gower, the so-called first English poet. At the east end of the cathedral there is an Aids memorial chapel and at the west a large marble slab inscribed with the names of the people who died in the *Marchioness* boat disaster in 1989.

Southwark has both a boys' and girls' choir, which sing five services a week; applicants are always welcome. *Buggy access. Lifts. Nappy-changing facilities. Restaurant. Shop.*

Tate Modern
Bankside, SE1 (7887 8000/www.tate.org.uk). Southwark tube. **Open** 10am-6pm Mon-Thur, Sun; 10am-10pm Fri, Sat. Closed 25, 26 Dec. *Tours* 11am, noon, 2pm, 3pm daily. **Admission** free. *Tours* free. **Map** p320 O7.

In Shakespeare's footsteps

You can easily fill a day pursuing Shakespearean activities in Southwark, just as you could in Shakespeare's day – although many of the pastimes then available were of a disreputable, if not actually illicit, nature and some have even been banned completely in the interim (bear-baiting, for instance).

The huge stuffed carcass of a former fighting bear stands in the fascinating and extensive museum at **Shakespeare's Globe** (*see p40*), which contains costumes, props and other Bard relics as well as touch-screens and displays. Guided tours of the centre begin at the museum exit. In summer, you can take a tour or participate in a workshop in the morning and watch a performance on the open stage in the afternoon. Pay for a groundling's ticket – the informality makes it fun.

Outside, the cobbled streets still bear Elizabethan names. Bankside was full of brothels or 'stewes', which were convenient for the arriving sailors as well as theatre-goers. Bear Gardens was the noisy scene of gambling and bear-baiting and Rose Alley was where the **Rose Theatre** (*see p39*) was built. The entrance to its excavated remains is in Park Street. If you walk under the railway bridge you will find the ancient site of the original Globe, together with a small but informative display.

Walk on to **Southwark Cathedral** (*see p40*), which contains a monument to Shakespeare paid for by concerned Americans. His younger brother Edmond followed him down from Stratford but died aged 27 and was buried in the graveyard, which is now one of the most pleasant gardens in London.

Tate Modern, the South Bank's pride and joy. *See p41.*

Most people agree that the establishment of the Bankside Power Station as the new home of the Tate's collection of modern art from the last century was the most successful of London's millennium projects. Many children might add that the art has little to do with its attractions. The vastness of the space and the lure of the sloping runway into the Turbine Hall from the west entrance is irresistible to small people, who gallop down it in carefree fashion with their parents in hot pursuit. The hall is huge and awe-inspiring, and when it's not being used for exhibitions, the hall, with the gantries and pulleys from its past industrial life still hulkingly present, is left as an architectural space.

Galleries run along a slice of the building on its northern face, and are arranged thematically rather than chronologically or by place of origin. The shop should also be explored, for its trendy stationery, fridge magnets, quality books and so on. The top-floor restaurant, with its glorious views across the river, is generally packed at lunchtime, and the pastries, sandwiches and drinks in the cafés are good but pricey; save money and bring your own sandwiches to eat outside on the lawn. Shuttle buses and boats wend their way between the Tate Modern and Tate Britain (*see p88*). The café won the award for best interior design in the *Time Out Eating & Drinking Awards 2001*. There's also an outdoor coffee and ice-cream stall, open on north side of the building, which provides better refreshments than the dodgy ice-cream vans along the South Bank.

For more information on art, trails and activities, *see p218.*
Buggy access. Cafés. Lifts. Nappy-changing facilities.
Nearest picnic place: Tate Modern grounds.
Restaurant. Shops.

Winston Churchill's Britain at War Experience
64-6 Tooley Street, SE1 (7403 3171/
www.britainatwar.co.uk). London Bridge tube/rail.
Open *Apr-Sept* 10am-5.30pm daily. *Oct-Mar* 10am-4.30pm daily. Last entry 30min before closing. Closed 25,

26 Dec. **Admission** £5.95; £3.95 concessions; £2.95 5-16s; £14 family (2+2); free under-5s. **Credit** AmEx, MC, V. **Map** p321 Q8.
This 'real life' experience is actually nothing of the sort. Rather, this is a somewhat shabby attempt to evoke Blitz-time London, with rickety speakers blaring out '40s radio broadcasts and showtunes, and awkward-looking dummies dressed in period costumes. There is a lot of fascinating memorabilia, though, if you care to look for it among the muddled wall displays, and children might enjoy the atmospheric reproductions of an air raid shelter, a dance hall and a huge darkened bombsite.
Buggy access. Nearest picnic place: Southwark Cathedral Gardens/William Curtis Park. Shop.

Eating & shopping

The best restaurants in the area the two branches of **fish!**. There's one just beside Southwark Cathedral (Cathedral Street, SE1, 7234 3333; *see also p184*) and one near County Hall (3B Belvedere Road, SE1, same phone number). **Southwark Cathedral** now has its own refectory (7404 5740), where lunches are served from noon to 2.30pm (excellent pasta, innovative Modern European meat and vegetarian dishes) and the delightful home-made cakes are excellent for morning coffee, afternoon tea or indulgent pudding. High chairs are provided, but the atmosphere is sedate. There's a **Pizza Express** on London Bridge and a **Bella Pasta** at Hay's Galleria. While in the London Bridge area, foodie families should check out **Butler's Wharf Gastrodome** (36D& 36E Shad Thames, SE1, 7403 4030), where you can pick up baguettes and sweet pastries for a picnic, or take home handmade truffles, olives and cheese. The most welcoming restaurant here is **Cantina del Ponte** (Butler's Wharf Building, 36 Shad Thames, SE1, 7403 5403), where a children's menu at weekends includes pizzas, salads, chicken and chips and a variety of ice-cream.

The sandwich bars and pasta houses at Gabriel's Wharf enjoy the custom of workers at nearby London Weekend Television at all times of the day. The most popular lunch spot at Gabriel's Wharf is the **Gourmet Pizza Company** (56 Upper Ground, SE1, 7928 3188), where people are prepared to queue for ages (there's a no bookings policy) for a range of exotically topped bases (Chinese-style duck pizza, anyone?). There's a children's menu, high chairs and colouring-in activities, which is why you can't move for tomato-sauce-smeared toddlers at the weekend.

The main shopping street is **Borough High Street**, which runs from Borough tube station to London Bridge. Here you'll find a tobacconist's, newsagent's, chemist's, stationer's and banks. More interestingly, though, the northern end leads into **Borough Market**, a wonderful vegetable market of many centuries' standing, and a farmers' market for dairy and meat products, open Fridays and Saturdays. There is a cluster of upmarket shops at **Hay's Galleria** to the east of London Bridge, including the famous **Christmas Shop** (7378 1998), where you can buy tinsel all year round and chick-heavy merchandise around Easter. Children enjoy browsing in the community of crafty outlets at

Gabriel's Wharf (try **Ganesha** at 3 Gabriel's Wharf, SE1, 7928 3444, for hand-made textiles and artefacts from India) alongside the National Theatre. The studios and retail spaces of the sensitively renovated **Oxo Tower** (Oxo Tower Wharf, Barge House Street, SE1, 7401 2255) come under the Coin Street Community Association umbrella, and as such are open to the public to admire and buy, if they can afford them, the original designs by the lamp-makers, milliners and metalworkers. This is a lovely place to walk around and see the artisans' work, and the gallery here is free. The views from the swanky brasserie restaurant at the top are famous, but it's expensive and expects any young visitors to sit still and appreciate the food; under-fives may not be quite up to that. During the **Thames Festival** (the third weekend in September; hotline 7928 0011; *see also p28*), children can enjoy open workshops in a tent, in **Bernie Spain Gardens**, just near the Oxo Tower. Activities on offer include lantern-making workshops; the lights children create are for use in the after-dark Thames procession.

Just behind the Oxo Tower, a small group of shops including a cut-price stationer's and an art bookshop is trying to make its presence felt and cash in on the Tate Modern trade (the museum's own shop has plenty for kids to spend their pocket money on; *see p204*). The second-hand bookstalls beneath Waterloo Bridge conduct a healthy trade throughout the year.

Meet the teacher

Debs Callar is the Educational Co-ordinator at Shakespeare's Globe (*see p40*).

What do you do?
I organise visits to the Globe for groups of people aged from seven to 80. Everyone, old and young, does the same kind of things, though each visit is tailor-made to suit the group. You get a lecture or workshop and a tour of the theatre itself and maybe also the area. The group might want to look at costumes or weaponry, or how particular tricks were achieved on the Elizabethan stage. Education groups come all year round but, because of the weather, plays take place only during the summer months, just as they did in Shakespeare's day.

What activities do children request most?
Children don't really make requests but their teachers do!

The workshops on stage fighting are popular even with the girls – in fact, especially with the girls!

What other activities are there?
There's a Globelink scheme, which keeps schools in touch with what's going on here, and the adopt-an-actor-scheme, which allocates one actor to a specific school. Groups can tour the area to see what is left from Shakespeare's day. This might include visits to the remains of the Rose Theatre or Southwark Cathedral, which was called St Saviour's then. There are memorials to both Shakespeare and Sam Wanamaker there. This year, for the first time, we are producing 11am morning performances for schools.

What's the best part of your job?
I love the variety. I love the range of people who come here. I just love being involved in this wonderful project.

What was your favourite subject at school?
English and drama. Initially I thought about training to be a physiotherapist, but just as I was about to go down that route I discovered that I had been offered a place at university studying English and drama, which is what led me here.

Do you wear a uniform?
No, luckily I can wear my own clothes every day.

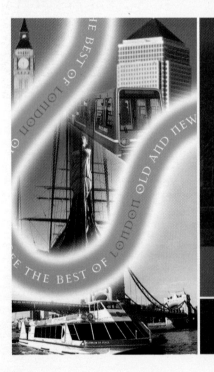

The City

Where the money is.

The City by the river: dominated, from this angle, by **St Paul's Cathedral**. *See p51.*

Dick Whittington was not much more than a boy when he set out for London with his possessions wrapped up in a handkerchief hanging on the end of a stick. He believed the streets would be paved with gold, and though he was wrong at the time, today he might feel vindicated at the sight of so much money being made here. The powerful banks and finance houses may be a turn-off to some young people, but to many others, they're an inspiration.

The district covered by the guide is the financial quarter of the capital. It is called the City of London because it is the original city as built and planned by the Romans. Evidence of their occupation still exists. Much of it is in the **Museum of London** but the ruins of the **Temple of Mithras** are in plain view and lengths of their wall still stand. You can investigate these on the gentle **London Wall Walk** (*see p50*).

The City might seem a rather grown-up place to take children, but it does offer plenty for families. In particular, the Tower of London goes out of its way to attract and entertain young visitors, and many of the present guides are former school teachers. And **St Paul's Cathedral** is of interest to children, particularly boys keen on getting into its world-famous choir.

Bank of England Museum

entrance on Bartholomew Lane, EC2 (7601 5545/cinema bookings 7601 3985/www.bankofengland.co.uk). Bank tube/DLR. **Open** 10am-5pm Mon-Fri. Closed bank hols. *Tours* by arrangement. **Admission** free; £1 audio guide. *Tours* free. **Map** p321 Q6.

The Bank of England Museum is the only part of the Bank of England that has any dealings with members of the public. Schoolchildren come in groups; primaries watch a film, *The Curious History of Money*, about how people engaged in the clumsy act of bartering before money existed. Goods could only be exchanged for other goods, a sheaf of corn for a cudgel, say, or a loaf of bread for an animal skin. At the end of the film the children are invited to dress up as fishmongers, farmers or arms manufacturers and then to try their own hand at bartering. GCSE scholars meanwhile watch the film *Ahead of the Game*, which drily explains the functions of the Bank of England and discusses the basics of economics. In the school holidays, staff supply families who visit with quiz sheets and badges. Screening times are ad hoc, so ring in advance for details. Phone, too, for opening times during seasonal holidays.

The museum is housed in several rooms of the original complex of buildings designed by the architect Sir John Soane. One room features a reconstruction of the original modest banking hall, complete with costumed dummies. Everywhere there are ancient heavy-framed pictures showing periwigged Georgians signing documents. There is a cheque for a million pounds. There are forgeries for which a 17th-century forger hanged (in the 13th century he would have had his testicles chopped off). The banking hall runs touch-screen tests on your fiscal know-how. In the central rotunda, a pile of 59 replica gold ingots holds no fascination, but two real ones, each worth £96,000, attract a crowd. In a separate room there is a display in humidified glass boxes of all the bank notes ever designed. Children can discomfit their parents by asking if they remember the ten-bob note.

Buggy access. Nearest picnic place: St Paul's Cathedral garden. Nappy-changing facilities. Shop.

Barbican Centre

Silk Street, EC2 (7382 7105/box office 7638 8891/ www.barbican.org.uk). Barbican tube/Moorgate tube/rail. **Open** 10am-6pm Mon, Tue, Thur-Sat; 10am-8pm Wed; noon-6pm Sun. **Admission** £7; £5 concessions, 12-16s; free under-12s. **Credit** AmEx, MC, V. **Map** p320 P5.
The Barbican is named for the ancient Roman fort upon whose site it sits. Long stretches of the old wall still stand – you can see them if you sit outside at the café tables by the lake of fountains or wander over to St Giles Church where a plaque on the railings describes their history. This huge arts centre, which also includes 6,500 state of the art flats, contains

Fashionable flats and an old wall in the **Barbican Centre**.

concert halls (home to the London Symphony Orchestra), a theatre (London base of the Royal Shakespeare Company), a cinema, art gallery, exhibition space, cafés and restaurants. The complex also incorporates one of the city's best museums, the Museum of London (*see p48*), the Barbican Art Gallery, with its wide-ranging exhibitions (*see p215*), the Guildhall School of Music and Drama and the City of London School for Girls. There's also a splendid library with an extensive children's section on Level 3 (*see p215*).

Local schools are invited to join the 'Adopt the Barbican' scheme, which helps them build up a long-term partnership with the centre. The education department collaborates with teachers in designing and managing projects. The Barbican is home to the Royal Shakespeare Company and the London Symphony Orchestra. The former organises backstage tours, make-up workshops and costume-making classes for keen young actors. The latter puts on monthly children and family fun concerts.

A large lottery grant has enabled the world-class orchestra to buy and renovate the derelict church of St Luke's just to the north of the Barbican. It is due to open as an education centre, small concert hall and recording studio in December 2002. Check the exhibition programme for closed days.

Bars. Buggy access. Cafés. Nappy-changing facilities. Nearest picnic place: Barbican Lakeside Terrace. Restaurants. Shops.

Broadgate Ice Rink

Broadgate Arena, EC2 (7505 4068/ www.broadgateestates.co.uk). Liverpool Street tube/rail. **Open** *Mid Oct-mid Apr* 12-2.30pm, 3.30-6pm Mon-Thur; 12-2.30pm, 3.30-6pm, 7-10pm Fri; 11am-1pm, 2-4pm, 5-8.30pm Sat; 11am-1pm, 2-4pm, 5-7pm Sun. **Admission** *per session* £7; £4 under-16s. **No credit cards. Map** p321 Q5.
The Broadgate arena becomes an open air ice-rink for six months of the year. The rink is open to adults and children. There are even skates for three-year-olds, or rather blades that are attached to the child's trainers. Skating sessions take place during the day and on Friday evenings. Other sessions are reserved for games of broomball, a form of ice hockey without skates. The ice is melted in April, after which the arena becomes a venue for other events such as concerts and theatre events. If all that exercise has worked up an appetite, there are restaurants and cafés in nearby Broadgate Circle and at Liverpool Street Station, or take a picnic to the broad expanse of **Finsbury Circus**, which is popular with local office workers.

Buggy access. Lift. Nearest picnic place: Finsbury Circus.

College of Arms

Queen Victoria Street, EC4 (7248 2762/ www.college-of-arms.gov.uk). Blackfriars tube/rail. **Open** 10am-4pm Mon-Fri. Closed bank hols. *Tours* by arrangement 6.30pm Mon-Fri; prices vary.
Admission free. **Map** p320 O7.
Despite the fact that this ancient institution, which dates from 1484 (the present building is from the 17th century), is very much concerned with families and their lineage, it's not the sort of place to visit with very young and/or noisy children. Royal heralds work here, granting and designing coats of arms and checking family pedigrees (the old-fashioned form of DNA testing). A large, roped-off throne bears the dark red Queen's Cushion, which, although at each of the last three coronations, is starting to look a little tacky. If you wish to trace your roots, ask to see the Officer in Waiting and expect to pay him a fee to look up the information (the price depends on how long it takes; if it's very quick it could be free). It helps to bring with you a family tree, going back as far as possible.

Nearest picnic place: St Paul's Cathedral garden. Shop.

Dr Johnson's House

17 Gough Square, off Fleet Street, EC4 (7353 3745/ www.drjh.dircon.co.uk). Chancery Lane or Temple tube (both closed Sun)/Blackfriars tube/rail. **Open** *May-Sept* 11am-5.30pm Mon-Sat. *Oct-Apr* 11am-5pm Mon-Sat. Closed 24-26 Dec, 1 Jan, bank hols. *Tours* by arrangement; groups of 10 or more only. **Admission** £4; £3 concessions; £1 under-14s; free under-5s; £9 family (2+unlimited children). *Tours* free. *Evening tours £5-£8 per head.* **No credit cards. Map** p320 N6.

The recently refurbished Dr Johnson's House presents artefacts and mementoes from the great lexicographer's life. No special arrangements are made to visiting children, but the curator does visit schools and libraries to present outreach workshop sessions on 18th-century life in general and Johnson's in particular.

Nearest picnic place: Lincoln's Inn Fields/The Temple. Shop.

Guildhall

Gresham Street, EC2 (7606 3030/tours ext 1463/ www.corpoflondon.gov.uk). Bank tube/DLR. **Open** *May-Sept* 10am-5pm daily. *Oct-Apr* 10am-5pm Mon-Sat. Last entry 4.30pm. Closed 25, 26 Dec, 1 Jan. *Tours* by arrangement; groups of 10 or more people only. **Admission** free. **Map** p320 P6.

For more than 800 years, Guildhall has been the centre of the City's local government (as well as the site of major trials such as those of Lady Jane Grey and Archbishop Thomas Cranmer in 1553). The stunning 15th-century Great Hall was gutted during the Great Fire and again in the Blitz, but has been sensitively restored. It is decorated with the banners and shields of the 100 Livery Companies; the windows record the names of every Lord Mayor since 1189; and there are monuments to Wellington, Nelson, Churchill and the two Pitts. Look out for the almost oriental-looking statues of legendary giants Gog and Magog guarding the West Gallery. They are post-war replacements for originals destroyed in the Blitz; the phoenix on Magog's shield symbolises renewal after fire.

Meetings of the Court of Common Council (the governing body for the Corporation of London, presided over by the Lord Mayor) are held here once a month on a Thursday at 1pm, except during August (visitors welcome; phone for dates). The hall is also used for banquets and ceremonial events. Below the Guildhall is the largest medieval crypt in London, which can be accessed as part of a guided tour only.

The buildings alongside house Corporation offices, the Guildhall Library (partly financed by Mayor Dick Whittington's estate and the first local authority-funded public library), as well as a shop with books on London and the Clockmakers' Company Museum. *See also below.*

Buggy access. Lifts.

Guildhall Art Gallery

Guildhall Yard, off Gresham Street, EC2 (7332 3700/ www.guildhall-art-gallery.org.uk). Mansion House or St Paul's tube/Bank tube/DLR/Moorgate tube/rail. **Open** 10am-5pm Mon-Sat (last entry 4.30pm); noon-4pm Sun (last entry 3.45pm). Closed 24-26 Dec, 1 Jan. **Admission** £2.50; £1 concessions; free under-16s. Free to all after 3.30pm daily, all day Fri. **Credit** *over £5* MC, V. **Map** p320 P6.

The Guildhall Art Gallery appeals to younger teenagers of an artistic bent. Nonetheless, school groups come not only to admire the art as art, but also for the history and sociology, as many of the paintings depict aspects of the capital's life. Teachers, applying in advance, receive a pack that tells them exactly how the exhibits accord with the national curriculum. The 250 paintings on display are part of a col-

It's as easy as falling over: **Broadgate Ice Rink**. *See p46.*

lection of 4,000 owned by the local council, the Corporation of London. A computerised search facility, the Collage System, lets visitors carry out searches of the collections, and is also available online on the website.

The gallery has three floors. One of the paintings, John Singleton Copley's *Siege of Gibraltar*, is two storeys tall and holds the record as the largest painting in Britain. You can see it from both the upper and middle levels. Although it records a naval victory over the Spanish, it also depicts scenes of improbable fair play and gallantry as the jolly British jack-tars haul from the water those luckless marineros whose ships they have just torched and sunk.

On the top floor are the pictures of London, including market, street, river, park and parliamentary scenes, dozens of cityscapes and portraits of dignitaries and former Lord Mayors of London. In the middle level (ground floor) there are contemporary paintings including two new rooms devoted to numerous works of Sir Matthew Smith (1879-1959), a follower of Matisse and the violently colourful Fauvists.

The basement houses the Victorian paintings that formed the bulk of the collection when the gallery was opened in the 19th century. It soon became renowned for daring and innovative exhibitions, especially of the Pre-Raphaelite Brotherhood, whom Dickens derided and accused of blasphemy. The collection still has a large number of Pre-Raphaelite paintings by Dante Gabriel Rossetti, William Holman Hunt and John Everett Millais, the founders of the movement.

The original gallery burned down during World War II, albeit with remarkably little damage to the collection. The excavations that were carried out for the new building in the 1990s revealed the remains of the ancient Roman 11,000-seat amphitheatre. Lines in the new courtyard show the curve of the gladiatorial arena. Plans to allow the public access to the ruins are still at the talking stage.

Buggy access. Lift. Shop.

A **Monument** to cowboy builders.

The Monument

Monument Street, EC3 (7626 2717). Monument tube.
Open 10am-5.40pm daily. Closed 25, 26 Dec, 1 Jan.
Admission £1.50; 50p 5-15s; free under-5s.
No credit cards. Map p321 Q7.
Children are quite easily persuaded of the excitement of climbing high towers, and the Monument, with its 311 steps, is one of the highest. Here you also get the added benefit of receiving a certificate of accomplishment once you've made it back down again. The tower commemorates the Great Fire of London in 1666. It was built by Sir Christopher Wren, who was the chief architect in the reconstruction of the City after the conflagration. At its head is a flaming urn of gilt bronze. Relief sculptures at the bottom depict souls in hell and enumerate the losses. Because few people came to any harm, the fire was soon recognised as a hellfire warning from God not, alas, of dodgy building practices but of Roman Catholic Popery. A Latin inscription alleging this was erased in 1860.
Nearest picnic place: riverside by London Bridge.

Museum of London

150 London Wall, EC2 (7600 3699/24hr info 7600 0807/ www.museumoflondon.org.uk). Barbican or St Paul's tube/Moorgate tube/rail. **Open** 10am-5.50pm Mon-Sat;
noon-5.50pm Sun. Closed 24-26 Dec, 1 Jan. **Admission** (tickets valid for 1 yr) £5; £3 concessions; free under-16s, registered disabled. Free for all after 4.30pm. **Credit** *Shop* AmEx, MC, V. **Map** p320 P5.
The approach to this museum, through the windswept city walkways above screaming traffic, is the most unattractive thing about it. It's built on the site of a Roman fort, in the middle of a roundabout where Aldersgate Street meets London Wall. Once you've found the entrance, however, locale difficulties are forgotten. This is a truly inspiring museum and a must-see for anyone wanting to trace the history of this city, from prehistoric times to the present day.

School groups of the Year 3 age group, studying the Roman Empire, vie for space around the galleries dedicated to Roman London: you see how they cooked, what they ate, what their houses were like, you even meet an actor in the guise of a Roman, chatting excitedly about the mod cons in her villa. Other popular galleries include the Cheapside hoard (a cache of fine jewels, dating from 1560 to 1640, found in a box under a shop); and the Great Fire Experience, an illuminated model with sound effects and commentary depicting the fire that destroyed four-fifths of London in 1666. Reconstructions of Newgate prison cells, the Lord Mayor's ceremonial coach, and shop/restaurant interiors from Victorian and Edwardian London all help to create an atmospheric and informative experience. A new gallery on the lower ground floor, called World City, is concerned with social history from 1789 to 1914; artefacts include Nelson's sword and Queen Victoria's parliamentary robe. Phone for details of tours.
Buggy access. Café. Lift. Nappy-changing facilities. Nearest picnic place: benches outside museum/grassy area by London Wall. Shop.

Museum of Methodism & John Wesley's House

Wesley's Chapel, 49 City Road, EC1 (7253 2262). Old Street or Moorgate tube/rail. **Open** 10am-4pm Mon-Sat. Closed 25 Dec-1 Jan, bank hols. *Tours* free; ad hoc arrangements on arrival. **Admission** £4; £2 concessions, under-16s; additional visits free within same month.
No credit cards.
Dressing-up clothes may be given to children who visit this lovingly cared-for museum, especially if they have booked their tour in advance. There is a preacher's rig for boys and a housekeeper's outfit for girls. Nowadays we might blanch at such gender stereotyping, but the 18th century was rigidly different. Indeed, the methodical non-conformist religion of prayer and fasting that was founded by John Wesley and his brother Charles was much less child-friendly then than it is now among its 50 million adherents. Highlights of the museum, which is in the crypt of the Chapel, include the pulpit that John used and a large oil portrait of the tender scene at his death bed. Museum guides can give religious, drama and music instruction if desired (the Wesley brothers wrote solemn hymns, many of which are still in use and the chapel here is the actual one that John Wesley built and preached in). Children aged from 7-11 are provided with colouring-in worksheets.

His house next door has been restored to its original Georgian interior design, right down to the paint that Wesley would have chosen. In the kitchen and study you can see his nightcap, preaching gown and, bizarrely, his personal experimental electric-shock machine. On the walkway to the Barbican above the southern end of Aldersgate Street stands the petrified tree under which John Wesley saw the light. Free tours can normally be arranged on arrival.
Nearest picnic place: enclosed courtyard at entrance. Shop.

Top: Picnic spots

It's not all concrete in the City. Take a packed lunch to eat in the gardens below.

Gardens of Barber-Surgeon's Hall
Monkwell Square, EC2. *See p50.*

Churchyard of St Botolph
Bishopsgate, EC2. *See p50.*

Finsbury Circus
EC2. *See p46.*

Postman's Park
King Edward Street, EC1. *See p50.*

Gardens of St Bartholomew-the-Great
West Smithfield, EC1. *See p51.*

Orange peals

The children's nursery rhyme *Oranges and Lemons* commemorates a number of London churches and their bells, most of which are in the City of London. Traditionally, people born within earshot of 'Bow Bells' (the bells of St Mary-le-Bow) are reckoned to be the only true cockneys.

'Oranges and Lemons, say the bells of St Clements'
St Clement Eastcheap, Clements Lane, EC4 (7626 0220). Monument tube/Bank tube/DLR. **Open** *8am-5pm Mon-Fri; by appointment Sat.* **Admission** *free.* **Map** *p301 Q7.*
Oranges and lemons were unloaded from ships moored at London Bridge and left in the church's porch as a gift, which all but guarantees the validity of its claim to be the original church in the rhyme. Sadly, its bells no longer ring. The church of St Clement Danes outside the City in the Strand, WC2, also reckons to be the oranges-and-lemons church, though its claim is probably bogus. Nevertheless, it does have a magnificent peal of bells, which periodically rings out the nursery rhyme tune, and the church holds an annual oranges-and-lemons children's service in March. *Buggy access.*

'You owe me five farthings, say the bells of St Martins'
St Martin-within-Ludgate, Ludgate Hill, EC4 (7248 6054). St Paul's tube. **Open** *11am-3pm Mon-Fri.* **Admission** *free.* **Map** *p320 O6.*
St Martin's has two bells, neither of which now ring. One is in the belfry, the other in the main body of the church standing on an iron chest. It was presented to the church by the Scriveners' Guild in 1683 to commemorate its reconstruction by Sir Christopher Wren after the Great Fire of London in 1666 in which its predecessor was destroyed. *Nearest picnic place: St Paul's Cathedral garden.*

'When will you pay me, say the bells of Old Bailey'
St Sepulchre-without-Newgate, Holborn Viaduct, EC1 (7248 3826). St Paul's tube. **Open** *noon-2pm Tue, Thur; 11am-3pm Wed.* **Tours** *free; by arrangement.* **Admission** *free; donations appreciated.* **Map** *p320 O6.*
St Sepulchre's, at the top of the street called Old Bailey, has a complete set of 12 140-year-old bells, which ring every Saturday morning and on frequent weekday evenings when the campanologists gather to rehearse. The church also possesses the execution handbell from old Newgate Prison, which would be rung slowly on the morning of a hanging but is now only tolled for visiting schoolchildren. While you're here, check out the glorious stained-glass windows (*pictured*). *Buggy access. Nearest picnic place: churchyard.*

'When I grow rich, say the bells of Shoreditch'
St Leonard, 120 Shoreditch High Street, E1 (7739 2063). Old Street or Liverpool Street tube/rail. **Open** *Oct-Mar noon-2pm Mon-Fri. Apr-Sept 10am-4pm Mon-Fri.* **Admission** *free.* **Map** *p321 R5.*
Shoreditch's line in the nursery rhyme reflects the poverty in the borough: the bells' answer is tantamount to 'never'. The 13 bells ring from 10am on most Sundays and often during the week. Each bell is named after one of the apostles, except that Paul replaces the traitor Judas and the 13th is named Messias. The present set was cast in 1997 and replaces an older peal of which the great tenor bell has been kept in the church below for the amazement of visiting schoolchildren. *Buggy access. Nappy-changing facilities. Nearest picnic place: church gardens. Lift.*

'When will that be, say the bells of Stepney'
St Dunstan & All Saints, Stepney High Street, E1 (7791 3545). Stepney Green tube. **Open** *by appointment only; phone for details.* **Admission** *free.*
The new set of ten bells at Stepney were looking for bellringers at press time. Sadly, the church has suffered at the hands of vandals so phone first. *Buggy access. Nappy-changing facilities.*

'I do not know, says the great bell of Bow'
St Mary-le-Bow, Cheapside, EC2 (7248 5139). Mansion House or St Paul's tube/Bank tube/DLR. **Open** *6.30am-6pm Mon-Thur; 6.30am-4pm Fri.* **Admission** *free.* **Map** *p320 P6.*
The Great Bell of Bow is the large tenor bell that often tolls alone among the full set of 12 Bow Bells. It is these that Dick Whittington is said to have heard calling him back to London: the 12 letters of D WHITTINGTON are stamped on them. From the 15th to the 19th centuries they were rung daily at 5.45am to wake everyone in London and again at 9pm to tell them it was time for bed. They were destroyed in the war and recast in the 1960s. *Buggy access. Café. Nearest picnic place: churchyard.*

This two-hour walk follows the course of the old Roman and medieval wall as marked by 21 tiled panels between Tower Hill and Blackfriars tube stations. Some have gone missing, which isn't exactly helpful as each panel tells you where the next is to be found. The walk includes various picnic places and sandwich bars and may be completed with a pushchair (just ignore the short high walkway section, which you can bypass at ground level).

▶ Start at **Tower Hill tube**. Walk the short underpass towards the Tower of London. Stop at the iron railing. **Panel 1** marks the site of a medieval city gate. Retrace your steps back through the underpass to find **panel 2**. There is a bench nearby, a statue of a Roman emperor and a slab with a Latin inscription. Visit the giant sundial on the mound where public executions took place. Continue along Cooper's Row. **Panel 3** is missing but the Roman wall is there.

▶ Walk under the railway bridge by Fenchurch Street Station. Turn right into Crosswall and left at the Angel pub into Vine Street. **Panel 4** is at Emperor House. Enter through the tradesman's gate. The Roman wall is in the cellar but visible from the outside through windows.

▶ At the end of Vine Street, turn left into India Street and right into Jewry Street. Go to the end and cross Aldgate. **Panel 5** is on the wall of the Sir John Cass Foundation Primary School. The Roman wall lies below the street. Descend to see **panel 6**.

Panel 7 is in Bevis Marks by the Spanish and Portuguese Synagogue (built 1700), which was a sanctuary for refugees from the Inquisition. **Panel 8** was blown up by an IRA bomb in 1993, which shattered Bishopsgate. The Roman wall was already rubble and ran through the beautiful churchyard of **St Botolph**. Continue into **London Wall**. The church of All Hallows is built against the medieval brickwork, which is built on the Roman wall. **Panel 9** should be at St Botolph-without-Bishopsgate but there is no sign of it. **Panel 10** is in the yard. **Panel 11** should be at the junction of Moorgate and London Wall but isn't.

▶ Climb the steps to the pedestrian walkway and follow St Alphage Highwalk. After a short distance descend into **St Alphage Garden**, where the ancient wall is long and sturdy. **Panel 12** is here. Water has seeped under the grouting and frost has burst the tiles. Walk on to Wood Street, where **panel 13** is tucked behind a motor cycle park. It marks the site of Cripplegate, which was the northern entrance to the Roman fort. Walk towards the Crewers Well pub and turn left into the pedestrian precinct around the church of St Giles Cripplegate. **Panel 14** is attached to railings beside a plaque commemorating the churchyard's victory in the 1972 Britain in Bloom competition. Gates prevent further progress. Return and pass panel 13 again. Ascend the steps at the western end of St Alphage Garden.

▶ Descend by steps to the gardens by **Barber-Surgeon's Hall**. **Panel 15** has escaped the vandals. Not so **panels 16** and **17**, which once recorded the history of the two west wall towers standing in this spacious park. Barber-Surgeon's Tower was built on to the Roman wall in the 13th century. The ruins now enclose a discreet herb garden, which is appropriate to the members' medical calling. **Panel 18** lies at the bottom of a service road. It describes the western gate into the Roman city, the ruins of which are in the subterranean car park.

▶ Cross London Wall and enter Noble Street. The Roman wall is long and impressive here. **Panel 19** has disappeared but **panel 20** looks down on to the ruined south-west corner of the fort. At the end of Noble Street, turn right into Gresham Street and right again into Aldersgate Street. Cross over and enter **Postman's Park**, which is famous for its Heroes' Wall, which commemorates suicidal acts of bravery usually involving rescuing children from burning buildings at the end of the 19th century. (Opposite the entrance to the park is **panel 21**.) Exit the park by its west gate and turn left into **King Edward Street**, where you can see St Paul's Cathedral from the north.

▶ Turn right into Newgate Street and left into **Old Bailey**. Avoid the paparazzi waiting for the arrival of a criminal outside the Central Criminal Courts. The Roman wall runs through the courtroom cellar but the public may not see it. They may, however, enter to watch British justice in action. Continue to the end of Old Bailey, then cross Ludgate Hill, enter Pageantmaster Court, walk through into Ludgate Broadway and straight on into narrow **Blackfriar's Lane**. Cross Queen Victoria Street and turn into **Puddle Dock**, where the Romans lined the embankment with wooden wharves and left a boat in the mud for us to discover, which we did in 1962, along with some coins from the reign of the Emperor Domitian (AD 81-96), which are now in the **Museum of London** (see p48). Here the Roman wall met the Thames and you meet Blackfriars railway station.

Old Bailey (Central Criminal Court)

corner of Newgate Street & Old Bailey, EC4 (7248 3277). St Paul's tube. **Open** *Public gallery* 10.30am-1pm, 2-4pm Mon-Fri. Closed Easter, Whitsun, 24 Dec-1 Jan, bank hols. **Admission** free. No under-14s; 14-16s accompanied by adults only. **Map** p320 O6.

Britain's most famous courts of law are open to anyone over the age of 14. There are 18 courts, and members of the public may attend any of them. Visitors should go to the front of the building in Old Bailey Street where a list of the courts and what trials are to be heard in them is fixed to the wall. Most of the high-profile trials in which the press are interested take place in Court no.1. Visitors for courts 1-4 then queue at the entrance in Newgate Street; those for courts 5-18 at the entrance in Warwick Place. Note that no one with electronic equipment, mobile phones, tape or CD players, large bags or food will be admitted.

Nearest picnic place: Greyfriars Gardens/Newgate Street.

St Bartholomew's Hospital Museum

West Smithfield, EC1 (7601 8152/tours 7837 0546). Barbican or St Paul's tube. **Open** 10am-4pm Tue-Fri. Closed 24 Dec-1 Jan, bank hols. *Tours* 2pm Fri. **Admission** free. *Tours* £4; £3 concessions; accompanied children free. **No credit cards**. **Map** p320 06.

GCSE school groups studying the History of Medicine and Nursing add this small but fascinating museum to the circuit that includes the Old Operating Theatre (*see p39*) and the Florence Nightingale Museum (*see p35*). It is situated on the ground floor of the north wing of St Bartholomew's Hospital, which, along with the beautiful church of St Bartholomew-the-Great, was built by Henry I's jester as a thanksgiving for his recuperation from malaria. The glass case of old gory instruments holds most fascination for young visitors.

It contains a wooden head on which student doctors practised their drilling technique. Early stethoscopes, instruments for bleeding patients and restraining trusses give a vivid idea of the crudity of bygone practices. A display of nursing uniforms shows how closely care and femininity were associated in previous decades.

Buggy access. Nearest picnic place: hospital grounds. Shop.

St Paul's Cathedral

Ludgate Hill, EC4 (7236 4128/www.stpauls.co.uk). St Paul's tube. **Open** 9am-5.15pm Mon-Sat; services only Sun, 25 Dec. *Galleries, crypt & ambulatory* 9.30am-4pm Mon-Sat. Closed for special services, sometimes at short notice. *Tours* 11am, 11.30am, 1.30pm, 2pm Mon-Sat. **Admission** *Cathedral, crypt & gallery* £5; £2.50 6-16s; £4 concessions; free under-6s. *Tours* £2.50; £1 6-16s; £2 concessions; free under-6s. **Audio guide** £3; £2 concessions. **Credit** MC, V. **Map** p320 06.

This astonishing landmark is thought to be built on the site of King Ethelbert's first wooden church, dating from AD 604. This burned down, as did two more Saxon cathedrals thereafter. The Normans constructed 'Old St Paul's' at the end of the 11th century, and that was the one destroyed in the Great Fire of 1666. The present building was built in 35 years by Sir Christopher Wren, with a bit of help from his master builder (Thomas Strong).

The climb to the Whispering Gallery in the dome is the highlight of any trip, for visitors of any age (provided they can make it up the stairs). Two people sitting diametrically opposite each other in the gallery will be able to hear each other even if they mumble. The uncomfortable feeling of vertigo is more acute here than it is higher up at the Stone Gallery or even the Golden Gallery, 530 steps above the street, both of which look out on to London spread out below. The treasures of St Paul's are many. Holman Hunt's famous Pre-Raphaelite

Suicidal selflessness is honoured in **Postman's Park**. *See p50*.

A day at: The Tower of London

William the Conqueror's stronghold has been the scene of some of the worst cases of child brutality in Britain's history. King Edward V, aged 13, and his little brother Richard were imprisoned and murdered in the Bloody Tower in 1483, presumably by their uncle the Duke of Gloucester, who was supposed to be looking after them. (Suspicion rests on him because he benefited by becoming King Richard III.) There is plenty to terrify young girls, too. Lady Jane Grey, the nine-day queen, was only 16 when she was beheaded on Tower Green in 1554. Indeed, five of the seven people ever dispatched here were women, two of them – Anne Boleyn and Katherine Howard – wives of Henry VIII.

Today, visits by families and schoolchildren are encouraged. At half-terms and holidays, 'Family Trail' booklets are available from the tent inside the main entrance at the West Gate. One, written in rhyme, is aimed at five- to nine-year-olds. It conducts them to the various parts of the tower and asks simple questions, which lead to a final riddle. The other, aimed at older children, similarly requires answers as it progresses around the site towards a denouement but

provides more factual information en route. Both include colouring-in cartoons drawn by one of the yeoman warders, or 'Beefeaters'. These are the uniformed guardians of the Tower who entertain groups of visitors with facts and anecdotes in booming military voices.

School visits take place throughout the day. Many of the children come from all over the world. Two-hour group sessions include a workshop and an activity. The workshops feature talks, slide shows and an opportunity to look at and examine historic objects. Infants look at castles and the relative security of different building materials in a session entitled 'Three Little Pigs'. Activities might be brass-rubbing, document-making or a re-enactment of a coronation. The education centre has its own replica crown jewels collection.

Children of a certain age show great interest in the real thing in the Jewel House. Younger visitors, meanwhile, are more taken with the moving walkways than the bejewelled crowns and coronets in glass boxes, which glide by like prizes in a game show. Older children find the whole castle with its many rooms a vehicle for fantasy, especially the Medieval Palace, which has a permanent staff of costumed historian-guides, most of them former teachers. Younger children take pleasure in the sentries, who occasionally jerk into life or bellow, 'Make way for the Queen's guard!' at idling tourists who wander into their path.

The ravens at the Tower hold a fascination for all ages, but the education department's session called Charlie the Raven is aimed at 3- to 7-year-olds. There is a legend that if the ravens leave the Tower, it will fall down. Some of the birds talk and all of them wear coloured ankle tags for identification. In the days of public execution, when the heads of traitors would be impaled on poles outside the gates, the ravens made themselves useful by picking off the flesh and swallowing the eyeballs. This has given them a bad reputation and accounts for the collective term that describes them – an 'unkindness'.

The Tower of London

Tower Hill, EC3 (7709 0765/www.hrp.org.uk).
Tower Hill tube/Fenchurch Street rail. **Open** *Mar-Oct* 9am-5pm Mon-Sat; 10am-5pm Sun. *Nov-Feb* 10am-4pm Mon, Sun; 9am-4pm Tue-Sat. Closed 24-26 Dec, 1 Jan. *Tours* Beefeater tours (outside only, weather permitting) free; half-hourly 9.25am-2.50pm daily. *Short talks* given by yeoman warder (40min) free; advance tickets from kiosk outside Lanthorn Tower 3 times a day. **Admission** £11.30; £8.50 concessions; £7.50 5-15s; family £34 (2+3); free under-5s. **Audio guides** £3.
Credit AmEx, MC, V. **Map** p321 R7.
Nappy-changing facilities. Café. Nearest picnic place: Trinity Square Memorial Gardens – riverside benches. Shop.

Sightseeing

painting of the *Light of the World* hangs in the south aisle. So-called 'super-tours' allow visitors access to the choir where the dark wooden stalls are carved by Grinling Gibbons. They are filled most evenings of the year by the choir. Be sure not to miss the crypt. Lord Nelson is buried there in a magnificent tomb alongside other British war heroes and Wren himself. The cathedral tea shop is conveniently placed down here. In the clock tower on the West Front hangs 'Great Paul', the heaviest swinging bell in England. It is tolled daily at 1pm.

St Paul's distinguishes itself among London's other 'visitor attractions' by its dearth of free trails, guides, workshops or other activities for young visitors. Everyone aged over six has to pay for the privilege of experiencing Sir Christopher Wren's masterpiece. A new guidebook, the *St Paul's Cathedral Maths Trail*, aimed at 11- to 14-year-olds, is available at the cathedral bookshop (£3.99). It requires children to visit specific locations in the building from where they must count spires, floor tiles, etc, or identify particular geometric shapes. Also available is the less-taxing *St Paul's Explorers' Guide* (£1.99), aimed at kids of all ages.
Café. Restaurant. Nearest picnic space: Cathedral garden. Lifts. Shop.

Temple of Mithras
on the raised courtyard in front of Sumitomo Bank/Legal & General Building, Temple Court, 11 Queen Victoria Street, EC4. Mansion House tube. **Open** *24hrs daily.* **Admission** free. **Map** p320 P6.
During the third century AD, the rival cults of Mithraism and Christianity were battling for supremacy. The worship of the macho Persian god Mithras appealed particularly to Roman soldiers, and the troops on the British frontier built the small temple to their champion near this spot (cAD 240-250). The reconstructed foundations (which haven't changed since they were unearthed in 1954) aren't much to look at, but you can stop and rest awhile on the park bench provided.

Tower Bridge Experience
SE1 (7403 3761/www.towerbridge.org.uk). Tower Hill tube/London Bridge tube/rail. **Open** *Apr-Oct* 10am-6.30pm daily. *Nov-Mar* 9.30am-6pm daily. Last entry 1hr 15min before closing. Closed 24-25 Dec, 16 Jan. **Admission** (includes guided tour) £6.25; £4.25 5-15s, concessions; £18.25 family (2+2); free under-5s. **Credit** AmEx, MC, V. **Map** p321 R8.
The 'experience' involves much stair-climbing up one tower and down the other, with excellent views over London from the high-level walkway between the two. Unfortunately, you have to go around as part of a group, which means that fractious minors who want to race ahead have to be restrained and made to listen to the series of presentations at each of the various levels detailing the different stages – political, financial, scientific – in the story of the famous drawbridge. These talks are mostly given by lifesize puppets mouthing to taped voices that are initially intriguing but which after a while imbue the whole experience with a feeling of neglect. There's also no opportunity to ask questions.

The tour ends in the engine rooms, which house the steam pump engines used to raise the bridge until 1976 (it's all done by electrics now). To find out when the bridge will next be

The glory of **St Paul's Cathedral**. See p51.

Take them to the **Tower of London**. See p52.

Eating & shopping

There are plenty of eating possibilities in the area. Any number of sandwich bars, and the ever-enticing **Pret a Manger**, will provide delightful picnic fare to eat in local spots (for the best of these, *see p48*).

The always-popular **Pizza Express** (125 London Wall, EC2, 7600 8880; *see also p185*) provides a decent lunch after a morning at the Museum of London. Noodles and more noodles are served at the authentically Japanese **Noto Ramen House** (Bow Bells House, 7 Bread Street, EC4, 7329 8056), although the atmosphere is a tad brusque for toddlers and pushchair laden families. **Café Flo** (38-40 Ludgate Hill, EC4, 7329 3900; *see also p184*), **Café Rouge** (140 Fetter Lane, EC4, 7242 3469; *see also p184*) and **Hillgate House** (Limeburner Lane, EC4, 7329 1234) all have a children's menu and the odd high chair. There are also plenty of branches of **EAT**, a great little lunch venue for soups, sandwiches, salads and takeaways, at Cornhill, Cannon Street, Fenchurch Street and London Wall.

Shops in the City tend to be of a rather grown-up nature. The most interesting, as far as children are concerned, are those irresistible money-magnets, museum gift shops, especially those at the **Tower of London** (*see p52*) and the **Museum of London** (*see p48*). **Leadenhall Market** (Whittington Avenue, off Gracechurch Street, EC3) is a charming place to wander around. It has been done up in recent years, and names such as **Jigsaw** and **Hobbs** have moved in to serve City fashion palates. The food stalls are worth a gander – check out the wet fish stall and its luxury lobsters. Otherwise, it's mainly well-heeled chains. The shops at Liverpool Street Station's mall include a cool **Space NK** and **Next**, and there are branches of **Books etc** all over the place.

lifted (usually at least once a day), and the name and type of vessel passing beneath, phone 7940 3984. There are one or two models of the bridge on the top level and, at the end of the descent, a glass case containing the silver London Marathon cup, because Tower Bridge is where the race ends each year.

Buggy access. Lifts. Nappy-changing facilities. Nearest picnic place: William Curtis Park/Tower of London gardens. Shop.

Meet the teacher

Liz Denton is Education Officer for the Royal Armouries at the Tower of London (*see p52*).

What do you do?
My job involves the delivery of teaching sessions to a wide range of schoolchildren, developing new teaching sessions, organising pubic events, answering enquiries and doing outreach in hospitals, schools or libraries.

What activities do children request most?
It's usually the teachers who do the requesting! In general,

though, children want to know about the Tower of London and the city as a whole and also about the Tudors. Teachers tend to request information to do with castles or the Tudors or armour.

What's the best part of your job?
The bit I like most is getting to handle really old objects. I love touching things that are hundreds of years old, and having my hands on real history. I had to deal with

Charles I's armour recently. Can you imagine that? The very helmet and breastplate he wore! That was very exciting.

Do you wear a uniform?
No. But we do have a smart-casual dress code, which means no jeans. We look exactly how a teacher would do in the classroom.

Sightseeing

Bloomsbury & Holborn

Best of British.

The tension that has long existed between spendthrift Westminster and the industrious City, the monarch and the merchants, is mediated by the lawyers in the middle – that is, in the WC (West Central) postcodes that this chapter covers. Bewigged judges in the **Royal Courts of Justice** preside over bankruptcies, libel cases and family disputes, while lawyers operate from chambers in quaint, quiet Gray's Inn, Lincoln's Inn and Temple, which have hardly changed since Dickens' day.

The great writer lived at three different addresses in this heterogeneous area, which he described in many of his novels (*see p59*). His was an era when London expanded greatly, when its gaps were filled in with beautiful stucco terraces and great railway stations that dispersed the wealth of empire, when history was consolidated in the magnificent **British Museum** and when former royal residences were turned over to the public good.

Victorian expansion was preceded by Georgian humanist philanthropy, of which there's no better example than **Coram's Fields**, once the site of Captain Coram's Foundling Hospital (1742), and now a vast, grassy playground for children. In an early form of private sponsorship, the Foundling Hospital was supported by various artists, whose works are now housed at the **Foundling Museum** (40 Brunswick Square, WC1, 7841 3600; closed for refurbishment until spring 2003). The Foundling Hospital's contemporary legacy is **Great Ormond Street Children's Hospital** (*see 57*).

This is also an area of contemplation, study and research: the **British Museum** and **British Library** occupy considerable acreages (they used to be in the same place but expansion of both resulted in the library moving to new premises at Euston); most of the buildings of University College London (UCL) are here; the aforementioned lawyers pore over tracts and documents in their chambers; and

Mummies (and daddies) at the **British Museum**. *See p57.*

there's **Somerset House**, which houses three stunning collections – the **Courtauld Institute Gallery**, the **Gilbert Collection** and the **Hermitage Rooms** (for all three, *see p58*). There are also children's events and workshops, plus, on the fun side, fountains to run through (*see p60*). Also in the area is the **Museum of the Royal College** of **Surgeons** (35-43 Lincoln's Inn Fields, WC2, 7869 6560; closed for redevelopment until spring 2003), which includes 3,500 exhibits of human and zoological anatomy, among them the skeleton of Caroline Crachami, alias the 'Sicilian Dwarf', who was only 18 inches (45 centimetres) tall when she died aged nine.

Walk: the famous fields of Holborn

▶ Start at Waterloo Bridge, and work out from the steel plaque in the middle of the bridge which buildings you can see on the London skyline, then walk north towards green-domed **Somerset House** (*see p61*), entering via the new glass footbridge from Waterloo Bridge. Turn into the middle of three arches and enter the grand courtyard, where you can relax as the children frolic among the lively water jets. Pass the statue of King George III and come out on to the Strand, which is full of buses heading west. Cross the road, and head straight over to Aldwych and turn right into Houghton Street then left into Clare Market, where the butchers' stalls have been replaced by the buildings of the London School of Economics.

▶ Continue along Portugal Street, where you'll find the **George IV pub**, the successor to the Magpie & Stump that Pickwick visits in Dickens' *The Pickwick Papers*. Turn left into Serle Street and cross Lincoln's Inn Fields, London's largest square. At the north-east corner take Newman's Row to **High Holborn**, where Dickens first had lodgings (now the Prudential Insurance Company, 271 High Holborn, WC1). Carry on for a while, past his old address, before turning left into Gray's Inn Road and eventually left into Gray's Inn Square itself, where you can walk around the lawns. Emerge on to **Theobald's Road**, cross it and continue north along John Street, which leads into Doughty Street, where **Dickens House Museum** (*see p59*) is situated. At the end, turn left into Guilford Street and walk along to the entrance to **Coram's Fields** (*see p57*), which you can enter as long as you haven't lost your kids along the way. Send them to play on the swings, slides and climbing frames. Lie on the grass and do not move until they return and start pestering you for an ice-cream.

Cadets from the Museum & Library of the Order of St John. *See p59.*

GOSH!

One of the most famous paediatric hospitals in the world, 350-bed Great Ormond Street Hospital at 31-35 Great Ormond Street, WC1, celebrates its 150th birthday in 2002.

British Library

96 Euston Road, NW1 (7412 7332/education 7412 7797/www.bl.uk). Euston or King's Cross tube/rail. **Open** 9.30am-6pm Mon, Wed-Fri; 9.30am-8pm Tue; 9.30am-5pm Sat; 11am-5pm Sun. Closed 22-26 Dec, 1 Jan, bank hols. **Admission** free; donations appreciated. **Map** p317 K3.

Not a library where you can borrow books, this is a reading room, research centre and repository of the nation's literary treasures. Works on display in the John Ritblat Gallery include the Magna Carta or 'Great Charter' of 1215, one of the first declarations of democratic rights; the Lindisfarne Gospels of AD 698 (with a special machine turning over the pages in the temperature-controlled glass case); *Alice's Adventures in Wonderland* by Lewis Carroll; the original *Jungle Book* by Rudyard Kipling and some scribbled Beatles' lyrics. There's also a hands-on gallery about the history of book production: the Workshop of Words, Sound & Images, and the Philatelic Exhibition, reckoned to be the finest of its kind in the world. This collection includes an Indian stamp of 1854 with the Queen's head on upside down, and one of only three 1847 penny orange-reds from Mauritius, worth a whopping £1 million. The King's Library, in the heart of the building, is the library of George III, and is housed in a six-storey glass tower beside the café.

The Education Office has an energetic staff devoted to dreaming up exotic workshops, activities and storytelling sessions for children aged 5 to 11 and their families to enjoy. The events are usually run during school holidays and half-terms and are always free, run on a drop-in basis. You can have advance notice of these by joining the Education Department's free mailing list: Education Service, British Library, 76 Euston Road, London, NW1 2DB, or by calling 7412 7797 or by logging on to www.education@bl.uk.

Buggy access. Café. Nappy-changing facilities. Lift. Nearest picnic place: St James' Gardens. Restaurant. Shop.

British Museum

Great Russell Street, WC1 (7636 1555/disabled info 7637 7384/textphone 7323 8920/www.thebritishmuseum.ac.uk). Holborn, Russell Square or Tottenham Court Road tube. **Open** *Galleries* 10am-5.30pm Mon-Wed, Sat, Sun; 10am-8.30pm Thur, Fri. *Great Court* 9am-6pm Mon, 9am-9pm Tue, Wed, Sun; 9am-11pm Thur-Sat; closed 24-26 Dec, 1 Jan. *Highlights tours (90min)* 10.30am, 1.30pm, 2.30pm, 3.30pm. *Focus tours (60min)* 11.30am, 12.30pm. **Admission** free; donations appreciated. *Temporary exhibitions* prices vary; phone for details. *Highlights tours* £7; £4 concessions, 11-16s; under-10s free. *Focus tours* £5; £3 concessions, 11-16s, under-10s free. **Credit** MC, V. **Map** p317 K5.

When visiting this venerable old museum, remember two cardinal rules: go early, and don't try to see everything. A good introduction for novices is the 90-minute tour of the museum's top treasures (they leave from the information desk), and the free 'Eye Openers' tours, which concentrate on specific aspects of the collections (such as 'Europe: Medieval to Modern' or 'Treasures of the Islamic World'). The world-famous Elgin Marbles are on the ground floor, in a gallery to the left as you walk into the Great Court from Great Russell Street. The Egyptian sculpture galleries are on the ground floor, and the Roxie Walker galleries of Egyptian funerary archaeology on the first floor. Glass cases full of mummies snatched from their resting places in the desert sand, are at the rear of the building (Montague Place) on the third floor. And if it's all too much for you before you even start, buy a souvenir guide (£6) and scrutinise the highlights, or try one of the four suggested tours on the leaflets (£2.50).

The light and airy Great Court, which was designed by Norman Foster at a cost of £100 million and opened in December 2000, is a wonder. In the centre is the old Reading Room, where scholars used to read, write and hatch plots to change the world (Karl Marx always sat in desk K1). Now the scholars have decamped to British Library on Euston Road (*see above*) and the Reading Room has become a computer-equipped public library focused on the collections of the museum.

The education department (*see p62* **Meet the teacher**) produces teacher packs on areas of study relevant to the national curriculum; in the Ancient Greek Daily Life room, for instance, kids are asked to draw a ground plan of a Greek house from what is on display. For families, trailsheets and 'Family Backpacks' are available from the information desk in the Great Court. The trailsheets cover, among other topics, human remains (including Egyptian mummies), Money, Greek and Assyrian sculpture, and Vikings, and encourage visitors to make drawings, write poems and consider why particular items have been included in the displays. The backpacks (which you have to return to the museum) relate to specific exhibitions and contain items for discussion – the Aztec pack includes cocoa beans and a piece of turquoise, for example.

The ever-popular sleepovers (based on different themes but children always doss down in the Egyptian sculpture gallery) are open only to Young Friends of the British Museum; the £17.50 annual membership also allows entry to Sunday sessions and receipt of the quarterly magazine *Remus*. See the website for enrolment details.

Buggy access. Cafés. Lifts. Nappy-changing facilities. Nearest picnic place: Russell Square. Restaurant. Shops.

Coram's Fields

93 Guilford Place, WC1 (7837 6138). Russell Square tube. **Open** *Apr-Sept* 9am-7pm daily. *Oct-Mar* 9am-6pm daily. Closed 25, 26, 31 Dec, 1 Jan. **Admission** free (adults only admitted if accompanied by child under 16). **Map** p317 L4.

This wonderful adventure playground was established by newspaper magnate Lord Rothermere on the site of the 18th-century Foundling Hospital, which was demolished in the 1920s (only the street gates remain). The site that the hospital occupied is now given over to lawns, huge sandpits, an astroturf football pitch, an asphalt basketball court, a toddlers' gym and fenced-off play areas with a three-storey wooden climbing tower, a helter-skelter chute, swings and an assault-course pulley (the ground is covered in soft bark to ensure pain-free landings). There's also a café, toilets, a band room, a scouts and guides room, a groundsman's office, and quarters for sheep, goats, geese and peacocks. Sporting activities, such as informal footie and cricket matches, are organised year round. For the under-threes there's a drop-in centre with daily painting sessions and occasional clowns' visits in summer. At the centre of the park a small bandstand is dedicated to the memory of two of Lord Rothermere's sons who died in World War I; in front of it a fountain pool provides welcome relief on hot summer days. Everything is free except the café, which runs to jacket spuds on cold days. *Buggy access. Café. Nappy-changing facilities. Shop.*

Courtauld Institute Gallery

Somerset House, Strand, WC2 (7848 2526/ education 7848 2922/www.courtauld.ac.uk). Covent Garden or Holborn tube. **Open** 10am-6pm daily (last entry 5.15pm); *31 Dec* 10am-4pm; *1 Jan* noon-6pm. Closed 24-26 Dec. **Tours** phone for details. **Admission** £4; £3 concessions; free under-18s, students. Free to all 10am-2pm Mon (not bank hols). *Annual ticket* £10. **Credit** MC, V. **Map** p319 M7.

The bulk of the Courtauld's collection is made up of the Impressionist and post-Impressionist works donated by textile magnate Samuel Courtauld, including Manet's *A Bar at the Folies-Bergère*, Cézanne's *The Card Players* and Gauguin's *Nevermore*. The first Saturday of the month, school holidays and half-terms are given over to family events For details, *see p216*.

The Courtauld throngs with school groups armed with packed lunches and overalls most days of the week in termtime. Those at Key Stages 1, 2 and 3 come from 10.30am until 2pm, enjoy a free guided tour and study paintings in connection with such themes as animals, Bible stories, weather, Greeks and Romans, and light and shade.

Buggy access. Cafés. Lift. Nappy-changing facilities (in Somerset House, near Gilbert Collection entrance). Nearest picnic place: Somerset House Courtyard/ Embankment Gardens. Restaurant. Shop.

Gilbert Collection

Somerset House, Strand, WC2 (7240 4080/ www.gilbert-collection.org.uk). Covent Garden, Holborn or Temple tube (closed Sun). **Open** 10am-6pm daily (last entry 5.15pm); *31 Dec* 10am-4pm; *1 Jan* noon-6pm. Closed 24-26 Dec. **Tours** phone for details. **Admission** £5; £4 concessions; free under-18s, students. Free to all after 4.30pm daily. *Annual ticket* £10. **Credit** AmEx, MC, V. **Map** p319 M7.

This 1,000-strong collection of decorative arts, which includes snuff boxes, silverware, mosaics and micro-mosaics from the 16th to 18th centuries, was given to the nation by Sir Arthur Gilbert, a British-born Californian businessman, who died in 2001. There are family events held regularly throughout the year, with tours of the collection, often with costumed guides. Schoolchildren at Key Stages 1-4 are encouraged to interpret the history of Somerset House in terms of the artefacts in the collection.

Buggy access. Cafés. Lift. Nappy-changing facilities. Nearest picnic place: Somerset House Courtyard, Embankment Gardens. Restaurant. Shop.

Hermitage Rooms

Somerset House, Strand, WC2 (info 7845 4630/ www.hermitagerooms.co.uk). Covent Garden or Temple tube (closed Sun). **Open** 10am-6pm daily (last entry 5pm); *31 Dec* 10am-4pm; *1 Jan* noon-6pm. Closed 24-26 Dec. **Admission** £6; £4 concessions; free under-5s. **Credit** MC, V. **Map** p319 M7.

The Hermitage Rooms in Somerset House (*see p61*) play host to rotating exhibitions from the famous State Hermitage Museum in St Petersburg. Displayed in rooms decorated in the style of the original, new exhibitions arrive every six to ten months. November 2001 sees French Drawings & Paintings: Poussin to Picasso. With each exhibition comes a programme of events. To find out about what's going on here, and in the Courtauld and Gilbert collections, be sure to

The leader of the pack at **Pollock's Toy Museum**. *See p60.*

Where the Dickens...?

Charles Dickens (1812-70) wrote some 15 novels, many of which place heavy emphasis on the lives of children in the Victorian era. The author's own childhood was spent in Chatham, Kent, where his father worked as a naval clerk. In 1823 Dickens senior took a post at **Somerset House** (see p61) and moved his family to Camden Town, where they lived at various addresses for the next ten years and which became the home of various Dickens characters, including Bob Cratchitt from A Christmas Carol and the likeable but unreliable Mr Micawber from David Copperfield. The latter is based on the author's impecunious father (during their time at Camden Town Dickens Senior fell into debt and spent time in prison).

After leaving home, Dickens first lived at Furnival's Inn on Holborn, now the offices of the Prudential Insurance Company. Here he began writing The Pickwick Papers for publication in monthly instalments. In 1837 he married and moved to 48 Doughty Street, WC1, a large, late Georgian house, where he finished writing the book, which was a huge success and largely paid for the house. He then wrote Oliver Twist, about a hungry orphan who falls in with a gang of London pickpockets; Nicholas Nickleby, about a penniless 19-year-old who goes around avenging the victims of abuse; The Old Curiosity Shop, set in the shop of the same name (see p62) near Lincoln's Inn Fields; and Barnaby Rudge, about the half-witted son of a murderer who becomes involved in the real-life anti-Catholic Gordon Riots of 1780, named after the ringleader Charles Gordon.

Dickens House Museum is the sole survivor of the author's various London residences. Only the drawing room has been restored to its original state, but the house is packed with Dickens' effects, including portraits of the author and his family. There is also the room in which his teenage sister-in-law, Mary Hogarth (with whom he had fallen in love), died. Every Wednesday night from April to July, a one-man show, 'The Sparkler of Albion', brings Dickens and his characters to life.

In 1839 Dickens moved to 1 Devonshire Terrace in Marylebone (now Ferguson House), where he wrote Martin Chuzzlewit, the story of a selfish brat who travels to America (as Dickens himself did while writing the book) and is cured of his greed and egocentricity; A Christmas Carol, in which a miser finally mends his ways after dreaming of the death of a poor crippled boy; Dombey and Son, in which an arrogant businessman is humbled by a series of disasters, including the death of his offspring; and David Copperfield, the partly autobiographical tale of a boy who is abused by both his stepfather and headmaster, marries the wrong girl and becomes a famous author. Dickens finally separated from his own wife in 1856.

In 1851 the author moved to Tavistock House in Bloomsbury (now BMA House). Here he wrote Bleak House, a satire on the legal fraternity; Little Dorrit, the story of a young girl who grows up in the debtors' prison where her father is incarcerated; A Tale of Two Cities, a study of child brutality in the French Revolution; and Great Expectations, the adventures of a boy with an unknown benefactor.

In his last decade, he moved to Gad's Hill in Kent, where he finished Great Expectations and wrote Our Mutual Friend, the story of a young man exiled by a harsh father. The Mystery of Edwin Drood, a bewildering story about orphans, was left incomplete at his death.

Dickens House Museum

48 Doughty Street, WC1 (7405 2127/ www.dickensmuseum.com). Chancery Lane or Russell Square tube. **Open** *10am-5pm Mon-Sat. Closed bank hols; phone to check. Tours by arrangement.* **Admission** *£4; £3 concessions; £2 5-15s; £9 family (2+2); under-5s free. Tours free.* **Credit** *Shop AmEx, MC, V.* **Map** *p317 M4.*

get yourself on the Somerset House mailing list (email info@somerset-house.org.uk or write in to request). *Buggy access. Cafés. Lift. Nappy-changing facilities. Nearest picnic place: Somerset House courtyard/ Embankment Gardens. Restaurant. Shop.*

Museum & Library of the Order of St John

St John's Gate, St John's Lane, EC1 (7324 4074/ www.sja.org.uk/history). Farringdon tube/rail. **Open** 10am-5pm Mon-Fri; 10am-4pm Sat. Closed 24 Dec-2 Jan, bank hol weekends; phone to check. **Tours** 11am, 2.30pm Tue, Fri, Sat. **Admission** free; suggested donations for tours £5; £3.50 concessions. **Map** p320 O4.

Though it's more Clerkenwell than Bloomsbury or Holborn, this crusading organisation should not be overlooked – it was out of the Order of St John that the St John Ambulance Brigade rose. Volunteers are trained in first aid and are often to be seen administering it at public events. Child recruits ('Little Badgers' and 'Cadets') are taught the rudiments of first aid and take exams in basic medicine, which like taxi drivers they call 'doing the knowledge'. On completion of their tests they visit the museum and library as a treat. The organisation also runs practical and adventure activities for children, including courses in animal welfare, mountaineering, canoeing and map-reading. Membership is free, though of course you have to buy the black and white uniform.

The museum traces the history of both the Ambulance Brigade and the Order of St John, which began in the 12th century when the crusading Knights Hospitallers acted as guards and superintendents at the Benedictine hospital next to the Holy Sepulchre in Jerusalem. Exhibits include pharmacy jars from the present-day hospital on the Gaza Strip. The magnificent gateway, which dates from 1504, was once the entrance to the Priory of St John of Jerusalem. The Chapter Hall, Council Chamber, Old Chancery, new church and Norman crypt (the sole survivor from the original building)

Marvel at the marbles in
Sir John Soane's Museum. *See p61*

can only be seen on a guided tour. All that remains of the priory's original circular church is its outline, traced in cobbles, in St John's Square just north of the gate. Note that there's buggy access for the ground-floor galleries only.
Buggy access. Shop.

Petrie Museum of Egyptian Archaeology

University College London, Malet Place, WC1 (7679 2884/www.petrie.ucl.ac.uk). Goodge Street tube. **Open** 1-5pm Tue-Fri; 10am-1pm Sat. Closed 24 Dec-2 Jan, Easter hols. **Admission** free; donations appreciated. **Map** p317 K4.
Archaeologist William Flinders Petrie's private collection, donated to UCL in the 1930s, includes the oldest piece of clothing in the world (from 2,800 BC) and an array of Roman mummy portraits, as well as a dazzling collection of the minutiae of Egyptian life, from jewellery and ceramics to games and grooming accessories. Macabre exhibits include an 4,500-year-old exhumed pot-burial and the coiffured head of a mummy, with eyebrows and lashes still intact. There are worksheets on clothing, burial and writing to aid personal research, while family backpacks (available in the summer holidays) lead visitors on trails of exploration. Exhibits are relevant to the study of Ancient Egypt in Key Stage 2. Phone for details of guided tours.
Buggy access. Café. Lifts. Nearest picnic place: Gordon Square.

Pollock's Toy Museum

1 Scala Street (entrance on Whitfield Street), W1 (7636 3452/www.pollocksweb.co.uk). Goodge Street tube. **Open** 10am-5pm Mon-Sat. Last entry 4.30pm. Closed bank hols. **Admission** £3; £1.50 3-18s; free under-3s. **Credit** Shop MC, V. **Map** p316 J5.

The home of thousands of children's toys from the last 150 years, from dolls as big as children, old teddy bears (Eric, stuffed and sewn in 1905, is apparently the oldest known surviving teddy in the world) and platoons of Action Men to miniature dolls' houses, clockwork tin railways and games of Pik-a-Styk, Snap!, Ring-My-Nose Quoits and Snakes & Ladders, all crammed into eight tiny rooms. It doesn't take much to imagine it all coming to life at night. Visitors pay at the old-fashioned till on the ground floor and go up through the house by one narrow, creaky staircase and down by another, finishing in the shop, which sells playing cards, jigsaws, marbles, magic sets and puppets. The toy theatre can be booked for parties (minimum ten children; admission charges as above) and school groups are welcome (call first). *Nappy-changing facilities. Nearest picnic place: Colville Place Gardens.*

Prince Henry's Room

17 Fleet Street, EC4 (7936 4004). Temple tube (closed Sun). **Open** 11am-2pm Mon-Sat. Closed bank hol weekends. **Admission** free; donations appreciated. **Map** p320 N6.
The eldest son of King James I of England and VI of Scotland, weakling Henry was only 14 when he became Prince of Wales in 1610, the same year the house containing this beautiful oak-panelled room, believed to have been used by the prince's lawyers, was built. Its magnificent plaster ceiling has the Prince of Wales' feathers at its centre, together with the initials PH. Henry died of typhoid at the age of 18, leaving his brother to succeed to the throne as Charles I and eventually have his head chopped off after a quarrel with Parliament.
The rest of the building was a tavern called the Prince's Arms that was frequented by Samuel Pepys. Some of the items the diarist left behind in the pub, including a letter he wrote, some model boats in glass cases, a number of framed pictures and a quill pen, are housed in Prince Henry's Room. *Nearest picnic place: Temple Gardens.*

Roman Bath

Strand Lane, WC2 (no phone). Temple tube (closed Sun). **Open** 10am-12.30pm Mon-Fri. **Admission** free. **Map** p319 M7.
Despite its name, no one knows the history of this intriguing relic in the basement of a building in an alley off the Strand. Dickens' hero David Copperfield bathes in it, and presumably the novelist did, too. No longer used as a bath, it has limited opening hours but is visible at other times through a window and by means of a light switch in the wall outside.

St Clement Danes Church

Strand, WC2 (7242 8282). Temple tube (closed Sun). **Open** 9am-4pm Mon-Fri; 9.30am-3pm Sat, Sun. Closed bank hols. **Admission** free. **Map** p320 M6.
Though almost certainly not the church that gave rise to the nursery rhyme 'Oranges and lemons say the bells of St Clements' (it was probably St Clement Eastcheap; *see p49*), this church behaves as if it were – its bells ring out the famous tune three times a day (9am, noon and 3pm), and an annual Oranges & Lemons service is held in April for the children of St Clement Danes Primary School, Drury Lane, WC2, who perform a short play in exchange for a free orange or lemon. The church's curious name dates back to the time of Alfred the Great, when it was used by Danes married to English wives who were allowed to stay in

Water palaver!

Every half hour, the water jets in the courtyard of Somerset House (see p61) perform choreographed displays that see them reaching up to 20 feet (six metres) high.

England after their fellow countrymen were expelled. It's now the central church of the RAF; there's a statue of Arthur 'Bomber' Harris outside (responsible for the raids on Dresden). *Buggy access. Nearest picnic place: Victoria Embankment Gardens.*

St Dunstan in the West

186A Fleet Street, EC4 (7242 6027). Chancery Lane tube. **Open** 10am-2pm Tue; 5-8pm Fri; 2-6pm Sat; 9am-2pm Sun. Closed bank hols. **Admission** free; donations appreciated. **Map** p320 N6.

You don't have to enter this church to see what's most interesting about it – the ancient clock on the outside, which was the first in London to acquire a minute hand, is attached to a great bell. This is struck at a quarter past the hour by two giant clockwork statues that emerge from the background with huge cudgels. Concerts are sometimes held on a Friday. *Buggy access.*

St Etheldreda

14 Ely Place, EC1 (7405 1061). Chancery Lane tube. **Open** 7.30am-7pm daily. Closed 26 Dec. **Admission** free; donations appreciated. **Map** p320 N5.

Britain's oldest Catholic church (built in the 1250s) is the only surviving building of the Bishop of Ely's London residence. Its simple chapel, lined with the statues of local martyrs, is London's sole remaining example (excepting parts of Westminster Abbey; *see p89*) of Gothic architecture from the reign of Edward I. The strawberries once grown in the gardens were said to be the finest in the city, receiving plaudits in Shakespeare's *Richard III*. Every June the church holds a 'Strawberrie Fayre' in Ely Place, which is also the scene of important episodes in Dickens' *David Copperfield*. *Café (closed Sat, Sun).*

Sir John Soane's Museum

13 Lincoln's Inn Fields, WC2 (7405 2107/ www.soane.org). Holborn tube. **Open** 10am-5pm Tue-Sat; 6-9pm 1st Tue of month. Closed bank hol weekends. **Tours** 2.30pm Sat. **Admission** free; donations appreciated. *Tours* £3; free concessions, children. **Credit** *Shop* MC, V. **Map** p317 M5.

One of the best museums in London, this house is full of the multifarious artefacts amassed by its architect-founder. In among the brilliant chaos, Cantonese chairs sit near vases dating from the fourth century BC; a tiny study is made smaller by the assortment of marble bits and pieces glowering from the walls; another wall is covered by Hogarth's *Rake's Progress* series but then opens up to reveal a stash of Piranesi drawings; and there's a huge 3,300-year-old Egyptian sarcophagus downstairs in the spooky crypt. Nothing is labelled and each room differs from the last in its architecture and interplay of light, shadows and reflections. The overall effect is stunning, especially on the first Tuesday of the month, when the house is lit by candles. Tickets for guided tours go on sale at 2pm in the library dining room, on a first-come first-served basis. Give generously; there are plans to open the house next door – also owned by Soane – in 2003. *Nearest picnic place: Lincoln's Inn Fields. Shop.*

Somerset House

Strand, WC2 (7845 4600/www.somerset-house.org.uk). Covent Garden, Holborn or Temple tube (closed Sun). **Open** 10am-6pm daily; extended opening hours for courtyard and terrace. Closed 25 Dec. **Tours** phone for details. **Admission** *Courtyard & terrace* free. Charge for exhibitions. **Credit** *Shop* MC, V. **Map** p319 M7.

The magnificent house was built in the 18th century. George III, whose statue stands inside the Strand entrance,

Wet play at **Somerset House**.

commissioned it after its dilapidated predecessor was pulled down. Inside the southern (riverside) building, the information desk offers six Family Trail leaflets directing the inquisitive to the various parts of the mansion and inviting them to answer questions on and make observations about what is to be found. There's also a full programme of free family events, including puppet performances, storytelling, dance masquerades and painting workshops in the various panelled rooms and the fountain courtyard, where children love to splash around in the water jets (*see p60*). In winter 2000, the courtyard was the venue for an ice rink, but this may not be a regular occurrence so call for details.

The east and west wings are home to the Inland Revenue and are not accessible to the public, but the north and south blocks house three of the most valuable art collections in the capital, the Courtauld Institute Gallery, the Gilbert Collection and the Hermitage Rooms (for all three, *see p58*).
Buggy access. Cafés. Lift. Nappy-changing facilities.
Nearest picnic place: Somerset House Courtyard/River Terrace/Embankment Gardens. Restaurant. Shop.

Eating & shopping

In terms of food, the **North Sea Fish Restaurant** (7-8 Leigh Street, WC1, 7387 5892) is one of the best places to take children for a great British plateful of fish and chips, while pint-sized pasta fans can enjoy reduced-price portions and a cheery atmosphere at **Spaghetti House** (20 Sicilian Avenue, WC1, 7405 5215). **Heal's** homewares shop (196 Tottenham Court Road, WC1, 7636 1666) has an excellent café for those who like to scoff and shop, and a healthy, noodle-based lunch is served by friendly staff at the local Japanese, **Abeno** (47 Museum Street, WC1, 7405 3211), where little ones are given high chairs. More Japanese-inspired nosh is on the menu at the nearby branch of **Yo! Sushi** (myhotel, 11-13 Bayley Street, Bedford Square, WC1, 7636 0076; *see also p185*).

You shouldn't leave the **British Museum** without a spot of retail therapy: pocket money-priced souvenirs (mock scarabs, Egyptian-theme stationery, jigsaws, games and trinkets) can be bought here and at the separate shop on 22 Bloomsbury Street, WC1, (7637 9449). In the streets around the museum there are lots of specialist and general bookshops; the most popular with teenagers is inevitably the schlocky **Forbidden Planet** (71-5 New Oxford Street, WC1, 7836 4179), which stocks all the *Star Wars* and *Buffy* memorabilia a diehard fan could ask for.

If they're into wizardry, visit the magicians' favourite, **International Magic Studio** (89 Clerkenwell Road, EC1, 7405 7324). Here you could spend more than £1,000 on the wherewithal to cut someone in half, though simple tricks cost just a few quid. At **Playin' Games** (33 Museum Street, WC1, 7323 3080), traditional pastimes such as chess and backgammon are sold alongside fantasy and role-play games and newer products such as the Harry Potter board game.

Model Zone (previously called Beatties; 202 High Holborn, WC1, 7405 6285) is deservedly the most successful toy and model shop in the capital. Some computer games are available but the shop keeps the emphasis on the traditional, including Hornby trainsets. The pedallers at **Bikefix** (48 Lamb's Conduit Street, WC1, 7405 1218; *see also p208*) undertake all reasonable repair jobs and custom-build bikes to suit the buyer's physique.

The rickety, low-ceilinged **Old Curiosity Shop** (13-14 Portsmouth Street, WC2, 7405 9891), famous as a result of Dickens' eponymous novel, is now a Japanese-owned fashion shop, selling mainly shoes but also clothing and bags. It's always full of literary-inspired tourists.

Meet the teacher

Madeleine Sarley-Pontin is the Primary Education Officer at the British Museum (*see p57*).

What do you do?
I undertake the development of core programmes for teaching primary schoolchildren. I also write some of the materials and supply the teachers for seminars and other sessions. Occasionally I go out to local authorities on outreach exercises. I also give gallery talks when I can. Pottery is my special subject.

What activities do children request most?
It's actually the teachers who request sessions and workshops

related to the national curriculum. We do our best to make study sessions fun and exciting. The most popular subject is Egyptology, followed by the Ancient Greeks, then the Anglo-Saxons and finally the Mayans and Aztecs. What the children really like to do is hold the statue of a god that's 3,000 years old. Can you imagine that? An ancient Egyptian handled this very object!

What's the best part of your job?
Seeing the children's faces as history comes alive to them just

as it came alive for me once – and still does. In summer 2001 we held a Mummy Show, when we were allowed to present some mummified human remains to the participants. It was very exciting! Outreach is important and rewarding. I recently did a project with Tower Hamlets schools, whose pupils had never been to the museum. I took some of the exhibits to show them.

Covent Garden & St Giles's

The arty heart of London.

Covent Garden is bordered by the Strand to the south, New Oxford Street to the north, Charing Cross Road to the west and Kingsway to the east. It's no surprise that the Bow Street Runners of the 18th century, London's first police force, started out here – at the time it was the most dangerous square mile in the capital, with many juveniles among its legions of criminals. Prior to that the area had been Westminster Abbey's convent garden (hence the name), and as well as a den of prostitution and lawlessness it went on to become London's main flower and veg market.

It was the sleaze and general degeneracy of the area that attracted low-lifers of all sorts, and actors in particular. The theatre world shifted here with the restoration of the monarchy in 1662; before that London's theatres had stood next to the brothels and gambling dens of Southwark, but the puritans shut them down and the playground south of the river went into decline during the Commonwealth. The first playhouse built in Covent Garden was the Theatre Royal Drury Lane, in 1663, and it's now the world's oldest theatre still in use.

Many of the long-running shows in the area's theatres appeal primarily to the young – Andrew Lloyd Webber's *Cats* (*see 227*), responsible for today's face-painting fad, has been running at the New London Theatre, Drury Lane, for nearly 30 years, while Disney's *The Lion King* (*see p228*), the musical of the film of the book, is performed at the Lyceum Theatre in Wellington Street. *Blood Brothers* (*see p227*), the story of twin boys separated at birth, still fills the Phoenix Theatre on Charing Cross Road. Behind it, **Phoenix Garden** is a leafy place for a picnic.

The story of London's theatrical heritage is told in an entertaining and interactive way at the **Theatre Museum** in Russell Street. Next door, **London's Transport Museum** allows members of the public to clamber on to buses, trams and trains that have been saved from the scrapheap. The latest addition to the museum scene is the **Impossible Microworld of Willard Wigan**, where the exhibits are so tiny they have to be observed through a microscope.

In terms of opera, the name Covent Garden is on a par with La Scala in Milan. The venue, which has occupied the same Bow Street site since 1732, is more properly known as the **Royal Opera House**.

Covent Garden's commercial fruit and flower market moved south of the river to Vauxhall in 1973, and its place around the piazza was taken over by shops, bars, cafés, restaurants, craft stalls and licensed street performers, many of whom like to get children involved. It's all very touristy, so expect to pay high prices for snacks and ice-creams.

English National Opera

The Coliseum, St Martin's Lane, WC2 (box office 7632 8300/www.eno.org). Leicester Square tube/ Charing Cross tube/rail. **Open** *Box office* 10am-8pm Mon-Sat. Closed 25 Dec, bank hol Mon. **Tours** 3.30pm 1st Sat of every month that company is in residence. **Admission** *Tours* £5. **Credit** AmEx, MC, V. **Map** p319 L7.

Look and do touch at **London's Transport Museum**. *See p64.*

All fired up in Covent Garden's **piazza**. See p63.

Guided tours of London's largest theatre focus on the front-of-house areas rather than backstage, and though one dressing room is included it only really serves to show how cell-like they are. The foyer is opulent, with mosaic ceilings and huge portraits, including one of the impresario Lilian Baylis. When the theatre was built, in 1904, it hosted a freak show that included appearances by Fräulein Brunnhilde, at almost 8ft (2.4 m) the tallest pianist in the world. In the 1960s it was a cinema; in 1974, it became home to the English National Opera.

Not guaranteed as part of the tour is a sighting of the purported resident ghost, said to be a young World War I soldier killed at Flanders. He spent his last night in London at the theatre and now periodically repeats the steps he took as he made his way to his seat at the front of the dress circle. *Nearest picnic place: churchyard of St Paul's. Shop.*

The Impossible Microworld of Willard Wigan

Lower Courtyard, 33-4 Covent Garden Piazza, WC2 (7240 2120/www.theimpossiblemicroworld.com). Covent Garden tube. **Open** 11am-7pm Mon-Sat; 11am-6pm Sun. Closed 25 Dec, 1 Jan. **Admission** £3.95; £3.45 concessions; £2.95 under-16s; £11.95 family (2+2), £12.95 (2+3); free under-6s. **Credit** MC, V. **Map** p319 L6. Micro-artist Willard Wigan sculpts and paints on an unbelievably small scale – Snow White and the seven dwarves line up in the eye of a needle; the Tower of London stands in all its detail on a grain of rice; a boxing match takes place on a pin-head. The 'wow' factor is all in the extraordinary size – if the sculptures were the size the microscopes blow them up to be, you'd think them rather poorly made. The shop sells the wherewithal to make your own tiny models: magnifying glasses, microscopic sculpting tools and other mini objects. *Nearest picnic place: churchyard of St Paul's. Shop.*

London's Transport Museum

Covent Garden Piazza, WC2 (7379 6344/ www.ltmuseum.co.uk). Covent Garden tube. **Open** 10am-6pm Mon-Thur, Sat, Sun; 11am-6pm Fri. Last entry 5.15pm. **Tours** 11am-4pm Sat, Sun. Check at cloakroom for times. **Admission** £5.95; £3.95 concessions; free under-16s when accompanied by an adult. *Tours* free. **Credit** MC, V. **Map** p319 L7. Nearly two centuries' worth of London buses stand in crimson splendour in the huge display area of this famous museum. The earliest are harnessed to life-size plastic work-horses that kids like to pat, while the most recent, the driver-only 'hopper', attracts queues of small enthusiasts keen to occupy the driver's seat. Most of the exhibits may be clambered on

Walk: to Cleopatra's Needle

▶ Starting at **Covent Garden's Piazza**, walk through the market buildings to **Southampton Street** and keep walking south to the Strand, which runs parallel to the Thames. In German and Old English, Strand means 'beach', and that's exactly what it used to be – a muddy bridle path by the river in any case – before the Victoria Embankment was built in the 1860s. Before you come to the river there are the pretty **Embankment Gardens** to admire. At the entrance to the gardens by Embankment tube station is a covered stage where brass bands, youth orchestras, wind ensembles and other groups play to a deckchair-slumped public all through the summer. Scottish poet Robert Burns is commemorated by a very large statue, as is wordsmith WS Gilbert, who stares up at the Savoy Hotel, which was the scene of his greatest triumphs, in collaboration with composer Arthur Sullivan. The gardens are an ideal place for a picnic.

▶ Across the main road from the gardens, right on the river, is the massive **Egyptian obelisk, Cleopatra's Needle**, which stands nearly 19 metres (60 feet) tall. Obelisks are carved from a single stone; the largest ones were highly revered by the ancient Egyptians. Cleopatra's Needle was quarried in Aswan, transported down the Nile to Helios in 1500 BC, and later taken further still, to

Alexandria, where it fell over in the sand and lay neglected until the Turkish viceroy Mohammed Ali made a present of it to the British in 1819.

No one even considered moving it to London until 1877, when the British decided they wanted it to come home. A special pontoon was designed for it, and it was towed away by ship, nearly sinking during a storm in the Bay of Biscay, where some of the unfortunate crew lost their lives. The obelisk finally made it to the Thames Estuary a year later, when it was erected where it now stands. Beneath it some mementoes of the time were interred: the day's newspapers, four Bibles in different languages, and photographs of 12 of the best-looking Englishwomen of the day (though we're not told who the judges were).

▶ The stone stairs beside Embankment tube station lead up to **Hungerford Bridge**, which takes you across the Thames to the South Bank. This is actually a railway bridge with a pedestrian walkway that is currently undergoing a grand and much-needed refurbishment. The plans include the construction of a second walkway on the other side of the railway tracks, so that there's one for the northwards flow and one for the south. There'll also be niches for buskers, corners for *Big Issue* vendors and lanes for fast and slow walkers.

BE MOVED

London's Transport
Museum

Covent Garden Piazza

Visit us at ltmuseum.co.uk
24 hr info (020) 7565 7299

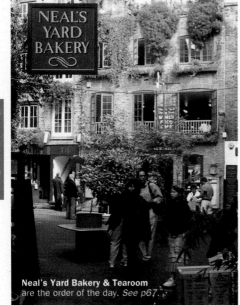

Neal's Yard Bakery & Tearoom are the order of the day. *See p67.*

to; you sit next to uncannily realistic mannequins in period dress. As well as buses there are trams, a steam engine with two carriages (including one ladies-only compartment) and a very old tube train upholstered like a padded cell.

Call for details of the free guided tours run in the school holidays, led by actors in period costume. The history tour, Victorians on the Move, and the science tour, Bright Sparks, include creative workshops and handling sessions. For three-to five-year-olds there are group sessions when they can make bus mobiles and and take turns to board the well-cushioned Fun Bus. Older kids enjoy the Numeracy Workshop involving games with bus numbers and timetables (see *p67* **Meet the teacher**). The shop, on the way out, stocks model buses among the other souvenirs.

Buggy access. Café. Lift. Nappy-changing facilities. Nearest picnic place: picnic area in ground floor museum gallery/churchyard of St Paul's. Shop.

Phoenix Garden
21 Stacey Street (entrance St Giles Passage), WC2 (7379 3187). Tottenham Court Road tube. **Open** 8.30am-dusk daily. **Admission** free. **Map** p317 K6.
This small, shady garden at the north end of Neal Street was established by the Covent Garden Open Spaces Association in 1984. Permanently staffed, it has slides and benches, one of which was contributed by Michael Palin. In the farthest corner willow trees surround a wildlife bog; the walnut, fig and cherry trees make it a real mini-Eden. A little kiosk sells plants that have been grown here.
Buggy access. Tea/coffee available for donation to garden.

Royal Opera House
Bow Street, WC2 (7304 4000/www.royaloperahouse.org.uk). Covent Garden tube. **Open** *Box office* 10am-8pm Mon-Sat. **Tours** 10.30am, 12.30pm, 2.30pm Mon-Sat. **Tickets** £7; £6 under-18s, concessions. **Credit** AmEx, DC, MC, V. **Map** p319 L6.

Guided tours of London's beautifully renovated opera house start in the pit lobby and include the Vilar Floral Hall, with its bars, restaurants, mirrors, escalators and rooftop garden, the ballet studio, the backstage area, a dressing room and the auditorium (or the crush bar if the latter is inaccessible). Booking is advised, though eight tickets are held each day for last-minute visitors.

Participants can also have a look around all the ROH treasures, among them props, hats and jewellery, and costumes for both revival and new productions. *See also p222.*
Buggy access. Café. Lift. Nearest picnic place: Covent Garden piazza/churchyard of St Paul's. Restaurant. Shop.

St Giles-in-the-Fields
60 St Giles High Street, WC2 (7240 2532). Tottenham Court Road tube. **Open** 9am-4pm Mon-Fri. **Open** for services Sun; phone for details. **Admission** free. **Map** p317 K6.
The leafy churchyard, where large numbers of Londoners were buried during the plague of 1665 (which started in the borough of St Giles's), has a well-equipped playground with swings, a roundabout, a basketball court, an alphabet frame and a hopscotch court, plus benches to rest on. The church dates back to 1101, when a leper colony stood nearby, and is named after the patron saint of outcasts. Condemned prisoners on the way to the Tyburn gallows at Marble Arch were given a drugged drink known as the St Giles Bowl here, and many were returned here to be buried. The present building was constructed in 1711 by the architect Henry Flitcroft, whose name is inscribed above the porch. The interior is a cool and calm venue for lunchtime concerts.
Buggy access. Nearest picnic place: Phoenix Garden.

St Paul's Covent Garden
Bedford Street, WC2 (7836 5221). Covent Garden tube. **Open** 9am-4.30pm Mon-Fri; 10am-12.30pm Sun. Closed bank hols, 1 Jan. **Admission** free; donations appreciated. **Map** p319 L7.
The real glory of this squat symmetrical church, built by Francis Russell, Earl of Bedford, in 1638, is its grassy, enclosed garden, accessible via either the main gates in Bedford Street or the tiny alleys in King Street and Henrietta Street. Its benches fill up with office workers at lunchtimes. Nicknamed 'the Actors' Church', St Paul's is closely linked with the theatre world – the vicar is chaplain to all the West End theatres, and on the walls inside are memorials to Charlie Chaplin, Boris Karloff, Vivien Leigh and many others.

There are services on certain days of the week and occasional concerts. Facing the Covent Garden piazza, the east end of the church, a bare wall behind a row of columns, has always presented itself as a natural stage to those outside. Pepys recorded seeing a Punch & Judy show under the portico, and in the 18th century it was the scene of unruly political hustings. Nowadays, musicians, jugglers, acrobats, fire-eaters, monocyclists, tightrope walkers, ventriloquists and magicians book the space to entertain the large passing crowds (all day, every day).
Buggy access. Nearest picnic place: churchyard.

Theatre Museum
Tavistock Street (entrance Russell Street), WC2 (7943 4700/group bookings 7943 4806/ www.theatremuseum.org). Covent Garden tube. **Open** 10am-6pm Tue-Sun. Last entry 5.30pm. Closed 24-26 Dec, 1 Jan, bank hol Mon. **Tours** 11am, 2pm, 4pm Tue-Sun. **Admission** £4.50; £2.50 concessions; free under-16s, over-60s. **Tours** free. **Credit** AmEx, MC, V. **Map** p319 L6.

The Theatrerites exhibition (on until June 2002), which allows visitors to pull levers and turn handles to operate mechanical stage props and puppetry devices with fascinating consequences, is brilliant for kids. The basement galleries offer more conventional museum fare – arranged in aquarium-style tanks lining long, gloomy corridors, the exhibits, which include permanent valuable collections of Fonteyn and Diaghilev costumes, props and set designs, chart the progress of theatre from 1576 (the opening of this country's first permanent theatre since Roman times) to the recent restoration of the Savoy Theatre and present-day productions.

For details of study sessions and workshops, *see p227. Buggy access. Nappy-changing facilities. Nearest picnic place: churchyard of St Paul's. Shop.*

Eating & shopping

Among the many places to eat in the area, the biggest and noisiest is **TGI Friday's** (6 Bedford Street, WC2, 7379 0585; *see also p173*), whose uncannily upbeat staff welcome children with balloons. **Rock & Sole Plaice** (47 Endell Street, WC2, 7836 3785; *see also p172*) offers both eat-in and takeaway fish and chips, and for pizzas there's **Pizza Express** (9-12 Bow Street, WC2, 7240 3443; *see also p185*) and **Pizza Paradiso** (31 Catherine Street, WC2, 7836 3609).

If there are veggies or vegans in the family, head for Neal's Yard, where both the **Neal's Yard Bakery & Tearoom** (no.6, 7836 5199; *see also p172*) and the **World Food Café** (Neal's Yard Dining Room, 1st floor, no.14, 7379 0298; *see also p173*) welcome kids. The **Great American Bagel Factory** (18 Endell Street, WC2, 7497 1115) has light snacks and ice-cream.

Covent Garden is known for its shops and stalls more than anything else. Londoners flock here for the hip clothes shops, especially on Floral Street and Long Acre. **Paul Smith for Children** (40-44 Floral Street, WC2, 7379 7133; *see also p200*) has fashions for the very small. On the same street is the **Tintin Shop** (no.34, 7836 1131). Pedestrianised, offbeat Neal Street has the **Kite Store** (No.48, 7836 1666). Neal's Yard (off Shorts Gardens) is a hippie haven of health food and natural remedies. In the Market, children will find plenty more to spend their pocket money on in **Benjamin Pollock's Toyshop** (no.44, 7379 7866; *see also p208*), **Peter Rabbit & Friends** (no.42, 7497 1777; *see also p209*) and the **London Doll's House Company** (no.29, 7240 8681).

Dress Circle (57-9 Monmouth Street, WC2, 7240 2227) has a huge range of soundtracks from all your favourite musicals. The **Royale Stamp Co** (110 St Martin's Lane, WC2, 7240 1963) is a philatelist's dream, with Penny Blacks for about £50 and unusual postcards for the less extravagant. Also on St Martin's Lane are **St Martin's Accessories Ltd** (no.95, 7836 9742), which sells collector's model cars and plastic kits, and ballet outfitters **Freed's** (no.94, 7240 0432), with a full range of leotards, crossover cardigans, tutus and silky pumps.

The Strand is full of chainstores, including **Top Shop** (nos. 60-4, 7839 4144) for fashion. Nearby, a place of particular interest to children is **Davenport's Magic Shop** (7 Charing Cross Underground Concourse, WC2, 7836 0408), where itching powder, black face soap, plastic dog turds and fart gas are the order of the day.

Meet the teacher

Janette Palmer is Senior Museum Information Assistant at London's Transport Museum (see p64).

What do you do?
I am operational supervisor for our Learning Centre Resource Desk, and am responsible for designing and organising the museum's programme of family activities.

What activities do children request most?
Children seem to enjoy the high level of interactivity in the museum. They love being able to clamber aboard the vehicles, and the 15 KidZones give them the chance to pull and turn various components to find out more about our exhibits. We also have actors who play a variety of gallery

characters, and a programme of craft workshops and gallery trails during school holidays, which are always very popular.

What's the best part of your job?
What I like most is when an activity I have helped design stands up to the ultimate test and captures the imagination – and attention – of the children. It's great to see them having fun and hopefully learning something at the same time.

Do you have a favourite bus in the museum?
My favourite bus is probably one of the most modern, the Optare

bus. Children are able to sit in the driving seat and take turns at pretending to drive the vehicle. We also have an actress who plays the character of a modern-day bus driver. Every time I go past there's a group of children acting out journeys with her.

Do you wear a uniform?
As museum information assistants, we wear museum-branded polo shirts and dark jeans to help the public identify us; it's a very friendly and approachable sort of uniform.

Kensington & Chelsea

Pirates at play and dinosaur days.

The Royal Borough of Kensington & Chelsea, to give it its full name, is one of the most desirable areas of London to live in. Former residents fortunate enough to have afforded to live here include Sir James Barrie, creator of Peter Pan, (there's a statue of the latter in Kensington Gardens), and Princess Diana, who lived in **Kensington Palace**. The nearby **Diana, Princess of Wales Memorial Playground** was created in her memory for the exclusive pleasure of young people.

Adjoining Kensington Gardens, **Hyde Park**, central London's largest park (one-and-a-half miles long and just under a mile wide) was the setting of the Great Exhibition of 1851; the £186,000 profit of the exhibition was used to finance the construction of great museums and colleges for the study of arts and sciences in an area known colloquially as 'Albertopolis'. It includes the **Natural History Museum**, the **Science Museum**, the **Victoria & Albert Museum**, the **Royal Albert Hall** (*see p222*), the Royal College of Art and the Imperial College of Science and Technology.

Chelsea, the wedge-shaped piece of land between Kensington and the river, is synonymous with posh shops and even posher houses, out of the realm of most Londoners. It may not have the attractions to rival other brasher parts of town, but its peaceful gardens, in particular the oasis that is the **Chelsea Physic Garden**, are well worth checking out, especially if you've exhausted the shopaholics' haven that is the King's Road.

Baden-Powell House
65-7 Queen's Gate, SW7 (7584 7031/ www.scoutbase.org.uk). South Kensington tube. **Open** 7am-10pm daily. Closed 22 Dec-3 Jan. **Admission** free. **Map** p315 D10.

Walk: Hyde Park & Kensington Gardens

▶ Start at the gloriously golden **Albert Memorial** opposite the Royal Albert Hall. Walk round the statue until Albert has his back to you, then head north into the park but almost immediately turn left into the shady **Flower Walk**, and admire the rhododendrons. Continue to the end of the walk and turn right into the paved **Broad Walk** running north–south across Kensington Gardens. Make a detour when you see the great iron gates of **Kensington Palace** (*see p69*) on your left. Cross the grass towards them. This was where Princess Diana's fans made a carpet of flowers in mourning when she died in 1997.

▶ Return to the Broad Walk but cross immediately to the **Round Pond**, where you see the swans and geese. Here, if you have time, you can sail a model boat on the lake, or just chill out in one of the deckchairs. Return to the Broad Walk and continue northwards until you see signs to the **Diana, Princess of Wales Memorial Playground** (*see p69*). Once you get to the garden, take your children in and allow them to run free for a while. On leaving the garden, walk eastwards following the northern boundary of the park until you come to the magnificent fountains at Marlborough Gate. Nearby is a gatekeeper's lodge, with a pets' cemetery.

▶ Walk south alongside the lake known as the **Long Water**. Eventually you'll come to a wooded clump, in the centre of which stands a statue of **Peter Pan** playing his pipe. The statue commemorates the book of the same name by JM Barrie, who used to walk his dog in the park every day. Continue following the Long Water round until you meet the north–south road that separates Kensington Gardens from Hyde Park. Cross the bridge spanning the lake and enter **Hyde Park**. Continue following the road along the northern flank of the lake, which is now called the **Serpentine**, where you can go rowing.

▶ When your time's up and you've handed the boat back, walk round the lake in a clockwise direction. You'll eventually come to a restaurant, which provides refreshments as well as the facilities for a swim in the lake. There is a club whose members swim here every day of the year, even in midwinter.

▶ A little further west from this second restaurant you will come to the dividing road again. Cross again and enter Kensington Gardens near the **Serpentine Gallery** (*see p73*). On emerging from the gallery, see if you can spot the Albert Memorial protruding above the trees to the south-west. To get to know the monument more intimately, book a guided tour (7495 0916/www.tourguides.co.uk).

Hyde Park & Kensington Gardens
W2 (7298 2100/www.royalparks.gov.uk). Hyde Park Corner, Knightsbridge, Lancaster Gate, Marble Arch or Queensway tube. **Open** *Hyde Park* 5am-midnight daily. *Kensington Gardens* 5am-dusk daily. **Map** p312 C7/313 E7.

Money raised by boy scouts and girl guides all over the world built this memorial hostel to Lord Baden-Powell (1857-1941), the founder of scouting. It was opened in 1961 and accommodates about 300,000 people from 30 different countries each year. A modest exhibition on the ground floor gives an entertaining account of the life of the Chief Scout. The canteen is open to all (parties of six or more should book in advance). *Buggy access. Café. Nappy-changing facilities. Nearest picnic place: Natural History Museum gardens. Shop.*

Chelsea Physic Garden
66 Royal Hospital Road (entrance in Swan Walk), SW3 (7352 5646/www.cpgarden.demon.co.uk). Sloane Square tube/11, 19, 22, 239, 319 bus. **Open** *Apr-late Oct* noon-5pm Wed; 2-6pm Sun. *Tours* 1.30pm, 3.30pm (check blackboard to confirm); phone for group tours. **Admission** £4; £2 5-16s, students (not incl OAPs). *Tours* free. **Credit** *Shop* MC, V. **Map** p315 F12.
This enchanting garden of discovery was established in 1673 and developed by Sir Hans Sloane in the early 18th century. Its 3.5 acres contain healing herbs and rare trees, dye plants, medicinal vegetables and plants for sale. The gardens enjoy a microclimate, as evidenced by some of the trees found growing here, including the largest fruiting olive tree in Britain.

The garden is primarily a research and education facility, hence the rather limited opening hours. Children, however, are encouraged to visit the garden in school groups or to take part in regular activity days during the holidays. The education department organises craft workshops, wildlife watching and microscopy, and reptile displays and storytelling/music sessions. *Buggy access. Nappy-changing facilities. Shop.*

Diana, Princess of Wales Memorial Playground
near Black Lion Gate, Broad Walk, Kensington Gardens, W8 (7298 2117/recorded info 7298 2141). Bayswater or Queensway tube. **Open** 10am-8pm or 1hr before dusk if earlier, daily. Closed 25 Dec. **Admission** free. All adults must be accompanied by a child. (Adults may view the gardens from 9.30-10am daily.) **Map** p312 C7.
'About as far from the municipal and as close to *Swallows and Amazons* as you can get' was how Rosa Monckton described the playground opened in memory of her friend Princess Diana in June 2000. Though Titty and her comrades may not have had to put up with loads of other children jostling for a place in the crow's nest, there's no denying that this is an enchanting place. The playground cost £1.7 million just to build, and upkeep is of prime importance. Watchful rangers see it stays pristine, and make sure that no unaccompanied adults enter.

Dominating the space is a pirate ship, in a sea of fine white sand (shoes fill up with it quickly, which can be a bit annoying). Older children have fun scaling the rigging to the crow's nest, little ones bring buckets and spades for the sand; all adore the ship's wheel, cabins, pulleys and ropes. Equally alluring, in warm weather at least, is the mermaids' fountain and rocky outcrops, beyond which is the tepee camp: a trio of wigwams, each large enough to hold a sizeable tribe. The tree house encampment provides walkways, ladders and slides.

The playground's attractions are designed to appeal to the senses: sensitive planting of scented shrubs, whispering willows and bamboo, metal dance chimes (tap your foot and hear the note) and touchy-feely sculpture are all carefully designed to engage visitors on every level. Much of the equipment has been designed for use by children with special needs, as befitting a playground built in Princess Diana's name.

It is well worth travelling to the playground from other parts of town, especially if your children are aged under ten (those after a more physically challenging adventure play-

He never grew up: **Peter Pan**. *See p68.*

ground may find this somewhat tame). The food in the café is good, and the loos, housed in a grass-roofed dome, are clean. Drinking water is thoughtfully provided for those long, hot afternoons playing pirates. All in all, a terrific, free day out. *Buggy access. Café. Nappy-changing facilities. Nearest picnic place: Kensington Gardens.*

Kensington Palace
W8 (7937 9561/www.hrp.org.uk). Bayswater, High Street Kensington or Queensway tube. **Open** 10am-6pm daily. Last entry 5pm. Closed 24-26 Dec. **Admission** (includes audio guide) £8.80; £6.30 5-15s; £6.90 concessions; £26.80 family (2+3). **Credit** AmEx, MC, V. **Map** p312 B8.
Living by the river at Whitehall aggravated William III's asthma, so in 1689 he and Mary, looking for a new home, bought this modest Jacobean mansion then known as Nottingham House. Wren and Hawksmoor (and, later, William Kent) were drafted in to redesign the building, which remained the favoured royal residence until the reign of George III (he preferred Buckingham Palace). The future

Man the lifeboats on the **Serpentine**. *See p68.*

A day at: the Natural History Museum

Opened in 1881 to display the natural history specimens of the late Sir Hans Sloane, the collection now runs to 68 million plants, animals, fossils, rocks and minerals. You'd never see them all in a day, of course, but the following gives some ideas about what you should definitely not miss.

For many children, the **Dinosaurs Gallery** (no.21) is London's best attraction. When the animatronic Tyrannosaurus Rex arrived at the museum in early 2000, he stole the show. Crowds wrapped around the vast, stately building to see him, even for just a few seconds. The initial hysteria generated by his arrival may have died down, but when a nervy child catches his beady eye and clocks those bloodstained teeth, screams ricochet around the galleries once again. The roaring beast will be in his enclosure, especially fragranced for that authentic, prehistoric odour (slightly vegetably, with a tang of the dry ice that makes him yet more scary), until at least summer 2002. Even before you get to the T-Rex things are a bit scary – you walk on a metal walkway over the Dinosaurs Gallery, guarded by three animatronic Deinonychus.

Until 6 May 2002 the Predators Exhibition is the centrepiece of the NHM's Year of the Predator. Featuring huge, moving models of a great white shark, a toxic spider and an interactive chameleon, as well as specimens such as a Harris Hawk swooping to kill, Predators examines the predation skills that decide whether an animal gets a meal or escapes being one. Suitable for children aged 7 to 12, the exhibition explores many fascinating scientific issues, such as the evolutionary 'arms race' – as predators get better at hunting, prey find new ways to hide and fight back, so strategies have to be rethought.

Other galleries worth checking out if you have kids with you include the one called, provocatively, **Creepy Crawlies** (gallery 33), which focuses on arthropods. It has a live ant colony, diverting displays about insects' domestic habits and the nauseating creepy crawly house. **Human Biology** (gallery 22) is noisily interactive and full of interesting tests and explorations, films and games. Some things have changed surprisingly little over the years – **Discovering Mammals**, in galleries 23 and 24, still has a vast blue whale model still dangling above lesser species, as it has done for the past 50 years or so.

Earth Galleries are approached via Exhibition Road. The escalator that takes you in through a suspended, revolving globe is a memorable experience, and that's even before you come across the interactive displays investigating the earth's treasures and natural disasters. **Gallery 61** has a re-creation of the Kobe (Japan) earthquake of 1995. Young visitors like to relive that floor-shaking supermarket experience an obscene number of times.

In addition to the above spectacles, the museum is highly committed to education. A new science education centre called **Investigate** opened in the Clore Education Centre in April 2000. The idea behind it is to encourage visitors to use equipment available to examine and find out about hundreds of specimens on display. There are also activity trails (available from the box office), half-term and school holiday events programmes and weekend workshops for families. The themes of these change frequently, so it's best to check the website or ring the bookings line (7942 5555) to find out what's on.

The museum is also continuing to expand: work progresses on the £100-million Darwin Centre, the first phase of which is scheduled for completion in summer 2002 (*see also p24*).

Natural History Museum

Cromwell Road, SW7 (7942 5000/ www.nhm.ac.uk). South Kensington tube.
Open 10am-5.50pm Mon-Sat; 11am-5.50pm Sun. Closed 24-25 Dec. *Tours* free, hourly; 11am-4pm daily. **Admission** £9; £4.50 concessions; free OAPs, under-16s. Free for all after 4.30pm Mon-Fri, after 5pm Sat, Sun, public hols.
Credit AmEx, MC, V. **Map** p315 D10.
Buggy access. Cafés. Nappy-changing facilities. Nearest picnic place: indoor eating area/museum grounds. Restaurant. Shops.

A day at: the Science Museum

A day spent in this seven-floor museum is an exhausting and stimulating experience, but make sure you catch these highlights.

The ultra-modern **Wellcome Wing**, named after the medical charity that contributed to the project, is accessed on the ground floor via a new display, **Making the Modern World**. Passing technological icons such as Stephenson's Rocket, the Apollo 10 command module and a 1970s Chopper bike, visitors arrive in the extension proper.

Pattern Pod, on the ground floor of the Wellcome Wing, is definitely one for the kids – designed for under-eights, it's out of bounds for unaccompanied adults. The Pod aims to impress upon children the importance of patterns in nature. Children are encouraged to explore questions like 'What gives honeycomb its strength?' through hands-on experiments and designing their own patterns.

Launch Pad is a technological adventure playground in the basement, where there's also the Garden, a stimulating area for three-

to -six-year-olds, dedicated to learning through water play, soft play, construction, dressing-up fun, adventures in sound and light and a variety of simple scientific concepts.

Would-be astronauts flock to the **Space** gallery on the ground floor. Similarly, children also adore the flight simulator on floor three, which also has a real Cessna to sit in and learn all about flying.

Health Matters, floor three, is an exploration of the history of medical technology, but it's not half as entertaining as the waxwork nurses, doctors and blood-spattered patients in tableaux displayed upstairs in a spooky darkened floor called **Glimpses of Medical History**.

The Wellcome Wing's five-storey **IMAX** cinema runs 40-minute 3-D shows. *T-Rex* is a roaring dinosaur movie; *Cyberworld* is a highly animated programme about computer bugs and viruses. *Blue Planet* focuses on geographical features on Earth. Unfortunately, the IMAX lacks the slick design of the rest of the gallery and access to it, via a tortuous set of stairs and corridors, is inconvenient. It's not cheap either: tickets cost an additional £6.75 for adults, and £5.75 for students, concessions, under-16s and OAPs. Also in the wing, on the ground floor, is **Virtual Voyages**, a 15-minute motion ride simulator, which takes you on a trip to Mars. The voyage costs £3.50 for adults and £2.50 for children.

While all these high-tech adventures are sure-fire hits with younger visitors, the more traditional exhibits should not be neglected: the **Secret Life of the Home** in the basement, for instance, includes a cut-away model of a flushing toilet with plastic poo accessory (invariably popular with kids).

And if a visit to the museum has fuelled your child's interest in all things scientific, treat them to one of the Science Night sleepovers (held once a month, except for August, for 8-11-year-olds). They consist of an evening of activities followed by a sleepover among the exhibits. Not surprisingly, they're extremely popular, so book one to two months ahead). Children's educational events and workshops are run every half-term and school holiday. They can't be booked in advance, so it's worth turning up early on the day (*see p74* **Meet the teacher**). For a list of forthcoming events for children ask to be put on the mailing list.

Science Museum

Exhibition Road, SW7 (7942 4454/4455/ www.sciencemuseum.org.uk). South Kensington tube. **Open** 10am-6pm daily. Closed 24-26 Dec. **Admission** £7.95; £4.95 students; free under-16s, concessions. Free for all after 4.30pm daily. **Credit** AmEx, MC, V. **Map** p315 D9. *Buggy access. Cafés. Lifts. Nappy-changing facilities. Nearest picnic place: indoors (basement) or outdoors/Hyde Park. Restaurant. Shops.*

Queen Victoria was born in the palace in 1819, and it has latterly been known as the last home of Princess Diana (only one of a number of royal residents). Princess Margaret and the Duke and Duchess of Kent both have apartments here. The palace is open for tours of the State Apartments, including the ground-floor room where Queen Victoria was baptised, the long King's Gallery, with its Tintoretto nudes and Van Dyck portrait of Charles I, and the exhibition of Diana's celebrated frocks (till April 2002).

Buggy access. Café. Nappy-changing facilities. Nearest picnic place: palace grounds. Restaurant. Shop.

London Oratory

Thurloe Place, Brompton Road, SW7 (7808 0900). South Kensington tube. **Open** 6.30am-8pm daily. Phone to check. **Admission** free; donations appreciated. **Map** p315 E10.

The Brompton Oratory is an awesome extravaganza of marble and mosaic designed to inspire reverential fear. Many of the ornate internal decorations predate the building, including Mazzuoli's late 17th-century statues of the apostles, which previously stood in Siena Cathedral. During the Cold War, the church was used by the KGB as a dead letter box.

The 'Brompton' Oratory's Junior Choir sings weekly Mass at 10am on Sundays. Schola, the boys' choir of the London Oratory School, performs Mass on Saturday evenings in term time.

Buggy access. Nearest picnic place: Holy Trinity Brompton churchyard. Shop.

National Army Museum

Royal Hospital Road, SW3 (7730 0717/ www.national-army-museum.ac.uk). Sloane Square tube/11, 19, 239 bus. **Open** 10am-5.30pm daily. Closed 24-26 Dec, Good Friday, 1st bank hol May. **Admission** free. **Map** p315 F12.

It's not just boys with a penchant for toy soldiers who love this museum – boys and girls of all ages warm to the story of British military endeavour. The life-size figures and model battlefields go down well with children, and they also love to stroke the nose of the full-size horse returning from battle during the English Civil War, then go and look at the skeleton of Napoleon's mount, Marengo. Permanent exhibits include Redcoats, a gallery that tells the story of the British soldier from the archers of Agincourt in 1415 to the redcoats of the American Revolution; the Road to Waterloo, which features a huge model of the battle, with 75,000 mini-soldiers; and the Nation in Arms, which charts the history of the army in two world wars and includes reconstructions of a trench in Flanders and a landing craft off Normandy.

School and family groups are given gallery trails to guide them round the various eras, and regular special events days throughout the year, and specal events weekends (the first one of each month) allow children to gain a more hands-on impression of the life of a soldier: they can try on helmets, touch weapons and pity the hapless sappers.

Buggy access. Café. Nappy-changing facilities. Nearest picnic place: benches outside museum/Chelsea Hospital grounds. Shop.

Serpentine Gallery

Kensington Gardens (near Albert Memorial), W2 (7402 6075/www.serpentinegallery.org). Lancaster Gate or South Kensington tube. **Open** 10am-6pm daily. Closed 25 Dec. *Tours* free; 3pm Sat. **Admission** free. **Map** p313 D8.

The Serpentine is housed in a tranquil former tea pavilion with French windows looking out on to Hyde Park, imbuing the exhibitions with varying qualities of natural light (depending on our notorious weather, of course). On Saturday mornings, the Children's Art Club offers tours of the artworks

Chelsea Physic Garden. *See p69.*

on display in this light and airy place, plus discussions of the techniques and practical workshops for participants' own creativity and expression.

Buggy access. Nappy-changing facilities. Nearest picnic place: Hyde Park/Kensington Gardens. Shop.

Victoria & Albert Museum

Cromwell Road, SW7 (7942 2000/www.vam.ac.uk). South Kensington tube. **Open** 10am-5.45pm Mon, Tue, Thur-Sun; 10am-10pm Wed. Closed 24-26 Dec. *Tours* daily; phone for details. **Admission** £5; free concessions. *Tours* free. Free for all after 4.30pm daily. **Credit** AmEx, MC, V. **Map** p315 E10.

Items pertaining to children were moved from here to the Museum of Childhood at Bethnal Green (see p117) a few years ago, though the curators seem to have missed a few. The Ironwork Gallery (Room 114) has a glass case containing a number of early 20th-century tin toys – a ship, a train, a tank – and the German stained-glass display (Room 117) includes a panel depicting the Murder of the Innocents in gory detail.

Other selected items at which some children might register a flicker of interest include Tippoo's Tiger (Nehru Gallery of Indian Art), a barrel organ inside the body of a tiger that is devouring a petrified European. Also St Thomas à Becket's casket (Medieval Treasury 400-1400), which was built for the murdered archbishop in 1180. The musical instrument room (no.40) is fascinating to all those who play one.

Children's activities take place at weekends. On Saturdays from 1.30pm, 5- to 11-year-olds may pick up a themed backpack with jigsaws, games, stories and puzzles. On Sundays from 10.30am, under-5s visit the Cart, which contains materials for drawing and model-making and is stationed in a room relevant to the Cart's activities. Half-terms are devoted to daily events such as workshops and fashion displays pertaining to current exhibitions. All children's activities are free.

In broader terms, the V&A houses the world's greatest array of decorative arts, as well as the national sculpture collection. The Art & Design galleries are arranged thematically by place and date, the Materials & Techniques galleries by type. The museum is also home to a huge photographic archive, and also hosts regular photographic exhibitions.

The British Galleries are due to open in November 2001, following a massive programme of modernisation: they tell the tale of Britain's ascent from a minor offshore island in 1500 to a major world power and cultural authority in 1900.

Be sure to pay a visit to the museum shop, which has a pretty good selection of books, various ornaments and jewellery. *Buggy access. Café. Nappy-changing facilities. Nearest picnic place: Holy Trinity Brompton churchyard. Restaurant. Shop.*

Eating & shopping

Visitors to the Exhibition Road museums who don't want to partake of their improved (but still pricey) menus should head back to the area around South Kensington tube. Here they'll find **Francofill** (1 Old Brompton Road, SW7, 7584 0087), a very serviceable French fast food joint (lovely *biftek* and frites), where children are welcomed with high chairs and drawing stuff. Kids are also treated kindly in the **Oratory** (232 Brompton Road, SW7, 7584 3493), a cheerful brasserie with an imaginative, international menu. Head over to Gloucester Road for the closest source of child-friendly pizza places and burger bars (ASK, Pizza Express, Tootsies). In Chelsea there's **Big Easy** (332-4 King's Road, SW3, 7352 4071; *see also p173*), a large-portioned, all-smiling, high-chair and children's-menu-toting American eaterie, and a more sober, Tex-Mex inspired restaurant, **Cactus Blue** (86 Fulham Road, SW3, 7823 7858), where the chimichangas are excellent

and the brownies even better. More American chow is available at the local branch of **Ed's Easy Diner** (362 King's Road, SW3, 7352 1956; *see also p175*). **Benihana** (77 King's Road, SW3, 7376 7799; *see also p173*) is a link in a particularly child-friendly Japanese chain, where food is cooked in front of you on a *hibachi* grill. Other well-known, welcoming restaurants on the King's Road include Café Rouge and Pizza Express.

The prosperous streets of South Kensington and Chelsea are shopping heaven. Chelsea has the King's Road, which is full of top fashion and lots of chi-chi children's boutiques and toy shops: **Brora** (no.344, 7352 3697; *see also p196*); **Daisy & Tom** (no.181-3, 7352 5000; *see p191*); nearby is **Traditional Toys** (53 Godfrey Street, SW3, 7532 1718; *see also p209*). Not far away, on and around impossibly smart Walton Street, are baby boutiques and nursery shops: **Butterscotch** (172 Walton Street, SW3, 7581 8851; *see also p196*); **Caramel** (291 Brompton Road, SW3, 7589 7001; *see also p196*); and **Nursery Window** (83 Walton Street, SW3, 7581 3358; *see also p195*). Exclusivity is up the road in Knights-bridge, where **Harrods** (87-135 Brompton Road, SW1, 7730 1234; *see also p192*) impresses shoppers of all ages. And Chelsea **Gap** (122 King's Road, SW3, 7551 9720; *see also p206*) has a particularly good permanent sale in the children's department.

Meet the teacher

Sarah Leonard is the Education Manager at the Science Museum (*see p72*).

What do you do?
All sorts of things. I run INSET training for teachers and present video-conference sessions to pupils in schools. I develop and present workshops and demonstrations for school groups in the museum, and research and write pupils' activity sheets and teachers' notes about the galleries. When we are developing a new exhibition I might give advice on making the displays more useful for school groups. I also answer enquiries from people wanting to know about the museum.

What activities do children request most?
In addition to the hands-on exhibits, children like the fantastic science shows and demonstrations such as the rocket demo. And, of course,

there's the IMAX cinema. The Science Night sleepovers are very popular, too.

What other activities are there?
There are drama characters who explain how changes in science and technology have affected people's lives. For example, you might meet 'Thomas Crapper' extolling the virtues of his syphonic flush toilet or NASA astronaut 'Gene Cernan' describing his space flights on the Apollo 10 mission. There's the Biometric Trail, which allows you to create your own web page and store information on it, which you collect during your visit ready for you to download after you leave the museum. There are exciting simulator rides, and there are lots of workshops, talks, shows and events, especially during school holidays.

What's the best part of your job?
For me the most satisfying aspect is seeing children and teachers enjoying themselves.

Do you wear a uniform?
I don't usually wear a uniform, although other people, such as the Explainers in the hands-on galleries, wear blue Science Museum T-shirts. When I work on Science Nights I wear one, too.

Do you have a favourite part of the museum?
My favourite bit is the Who am I? gallery, which looks at the ways in which developments in brain science and genetics are helping us to understand our identity. There are some exhibits that really make you think.

West End

Out on the town.

When Londoners talk of the West End, they mean a loosely defined district of shopping and entertainment, which for the purposes of this chapter includes Soho, Mayfair and St James's. This area is bordered by Park Lane to the west, Oxford Street to the north, Charing Cross Road to the east and Pall Mall to the south. It is actually all rather adult in appeal but there are certain aspects of it that bear upon the young.

At the heart of the West End is **Shaftesbury Avenue**. Famous theatres dominate its northern side, while **Chinatown** lies along its southern flank. The street takes its name from the 7th Earl of Shaftesbury, aka Anthony Ashley Cooper (1801-85), who was prominent in the Ragged Schools movement (*see p120*), which provided free education and clothing for deprived children.

The statue of the boy Cupid, or **Eros**, at Piccadilly Circus at the western end of Shaftesbury Avenue is dedicated to the philanthropic earl. Young people from around the world congregate, not necessarily in his memory, on the steps of the fountain. Many are

attracted into the dark and noisy **Trocadero** across the road. It's not much, but it's the only specifically youth-oriented entertainment site in the West End.

Next to Piccadilly Circus is **Leicester Square**, home of London's great cinemas. On prestigious opening nights, young starstruck autograph hunters strain at the crowd-control barriers screaming for attention from the latest here-today-gone-tomorrow celebrities. But this isn't the only square in this part of town – each of the great squares of the West End has its own individual character (*see p78*).

Soho is the centre of sleaze. There are sights here from which you may wish to shield innocent eyes. Buzzing **Carnaby Street** poses no great threat as long as you keep a rein on your purse. **Berwick Street Market** is a bit seedy but friendly enough.

Mayfair is best known for its reputation as the costliest property on the Monopoly board. It's no different in real life. The roads are broad and the trees are tall, and liveried footmen stand at the entrances of its grand hotels. Famously expensive

A proper Charlie in **Leicester Square**.

Could this be the prettiest tool shed in London? **Soho Square**. *See p78.*

shopping streets feed its reputation. **Regent Street** is home to **Liberty** and the world-famous toy shop **Hamleys**. **Bond Street** is for quality fashions, antiques, jewellery and fine art. **Savile Row** purveys handmade suits for a bob or two. Not much here for the kids.

St James's is still the official name of the monarch's court, despite the fact that the royal family moved out of St James's Palace and into Buckingham Palace nearly 300 years ago.

Apsley House: The Wellington Museum
149 Piccadilly, W1 (7499 5676/www.vam.ac.uk). Hyde Park Corner tube. **Open** 11am-5pm Tue-Sun. Closed 24-26 Dec, Good Friday, 1st bank hol.May **Admission** £4.50 (includes audio guide); £3 concessions; free under-18s. *Tours* £2.50 per person (min 10); by arrangement. **Credit** AmEx, DC, MC, V. **Map** p318 G8.
This grand house (once known as 'No.1 London' because it was the first building you came to en route from the village of Kensington to London) was built by Robert Adam in the 1770s. The house was the London residence of Arthur Wellesley, the Duke of Wellington from 1817 until his death in 1852. The duke's descendants still live here, but ten rooms, restored to their original state, are open to the public. There are gilt-framed paintings by Velázquez, Caravaggio and Rubens in the Waterloo Room and portraits of kings and popes in the Piccadilly Room. In the China and Plate Room, the Egyptian dinner service sits around a gigantic plaster

model of the Temple at Karnak and in the stairwell stands an extraordinary 14-foot-4-inch (4.4-metre) marble statue of Napoleon in the fig-leafed nude by Canova.

Wellington's statue is outside on Hyde Park Corner. He sits with his medals and his boots on astride his horse Copenhagen (which died in 1836 at the age of 28 and was buried with full military honours), surrounded by sleeping representatives of his regiments, one from each of the United Kingdom's kingdoms – Guards, Royal Highlanders, Inniskilling Dragoons and Welsh Fusiliers. *See p80* **Meet the teacher.**
Buggy access. Lift. Nearest picnic place: Hyde Park. Shop.

Faraday Museum
Royal Institution, 21 Albemarle Street, W1 (7409 2992/www.ri.ac.uk). Green Park tube. **Open** 9am-5pm Mon-Fri. Closed 24-26 Dec, 1 Jan. *Tours* by arrangement. **Admission** £1. *Tours* £5. No child reductions. **Map** p318 J7.
This small, eccentric, public museum is part of the Royal Institution, where Michael Faraday (1791-1867), 'father of electricity', worked for 30 years. Exhibits include a re-creation of the lab where Faraday discovered the laws of electromagnetics and identified the compound benzene. The Royal Institution itself is responsible for making science a subject of interest to the public. The annual Christmas lectures have gained wide appeal in recent years – the 2001 series The Rise of the Robots attracted a large and youthful audience already inspired by other robotic television initiatives. The Institution guards its position at the forefront of technology jealously. Over the years, ten chemical elements have been discovered here and 14 Nobel prizes won. The programme of schools visits and lectures is extensive and serious. The Institution runs a maths masterclass for gifted mathematicians aged 11 and over.
Buggy access. Lift. Nearest picnic place: Berkeley Square.

Handel House Museum
25 Brook Street (entrance at rear), W1 (7495 1685/ www.handelhouse.org). Bond Street tube. **Open** *from 8 Nov 2001* 10am-6pm Tue, Wed, Fri, Sat; 10am-8pm Thur; noon-6pm Sun. Closed 24-26 Dec, 1 Jan. **Admission** £4.50; £3.50 concessions; £2 children. **Credit** MC, V. **Map** p318 H6.
The composer George Frideric Handel lived in this house for nearly 40 years. Belatedly, it (and no.23 next door where Jimi Hendrix lived) have now been turned into a commemorative museum. The two harpsichords on display are not originals but authentic modern-day copies. The documents, including correspondence with the *Messiah* librettist Jenners, are genuine. Phone for details of group guided tours.
Buggy access. Lifts. Nappy-changing facilities. Nearest picnic place: Hanover Square. Shop.

Royal Academy of Arts
Burlington House, Piccadilly, W1 (7300 8000/ www.royalacademy.org.uk). Green Park or Piccadilly Circus tube. **Open** 10am-6pm Mon-Thur, Sat, Sun; 10am-10pm Fri. *Tours* times vary. **Admission** varies. *Tours* free. **Credit** AmEx, MC, V. **Map** p318 J7.
Britain's first art school – it opened in 1768 – the Royal Academy also held the country's first annual open exhibitions of living artists. This persists as the Summer Exhibition (June-August each year); anyone of any age or nationality may submit a painting, sculpture or piece of architecture (in model form) for entry. Application forms are available in February each year. Cost of entry is £18 per item but only about 10% of the works submitted are chosen for display.

Though there is a permanent collection at the RA, only a few works from it are on show at any one time). But in any

IAN FLEMING'S

"CHITTY CHITTY BANG BANG"

The most FANTASMAGORICAL stage musical in the history of everything!

PERFORMANCES FROM 19 MARCH 2002

BOOK NOW

BOX OFFICE AND 24 HOURS CC WITH BOOKING FEE

020 7494 5572 · 020 7344 4444

GROUPS: 020 7494 5454 · BOOK ON-LINE: www.chittythemusical.co.uk

LONDON PALLADIUM

Argyll Street, London W1

Walk: Square bashing

Sightseeing

▶ This walk takes you to six of the West End's squares – St James's, Berkeley, Grosvenor, Hanover, Soho and Leicester. All of them are green.

▶ Start at Charing Cross Station. Walk up Duncannon Street, across Trafalgar Square and west into Pall Mall. Consult the Westminster chapter (*pp81-90*) for ideas of how to spend time here. Head west along Pall Mall past the Ministry for Culture, Media and Sport and the National Lottery office on the left. Cross Haymarket and turn right into Royal Arcade. Turn left at the end, walk along Charles II Street until you come to **St James's Square**. Enter the gardens by the iron gate. In the centre is a statue of Guglielmus III, which is Latin for William the Third. He signed the Bill of Rights (1689), which obliged the monarch to rule subject to parliament and the law. Sit in John Nash's tiny pavilion by the spreading fig tree. Admire the symmetry formed by you, the statue and the church of **St James's Piccadilly** (*see p79*) beyond.

▶ Leave the gardens and walk up to the church, which has a café under the tower. Go in, listen to a lunchtime concert if there is one, toss a coin in the poor box and exit by the north entrance into the craft market.

▶ Saunter down Piccadilly to doughty old department store **Fortnum & Mason** (*see p80*), and watch the clock on the outside. It does wacky things as the hour strikes. Cross over and turn into Burlington Arcade.

▶ Turn left at the top and right into **Old Bond Street**. Ask the time of the two men on the park bench where Old Bond Street becomes New Bond Street (there's actually no Bond Street as such). They will not answer you. They are only statues. Turn left here into Grafton Street and follow it round until you come to Hay Hill on the right. It emerges at the southern side of **Berkeley Square**.

▶ Cross to the gardens. Stroll up the gravel aisle under the tallest, oldest, most graceful plane trees in London. Plaques on the benches record the names of those who loved sitting on them. Americans who were stationed here during World War II popularised the square in the ballad *A Nightingale Sang in Berkeley Square*. They even took some of it home. Aspects of Lansdowne House, which once dominated the square, are still visible across the Atlantic. The drawing room is in the Philadelphia Museum of Antiquities and the dining room in the Metropolitan Museum in New York.

▶ Leave the gardens by the western gate, cross the road and walk up the hill. Pass 44 Berkeley Square, which has been described as the most beautiful house in London. Now it is a casino. The interior is intact and has not been shipped to the States when no one was looking.

▶ Turn left into **Mount Street** and enter Mount Street Gardens, whose rare trees include Australian mimosa, Canary Island palm and Chinese redwood. Leave the gardens by the western gate. Turn right into South Audley Street, pass Grosvenor Chapel and Richoux Chocolates tea shop before entering the great expanse of **Grosvenor Square**.

▶ The American Embassy looms over it. Eisenhower stands on the north-western corner, Roosevelt in a pond in the middle of the park and a golden eagle on a plinth by the southern gate.

▶ Leave the square at the north-east corner and walk east along **Brook Street**. Pass the 250-room Claridge's Hotel on the right. Cross New Bond Street and enter Hanover Square, once the centre of London's musical life. The composer Handel lived at 25 Brook Street, which is now the **Handel House Museum** (*see p76*). Next door and in a different era lived Jimi Hendrix. They both have plaques. In 1780 the Hanover Square Rooms became London's first public concert hall. Haydn, JC 'London' Bach, Paganini and Liszt played here, superstars of their day.

▶ Leave the square by Hanover Street. Cross Regent Street and continue along Great Marlborough Street passing the **Liberty** department store (*see p80*) on the right. Cross Poland Street into Noel Street, turn right at the end into Wardour Street and left into Carlisle Street, which leads into **Soho Square**, which packs out with sprawling office-workers and other Soho types in summer. The quaint hut in the middle is a genuine antique gardeners' shed built in 1875.

▶ Leave the gardens, pass the offices of 20th-Century Fox and the British Board of Film Censors and turn down **Greek Street**. Continue to the end, and cross Old Compton Street and Shaftesbury Avenue and follow the whiff of soy sauce into Gerrard Place and Gerrard Street. This is **Chinatown**. Glazed ducks hang in the windows of many Chinese restaurants. Turn right into Newport Place, then into Lisle Street and left into Leicester Place, which leads into grubby **Leicester Square**.

▶ At the north-west corner of the square is the **Swiss Centre**, which entertains the crowds with an extended peal of Alpine cow bells daily at noon. On the south side is **Tkts**, the cut-price ticket booth marked by its snaking, orderly queues. The square is surrounded by huge cinemas, which are the usual venues for film premières in the UK. Glamorous darlings of the screen alight from stretch limousines on to red carpets on opening night. The nations of the former empire and present Commonwealth are celebrated in a ring of brass plaques set into the cobbles around the statue of Shakespeare at the centre of the gardens.

Smile! You're in **Piccadilly Circus**. *See p75.*

case, almost everyone who visits does so to see one of the temporary exhibitions: the most visited of any London gallery, booking for them is sometimes a necessity. Shows to look out for in the near future include Rembrandt's Women (22 Sept-16 Dec 2001) and Paris, Capital of the Arts 1900-1968 (26 Jan-19 Apr 2002). *See also p218.*
Buggy access. Café. Nappy-changing facilities. Lift.
Nearest picnic place: Green Park/St James's Square.
Restaurant. Shop.

St James's Church Piccadilly

197 Piccadilly, W1 (7734 4511/
www.st-james-piccadilly.org). Piccadilly Circus tube.
Open 8am-7pm daily (phone for details of evening events). Closed 24-26 Dec, some bank hols (phone to check). **Map** p318 J7.
The handsome 2,000-seat Christopher Wren church is known for its churchyard market (antiques and collectors' stuff on Tuesdays, arts and crafts Wednesdays to Saturdays, closed on Sundays and Mondays), its modest café, its lectures and its lunchtime concerts. Its interior is cool and calm and perfect for silent contemplation. Grinling Gibbons carved much of the woodwork (also white marble font) and Henry Purcell tested the organ. The church was badly bombed during World War II but beautifully repaired afterwards. The new spire is made of fibreglass.
Buggy access. Café. Nearest picnic place:
St James's Square.

Spencer House

27 St James's Place, SW1 (info 7499 8620/
www.spencerhouse.co.uk). Green Park tube. **Open**
House *Feb-July, Sept-Dec* 11.45am-5.30pm Sun. Last

entry 4.45pm. Restored gardens *specific days, spring, summer*; phone or check website. **Admission** *Tour only* £6; £5 10-16s. No under-10s. **Map** p318 J8.
The compulsory guided tours of one of the capital's most splendid Palladian mansions take in eight restored state-rooms, which are now used mainly for corporate entertaining. Apart from its being the ancestral London house of Princess Diana's family, the most notable features of Spencer House are the extravagant murals of the Painted Room, the beautiful painted ceiling in the Great Room and the impressive collection of 18th-century paintings. James Vardy, James Stuart and Robert Adam all worked on the opulent interior, which was completed in 1766 for Earl Spencer.
Nearest picnic place: Green Park.

Trocadero

1 Piccadilly Circus, W1 (7439 1711/www.troc.co.uk).
Piccadilly Circus tube. **Open** 10am-midnight daily.
Admission free; individual attractions vary.
Credit varies. **Map** p319 K7.
This long-suffering building overlooking Piccadilly Circus is the home of Funland, a dark and extremely noisy indoor funfair. The central attraction is the Pepsi Max Drop Ride (£3), which involves being strapped into a chair and plunging from the top of the building six floors up to the basement in a couple of seconds. Cheaper but less thrilling attractions flash at you from every corner of the building. There are dodgems and a ten-lane, ten-pin bowling alley with a snack bar attached. There is a small-scale shooting range and a fighting machine, where young toughs pay to attack with their fists.
Less aggressive but just as strenuous is the Pump Pump Feel the Beat International Dance Floor machine, on which the correct steps earn points but no prizes. Still, it attracts a

big audience, which is probably the main thing. The Ridge Racer game is played by contestants in life-size red open-top sports cars hurtling round on-screen cliff-top bends like amateurish, old-fashioned film effects. Dynamo Hockey is a sort of space-age shove-ha'penny and the Cybersled, a two-seater capsule that spins you up and down, makes you feel queasy just watching. There are also computer games, on level one; not surprisingly, they're very popular. The pool hall bar, on level 2, is available to over-18s only.

The ground floor is dominated by shops, among them HMV, Baskin Robbins, Claire's Accessories and a bunch of tacky novelty and souvenir stores hawking everything from Union Jack towels to fake-blood squirters.

The Trocadero isn't everyone's cup of tea, but it's cool in the heat and dry in the wet, which is something.

Cafés. Lift. Nappy-changing facilities. Nearest picnic place: Leicester Square/Trafalgar Square. Restaurants. Shops.

Eating & shopping

The West End is full of excellent restaurants of all price brackets, many of which are reviewed in the Eating chapter on pages 170-190. Suffice to say that **Ed's Easy Diner** (12 Old Compton Street, W1, 7434 4439; *see also p175*) is cheap and fun and **Maison Bertaux** (28 Greek Street, W1, 7437 6007) sells the most exquisite French cakes.

For upmarket lunchables and picnic fare, even the wicker hampers to put them in, it has to be **Fortnum & Mason** (181 Piccadilly, W1, 7734 8040). Nearby **Pret a Manger** (163 Piccadilly, W1, 7629 5044) is a cheaper option.

Hamleys (188-96 Regent Street, W1, 7494 2000; *see also p208*) is an Aladdin's cave of goodies, but avoid the queues for Santa's Grotto at Christmas time. If you are in town over the festive period, department store **Liberty** (210-20 Regent Street, W1, 7734 1234) is a better bet. The **Disney Store** (140-4 Regent Street, W1, 7287 6558; *see also p208*) is a must-see for fans of the Corp's characters. **Lillywhite's** (24-36 Lower Regent

Eisenhower is president of all he surveys outside the US Embassy in **Grosvenor Square**. *See p78.*

Street, W1, 7930 3181; *see also p207*) has all sorts of sports equipment and clothing, while **Lonsdale Sports Equipment** (47 Beak Street, W1, 7437 1526), is one for budding boxers. Music lovers head to **Tower Records** (1 Piccadilly Circus, W1, 7439 2500). Back in Soho, the haberdasher **Kleins** (5 Noel Street, W1, 7437 6162) is full of glamour: sequins, fringing and diamante; downstairs sells craft supplies.

Meet the teacher

Lucy Ribeiro is Schools and Access Officer at Apsley House (*see p76*).

What do you do?
I organise the programme for schools, teach workshops and co-ordinate access for disabled visitors.

What activities do children request most?
Children especially enjoy the art activities and costumed characters during our special events for Waterloo Week in June and Victorian Christmas in December.

What other activities are there?
Trails (there are two available, one for 3-5 years and one for 6-11 years) and special sound guides are available for families all through the year. The Schools Service is also extremely popular.

What's the best part of your job?
The variety. During one day I might teach a number of workshops on numeracy, literacy or art to children ranging from 5 to 18 years, create raised images

of the paintings in the collection for visually impaired visitors, or take school bookings!

Do you wear a uniform?
No I don't, I just wear everyday clothes.

Do you dress up?
Some of our freelancers dress up as a Victorian housekeeper for our Schools Service.

Westminster

Ruling passions.

Four palaces have been built in this area where royalty and government meet – **Buckingham**, **St James's**, **Whitehall** and **Westminster**. Queen Elizabeth II lives in the first, and bore four children in one of its wings; Elizabeth I lived in the second and had none. Henry VIII lived in the third, which but for its **Banqueting House** no longer exists, and the last is the home of the so-called Mother of Parliaments, revered by many as a model of democracy. Nearby Downing Street is the home of Prime Minister Tony Blair and his wife and four children. Well travelled as the Blairs may be, there's plenty to occupy them on their own doorstep.

Trafalgar Square is the centre of London and an obvious playground – kids can enjoy the fountains and climb the bronze lions, though feeding the pigeons is now banned (not that that stops some people). When they're bored with this or if it rains, pay the **National Gallery** a visit, or try guessing the famous faces at the **National Portrait** Gallery next door. On the east side of the square, **St Martin-in-the-Fields** houses the London Brass Rubbing Centre.

The Changing of the Guard at **Buckingham Palace** (*see p82*), with its displays of synchronised marching, stamping and shouting orders, draws huge crowds. **St James's Park** (*see p82*) and **Green Park** were once exclusively for royalty but over time have been turned over to the riff-raff for deckchair-dozing and frisbee throwing. The former has a lake and a pleasant children's playground with swings, slides and a huge sandpit.

Until the time of Charles I, it suited monarchs to believe that they were chosen by God, and it's no coincidence that their palaces are next to **Westminster Abbey**, which is convenient for coronations and funerals, if not the shopping scene. Unfortunate royal infants such as the so-called Princes in the Tower are buried in Innocents' Corner. The campanile of **Westminster Cathedral**, meanwhile, offers vertiginous views.

Pigeons need no encouragement: **Trafalgar Square**. *See p88.*

Walk: around the park

▶ Start at St James's Park tube just before 10am (when rush hour is largely over), emerging into Palmer Street then proceeding towards the **Adam & Eve** pub and turning right into **Petty France**. Walk alongside the Home Office and turn left into Queen Anne's Gate, where you'll see the grass and trees of **St James's Park**. Pass through the gate and turn left into **Birdcage Walk**; after a short distance you'll get to the entrance of the Guards' Museum on the left (*see p83*), which opens at 10am. If you arrive early, sit on the stone benches beside the goldfish pond just inside the gate. When you've visited the museum, head for the shop, where you can stock up on tin grenadiers and other model soldiers.

▶ Turning left out of the museum, cross Birdcage Walk to the children's playground, which you'll only be allowed to enter if you have a child with you. It has swings and a slide, a sandpit, a well-kept toilet and an ice-cream stall. At 10.45am you can watch through the railings as a company of guardsmen turn out onto the parade ground in front of **Wellington Barracks** back across Birdcage Walk, together with a military band (*see p85*). At 11.25am the soldiers march smartly out of the barracks towards **Buckingham Palace**, accompanied by mounted police constables, and go to change places with guardsmen at the end of their watch at the palace. If you walk along with them as far as the Victoria memorial at the western end of the Mall, you can watch a squadron of horseguards move slowly towards you from the eastern end, accompanied by policemen on motorbikes.

▶ Enter St James's Park and cross the grass towards the ornamental lake, with its assortment of exotic waterfowl, including ducks, swans and pelicans (the latter are fed daily at 3pm). Follow the lakeside path or stop for a rest in a green-striped deckchair (an attendant will soon appear to take your pennies). At the end of the lake, head for the green restaurant building at the **Trafalgar Square** end, the Cakehouse Café, a cheap and cheerful open-air place, good for baked potatoes and sandwich lunches, with trestle tables outside. After lunch, continue down the Mall to Trafalgar Square and dip your toes in the cool fountain pool or scale one of the four lions.

▶ Afterwards, walk south along **Whitehall** towards Big Ben but turn right into **Horse Guards Parade** when you come to the soldier in a sentry box and pose for a picture with him (see if you can make him smile). Go through the arch and cross the Parade, which was Henry VIII's jousting yard, then turn left into Horse Guards Road. Pass the end of **Downing Street**, where the prime minister and his family lives, and turn right into Birdcage Walk once again. From there return to Queen Anne's Gate and to St James's Park tube on Petty France.

Banqueting House

Whitehall, SW1 (7930 4179/www.hrp.org.uk). Westminster tube/Charing Cross tube/rail. **Open** 10am-5pm Mon-Sat (last entry 4.30pm); sometimes closes at short notice; phone to check. Closed bank hols. **Admission** £3.90; £2.30 5-15s; £3.10 concessions; free under-5s. **Credit** MC, V. **Map** p319 L8.
Before they acquired Buckingham Palace, British kings and queens lived at Whitehall Palace. All of it was destroyed by fire in 1698, except the Banqueting House, a beautiful ceremonial hall commissioned by James I and built by Inigo Jones between 1619 and 1622. The glory of the building is the Rubens ceiling, commissioned by Charles I in 1636, and it is with this king that the hall is most famously associated. It was from its tall windows that he stepped on to a wooden platform, made a short speech calling himself 'martyr of the people' and bent over a chopping block for his execution. Rubens painted the nine panels on to canvas, which was then stuck to the ceiling. The central section is entitled 'The Apotheosis of James I', as the whole was intended as a tribute to Charles's father. In it James is seen ascending to heaven surrounded by well-nourished cherubs, some of whom are spiriting away his earthly symbols of orb, sceptre and crown, while others announce with fanfares his entry into paradise.

A visit to the Banqueting House is preceded by a video presentation of the history of the house. From 1700 the hall was used first as a chapel, then as a museum. Nowadays it's primarily a tourist attraction, but classical concerts are performed with increasing frequency.
Nearest picnic place: St James's Park. Shop.

Buckingham Palace & Royal Mews

SW1 (7930 4832/recorded info 7799 2331/credit card bookings 7321 2233/Royal Mews 7839 1377/ www.royalresidences.com). Green Park or St James's Park tube/Victoria tube or rail. **Open** State Rooms *early Aug-Sept* 9.30am-4.15pm daily. Royal Mews *Oct-July* noon-4pm Mon-Thur. *Aug, Sept* 10.30am-4.30pm Mon-Thur. Last entry 30mins before closing. Closed 25, 26 Dec. **Admission** £11; £5.50 5-17s; £9 concessions; £27.50 family (2+2); free under-5s. *Royal Mews* £4.60; £2.60 5-17s; £3.60 concessions; £11.80 family (2+2); free under-5s. **Credit** AmEx, MC, V. **Map** p318 H9.
Buck House was originally bought from the Buckingham family by the Queen's great-great-great-grandfather George, and it was he who commissioned the extensions that constitute the formal parts that the public sees when the palace opens as a showhome for part of the summer (when Liz and

Phil get away from it all in the country) and not those where the Windsors eat breakfast, watch TV, have rows, kennel the dogs, go to the loo and sleep. Visitors queue from 9am at the box office on Constitution Hill for tickets to view 18 State Apartments, including the Music Room, which was used for the christenings of Charles, Anne, Andrew and Edward, with water brought from the River Jordan; and the Ballroom, which is occasionally used for sit-down meals and banquets when the number of guests demands (the Queen's great-grandmother Victoria, who brought up 11 children under this roof, used to complain about the lack of space in the palace and insisted that the Ballroom be able to accommodate the very wide skirts that were fashionable among 19th-century debutantes).

The Queen's Picture Gallery was closed for a facelift as we went to press (it's scheduled to reopen in May 2002) but there are hundreds of antique framed paintings on other walls. The shop, on the way out, has special Windsor Family chocs, tea towels, mugs, replica jewellery, jigsaws and tin soldiers modelled on the ones who stamp up and down outside.

Just around the corner from Buckingham Palace, on Buckingham Palace Road, are the Windsors' garages and stables. The family keeps one or two limousines powered by internal combustion engines but otherwise travels around in horse-drawn coaches, of which they have made something of a collection, including the Coronation Coach, the Glass Coach and the fairytale-like gold State Coach built in 1761. The horses, which are beautifully groomed by loving servicemen, have their own exercise and dressage arena. The Mews is closed during Royal Ascot and on state occasions.

Buggy access (Royal Mews). Lift (Buckingham Palace). Nappy-changing facilities (Buckingham Palace). Nearest picnic place: Green Park. Shop.

Cabinet War Rooms

Clive Steps, King Charles Street, SW1 (7930 6961/ www.iwm.org.uk). St James's Park or Westminster tube. **Open** *Oct-Mar* 10am-6pm daily. *Apr-Sept* 9.30am-6pm daily. Last entry 5.15pm. Closed 24-26 Dec. **Admission** £5; £3.90 OAPs, students; £2-£2.70 concessions; free under-15s. **Credit** AmEx, MC, V. **Map** p319 K9.

During World War II the then prime minister Winston Churchill actually lived in these bunkers, and though it's the chamberpot under his bed that sticks in the memory of most kids, decisions were made here that bear on our lives today. The bomb-proof underground structure has been preserved largely as it was left when it closed down on 16 August 1945, with the very book, chart and pin in the Map Room occupying the same space it did then. The thorough and wide-ranging schools programmes include a tour, a talk and an educational element focusing on the Home Front, World War II and the subsequent Cold War (in which Churchill but not the bunker was involved). In the workshops (which take place in all school holidays except summer, when the volume of tourist traffic is too high), scouts, guides and students investigate rationing, operate stirrup pumps, wear gas masks, handle items in an evacuee's suitcase or spend an afternoon 'making do and mending'.

Buggy access. Lift. Nappy-changing facilities. Nearest picnic place: St James's Park. Shop.

Guards' Museum

Wellington Barracks, Birdcage Walk, SW1 (7414 3271). St James's Park tube. **Open** 10am-4pm daily. Last entry 3.30pm. Closed 25 Dec, 1 Jan. *Tours* by arrangement. **Admission** £2; £1 concessions; free under-16s; £4 family (2+unlimited children). **Credit** *Shop* AmEx, MC, V. **Map** p318 J9.

Very grand. **Buckingham Palace.** *See p82.*

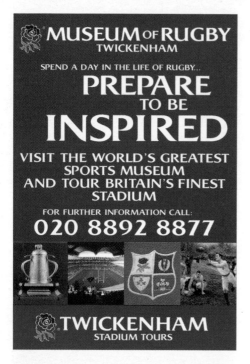

A small armoured vehicle, called a Ferret scout car, marks the entrance to this museum dedicated to the history of the British Army's five Guards regiments, founded in the 17th century under Charles II. Among the medals, tunics and weaponry filling most of the display cases is a miniature Guard's uniform tailored for nine-year-old Prince Arthur, son of Queen Victoria. There's also a large picture of George II at the Battle of Dettingen in 1743 – this was the last time a British monarch actually fought in a war. The oldest medal displayed here was awarded by Oliver Cromwell to officers of his New Model Army at the Battle of Dunbar in 1651.

Mementoes collected from the regiments' many actions over the centuries include the gateposts from the farm at Le Caillou where Napoleon encamped the night before Waterloo and a Nazi propaganda document in English entitled 'Hitler's Last Appeal to Reason' and signed by the Führer himself. There's also a bottle of Iraqi whisky captured in the Gulf War. The Guards can be seen in ceremonial action performing the Changing of the Guard. The toy soldier shop at the museum, the largest of its kind in London, sells all kinds of miniature models, including farm animals.

Note that the museum is closed from 20 Dec 2001-20 Feb 2002 for gallery changes.
Buggy access. Lift. Nearest picnic place:
St James's Park. Shop.

Houses of Parliament

Parliament Square, SW1 (Commons info 7219 4272/Lords info 7219 3107/tours 7344 9966/ www.parliament.uk). Westminster tube. **Open** (when in session) *House of Commons Visitors' Gallery* 2.30-10pm Mon-Wed; 11.30am-7.30pm Thur; 9.30am-3pm Fri. Closed bank hols. *House of Lords Visitors' Gallery* 2.30pm Mon-Wed; from 3pm Thur; from 11am Fri. *Tours* summer recess only phone for details. **Admission** *Public gallery* free. *Tours* £3.50; under-2s free. **Map** p319 L9.

Citizenship will be studied as part of the national curriculum in 2002, but school groups visiting the Houses of Parliament are already having the C-word impressed on them – a tour of the building is followed by a talk on 'needs and wants and how we can help'. The first Parliament was held here in 1275, but Westminster did not become Parliament's permanent home until 1532, when Henry VIII made his home at Whitehall Palace. Parliament was originally housed in the choir stalls of St Stephen's Chapel, where members sat facing each other; the tradition continues today. The only remaining parts of the original palace are Westminster Hall, with its hammer-beam roof, and the Jewel Tower (*see p86*); the rest burned down in a fire (1834) and was rebuilt in neo-Gothic style by Charles Barry and Augustus Pugin. The mammoth structure comprises 1,000 rooms, 100 staircases, 11 courtyards, eight bars and six restaurants (none of which is open to the public).

Families can queue up to visit any session of both the Commons and the Lords, though there's such demand for places at Prime Minister's Questions in the Commons (3pm on Wednesdays) that prospective visitors have to apply to their MP in writing. In general, it's easiest to gain access in the evening when even many MPs find it hard to raise the enthusiasm for debate. There's no minimum age for visitors but children must at least be able to sign their name in the visitors' book. Parliament goes into recess at Christmas, Easter and during the summer just as schools do; at these times the galleries are open only for pre-booked guided tours (call for details).

Always phone to check opening times before making a special journey.
Nearest picnic place: Victoria Tower Gardens. Shop.

Guard duty

The Changing of the Guard, a splendidly futile ceremony that was made famous in a poem by AA Milne (who described a visit made by his son Christopher Robin), involves soldiers marching up and down on the parade ground outside Buckingham Palace.

The Guards are stationed at Wellington Barracks on Birdcage Walk. The fresh set of Guards carries out marching practice on the square in front of the barracks before setting off for the palace to the accompaniment of a military band, which nowadays plays Beatles hits as well as standard military marches. The band and the new Guard start marching at Wellington Barracks at 10.45am, but be sure to arrive early, as thousands of tourists turn up for the spectacle, which takes about an hour and can be seen daily in some months and every other day in others: the authorities cannot say from month to month how frequent it will be, so it's best to ring Buckingham Palace before you set out.

Picture this

If you arrive at the **National Gallery** (*see p87*) with no idea of what to look at among the thousands of pictures, why not check out the following eight paintings, which are of or about families? Pick up a floor plan from the information desk and follow them in sequence clockwise around the gallery.

● Veronese's *Family of Darius before Alexander* (Room 9). The Pisani family, as the family Darius, mistakenly salute Alexander the Great's general.

● Judith Leyster's *A Boy & Girl with a Cat & an Eel* (Room 25). Two children teach us a lesson.

● Rubens' *Minerva Protects Pax from Mars* (Room 31). Political allegory on war and peace using the family of the artist's London landlord as models.

● Michiel Nouts' *Family Group* (lower-floor Gallery A, screen 29). Solemn parents and four buttoned-up children gaze out seriously.

● Frans Hals' *Family Group in a Landscape* (Room 24). Unknown Dutch family of ten.

● Rembrandt's *Margaretha Trip* (Room 23). Portrait of a 78-year-old woman who had at least a dozen children to light up her life.

● Gainsborough's *Mr & Mrs Andrews* (Room 35). Much-loved but unfinished painting of an English farmer and his wife, with space for children.

● Stubbs' *Melbourne & Milbanke Families* (Room 35). English aristocrats with their animals.

ICA Gallery

The Mall, SW1 (box office 7930 3647/membership enquiries 7766 1439/www.ica.org.uk). Piccadilly Circus tube/Charing Cross tube/rail. **Open** *Galleries* noon-7.30pm daily. Closed 24-26 Dec, 31 Dec, 1 Jan. **Membership** *Daily* £1.50, £1 concessions Mon-Fri; £2.50, £1.50 concessions Sat, Sun; under-14s free. *Annual* £25; £15 concessions. **Credit** AmEx, DC, MC, V. **Map** p319 K8.

Though computer screens and digital technology befuddle many parents, kids seem to intuitively know what to do at a terminal. The Institute of Contemporary Arts recognises this, hence its 'Summer University' for 11-16-year-olds, offering free fortnightly digital courses in areas such as web design, web movie making and computer game creation. Of a more traditional nature are the sixth-form conferences in which arty teenagers can meet professional artists, and the workshops attended and run by contestants in the annual Beck's Futures exhibition (an art competition sponsored by Beck's beer).

Temporary exhibitions provide ready-made subjects for discussion. Half-term breaks are filled with workshops in drawing or sculpture and there are plans for a primary school programme with dance, art appreciation and computer animation strands.

Café. Nappy-changing facilities. Nearest picnic place: St James's Park. Shop.

Jewel Tower

Abingdon Street, SW1 (7222 2219/ www.english-heritage.org.uk). Westminster tube. **Open** *Apr-Sept* 10am-6pm daily. *Oct* 10am-5pm daily. *Nov-Mar* 10am-4pm daily. Last entry 30min before closing. Closed 24-26 Dec, 1 Jan. **Admission** (EH) £1.60; 80p 5-16s; £1.20 concessions; free under-5s. **Credit** MC, V. **Map** p319 L9.

Along with Westminster Hall, the moated Jewel Tower is a survivor from the medieval Palace of Westminster. It was built in 1365-6 to house Edward III's gold and jewels but

Heirs & graces

Forty-one monarchs have reigned since the illegitimate French duke William the Bastard of Normandy was crowned William I of England at Westminster Abbey on Christmas Day 1066. Only 28 of them produced male heirs, or Princes of Wales as the eldest son of the British sovereign has been known since 1301, when Edward I defeated the last native Prince of Wales, Llewellyn ap Gruffydd, and annexed the principality. Of these 28 kings-in-waiting, just 14 acceded to the throne, including two who barely count – 12-year-old Edward V, murdered (allegedly) by his uncle Richard, who became king in his place, and Edward VIII, who abdicated in 1936 after 11 months on the throne for the love of Wallis Simpson, an American divorcée.

So what's the outlook for the current Prince of Wales? Well, there are certain factors that enhance Charles's chances of eventually making it to the throne. At over 50, he may be considered well past the danger period of youth. But for infantile illnesses, there would have been English

kings called Eustace, Albert and Frederick; Queen Anne, the last of the Stuarts, gave birth to 17 heirs of either sex, only to see them die one by one. Charles is unlikely to die in battle, which is what happened to the son of Henry VI, Edward, at Tewkesbury in 1471; nor is he likely to drown at sea, as Henry I's heir William did in 1120.

Princes of Wales seem to have had most to fear from members of their own family – was Henry I responsible for his brother William II's 'freak' accident with a crossbow in the New Forest in 1100?, for instance – but Charles's family seems unlikely to stage any coups. In fact, it's Charles himself who could be his own worst enemy – is the ecologically minded prince simply too caring and sensitive to take on the mantle of kingship?

The sort of kings whom British subjects have tended to respect are the foreign ones who couldn't give a damn about the place – William the Conqueror didn't consider Britannia worthy of his eldest son Robert, who inherited comfortable, sophisticated Normandy, while two of the Georges (I

there are no jewels here now. Instead, the museum, which welcomes school groups, features an exhibition on the past and present of Parliament. Of most interest to children is a Saxon sword that was dug up during excavation of the moat in 1948.
Nearest picnic place: Victoria Tower Gardens. Shop.

Bathe in glory in **Trafalgar Square**. *See p88.*

National Gallery
Trafalgar Square, WC2 (info line 7747 2885 www.nationalgallery.org.uk). Leicester Square tube/Charing Cross tube/rail. **Open** 10am-6pm Mon, Tue, Thur-Sun; 10am-9pm Wed. *Micro Gallery* 10am-5.30pm Mon, Tue, Thur-Sun; 10am-8.30pm Wed. *Sainsbury Wing* 10am-6pm Mon, Tue, Thur-Sun; 10am-9pm Wed. Closed Good Friday, 25 Dec. *Tours* free; times vary; check info line. **Admission** free; temporary exhibitions prices vary. **Credit** *Shop* MC, V. **Map** p319 K7.
This great collection of Western European painting from the mid 13th century to 1900 started from small beginnings. When the National Collection of Paintings was started in 1824, it consisted of just 38 pictures. Hung in light, airy galleries, especially in the Sainsbury Wing, the collection includes famous masterpieces that children, as well as their parents, will recognise: Constable's *Hay-Wain*, Van Gogh's *Sunflowers* and Seurat's *Bathers at Asnières* to name but a few. Among the temporary exhibitions planned for the near future are Goya: The Family of the Infante Don Luis (1 Dec 2001–3 Mar 2002) and Baroque Painting in Genoa (13 Mar–16 June 2002).

The National's family events are the talk of every cultured family: there are special audio guides, drop-in activities every second Saturday and a whole range of educational workshops to encourage a love of art (*see p217*). See also *p86.*
Buggy access. Café. Lift. Nappy-changing facilities. Nearest picnic place: Leicester Square/Trafalgar Square. Restaurant. Shops.

National Portrait Gallery
2 St Martin's Place, WC2 (7306 0055/www.npg.org.uk). Leicester Square tube/Charing Cross tube/rail. **Open** 10am-6pm Mon-Wed, Sat, Sun; 10am-9pm Thur, Fri.

and II) hated Britain, had no interest in speaking English and spent more time in Hanover. And Richard the Lionheart spent no more than six months here during his ten-year reign.

Breaks in the chain, when monarchs fail to produce heirs or heirs fail to succeed monarchs, generally occasion a change of royal house and new coats of arms, as happened with the successive rules of the Normans, Plantagenets, Lancastrians, Yorkists, Tudors, Stuarts, Hanoverians, Saxe-Coburg-Gothas and Windsors. No branch since the Tudors has managed to provide more than five monarchs and the trend has been towards fewer and fewer – the Saxe-Coburg-Gothas only numbered two (Victoria and her son Edward VII) before their diplomatic adoption during World War I of the English-sounding surname Windsor. There have now been three Windsor kings and one Windsor queen, so it's about time for change. Perhaps Charles should relinquish his claim to the throne in favour of his studious elder son, William.

Closed 25, 26 Dec, 1 Jan. *Tours* Aug free; times vary; phone for details. **Admission** free; selected exhibitions £5; £3 concessions. **Credit** AmEx, MC, V. **Map** p319 K7.
Before photography came along, families who wanted to record their images for posterity had to turn to portraitists for help. You'll find no better evidence of that than at the National Portrait Gallery. All the portraits in the Gallery are of people who have contributed in some way to the life of Great Britain over the years.

The main collection hangs in the new Ondaatje Wing (named after a major contributor, Christopher Ondaatje) at the top of a long escalator. Picture 5511, in Room 1, shows the boy-king Edward VI looking serious as he carries the weight of his father Henry VIII's ambitions on his tiny shoulders, while in Room 2 (picture 3914) Walter Raleigh and his son (also named Walter but known as Wat) adopt identical poses, and in Room 5 (picture 4759) Cornelius Johnson immortalises the Royalist Capel family shortly before the father's execution in 1640. Items from the photograph collection change frequently because of their sensitivity to light, which means that Howard Coster's snapshot of AA Milne with his son Christopher Robin and the original Winnie the Pooh may or may not be on display (though you can always buy a postcard of it in the well-stocked shop). The extension also boasts the Portrait, a swanky restaurant with views west beyond Nelson's Column and across a sea of sloping rooftops to Westminster.

Art house. **Tate Britain.**

In the main building, in Room 21 (picture 1833), Henry Jamyn Brooks' painting of the Old Masters Exhibition at the Royal Academy in 1888 focuses on a family visiting an art exhibition, just like you.
Buggy access. Café. Lift. Nappy-changing facilities. Nearest picnic place: Leicester Square/Trafalgar Square. Restaurant. Shop.

St Martin-in-the-Fields

Trafalgar Square, WC2 (7766 1100/Brass Rubbing Centre 7930 9306/box office evening concerts 7839 8362/www.stmartin-in-the-fields.org). Leicester Square tube/Charing Cross tube/rail. **Admission** free. *Brass rubbing* £2.90-£15 (special rates for groups and families). *Evening concerts* £6-£16 (7.30pm Thur-Sat). **Open** *Church* 8am-6pm daily. *Brass Rubbing Centre* 10am-6pm Mon-Sat; noon-6pm Sun. **Credit** MC, V. **Map** p319 L7.
This is Buckingham Palace's local church, and it has a royal box in the gallery, though not many members of the monarchy have visited its beautiful interior since it really was 'in the fields' between Westminster and the City. Nowadays it's chiefly famous for its cheap café in the crypt, its soup kitchen for down-and-outs and its free lunchtime concerts on Mondays, Tuesdays and Fridays, at 1pm. Its chief attraction as far as children are concerned is the city's only brass rubbing centre, with 90 brasses from all over the world. Many are scaled-down replicas and some have been designed specially for the tourist market. Particularly popular are the two beautifully ornate Flemish dragons from the late 14th century. Rubbings, which are supervised, take about half an hour to complete. All materials are supplied.
Café. Nearest picnic place: Leicester Square/ Trafalgar Square.

Tate Britain

Millbank, SW1 (7887 8000/www.tate.org.uk). Pimlico tube/C10, 77A, 88 bus. **Open** 10am-5.50pm daily. Closed 24-26 Dec. *Tours* free; 11.30am, 2.30pm, 3.30pm Mon-Fri. **Admission** free; prices for special exhibitions vary. **Credit** MC, V. **Map** p319 K11.
Since the establishment of Tate Modern downriver in Southwark (*see p41*), Tate Britain has dedicated its galleries to British art from the 16th century to the present, with displays of Blake, Constable, Spencer and Bacon et al expanded to fit the greater space. To mark 100 years since the Tate opened, the Centenary Development was unveiled on 1 November 2001. The project has created extra space for the collections – new galleries on the main floor plus six new Linbury Galleries on the ground floor. The latter will host temporary exhibitions – look out for American Sublime (20 Feb-19 May 2002) and Lucian Freud (20 June-15 Sept 2002). A grand staircase and increased visitor facilities (another shop, more talks and conferences) complete the upgrade.
Every Sunday is children's day, with Art Trolley (creative play) for the under-11s and the less messy Art Space for older kids, with jigsaws and other activities. For more on these and on family workshops in the school holidays, *see p218*.
Buggy access. Café. Lift. Nappy-changing facilities. Nearest picnic place: lawns on either side of gallery/Riverside Gardens by Vauxhall Bridge. Shop.

Trafalgar Square

SW1. Charing Cross tube/rail.
In many ways Trafalgar Square is both the emotional and geographical heart of the capital – it's to its statue of Charles I that mileposts measure distances to the centre of London, and it's

here that many revellers come to welcome in the New Year, while the fountains are popular with frolicking children on summer days. Feeding the hundreds of pigeons, despite Mayor Ken Livingstone's termination of the last feed-seller's licence in 2000, is carried on by many tourists.

Nelson's Column, which dominates the square and is one of London's best-known landmarks, commemorates the former admiral's naval victories over the French, most famously at the Battle of Trafalgar in which he died. The column is guarded by four huge bronze lions that youngsters like to clamber on and pet, and on either side of it are bronze statues of generals Napier and Havelock. In the north-east corner of the square is an equestrian statue of George IV, who as Prince Regent defined the elegant Regency period. The plinth in the north-west corner of the square has hosted various temporary works in recent years; it currently bears a resin cast of itself by sculptor Rachel Whiteread, which will stay in place until late spring 2002 (a replacement is yet to be decided).

Westminster Abbey

Dean's Yard, SW1 (7222 5152/tours 7222 7110/www.westminster-abbey.org). St James's Park or Westminster tube. **Open** *Nave & royal chapels* 9.30am-4.45pm Mon-Fri; 9am-2.45pm Sat. *Chapter House* Nov-Mar 10am-4pm daily. Apr-Sept 9.30am-5pm daily. Oct 10am-5pm daily. *Pyx Chamber & Abbey Museum* 10.30am-4pm daily. *College Garden* Apr-Sept 10am-6pm Tue-Thur. Oct-Mar 10am-4pm Tue-Thur. Last entry 1hr before closing. Closed 24, 25 Dec, Good Friday. **Tours** phone for details. **Admission** *Nave & royal chapels* £6; £3 11-15s; £3 concessions; £12 family (2+3); free under-11s with paying adult. *Chapter House, Pyx Chamber & Abbey Museum* (EH) £2.50; £1 with main entrance ticket; free with £2 audio guide. **Credit** MC, V. **Map** p319 K9.

Power house. **Houses of Parliament**. *See p85.*

God's house. **Westminster Abbey**.

Visitors to Westminster Abbey are greeted by Richard II, whose portrait hangs inside the porch overlooking the Tomb of the Unknown Warrior, the most haunting memorial in a building full of them. Ever since Edward the Confessor built his church to St Peter (consecrated in 1065) on the site of the Saxon original, the abbey has been linked with royalty – with two exceptions, every English monarch since William the Conqueror (1066) has been crowned here, and many are buried here, too, along with poets, musicians, scientists and others who have played significant roles in the history of the nation.

Of special interest to children is Innocents' Corner, part of the north aisle of Henry VII's chapel; in it are buried the skeletons of the two small boys found in the Tower of London, believed to be Edward V and his brother Richard, who were thought to have been murdered by their uncle Richard, later Richard III. Here, too, are the tombs of two of the children of James I: the effigy of Princess Sophia, who lived only three days, lies in a stone cradle, and Princess Mary, who died when she was two, reclines on top of a miniature mausoleum.

In 1998 ten niches on the west front of the abbey, which had been empty since the Middle Ages, were filled with new statues of selected 20th-century martyrs, including Archbishop of San Salvador Oscar Romero, Polish Catholic Maximilian Kolbe, Dietrich Bonhoeffer, who was murdered by the Nazis and black rights activist Martin Luther King Jr.

The boys' choir, one of the world's most famous, is as old as the abbey itself. Auditions for boys aged eight to ten of any religion take place regularly, with successful applicants educated at Westminster School in Dean's Yard beside the abbey. The luckiest choristers get to sing at coronations (admittedly few and far between), royal weddings and state occasions. *Buggy access. Café. Nearest picnic place: Dean's Yard. Shop.*

Sightseeing

Westminster Cathedral

Victoria Street, SW1 (7798 9055/tours7798 9064/ www.westminstercathedral.org.uk). Victoria tube/rail.
Open 7am-7pm Mon-Fri, Sun; 8am-7pm Sat. *Tours* by arrangement. **Admission** free; donations appreciated. *Campanile* £2, £1 concessions; £5 family (2+2). *Audio guide* £2.50; £1.50 concessions. **No credit cards.** **Map** p318 J10.

Worksheets available at the gift shop familiarise the young with this beautiful late Victorian cathedral, whose vaulted pitch-black ceiling is still waiting to be decorated. Sheets for the under-tens require kids to study the architecture and spot butterflies in the mosaics; those for the over-tens ask questions on subjects such as the martyrs and saints commemorated in the building. It's worth the climb to the viewing platform at the top of the campanile.

The boys' choir, one of the finest choirs in the country, sings daily Vespers (5pm) and Mass (5.30pm; more on Sundays) all year except August. Roman Catholic boys aged eight to ten can apply to the headmaster of the choir school for auditions, which are held regularly.

Buggy access. Café. Nearest picnic place: Ashley Gardens off Howick Place. Shop.

Eating & shopping

Burger chains proliferate all round Trafalgar Square. More adventurous visitors should try **Texas Embassy Cantina** at the back of Trafalgar Square (1 Cockspur Street, SW1, 7925 0077; *see also p177*), where staff welcome children with balloons, crayons, a special menu and a cheery hello. The **Cakehouse Café** in St James's Park serves hot savouries (sausages, jacket potatoes, soups). There are also a number of Internet cafés and cheap restaurants around Victoria Station, including **easyEverything** (9-13 Wilton Road, SW1, 7233 8456) and **Café Internet** (22-4 Buckingham Palace

Road, SW1, 7233 5786). Branches of **ASK** (7630 8228) and **Pizza Express** (7828 1477; *see p185*) can be found on Victoria Street.

Crivelli's Garden (7747 2869), the National Gallery's ultra-smart restaurant, has high chairs for babies but rather fancy Mediterranean food. Snacks, salads, soups and chunky main courses are cheap and cheerful in **Café in the Crypt** (Crypt of St Martin-in-the Fields, Duncannon Street, WC2, 7839 4342) if all that brass rubbing has worked up an appetite.

Most of the decent shopping that's to be done in Westminster is in the area around Victoria. The **Army & Navy Stores** (101 Victoria Street, SW1, 7834 1234) is a slightly neglected close relative of the more upmarket House of Fraser, but it's useful for clothes and home necessities. **Game** (106 Victoria Street, SW1, 7931 7631) has a huge number of computer games, plus consoles.

Those about to throw a party will want to visit **Just Balloons** (127 Wilton Road, SW1, 7434 3039; *see also p245*), books, games and gifts can be found at the **National Trust Gift Shop** (Blewcoats School, 23 Caxton Street, SW1, 7222 2877) and bikes are sold (no rentals) at **Action Bikes** (19 Dacre Street, SW1, 7799 2233; *see also p207*). Head out west toward Sloane Square and you're in Belgravia, where the shops are posher; here's Emma Forbes' pretty childrenswear shop, **Semmalina** (225 Ebury Street, SW1, 7730 9333; *see also p200*), for example.

Victoria Station's shopping centre is good for chain stores and has a **Café Rouge** (7931 9300; *see also p184*). Elsewhere in Westminster, and especially as you go in the direction of Piccadilly, the shops are either bookish or smart and country gentish.

Meet the teacher

Jo Hunt is Education Officer at the Cabinet War Rooms (*see p83*).

What do you do?
I co-ordinate and organise school visits and I address the children when they arrive. My full name is Jocelyn Hunt, but I only use it when I write A-level history textbooks for Routledge.

What activities do children request most?
They don't really request things themselves, but what they like most of all is the Blitz workshop, when they can handle lots of World War II stuff, and the Propart workshop, in which they study propaganda posters, mostly British ones, and then design their own.

What other activities are there?
All sorts of things. We try to get the children to understand what life was like in wartime Britain. They can darn a sock for an RAF pilot or make a meal using only rationed items.

What's the best part of your job?
The fact I get to handle and talk about all these fascinating and wonderful relics of a bygone era, and I have the chance to make history come alive. What I like is the opportunity to engage with pupils and for them to engage with the museum. It's a wonderful place if you let it fire the imagination.

Do you wear a uniform?
No, just a security badge on my everyday clothes.

Do you dress up?
No, but the children do sometimes. One activity has them all going round dressed as 1940s evacuees for a day. It really brings home to them what war must have been like. Suddenly they see that history isn't just a matter of reading dry old textbooks, although being a writer means I am responsible for that aspect of it as well.

Marylebone

Wild animals couldn't drag you away.

Enclosed by the thundering thoroughfares of Oxford Street, Edgware Road, Marylebone Road and Great Portland Street, Marylebone used to comprise two ancient manors, Lileston (Lisson) and Tyburn (named after a stream that flowed through the area and the site of a famous gallows from 1388 to 1783; the site is marked by a plaque on the traffic island at Marble Arch). The area was a hotbed of violence and criminal activity, and after frequent ransacking of the parish church, which stood in what is now Oxford Street, a second was built about halfway up what has since become **Marylebone High Street**. The church was named St Mary's by the Bourne, which came to designate the entire area, eventually being shortened to Marylebone.

Though nothing remains of the first two parish churches, you can see the foundations of the third (which was demolished after damage sustained during World War I) towards the top of the high street, in the **Memorial Garden of Rest**. Connected with many famous figures (including Lord Byron, who was baptised here in 1788, and Lord Nelson, who worshipped here and whose only child Horatio was christened here in 1803), the garden is a pleasant place to sit and take stock of the places to go and people to see in this diverse area, which covers villagey Marylebone High Street and the tourist-heavy sights of Marylebone Road and its environs.

Among those people are the myriad waxen images of **Madame Tussaud's**, the area's biggest draw for foreign tourists. British families tend to be more enamoured of **London Zoo**, across the park from Tussaud's. It's hard to believe that **Regent's Park**, home of the zoo, is just a brisk walk from the chaos of Oxford Street. It marks the northern reaches of Marylebone, covering an area that was once royal hunting ground.

The southern half of Marylebone was developed into an elegant sweep of streets and squares by the Portman family in the 18th century. Dignified Manchester Square, is home to the paintings, armour and other goodies of the **Wallace Collection**.

Stately **Portland Place**, leading up to Regent's Park, was the glory of 18th-century London, and although many of its houses have been rebuilt, its spacious proportions have been maintained. At its kink, where it links with architect John Nash's Regent Street at Langham Place, is the BBC's HQ, **Broadcasting House**, which is set for expansion over the next few years – though the family-friendly BBC Experience is unlikely to be resurrected, there are plans for a 'new landmark broadcasting centre'.

London Planetarium

Marylebone Road, NW1 (0870 400 3000/ www.london-planetarium.com). Baker Street tube. **Open** *June-Aug* 10am-5pm daily. *Sept-May* 12.30-5pm Mon-Fri; 10am-5pm Sat, Sun. Closed 25 Dec. **Admission** £7; £4.85 5-15s; £5.60 concessions. Under-5s not admitted. *Combined ticket with Madame Tussaud's* £14.45; £10 5-15s; £11.30 concessions; £49 family (2+2 or 3+1). **Credit** AmEx, MC, V. **Map** p316 G4.

The main event here is a thrilling star show projected on to a screen on the ceiling of the dome. Choose a seat in one of the back rows, sit back and enjoy an outer-space experience, with meteorite showers and exploding planets, plus a soundtrack that's corny but delivers the right atmosphere. The 20-minute film plays every 40 minutes; if you just miss one, you have to wait in the lobby area, which is done up to look space age (with models of planets and astronauts, a zero-gravity weighing machine and other gravity-inspired games) but has little to hold the attention of children. Book ahead to avoid queues. *Café. Lift. Nappy-changing facilities. Nearest picnic place: Regent's Park. Shop.*

Marylebone High Street – blooming marvellous.

Squirrel charms child in **Regent's Park**. *See p93.*

Madame Tussaud's

Marylebone Road, NW1 (0870 400 3000/
www.madame-tussauds.com). Baker Street tube.
Open *May-Sept* 9.30am-5.30pm daily. *Oct-June* 10am-
5.30pm Mon-Fri, 9.30am-5.30pm Sat, Sun. Times vary
during hols; phone to check. Closed 25 Dec. **Admission**
£12; £8.50 5-15s; £9.50 concessions; £39 family (2+2
or 3+1; timed tickets only); free under-5s. *Combined ticket
with Planetarium* £14.45; £10 5-15s; £11.30 concessions;
£49 family (2+2 or 3+1; timed tickets only). **Credit**
AmEx, MC, V. **Map** p316 G4.
London's most popular fee-paying attraction, Madame
Tussaud's has always been distinguished by the queues of
foreign tourists wrapped round it, though a new hotline giving visitors timed entry is intended to put paid to all that.
Sadly, children are more charmed by the idea of Tussaud's
than the reality – once they've stuck their fingers up Pierce
Brosnan's nose and peeked up Darcey Bussel's tutu, they're
clamouring for the Chamber of Horrors, where waxen guts
spill out of bloody corpses and royal heads sit on spikes.
These Horrors are reached through a gloomy passageway,
and include a truly horrible Jack the Ripper section and
a nasty, screaming soundtrack. They're certainly alarming
enough for the under-eights, but incite scoffs and giggles from
more experienced blood-and-guts aficionados, especially
those lucky kids who have witnessed the horrors of the
London Dungeon (*see p38*).
Additions to the main collection such as Ken Livingstone
and Alan Titchmarsh are hardly going to set the kids alight:
you'd be better off making for the new Superstars section,
where you'll find a motley crew including a suitably moody
Samuel L Jackson, Chris Tarrant and David Beckham (hopefully to be joined by his Posh lady wife Victoria, who's mov-

A boat to the Zoo

London Waterbus Company

*Camden Lock Place, off Chalk Farm Road, NW1
(7482 2550). Camden Town tube. **Open** Apr-Oct
10am-5pm daily. Nov-Mar 11am-4pm Sat, Sun.
Closed 25 Dec, 1 Jan. **Return trips** Little
Venice–Camden Lock £5.60; £3.60 3-15s;
free under-3s. **One-way trip with zoo admission**
Little Venice–London Zoo £11; £8.20 3-15s; free
under-3s. Camden Lock–London Zoo £10.50;
£8 3-15s; free under-3s. **No credit cards**.
Buggies must be folded prior to boarding.*

ing here, along with a bunch of other glittering popster celebs,
from the now-defunct Rock Circus). The finale, a ride in
London 'time taxi' through the sights and sounds of London's
history, is short and rather baffling.
Buggies aren't allowed but baby carriers are provided.
*Café. Lifts. Nappy-changing facilities. Nearest picnic place:
Regent's Park.*

Regent's Park

*NW1 (7486 7905/tennis courts 7486 4216/
www.royalparks.co.uk). Baker Street, Camden Town,
Great Portland Street or Regent's Park tube. **Open** Park
& Queen Mary's Gardens 5am-30mins before dusk daily.
Tennis courts Mar-Oct 9am-dusk daily. Apr-Sept 7am-
dusk daily. Playgrounds 10am-30min before dusk daily.*
Map p316 G2.

Walk: around Regent's Park

▶ Come out of Regent's Park tube and head
towards the park. Cross busy Marylebone Road
and walk up Park Square West. Cross Outer Circle;
just inside the park is the first well-kept children's
playground on this walk. Once you've managed to
extricate the kids from its delights, head due west
along the Outer Circle until you reach York Bridge
on your right, then walk over it to the Inner Circle.
Across this circle – inside it, in fact – are Queen
Mary's Gardens, the flowery heart of the park.
There's a small lake here, a fragrant rose garden
and, behind the trees in the north-western corner,
the famous and atmospheric **Open Air Theatre**
(*see p225*), where there's a show for families every
summer, as well as Shakespeare in the evenings.
Queen Mary's Gardens contain the Rose Garden
buffet, which has an impressive ice-cream
selection, a function room and a private playground
that can be hired for children's parties.

▶ Return to the Inner Circle to admire the Holme,
another beautiful Nash villa, just south-west of the
theatre, before striking out in a westerly direction
for the lake and Hanover Island, where herons
live and breed. The café at the boat house has
a decent menu of barbecue-type lunches and
snacks. In good weather its terrace, where there is
weekly free entertainment for young children during

the summer holidays, is packed to capacity.
Tired parents will like the children's boating lake
with pedalos (£2 per 15-minute ride); otherwise
you can man the rowlocks on the main Boating
Lake, where a rowing boat for a small family
group can be hired for £2 for 30mins per child
or £4 an hour per adult.

▶ The second children's playground is just to the
west of the children's boating pond, and just over
the Outer Circle from that the 43-metre (141-foot)
minaret of the Central London Mosque is visible
right across the park. When the playground has
been fully investigated, walk across the sports field
to **London Zoo** (*see p94*), or at least its boundaries.
When you rejoin the Outer Circle, where the zoo's
main gate is situated, either go and meet the
animals or settle for a glimpse of the various fauna
and their urban habitat as you stroll to Gloucester
Green and the third children's playground.

▶ The last bit of the walk is south along the
Broad Walk, past the newly restored Readymoney
Drinking Fountain. There's more refreshment
(soups, pastries, drinks) at the chalet-like building
by the Broad Walk or further south at the Chester
Gate park café. Duly refreshed, head back south
to Marylebone Green and the first playground,
before returning to the tube station.

A day at: London Zoo

Well aware that gawping at wild animals in enclosures offends modern sensibilities, the Zoological Society of London has gone all out to publicise the breeding programmes it runs for endangered species, which are pivotal to wildlife conservation in the natural world. To make the best of the zoo's 36 acres – which you'll need at least a day to cover (children can easily fritter away an hour, and plenty of pocket money, in the shop alone) – pick up a guide from the front desk and make a plan of action. Popular attractions include feeding times for some of the stars (pigs, pelicans, fish), hands-on experiences with reptiles and various events in the Web of Life and Lifewatch centres. You're bound to miss something, but if everyone chooses a 'must see' you can work out your tour accordingly.

The £4.4 million invested in the Web of Life was money well spent. Set in a light, bright, ecologically inspirational building called the Millennium Conservation Centre, it is a monument to biodiversity, which is presented, explained and celebrated in a delightful fashion. Children invariably spend a long time with the cockroaches and other insects living the life of Riley in glass-fronted luxury homes.

Much entertainment can be had from the penguins diving and waddling in their cool, white, elegant home, designed by Tecton and Lubetkin. The Reptile House is another popular haunt, and no child should be denied the pleasure of cuddling goats and sheep in the spick and span Children's Zoo, which shows how hamsters, gerbils, mice and rats should be kept as pets, in spacious enclosures (experts also occasionally give talks on keeping small pets).

When it comes to feeding the family, the Fountain Café has a small range of meals, including half-price portions of hot dishes and special lunchboxes with sandwiches, crisps, fruit, biscuits and juice, for the children. There are also indoor and outdoor seating areas for picnics, and, in peak season, ice-cream, drink and snack vendors dotted all around. The shop, which has been a high point for more than 30 years, is now even better than ever, with lots of stuff for pocket-money prices.

A trip to the zoo is a fine birthday treat in itself, but if you're bent on spoiling the birthday boy or girl rotten, contact aka Rampage (7722 5909), a company affiliated to the zoo, which organises activities, games and tea here; *see also p247*.

If you're planning a winter visit, it's worth booking ahead for a 'Christmas Experience', which houses the best living nativity scene in London (real reindeer and walk-on parts by the stars of the children's zoo), mulled wine, mince pies and Christmas dinners.

In spring and summer, and on winter weekends, you can get to the zoo by canalboat from Little Venice or Camden Lock (*see p93*); the all-inclusive

ticket allows you into the zoo without queuing. If you're feeling particularly energetic, walk to the zoo along the canal from Regent's Park, though you should bear in mind that you'll be doing a great deal of walking and standing once you're in the zoo itself.

London Zoo

Regent's Park, NW1 (7722 3333/ www.londonzoo.co.uk). Baker Street or Camden Town tube, then 274 or C2 bus. **Open** *Nov-Mar 10am-4pm daily. Apr-Oct 10am-5.30pm daily. Closed 25 Dec.* **Admission** *£10; £7 3-15s; £8.50 concessions; free under-3s.* **Credit** *AmEx, MC, V.* **Map** *p316 G2.*

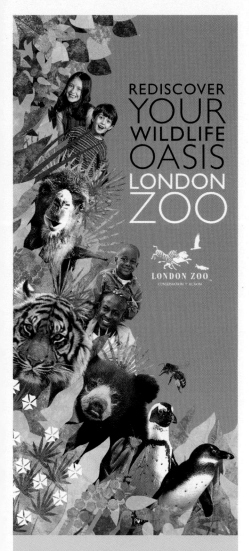

Factfile: London Zoo

- More than 600 species live at London Zoo.

- Of these, an amazing 150 are listed on the IUCN (the World Conservation Union) Red List of the world's most threatened species.

- Though the zoo has welcomed paying visitors since 1847, it first opened in 1826, celebrating its 175th birthday in 2001.

- The zoo's food bills are massive, as the animals get through 23 tons of bananas a year (not surprisingly, the monkeys and apes eat most of them). A whopping 35 tons of carrots, 31 tons of potatoes, 26 tons of apples, 11 tons of oranges and 40 tons of meat are also consumed annually.

- Guy the gorilla, one of London Zoo's best-loved characters, ate quite a few bananas in the 31 years he lived there. When he died in 1978 London went into mourning. You can visit the bronze sculpture of Guy by the Apes & Monkeys section.

- The smallest celebrity resident was probably Belinda the Mexican red-kneed bird-eating spider, who died aged 22 in 1993. She made many TV appearances and because of her 'cuddliness' was often used to help people overcome their arachnophobia, through the zoo's Friendly Spider Programme.

- Today's animal celebs include another Mexican red-kneed bird-eating spider called Frieda, Dana the lemur and Max the eagle owl. The last two feature in the 'Animals in Action' displays.

- Some of the more 'misunderstood' animals at London Zoo include black rats, which carried the bubonic plague in the Middle Ages, as well as cockroaches, snakes, scorpions and bats.

- London Zoo runs an adoption scheme to raise money to care for the animals (from £25; phone or check out the website for details). Penguins and tigers are the most commonly adopted animals.

- Some of the species found at the zoo are extinct in the wild, and others are on the verge of disappearing forever. These include the Asiatic lions (just 300 are left in the wild) and the Sumatran tigers (400).

- The children's zoo was opened by the young Robert and Edward Kennedy in 1938. It was redeveloped in 1995 and reopened as the Ambika Paul Children's Zoo, dedicated to the memory of Ambika Paul, who died of leukaemia aged four in 1968. Ambika loved coming to the children's zoo, and it was her father, Lord Paul, who donated £1 million for its redevelopment.

Central London's cleanest green lung, Regent's Park has three playgrounds, the best boating in London, well-kept sports facilities, London Zoo (see p94), an excellent open-air theatre and oodles of class. It started life as a royal hunting estate in the Forest of Middlesex, until it was laid out as parkland by John Nash, the Prince Regent's friend and chief architect, in the 19th century. Walking the Outer Circle, the 2-mile (3.2km) main road round the park, brings you to some of London's most popular sights. South of the park, amid the fumes of Marylebone Road, are Madame Tussaud's (see p93) and London Planetarium (see p91), as well as Nash's elegant Park Crescent, which was originally intended to be a full circus. To the west is the London Central Mosque, built in 1978 to service the spiritual needs of many of the city's Muslims, while east are the plush Palladian mansions of Nash's Cumberland Terrace. Further north is the Grand Union Canal and, across Prince Albert Road, Primrose Hill (see also p99), which affords great views of the city and has its own playground (of the swings and slides variety), where the children of both the minor Britpack celebs who have colonised the area and ordinary mortals can de-stress. See also p93.

Sherlock Holmes Museum
221B Baker Street, NW1 (7935 8866/ www.sherlock-holmes.co.uk). Baker Street tube. **Open** 9.30am-6pm daily. Closed 25 Dec. **Admission** £6; £4 6-16s; free under-6s. **Credit** AmEx, DC, MC, V. **Map** p313 F4.
The people handing out flyers near the statue of Holmes outside the tube station will direct you to this lovingly recreated 'home' of someone who never existed. Although the front door says 221B to keep the Holmes fantasists going, it is, in fact, at 239 Baker Street. The real 221B is a few doors down the road, now the site of an Abbey National, where the task of opening all the post sent to 'Holmes' is so cumbersome it requires a full-time job. Visitors can see the sleuth's putative hat and pipe, leather briefcase, books and toiletries, and mannequins depicting scenes from Conan Doyle's works. Not really worth shelling out for unless someone in the family is a Sherlock fiend.
Nearest picnic place: Regent's Park. Shop.

Wallace Collection
Hertford House, Manchester Square, W1 (7935 0687/ www.the-wallace-collection.org.uk). Bond Street tube. **Open** 10am-5pm Mon-Sat; noon-5pm Sun. Closed 24, 25 Dec, Good Friday. **Admission** free. **Credit** *Shop* MC, V. **Map** p316 G5.
One of London's most splendid collections – and all the more gorgeous for being free – the Wallace resides in Sir Richard Wallace's late 18th-century house.The illegitimate son of the Marquis of Hertford, Wallace inherited the extraordinary array of furniture (including a writing desk belonging to Marie Antoinette), paintings and porcelain that was purchased for safekeeping in London after the Revolution. Old Masters, including Frans Hals's *The Laughing Cavalier*, vie for space with magnificent European and Asian arms and armour and a display of Catherine the Great's crockery. The addition of a new basement space, designed and opened in time for the museum's centenary in 2000 and including the Watercolour Gallery, an interactive Materials and Techniques Gallery and the entire Reserve Collection, has proved a major boon, as has the glass-roofed Sculpture Garden with its delightful café.
Families are very welcome: children are given a 'trail' workcard to follow (a sort of 'I spy'), and a programme of events is devised for every school holiday and half-term (see p218). There's also an 'Eighteenth Century Family Day' every

Sightseeing

February; participants dance, take tea, play games and generally behave in a thoroughly Georgian manner. *Buggy access. Café. Nappy-changing facilities. Lift. Nearest green space: space in front of museum. Restaurant. Shop.*

Eating & shopping

As well as the multitude of cafés in Regent's Park, Marylebone is pretty well served with the burger and pizza chains, on Portland Street and Baker Street. Local parents are fond of Baker Street's huge and friendly **Pizza Express** (133 Baker Street, W1, 7486 0888; *see also p185*). For more exotic options, head for Marylebone High Street, where environmentally conscientious parents swear by the **Quiet Revolution** inside Aveda (nos. 28-9, 7724 3157). Try a cake from **Pâtisserie Valerie at Maison Sagne** (no.105, 7935 6240) for pudding, or linger for croques monsieurs and baguettes.

Substantial meals such as noodles with tomato sauce and chicken and chips are on the children's menu at the bright and breezy **Giraffe** (6-8 Blandford Street, W1, 7935 2333; *see also p178*), which won the 'Kids Out Best Family Restaurant Award' in 2001. Reduced-price half portions from the adults' international menu can also be ordered. Noodle joint **Wagamama** (101A Wigmore Street, W1, 7409 0111; *see also p177*) offers high chairs, friendly staff and smaller portions for children.

Staff at restaurant-cum-deli **Villandry** (170 Great Portland Street, W1, 7631 3131) are happy to serve well-behaved kids, though child-size portions aren't on the menu. If you're on Baker Street in need of refreshment, **Baskin Robbins** (no.208, NW1, 7224 6298) has some cool varieties worth investigating.

The design emporium **Conran Shop** (no.55; 7723 2223), has gorgeous toys and kids' clothes, furniture and books, and **Shaker** (nos.72-3, 7935 9461), where

For the **Wallace Collection**, apply within. *See p96.*

you can buy smart items to make over the nursery. The lovely **Daunt Books** (no.83-4, 7224 2295) has a reasonable range of books for children, though travel is its speciality. Those with little princesses in tow should check out **VV Rouleaux** (no.6, 7224 5179) for ribbons, fun fur, feathers and sequins.

Down on Marylebone Lane, with its old deli, sausage specialist, vintage clothes shop and dressmakers' delight **Button Queen** (no.19, 7935 1505), time seems to have stood still. Would-be gourmets should gallop along to Marylebone Road, where **Le Cordon Bleu** cookery school (no. 114, 7935 3503; *see also p230*) runs courses for children who have a yen to make Christmas dinner this year. Ballet outfitter **E Gandolfi** (150 Marylebone Road, W1, 7935 6049) provides shoes, tights and tutus.

Older children and teenagers like London's most famous shopping thoroughfare, clogged-up **Oxford Street**, with its chains (Gap, Top Shop, Hennes). Big toy selections are to be found in the department stores (John Lewis, Selfridges, Debenhams), but Oxford Street is no place for tots. *See also p206.*

Meet the teacher

Emma Bryant is the Education Assistant at the Wallace Collection (*see p96*).

What do you do?
I organise and run family programmes during half-terms and holidays. This might involve planning activity weeks; employing artists and drama specialists to run workshops, and devising appropriate activities according to the Wallace Collection's quarterly 'theme'.

What activities do children request most?
They flock to armour handling sessions with our armoury

curator, David Edge. They can try on real original armour, as worn by a sweaty knight of long ago.

What other activities are there?
Arts and crafts sessions are also very popular. Children can make puppets, masks or miniature gardens, and they come away with some beautiful creations.

What's the best part of your job?
I love every aspect of my job, but it's great to see how creative children can be, and to hear what

they say about the paintings in our collection. A little boy said the other day that he thought the *Laughing Cavalier* was so happy because he had a sweet in his mouth!

Do you wear a uniform?
No, but I have a special badge to wear.

Do you dress up in the armour?
Yes. All the time – it's great fun!

North London

Northern sights.

North London encapsulates all that is best and worst about the capital. Its most desirable bits have retained a sense of identity and a villagey atmosphere. These places rejoice in vast tracts of woodland and park, such as **Hampstead Heath** and **Waterlow Park**; spectacular vistas (there's nothing to beat the exhilarating view from **Primrose Hill**); great markets (**Camden Market** is London's trendiest tourist attraction); grand houses (the grandest of which is **Kenwood House**) and too many exotic restaurants to list. North London has come to be synonymous with sophistication and culture, qualities that used to be associated just with wealthy Hampstead.

North London has, however, a big traffic problem. Many of the attractions we list, such as the serene **Shri Swaminarayan Mandir Temple**, are accessed via thundering arterial roads, and a vague vehicular drone seems to accompany you wherever you go (all the more reason for exploring the green and pleasant heath). Traffic has increased with creeping gentrification, and on some streets you can scarcely move for 4X4s. Nonetheless, north London still feels more urban, buzzy and, yes, sophisticated than the southern boroughs, but don't tell the trendy Brixtonians we said that.

Camden Town & around

At weekends it seems as if every tourist, as well as many a local, comes here to trawl for bargains in the market – now officially London's fourth most popular tourist attraction. Before you join them, take a peek down Parkway for another view of Camden Town – this characterful street has some lovely places to eat, drink and browse. It's also the way to the excellent **Jewish Museum**.

It's fashionable among Londoners to say that **Camden Market** has been ruined by its success, and certainly many of the stalls you join the crush to browse over are laden with ethnic tat seen in craft markets everywhere, and the once cutting-edge fashion and retro clothes now seem hackneyed. There are plenty of interesting stalls, however, particularly in the original market building at Camden Lock beside the canal. In any case, it's great for people-watching, and there's no getting away from the fact that the market as a whole has a lurid attraction for older children and teenagers, who love the quirky gifts, clothing and jewellery.

With small children you'd be well advised to arrive early and beat the crowds. **Camden Lock**, where you're most likely to be, is no picnic with a buggy, as some of it is cobbled and spread out over different levels accessed via narrow stairs. The proximity of deep water also makes keeping a firm hold on youngsters essential.

When the crowds get too much, follow the towpath down to Regent's Park and London Zoo (*see p94*), or hop on one of the narrow boats that ply the canal to Paddington. If the idea of life on a narrow boat grabs your child's imagination, check out the **Canal Museum** in King's Cross. Apart from platform nine and a half at the train station (the departure point for Hogwarts Express in the *Harry Potter* stories), King's Cross isn't an area in which to linger, but an oasis of calm can be

Thank God for **Hampstead Heath**. *See p103*.

found beside the canal in the shadow of the gasholders, in the wildlife-friendly **Camley Street Natural Park**.

You'll need to hop on the tube to visit **Kentish Town City Farm**, another rural retreat in the area.

Camley Street Natural Park
12 Camley Street, NW1 (7833 2311). King's Cross tube/rail. **Open** *May-Sept* 9am-5pm Mon-Thur; 11am-5pm Sat, Sun. *Oct-Apr* 9am-5pm Mon-Thur; 10am-4pm Sat, Sun. Closed 25 Dec-1 Jan. **Admission** free. **Map** p317 L2.
The London Wildlife Trust's flagship reserve, Camley Park has marshlands and flower meadows, ponds and woodland glades. There's a visitors' centre where you can study the park's history and book places on school holiday play-schemes. Staff also organise an annual summer festival and run an education scheme (*see p231*).
Buggy access. Nappy-changing facilities.

Jewish Museum, Camden
129-131 Albert Street, NW1 (7284 1997/ www.jewmusm.ort.org). Camden Town tube. **Open** 10am-4pm Mon-Thur; 10am-5pm Sun. Closed bank hols, Jewish festivals. **Admission** £3.50; £2.50 OAPs; £1.50 5-16s, concessions; free under-5s. **Credit** MC, V.
Of more interest to teenagers, particularly those studying for history, RE or sociology GCSEs, this impressive museum offers an extensive look into the history of Jewish religion in Britain. This Camden branch (there's another in Finchley, *see p110*) includes a display of objects used in religious ceremonies, including Hanukkah lamps and an incredible 16th-century Venetian synagogue ark. Staff take the time to explain the exhibits to visitors. Children aged 4-14 can make use of the activity sheets and trails; phone for details of the craft and drama workshops.
Buggy access. Lift. Nearest picnic place: Regent's Park. Shop.

Kentish Town City Farm
1 Cressfield Close, off Grafton Road, NW5 (7916 5420). Chalk Farm or Kentish Town tube. **Open** 9.30am-5.30pm Tue-Sun. Closed 25 Dec. **Admission** free; donations appreciated.
Though relatively small, this is one of the busiest farms in town, with local children aged 8-16 clamouring to join its pony club and holiday play-schemes (open to Camden residents only). Visitors can admire the ducks, chickens, geese, ponies, cows and large black pig.
Buggy access. Nappy-changing facilities. Nearest picnic space: Hampstead Heath.

London Canal Museum
12-13 New Wharf Road, N1 (7713 0836/ www.canalmuseum.org.uk). King's Cross tube/rail. **Open** 10am-4.30pm Tue-Sun, bank hol Mons. Closed 24-26 Dec. **Admission** £2.50; £1.25 concessions, 8-16s; free under-8s. **Credit** MC, V. **Map** p317 M2.
The warehouse containing this small museum on the Regent Canal's Battlebridge Basin was built in the 1850s by Carlo Gatti, an Italian immigrant who made his fortune importing ice from Norway. The blocks were carried from the docks on canal boats and stored here in huge ice wells. The museum tells the story of Gatti and the families who made their living on the canals, supplementing permanent displays with lectures and temporary exhibitions. Regular activity days for 6-to 12-year-olds include model-making, plate-painting, and study sessions on wildlife and boat people. Sailings to Three Mills Island (*see p121*) occasionally depart from here.
Nearest picnic place: museum terrace/canal towpath. Shop.

Fancy a dip? Camley Street Natural Park

Primrose Hill

West of Camden, charming, photogenic Primrose Hill provides green relief. Even if you've never been here, there's a good chance you'll have seen it on the big or small screen – it's beloved of directors and photographers, with its slightly wonky streetlamps silhouetted against the sky, the asymmetrical cage of London Zoo's Snowdon Aviary (*see p94*) and the fabulous views over the city. It was from the top of the hill that the twilight call sent out an SOS for the lost puppies across the land in Dodie Smith's children's classic *One Hundred and One Dalmatians*.

American poet Sylvia Plath lived with her husband Ted Hughes and their children round the corner from Regent's Park until her suicide in 1963. In July 2000 a blue plaque was finally unveiled on the house at 3 Chalcot Square where the literary couple lived for two years (though Plath actually killed herself in a flat around the corner in Fitzroy Road, where she wrote her last collection, *Ariel*).

Today's roll-call of media celebs who have chosen to make the area their home includes Martin Amis, Harry Enfield, Jude Law, Neneh Cherry, Ewan McGregor and Ben Elton, so you're more than likely to spot at least one famous face. Primrose Hill's hub is on Regent's Park Road, with its cafés and boutiques. **Chalcot Square** has fine stucco-fronted terraces and a play area in the centre, while cul-de-sacs hold

Camden Market (see p98) – refreshment

fascinating office developments such as 'Utopia Village' (once a piano factory). It's a small area but its attractions, from kite-flying at the top of the hill to local café society, are many.

Primrose Hill is one of the best bonfire night venues (the event takes place on the Saturday closest to 5 November), with an enchanting display and a traffic-free zone to accommodate the crowds. Local restaurants are booked solid from two weeks in advance. One of the best viewing points is from the tiny terrace of the Queens pub on Regent's Park Road. If you're thinking of going, leave the car at home and walk from Chalk Farm tube. *See also p30.*

Just over the railway footbridge in Chalk Farm is the **Roundhouse** (7424 9991), a former train turning shed now ingeniously used as a circular theatre. Many of the musical presentations are suitable for older children; the Chinese State Circus usually does a week here when it visits town.

Eating & shopping

For hungry kiddies, there's a branch of **Wagamama** at 11 Jamestown Road, NW1 (7428 0800; *see also p177*), and children are welcomed at the **Mango Room** (10 Kentish Town Road, NW1, 7482 5065), which serves top-notch Caribbean food. That old standby **Pizza Express** has a branch (187 Kentish Town Road, NW5, 7267 0101; *see also p185*),

housed in a former lecture theatre of the old North London Polytechnic; it's roomy, and popular with local families at weekends.

Almost every other shopfront on Regent's Park Road seems to be a café of some description, and at weekends their pavement tables are an assault course of baby buggies, dogs, chocolate-smeared toddlers and breastfeeding mothers. **Primrose Pâtisserie** (no.136, 7722 7848), the most well established, has irresistible apple pastries and almond croissants.

Manna (4 Erskine Road, NW3, 7722 8028), a long-established and excellent vegetarian restaurant, is a lovely place for a family meal, though the best place of all for children to feed their faces is **Marine Ices** (8 Haverstock Hill, NW3, 7482 9000; *see also p182*) opposite Chalk Farm tube, whose delicious Italian ice-creams and sorbets (take away or eat in) have been refreshing punters since 1913; it also serves up more substantial nosh of the cheap 'n' cheerful pasta and pizza variety.

Camden High Street has the usual chain stores, but computer games fans recommend **Gamestation** (no.43, 7380 0161) for new and used Playstation and Nintendo games. **Escapade** (no.150, 7485 7384) sells all sorts of lurid hair gels, greasepaint, stage blood, wigs, caps and rude jokes, as well as fancy-dress costumes. Around the corner, opposite Sainsbury's, **Fantasy Fayre** (22 Camden Road, NW1, 7916 2100) has a wonderful selection of buttons, feathers and

fringes. **Dot's** in St Pancras Way (no.132, 7482 5424) is much loved by musical families; Dot, an experienced music teacher, is happy to offer information and advice on musical education and puts on a programme of events at the shop.

Shops in Primrose Hill tend to reflect the stylish and wealthy nature of its residents. There's an outpost of **Graham & Green** (164 Regent's Park Road, NW1, 7586 2960), familiar to denizens of Notting Hill and stocking lovely sleepwear alongside bed linen and ethnic furniture. **Primrose Hill Books** (134 Regent's Park Road, NW1, 7586 2022) has both new and second-hand children's books, while many of the gift shops along the same street have kids' stuff such as cuddly animals and booties.

St John's Wood

A stone's throw from Regent's Park, this cosmopolitan little enclave is the very picture of affluence. Most visitors come for the cricket rather than the high street, but the shopping and eating prospects here are quite good. Expensive clothes shops and interior-design studios predominate but there are several shops catering to children's needs: **Tiddlywinks** (23 St John's High Street, NW8, 7722 3033), an upmarket kids' clothes shop, is conveniently next door to Joseph, and there's a good little toyshop, **JJ's Toys** (138 St John's Wood High Street, NW8,

7722 4855). You can buy great bagels and other Jewish nosh at **Panzer's** deli (13-19 Circus Road, NW8, 7722 8596), or coffee and wonderful cake and pastries at **Richoux** (3 Circus Road, NW8, 7483 4001). A hearty oriental meal is yours at the branch of Yellow River Café (7 St John's Wood High Street, NW8, 7586 4455; *see p185*). A short stroll away are **Lord's** cricket ground and the **Saatchi Gallery**.

A little further north is **Abbey Road**, where tourists can often be seen risking life and limb on the zebra crossing to re-enact the cover of the Beatles album of the same name (recorded at the studio here). At no.127 is **Oscar's Den**, one of the best party shops in London; it can provide everything from balloons to a real-life baby elephant (*see also p245*).

Lord's & MCC Museum

St John's Wood Road, NW8 (7432 1033). St John's Wood tube. **Open** *Tours* Oct-Mar noon, 2pm daily. *Apr-Sept* 10am, noon, 2pm daily. Closed Christmas Easter period, bank hols, all major matches; call to check. **Admission** *Tours* £6.50; £5 concessions; £4.50 5-15s; free under-5s. **Credit** MC, V.

The home of Marylebone Cricket Club has a museum that includes, among the paintings, photos and battered bats, a reconstruction of the shot that killed a passing sparrow in 1936, complete with the stuffed bird and the ball. The Ashes reside here, too. The guided tour takes visitors into the Mound stand, the pavilion, the visitors' dressing room and the historic Long Room. Among the cricket-related souvenirs in the shop are child-sized replica shirts, cricket balls and caps. Across the road, St John's Churchyard playground is a heaven-sent letting-off-steam point. Phone to book a guided tour. *Buggy access. Lifts. Shop.*

Saatchi Gallery

98A Boundary Road, NW8 (info 7624 8299/7328 8299). St John's Wood or Swiss Cottage tube. **Open** during exhibitions noon-6pm Thur-Sun. Phone to check exhibition dates. **Admission** £5; £3 12-16s, concessions; free under-12s. **Credit** MC, V.

This fantastic whitewashed space puts on temporary exhibitions of cutting-edge art from ad-man Charles Saatchi's collection. Much of the work is accessible to children, but it's best to phone first so you know whether to expect dissected cows or mutated children (Damien Hirst and the Chapman brothers have been shown here, as have Tracey Emin and Sarah Lucas). *Shop.*

Playground at **Primrose Hill**. *See p100.*

Don't fence me in. **Kenwood House**.

Hampstead & around

Hampstead still likes to see itself as the centre of affluent, liberal north London, though the truth is that nowadays the left-wing bohemians, if they ever existed, are unlikely to be able to afford its house prices. In fact, the area is in many ways the archetypal London 'village', with its pretty cottages and churches strung along a steep hill. Its roots as a spa, to which Londoners fled for fresh air and health-inducing water, can be seen in the old drinking fountain in Wells Walk near the Wells Tavern.

Hampstead is packed with smart houses, some of which you can nose around, including **Burgh House** (New End Square, NW3; 7431 0144), a small museum charting the area's history. Many of the gracious mansions of Fitzjohn's Avenue have been converted into prep schools, so give the area a wide berth during school dropping-off and pick-up times.

Weekends see the cosmopolitan locals and their chicly clad offspring hanging out over newspapers, coffee and croissants, waiting for the shops to open (many don't do so until 11am or noon on Sundays), but the main reason families with young children visit the area is glorious **Hampstead Heath**. Older kids of a poetic bent should pop into **Keats' House**. **Fenton House**, eclectic and interesting, is also a pleasure to explore. The smartest house of all is **Kenwood House** overlooking the heath; it's jammed with art treasures and is the picturesque setting for many summer concerts.

Fenton House

3 Hampstead Grove, NW3 (7435 3471/info 01494 755563/www.nationaltrust.org.uk). Hampstead tube. **Open** *Mar* 2-5pm Sat, Sun. *Apr-Oct* 2-5pm Wed-Fri; 11am-5pm Sat, Sun. Last entry 4.30pm. *Bank hols* 11am-5pm. *Tours* £10; call for details. **Admission** (NT) £4.40; £2.20 5-15s; free under-5s. **No credit cards**.
Built in 1693 in the William and Mary style, this is one of the earliest and largest houses in Hampstead. It houses the excellent Benton Fletcher Collection of early keyboard instruments, which can be heard in action during the summer at fortnightly baroque concerts (phone for details). Other exhibits include a

quirky range of pottery poodles in the Rockingham Room. The four attic rooms have retained the atmosphere of a 17th-century property with impressive views over London. Entry to the garden (one side is beautifully landscaped, the other contains an orchard and vegetable patch) is free. Note that tours are of the instruments and porcelain only.

Freud Museum

20 Maresfield Gardens, NW3 (7435 2002/ www.freud.org.uk). Finchley Road tube/Finchley Road & Frognal rail. **Open** noon-5pm Wed-Sun. Closed 24-26 Dec, bank hols. **Admission** £4; £2 concessions; free under-12s. **Credit** MC, V.
Here you'll find the famous couch that was brought from Austria when the father of psychoanalysis fled the Nazis in 1938. The ground floor houses a reproduction of Freud's Vienna study. A selection from his collection of art and antiquities is also displayed. The upstairs is devoted to the belongings of his daughter Anna, a child analyst who lived here until her death in 1982.
Nearest picnic place: Regent's Park.. Shop.

Keats' House

Keats Grove, NW3 (7435 2062/www.keatshouse.org.uk). Hampstead tube/Hampstead Heath rail/24, 46, 168 bus. **Open** *Easter-Oct* noon-5pm Tue-Sun. *Nov-Easter* 10am-4pm Tue-Sun. Closed 25, 26 Dec, 31 Dec, 1 Jan. *Tours* 3pm Sat, Sun. **Admission** £3; £1.50 concessions; free under-16s.
Poet John Keats lived for two years in this romantic Regency cottage before, weakened by TB, he travelled to Italy and died, aged just 24, in 1821. It was in this romantic setting that he wrote some of his most popular poems, and here also that he fell in love with Fanny Brawne. A plum tree in the garden marks the site of the original tree beneath which he is thought to have penned his 'Ode to a Nightingale'. Cabinets contain original manuscripts, and visitors can nose round Keats' bedroom, living room and kitchen. A tour of the house is included in the admission price. Note that the house may close from late 2002; phone to check.
Buggy access (ground floor only). Nearest picnic place: house gardens. Shop.

Kenwood House/Iveagh Bequest

Kenwood House, Hampstead Lane, NW3 (8348 1286). Hampstead tube/Golders Green tube then 210 bus. **Open** *Apr-Sept* 10am-6pm Mon, Tue, Thur, Sat, Sun; 10.30am-6pm Wed, Fri. *Oct* 10am-5pm Mon, Tue, Thur, Sat, Sun; 10.30am-5pm Wed, Fri. *Nov-Mar* 10am-4pm Mon, Tue, Thur, Sat, Sun; 10.30am-4pm Wed, Fri. Closed 24-26 Dec, 1 Jan. *Tours* by appointment. **Admission** (EH) free; donations appreciated. *Tours* £3.50; £2.50 concessions, £1.50 under-16s.
No credit cards.
This elegant mansion overlooking Hampstead Heath from its northern fringe was rebuilt in the classical style for the Earl of Mansfield by Robert Adam in 1767-9 and bequeathed to the nation in 1927. Today, its chief attraction is the Iveagh Bequest, a collection of paintings that takes in works by Reynolds, Turner and Van Dyck, a Rembrandt self portrait tucked into a darkened corner of the Dining Room and a rare Vermeer (*The Guitar Player*). Botticelli, Guardi and a couple of classic flirtatious Bouchers round out the wonderful collection. The sumptuous library is worth a gawp. The fragrant Brew House café is perfect for tea and luscious cakes after a walk on the heath, which means it's often jammed with pushchairs at weekends.
Buggy access (limited in house). Café. Nappy-changing facilities. Shop.

A day at: Hampstead Heath

It's difficult to get an idea of how big the heath is until you're lost on it. The best points of entry are Parliament Hill Lido (see p265), which has a car park and is next to Gospel Oak station, and South End Green, which is handy for Hampstead Heath station and also has a large car park. If you're coming by tube, Hampstead is your best bet, but it's at least a 15-minute walk from there.

Coming on to the heath from Highgate Road you feel as if you're in an ordinary park – there are tennis courts, a boules court, a bowling green, a drinking fountain, a bandstand and a café. Turn left here and head for the athletics ground and lido, which is recommended for competent swimmers only. It's an enormous pool, the water is very cold even at the height of summer and even the shallow end is too deep for toddlers. Tinies are better off dabbling about in the paddling pool in the play area next to the athletics ground.

Next to the lido is an information centre with exhibits on the history of the heath – learn about the battles that were fought to keep it a public space, and how its bushes were useful places to dry laundry.

Parliament Hill, the name of this stretch of the heath, is one of the best spots in London for flying a kite, but watch out: some of the stunt flights hit the ground at great speeds. From the hill you can see right across London on a clear day, with Canary Wharf to the east, the London Eye, Big Ben and St Paul's straight ahead, the white chimneys of Battersea Power Station to the west and the Crystal Palace mast away in the far distance.

Looking north towards Highgate from here you'll see a string of willow-fringed ponds below you; the path alongside these is a less strenuous walk for little legs. It was here, so the story goes, that CS Lewis was inspired to write The Lion, the Witch and the Wardrobe as he walked by the ponds one snowy morning and came across a lamp-post that seemed to belong to an entirely different world.

The ponds may look decorative but they have all been designated a specific purpose – one is dedicated to birdlife, with swans, moorhens and herons building nests on or around it; others are for fishing or sailing model boats. Best of all are the bathing ponds, one for men (with a reputation as a gay hangout), one for women and one for mixed bathing. Children of eight and over can use them with an adult, but the ponds are deep and murky, so good swimming skills are needed. It's a wonderful experience to dip into a cool pond and then dry off on a grassy bank, especially knowing you're in one of the busiest cities in the world. Better yet, it's free. See also p265.

From Parliament Hill it's a pleasant walk through woods full of fallen trees that are perfect for climbing up to **Kenwood House** (see p102). Have lunch or a snack on the sunny patio of the Brew House café (8341 5384), then visit the beautifully restored Romany caravan nearby. On summer Saturday evenings, the lawns sloping down to the lake at Kenwood become an outdoor auditorium, with concerts of popular classics that often climax with a firework display. Don't shell out for a ticket, though – just take a rug, a picnic and some warm sweaters and enjoy the music from outside the enclosure without worrying about the children annoying music buffs.

Head north across Spaniards Road to reach the Spaniards Inn (8731 6571), an ancient coaching inn that was once a favoured drinking place of highwayman Dick Turpin. It has a pleasant garden for lunch or a drink on a summer evening.

For those wanting to cycle here, there are designated tracks, but they're not always on the most obvious and direct routes. Don't be tempted to forge your own passage through the undergrowth – small children with training wheels are allowed more or less anywhere, but older ones on bigger bikes, especially if not accompanied by adults, are likely to get a telling off if they cycle anywhere other than on the marked paths.

The heath has all kinds of activities throughout the year, including birdwatching walks, free puppet shows, classical concerts, track events, football, angling and tennis lessons and a travelling funfair that pitches up on bank holiday weekends. To find out what's going on, pick up a free diary from the office near the drinking fountain next to the Italian café at the Parliament Hill entrance.

Hampstead Heath

NW3 (Parliament Hill 7485 4491/Golders Hill 8455 5183). Belsize Park or Hampstead tube/Gospel Oak or Hampstead Heath rail/24, 46, 168, 214, C2, C11 bus. **Open** 24hrs daily.

Golders Hill Park

Whether it's technically in Golders Green or part of Hampstead Heath, this is one of the most family-friendly parks in London. As well as carefully tended flowerbeds and shrubberies and sports facilities (tennis courts and a putting green), there's a small zoo, which was recently restocked with many varieties of poultry, deer and goats, and a large sandpit full of wooden boats and trucks for imaginative play. Staff here believe children come first: in the summer holidays little ones are treated to the full bouncy castle, singalong, storytelling, conjuring and clowning experience.

Many people come for **Arte Gelato** (*see also p182*), a café that makes its ice-cream on the premises, in a huge variety of flavours. It's so good that the *Wall Street Journal* has run a feature on it. Its more substantial meals (home-made pasta, soups and salads) are also terrific.

Golders Hill Park

North End Road, NW3 (8455 5183).
Golders Green or Hampstead tube. **Open**
Park 7.30am-dusk daily. Arte Gelato (8455
8010) Mar-Nov 10am-8pm or dusk if earlier.
Nov-Mar 10am-dusk daily.
Buggy access. Nappy-changing facilities.

Eating & shopping

Zen (83 Hampstead High Street, NW3, 7794 7863) is a classy Chinese restaurant that's popular with local families. **Giraffe** (46 Rosslyn Hill, NW3, 7435 0343), which won the *Kids Out* Best Family Restaurant category at the *Time Out* Eating & Drinking Awards 2001, is a stop-off point for smoothies, noodles, stir fries and the like. Japanese grub is served with a flourish at the branch of **Benihana** (100 Avenue Road, NW3, 7586 1303; *see p173*). More Japanese dishes are available at **Hi Sushi** (16 Hampstead High Street, NW3, 7794 2828), or grab a delicious crêpe, from the stall by the William IV pub before heading down to the Heath for a bracing walk.

Nature walk in **Highgate Woods**. *See p105.*

On the way to Parliament Hill, you can stop for coffee and sandwiches at **Polly's** (55 South End Road, NW3, 7794 8144) or cakes and sticky buns at **Rumbolds'** bakery (45 South End Road, NW3, 7794 23244), or stock up on the makings of a delicious picnic at **Cucina** (45A South End Road, NW3, 7435 7814). At **Giacobazzis** (150 Fleet Road, NW3, 7267 7222), you can buy the best fresh tortelloni in London (and if you're lucky watch the deft-fingered chap who makes it at work through the window). **Craftworks** (31 South End Road, NW3, 7431 4337) has lots of interesting and unusual presents, including chocolate skeletons.

Long-term residents bemoan the fact that high rents have pushed out small, independent shops, with the result that despite its village atmosphere, Hampstead is beginning to look like any other high street (though it's considerably steeper in terms of both gradient and prices). Even McDonald's finally won a long battle to open a branch, though its golden arches have been tastefully toned down so as not to offend local sensibilities. For the children, there are branches of **Baby Gap** and **Gap Kids** (both 36 Hampstead High Street, NW3, 7794 9182). On Heath Street are **Jigsaw Junior** (no.83, 7431 0619; *see also p199*) and **Look Who's Walking** (no.78, 7433 3855), the latter stocking indispensable labels for fashionable villagers aged 12 and below, including Oilily, DKNY and Kenzo.

In delightful Flask Walk, **Humla Children's Shop** (no.9, 7794 8449; *see also p193*) has a colourful selection of clothes and tasteful wooden toys. A few doors down at no.15 (7431 3314), **Verde** sells an irresistible range of aromatherapy products for adults and children (its Clarity Headache Gel may come in especially handy). **Happy Returns** (36 Rosslyn Hill, NW3, 7435 2431) stocks a basic if unimaginative range of well-known brands of toy (Galt, Brio, Lego…) but not much in the way of pocket-money toys or stocking fillers. The large Waterstone's branch has a well-stocked kids' section.

Highgate & Archway

Highgate is another delightful London 'village', though it's marred a little by the traffic roaring down its high street to Archway. Many famous people have been associated with the area, including Sting, Annie Lennox, George Michael and Pierce Brosnan. Further back, Samuel Coleridge, JB Priestley and the ubiquitous Charles Dickens all lived here.

The best reason for visiting Highgate with kids is **Waterlow Park**, which looks like it's straight out of a storybook; indeed, some locals claim that it inspired the illustrations for Nick Butterworth's Percy the Park Keeper books. Next door, **Highgate Cemetery** is too picturesque to miss.

A little down the hill from the tube station is Shepherd's Close, from where you can access the Parkland Walk, (*see p108*). **Highgate Woods** has one of the best-designed adventure playgrounds in the city, plus nature trails and open spaces that are ideal for football, cricket, frisbee, learning to ride bikes, and picnics. The old cricket pavilion is now **Oshobasho** (8444 1505), a thriving and highly recommended vegetarian café that, despite high prices and occasional grumpy notices announcing it is 'not a playground', is popular with families – so be prepared to join the queue at weekends.

Hornsey Lane, on the other side of Highgate Hill, leads you to the Archway, a Victorian viaduct that now spans the A1 and offers views of the City and the East End. **Jackson's Lane Community Centre** (8340 5226; *see also p224*) off Archway Road has shows for children every Saturday.

Highgate Cemetery

Swain's Lane, N6 (8340 1834). Archway tube/C11, 271 bus. **Open** *East Cemetery* Apr-Oct 10am-5pm Mon-Fri; 11am-5pm Sat, Sun. *Nov-Mar* 10am-4pm Mon-Fri; 11am-4pm Sat, Sun. *West Cemetery tours* Apr-Oct noon, 2pm, 4pm Mon-Fri. 11am, noon, 1pm, 2pm, 3pm, 4pm Sat, Sun, bank hols. *Nov-Mar* 11am, noon, 1pm, 2pm, 3pm Sat, Sun. Closed 25, 26 Dec. **Admission** *East Cemetery* £2. *West Cemetery tours* £3; £1 8-16s (reduced rate for 1st child in group only, other children pay full rate). No children under 8 admitted. *Camera fee* £1. No camcorders permitted. **No credit cards**.
Though the newer East Cemetery is famous for the impressive granite head of Karl Marx, who is buried there, the West Cemetery across the road is far more exciting, with its overgrown tombs and catacombs. It was here that Dante Gabriel Rossetti romantically buried some of his poems in the coffin of his wife Lizzie Siddell but later had it opened so he could retrieve them. The cemetery has also provided an atmospheric set for Dracula films. Children should look out for the sleeping lion that guards the grave of a former ringmaster. Other interesting stories are told on the regular guided walks, which are the only way you're allowed to see the mysterious West Cemetery.
Nearest picnic place: Waterlow Park.

Lauderdale House

Waterlow Park, Highgate Hill, N6 (8348 8716/café 8341 4807). Archway tube. **Open** 11am-4pm Tue-Fri; 1.30-5pm Sat, noon-5pm Sun; phone to check weekend openings. Closed 24 Dec-mid Jan. **Admission** free. **No credit cards.**
The 16th-century former home of Nell Gwynne now offers interesting after-school and holiday courses for kids, plus Saturday morning puppet shows, craft fairs, musical events, exhibitions by local artists and other events (for further details, *see p224*). In summer the park often hosts promenade performances from the travelling Bubble Theatre company. Sit on the terrace of the adjoining café and admire the view over a coffee and ice-cream, or an Italian meal. Waterlow Park, in which the house is set, is beautiful, with several lakes, a toddler's playground, an aviary and gentle grassy slopes that are great for picnicking.
Buggy access (ground floor only). Café. Nearest picnic place: Waterlow Park.

Roses in bloom at **Waterlow Park**. *See p104.*

Eating & shopping

In addition to the cafés in Highgate Woods and at Lauderdale House, Highgate has a branch of **Café Rouge** (6-7 South Grove, N6, 8342 9797; *see also p184*), which has a kids' menu and is popular with families at weekends. **Café Mozart** (17 Swains Lane, N6, 8348 1384) is recommended for its fresh food and laid-back atmosphere, and there's a **Pizza Express** on the High Street (no.30, 8341 3434; *see also p185*).

In Archway, the **St John's** pub (91 Junction Road, N19, 7272 1587) has a restaurant that's popular for Sunday lunch. **Papa Del's** pizzeria (347 Archway Road, N19, 8347 9797) at the top of the hill is a good place for lunch.

On Highgate High Street, the tiny **Highgate Bookshop** (no.9, 8348 8202) has a popular children's section at the back, while **Notsobig** (no.31A, 8340 4455) is a stylish kids' clothes shop (*see also p199*). Further up the hill, **Ripping Yarns** (355 Archway Road, N6, 8341 6111) is a brilliant and unmissable second-hand book store for children's literature.

Also on the Archway Road are the two branches of **Rainbow** (nos.249 & 253, 8340 8003; *see also p203*), one crams an interesting range of toys, cards, beads, jokes and designer clothes into its tiny space; the other has a good selection of second-hand clothes and baby and children's equipment.

Highbury Fields forever.
See p107.

Tony Blair might have left for pastures new, but elegant Islington is still one of the most sought-after postcodes in London. The gentrification of the Georgian and Victorian terraces began as far back as the 1960s; since then Upper Street has become a lively mixture of theatres, shops, cafés, pubs and restaurants, as well as a bit of a culture hub. Every June the area hosts a two-week festival of music, theatre and art, and there are regular exhibitions at the Business Design Centre. The area is home to 11 theatres, including the ground-breaking Almeida, and it's also the home of the Anna Scher Theatre School, which has turned many local working-class kids into thesps, including actress Kathy Burke and half of the cast of *EastEnders* (there's currently a five-year waiting list). The **Little Angel Theatre** in Dagmar Passage (*see p228*) is a famous name in London. This purpose-built puppet theatre has an excellent reputation for top quality shows for children aged from four.

No playground-loving child should miss **Highbury Fields**, where the climbing equipment is second to none. If weather puts paid to parklife, the Playhouse indoor adventure playground (The Old Gymnasium, Highbury Grove School, corner of Highbury Grove and Highbury New Park, (7704 9424; *see p248*) is popular. Footie fans of the Gunner variety may like to tour Arsenal Football Club.

If you crave the smell of the countryside, commune with the pigs at **Freightliners City Farm**, or find out about green activities and events at the **Islington Ecology Centre**. If you crave the taste of the countryside, bear in mind that the Islington Farmers' Market sets out its wares every Sunday from 10am to 2pm.

Arsenal Football Club

Arsenal Stadium, Avenell Road, N5 (7704 4000/tickets 7413 3366/www.arsenal.co.uk). Arsenal tube/Finsbury Park tube/rail. **Open** *Shop* 9.30am-6pm Mon-Sat. *Tours* 11am, 2pm Mon-Fri. **Admission** *Tours* £4; £2 concessions, under-16s; £1 junior Gunners. **Credit** *Shop* MC, V.
Gunners fans can pre-book a tour of the ground, changing rooms and museum; the latter has a Gunner-glorifying video, info about the club's early days and memorabilia. The shop sells a red and white replica kit and souvenirs.
Nearest picnic place: Gillespie Park. Shops.

Freightliners City Farm

Paradise Park, Sheringham Road, off Liverpool Road, N7 (7609 0467). Holloway Road tube/Highbury & Islington tube/rail. **Open** *Termtime* 10am-1pm, 2-5pm Wed, Sat, Sun. *Holidays* 10am-1pm, 2-5pm Tue-Thur, Sat, Sun. Closed 25, 26 Dec, 1 Jan. **Admission** free; donations appreciated.
Islington's farm has a close working relationship with local schools, with children either helping out or joining summer play-schemes. On its small site Freightliners sustains

several varieties of sheep, as well as cows, poultry, pigs and goats. Free-range eggs are usually available. Its meat, in particular Gloucester Old Spot and Berkshire pork, is sold at accredited butchers in London.
Buggy access. Nappy-changing facilities. Nearest picnic place: picnic area in farm. Shop.

Highbury Fields
Highbury Crescent, N5 (7527 4971). Highbury & Islington tube/rail. **Open** *Park open access. Playground* 8am-dusk daily.
Islington's largest open space has a showpiece playground with climbing frames, ropes and swing bars designed to challenge older children, in addition to safe areas of play for little ones. There's also a café, tennis courts and open spaces for football, plus an excellent swimming pool next door.
Buggy access. Café.

Islington Ecology Centre
191 Drayton Park, N5 (7354 5162). Arsenal tube. **Open** *Park* 8am-dusk Mon-Fri; 9am-dusk Sat; 10am-dusk Sun. *Centre* drop-in advice sessions 10am-noon Tue; 2-4pm Thur; for other times phone to check. **Admission** free; donations appreciated.
The Ecology Centre, where visitors can find out about all things green and pleasant in the area, is part of the Gillespie Park Local Nature Reserve, which is the largest reserve in the borough, with a range of wildlife habitats (woodland, meadow, wetland and ponds). There's an organic café, though it's not open year-round. Call for details of walks, talks and activities, in particular children's ones held during the holidays.
Buggy access. Café.

Eating & shopping

Cafés, restaurants and bistros abound, including Pizza Express and Café Flo. The rather more swanky **Granita** (127 Upper Street, N1, 7226 3222) welcomes children and babies to lunch, offering small portions of the delicious grown-up food on offer. **Frederick's** (106 Islington High Street, N1, 7359 2888) makes a concession to well-heeled parents with a children's menu at Saturday lunchtimes.

For cheaper, more relaxed meals, try the Islington branches of the award-winning **Giraffe** (29-31 Essex Road, N1, 7359 5999; *see also p178*) or **Wok Wok** (67 Upper Street, N1, 7288 0333; *see also p185*). At **Tiger Lil's** (270 Upper Street, 7226 1118; *see also p180*) children choose the ingredients they want the chefs to stir-fry and at **Santa Fe** (75 Upper Street, 7288 2288; *see also p178*) there's a warm Tex Mex welcome for kids of all ages, who can choose chicken, spaghetti, quesadillas and other goodies from their own menu (£3.95 with soft drink).

The pedestrianised area around **Camden Passage** has more than 40 shops for antiques and collectibles, and Chapel Street's market stalls (clothes, flowers, vegetables and household goods) are fun to explore. While in Chapel Street, pop into **Tiddlywinks** (no.84, 7278 5800) and **Kids Boutique** (no.14, 7837 4889) for upmarket kids' fashion. The **Crafts Council Gallery Shop** (44A Pentonville Road, N1, 7806 2559) sells innovative homewares, jewellery and

books, including some for kids. **Jakss** (319 Upper Street, N1, 7359 4942) has rails of expensive childrenswear by the likes of Paul Smith and Oilily. Unusual and striking girlswear is the mainstay of **Gotham Angels** (23 Essex Road, N1, 7359 8090; *see also p198*). **Green Baby** (345 Upper Street, N1, 7359 7037; *see also p193*), the ecologically responsible babycare shop, could only be in Islington.

Stoke Newington

Less expensive but funkier than its near-neighbour Islington, 'Stokey' is an enclave of middle-aged alternative families, though it's no less charming for that. The heart of the area, which has a respectable literary history (Daniel Defoe wrote *Robinson Crusoe* here) is **Stoke Newington Church Street**, which hosts a street festival every June.

Stoke Newington is blessed with two of the finest green spaces in London – **Clissold Park**, where local families congregate, and the rambling old boneyard of **Abney Park Cemetery & Nature Reserve**.

Abney Park Cemetery & Nature Reserve
Newington Church Street, N16 (7275 7557). Stoke Newington rail/73 bus. **Open** dawn-dusk daily. Closed 25 Dec. **Admission** free.
Eerily quiet except for the twittering of birds, this large cemetery with its crumbling statues and derelict church is home to an impressive number of animal and bird species. It's a peaceful place for a walk and a picnic: you'd never know you were in central London. Call for details of guided tours.
Buggy access. Shop.

Clissold Park
Stoke Newington Church Street, N16 (7923 3660/tennis courts 8806 2542/café 7923 3703). Bus 73. **Open** *Park* 7.30am-dusk daily. *Café* 10am-dusk daily.
This park has three ponds (fishing; paddling; ducks), pleasant tree-lined walks with plenty of room for ball games, and a well equipped playground popular with local families. The mini-zoo has fallow deer, a butterfly tunnel and an aviary. Clissold Park is set around a mansion housing a friendly café serving reasonably priced vegetarian food and snacks. During the Stoke Newington Festival (*see above*), this delightful park becomes a hive of activity. A stage is set up for bands, there are numerous stalls and the odd bouncy castle for family fun and face-painted children mill about merrily.
Buggy access in park, steps at café. Café.

Eating & shopping

There are many places to eat on **Church Street**, though some, including the superb South Indian vegetarian restaurant **Rasa** (no.55, 7249 0344), are quite small and can't easily accommodate buggies. **Il Bacio** (no.61, 7249 3833) is dependable for good Italian pasta and pizza, or tuck into delicious sandwiches at the **Cooler** (no.67, 7275 7266).

Vortex (no.139-41, 7254 6516) is a grown-up jazz venue that serves excellent veggie food to cool cats of all ages during the day.

Stoke Newington Church Street is one of the few places not to have succumbed to the invasion of London by huge multinationals, retaining instead a range of interesting independent shops. **Stoke Newington Bookshop** (no.159, 7249 2808) has a good selection of kids' books, while **Encore** (*no.53, 7249 5329; see also p203*) sells second-hand clothes, including well-known children's makes such as Oilily and Osh Kosh. **Route 73 Kids** (no.86, 7923 7873; *see also p211*) sells thoughtfully chosen toys, including lots of interesting pocket-money treats.

Crouch End & Muswell Hill

Spacious Victorian and Edwardian houses, excellent shops and restaurants, wonderful parks with lovely views – it's no wonder many Londoners take to these parts as soon as the baby starts walking. A few years ago it seemed that everyone knew someone who had almost sold their house to Bob Dylan, who is said to have fallen in love with the area while working at Dave Stewart's recording studio in a converted church, and Stephen King wrote a short story called 'Crouch End' after visiting a friend here.

These suburban enclaves are often passed through by people en route to **Alexandra Park & Palace**, but being family-friendly they have plenty of delightful green spaces of their own – **Priory Park** in Middle Lane is great for cycling, Rollerblading and football, and has a paddling pool, formal gardens and tennis courts (its Rainbow Café is good for snacks), while Stationers Park between Mayfield Road and Denton Road has a challenging adventure playground, a pre-school children's play area, and tennis courts. **Park Road** (8341 3567; *see also p265*) has both indoor and outdoor swimming pools, though the latter gets pretty crowded on warm weekends.

Alexandra Park & Palace

Alexandra Palace Way, N22 (park 8444 7696/palace 8365 2121/info 8365 2121/boating 8889 9089/www.alexandrapalace.com). Wood Green tube/Alexandra Palace rail/W3, W7, 84A, 144, 144A bus. **Open** *Park 24hrs daily. Palace times vary depending on exhibitions.* **Admission** free.

The ill-fated Ally Palace (it has burned to the ground several times) is at the top of this steep park and affords impressive views on a clear day. It once housed the BBC's first TV studio; now it's an entertainment and exhibition centre with an indoor ice rink where children can take lessons. It boasts a junior ice-hockey team that plays all over the country. The public gardens have plenty of children's attractions and sports facilities, including a pitch-and-putt course, a boating lake with

Walk: on the line

► Finsbury Park, with its busy schedule of booze-fuelled concerts (the most famous of which is the annual Fleadh), might not be the most child-friendly green space in London, but it's worth visiting for the **Parkland Walk**, London's longest nature reserve, alone. The pretty, peaceful woodland path, home to lots of species of flora and fauna, is actually a disused railway line about three miles (five kilometres) long, stretching all the way to Queens Wood in Highgate.

► Escape the rather unsavoury surroundings of Finsbury Park's rail and bus stations by turning right at the Wells Terrace exit at the back of the station, through the small bus depot and walk up **Stroud Green Road**. Turn right into Woodstock Road, cross over Oxford Road, and at the end of Florence Road are some steps up to the start of Parkland Walk. You can also walk in a northerly direction on the western edge through the park, past the small children's play area until you come to the tennis courts. Cross the bridge on the left just past the tennis courts, and you're at the start of the walk, at **Florence Road**.

► Head up a gentle incline to reach the former railway line, where hawthorns, blackthorns, dogwoods and chestnuts blossom in spring and blackberries grow in summer. Rough and ready

benches can be found at intervals, and where the path crosses Stapleton Hall Road the bridge is adorned with a scruffy little **Millennium Mural**, painted by the Stoud Green Elfins playgroup. This used to be the old Stroud Green rail station. Further on, the **Wooden Bridge Youth Centre** has slides built into the embankment and rope swings hanging from the trees. Those who've remembered to bring their skateboards can test their skills on the U-shaped, fibreglass ramp.

► Next comes an abandoned and overgrown platform of what was the old Crouch End station, where you can imagine the shriek of the night train as it brought Victorian city gents back to the suburbs. Even more spine-chilling is the long, pitch-black train tunnel with more than a suggestion of rat habitation. Your journey ends in bird-filled north London woodland, where the path peters out, bringing you to Shepherd's Hill and Highgate tube station. **Highgate Woods** (*see p105*) is nearby if you want to explore further.

► For refreshments, there's the **Crouch Hill Community Centre**, about halfway along opposite Mountview Road, or the **Crescent Café**, accessed via some rickety wooden steps from the path, which can be relied upon for bacon sarnies, all-day breakfasts and cold drinks.

mini-pedaloes for hire, a deer enclosure, cycle routes, a café and hills that are perfect for kite-flying. On the Saturday nearest to 5 November it's the site of one of the biggest firework parties in London, organised by the local council. Bank holiday funfairs are another draw.

Buggy access. Café. Nappy-changing facilities. Nearest picnic place: picnic area by boating lake.

Eating & shopping

Restaurants are in plentiful supply in the area – the **World Café** (130 Crouch Hill, N8, 8340 5635) has interesting global food at very reasonable prices; **Banners** (21 Park Road, N8, 8292 0001) is relaxed but crowded, so book in advance. Offering everything from fried breakfasts to exotic fish dishes, it's famous for its extensive under-10s menu. **Pizza Bella** (4-6 Park Road, N8, 8342 8541) is also child-friendly, and is popular for birthday parties. Terrific chips and super fresh fish are on the menu at **Toff's** (38 Muswell Hill Broadway, N10, 8883 8656). The Broadway is your best bet for family dining in Muswell Hill; there's a well loved **Pizza Express** at no.290 (8883 5845; *see also p185*) and children eat their favourite Italian dishes for free at Sunday lunchtimes at **Caffé Uno** at no.348 (8883 4463).

There are more interesting shops for children's toys, clothes and books here than in some parts of the West End. Muswell Hill is the home of the well-stocked **Children's Bookshop** (29 Fortis Green Road, N10, 8444 5500; *see p196*) and **Fagin's Toys** (84 Fortis Green Road, N10, 8444 0282; *see p209*). **Early Clothing** (79-85 Fortis Green Road, N10, 8444 9309; *see p198*) is strong on big name designers and children's streetwear. Crouch End has **Word Play** for toys (1 Broadway Parade, N8, 8347 6700; *see p211*), and **Soup Dragon** (27 Topsfield Parade, Tottenham Lane, N8, 8348 0224; *see also p209*) for original British knitwear in strong colours and traditional, tasteful, wooden toys.

Finchley

Sprawling in three sections (North, East and Central) across the great divide of the North Circular, Finchley is hard to pin down – its cosmopolitan background (it has a large Jewish community and a growing Japanese population) and air of general prosperity make it an attractive place to visit, yet it suffers the blight of dull suburbia and visitors feel confused by its geography (it's a long way from Finchley Road tube station, which is actually in West Hampstead).

Given its proximity to major roads, Finchley is the setting for a surprisingly peaceful walk, the **Dollis Valley Green Walk** that runs for 16 kilometres (10 miles) beside the brook from Hampstead Heath Extension in the south to Moat Mount in the north.

Oshobasho. *See p105.*

It forms a green corridor that runs through Barnet and provides a habitat for a wide variety of wildlife, including dragonflies and kingfishers. Opened in 1992 by Barnet Council, it's now part of the London Walking Forum's walker's web, a city-wide network of footpaths (for information call 8359 3052/www.londonwalking.com).

Around Church End, Central Finchley, the true heart of what was once a village, was the childhood home of Baby Spice and formed part of Maggie Thatcher's constituency. **Avenue House** and its beautifully landscaped gardens were given to the populace in 1918.

College Farm (45 Fitzalan Road, N3, 8349 0690), a picturesque landmark with farm animals to pet, has been closed by the recent foot and mouth crisis; phone to find out if and when it's reopening.

Victoria Park, just off Ballards Lane between Finchley Central and North Finchley, has a useful children's playground, bowling green and tennis courts. In July the Finchley Carnival takes place here.

The **Great North Leisure Park** (Leisure Way, High Road, N12), better known locally as Warner Village, is a US-style entertainment complex built, rather unimaginatively, around its car park. The cinema, **Finchley Warner Village** (0870 240 6020), has a Saturday morning kids' club. There's also an extremely popular swimming pool, with a lido next door, which really comes into its own on warm summer days. The bowling alley (Hollywood Bowl *see also p262*) has its own micro-brewery and burger bar. Next door to the Bowl is an amusement arcade with driving games and shoot-the-limbs-off-rotting-zombie computer games. A couple of rowdy games here followed by pizza and pop next door at **ASK** (8446 0970) is a tried-and-tested children's party combination in these parts.

Across the North Circular in East Finchley the **Phoenix Cinema** (*see p221*) has children's films on Saturdays. In East End Road the Old Manor House has been transformed by the Sternberg Centre into a cultural centre, which includes ritual baths, a school and the **Jewish Museum**.

Chocks in place at the **Royal Air Force Museum Hendon**. *See p111.*

Avenue House

15-17 East End Road, N3 (8346 7812). Finchley Central tube. **Open** *Ink Museum* 2-4.30pm Tue-Thur. Closed 24 Dec-1 Jan, bank hols. **Admission** free; donations appreciated.

The tiny Ink Museum commemorates 'Inky' Stephens, whose father invented ink and once owned Avenue House. Some of the beautiful rooms can be hired out and it's a popular venue for children's parties . Outside, there's a playground, café and a tree trail accessible to wheelchairs and buggies.

Buggy access. Nappy-changing facilities. Nearest picnic place: Avenue House grounds.

Jewish Museum, Finchley

Sternberg Centre, 80 East End Road, N3 (8349 1143/ www.jewmusm.ort.org). Finchley Central tube/13, 82, 112, 143, 260 bus. **Open** 10.30am-5pm Mon-Thur; 10.30am-4.30pm Sun. Closed bank hols, all Jewish hols, Sun in Aug. **Admission** £2; £1 concessions, 12-16s; free under-12s. **No credit cards.**

The Finchley branch of Camden's Jewish Museum (*see p99*) has fascinating displays on aspects of Jewish social history. It's not really the place for young children, though – the Holocaust exhibition may be too much for them. On the ground floor a functional sewing workshop gives the feel of sweatshop life at the turn of the 19th century, while upstairs an exhibition traces the life of Leon Greenman, a British Jew who, alone of his family, survived Auschwitz. This branch also has a 12,000-strong photographic archive augmented by 2,000 oral history tapes. Note that the café is open only at lunchtimes, Monday to Friday.

Café. Nearest picnic place: museum garden/Avenue House gardens. Shop.

Eating & shopping

Many of Finchley's decent grubstops fall over themselves to please pint-sized customers. **Two Brothers Fish Restaurant** (297-301 Regent's Park Road, N3, 8346 0469) is always full of smart people eating fab fish and chips; grab a takeaway next door if you can't get in. **Frankie & Benny's** (Great North Leisure Park, Leisure Way, N12, 8445 2895) has a children's menu, a party package and wacky staff. At **Chorak** (122 High Road, N2, 8365 3330) the cakes (including themed party cakes) are baked on the premises (*see also p239*).

Rani (7 Long Lane, N3, 8349 4386), a well-known vegetarian Indian, attracts people from a wide area. There's a £4.90 under-12s' menu. The **Old Europeans** (106 High Road, N2, 8883 3964) welcomes children with open arms, high-chairs and half-portions of hearty Hungarian grub.

The proximity of Brent Cross Shopping Centre *(see p210)*, together with parking problems, has had a rather depressing effect on local shopping, though children are happy enough with **Leisure Games** (91 Ballards Lane, N3, 8346 2327), which stocks boxed games from around the world, **Football Crazy** (20 Hendon Lane, N3, 8343 1121), which has official club gear and runs a useful mail-order service, and **Action Bikes** (64 Ballards Lane, N3, 8346 2046) for children's bikes and repairs of same.

At the North Finchley end of the High Road, **Tally Ho** (749 High Road, N12, 8445 4390) is excellent for bargain toys and games. At Tally Ho Corner proper there's a Tuesday, Friday and Saturday market where you can get your hands on even cheaper toys. **All Seasons** (654-6 High Road, Tally Ho Corner, N12, 8445 6314) is good for baby and nursery essentials. Much further down, near East Finchley tube, is **Teaching Trends** (160 High Road, N2, 8444 4473), an educational games and toys shop.

Further north

Go north from Finsbury Park up to Haringey and Tottenham and you're on Green Lanes, where London's main Greek Cypriot and Turkish Cypriot communities live and work. For honey pastries and lamb kebabs, the area can't be beaten. Many people beat a path up here to visit the less mouthwatering **Tottenham Hotspur Football Club** on White Hart Lane, a tour of which is much easier to arrange than scoring a ticket to a home match.

Further west, the North Circular, which thunders out of London into the somnolent suburbs, is well travelled by Londoners looking for fashion and a handy crèche at **Brent Cross Shopping Centre** (*see 210*). Nearby is the serene and stunning **Shri Swaminarayan Mandir Temple**, an oasis of Hindu spirituality in the suburbs.

Roaring Edgware Road might not have much to recommend it as a haven for recreational pursuits but just off it is the peaceful **Welsh Harp reservoir** (Cool Oak Lane, 8205 1240), where many Londoners and their kids skim across the water in sailing dinghies, blissfully unaware of the thundering traffic not so far away. It offers RYA-approved sailing courses all year round.

Carry on up this major thoroughfare and you'll reach **Oriental City** (399 Edgware Road, 8200 0009), a Japanese mall with several good places to eat, including a huge self-service buffet. The shops are fascinating, though it's the state-of-the-art amusement arcade that turns children Japanese – it's a lot less seedy than its counterparts in central London.

Further on, the North Circular swoops on to Hendon, home to the impressive, action-packed **Royal Air Force Museum Hendon**.

Royal Air Force Museum Hendon

Grahame Park Way, NW9 (8205 2266/ www.rafmuseum.com). Colindale tube/Mill Hill Broadway rail/32, 226, 292, 303 bus. **Open** 10am-6pm daily. Closed 24-26 Dec, 1 Jan. *Tours* daily; times vary, phone for details. **Admission** £7.50; £4.90 concessions; free OAPs, under-16s accompanied by an adult. *Tours* free. **Credit** MC, V.

Learn about the history of the flying machine at the birth-place of aviation in Britain (book in advance for guided tours). Of particular note is the spectacular sound and light show 'Our Finest Hour', which tells the story of the Battle of Britain. There's also a Red Arrows flight simulator, a 'touch and try' Jet Provost cockpit and a walk-through Sunderland flying boat. Activities for children and adults take place year-round: recent workshops have included hot air balloon making, rocket science, and dressing up in RAF uniform. The workshops are always very popular, so do book ahead. Call for details of special events in the school holidays. The museum plans to expand by a third in the next few years.

Buggy access. Café. Lift. Nappy-changing facilities. Nearest picnic place: picnic ground on site. Restaurant. Shop.

Shri Swaminarayan Mandir Temple

105-15 Brentfield Road, NW10 (8965 2651). Wembley Park tube then BR2 bus. **Open** 9.30am-6pm daily. **Admission** free.

Europe's first traditional Hindu temple is one of the city's least publicised treasures. This gorgeous building is decorated with marble that was carved by master artisans in India before being shipped to London and reassembled. As it's a place of worship, you have to remove your shoes and remain silent while inside. It's a soothing and inspirational place to visit. The 'Understanding Hinduism' exhibition is presented in a style that even young children can understand. It's especially suitable for those in year 6 studying world religion. Stock up on incense sticks at the shop and sample Indian delicacies at the small café. Ask at the entrance about a free tour. *Café. Nappy-changing facilities. Shop.*

Tottenham Hotspur Football Club

Bill Nicholson Way, 748 High Road, N17 (8365 5000/ www.spurs.co.uk). White Hart Lane rail. **Open** *Tours* 11am-Mon-Fri; 11am, 1pm Sat. **Admission** *Tours* £7.50 adults; £4.50 under-16s, OAPs. **Credit** MC, V.

A place of pilgrimage for Spurs fans – the Saturday tours were booked up three weeks ahead when we last called. They last about an hour, depending on how chatty the punters are, and take in board rooms, changing rooms, press rooms, pitch-side and tunnel. Marvel at the showers where Ginola once conditioned his hair, sneer at the bench where treacherous Sol Campbell removed his boots for the last time, and finish in the megastore, where you can blow £50 on a shirt or 50p on a souvenir pencil.

Buggy access. Nearest picnic place: Shop.

Meet the teacher

David Keen is Education Officer at the Royal Air Force Museum Hendon (*see above*).

What do you do?
I organise educational activities for school groups, take guided tours and give talks on all sorts of subjects. They might be on the story of flight, the development of air power or on World War II. I also arrange school half-term and holiday activities such as making rockets, dressing up in pilot gear or Search and Rescue, an exciting simulation involving a life raft, radios and a rescue co-ordination centre.

What activities do children request most?
The most popular education programme is the Evacuees Experience, which we also offer to all visitors during the October half-term. Having made a replica gas mask case, children have a lesson similar to one they would've had in 1939, and then an air raid signal is given, and

they all have to dive under the desk. The lesson often ends with someone getting the cane for playing on a bomb site. It's a hugely enjoyable way of finding out what it was like to be a child during the war years.

What other activities are there?
We help children to make a hot-air balloon that really flies to take home with them. We also give them the chance to wear real RAF uniforms, many dating from World War II and flight clothing ranging from World War I leather coats and hats with goggles to G-suits of the fast jet age.

Our Search and Rescue activity teaches people about survival at sea in an emergency situation and how the RAF and other agencies carry out rescue operations. The museum also has an interactive science gallery called Fun'n'Flight, which is full

of hands-on exhibits enabling children to discover the science behind aviation.

What's the best part of your job?
I love all of it! It's a great privilege to meet Battle of Britain pilots and others who served with the RAF during the war. In addition, it's rewarding to get to know today's schoolchildren, especially when they respond to our exciting and dramatic aeroplanes. I also like the fact that every time I look at the exhibitions here I learn something new.

Do you wear a uniform?
No, but I do dress up as an old-fashioned teacher for the Evacuees Experience and I wear a flight suit for the Search and Rescue activity.

East London

Go to the dogs. Or the Docks. Or Georgian squares and unbeatable markets.

Though it may not hold the instant attractions of more central and western areas of the capital, there's more in characterful east London for families than first meets the eye. Highlights include the Museum of Childhood, the Whitechapel Art Gallery, the markets at Spitalfields, Brick Lane and Columbia Road and, further out, leafy Epping Forest.

Whitechapel & Spitalfields

After absorbing all the sights of the City, you might think the streets of Whitechapel and Shoreditch provide little in the way of great days out for the family, but never underestimate local colour – with its weekend street markets, city farm and one of the most happening art galleries in London (especially where children are concerned), Whitechapel and its trendier sister are definitely worth exploring.

Brick Lane, for bargains. *See p115.*

This area has always been lively. As the City's poor neighbour offering cheap rents on slum housing, the heart of the East End has been enriched by waves of immigrants over the centuries. In the 18th century came the Huguenots (French Protestant refugees), whose prowess in fine silk weaving gained the area a reputation for fine cloth and fashionable clothes. Nicholas Hawksmoor's huge and now rather crumbly **Christ Church** on Commercial Street, E1 (7247 7202) was built in 1714 to provide a place of worship for the weavers. It's currently undergoing restoration to bring it back to its former glory.

Irish and German immigrants built communities here in the early 19th century, followed, from 1880 onward, by Jews. Jewish success in the 'rag trade', as it became known, attracted unwanted attention from the British Union of Fascists before World War I, with enmity coming to a head in 1936 with the 'Battle of Cable Street'. From the 1950s to the '70s Indians and Bangladeshis took over the textile businesses on Commercial Street and Commercial Road, and the East End is still associated with the Asian clothes trade today.

For some people the mention of the East End brings to mind the unsavoury thought of Jack the Ripper, who stalked and murdered women on these streets more than 100 years ago (*see p113*), but as far as children are concerned the main attractions are quite rightly the farms: **Spitalfields City Farm** and, a short bus or tube journey away, **Stepping Stones Farm**.

Between Commercial Street and Brick Lane runs elegant Fournier Street, with its beautifully preserved early Georgian houses, once inhabited by Huguenot silk barons and now owned by wealthy new East Enders. On nearby Folgate Street is **Dennis Severs' House**, a lovingly recreated Georgian residence.

Whitechapel Road has two main points of interest: **Whitechapel Bell Foundry**, where bells have been cast since 1570; and, at no. 82, **Whitechapel Art Gallery**, one of London's best exhibition spaces, which has just celebrated its centenary.

Hospital-drama fans and connoisseurs of the macabre may be drawn to the **Royal London Hospital Museum**, which is famous for its tragic inhabitant Joseph (or John) Merrick, better known as the 'Elephant Man'. Merrick was a patient here in the late 1800s and part of the museum is devoted to an exhibition about his life.

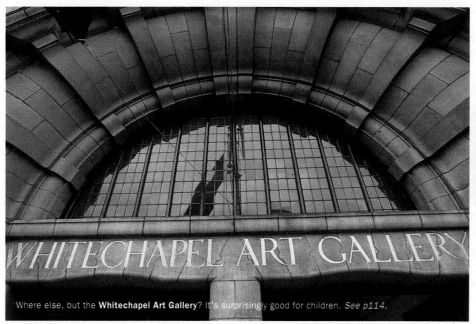

Where else, but the **Whitechapel Art Gallery**? It's surprisingly good for children. *See p114.*

Dennis Severs' House

18 Folgate Street, E1 (7247 4013/
www.dennissevershouse.co.uk). Liverpool Street tube/rail.
Open noon-2pm Mon; Mon evenings (times vary, phone
to book); 2-5pm 1st Sun of mth. Closed bank hols. *Tours*
phone for details. **Admission** £7 Mon afternoon, Sun;
£10 Mon eve. **No credit cards. Map** p321 R5.

Half museum, half piece of performance art, this place must
be experienced to be understood. Dennis Severs, who died in
2000, converted the huge terraced house (built in 1724) into a
tribute to London living through the ages. Visitors move
upwards through the building on a tour that starts in the early
1900s and goes back in time to the 18th century. Though it's
fascinating, it's only suitable for older (and well-behaved) children, or those studying the relevant periods in history: staff
add greatly to the experience, but are zealous in ensuring the
appropriate (calm) atmosphere.

Royal London Hospital
Archives & Museum

St Philip's Church, Newark Street, E1 (7377 7608/
www.bartsandthelondon.org.uk). Whitechapel tube.
Open 10am-4.30pm Mon-Fri. Closed bank hols &
adjacent days. **Admission** free.

Part of this museum is devoted to the tragically deformed
Joseph Merrick or the 'Elephant Man', who lived in the area
and was treated here; the rest charts the history of the hospital and of medicine in general, as well as famous nurses who
practised here, including Edith Cavell, who was executed by
the Germans in 1915 for helping Allied soldiers escape from
occupied Belgium. There are documents and exhibits relating to her training period at the Royal London, plus a blue
plaque (there's a statue to her memory in St Martin's Place
near the National Portrait Gallery).

Buggy access. Café. Nappy-changing facilities. Nearest
picnic place: hospital garden. Shop.

Jack the Ripper

Though the Ripper murders took place more than
a century ago, 'Jack' can still pull in the punters.
Notorious for preying on prostitutes in the East
End area of Whitechapel, he was never caught,
and even today speculation is rife with regard to
his identity. Possible identities of the murderer
include a mad midwife and a royal physician –
there are even suggestions that Queen Victoria's
grandson Albert was implicated in the crimes.

While it's feasible to visit any of the killer's
stamping grounds on your own, by far the best
way is to join a walking tour, where the grisly
scene will be set for you. It hardly need be said
that such tours are unsuitable for small children,
but it's bound to brighten up the day of any
moody teenager with a fascination for all
things gruesome, with its mixture of historical
commentary and fanciful speculation. For the
seriously ghoulish, guides supply pictures of
crime scenes and victims. They're so confident
you'll have a rip-roaring time that you don't pay
until after the tour has taken place.

Ripping Yarns Jack
the Ripper Walk

(7488 2414/www.rippingyarns.8m.com).
Time 6.45pm daily (meet at exit of Tower Hill
tube; guide will be holding a Ripping Yarns
brochure). **Tickets** £5; £4 concessions; 12-16s.
Not suitable for under-12s. **No credit cards**.

Sightseeing

Spitalfields City Farm

Weaver Street, off Pedley Street, E1 (7247 8762/ www.spitalfieldsfarm.htmlplanet.com). Whitechapel or Aldgate East tube/Liverpool Street tube/rail. **Open** 10.30am-5pm Tue-Sun. Closed 25, 26 Dec, 1 Jan. **Admission** free; donations appreciated.

Spitalfields' chickens, cows, geese, sheep and goats provide fertiliser for the farm's allotments, which in turn yield boxloads of well-nourished veg and herbs that are sold to the public. Staff are keen to deliver a decent agricultural education to city-bred young 'uns, and children can enjoy school holiday play-schemes and education programmes.
Buggy access.

Stepping Stones Farm

Stepney Way (junction with Stepney High Street), E1 (7790 8204). Stepney Green tube. **Open** *Apr-mid Oct* 9.30am-6pm Tue-Sun; bank hol Mon. *Mid Oct-Mar* 9.30am-dusk Tue-Sun; bank hol Mon. **Admission** free; donations appreciated.

A short bus or tube away from Spitalfields, this further example of small-scale agriculture is run by hard working volunteers, who look after part-bred Bagot, Windsor White and pygmy goats, as well as cows, donkeys, sheep, poultry and small pets. Eggs, jams and chutneys are sometimes sold.
Buggy access. Café. Nappy-changing facilities. Shop.

Whitechapel Art Gallery

80-82 Whitechapel High Street, E1 (7522 7888/ recorded info 7522 7878/www.whitechapel.org). Aldgate East tube/15, 25, 253 bus. **Open** 11am-5pm Tue, Thur, Fri; 11am-8pm Wed; 11am-6pm Sat, Sun. Closed 24-26 Dec, 1 Jan. *Tours* 2pm Sun. **Admission** free. *Tours* free. **Map** p321 S6.

The Whitechapel boasts a strong education and community programme, so local schoolkids have a hand in many of the exhibits. Its founder, a schoolteacher, insisted that every exhibition have its own educational programme for children and as a result the education department is one of the busiest in the gallery world. *See also p220.*
Buggy access. Café. Nappy-changing facilities. Nearest picnic place: grassy area opposite. Shop.

Whitechapel Bell Foundry

34 Whitechapel Road, E1 (7247 2599/ www.whitechapelbellfoundry.co.uk). Whitechapel tube. **Open** 8am-5pm Mon-Fri. Closed 24 Dec-1 Jan, bank hols. *Tours* 10am, 2pm select Sats, phone for details. No under-14s. **Admission** free. *Tours* £8. **Map** p321 S6.

This is where Big Ben was made (it's the largest bell ever cast here), as were the clock bells at St Paul's Cathedral and the American Liberty Bell. A special tour takes visitors round the working parts; the tiny museum charts the foundry's history. The small shop has bell-related fripperies and literature, and some delightful hand bells.
Nearest picnic place: St Mary's churchyard. Shop.

Eating & shopping

The best eating options in the area are traditional, and, on the whole, great value, though curry, eels and black pudding may be a bit of an acquired taste. There's a refreshing lack of big-name fast food outlets (aside from a KFC and a Burger King on Whitechapel High Street, that is) but you'll find something for everyone at the 24-hour **Brick Lane Bagel Bake** (159 Brick Lane, E1, 7729 0616), where combinations start at 85p. There are sweet pastries or biscuits for afters.

Alternatively, a traditional Brick Lane curry will set you back less than a tenner at **Preem** (no.120, 7247 0397), which has high chairs. Staff here are happy to let children pick the best bits out of the masala dosai. **Café Spice Namaste** (16 Prescot Street, E1, 7488 9242) is somewhat pricier but has a wide range of colourful dishes to entice conservative kids. Those who still insist on plain English grub should sample pie and mash or order meat and two veg at the **Market Café** at 5 Fournier Street.

Pie in the sky

For a real taste of the East End, there's nothing like a pie and mash shop, a cockney institution that has never exactly been at the height of fashion. Hot pies have been a tradition since Victorian times, when eel pies (made from eels caught in the Thames Estuary) were the norm. When fish became scarce in the wars, mince was substituted, and it's now the usual filling.

Pie and mash shops are becoming scarce, but they're worth visiting for their interiors alone, which normally consist of blue and green tiles, wooden benches and tiled floors. Food-wise, don't go expecting much of a choice – there's pie, fruit pie, mash and 'liquor', a sort of green (parsley) gravy that's ladled over the top. Side dishes include stewed eels, which are not as bad as they sound (they're a bit like pickled herrings). A filling meal of pie, mash, liquor and a cup of tea usually comes in at less than a fiver, which must make it one of the best bargains in the city.

F Cooke
9 Broadway Market, London Fields, E8 (7254 6458). Bus 55, 106, 236. **Open** 10am-7pm Mon-Thur; 10am-8pm Fri, Sat. **No credit cards.**

J Gooding
257 Well Street, E9 (8985 4900). Bus 26, 30, 277. **Open** 10am-3pm Mon-Thur; 10am-6.30pm Fri; 10am-6pm Sat. **No credit cards.**

G Kelly
414 Bethnal Green Road, E2 (7739 3603). Bethnal Green tube/rail/8 bus. **Open** 10am-3pm Mon-Thur; 10am-6.30pm Fri; 10am-4.30pm Sat. **No credit cards.**

L Manze
76 Walthamstow High Street, E17 (8520 2855). Walthamstow Central tube/rail. **Open** 10am-4pm Mon-Wed; 10am-5pm Thur-Sat. **No credit cards.**

The much-fêted **Spitalfields Market**, which takes place in a huge, draughty structure that was once the home of the eastern fruit and veg wholesale market, has become extremely hip with young, ecologically aware parents at weekends, with its ever-expanding range of organic food stalls. It's also a general market during the week, though the buzz is best on Sunday.

It's here that many of London's artists and designers sell their wares. The Hello Kitty merchandise goes down well with teenagers, while their younger siblings love the knick-knacks at pocket-money prices and the irresistible food stalls (doughnuts, sweets, curries…). Performance artists sometimes take centre stage in the market building, and there's usually a football game in progress on one of the indoor pitches. However, with redevelopment programmes under way as we go to press, this wonderful market looks like it may be squeezed out by flashy office blocks and luxury flats.

For a long time the East End's favourite rough diamond was **Brick Lane Market** (8am-1pm Sun). Although nowadays it's becoming alarmingly 'designer', there's still a happy mish mash of stalls – second-hand bikes around Slater Street Yard; junk at the Bethnal Green end; second-hand clothes (cool streetwear for skateboard-fixated adolescents) and customised jeans in the covered bit called Laden Market; and electrical and household goods around Grimsby Street.

Petticoat Lane Market (9am-2pm Sun; Wentworth Street stalls also open 10am-2.30pm Mon-Fri), which sprawls over Goulston Street and Middlesex Street and envelops Cobb and Leyden streets (among others), has a famous name but no designer pretensions. Bargain-hunters love it for the imitation designer togs, dodgy toys and cheap rugs, jewellery and household goods. Children love the buzz but take care they don't get lost in the mêlée.

Shoreditch & Hoxton

Shoreditch used to be known for its music halls (James Burbage is said to have founded London's first theatre here in 1598, though it was moved to Southwark 20 years later and is now known as Shakespeare's Globe; see p40), while newly trendy Hoxton, the area of Shoreditch north of Old Street and west of Kingsland Road, has a more macabre claim to fame – playwright Ben Jonson fought and killed the actor Gabriel Spencer in Hoxton Fields (now Hoxton Square). Jonson managed to escape the gallows because he was a clergyman, but he had his thumb branded for the crime.

From Victorian times on the area was infamous for its slum housing, which was replaced in the 20th century by blocks of flats. Drawn by its rawness and

Reflect on the history of design at the **Geffrye Museum**.

low rents, artists and bohemian types have flocked here, and the main attractions are bars and clubs, centred around **Hoxton Square**, home of the **Lux Cinema** (7684 0201), which has a summer children's film festival plus occasional half-term events, too. Also worth a visit en famille are the **Geffrye Museum**, which is an oasis of loveliness, and **Hoxton Hall**, the arts centre and theatre, which provides entertainment for kids.

Geffrye Museum
Kingsland Road, E2 (7739 9893/recorded info 7739 8543/www.geffrye-museum.org.uk). Liverpool Street tube/rail then 149, 242 bus/Old Street tube/rail then 243 bus. **Open** 10am-5pm Tue-Sat; noon-5pm Sun, bank hol Mon. Closed Good Fri, 24-26 Dec, 31 Dec, 1 Jan. **Admission** free; donations appreciated. Under-8s must be accompanied by an adult.
Built in 1715 as an almshouse, the Geffrye was converted into a furniture and interior design museum in 1914, with rooms representing different periods in design and interior history, from the Elizabethan era to the present day. There's an imaginative (but often far-too-popular) programme of school holiday and weekend events for children: making potions from the fragrant vegetation in the pretty herb garden is a firm favourite with the over-fives. Call the museum for more information about the courses, workshops and other messy, arty stuff to occupy bored kids in the holidays. On summer weekends a jazz band sometimes plays on the lawn, while the airy restaurant is a pleasure to visit year round. Christmas is also a good time to come – every room is lovingly and evocatively decorated in period festive style, so you can trace the develop-

ment of the modern Christmas and find out how indebted we are to the Victorians for so many of our festive traditions. *Buggy access. Café. Lift. Nappy-changing facilities. Nearest picnic place: museum grounds.*

Hoxton Hall
130 Hoxton Street, N1 (7739 5431/www.hoxtonhall.co.uk). Old Street tube/rail. **Shows** times depend on season. **Tickets** £5; £3 under-16s. **No credit cards.**
Dance, music, arts and crafts and drama classes are held every week. The theatre is given over to children's shows on Saturday afternoons (*see also p229*).
Buggy access. Café. Nearest picnic place: Hoxton Community Garden.

Bethnal Green & Hackney

Like much of the outer east, these once-poor areas are experiencing regeneration, gentrification and new-found cool, yet they remain, for the most part, pretty scruffy. Bethnal Green, in Victorian times, held the shameful title of 'poorest district in London' and, despite wholesale slum clearance in the 20th century, there's still a great deal of work needed. The area does boast an important attraction, however: the free **Bethnal Green Museum of Childhood**. Further north, little gems such as **Sutton House**, the **Hackney Empire** and the **Clowns International Gallery** make faffing with buses around the tube-free bits of Hackney worthwhile.

Urban roosting at **Hackney City Farm**. *See p117.*

The beautiful old **Hackney Empire** (291 Mare Street, E8, 8985 2424) was once one of London's great music halls and has seen the best in family entertainment over the years. Its funding is continually in a state of crisis, though it has somehow managed to keep its head above water. As well as the infamous adults-only comedy nights, there's a year-round family programme; call for details. As we went to press, the Empire was closed for refurbishment as part of Hackney's exciting plan to create a 'cultural quarter' around the Town Hall Square (Mare Street), which is due for completion in April 2002. Central to the quarter will be Hackney Museum, in a shiny new building with plenty of interactive ways of charting the last 1,500 years in Hackney. The Central Library will at last be given lovely new premises. Shops, restaurants and a gym will join Ocean, a hot local music venue.

There are many places to run wild here: **Hackney Downs** (Downs Park Road, E8, 7241 6344) has three tennis courts, floodlit basketball courts, a bowling green and a kids' playground; while **Hackney Marshes**, a large expanse of grassland between Clapton and Leyton, north of Victoria Park, is known as the often extremely muddy home of English Sunday league football, with 88 pitches in all. Teams welcome amateurs and professionals. This windy eastern reach of Hackney Marshes is a favourite unravelling place for kite-fliers, and kite festivals take place in summer. Further activities include remote-control aircraft shows, American and Gaelic football, rugby and cricket.

London Fields (Westside, E8, 8806 1826) has attracted cricketers since 1802. As well as sports and play facilities, the park has an intriguing sculpture of a seated couple surrounded by pretty, inset mosaic pictures – it's a real favourite with children (and winos), as is a game of pétanque (similar to boules) at the Pub on the Park.

Springfield Park (8806 1826) in Clapton is a picturesque green space overlooking the River Lea and Springfield Marina. Its drawing-room café, which opens every day in summer, has huge French windows looking out on to the gardens.

Green space and agriculture come together at the pastoral **Hackney City Farm** (*see p117*), next door to which is **Haggerston Park**, E2 (8806 1826), with pretty gardens, a softball pitch, a cycle track and astroturf for ball games.

Clowns International Gallery
(7608 0312). **Open** phone for details. **Admission** free.
The oldest established organisation for clowns in the world is not open often, and was aiming to be up and running in a new venue by January 2002. When it does open, however, it's a fine place to visit. There's a gallery of famous clowns, and information on the history of madcap acting from the *commedia dell'arte* of the 16th century to present-day loons

A day at: the Bethnal Green Museum of Childhood

Nostalgic adults love the Bethnal Green Museum of Childhood as much, if not more, than children. Established in 1862 and originally the National Museum of Childhood (the East London branch of the V&A), this enchanting archive holds the largest collection of toys and childhood paraphernalia in the UK, and one of the largest in the world, including more than 80,000 toys and games. Among the oldest toys is one of only two surviving Nuremberg dolls' houses dating back to 1673. Permanent exhibitions include teddy bears, toy soldiers, train sets, puppets and board games. The museum also houses a history of children's costume, plus the Renier Collection and the Book Trust Collection, the largest selection of children's literature in the UK. The 21st-century part of the collection stays bang up to date with Gameboys.

Staff hold art workshops for children at the weekends and school holidays, as well as soft-play sessions on Sundays (call for details). A new, permanent play area for under-fives make this an excellent place to bring pre-schoolers. How long you spend here depends on the age and character of your children – there's not a great deal in the way of hands-on fun, but many young kids are entranced by the dolls' houses and spend ages spotting tiny details in the rooms. Be sure to set aside at least half a day.

Most children come to rest at the shop, where pocket money goes a long way, thanks to an imaginative collection of toys, stationery and gadgets for under £1. The licensed museum café makes for a welcome break from toy-spotting, and has special lunchboxes for children alongside cakes, crisps and sandwiches. If you've been organised enough to bring your own picnic you can eat it outside in the gardens.

Postman Pat fans should note that there's an exhibition on from 3 December 2001 till 7 March 2002, including a mock-up of Greendale.

Bethnal Green Museum of Childhood

Cambridge Heath Road, E2 (8983 5200/recorded info 8980 2415/www.museumofchildhood.org.uk). Bethnal Green tube/rail. **Open** *10am-5.50pm Mon-Thur, Sat, Sun. Closed 24-26 Dec, 1 Jan, Good Friday.* **Admission** *free; donations welcome. Under-8s must be accompanied by an adult. Buggy access. Café. Lift. Nappy-changing facilities. Nearest picnic space: museum gardens. Shop.*

in big trousers. Children like the clown car, costumes and audio-visual displays, plus the cases of long-gone clowns' treasures. The shop sells anything with a clown on it, plus tricks, jokes and squirty flowers.

Hackney City Farm

1A Goldsmiths Row, E2 (7729 6381/ www.hackneycityfarm.co.uk). Bethnal Green tube/Cambridge Heath rail then 26, 46, 55 bus. **Open** 10am-4.30pm Tue-Sun. Closed 25, 26 Dec, 1 Jan. **Admission** free; donations appreciated.
This cobbled farmyard is a pleasant place to while away an afternoon in the company of pigs, geese, turkeys, sheep and cattle. Staff run pottery and weaving classes and a popular play-scheme in the summer holidays, and regularly dream up farming-inspired fun days. Parents can appreciate the idyll from the shelter of the café, or stock up on fresh honey and eggs from the shop.
Buggy access. Café. Nappy-changing facilities. Nearest picnic place: Haggerston Park. Shop.

Sutton House

2 & 4 Homerton High Street, E9 (8986 2264/ www.nationaltrust.org.uk). Bethnal Green tube then 253, 106, D6 bus/Hackney Central rail. **Open** *Historic rooms* Feb-Nov 11.30am-5.30pm Wed, Sun, bank hol Mon. Last entry 5pm. *New opening times from 5 Feb 2002:* 2-5pm Fri-Sun, bank hol Mon, 4 June (Jubilee Day). *Tours* usually last Sun of mth; phone for details. **Admission** (NT) £2.10; 50p 5-16s; £4.70 family (2+2); free under-5s. *Tours* free. **Credit** MC, V.
The oldest house in east London, this was built in 1535 for Henry VIII's secretary of state. Much more recently, in the late 1980s it was used as a community centre (a protected graffiti-daubed wall is testament to the period), before the National Trust got hold of it. A grand restoration project saved the building's many original charms, as well as elegant Tudor, Jacobean and Georgian interiors. Don't forget to look in on the 16th-century garderobe, London's oldest loo. There are a few multimedia exhibits, and changing art exhibitions and themed events for children during school holidays, which

Off the rails

Docklands Light Railway is as much a tourist attraction as a transport system – in fact, many East Londoners see it more as the former, given that the trains aren't known for their reliability. But for visitors with time to kill and small children to entertain, the DLR is a treat. Kids love the fact that the trains are driverless – sitting in the front is a bit like being on a rollercoaster. En route you can see ponies grazing on Mudchute's fields, water in the docks glistening in the sun and Cesar Pelli's impressive Canary Wharf Tower at close quarters.

A word of warning, though: be sure to buy your tickets at the station before boarding the train – the inspectors are merciless.

have included historic cookery workshops, Tudor and Victorian games, dressing-up and ghost story events. Light meals, home-made cakes and drinks are served in the Brick Place Café (11.30am-5pm Wed-Sun).
Café. Nappy-changing facilities. Nearest picnic place: St John's churchyard. Shop.

Eating & shopping

The eating is exotic around Hackney. A favourite for inexpensive fuel food is **Café Alba** (183 Mare Street, E8, 8985 5927), with Indian-inspired dishes and comforting puddings. You have to book at weekends for the popular Vietnamese caff **Hai-Ha** (206 Mare Street, E8, 8985 5388). At **Little Georgia** (2 Broadway Market, E8, 7249 9070), dishes from the meze menu are £1.50 each.

It's not known as a shoppers' paradise, but Hackney and Bethnal Green both boast lively and excellent markets. Hackney's pride is the great **Ridley Road Market** (8.30am-6pm Mon-Sat); it's more Dalston really, but people come from all over the borough for this classic East End market, where Asians, Turks, Jews and people from the Caribbean come together in a loud and lively way. It's usually pounding with reggae music and full of canny shoppers buying exotic

fruit and veg, bagels (there's a 24-hour bagel shop), fresh herbs and spices, 'designer' and household goods.

Bethnal Green has **Columbia Road Market** (between Gosset Street and the Royal Oak Pub, 8am-1pm daily), where horticultural stalls heave with bedding, shrubs, bulbs, pots and cut flowers for the house. Enjoy the spectacle. There are plenty of eating opportunities nearby – **Jones Dairy Café** (23 Ezra Street, E2, 7739 5372; *see also p181*) and, on Columbia Road itself, **Perennial** (no.110, 7739 4556) and **Laxeiro Tapas Bar** (no.93, 7729 1147).

If you're around Victoria Park, look in on the delightfully named **Chocolate Crocodile** (39 Morpeth Road, E9, 8985 3330; *see also p203*) for second-hand clothes, toys, books and equipment. There's also a play area.

Docklands

From its heyday in the 18th and 19th centuries, when boats from all over the world unloaded their treasures here, to the breakdown of empire and the modern regeneration of the area into a riverside retreat for the well-off, Docklands has seen it all. Stretching from Tower Bridge to the Isle of Dogs and beyond, it has plenty to keep daytrippers occupied, especially if you buy a Travelcard and hop on and off the driverless Docklands Light Railway (DLR) trains, which is part of the fun (*see opposite*). Now that the Jubilee tube line connects with several DLR stations, Docklands is not such a chore to get to, though an alternative, and amusing, route to the area is the Greenwich foot tunnel, which takes you under the river from the *Cutty Sark* in Greenwich to Island Gardens in Docklands. Children are intrigued by the idea of Old Father Thames flowing over their heads. Recent developments such as bridges and walkways make the area slightly more appealing to pedestrians, but Docklands is still a confusing sprawl, so plan your route before you leave.

The area gained a reputation as a yuppie haunt in the '80s, when the Conservative government set up the London Docklands Development Corporation (LDDC) to regenerate derelict land by building upmarket offices and new homes to attract business to this once-poor part of London. By the time recession came in the '90s, the LDDC was in bad shape, accused of pandering to the wealthy instead of real East Enders. It ceased operations in 1998, when other bodies took over the task of making the Docklands a proper community.

It's certainly more visitor-friendly now, and if the apartments and homes are too swish for ordinary folk to afford, there's still plenty of fun to be had here, particularly on the **Isle of Dogs**. People disagree about the name given to this peninsula sticking out into the deepest loop of the Thames – it's an isle because the stretch of water making up the West India Docks cuts it off from the mainland, but where are, or were, the dogs? Some people think there may once have been royal kennels here, others think 'dog' is a corruption of 'dykes', which were built here by Flemish engineers in the 19th century.

Though many still fume about the area being a playground for the rich, strolling around Docklands with the family on a sunny day makes you feel good about London. If the water looks just too inviting, visit the **Docklands Sailing & Watersports Centre** (Millwall Docks, 235A Westferry Road, E14, 7537 2626; *see also p262*). If that seems a bit soggy, board the DLR bound for Mudchute, at the undeveloped southern tip of the Isle. Here, the unfamiliar whiff of llama droppings assails your nostrils as you hike over the meadow to **Mudchute City Farm**.

For something a little more fast-paced, join the large-salaried office workers who enjoy removing their jackets and making like Michael Schumacher during their lunch break at **Docklands F1 City** kart track (Gate 119, Connaught Bridge, Royal Victoria Dock, E16, 7476 5678; *see also p259*).

Due to open in early 2002 at West India Quay is the **Museum in Docklands**. Located in a Grade I-listed warehouse, the museum will chart the history of the Port of London and Docklands with an array of multimedia presentations, including reconstructed scenes, engravings and artefacts. For more information, log on to the website at www.museumindocklands.org.uk.

Mudchute City Farm

Pier Street, Isle of Dogs, E14 (7515 5901). Crossharbour or Mudchute DLR. **Open** *9am-4pm daily. Closed 25 Dec-1 Jan.* **Admission** *free.*
This farm, which has the Canary Wharf Tower looming anomalously in the background, is home to ducks, chickens, goats, pigs and llamas, plus a small flock of sheep and a cattle herd. Local children learn to ride at the British Horse Society, an approved riding school; others come to the Nature Studies resource centre to find out about our green and pleasant land and discover how to shear a sheep.
Buggy access. Café. Shop.

Eating & shopping

There are plenty of pretty good eating options nearby, many of them remarkably child-friendly, although in the week family groups have to elbow office workers out of the way between noon and 2pm around Canary Wharf. **Yellow River Café** (10 Cabot Square, E14, 7715 9515; *see also p185*) is one of a mini-chain of appealing Asian restaurants; here the good-value children's bento boxes (£4.95) can be eaten with child-size chopsticks and followed by ice-cream. **Café Rouge** (20 Cabot Square, E14, 7537

9696; *see also p184*) has a children's menu with a good line in fuel food (sandwiches, chips, steaks and salads) and provides high chairs.

There are pizzas galore at the **Gourmet Pizza Company** (18-20 Mackenzie Walk, E14, 7345 9192). Alternatively, pick up some veggie treats at **Cranks** (Concourse Level, 15 Cabot Place, E14, 7513 0678) and picnic on a bench in the square (if you can find a free one at lunchtimes). **Hubbub** (269 Westferry Road, E14, 7515 5577) is a quiet place for a light pasta meal, sandwiches and cakes. For a rowdy lunch on the way back from Docklands, stop off in Wapping at **Babe Ruth's** (172-6 The Highway, E1, 7481 8181) for ribs, burgers and large platefuls of American-style food. There's also a children's area where they can run their lunch off. If you're treating older kids (the gorgeous food is too pricey for little ones to chuck about), the atmospheric **Lotus Chinese Floating Restaurant** (38 Limeharbour, Inner Millwall Dock, E14, 7515 6445) is moored to the bank of Millwall Dock and looks lovely lit up in the early evening. Another treat is **Baradero** (Turnberry Quay, off Pepper Street, E14, 7537 1666; *see also p180*), a tapas bar overlooking the river.

The **Docklands Sailing & Watersports Centre** will provide the canoe and paddles. You find the creek.

Canary Wharf: a good place for elevenses.

The smart shops around **Canada Square** are aimed at office workers with disposable income – boutiques, grooming salons and stores selling personal organisers and stationery, posh wine and food, and lifestyle accessories are very much the order of the day.

Mile End to West Ham

Mile End, which was mostly common land until the 16th century, became increasingly built up in the 1800s as industrialisation demanded more homes for workers. A confusing sprawl of busy roads and urban housing developments, it would have little charm were it not for its parklife: **Mile End Park** is in the midst of an ambitious regeneration project, while **Victoria Park** is handsome following the recent completion of a £2-million restoration project. The **Ragged School Museum** is another family attraction worth heading east for.

Stratford ('street by the ford') has opened up in recent years thanks to the Jubilee Line extension, which links it to the West End. Its busy centre is focused around Broadway, a typical high street with the usual fast food and shopping chains. Its real star is **Theatre Royal Stratford East** (Gerry Raffles Square, E15, 8534 0310), a delightful old theatre, which is scheduled to re-open in December 2001 (perhaps in time for its jolly family pantos), after a programme of refurbishment that has added a café-bar, improved disabled access and generally spruced-up the atmospheric Grade II-listed auditorium.

The old theatre has a new neighbour in the state-of-the-art **Stratford Circus Arts Centre** (8279 1000), which runs a full programme of activities, including children's performances and classes and workshops in dance, music and drama for all ages. It has a café, bar and crèche, making it a welcome new resource for families in the area.

There are two good reasons to travel east from Stratford. The first is **West Ham Park**, which was designed as part of the Borough of Newham. An 1886 *Times* article stated that 'the whole area of the new borough will be covered with human habitations, save that blessed oasis West Ham Park'. The other big attraction is **West Ham United Football Club**, known across the country as the little London club with the big heart.

Mile End Park
Locksley Street, E3 (8525 9416/www.mileendpark.co.uk). Mile End tube. **Open** 24hrs daily.
This long, thin stretch of green, previously known by locals as 'dog toilet', is enjoying the fruits of a £25-million makeover, which should be completed by autumn 2002. Partly funded by the Millennium Commission, the scheme divides the park into a series of themed areas and adds a state-of-the-art children's playground (until then, kids have to make do with a rather ordinary one at the north end). The electric go-kart track is probably the biggest draw for older children; those looking for something gentler will enjoy the ecology park with its indoor and outdoor education centres, paddling lake and 850-plus species of plants. New park rangers have been trained to keep the revamped park buzzing, and they're certainly doing their job – there are outdoor sculpture and cutting-edge community arts initiatives (which take place in a purpose-built arts pavilion), plus all kinds of events and exhibitions on the theme of 'greening your environment'. Piers Gough's tree-lined Green Bridge spans Mile End Road, providing a link between the two sides of the park. The park incorporates Mile End Stadium (Rhodeswell Road, E14, 8980 1885), which has athletics tracks, football and hockey pitches, and aerobics, weight training, tennis and cricket facilities.
Buggy access. Nappy-changing facilities.

Ragged School Museum
46-50 Copperfield Road, E3 (8980 6405/ www.raggedschoolmuseum.org.uk). Mile End tube. **Open** 10am-5pm Wed, Thur; 2-5pm 1st Sun of mth. Closed 24 Dec-1 Jan, bank hols. *Tours* by arrangement; phone for details. **Admission** free; donations welcome.
Ragged schools were charity schools that provided a basic education for orphaned, poor or down-and-out children. Opened in 1900, this converted warehouse, which was previously used by Dr Barnardo, became the largest ragged school in London. Its sparse Victorian classroom has been recreated, and school groups come from all over London to don Victorian togs and sit in it. Their own teachers give the kids old-fashioned names such as Walter and Agatha and hand them over to a hatchet-faced 'schoolmistress' (a museum actress) for some serious learning. There are also exhibitions on local history and temporary exhibitions and workshops, treasure hunts and canal walks.
Café. Nappy-changing facilities. Nearest picnic place: Mile End Park. Shop.

Victoria Park

Old Ford Road, E3 (8533 2057). Mile End tube/
Cambridge Heath or Hackney Wick rail/8, 26, 30, 55,
253, 277, S2 bus. **Open** 6am-dusk daily. Closed 25 Dec.
The largest area of formal parkland in east London, which
opened in 1845 after demands for more public space, has a dramatic history – it was the scene of riots during the 19th century, and it contained Bonners Fields, where heretics were burned
for daring to speak their mind. Today, it has an aura of peaceful grandeur. It was originally conceived as the Regent's Park
of the East End, but the poor inhabitants had no carriages to
drive through the tree-lined drives or around the park's smart
villas. In fact, the slum-dwellers, having no running water of
their own, used the park's two lakes as baths. Nowadays,
they're used for leisure rather than hygiene purposes – the
Western Lake is fished for carp, tench, perch and roach by
licensed anglers, while the country's oldest Model Boat Club
convenes around the lake near Crown Gate East every second
Sunday for its regattas, when model steamboats take to the
water, deftly controlled by their captains, young and old.
   The park's animal enclosure is dedicated to goats and fallow deer. Tennis courts and a bowling green entice those with
a yen for sports, and kids can get stuck into the popular
adventure playground in the centre of the park. The Lakeside
Pavilion Café is one of the prettiest places for miles around to
stop for lunch after a frenetic morning in the playground.
Café. Nappy-changing facilities.

West Ham Park

Upton Lane, E7 (8472 3584). Stratford tube/rail/
104, 238, 325 bus. **Open** 7.30am-dusk daily.
Officially opened in 1874 (though documents relating to it go
back to 1566), this Corporation of London-run park includes
12 tennis courts, two cricket squares, two football pitches,
a running track and a rounders area. Children's sport is
taken so seriously at West Ham Park that several schools
have their sports days here, and visiting professionals
give tuition in cricket and tennis. The children's playground
has a full-time attendant and a full quota of swings, roundabouts and climbing frames. On summer weekday afternoons
it has been known for more than 300 children to turn up to
see the clowns, ventriloquists and magicians who put on
shows in and around the bandstand. There's also a paddling
pool and, at times, a bouncy castle. The rose garden is a
beautiful oasis complete with eight computer-controlled
greenhouses. Out of season, staff offer botanical tours to suit
both children and adults.
Nappy-changing facilities.

West Ham United Football Club

Boleyn Ground, Green Street, E13 (8548 2748/
www.westhamunited.co.uk). Upton Park tube. **Open**
Shop 9am-5pm Mon-Sat. *Museum* no times yet. Closed
25 Dec, bank hols. **Admission** *Tours* phone for details.
Credit MC, V.
All West Ham supporters are very excited about the £35-million redevelopment of this family club, and the opening of
the new Doctor Marten West Stand. A West Ham megastore,
a smart hotel, cafés, bars and themed restaurants were
all scheduled to open as this guide went to press, as was a
museum telling the story of the club from 1865 to the present,
through displays of medals, caps and shirts from the late
Bobby Moore, Sir Geoff Hurst's medals, caps and memorabilia and similar treasure that belonged to Martin Peters.
Bars. Café. Nappy-changing facilities. Restaurant.
Shop.

Milling around

Hidden away in the heart of East London, Three
Mills (near where *Big Brother* was filmed), is a
group of historic industrial buildings standing amid
a complicated network of tidal channels. The site's
industrial heritage goes back as far as the 11th
century. The House Mill, built in 1776 in the Dutch
style and the oldest and largest tidal mill left
standing in Britain, was used to grind the grain for
gin distilling. Its stones stopped their grinding in
1941 and it was taken over in 1989 as part of a big
restoration project by the River Lea Tidal Mill trust.
   There's a visitors' centre that provides a history
of the area and map-leaflets detailing walks in the
area: nearby Riverside Green and Three Mills
Green are pleasant for picnicking and strolling. Or
wander along the network of the Bow Back rivers
and enjoy the wildlife that thrives in this pocket of
peace and quiet. Note that there are no toilets
nearby, and that those with pushchairs might find
the cobbled walkways a little hard going, though
the towpaths are easily accessible.
   There may not be any loos, but don't miss the
great 'Cathedral of Sewage', the Victorian-built
Abbey Mill Pumping Station. This is one of the
highlights of the various Bow Back rivers walks;
brochures can be picked up at the **Lower Lea
Environmental & Educational Team**; also see the
Time Out Book of London Walks Vol II. On the first

Sunday of every month, the Mill hosts a popular
craft market (ornaments, wind chimes, corn
dollies and the like), and children can take part in
absorbing workshops with a broadly environmental
theme (paper-making, bread-making and willow-
weaving are popular). All the activities are free
and are run on a first-come first-served basis.
   Also on the first Sunday of the month, the team
organises one-hour boat trips on the *Pride of Lee*
to Limehouse Basin and back (*see p123*). Narrow
boat enthusiasts also flock here for the
occasional rally.
   The Lower Lea project, a registered charity,
is extending its range of activities for children.
Ring or write in with an SAE for walking routes
and events info. The visitors' centre and tours of
the mill are open for pre-booked school groups
during the week.

Lower Lea Environmental & Educational Team

*The House Mill, Three Mill Lane, E3 3DU (8983
1121). Bromley-by-Bow tube.* **Open** *House Mill* May-
Oct 2-4pm Sun. Call for details of group/school
visits in week. Craft market/children's activities
11am-4pm 1st Sun of mth.
*Buggy access. Nearest picnic place: Lee Valley
Park. Refreshments.*

Walthamstow

Situated at the northern end of the Victoria Line, Walthamstow provides a quaint country village ambience that exists cheek-by-jowl with the bustle of city life. Listed in the Doomsday Survey as 'Wilcumestou' (when the few scattered farm buildings were valued at £28 and two ounces of gold), today it retains many historic buildings. Picturesque Walthamstow Village was designated a conservation area by Waltham Forest Council in 1967.

Walthamstow High Street hosts what is claimed to be the longest daily street market in Europe (it has 450 stalls); its costers wet their whistles at the numerous untrendy pubs and caffs that give the street its genuine East End feel. To the north lies Lloyd Park and the **William Morris Gallery**, while to the west **Walthamstow Marshes** is the perfect location for a picnic or a leisurely stroll through the wilds by the River Lea.

Though it's relatively small, **Lloyd Park**, on Forest Road, is more than your average park – not only is it the site of the **William Morris Gallery** and the **Changing Rooms Gallery**, it also contains the **Waltham Forest Theatre** (call 8521 7111 for programme details), which is surrounded by an ornamental moat. There's a children's play area at the far end of the park, attractive gardens throughout and an aviary containing budgies and cockatoos. A short tree trail, detailed in leaflets available from the William Morris Gallery, takes in some 20 different species.

It's wise to take the car or cycle to **Walthamstow Marshes** at the end of Coppermill Lane (otherwise it's a brisk 15-minute walk from St James Street rail station). Past the railway bridge there's a special site noted for its rare plants. There are occasional open days at the old copper mill itself, plus various rambles and boat trips from Springfield Marina. These trips are free but booking is essential with the Lower Lea Project (7515 3337; it also gives info on other events at the marshes). More environmental advice is available at the **Hornbeam Centre**.

The revamped **Theatre Royal Stratford East**. See p120.

Five minutes from Walthamstow Central tube and rail station lies the village of Walthamstow. Wandering round this area, you'll find it hard to believe you're still in London and haven't been transported back in time. Opposite St Mary's Church is the **Ancient House** – a 15th-century 'hall' house – while nearby the Squire's Almshouses, erected by Mrs Mary Squires in 1795 'for six decayed tradesmen's widows', are still standing. Extensive guides to the village and to other historic buildings in the area are available at the **Vestry House Museum**, which provides an overview of the borough's history.

The big cheeses of greyhound racing have long tried to market the sport as a fun day out for the family – find out for yourself at **Walthamstow Greyhound Stadium**, just north of the town centre.

Changing Room Gallery
Averling Park, Forest Road, E17 (8496 4563/ www.lbwf.gov.uk/crg). Walthamstow Central tube/rail. **Open** *Exhibitions Apr-Nov* 10am-5pm Sat, Sun; weekdays varies depending on exhibitions. **Admission** free.
This exhibition space for contemporary arts and crafts has a New Agey feel. As well as the changing programme of exhibitions hosted by the gallery, there's studio space for local artists, regular artists' seminars and a popular café.
Buggy access. Café. Nearest picnic place: Averling Park.

Hornbeam Centre
458 Hoe Street, E17 (8558 6880). Walthamstow Central tube/rail. **Open** noon-3.30pm Mon-Thur; noon-3.30pm, 7-10pm Fri; 10am-4.30pm Sat. Closed 25 Dec-1 Jan, bank hols.
The home of nature studies in the Walthamstow area, with frequent exhibitions in the gallery, a library and Gannets Café, where a generous plateful of wholefood vegetarian grub costs about a fiver.
Nappy-changing facilities.

Vestry House Museum
Vestry Road, E17 (8509 1917/www.lbwf.gov.uk). Walthamstow Central tube/rail. **Open** 10am-1pm, 2-5.30pm Mon-Fri; 10am-5pm Sat. Closed 24-26 Dec, 1 Jan, bank hols. *Tours* groups only, by arrangement. **Admission** free.
This museum includes one of the original police cells constructed in 1840, a gallery of toys and games, and the Bremer Car, built by local engineer Frederick Bremer in 1892-4 and said to be one of the first cars ever built in Britain (it was certainly the first in London). There's also a section devoted to local lad Alfred Hitchcock.
Nearest picnic place: museum garden.

Walthamstow Greyhound Stadium
Chingford Road, E4 (8531 4255). Walthamstow Central tube/rail then 97, 357, 215 bus. **Times** *Race days* 1pm Mon. *Race nights* 6.30pm Tue, Thur, Sat (first race 7.30pm). **Tickets** prices vary; call for details. **No credit cards.**
With regular appearances from diamond geezers such as Vinnie Jones (who turned up with Claudia Schiffer one week), there's no denying that going to the dogs, with all its boisterous charm, is de rigueur these days. There's a children's play area for those who don't want to watch the canine capers, and a bar for parents who do. Arrive at least an hour before the races start if you want to bag a table.
Nappy-changing facilities. Restaurant.

It's a dog's life at **Walthamstow Greyhound Stadium**. See p122.

William Morris Gallery

Lloyd Park, Forest Road, E17 (8527 3782/ www.lbwf.gov.uk/wmg). Walthamstow Central tube/rail. **Open** *10am-1pm, 2-5pm Tue-Sat; 1st Sun of mth. Closed 25, 26 Dec, 1 Jan, bank hols. Tours phone for details.* **Admission** *free.*

The childhood home of the famous designer and socialist, who was born in Walthamstow in 1834, is a must-see for those interested in design or who are taking GCSE Art. Examples of Morris's work, from textiles and wallpapers to fine printing, are displayed in four ground-floor rooms alongside work by his peers and collaborators, including Ford Madox Brown and Dante Gabriel Rossetti.

Nearest picnic place: Lloyd Park. Shop.

Eating & shopping

For something beyond the ubiquitous pie and mash, **Central Kitchen** (226 Hoe Street, E17, 8521 9432) and **Village Kitchen** (41 Orford Road, E17, 8509 2144) provide ciabattas and baguettes for £2 and hot lunches such as char-grilled chicken and couscous, lasagne or pasta for around £3.75. Village Kitchen becomes a more formal restaurant in the evenings.

Central to the Walthamstow shopping experience is the market on the High Street, packed with more than 450 stalls. A whole morning can be whiled

away here poring over everything from cut-price trainers, children's clothes, fruit and veg, cosmetics, music, computer games, toys and kitchenware. The market also provides the focus for street entertainers at weekends (even pop stars have made an occasional appearance).

Walthamstow residents are also proud of their bookshop, **Hammicks** (259 High Street, E17, 8521 3669), claimed (by its management) to be the biggest bookshop in the East End. Its extensive children's section has a train for them to sit in while they browse the books. Tucked away in an otherwise residential area at 29 Haroldstone Road is a real cottage industry, the **Handweavers Studio and Gallery** (8521 2281), where spinning and weaving equipment can be found to suit those of all ages and levels of experience. There's also tuition and demonstrations available.

Further east

South of Walthamstow are its poor relations, **Leyton** and **Leytonstone**. The largest area of public open space here is **Marsh Lane Fields**, enthusiastically used by local people for picnics, walks, sports activities and nature studies. Part of the Dagenham Brook 'green corridor', the Fields are what remains of the original Lammas Lands (fertile strips of land alongside the River Lea) of the rural village of Leyton, which until 1864 had nothing to do with London at all.

Despite being enveloped by the city, the area has its own Nature Conservation Officer (8527 5544). More information about this charmingly countrified area and its near relation, the Lee Valley Park, can be obtained by calling the helpful Lower Lea Project (8983 1121).

The Pride of Lee

This wide-beam boat, which seats 40, runs from the pretty Three Mills along the River Lea and through Hertford Union Canal and Regent's Canal to Limehouse Cut. It's a relaxing way to spend a spare hour on a summer's afternoon, as well as giving you the chance to see a side of London that's normally hidden to the tourist eye. The *Pride of Lee* is used for all kinds of themed cruises, including a spooky Hallowe'en cruise, a fish and chip special and various longer trips to far-flung beauty spots. Call for a brochure.

Pride of Lee

Three Mills, Bromley-by-Bow, E3 (8983 7476). Bromley-by-Bow tube. **Times** *vary; call for details (cruises run Apr-Oct).* **Tickets** *adults from £4, under-16s from £3, depending on length of trip.*

Heading east along the river to the furthest outpost of the DLR takes you to **Beckton**, famous for its 'Alp', a dry ski slope, which is great fun for kids of all ages. As this guide went to press it was closed for a revamp and was due to re-open as a real 'snow dome' in late 2002 (call the Ski Club of Great Britain on 8410 2000 for further details).

While you're in this part of Newham, you could spend lots of money in the rather run-of-the-mill out-of-town shopping centre, **Beckton Retail Park**, on Alpine Way, or enjoy more countrified pursuits, such as riding at **Docklands Equestrian Centre** (2 Claps Gate Lane, E6, 7473 4951), rambling at **East Ham Nature Reserve** or visiting livestock at **Newham City Farm**.

South of this lies unprepossessing **Silvertown**, which now boasts an exciting piece of modern landscaping, the delightful **Thames Barrier Park** (North Woolwich Road, E16), with its concrete tea pavilion, playground and fountains that kids can't wait to get stripped down to their trunks for.

If outdoor pursuits are your children's thing, it pays to travel way out east: there are several bird sanctuaries and open spaces in the Lee Valley Park and Chingford areas, while **Epping Forest** (*see p126*) is great for walkers, riders and cyclists. The forest is accessible on foot from several underground stations, but to fully explore these areas and the pretty Essex villages that lie beyond them, with their country pubs, a car may be the best option.

East Ham Nature Reserve

Norman Road, E6 (8470 4525). East Ham tube/ Beckton DLR. **Open** *Grounds & museum* Mar-Oct 10am-5pm Tue-Fri; 2-5pm Sat, Sun. Nov-Feb 10am-5pm Tue-Fri; 1-4pm Sat, Sun. Closed bank hols. **Admission** free.
Pick up a nature trail, or visit the museum, which combines natural and local history. There's a Victorian schoolroom to terrify the kids and a war time kitchen showing how people cooked up their spirits during the Blitz.
Buggy access. Nappy-changing facilities. Shop.

Newham City Farm

Stansfeld Road, E6 (7476 1170). Royal Albert or Prince Regent DLR. **Open** *mid Oct-mid Feb* 10am-4pm Tue-Sun. *Mid Feb-mid Oct* 10am-5pm Tue-Sun. Closed 25 Dec, 1 Jan. **Admission** free.
The farm's visitor centre welcomes families and school groups wanting to find out more about city farming. The Berkshire and Kune Kune pigs are popular residents, but there are also a number of cows, ducks, ferrets, geese, goats and guinea pigs to cuddle as well. Note that the on-site café is only open during the school holidays, so you might want to bring your own refreshments if you visit at other times.
Buggy access.

Twitching

At Chingford Reservoirs, look out for tufted ducks, winter goosanders, goldeneyes, great crested grebe, meadow pipits, green sandpipers, yellow wagtails and terns.

Lee Valley Park

Covering a vast area on either side of the River Lee between Waltham Abbey (Essex) and Broxbourne River Lee Country Park (which starts in Hackney and goes all the way to Hertfordshire), this network of lakes, waterways, parks and countryside areas makes a great getaway from east London's concrete acres. There's plenty to do, though a gentle guided walk (call the **Lee Valley Park Information Centre** for walk info and leaflets) is a good way to set about it. Some walks can easily be tackled with pushchairs.

Lee Valley Park is great for birdwatchers – more than 200 species have been seen here, despite its proximity to London. Of the birds that fly here from thousands of miles away, some come to breed, many just rest and feed, and others stay through the winter, retreating from much harsher weather.

The Middlesex Filter Beds on the Hackney side of Lee Valley, not too far from the **Lee Valley Ice Centre**, are now a nature reserve with great birdwatching potential. The beds, once part of a sewerage plant, now have the rather more savoury purpose of creating valuable marshland for flora and fauna. Nearby are three riverside pubs.

The best site for birdspotting, way up at the northern (countrified) end of the park toward Ponders End, is the series of watery expanses known as **Chingford Reservoirs**, but public access is restricted to the King George V Reservoir, and children under the age of eight aren't allowed in.

Lee Valley Riding Centre (8556 2629) just off Lea Bridge Road, a strangely un-rustic stables that looks more like a sports centre, welcomes riders of all ages and abilities and has a floodlit manège for after-work winter riding, as well as an indoor school and a cross-country course (*see also p256*).

Lee Valley Cycle Circuit (Temple Mill Lane, E15, 8534 6085) is set in open parkland and offers mountain bike, BMX and cyclo-cross courses. The rowdiest entertainment comes in the form of the **Lee Valley Ice Centre** (Lea Bridge Road, E10, 8533 3155), which has a frenetic disco soundtrack, a shop and a fast food café. It also hosts ice ballet shows, pantomimes and competitions throughout the year (*see also p258*).

Chingford Reservoirs

Lea Valley Road, E4 (info 8808 1527). Ponders End rail. **Open** 7am-dusk daily. **Admission** free.
Given its highly urban location, an extraordinary number of species of birds nest, feed and breed in the Reservoirs, many staying throughout the winter months. Serious birdwatchers aged eight and up should call ahead to gain access to this avian paradise.

Walk: in the woods

▶ **Epping Forest Tree Trail**, a Corporation of London walk (contact the Information Centre for details, *see p126*), covers about two kilometres (a little over a mile) and is a good walk for children, encouraging them to identify different types of tree. It's suitable for children over five, and points 1-9 are fine for pushchairs and wheelchairs. A map of the walk, with information on Epping's flora and fauna, is available at the Information Centre or the Field Studies Centre next door, where teachers and helpers run various outdoors activities for school-age children in the holidays (call 8508 7714 for details).

▶ Beginning just outside Epping Forest Information Centre (**point 1**), you're invited to spot the trees that have been pollarded (chopped at the top to encourage new growth). You then carry on past the pond (**point 2**), where water plants thrive year round. You may be able to see frogs leaping and newts paddling, and even snakes basking on hot days. The pond is also home to several species of dragonfly, which flit past as ducks dabble in the chickweed. This delightful spot is worth lingering at. Beech trees provide shade to the right (**point 3**), and there's a seat further on where you're instructed to engage in a bit of tree-hugging as a way of recognising oak by its bark.

▶ Further down on the left, groups of Turkey oak, English oak and holly give you further opportunity to memorise the individual features of native trees and examine their very different leaves (**point 6**). At **point 8**, the hornbeam trees (rare in the UK) are dotted with holes – in spring you might hear a woodpecker drilling into the bark. Knopper galls, the larvae of the gall wasp, can be spotted on the forest floor at **point 9**.

▶ From this point, follow the bridlepath, where in springtime the pussy willow is covered with downy buds. At **point 10**, study the gnarled and scarred bark of the ancient beeches. Continue in a westerly direction to Conservators Green (**point 12**), where the specimens, seeded by energetic Victorian plant-finders in the 19th-century nursery, are now huge: they include a collection of elegant Japanese maples, all burnished and coppery as summer gives way to autumn, towering rhododendrons, hollies and silver birches.

▶ After the green you're once again at the Information Centre; at the back are elder and sycamore trees, and further down are lime and sweet chestnut, introduced to this country by the Romans, who probably needed to roast chestnuts to see them through the interminable English winters. Follow the line of the fence, rejoin the path and turn left to see coppices of beech trees and lots of cheeky squirrels.

▶ Finish with another lovely oak – the King's Oak pub, where cold beers and hot food is the order of the day. There's a kids' playground here, and a café selling ice-creams next door.

Lee Valley Park Farms

*Stubbins Hall Lane, Crooked Mile, Waltham Abbey, Essex
(01992 892781/www.leevalleypark.org.uk). Waltham Cross
or Broxbourne rail.* **Open** 10am-4.30pm Mon-Fri; 10am-
6pm or dusk if earlier Sat, Sun. **Admission** £3.10; £2.05
concessions, 3-16s; free under-3s. **Credit** MC, V.

Hayes Hill Farm is a rare breeds centre, with a Tudor barn, a
restored gypsy caravan and plenty of space in which to play.
Nearby Holyfield Hall is a commercial farm where visitors
can watch the milking of cows (2.45-4pm). There are guided
tours for school parties, when city children can learn all about
agricultural ways.

Buggy access. Café. Nappy-changing facilities. Shop.

Lee Valley Park Information Centre

*Abbey Gardens, Waltham Abbey, Essex EN9 (01922
702200/www.leevalleypark.org.uk).* **Open** *Nov-Mar* 10am-
4pm Tue-Sun. *Apr-Oct* 9.30am-5pm daily. **Admission** free.

This has racks of literature about the various activities available to visitors to the park, including messing about on the
reservoirs in passenger boats, cruise boats and canoes.
Fishing permits can be obtained here, and there are maps for
cycle routes and information about scenic riverside pubs.

The old abbey church, parts of which date back to the 14th
century, is the centrepiece of Waltham Abbey town. The
Augustinian abbey was once one of the largest in the country, with its own farm, fishponds and brewery. Its remains
(the gateway, a few walls and a stone bridge) and surrounding parks are now managed by English Heritage and are
famous as the reputed burial site of King Harold, who died in
1066. You can still visit the church and the accompanying gardens. The gardens contain various public artworks and
there's a 'Sensory trail' (available from the centre) that highlights the natural history of the area.

*Buggy access. Nappy-changing facilities. Nearest picnic
place: information centre gardens. Shop.*

Epping Forest

At 19 kilometres (12 miles) in length and four
kilometres (2½ miles) in width, Epping Forest is the
biggest public space in London. In 1878 an act was
passed giving ownership to the Corporation of
London in order to stop development. Today, in
addition to its two listed buildings – the restored
Queen Elizabeth's Hunting Lodge in Chingford
(Rangers Road, E4, 8529 6681; under-16s must be
accompanied by adults) and the Temple in Wanstead
Park – and the remains of two large Iron Age
earthworks, there is a whole range of services.

Footie fans can have a kick-around on one of about
50 pitches, while cricketers have the choice of three
pitches. Riders have a huge amount of track space,
and there are more than eight riding schools in the
vicinity (contact the **Epping Forest Information
Centre** to find one to suit your needs). Those who
prefer wheels to hooves can hire bikes (it's best to
pre-book) at **Top Banana** cycle shop in Woodford
Green (7B Johnston Road, IG8, 8559 0170) or **Heales
Cycles** in Highams Park (477 Halend Road, E4, 8527
1592). Golfers may fancy a swing at the **Pitch &
Putt** course at High Beech (8508 7323) towards the
centre of the forest.

Also at High Beech is the **Green Tea Hut**, which
is good for snacks and drinks. For fuller cooked
meals there's the **King's Oak Pub**, which has
children's play areas.

An important wildlife and conservation centre,
the forest is home to woodpeckers, nightingales,
treecreepers and nuthatches, plus unusual waterfowl
species such as great crested grebes, goosanders and
widgeons. There are also 650 flower species and
more than 1,000 types of fungi. For a real back-to-
nature feeling, there's a campsite at **Debden House**
(Debden Green, Loughton, Essex, 8508 3008).

If you're coming to the forest by public transport,
Theydon Bois (Central Line) is the nearest tube stop,
though from there it's an uphill walk to the entrance,
which will be a bit of a struggle if you've got small
children in tow or buggies to push. Visitors are
advised to obtain a map and plan their route around
the forest in advance. The *Official Guide to Epping
Forest* (£1.50) is available from the Guildhall Library
Bookshop (7332 1858).

Epping Forest Information Centre

*High Beech, Loughton, Essex (8508 0028/
www.eppingforest.co.uk). Loughton or Theydon Bois
tube then 2-mile walk or 5-min taxi ride.* **Open** *Apr-Oct*
10am-5pm Mon-Sat; 11am-5pm Sun. *Nov-Mar* 11am-3pm
Mon-Fri; 10am-dusk Sat; 11am-dusk Sun.

Buggy access. Shop.

Meet the teacher

Peter Kinsey is Education Manager
at the Bethnal Green Museum of
Childhood (*see p117*).

What do you do?
I organise a programme for schools that visit us
in term time and activities for children and
families at the weekend and in the holidays.

What activities do children request most?
Well, they like to get their hands on anything they
can play with. That goes for the grown-ups, too!
The Art Cart, with things to make and draw, is
also very popular.

What other activities are there?
We are changing the museum a lot at the
moment and hope eventually to have a surprise
around every corner. In 2001 we opened a new
games area, where children can play all sorts of
board games, as well as a special under-fives
play space.

What's the best part of your job?
What I like most is working and
playing with our visitors and not
sitting at my desk too much.

Do you wear a uniform?
No, but I make sure I dress up
in some of the costumes!

South-east London

From big guns to beautiful beasties.

Historic **Greenwich** is the most obvious draw on the south-eastern trail, but there are lesser-known – and much-maligned – corners of south-east London that still have their charms: tough but endearing **Peckham** has the smartest library this side of the British Library (see p57), chi-chi **Dulwich Village** has an enchanting art gallery set in parkland, and **Crystal Palace** has the National Sports Centre next to a dinosaur-filled green space, recently saved from the developers' bulldozers. Meanwhile, open spaces such as **Blackheath** and **Oxleas Wood**, and unique attractions such as the **Horniman Museum** make this a diverse and diverting part of the world.

The lack of tube lines makes tourists tremble, but most places that we've included are within a short train ride of Charing Cross or London Bridge. And transport matters have improved with the extension of the Jubilee Line south of the river, the Docklands Light Railway (DLR; see p118) to Lewisham, and the new multi-million-pound tram system in Croydon (trams and driverless DLRs are a big hit with children – they're easy to get on and off and small people enjoy a great view of where they're going).

Greenwich

Greenwich has a regal background. Henry VIII loved his palace here above all others – his daughters Elizabeth and Mary were born there, and his hunting ground was **Greenwich Park**. On the site of Greenwich Palace, which fell into disrepair during the Civil War, a new building was erected that was to have been a new palace for Charles II, once Cromwell was safely dispatched, but under his successors William and Mary, it was turned into a naval hospital. It is better known today as the **Old Royal Naval College**, the noble façade of which you can see from the river. The navy left in 1998.

Greenwich: the pride of south London.

Behind it is the **Queen's House**, now part of the **National Maritime Museum**). It was here, they say, that Sir Walter Raleigh lay down his cloak over a puddle for Eizabeth I.

On top of Royal Greenwich Park looms the magnificent **Royal Observatory**, designed by Sir Christopher Wren (*see also p129*).

Cutty Sark
King William Walk, SE10 (8858 3445/ www.cuttysark.org.uk). Cutty Sark DLR/Greenwich DLR/rail. **Open** 10am-5pm daily (last entry 4.30pm). Closed 24-26 Dec. *Tours* dependent on availability of volunteer. **Admission** £3.50; £2.50 concessions; £8.50 family (2+2); free under-5s. *Combined ticket with National Maritime Museum & Royal Observatory* £12; £9.60 concessions; £2.50 under-16s. *Tours* free. **Credit** MC, V.
This lovingly restored ship, designed by Hercules Linton in 1869 with speed in mind, is the world's only surviving tea and wool clipper. It's fun to roam the restored decks and crew's quarters, and to gaze up at the rigging. Inside are displays of prints and naval relics, plus the world's largest collection of carved and painted figureheads. Children are intrigued by the hands-on exhibits, such as a knot-tying board and a hammock. On summer weekends there are shanty singers and popular costumed storytelling sessions that allow you to relive life aboard ship.
Nearest picnic place: Cutty Sark Gardens. Shop.

Fan Museum
12 Crooms Hill, SE10 (8305 1441/www.fan-museum.org). Cutty Sark DLR/Greenwich DLR/rail. **Open** 11am-5pm Tue-Sat; noon-5pm Sun. Closed 25 Dec. **Admission** £3.50; £2.50 concessions; free under-7s. Free entry OAPs, disabled 2-5pm Tue. **Credit** MC, V.
This rather beautiful museum houses one of only two permanent exhibitions of hand-held folding fans in the world. Only part of the huge collection is on view at any one time: the fans' elasticity necessitates periodic rest. The fans are displayed by theme, such as design, provenance or social history, and exhibitions change regularly so call for details. There are occasional talks and classes for art students, while the over-12s may be interested in the fan-making workshops on the first Saturday of every month.
Lift. Shop.

Greenwich Park
King William Way, SE10 (visitors' centre 8293 0703). Cutty Sark DLR/Greenwich DLR/rail/Maze Hill rail/ 1, 53, 177, 180, 188, 286 bus/riverboat to Greenwich Pier. **Open** 6am-dusk daily.
Some say this is the most beautiful royal park; it's certainly the hilliest. Spectacular views across the city from the Wolfe Monument at the top are snapped enthusiastically by tourists, though many prefer to capture their friends and relatives straddling the Prime Meridian Line. Small children like the lower reaches of the park, where the playground and boating lake attract crowds in good weather. Walks up the hills are bracing, and the deer enclosures and shrubberies are fine places for picnics. In summer the London Bubble theatre company's promenade shows spend a week here. Sadly, the free car park has been replaced by pay and display machines.
Buggy access. Cafés. Nappy-changing facilities.

National Maritime Museum
Romney Road, SE10 (8858 4422/info 8312 6565/tours 8312 6608/www.nmm.ac.uk). Cutty Sark DLR/Greenwich DLR/rail. **Open** 10am-5pm daily. Closed 24-26 Dec. *Tours*

phone for details. **Admission** £7.50; £6 concessions; free under-16s, OAPs. *Combined ticket with Cutty Sark & Royal Observatory* £12; £9.60 concessions; £2.50 under-16s, OAPs. **Credit** AmEx, MC, V.
This museum, which put its £20-million lottery handout to good use, is a thrilling place to visit for those of all ages, whether landlubbers or sea dogs. Its themed galleries combine traditional exhibits with interactive elements so as to be entertaining and educational in equal measure. The galleries, arranged around three sides of the central atrium – Neptune Court – are not meant to be seen in any particular order, and you may do well to ignore the bewildering colour-coded floor plan and explore the museum at your leisure.
On level one, the Explorers Gallery examines pioneering sea travel, while the Passengers Gallery looks at the more passive participants in marine expeditions, concentrating on those involved in the mass migration of the early 20th century. Maritime London brings old prints and lithographs together with video installations to present London's nautical past. On level two, the new Seapower exhibition concentrates on the Navy and sea trade in the 20th century, from World War I to the Gulf War. Level three is home to All Hands and The Bridge, two interactive galleries where younger visitors can learn to send a distress signal using Morse code, flags or radio, and try their hand at steering a Viking longboat, a paddle steamer and a modern passenger ferry. Just as popular as the hands-on stuff are the Nelson Gallery, a comprehensive monument to Britain's most celebrated naval hero, and the 17th- and 18th-century models in the Ship of War gallery.
Buggy access (limited for Royal Observatory). Café. Nappy-changing facilities. Nearest picnic place: Greenwich Park. Restaurant. Shop.

Old Royal Naval College
King William Walk, SE10 (8269 4747/ www.greenwichfoundation.org.uk). Cutty Sark DLR/ Greenwich DLR/rail. **Open** 10am-5pm daily (last entry 4.15pm). Closed 25, 26 Dec. **Admission** £3; £2 concessions; free accompanied under-16s. Free for all from 3.30pm daily; free to all all day Sun. *Tours* subject to staff availability. **Credit** MC, V.
Fine examples of monumental classical architecture in England, these spectacular riverside buildings, designed by Sir Christopher Wren, were begun in 1696. The college is split in two to give an unimpeded view of Queen's House (*see below*) from the river and vice versa. Intended as a palace, then turned into a grand almshouse for former Royal Navy seamen, it was adapted for use as a naval college in 1873. After 125 years in residence, the Navy vacated the buildings in 1998 and the University of Greenwich moved in. The spectacular Painted Hall (decorated by James Thornhill in 1708-27) and the chapel are still open to the public, and a space has been created for temporary exhibitions (call the above number for details).
Café. Nappy-changing facilities. Nearest picnic place: Naval College grounds. Shop.

Queen's House
Romney Road, SE10 (8312 6565/www.nmm.ac.uk). Cutty Sark DLR/Greenwich DLR/rail. **Open** 10am-5pm daily. Closed 24-26 Dec. **Admission** £1; free under-16s, OAPs. **Credit** AmEx, DC, MC, V.
Designed by Inigo Jones in 1616 for James I's wife, Anne of Denmark, the Queen's House was one of the first truly classical buildings in Britain. Anne died before it was finished and it was completed at the order of Queen Henrietta Maria in 1629. After refurbishment, the house reopened in spring 2001 with 'A Sea of Faces', an exhibition of more than

130 portraits of sea captains and shipwrights from the 17th century to the present day, including work by the likes of Reynolds and Hogarth.

Buggy access. Nappy-changing facilities. Nearest picnic place: Greenwich Park.

Royal Observatory

Greenwich Park, SE10 (8312 6565/www.rog.nmm.ac.uk). Cutty Sark DLR/Greenwich DLR/rail. **Open** 10am-5pm daily. Closed 24-26 Dec. *Tours* daily; phone for details. **Admission** £6; £4.80 concessions; free under-16s, OAPs. *Combined ticket with Cutty Sark & National Maritime Museum* £12; £9.60 concessions; £2.50 under-16s, OAPs. **Credit** AmEx, DC, MC, V.

This observatory was founded when Charles II appointed the first astronomer royal, John Flamsteed, to find out 'the so much desired longitude of places for the perfecting of the art of navigation', and several of the museum's galleries tell of the search for a means of determining longitude at sea. They include a collection of instruments that failed to solve the problem, as well as the one that finally did – John Harrison's marine chronometer. The rest of the museum includes exhibits on the development of ever-more-accurate timepieces and an extensive history of the buildings as a working observatory, including the Octagon Room, a faithful restoration of Sir Christopher Wren's original interior.

This working observatory is a fascinating place to take children: most are bowled over by the biggest refracting telescope in the world, even if they can't look through it. There's also the astro web: a website children can explore for news and

A day at: Greenwich

Daniel Defoe described Greenwich as 'the most delightful spot of ground in Great Britain', but then he didn't experience its congested one-way system and the vast numbers of tourists that converge here in high season. Yet you only have to climb one of the hills in **Greenwich Park** to see what he was on about – the view takes your breath away. Stretching out before you is the magnificent baroque **Old Royal Naval College**, the palatial **Queen's House**, the **National Maritime Museum**, the masts of the *Cutty Sark*, and the Thames winding its way through the cityscape.

On a sunny day, Greenwich Park, with its playground, boating lake, flower garden and deer enclosure, can take up several hours. Your only expense will be ice-creams and snacks from the cafés, and maybe a rowing-boat circuit round the pond. In the summer holidays there are free puppet and theatre shows for children (call Royal Parks Agency on 8858 2608/ www.royalparks.co.uk for details).

On a wet and windy afternoon you'll probably spend time in the nautical museums or the Royal Observatory, whose Telescope Dome houses Britain's largest telescope. As is the case with most attractions these days, you exit via the shop. Next door is the Planetarium, with shows every half hour. Diagonally across the park is the Rangers House, an early 18th-century red-brick villa now in the loving hands of English Heritage and undergoing major restoration work as this guide went to press, though it should be open to the public again around April 2002 (call 8853 0035 nearer the time).

Going back down the hill into Greenwich you'll pass the **Fan Museum** (*see p128*) on Crooms Hill, only suitable for older, aesthetically minded children. Many visitors spend a good chunk of their time at the Maritime Museum, with its 'All Hands' section bristling with interactive exhibits and a variety of holiday and weekend workshops, and the recently refurbished Queen's House next door.

The **Old Royal Naval College** (*see p128*), which is situated right on the river, is free on Sundays or after 3.30pm every day. Wander at your leisure or pre-book a tour (£4 per person). Family events take place during holidays and half-terms; phone for details.

Children also get special treatment at the *Cutty Sark*, back where you started: on Wednesdays in the holidays there is a costumed storyteller, and there are also 'Sailor for a Day' events for schools and other groups, in which kids aged 8-11 can have a go at being a Victorian seaman.

Maritime Greenwich was designated a UNESCO World Heritage Site in 1997, and since then its various sights and landmarks have been packaged for the tourist trade in a rather more coherent fashion than before. The new **Tourist Information Centre** makes it easier to plan your day out, so you'd be well advised to kick off proceedings there with an armful of free leaflets and maps. If you want to be led rather than explore under your own steam, sign up for a guided walk from here (£4 adults, free under-16s; call Greenwich Tour Guides Association on 8858 6169 for more details. Tours leave at 12.15pm and 2.15pm daily from the Tourist Information Centre in Cutty Sark Gardens).

The quickest way to reach Greenwich is by train from Charing Cross or via the new DLR link through Docklands, but the most pleasant way to appreciate Wren's architecture is to take a boat – try **Catamaran Cruises** (7987 1185) or **City Cruises** (7930 9033). For more riverboat companies, *see p299*. It's perfectly pleasant to walk between the various sights at Greenwich, but there is a shuttle bus, which runs from Greenwich Pier to the National Maritime Museum and the Royal Observatory every 15 minutes or so. Tickets (which last a day) cost £1.50 for adults and 50p for kids.

Tourist Information Centre

2 Cutty Sark Gardens, SE10 (8858 6376/ www.greenwich.gov.uk). Cutty Sark DLR. **Open** 10am-5pm daily. Closed 25, 26 Dec. **Credit** *Shop* MC, V. *Buggy access. Café. Nappy-changing facilities. Nearest picnic place: Greenwich Park/grounds of Old Royal Naval College. Shop.*

information from the world of astronomy. The planetarium show (£2 adults, £1.50 children) for everyone aged from four is an atmospheric way to see stars, and runs frequently during school holidays and weekends. The programme of events for children set up for every holiday includes role playing opportunities, talks, stories and workshops. Ring for details. *Buggy access (not in Telescope Dome).* *Nappy-changing facilities. Nearest picnic place: Greenwich Park. Shop.*

Eating & shopping

With its daily influx of visitors, Greenwich has its fair share of burger, pizza and fry-up refuelling stations. Salubrious places include **Time** (7A College Approach, SE10, 8305 9767), overlooking the market, which has a friendly attitude to children and a smart, fish-biased Modern European menu. The **Spread Eagle** (1-2 Stockwell Street, SE10, 8853 2333) has a rather pricey French menu but provides high chairs and plenty of bread for nibblers. A little further out of the centre, **Inside** (19 Greenwich South Street, SE10, 8265 5060) is a small but popular local restaurant with an excellent brunch menu on Saturdays and Sundays (10am-3pm).

Many local pubs, including the **Trafalgar Tavern** on the river (Park Row, SE10, 8858 2437), have a children's menu. The **North Pole** (131

Greenwich High Road, SE10, 8853 3020) is a trendy, clubby place during the week but on Sundays goes mellow, dishing up a family lunch menu in the restaurant upstairs (noon-4pm).

The most exciting shopping is to be had at **Greenwich Market** (mostly weekends, though the crafts market is open for antiques on Thursday and general trading on Friday). The covered bit, in particular, has some alluring stalls, with fudge, jewellery, hand-crafted toys and witty clothing all proving a hit with kids. **E sharp minor** (6 Earlswood Street, SE10, 8858 6648; *see also p198*) has Ella Sharp's knitwear for children. **Compendia** (10 Greenwich Market, SE10, 8293 6616) is a specialist board game shop that's good for smart backgammon, roulette and cribbage sets. The **South London Book Centre** (11-17 Stockwell Street, SE10, 8853 2151) has old books, annuals, magazines, comics and postcards enough to fill a former garage.

Blackheath

The windswept heath, which got its name from the darkness of its soil rather than anything more sinister (no plague victms were buried here, contrary

Take a hike on **Blackheath**.

to popular myth), is up Maze Hill from Greenwich Park (*see p128*) and, though criss-crossed with often busy roads, it's a fabulous open space where weekend footballers, kite-fliers and strollers converge (though you should avoid the weekend of the London Marathon, when the area is solid with runners and their families; *see p25*). Blackheath also plays host to regular kite festivals, bank holiday funfairs and the annual Blackheath Village Fair. After a bit of exercise, the village, as locals quaintly call it, is a good place for a meal or a snack and a nose round the shops (delis, cookshops, and gift and craft shops abound).

Parents flock to **Pares Children's Shoes** (24 Tranquil Vale, SE3; 8297 0785), but families should also pop into the **Age Exchange Reminiscence Centre** (11 Blackheath Village, SE3, 8318 9105), a museum/shop that constitutes a pleasant informal history lesson. Children like it all the more for the jars of sweets and lollipops and selections of wooden toys and games. Just through the village past the station, **Blackheath Halls** (23 Lee Road, SE9, 8463 0100) offer Saturday afternoon children's shows in winter; booking is advisable.

On Sundays Blackheath Station Car Park is home to a farmers' market, where you can usually sample all kinds of cakes and breads before you buy.

You're spoilt for choice when it comes to eating options here, with brasseries and café/bars all over the place. For a special family meal, try **Chapter Two** (43-5 Montpelier Vale, SE3, 8333 2666), whose views over the heath, colourful Modern European food and cheery service come highly recommended. A branch of **fish!** flapped into Blackheath in 2001 (1 Lawn Terrace, SE3, 7234 3333); its £6.95 children's menu, colouring books and toys keep tiddlers fed and entertained.

If you want to know more about the area, Greenwich Council has produced a 'Heritage Trail' with maps, information and suggestions for lunch stops. Others in the set (available from the Tourist Information Centre in Greenwich; price £2) include Eltham, Greenwich, and Woolwich and Deptford.

Charlton, Woolwich & Eltham

In centuries past, the steep Shooters Hill Road that takes you from Greenwich towards Kent was a lurking place for highwaymen after rich pickings from carriages heading out of town; if they were caught, they were taken straight to the gallows at the bottom of the hill. Some say Shooters Hill is so named because of the trigger-happy highwaymen, others reckon it's because the area was used for archery practice by that great sports enthusiast Henry VIII (he was born at Greenwich and spent a lot of time in the area).

Off Shooters Hill is **Hornfair Park**, which is popular among Charlton folk in hot weather for its cool blue lido (8856 7180) and its children's pool (*see also p264*). Further east lies **Oxleas Wood** (*see p140*). Eltham, a suburban enclave surrounded by more woods, parkland and golf courses, is not very interesting in its own right, unless you're bound for **Eltham Palace** for a shot of art deco splendour and a picnic in the grounds.

Due north of Shooters Hill, across Charlton's parkland, the redundant dockyards and industrial estates around Woolwich lead you to the astonishing **Thames Flood Barrier** (*see p132*), London's lifebelt. Woolwich has never been a big player on the tourist scene, but its noisy new **Firepower Museum** should make its mark. During World War I, 72,000 people worked in a weapons-development complex that stretched for three miles down the river. Now there are plans to regenerate the whole of the former MOD site – eventually there'll be swish flats and offices, a multiplex cinema, restaurants and other family facilities.

Woolwich is a satisfying place to visit even if you don't like guns: its shopping centre is better than most in the area, and its riverside architecture is spectacular in certain lights. Children can't get enough of the **Waterfront Leisure Centre** (Woolwich High Street, SE18, 8317 5000), with its flume-filled pools and large indoor adventure playground (*see also p265*). A wonderful place to sit and watch the river at work is outside the leisure centre, at the Woolwich Ferry terminal. The ferry, which runs from the Waterfront Leisure Centre in south Woolwich to the pier across the river, is free, runs every quarter-hour or so and takes four minutes to get you over to the **Old Station Museum**.

Eltham Palace

Court Yard, off Court Road, SE9 (82942548/ www.english-heritage.org.uk). Eltham rail. **Open** *Apr-Sept* 10am-6pm Wed-Fri, Sun. *Oct* 10am-5pm Wed-Fri, Sun. *Nov-Mar* 10am-4pm Wed-Fri, Sun. Closed 24-26 Dec, 1-15 Jan. **Admission** (EH) *House & grounds (incl audio tour)* £6; £4.50 concessions; £3 5-16s; free under-5s. *Grounds only* £3.60; £2.70 concessions; £1.80 5-16s; free under-5s. **Credit** MC, V.
Incongruously set just a few hundred yards off a suburban high street, this English Heritage property is full of surprises. It consists of a medieval great hall with a magnificent restored oak roof, but grafted on to the side of it is a stunning 1930s art deco house with exotic wood veneer and every mod con, including underfloor heating, a centralised vacuum cleaning system and specially designed quarters for the owners' pet lemur. The dream home was created by arts patron Stephen Courtauld and his wife Virginia, who bought the crumbling palace in 1933. Now you can tour its rooms while listening to a commentary on hand-sets.
Unlike most English Heritage properties, Eltham doesn't put on any special family events, and many visitors with younger children in tow tend to opt for the garden-only tickets. The grounds are beautifully laid out, with views across to the city and out to the greenery of Kent. It's a great place

for a picnic without the hassle of a long drive out to the country, and there's plenty of space to run around and play hide and seek (though be careful of the easily accessible moat). *Café. Lifts. Nappy-changing facilities. Nearest picnic place: palace grounds. Shop.*

North Woolwich Old Station Museum

Pier Road, E16 (7474 7244). Beckton DLR/North Woolwich, Woolwich Dockyard or Woolwich Arsenal rail, then ferry or foot tunnel to North Woolwich Pier. **Open** *Jan-Nov* 1-5pm Sat, Sun. *Half-term, school hols* 1-5pm daily. **Admission** free.

Here friendly train enthusiasts let you admire old engines, ticket machines, signs and relics from the age of steam. On Sundays you can see the traction engine in action, as well as the Coffee Pot and Pickett steam engines if they're up to it. Refreshments are provided and children are encouraged – during the school holidays, Wednesday afternoon fun and games keep little people amused. The museum is free, but there's a small shop where you might be persuaded to part with your pennies.

Firepower

Royal Arsenal, SE18 (8855 7755/www.firepower.org.uk). Woolwich Arsenal rail. **Open** 10am-5pm daily (last entry 4pm). Closed 25 Dec. **Admission** £6.50; £5.50 concessions; £4.50 5-16s; £18 family (2+2 or 1+3); free under-5s. **Credit** MC, V.

This £40-million military museum in the old Royal Arsenal opened with a bang in May 2001, after 15 years of planning and fundraising and five years of rebuilding. It tells the story of the Royal Artillery, or Gunners, in an interactive and dramatic way – family appeal is high on the management's agenda (though very young children may find the constant bangs and some of the images distressing). The exhibition areas include a Gunnery Hall and a hands-on Real Weapon Gallery, which isn't as alarming as it sounds – this is all about firing ping-pong balls and hitting targets rather than playing with guns. Other would-be gunners practise their marksmanship on a computerised version of a light artillery piece.

The centrepiece of the museum is 'The Field of Fire', a multimedia presentation that puts visitors in the midst of the battlefield with bombs and shells whizzing overhead as soldiers share their thoughts on campaigns as recent as Bosnia and Iraq. Some of their testimonies are sobering; kids nonetheless enjoy raiding the shop for books on the SAS, camouflage gear, toy tanks and guns and even bullets. *Buggy access. Café. Lift. Nappy-changing facilities. Nearest picnic place: riverside. Shop.*

Thames Barrier Visitors' Centre

1 Unity Way, SE18 (8305 4188). North Greenwich tube/Charlton rail/riverboats to & from Greenwich Pier (8305 0300) & Westminster Pier (7930 3373)/177, 180 bus. **Open** *Apr-Sept* 10.30am-4.30pm daily. *Oct-Mar* 11am-3.30pm daily. Closed 24-26 Dec. **Admission** *Exhibition* £1; 75p concessions; 50p 5-16s; free under-5s. **Credit** MC, V.

The strange silver hoods of the Thames Barrier protect the capital from flooding – precisely how this is achieved is explained by models and videos at the visitors' centre overlooking the river. The centre caters mostly for school parties, though members of the public are also welcome. One of the

Military might at **Firepower**.

Best: Animal sights

For 'dinosaurs'
Crystal Palace Park. *See p138.*

For newts
London Wildlife Trust Centre. *See p140.*

For stag beetles
Peckham Rye Common. *See p135.*

For bats
Dulwich Park. *See p137.*

For butterflies
Nunhead Cemetery. *See p135.*

most popular times to visit is when they set the magnificent structure in motion as they test it (once a month; call for dates and times but it's usually a weekday). The best way to appreciate the barrier, however, is from the water – Campion Cruises (8305 0300) run trips from Greenwich three times daily. If you're feeling energetic, you could also walk or cycle to the barrier from Greenwich (*see p135*).
Buggy access. Café. Lift. Nappy-changing facilities. Nearest picnic space: riverside. Shop.

Rotherhithe & Surrey Docks

Situated where the river bends as it meanders towards Greenwich, the mainly residential areas of Rotherhithe and Surrey Docks are relatively undisturbed by tourists, though some make it to one of the oldest and most atmospheric pubs in London, the **Mayflower**, and are impressed by the river views when they do. On the other side of the Rotherhithe Peninsula, looking out across the river at the Isle of Dogs, lies **Surrey Docks Farm**, always a hive of activity during school holidays. Inland, the area's green heart reveals itself at sites given over to urban ecology: **Lavender Pond** (Rotherhithe Street, SE16, 7237 9165), which was created from an old dock inlet in 1982 and now supports newts, frogs and dragonflies and attracts heron and tufted ducks to its shores; and the green and pleasant **Russia Dock Woodland** and **Stave Hill Ecological Park**, which are great for walks and picnics.

The largest green space in the area is **Southwark Park**, which was set up 130 years ago and is London's oldest municipal park. Though rather shabby of late, and of little interest to anyone other than dog walkers and athletes using the running track and stadium, the park is all set for a revamp in 2002 – the defunct playground will be transformed into a state-of-the-art play area with a giant slide, there'll be a new boating pond, and the café and gallery building will be refurbished.

It's not clear how long the transformation will take, so be sure to call the park rangers (7232 2091) before setting out.

At Surrey Quays, the **Hollywood Bowl** (Redriff Road, SE16, 7237 3773), complete with a Burger King next door, is heaven on earth for many kids. The **Discovery Planet** indoor adventure playground (Surrey Quays Shopping Centre, Redriff Road, SE16, 7237 2388) appeals to a younger age group (and parents appreciate the crèche run here in term time). The **Surrey Docks Watersports Centre** (Rope Street, SE16, 7237 5555) runs sailing and canoeing courses run for children aged from eight in school holidays and half terms (*see also p262*).

Russia Dock Woodland
Redriff Road & Salter Road, SE16 (info 7525 1050). Rotherhithe or Surrey Quays tube. **Open** 24hrs daily. **Admission** free.
Planted back in 1980, the woodland is a good place for nature walks and picnics. The willows, birches and ash trees are set around a stream and a series of ponds, in which you may spot eels and other fish. Kingfishers and heron have been known to come here for a snack.
Buggy access.

Stave Hill Ecological Park
Timber Pond Road, SE16 (info 7237 9165). Rotherhithe tube. **Open** 24hrs daily. **Admission** free.
Situated next to Russia Dock woodland, this meadow is bordered by wildlife-rich scrub and trees, providing a haven for birds, insects and butterflies and a welcome breath of fresh air for human visitors.
Buggy access.

Surrey Docks Farm
Rotherhithe Street, SE16 (7231 1010). Surrey Quays tube. **Open** 10am-1pm, 2-5pm Wed, Thur, Sun. **Admission** free (except school parties and play-schemes; phone for details).
This thriving organic farm has been part of the local community for more than 25 years and is home to a herd of milking goats, sheep, cows, pigs, poultry, donkeys and bees. There are also herb, vegetable and willow gardens and an orchard. Holiday play-schemes and workshops are very popular with local kids, so book ahead. The splendid riverside location makes the farm a good starting point for a walk along the Thames, and children love playing on the sculptures of farm animals just outside its river exit (see if you can spot the mouse that the cat is chasing).

Eating & shopping

In terms of child-friendly restaurants, the huge **Spice Island** (163 Rotherhithe Street, SE16, 7394 7108), located in a former spice warehouse, welcomes kids until 8pm, providing high chairs for tots and offering half-portions of most dishes (soups, pasta, grills, Tex Mex). **Arbuckles** (Mast Leisure Park, Surrey Quays Road, SE16, 7232 1901), which dishes up burgers, fries and pizzas, will only really appeal to the kids. Much more congenial, if you can fight your way through the American tourists on the heritage trail, is the **Mayflower** (117 Rotherhithe

Street, SE16, 7237 4088), with its creaky woodwork, poky bar area and delightful jetty. This ancient watering hole is where the Pilgrim Fathers' ship was moored before it set off on its fateful journey. Pub grub is served, and though there are no special menus or concessions for children, they're welcome to share adults' platefuls.

The **Surrey Quays Shopping Centre** has all the chains a local community could need, including a Mothercare and an Adams. Nearby is the exciting, trainer-filled French sports superstore **Decathlon** (Canada Water Retail Park, Surrey Quays Road, SE16, 7394 2000; *see also p206*).

Kennington & the Elephant

Kennington's proximity to central London and attractive residential squares, including Cleaver Square and Courtney Square, make it a desirable place to live, though Newington Butts, a pretty vile street, and, worse still, the Elephant & Castle (south London's ugliest landmark), are just a walk away. In fact, the Elephant is constantly undergoing cosmetic surgery, and by 2015 this gateway to south London will be a plaza that aims to raise everyone's spirits instead of depressing them.

In the streets around the charmless shopping centre, however, are several venerable institutions to take comfort in: **Pizzeria Castello** (20 Walworth Road, SE1, 7703 2556; *see also p181*), which does the best garlic bread in south London and welcomes children; the ancient herbalist **Baldwins** (171-3 Walworth Road, SE17, 7703 5550), which has an astounding range of tinctures, potions and remedies, including the famous sarsaparilla concoction, served in half-pint jugs, that you drink at the counter (it's supposed to be a pick-me-up); the **Geraldine Mary Harmsworth Park**, with its serene Tibetan peace garden; and a landmark with rather more bombastic origins, the **Imperial War Museum**. Make for the **AMP Oval**, further down Kennington Road, if you're a cricket fan.

AMP Oval
Kennington Oval, SE11 (ticket office 7582 7764/ 6660/tours 7820 5750/www.surreycricket.com). Oval tube. **Open** *Ticket office 9.30am-4pm Mon-Fri. Tours* by arrangement; phone for details. **Admission** *varies; depending on match.* **Credit** MC, V.
The home of Surrey County Cricket Club traditionally hosts the final test of the summer, as well as county and league matches. It runs a busy programme aimed at encouraging more youth into the sport: there are education projects for keen under-16s year-round (check the website for more info; under-16s also have free access to all Surrey's League Games). Tours have to be pre-booked and can be taken on match days; you get a ticket covering both match and tour. They include peeks inside the changing rooms (if not in use!), the broadcast and media studios and the indoor school. *See also p263.* *Shop.*

Imperial War Museum
Lambeth Road, SE1 (7416 5000/www.iwm.org.uk). Lambeth North tube/Elephant & Castle tube/rail. **Open** 10am-6pm daily. Closed 24-26 Dec. **Admission** £6.50; £4.50 concessions; £3.25 disabled; free under-16s, OAPs, free to all 4.30-6pm daily. **Credit** MC, V.
This memorial to the wars of the 20th century, housed in what used to be Bedlam, the notorious 19th-century lunatic asylum, strikes a careful balance between acknowledging the horror and waste and proudly exhibiting the weapons, vehicles and equipment that helped the forces get through them. One of the most sobering exhibits is the rotating clock hand in the basement, symbolising the cost of war in terms of human lives – it's now gone over the 100 million mark.

In the main hall, you can see restored and cut-away examples of a selection of hardware, including a Polaris, a V2 rocket and a Spitfire. There's a periscope giving views over the museum's roof and a warplane kids can climb into. The lower ground-floor galleries house the excellent four-part permanent exhibition of the history of warfare in the 20th century; two of the most popular 'experiences' are the Blitz and the Trench, which may bring history to life rather too vividly for some young visitors. Secret War, on the first floor, sheds some light on the clandestine world of espionage from 1909 to the present day; exhibits range from Brezhnev's uniform to an original German 'Enigma' encrypting machine. The second floor is devoted to art collections.

The museum has a new £17-million, five-storey extension housing a two-floor permanent exhibition on the Holocaust. The documents, artefacts, photographs and survivors' testimonies make for a moving display that's suitable only for those aged 14 and above.

The 1940s House, a full-scale re-creation of a typical wartime home (as seen on TV), has proved so popular that its run has been extended at least to the end of January 2002: it may even become permanent. A Spanish Civil War exhibition began in October 2001, as we were going to press, and was expected to run all winter, while spring 2002 sees the opening of a new Women in Uniform exhibition, about the role of women in the wars of the 20th century.

The education department runs a full term-time programme of school-party visits and classes. Young visitors can be furnished with free quiz sheets, including the popular 'spy quiz'. During the holidays, children aged 7-11 are treated to workshops and events, often linked to the temporary exhibitions. These may include art work, imaginative play and dressing up. Most workshops are free but book in advance. There is also a cinema at the museum, which is used for showing films to school groups and adults.
Buggy access. Café. Lifts. Nappy-changing facilities. Nearest picnic place: Geraldine Mary Harmsworth Park. Restaurant. Shop.

Camberwell & Peckham

For many years Camberwellians have tried to dissociate their arty and increasingly gentrified neighbourhood from Peckham, whose reputation for roughness was compounded by the fatal stabbing of a ten-year-old boy in November 2000, though it has benefited from a recent influx of public money – £280 million, to be precise.

Camberwell was the first local authority in London to own an art gallery, museum and college of arts; students from Camberwell Art College add a touch of glamour to the area, as does the **South London Gallery** (*see p136*) a few doors away. The other major landmark is St Giles, one of the largest parish churches in London.

To create the sprawling green lung of **Burgess Park**, which stretches from Camberwell Road all the way to Peckham, a built-up area was bulldozed and the Grand Surrey Canal was filled in. Over the decades the artificial look of the park has been a source of embarrassment to locals, but these days it seems to be growing into itself, and the area round Chumleigh Gardens is a delightful place to be.

You can walk a path that used to be the canal down to the newly created Peckham Town Square. Here the highly acclaimed and fashionable architecture of **Peckham Pulse Sports Centre** and Will Alsop's prize-winning, multi coloured **Peckham Library** (*see p136*), both symbols of Peckham's regeneration, gleam at each other across the rollerblade- and bike-friendly plaza, where a farmers' market takes place every Sunday morning. Rye Lane still looks pretty jaded, and **Peckham Rye Common**, at its top, hasn't much in the way of a playground, though the central pond sustains perch and waterfowl, the occasional heron and much of the local rat population, who blatantly dine out on bread left for their feathered neighbours.

Rats also scurry in the rampant undergrowth that (otherwise) makes **Nunhead Cemetery** so lovely, but wildlife fans will be enchanted by the range of beetles and butterflies, bird- and plantlife that thrives here.

Burgess Park

Albany Road, SE5 (park rangers 7525 1066/adventure playground 7277 1371). Elephant & Castle tube/rail, then 12, 42, 63, 68, 171, 343 bus. **Open** 24hrs daily. *Adventure playground* termtime 3.30-7pm Tue-Fri, 11am-5pm Sat. School holidays 10.30am-6pm Mon-Fri. **Admission** free.

Thanks to the planting of hundreds of trees and the creation of Chumleigh Gardens (in which the old almshouses of Chumleigh flank a beautiful series of five gardens created in different styles: English cottage, Mediterranean, Caribbean, oriental and Islamic), this park is beginning to blossom. The botanical gardens have a café and are the HQ for Southwark's park rangers, who run a busy education programme for local schools. As well as a huge boating and fishing lake, football pitches and tennis courts, there's a play park, a newly refurbished adventure playground and a go-kart track for children aged from eight (call 7525 1101 to book).

Nunhead Cemetery

Limesford Grove, SE15 (info 7732 9535). Nunhead rail. **Open** *Summer* 8.30am-7pm daily. *Winter* 8.30am-dusk daily. **Admission** free; donations to FONC welcome.

The Friends of the Nunhead Cemetery (FONC) have seen to it that this once-neglected old cemetery receives the TLC it deserves – its woodland paths have been resurfaced, its toppling monuments restored and the central chapel rebuilt. Those who love its wild, overgrown beauty needn't worry, however: this wonderful place will never be manicured, ivy

Walk: The Thames Path

▶ The **Thames Path** is a 44-mile (70-kilometre) route from Dartford in the east through London and all the way out to Hampton Court in the west. The small section covered here, from Greenwich to the **Thames Barrier**, is a good choice for a gentle family walk or cycle ride because it's mainly away from roads.

▶ The section, which is about three miles (five kilometres) one way, takes you out along the river at Greenwich, past the **Old Royal Naval College** (*see p128*), the **Trinity Almshouses** and the **Greenwich Power Station**, taking in some bleak industrial landscapes before heading out to the Greenwich Peninsula, towards the rather sorry-looking **Millennium Dome**. The path cuts across towards the Greenwich Yacht Club before you reach the Dome, but there are apparently plans to re-route the walk around the site of the Millennium Experience.

▶ Just when the children are saying they're tired, hungry or both, you'll come across signs for the **Pilot Inn** (68 River Way, 8858 5910), which is open for sandwiches all day every day (proper meals are available noon-2pm and 6-9pm). It has a large garden and backs on to the **Millennium Park**. After a rest, carry on to the steely gates of the **Thames Barrier** (*pictured*), where the visitors' centre's café is another refreshment option.

▶ This is where you turn around and head back to Greenwich (or take the train from Charlton). Soon you should be able to follow the river as far as the Royal Arsenal in Woolwich and the new **Firepower Royal Artillery Museum**, housed in the old military complex and armaments factory.

▶ A free map is available from the helpful **Greenwich Tourist Information Centre** (0870 608 2000) or **Thames Barrier Information Centre** (8854 1373).

still romps attractively around the enchanting stone angels and crumbling carved headstones (a subject of many a FONC postcard) and the ancient mausoleums are as spookily neglected as ever.
Nearest picnic place: benches in cemetery garden.

Peckham Library
122 Peckham Hill Street, SE15 (7525 0200). Peckham Rye or Queens Road Peckham rail/12, 36, 63, 171 bus. **Open** 9am-8pm Mon, Tue, Thur, Fri; 10am-8pm Wed; 9am-5pm Sat; noon-4pm Sun.
The best-looking library in London has a large and lively children's section, up on the fourth floor. Children love pressing their noses against the pink glass that looks out over developments in progress around Peckham and Camberwell. Kids activities and arts workshops take place during the school holidays, in funny little pod rooms up spiral staircases. Under-fives-activity and storytelling sessions take place on Tuesday mornings, from 10am. Call for details of activities, computer clubs and homework clubs.
Buggy access. Nappy-changing facilities.

Peckham Pulse Sports Centre
10 Melon Road, SE15 (7525 4999). Peckham Rye or Queens Road Peckham rail/12, 36, 63, 171 bus. **Open** 7am-10pm Mon-Fri; 8am-8pm Sat, Sun. Closed 25, 26 Dec. **Admission** varies. **Credit** MC, V.
The Pulse's futuristic exterior promises much, and indeed, the gym, pools, soft playroom and café are state-of-the-art and frantically popular. It was designed as an all-round healthy living centre, after the style of the famously philanthropic Peckham Experiment, a health programme created to pep up the community after World War II. On Sunday mornings, the smaller hydrotherapy pool is used for parent-and-toddler swimming sessions, which are always crowded. There's a creche for those little ones who don't want to get their feet wet. Drop-in child-health clinics, and a homeopathic clinic take place weekly: call for details.
Buggy access. Café. Lifts. Nappy-changing facilities. Nearest picnic place: Peckham Square.

South London Gallery
65 Peckham Road, SE5 (7703 6120/www.southlondongallery.org). Bus 12, 36, 171. **Open** 11am-6pm Tue, Wed, Fri; 11am-7pm Thur; 2-6pm Sat, Sun. Closed 25, 26 Dec, bank hols. **Admission** free.
Exhibitions in this cavernous space change every six weeks, with a fortnight's setting up in between; phone for details of the next one, especially whether or not it's suitable for children, or you could find yourself having to make a hasty exit from a Gilbert & George show. Keith Tyson exhibits in January and February 2002.
Nearest picnic place: Camberwell Green/Lucas Gardens.

Eating & shopping

Camberwell is pretty good for restaurants. Eating out *per la famiglia* is best attempted at its Italian restaurants – **La Luna** (380 Walworth Road, SE17, 7277 1991), a good, affordable place to enjoy pizzas and pasta, has high chairs and is open for Sunday lunch, while **Mozzarella E Pomodoro** (21-2 Camberwell Green, SE5, 7277 2020), which serves pasta, pizza and fish dishes, welcomes children and produces half-portions for them, though there are no high chairs for babies.

Have a good read at **Peckham Library**.

For lunch, **Seymour Brothers** (2-4 Grove Lane, SE5, 7701 4944) is a lovely, but often crowded, deli and sandwich bar. In summer its garden is popular with the pushchair brigade. The **Sun & Doves** (61-3 Coldharbour Lane, SE5, 7733 1525) is a trendy pub and restaurant that doubles as an art gallery. Its half-portions and south-facing garden make it a favourite with families.

Peckham has McDonald's, a very smart Burger King and a decent café in the Peckham Pulse Sports Centre. The newly established arty area of Peckham, Bellenden, has a right-on, friendly café, **Petitou** (63 Choumert Road, SE15, 07932 508450), with toys and sticky cakes for the children.

East Street Market (8am-5pm Tue, Wed, Fri, Sat; 8am-2pm Thur, Sun) between Camberwell and Elephant & Castle is a bona fide sarf London market. It's big, and everything – toys, clothes, flowers, food and household wares – is sold at rock-bottom prices.

Camberwell College of Arts (Peckham Road, SE5; (7514 6300), London's oldest art college, is worth visiting for the shop alone, where art materials and stationery are heavily discounted and provide essential rainy-day activities for children. Designer kidswear at **Peppermint** (321-3 Walworth Road, SE17, 7703 9638) includes Paul Smith, Versace and Ben Sherman. For a healthier way to treat the kids, stop off at **Edwardes** (221-48 Camberwell Road, SE5, 7703 3676; *see also p207*), which has a huge selection of new and second-hand bikes for all ages.

Peckham's main shopping street, **Rye Lane**, is characterised by pawn shops, cheap food and household goods stores – Woolwort's and Argos are the posh shops around here.

Dulwich & Herne Hill

Smart, villagey Dulwich, its trendy little sister East Dulwich and its near-neighbour Herne Hill are blessed with delightful parks and open spaces and with gracious residential roads. At their heart is well-kept **Dulwich Park**, with its acres of playing fields and woodland belonging to the Alleyn estate, and historic Dulwich College. Dividing Herne Hill from sassier Brixton is **Brockwell Park**.

It's hard to escape the call of the wild in this environmentally sound corner of south-east London. The **London Wildlife Trust Garden Centre** started life as a derelict bus depot and is now the focus for all wildlife gardeners, while Sydenham Hill Wood, just across the South Circular from Dulwich Park, is a hangout for bats, hedgehogs, rare hawfinches, tawny owls and all sorts of other birdlife. The London Wildlife Trust's warden for Sydenham Hill Wood (8699 5698) has his office up the road at the **Horniman Museum** in Forest Hill. The latter is a free museum that's worth crossing town for (even if it never finishes its seemingly endless refurbishment programme).

Brockwell Park
Dulwich Road, SE24 (7926 6200/tennis courts 7926 0105/www.brockwellpark.com). Herne Hill rail. **Open** 7.30am-dusk daily.

Brockwell Hall and the surrounding land were purchased for £117,000 by the local council in 1891 and extended in 1901, when four large houses were demolished – the recently rechristened Evian Lido was built where they once stood. The park has a flat area for play (unfortunately not a dog-free zone) and to the west duck ponds, tennis courts and a bowling green. For older kids there's a basketball court, football pitch and BMX track. The park hosts a big annual festival, the Lambeth Country Show, in July. In 2002, it will probably be 20 and 21 July, but ring to check nearer the time.

At the top of the hill, the attractive old hall houses the family-run First Come First Served café, a cheap and pleasant place for Sunday roasts or weekday lunches. The menu includes all-day fried breakfasts, chips, sarnies, pastries, gingerbread men, ice-cream and pop. It's bright and spacious enough for a birthday tea (staff provide cake and jolly tea-time boxes for £4 per child; 8671 5217).

In the summer Brockwell Park comes into its own with families from far and wide scrambling for their own piece of paradise around the picturesque **Lido** (Dulwich Road, SE24, 7274 3088).which is now working with the French drinks giant Evian in a bid to improve maintenance and secure its future. *See also p231.*
Buggy access. Café.

Dulwich Park
College Road, SE21 (rangers 8693 5737). North Dulwich or West Dulwich rail. **Open** 8am-1hr before dusk daily. **Admission** free.

The land that was presented to the people of London by Dulwich College in 1885 is everyone's favourite park in the area, not least because its smart playground has a brilliant 'spider web' climbing frame built of taut ropes that children love hanging about in. The newly resurfaced tennis

Social climbers in **Dulwich Park**.

Crystal Palace Park

This park was created by the famous Victorian landscape designer Sir Joseph Paxton in 1853-4 as a permanent home for the huge glass and cast iron building that was used for the Great Exhibition in Hyde Park and then re-erected here. The structure burnt down in 1936 but the stone terraces and many other original features remain, including a unique model dinosaur park (currently under restoration) around the lower lake. The park's future was recently threatened when Bromley Council announced plans to build a vast leisure complex on the site, but local opposition finally put the kibosh on those last year.

If you're a first-time visitor to the park, it's best to start off at the main (Penge) entrance at the bottom of the park on Thicket Road, SE20 – it has free parking and an **information centre**, where you can get free photocopied maps that include kiosks and toilets. There are also more detailed Paxton Heritage Trails that may appeal to older children (from 15p).

At this side of the park lies the much-loved children's fairground, with its pleasantly tame cup-and-saucer ride, merry-go-rounds and rollercoasters. It's open for most of the school holidays, weather permitting. You buy tokens from the kiosk to pay for each ride. The miniature railway, which also runs in good weather, costs £1.50 a go.

Unfortunately, the train won't run you up the hill to the site of the original palace, but the magnificent views over south London and the surrounding countryside make it worth the climb. The quickest way through the park is straight up the steps through the **National Sports Centre** (*see p267*) but it's far more interesting to meander round the members-only fishing lake and slightly rusted **Concert Bowl**, where a variety of open-air summer concerts take place. The Crystal Palace Park maze, grown of hornbeam, is just nearby. It's the biggest maze in London. In fact, it's the only maze in London, Hampton Court, (*see p156*), being in Surrey. Boy and girl racers on scooters and bikes make use of the broad tarmac paths round the area; these were once part of the park's motor-racing circuit, patronised by racing driver Stirling Moss and his contemporaries until the '70s. The farmyard is temporarily closed (*see below*) but the playground makes up for this. Adults and older children can gen up on local history in the museum (open Sun and bank hols, 11am-5pm) or head for the boating lake, where two to four people can hire a pedal-boat for £3.50 per half hour (though watch out for the timid but fairly energetic rats that congregate here in mild weather).

The park's famous model dinosaurs will be back, refurbished, in spring 2002. The farm, with its pigs, goats, poultry and other residents, should be open again by then, but it's best to call the Information Centre for the latest detailsg.

Crystal Palace Information Centre

Crystal Palace Park, Thicket Road, SE20 (8778 9496). Crystal Palace rail/bus 2, 3, 63, 108B, 122, 157, 227 bus. **Open** *Information Centre 9am-5pm daily (later in summer). Park dawn-dusk daily.* **Admission** *free.*

Little gem: **Horniman Museum**.

courts are equally popular, together with the steamy little restaurant/café, which is excellent for hot chocolate and chips on chilly winter afternoons and Slush Puppies and ice-creams on hot ones. The boating lake is open during school holidays and in warm weather, and there's a bridleway for those on horseback. The Rangers Yard is the home of London Recumbents (8299 6636), where you can hire (or even buy) bikes and trailers, trikes, tandems and the eponymous horizontal bikes. Its founders run one-to-one safety courses for nervous cyclists of all ages. The rangers are always in evidence, arranging rustic activities such as bat-watching and fungus identification walks for urban bumpkins of all ages.
Buggy access. Café.

Dulwich Picture Gallery

Gallery Road, SE21 (8693 5254/ www.dulwichpicturegallery.org.uk). North Dulwich or West Dulwich rail. **Open** 10am-5pm Tue-Fri; 11am-5pm Sat, Sun, bank hol Mon. Closed Good Friday, 24-26 Dec, 1 Jan. *Tours (included in entry fee)* 3pm Sat, Sun.
Admission £4; £3 concessions; free under-16s; free to all Fri. **Credit** MC, V.
Dulwich Picture Gallery, an object of great beauty in itself, is set between the glorious Dulwich and Belair parks and is the perfect art gallery to visit with children, especially now that, after a big revamp for the millennium, it has an imaginative educational programme that brings art to life for young visitors. Recent school holiday courses for children aged from five have included Telling Stories through Pictures, based on the permanent Old Masters, and a colourful workshop inspired by the paintings of Howard Hodgkin, which had an airing at the gallery in summer

2001. On Fridays, when admission is free to all, the gallery, café (where a cream tea is £5) and gardens are packed with cultured young families.

The magnificent collection of European Old Masters was assembled for the King of Poland in the 1790s; a new home was found for them in Dulwich after Poland was partitioned. The gallery, designed by Sir John Soane, was recently extended by Rick Mather Architects to include a glass and bronze cloister linking the original building with the new art studio, the Linbury Room and the café. The outstanding array of 17th- and 18th-century paintings includes works by Rembrandt, Van Dyck, Poussin, Canaletto and Gainsborough. Upcoming temporary exhibitions include The Golden Age of Watercolours (Turner, Ruskin, de Wint and others) until 6 January 2002, and Dutch Landscape Painters (22 May-26 Aug 2002). *See also p217.*
Buggy access. Café. Nappy-changing facilities. Nearest picnic place: gallery gardens. Shop.

Horniman Museum

100 London Road, SE23 (8699 1872/ www.horniman.ac.uk). Forest Hill rail/63, 122, 176, 185, 312, 352, P4 bus. **Open** 10.30am-5.30pm Mon-Sat; 2-5.30pm Sun. Closed 24-26 Dec. **Admission** free; donations appreciated. **Credit** *Shop* MC, V.
This singular museum, which celebrated its centenary in 2001, is partway through an extended programme of refurbishment (not scheduled to finish until some time in late spring 2002). Yet even with its Centre for Understanding the Environment and its Music Collection closed, the Horniman is an involving experience for all ages, especially in summer, when you can wander through the extensive gardens with their excellent planting schemes, fenced-off animal enclosure

(check out the obese goats and lazy wallabies) and bandstand for summer concerts. The picnic tables next to the animals have superb views over London.

The museum was built in 1901 by Frederick Horniman, a tea trader with a passion for collecting anything from stuffed birds to shrunken heads. Children enjoy the glassy-eyed wildlife specimens, petrified insects and huge stuffed walrus. A major extension is due to open in spring 2002, with new exhibition galleries and an interactive gallery with special appeal for children. Living Waters, one of the oldest free aquaria in London, consists of a series of tanks and pools, each recreating a miniature underwater world. There are sea-horses and crustaceans, exotic coral reef fish, rockpools and British pond specimens. Since its refurbishment in 2000/1, Living Waters has become a focal point for many activities for visiting children.

Art and craft, ecology and music workshops involving the museum's treasures run throughout school holidays and half-terms, and there are many activities for children during term-time weekends. Saturday music classes usually cost £1.50 per session (*see also p225*). Many sessions are based on a first-come first-served basis and will appeal to kids as young as three. On some summer afternoons there are free children's entertainments at the bandstand (call for details).

Nappy-changing facilities. Café (hot-drinks machines only till spring 2002). Nearest picnic place: piazza at museum entrance/Horniman Gardens. Shop.

London Wildlife Trust Centre for Wildlife Gardening

28 Marsden Road, SE15 (7252 9186/ www.wildlondon.org.uk). East Dulwich rail. **Open** 10.30am-4.30pm Tue-Thur, Sun. **Admission** free. This wild, wooded garden, with its pond, marsh and meadow areas, is the London Wildlife Trust's southern outpost. Visitors can tour the garden for ideas, ask advice from the knowledgeable staff and take away free plants and saplings (donations are gratefully accepted). There's a busy programme of gardening events for all ages – for young children there's the 'Acorns' toddler group; for older ones there are school holiday courses, which vary according to season but can involve, in different measure, tadpoles, frogs, newts, herbs, wildflowers and mud.

Buggy access. Nappy-changing facilities.

Eating & shopping

If you're looking for special family celebrations, particularly Sunday lunches, try the grand **Belair House** in Dulwich (Gallery Road, SE21, 8299 9788). It has a kids' menu and high chairs, and you can take fidgety children for a runaround in Belair Park after. Welcoming Dulwich pubs include the **Crown & Greyhound** (73 Dulwich Village, SE21, 8693 2466; *see also p188*), which does a children's teatime menu plus half-portions of fuel food at lunchtime. It has a garden with play equipment.

The hippest cafés in Dulwich are within croissant-lobbing distance of each other in Northcross Road – the **Blue Mountain Café** (no.18, 8299 6953) has fantastic coffee, cakes and pastries, while the more spacious **Grace & Favour** (no.35, 8693 4400) provides good, light meals and has a nappy-changing table in the loo.

Spaghetti Western (121 Lordship Lane, SE21, 8299 2372) has a buffet until 5pm on Sundays and high chairs for little ones. **Café Noodles** (159 Lordship Lane, SE21, 8693 4016) is great for a cheap teatime noodle fix.

Shopwise, **Biff** (43 Dulwich Village, SE21, 8299 0911; *see also p196*) offers unusual continental childrenswear, while staff at **Dulwich Music Shop** (2 Croxted Road, SE21, 8766 0202) can match a child with the correct instrument, new or second-hand. They also take in instruments for repair, sell all accessories and sheet music, and advertise music lessons, instruments for sale and the like. **The Dulwich Trader** (9 Croxted Road, SE21, 8761 3457) is good for witty gifts, home accessories, toys and novelties, while **Duo Dance** in Herne Hill (11 Half Moon Lane, SE24, 7274 4517) is much used by those seeking pink pumps and leotards.

Lordship Lane, the main shopping thoroughfare in East Dulwich, seems entirely geared to the needs of young families, with second-hand prams and pushchairs at **C&G Baby Shop** (nos.15-17, 8693 4504), footwear at **John Barnett Shoes** (no.137, 8693 5145) and colourful children's clothes and toys at the local branch of **Soup Dragon** (no.106, 8693 5515; *see also p209*). The latter shares a building with the Family Health Centre, which offers shiatsu, homoeopathy, osteopathy, reflexology and other natural therapies.

Further south-east

Oxleas Wood (Off Shooters Hill Road, SE18; Green Chain Project 8921 5028/www.greenchain.com) is an 8,000-year-old area of woodland, which was destined for the developers' bulldozers back in the 1990s, in order to build a new London river crossing. But local residents and conservationists rightly put up a fight, and today, with its wonderful views out towards Kent, it's as big an attraction as ever for families, joggers and cyclists, especially during the bluebell season (May).

The area is a network of footpaths that can be tricky to navigate, especially once you get into the depths of the woods. If you're feeling energetic, some of the paths link up with the **Green Chain Walk**, a 40-mile (65-kilometre) network of footpaths, which means you can walk from here down to Woolwich and the Thames Barrier as well as to Crystal Palace Park and Chislehurst Common.

On summer evenings and at weekends most people congregate around the café overlooking Oxleas Meadow (off Crown Woods Lane; open 9.20am-4pm daily, later in the summer). It looks pretty tatty from the outside but is warm and friendly within. There's limited free car parking at Crown Woods Lane and along the Welling Way.

Croydon and **Bromley,** prosperous suburbs both, are most attractive to families. Croydon boasts trams and an excellent arts centre (*see below*), while sports, shopping and cultural facilities are strong in both places: the Glades Shopping Centre in Bromley and the Whitgift Centre in Croydon are as highly rated by the people of Dulwich and Peckham as the West End. A trip to **Bluewater** is as much a family day out as a shopping trip (*see p210*); if you don't have a car, take the train from London Bridge to Greenhithe in Kent. If you can tear yourself away from the shops, pretty **Chiselhurst,** another Kentish suburb, is famous for its dark and creepy caves. Tours cost £4 for adults; £2 for children (Wednesday to Sunday; phone 8467 3264 for details).

In 2002 Croydon is applying for city status for the third time. Whether it's successful or not, it deserves recognition for many reasons, among them its £200-million Tramlink, its green credentials (it's the third greenest London borough) and the Croydon Clocktower. This handsome Victorian building, which was modernised in 1996 to accommodate three galleries, an outstanding library, a theatre space, a cinema and a smart café, is a dream for young families, especially as many of the activities are free and many exhibitions have related events for kids.

Croydon Clocktower

Katharine Street, Croydon, Surrey (info 8760 5400/box office 8253 1030/shop 8253 1035/ tourist info 8253 1009/www.croydon.gov.uk). East Croydon or West Croydon rail/George Street tram. **Open** *Clocktower & library* 9am-7pm Mon; 9am-6pm Tue, Wed, Fri; 9.30am-6pm Thur; 9am-5pm Sat; 2-5pm Sun. *Café Opera* 9.30am-5.30pm Mon-Sat; 1-5.30pm Sun. *Shop* 10am-7pm Mon, 10am-5pm Tue-Sat. *Tourist Information Centre* 9am-6pm Mon, Wed, Fri; 9.30am-6pm Thur; 9am-5pm Sat; 2-5pm Sun.

Lifetimes is a free interactive exhibition that takes as its subject the history and the future of Croydon. The displays are extremely child-friendly, with touch-screen computer terminals providing additional information about the artefacts and relaying the real-life stories of local people. There's also a dressing-up corner, with shoes, fairy dresses and headgear, and the David Lean cinema, which, though quite art housey at times, holds the Tick Tock children's cinema club every Saturday (11am), and puts on extra screenings of family favourites during the school holidays.

The Braithwaite Hall hosts regular weekend and holiday theatre productions for children, while the library holds Bookstart Baby Rhymetime song and rhyme sessions for babies and pre-schoolers and drop-in mornings of stories, music and art for kids of all ages. On Saturday mornings a crèche allows parents to use the library, wander round the displays or slurp double lattes in Café Opera in peace. *Café. Nappy-changing facilities. Nearest picnic place: Queens Gardens. Shop.*

Meet the teacher

Helena Stride is Head of Education at the Imperial War Museum (*see p134*).

What do you do?
I'm part of a team that arranges the programme of activities for school groups in term time and for family groups in holiday time. We find out what pupils are studying at school and college so that we can provide an education service that is relevant to the national curriculum and to exam syllabuses.

What activities do children request most?
Children (and adults, whether teachers or parents) enjoy activities where they get to handle the 'real thing', whether it is a helmet or an incendiary bomb. We also have a variety of active sessions where children have a chance to take part in drama activities in which they have to make their own decisions about certain dilemmas that people in the past were forced to face. And our half-term adventures

feature actors in a variety of roles from escapees from Colditz to secret agents.

What other activities are there?
We have a range of study sessions for secondary school students. For younger children there is an activity called the Model House Project, which focuses upon a model of a real house furnished and set up as though it were the 1940s, with an Anderson shelter, blackout curtains and so on.

We also have a poetry hunt devised by our former poet-in-residence Mario Petrucci, and we run poetry and literacy workshops. A fairly new part of the service is our Holocaust Education Service, which offers support to all school groups using this exhibition.

What's the best part of your job?
My favourite bit is working with a wide range of children, students and adults in the workshops and teaching sessions.

Do you wear a uniform?
No. We can wear what we like, within reason.

Do you have a favourite part of the museum?
The Large Exhibits Gallery in the central atrium has a big 'wow' factor. There are some amazing exhibits there, such as the wonderful 'Ole Bill' double-decker bus used in World War I to transport soldiers to the trenches on the Western Front, the gigantic V2 rocket and some handsome aircraft. I also like the art galleries, which tend to be quiet places suitable for contemplation. There are some wonderful paintings on show, such as the impressive *Gassed* by John Singer Sargent.

What was your favourite subject at school?
Art, followed very closely by history.

South-west London

To Nappy Valley and beyond!

As you wander deeper into the south-western reaches of London, park squares and playgrounds give way to commons whose grassy acres, once grazing land for the poor, provide open air and exercise space for local families who live in flats and terraced houses. Wandsworth Common, Tooting Common and Wimbledon Common have all helped to make the bits of London that border them desirable places in which to bring up children – in fact, one part of Wandsworth now cringes under the nickname Nappy Valley.

London becomes greener the further south you get, and suburbia takes hold. Wimbledon is synonymous with tennis, Putney with rowing and Twickenham with rugby, while Richmond used to be famous for its hunting. Its deer, once targets for royal arrows, are now protected; they rule the 2,500 acres (1,012 hectares) of parkland annexed by Charles I in 1637.

Vauxhall & Stockwell

Though Vauxhall is considered by many as a pedestrian nightmare, with its chaotically busy roads, and though it's primarily famous for the MI6 building that overlooks the Thames beside Vauxhall Bridge, it also boasts many hidden spots and has an interesting history. Known at different times as Fulke's Hall, Faukeshall and Foxhall, it was a village for most of the 18th century and was home to the much-admired Vauxhall Gardens: a fashionable park that was used for concerts, shows, displays and general public voyeurism. It closed in 1859 for financial reasons and the only reminder of it now is the mid-sized **Spring Gardens**.

Stockwell's green spaces are few and far between, though **Slade Gardens** on Robsart Street has an adventure playground, play areas and a one o'clock club. Over on Stockwell's west side, **Larkhall Park**, on Larkhall Rise, is quite a peaceful open space, with a one o'clock club, picnic and seating areas, a café, two multi-purpose ball-game areas, tennis courts, a walled garden, a playground and nappy-changing facilities.

At the beginning of Stockwell Road as you leave Brixton, the skate park attracts gangs of kids, particularly in summer. The graffitied area with its graded concrete bumps allows dextrous skaters and bladers to show off their skills. It's an eyesore to some people, perhaps, but it's popular with spectators.

Vauxhall Park (South Lambeth Road junction with Fentiman Road, SW8) has some well-manicured areas for quiet contemplation, as well as tennis courts, a bowling green, a play area, a one o'clock club and a fenced ball-game area. Opposite Spring Gardens is **Vauxhall City Farm**, which is a brilliant place to take kids.

Bonnington Square's **Pleasure Garden** started life as a play area during the 1970s but subsequently lay neglected and prey to vandals for years, until local residents pulled away the nettles to form the latest venture, a lovely secret garden with a restored Victorian water wheel.

Vauxhall City Farm
24 St Oswalds Place, Tyers Street, SE11 (7582 4204). Vauxhall tube/rail. **Open** 10.30am-4.30pm Tue-Thur, Sat, Sun. **Admission** free.
The farm's enthusiastic programme of educational and recreational activities for groups and individuals of all ages is a perfect antidote to this heavily urbanised area. Activities include pony and donkey rides (£2.50); all riders must be farm members and rides aren't every day so phone for details.

Down on **Vauxhall City Farm**.

Other activities include mosaic and mural painting, and music lessons. For those who can't make it to the farm, a lorry carries the animals in comfort and safety to school and nursery groups. Other farm residents include pigs, goats, poultry and small cuddly animals such as rabbits and guinea pigs. *Buggy access.*

Eating & shopping

A welcome newcomer on Vauxhall's rather limited culinary scene is **Lavender** (112 Vauxhall Walk, SE11, 7735 4440), which overlooks Spring Gardens and serves brasserie-style food in adult and children's portions.

The experience of eating out in Stockwell is much influenced by its large Portuguese community, whose cafés and bakeries along the Stockwell Road really come alive on summer evenings. Babies and children are welcome at all the following cafés and restaurants, and there are usually high chairs available. **O Cantinho de Portugal** (135-7 Stockwell Road, SW9, 7924 0218) is a bar/restaurant where you can spoil yourselves with a long Mediterranean-style lunch. **Bar Estrela** (113 South Lambeth Road, SW8, 7793 1051) draws families with its well-priced seafood-based snacks and tapas menu. For more tapas head along the road to **Rebatos** (169 South Lambeth Road, SW8, 7735 6388), a long-established Spanish-run tapas bar that attracts everyone from children and students to elderly couples. **Café Portugal** (5A-6A Victoria House, South Lambeth Road, SW8, 7587 1962) is a double-fronted café/bar and restaurant with good snacks and a sociable atmosphere though slightly over-priced main meals. Yet another Portuguese favourite, tucked away on a quiet backstreet, is **O Barros** (168A Old South Lambeth Road, SW8, 7582 0976), serving tapas and a good range of snacks.

Vauxhall is dominated by an enormous Sainsbury's and by **New Covent Garden Market** (Nine Elms, SW8, 7720 2211), so it's great for shopping if you're throwing a dinner party. The market, which relocated from Covent Garden to Vauxhall in 1974, is the most important fruit, flower and vegetable wholesale market in the UK.

Brixton

Brixton's chameleon character has never been more pronounced. Though the gentrification of the area is constantly rumoured and there are certainly parts of Brixton that can give Dulwich and Clapham a run for their money, real evidence of any general upmarket surge is hard to come by. It's true that the feel of the area has changed over the last decade or so, but Brixton is still edgy enough to have a distinctive urban vibe of its own.

Kew Gardens, an ideal mix of educational and outdoor. *See p151.*

Sightseeing

The **Ritzy** cinema, one of Brixton's assets.

3021) has perfect pizzas, but you'll need to go early or late to avoid queuing), while the friendly and relaxing **Jacaranda Garden** (11-13 Station Road, SW9, 7274 8383) serves great focaccia sandwiches and big slices of cake. Within the market area are **El Pilon Quindiano** (no phone), for both Colombian fare and plainer English food; bright and chirpy **Pangaea** (15 Atlantic Road, SW9, 7737 6777) with its tempting pasta dishes and lovely pizzas; and at 15 Market Row, **Kim's Café** (no phone), which is as straightforward as its name and has lovely wide aisles for those with pushchairs.

Older children should enjoy the beat at sassy **Bamboula** (12 Acre Lane, SW2, 7737 6633), where delicious 'sudden-fried chicken', rotis, plantains, barbecued fish and other Caribbean delights are served with attitude. Reduced-price portions for youngsters should be requested, as servings are huge.

Streatham

The further south you venture, the slower the pace and the bigger the houses, which is why Streatham is increasingly popular with families, who also appreciate the wide open spaces of Tooting and Streatham commons. It's hard to imagine it these days, but in its heyday Streatham was a hotbed of intellectual and artistic activity – Edmund Burke, Dr Johnson, Joshua Reynolds, Fanny Burney and David Garrick all lived here, which hoisted the village upmarket. Such exclusivity couldn't last, however, and the advent of the railways saw Streatham expand at a frightening rate at the end of the 19th century. Inter-war development and post-war bombsite infill completed the picture in the 20th century, making Streatham what it is today – a big, sprawling neighbourhood bisected by the A23, aka Streatham High Road.

The High Road is the gateway to the best that Streatham has to offer families – at the top, near Streatham Hill station, is **Streatham Megabowl** and further down the High Road by Streatham Station is **Streatham Ice Rink** (no.386, 8769 7771; *see also p259*), offering skating (including reasonably priced six-week courses) and spectator ice hockey; it's also a good venue for birthday parties. Speed fiends aged from eight love karting at **Playscape Pro Racing** (no.390, 7801 0110; *see also p259*), where they can savour their first taste of motor racing.

To the east, Streatham Common is initially unpromising – the windswept slope is bordered on all sides by busy roads and has a view south over Thornton Heath to Croydon. But carry on to its hidden treasure, the **Rookery** (8679 1635), a beautiful little formal garden that allows you to feel a million miles from the traffic. It's a lovely place to picnic and enjoy views over London, and in summer

Brixton's relatively affordable housing ought to make it a magnet for young families, but it seems that most of those with their foot on the property ladder in the area get out fast when they hear the distant pitter-patter. Lambeth has a poor reputation as far as state education is concerned, and as the school bell tolls, parents tend to head for the hills (Forest, Gipsy and Herne). There's a dearth of decent green spaces here, and indeed, most locals claim Brockwell Park, which joins Herne Hill to Brixton, as their green lung (*see p137*).

Brixton's star turn is the **Ritzy** cinema (Brixton Oval, SW2, 7733 2229; *see also p222*), whose Saturday morning Kids' Club is one of south London's best bargains: children's tickets are only £1 and the cinema shows two films, one aimed at seven-year-olds and under, the other at those aged eight and over. For parents there are free newspapers and tea and coffee in the Ritzy Crush Bar during the show.

Eating & shopping

Souk-like **Brixton Market** seduces the eye with its African fabrics, spices and exotic vegetables, as well as plenty of fashionable tat for kids to spend their pocket money on. It's also a good place to stop for a meal or a snack: **Eco** (4 Market Row, SW9, 7738

Nappy Valley

The southern tip of Battersea just before it turns into Balham is known to estate agents as 'Between the Commons' or 'Betwixt the Commons' (the commons in question are Clapham and Wandsworth), but the area also has the rather less appealing nickname of 'Nappy Valley', which came about because it's said to have the highest population density of under-fives anywhere in Western Europe. It's hard to find the source of this extraordinary statistic, but locals are proud of it.

The commons are the obvious playgrounds for the neighbourhood. There's a one o'clock club on the corner of Wandsworth Common and Chivalry Road, right beside a small playground that's suitable for pre-schoolers, with climbing frames and swings, and an adventure playground for children with disabilities (open to all in the summer holidays). On the far side of the railway tracks that cut Wandsworth Common in two, there's also a well-stocked pond that has been landscaped and edged with walkways on stilts to provide a more interesting bird habitat.

Wandsworth Common is big on Mother Nature, with a purpose-built **Nature Study Centre** (8871 3863) whose ecology officer is on hand to answer wildlife-related questions during opening hours (2-4pm Wed; 2.30-4.30pm Sun). It offers children's activities during school holidays – call for details. Children's football clubs dominate the common along Bolingbroke Grove on Saturday mornings, while there's indoor creativity at **Brush and Bisque-It** (41 Northcote Road, SW11, 7738 9909), a ceramics workshop where children (and many adults) paint their own crockery and have it glazed.

The floor of Nappy Valley is **Northcote Road**, a buzzy street full of independent shops and restaurants, many of which cater for the legions of families that live on the roads leading back to the commons. Chains such as Starbucks and All Bar One have started to stake their claim here, but the indigenous establishments are holding their own. There's also a fine range of specialist food stores selling, variously, free-range meat, stinky cheeses, organic veg and honey – the **Hive Honey Shop** (no.93, SW11, 7924 6233), with its wall of bees and honey to taste, is a favourite with kids. At the southern end of the road, **Quackers** (no.115D, 7978 4235) specialises in upmarket French childrenswear, and a few yards away **Lizzie's** (no.143, 7738 2973) sells nursery knick-knacks and hand-made clothes. **QT Toys** at no.90 (7223 8637) is a useful little toyshop that spares locals the indignities of Toys 'R' Us.

During the week Northcote Road is home to a small market of fruit, vegetable and flower stalls. At weekends they're joined by a magnificent stall selling French and Italian bread, cakes and pastries; a Provençal-style stall loaded with olives and oils; a chi-chi fabric stall draped in silks and sarongs; and a topiary stall.

When small appetites need sating, Northcote Road is a godsend, particularly at the north end where it runs up towards Battersea Rise. **Wok Wok** at nos.51-53 (7978 7181; *see also p185*), a branch of the oriental fusion chain, is popular with families because of its unthreatening eastern flavours, children's menu, high chairs, toys, drawing materials and Sunday-afternoon family sessions with the occasional kids' entertainer. The ubiquitous **Starbucks** at no.33-8 (7350 2887) has become an unofficial mother and toddler group that's crammed with babies and pushchairs every weekday morning.

More individual are two cafés: **Boiled Egg & Soldiers** at no.63 (7223 4894; *see also p181*) is also taken over by families during the week, who come for its justly popular old-fashioned menu with its nursery-tea offerings. Across the road, **Deli-Organic** (no.60, 7585 0344; *see also p182*) has organic baby purées on its menu and will host toddlers' tea parties for only £2.50 a head. Both of these places are too small to accommodate buggies, but you can leave them outside, and in dry weather there's a cluster of tables out on the street.

Wandsworth Common

Wok on at **Tiger Lil's**. *See p147*.

music wafts over from the seasonal open-air theatre. There's also a café. When you've restored your soul and the children are screaming out for something more exciting, let them loose in the woods and commons of **Norwood Grove**, where if you keep your eyes peeled you may even see the celebrated population of ring-necked parakeets.

Eating & shopping

As on most high streets across the country, the big pizza names line up: **Pizza Hut** (114-8 Streatham Hill, SW2, 8671 7311) and **Pizza Express** (34-6 Streatham High Road, SW16, 8769 0202) are always busy, while the **Waterfront** bar and restaurant (426-8 Streatham High Road, SW16, 8764 3985) offers stone-baked varieties For more adventurous souls there's **Trini's** (13 High Parade, Streatham High Road, SW16, 8696 9669), where family groups noisily appreciate Trinidadian classics such as goat curry, roti, callaloo and sweet barbecue chicken. Prices are low and high chairs are available.

Apart from charity shops, big-name chains tend to dominate Streatham's shopping scene, though skating fiends are richly served by **Streatham Skates** (386 Streatham High Road, SW16, 8677 8747), where end-of-line skates can be bought cheaply, and ice hockey, figure and in-line varieties are stocked.

Tooting & Balham

West Streathamites share **Tooting Common** (Tooting Bec Road, SW17) with the denizens of Balham. It's a wide open space with woods, tennis courts, ponds, football pitches, a couple of good playgrounds for the under-eights, riding, Tooting Bec athletics track and **Tooting Bec Lido** (8871 7198), where up to 2,000 people a day gather in summer to enjoy the open-air pools and the 1930s café.

As Clapham rose into the house-price stratosphere through the 1990s, Tooting and Balham soaked up the overspill. Nowadays they're as sought after and almost as fantastically expensive as their prettier neighbour, though thanks to their resistance to wholesale gentrification they're more interesting.

Tooting is home to a well-established Asian community, and the annual Diwali Festival of Light (October/November) is celebrated with a street party and lights strung along Tooting High Street and Upper Tooting Road. The area around and between Tooting Bec and Tooting Broadway has a number of excellent restaurants serving South Asian food, though their proprietors don't go out of their way to woo those with kids – only **Masaledar** (121 Upper Tooting Road, SW17, 8767 7676), a modern café-style Indian restaurant, supplies high chairs and toys. Babies and children are welcome in most places, however, and smaller portions are available on request.

Younger kids enjoy the simple, sing-along puppet shows put on by **Nomad Puppets** (37 Upper Tooting Road, SW17, 8767 4005) on Sundays (except during the summer holidays), while up on Balham High Road the **Art of Health & Yoga Centre** (no.280, 8682 1800; *see also p263*) promises to give you serenity, flexibility and muscle tone.

Clapham

The 'village on the hill' became fashionable in the 18th century because of its clean air and health-giving springs. East of the common, **Clapham Old Town** is a cluster of pubs, shops and restaurants around what might resemble a village green if it weren't for all the 88 buses (rather tweely known as the Clapham Omnibus) revving up by the bus terminal.

The **Clapham Picture House** (Venn Street, 7498 3323; *see also p220*), a rep cinema with a busy Saturday morning Kids' Club, is a godsend on a rainy weekend, but most families head for **Clapham Common** for leisure activities, whatever the weather. This flat, windy space has a chequered history – in the 18th century it was infested with vermin such as hedgehogs and polecats, and a raid was ordered; during World War I it was turned over to the cultivation of food; and in World War II tunnels and caverns were dug beneath it as training posts for army radio operators (these underground mazes were pressed into service as reception centres for immigrants from the Caribbean in the 1940s). Now the common is south-west London's recreation ground – dozens of sports clubs congregate here, and at weekends you'll see people playing Australian-rules football, camogie (Gaelic hurling), netball and even lacrosse. On Sundays the football pitches on the west side of the common are turned into a London outpost of the South American football league, with teams representing Chile, Colombia and the like fighting passionate battles while their families cook lunch, gossip and play on the touchlines.

Local children learn to ride their bikes here, play football and tennis, picnic in summer and just generally hang out. There are two playgrounds – the one by the corner of Battersea Rise is best for smaller kids, although broken equipment takes an age to fix and there are no loos within easy reach, while the one over by the Windmill on Clapham South Side was refurbished early in 2001 and has more facilities for older children, as well as loos beside the one o'clock club. A rightly popular spot for parents and toddlers is the **Bowling Green Café** beside the tennis courts on the west side of the common (it's here that you book and pay for the tennis courts, in person on the day of play).

Bowling Green Café
Clapham Common West Side, corner of Thurleigh Road, SW4 (7801 0904). Clapham South tube. **Open** *Apr-Oct* 9am-6pm daily. *Nov-Mar* 9am-5pm daily. **No credit cards.**
In sunny weather there are slides, playhouses, tractors and bikes to play on near this café, which does a good line in comfort food (bangers 'n' mash, fish fingers, pasta) costing from £1.55 for a child's portion. Sandwiches are fine and fresh, and the cakes go down a treat after an afternoon on the common. Children's parties are catered for in summer.
Buggy access.

Eating & shopping

Clapham High Street is a mixed bag, with its unreconstructed south London shops and rapidly gentrifying range of restaurants.

For eating out, the often frenetic **Eco** (162 Clapham High Street, SW4, 7978 1108) has great pizzas, though it's loud and crowded in the evenings, and its staff are not the most attentive at any time of day. **Tiger Lil's** (16A Clapham Common South Side, SW4, 7720 5433; *see also p180*) is great fun for kids as they get to choose their own ingredients then hand them to a chef to wok in front of them.

The Pavement is a good place to stop for tea, with the imaginatively named the **Pavement** (no.21, 7622 4944) and **Café Des Res** (no.8, 7622 6602). **Café Wanda** further down the High Street (no.153, 7738 8760) has superior cakes, scones and sandwiches to eat in or take over to the paddling pool on the common for a picnic. **Pizza Express** (43 Abbeville Road, SW4, 8673 8878) is as solidly child-friendly as ever – pizzas come sliced for children to share, and staff have even been known to warm babies' bottles or sterilise them with water from the espresso machine after they've fallen on the floor. For a slightly more exotic dining experience

Talk to the animals

One of the delights of **Battersea Park** is the **Children's Zoo**. Established during the Festival of Britain in 1951, it was meant to be a temporary feature, but was such a hit that it's been there ever since. Nowadays it's home to a motley collection of animals – wallabies and rheas keep company with meerkats, otters, kookaburras, tortoises, cows, various monkeys and a reclusive Vietnamese pot-bellied pig.

There's something to see all year round, but you're more likely to get your money's worth in the summer, when all the animals are back from their winter quarters. For children there are pony rides, a mini-roundabout and a contact area where they can pet and feed rabbits and goats. There's also an Animal Adoption scheme, which for a small fee will allow you two tickets to the zoo and a name plaque beside the animal's enclosure.

The exit takes you via the gift shop, which you'll be lucky to leave without, at the very least, a stuffed toy or souvenir pencil sharpener.

Battersea Park Children's Zoo
Battersea Park, SW11 (8871 7540/ www.wandsworth.gov.uk). Sloane Square tube then 19, 137 bus/Battersea Park or Queenstown Road rail. **Open** *Apr-Sept* 10am-5pm daily (last entry 4.30pm). *Oct-Mar* 11am-3pm Sat, Sun. Closed 29, 30 Dec. **Admission** £2; £1 3-16s, under-2s free. **No credit cards.** *Buggy access. Café. Nappy-changing facilities. Nearest picnic place: zoo grounds. Shop.*

Walk: Wander the Wandle

▶ Summer 2000 saw the launch of London's first new tramline since the 1950s, which links Wimbledon to Croydon. Use it to travel from Wimbledon station to Phipps Bridge (90p), then walk through **Morden Hall Park** to **Merton Abbey Mills** to start this two-mile (three-kilometre) walk, which is fine for little legs.

▶ Start with a potter round the heritage centre at **Morden**, where you can see artisans at work in jewellery and carpentry workshops. Refreshments (drinks, sandwiches, cakes) are available at the café beside the garden centre. Make a detour to the glade where hives are kept before following the Wandle along a rough path through boggy land and over the tramline to **Deen City Farm** (*see p153*).

▶ Keep walking along the Wandle track until you reach a huddle of old textile buildings in the shadow of the giant Savacentre. **Merton Abbey**

Mills has an illustrious Arts and Crafts history – Arthur Liberty of the Regent Street store started having his prints made here in the late 19th century, while a few years later Arts and Crafts pioneer William Morris opened a works just downstream from the Liberty mills. Now the mills keep up the tradition by filling at weekends with stallkeepers flogging handmade hats, lace, pictures, prints, jewellery and more. Children will enjoy the miniature steam train that chugs around the mill buildings.

▶ Food is available at various ethnic food stalls and at the **Gourmet Pizza Company**. At weekends, the **Colour House Theatre** usually has a madcap children's show for kids aged from about three (*see p224*).

▶ From here it's time to decide whether to retrace your steps or negotiate the busy roads to Colliers Wood tube station.

(for parents, at least), **Sash Oriental** (32 Abbeville Road, SW4, 8673 9300) has an extensive children's menu that includes chicken noodles, rice dishes, burgers and fish fingers.

Down by Clapham North rail station, **Apex Cycles** (nos.40-42, 7622 1334; *see also p207*) sells new and reconditioned bikes for kids and adults. The Clapham branch of the reliable **Wordsworth** bookshop chain (no.120, 7627 2797) has a small but culturally diverse kids' section.

On the Pavement there are two shops that teenagers can lose hours in looking for odd presents for friends: **Zeitgeist** (no.17, 7622 5000) has plenty of candles, jewellery and other trinkets, while **Kitschen Sync** (no.9, 7652 1070) is packed with wacky household objects made of Day-Glo plastic and any amount of inflatable knick-knacks. In both it's possible to find cheap and cheerful things among the expensive kit.

At the top end of Abbeville Road, a branch of parent-friendly toyshop **Cheeky Monkeys** (no.24, 8673 5215; *see also p208*) sells wooden toys and educational games. Beautiful heirloom dolls' houses and castles, plus a good range of items at pocket-money prices, ought to please both generations.

Battersea

Not all of Battersea is as cosy as Nappy Valley (*see p145*) – just across Battersea Rise lies the more down-to-earth St John's Road, where high-street chains predominate all the way down to Arding & Hobbs on the corner of Lavender Hill. The latter marks the beginning of Battersea proper – with

Clapham Junction at one end and Queenstown Road at the other, it's really nothing but a long drag of fairly uninspiring shopping.

One thing worth stopping for is **Battersea Arts Centre** on Lavender Hill (7223 2223; *see also p223*), in what used to be Battersea Town Hall. One of

A resident...

London's best alternative venues, the BAC also runs a variety of dance and drama workshops, as well as Saturday afternoon theatre for over-threes. The café is a good pitstop before a show.

Three other Battersea landmarks rate a mention before the park itself – the pool at **Latchmere Leisure Centre** (Burns Road, SW11, 7207 8004; *see also p264*), which is great for children to splash around in; **Lilliput** (255-9 Queenstown Road, SW8, 7720 5554; *see also p192*), a vast children's equipment warehouse housed in a railway arch and selling the largest range of nursery equipment, prams and buggies for miles around (it also has a hire service for visitors or for things you'll only need for a short while); and the world-famous **Battersea Dogs' Home**, where unwanted dogs and cats await the human of their dreams.

Five minutes' walk from the dogs' home is **Battersea Park**, which is an excellent place to play and pray. It came about after, some time at the beginning of the last century, a London clergyman stumbled, white-faced and trembling, away from Battersea Fields, calling it 'a place out of Hell worse than Sodom and Gomorrah in its ungodliness and abomination' and demanding that a public park be set up in the area to 'promote social and domestic happiness'. A century later, the park is a godsend for all those south Londoners who haven't room to

swing a cat in their back gardens, and it even lures the clued-up of Chelsea and Pimlico across the river.

Battersea Dogs' Home

4 Battersea Park Road, SW8 (7622 3626/ www.dogshome.org). Sloane Square tube then 19, 137 bus/Battersea Park or Queenstown Road rail. **Open** *Viewings* 10.30am-4.15pm Mon-Wed, Fri; 10.30am-3.15pm Sat, Sun (café closes 1hr earlier). **Admission** £1; 50p concessions, under-16s. **Credit** *Shop* MC, V.

If you're looking for a pet, there are around 80 dogs in search of a new home here at any one time, though if you fall madly in love you'll need to undergo a grilling from the rightly circumspect staff before you can take one home. It's worth coming for a few visits before reaching any serious adoption conclusions, anyway, and bear in mind that weekends get very busy, so try to come on a weekday. The shop is also a good source of unusual presents, with its doggy stationery, souvenirs and toys, and there's a café for drinks and snacks. *Buggy access. Café. Nearest picnic place: Battersea Park. Shop.*

Battersea Park

SW11 (8871 7530/7531/www.wandsworth.gov.uk). Sloane Square tube then 19, 137 bus/Battersea Park or Queenstown Road rail. **Open** *Adventure playground* School hols 11am-6pm daily. Term time 3.30-5pm Tue-Fri; 11am-6pm Sat, Sun. **Admission** *free.*

One of Battersea Park's most famous features is the remains of Festival Gardens, one of the attractions of the 1951 Festival of Britain. The children's zoo (*see p147*) is also here, along with a preponderance of playgrounds. There's a one

...and visitors at the **WWT Wetland Centre**. *See p152*.

o'clock club (8871 7541) for the under-fives, a playground for under-eights, and, for 5- to 15-year-olds, the biggest adventure playground in London. Children will also enjoy the Affordable Art Fair (Tony Hart was a guest in October 2001; the next one is 28 Feb-3 Mar 2002) and the fireworks displays for Bonfire Night.

The concrete foundations of the original Festival Gardens are good terrain for skateboarding and Rollerblading, and there's a branch of London Recumbents (next to the athletics track, 7498 6543), from whom you can hire horizontal bikes as well as bikes with trailers for tiddlers. Staff also guarantee to teach the least co-ordinated of children (or adults, for that matter) to ride a bike (£25 per one-to-one session).

On a sunny weekend, half an hour's drifting in a rowing boat allows you to imagine yourself back in Edwardian London in the park's heyday (under-tens must be accompanied by an adult). For the sportier among you, Battersea Park has 21 tennis courts, three football pitches, four softball pitches, one rugby pitch, three cricket squares, all-weather sports pitches, boules grounds, a bowling green and an athletics track with facilities for all major track and field events.

One of the Battersea Park's more recent landmarks and certainly its most eye-catching and incongruous addition is the Peace Pagoda, overlooking the Thames. With its four golden Buddhas, this was built by Buddhist monks in 1985 and donated to the people of London in the name of universal peace.

The café by the lake is an essential port of call; it has a licensed bar and a sturdy menu with sandwiches, coffee and cake, plus hot food of the lasagne, curry, and sausage and chips variety. Children's portions are smaller and cheaper, and there are tables outside right down to the lake's edge (which is fenced off).

Buggy access. Café. Nappy-changing facilities.

Round and about in **Putney**.

Putney

If you ask the locals what they like about this stretch of south-west London, chances are they'll say the river, which takes on a semi-rural aspect at **Putney Bridge** – looking back down the Thames you can catch glimpses of London's skyline but upstream the Putney treeline is pretty well all you can see. The scene is familiar to many as the starting point of the Oxford and Cambridge Boat Race; indeed, the stretch of river between Putney and Barnes is lined with boathouses belonging to London schools and the university and with various corporate boatclubs. Spring Saturdays are particularly busy as boatloads of strapping punters and rowers take to the water.

Back from the river, Putney has a number of green spaces – **Putney Heath** is the eastern edge of the huge piece of common land that eventually peters out where Wimbledon Common joins Richmond Park. In total, it's three times the size of Hampstead Heath but has much less glamour, and there are no areas set aside for children's play. As with all London heath and common land, it's best avoided after dark.

Infinitely tamer, but with more to entertain kids, is **Leaders Gardens** at the end of Asilone Road. This dainty little riverside park is a delight for all the family, with two play areas and tennis courts. The café (Loo Loos, 8246 6847, so called because it used to be a loo) enjoys views across the river to Fulham Palace and the football stadium. It's strong on child-friendly meals, which cost from £2.75 to £3.50 with unlimited squash and ice-cream. Children's parties start at £5.75 a head. This also the place to come to book a tennis court (no bookings are taken by phone). In a small open area of the gardens is Beverley Brook, which runs from Putney Heath to Wimbledon.

Eating & shopping

There are lots of places to eat, and even among restaurants that don't cater specifically to junior customers, few will make you feel like a pariah if you bring one or two through the door. The **Phoenix Bar & Grill** (162-4 Lower Richmond Road, SW15, 8780 3131) has a Modern European menu and a special kids' menu that includes old favourites such as chicken and chips or roast beef for £6.50 and up, including ice-cream. Staff provide crayons, comics and high chairs, and there's a lovely sun terrace for summer. Lively Italian **Del Buongustaio** (283 Putney Bridge Road, SW15, 8780 9361) also has high chairs and a children's menu that includes pasta and vegetable dishes and ice-cream. Just before Putney Heath, the **Spencer Arms** (237 Lower Richmond Road, SW15, 8789 5126) allows children in the bar area, where they can feed on nuggets, chips and the like from as little as £1.49.

A day at: Kew

The main reason for going to Kew is to see the world-famous **Royal Botanic Gardens**, but interest need not be purely horticultural. If you're looking for something educational, the Education & Visitor Centre in the **Public Record Office** is an odd hoard of national treasures ranging from the Domesday Book to the deed poll that records Reginald Dwight's decision to change his name to Elton John. Regular events in the Visitor Centre include tours by a costumed guide, who tells the stories surrounding various documents in the archive. There are also calligraphy workshops, lectures and poetry readings – call for an events leaflet or see the website for more details.

After leaving the Record Office, hotfoot it through residential Kew to the Victoria Gate of the Royal Botanic Gardens. You don't have to be a botanical expert to enjoy a day here, nor will that be sufficient to see half the wonders it has to offer, so either choose a section to explore or join one of the free guided tours that leave the Victoria Gate at 11am and 2pm daily. The whistle-stop, one-hour tours take in some of the more accessible highlights. If you're visiting with elderly relatives or small children, the Kew Explorer bus provides a hop-on hop-off service to the furthest reaches of the gardens for £2.50 (adults) and £1.50 (children).

The colour-coded maps are invaluable for planning your route and locating the nearest food or toilet stops. Of the six places to eat spread through the gardens, none is particularly cheap, though between them they cater for all appetites, providing everything from full hot meals to snacks, cakes and coffee. The Baguettery and the Barbecue are best for takeaway picnics, while the **Orangery**, beside the Main Gate, and the **Pavilion**, beside the Pagoda, are licensed, self-service restaurants. The Pavilion is generally more family-friendly, but the gift shop at the Orangery is your best bet for botanical knick-knacks on which the kids can spend their pocket money. The various cafés are the best places to go for loos and nappy-changing facilities.

If mobility isn't a problem, pick up one of the self-guided trails at the visitors' centre. 'Kids' Kew' has checklists of plants to find and a timeline of buildings to plot a course round; other trails designed to appeal to families tie in with seasonal themes. Alternatively, you could construct your own route round some of the reliable children's favourites. For example, you could take a trip back three billion years to experience plant evolution through the Silurian, Carboniferous and Cretaceous periods in the **Evolution House**, which contains some ancient species and puts on various special effects (smoking volcano, glowing lava flow, dinosaur footprints and so on).

The elegant **Palm House**, where the gallery affords an inspiring view of the dense, dripping foliage, contains plants with very early connections with Kew – breadfruit, for instance, was brought back from the South Seas by Captain Cook in the 18th century. Beneath the Palm House, the Marine Display's tanks contain fish, corals and primitive algae.

On the other side of the pond, opposite the Palm House, Museum Number 1 houses the **Plants & People Exhibition**, which, through displays and a variety of touch-screens, demonstrates the uses to which people have put plants through the ages. Nearby, the **Princess of Wales Conservatory** houses ten climate zones under one glass roof; the collection of carnivorous plants is reliably fascinating. The paths through the Conservatory are wide enough for buggies, but when it's very crowded it can be a bit stressful. If so, take the opportunity to construct a trail round some of the Greek temples and other decorative structures that punctuate the grounds. The **Pagoda** is probably Kew's most famous landmark, but there's not much to see when you get there – instead try the **Ice House**, which was used to stock ice when the latter was a great luxury (it was harvested from small ponds nearby).

When you've had enough of nature's wonders or want a break from the gardens (just tell the ticket officer at the gate before you leave), spend a lazy summer teatime watching the world go by on Kew's ridiculously pretty village green. If you're after a more industrious tea break, visit the **Ceramics Café** (1A Mortlake Terrace, Kew Green, 8332 6661; *see also p230*), where you can design your own tableware while taking tea. Tea is also served at the **Maids of Honour Tearooms** (288 Kew Road, 8940 2752; closed Sun) for an old-fashioned afternoon tea – try one of the famous Maid of Honour (vanilla custard) tarts. If the queues defeat you, buy some cakes from the shop and eat them on the green.

Kew Greenhouse (1 Station Parade, 8940 0183) serves generous portions of comfort food, including cakes, pastries and coffee. Sit outside if you want to leave the buggy up; otherwise high chairs are provided. The plant-filled back room is a pleasant reminder of the botanical treasures down the road.

Public Record Office
Ruskin Avenue, Richmond, Surrey (8392 5202/ www.pro.gov.uk/events). **Open** 9am-5pm Mon, Wed-Fri; 10am-7pm Tue; 9am-7pm Thur; 9.30am-5pm Sat. *Tours* 12.30pm 2nd Fri of mth. **Admission** free. *Tours* free.
Buggy access. Nappy-changing facilities. Nearest picnic place: grounds of Public Record Office.

Royal Botanic Gardens (Kew Gardens)
Richmond, Surrey (8332 5622/ www.rbgkew.org.uk). **Open** Feb, Mar 9.30am-5pm daily. *Apr-Sept* 9.30am-6pm Mon-Fri, 9.30am-7pm Sat, Sun. *Oct-Jan* 9.30am-3.45pm daily. **Admission** £5; £2.50 children; £13 family (2+ up to 4).

Yet more green space in Wimbledon – **Cannizaro Park**. *See p153.*

Barnes Buggy Repair occupies a space in the basement of the Putney branch of **Lilliput** (278 Upper Richmond Road, SW15, 8780 1682; *see also p192*).

High-street shoppers will find the usual brand names in Putney Exchange, and the top floor is given over to a **Gymboree Play & Music** (Putney Exchange Shopping Centre, SW15, 8780 3831; *see also p294*) activity room for toddlers and babies and a good coffee bar with plenty of crawling space, high chairs and helpful staff who will happily heat up bottles. Just round the corner is **Domat Designs** (3 Lacy Road, SW15, 8788 5715), which has a huge range of toys made by British artisans.

Barnes, Mortlake & Kew

Until early 2000 Barnes was only really a tourist destination for fans of '70s supergroup T Rex – it was on **Barnes Common** that lead singer Marc Bolan fatally crashed his Mini into a tree in 1977. Constantly decorated with wilting flowers and tacked-on notes, scarves and little tin hearts, the spindly tree is loathed by most locals, but at last they have something to be truly proud of – since May 2000 Barnes has been home to the **WWT (Wildfowl and Wetlands Trust) Wetland Centre**, a unique mosaic of wetland habitats

created from scratch from four concrete Thames Water reservoirs. Beyond the Wetland Centre, this entire stretch of Thames-side London is pretty and residential. Mortlake was a fashionable retreat from the 16th century on and remains a pleasant backwater on the way to the Royal Botanic Gardens at Kew (*see p151*).

WWT Wetland Centre

Queen Elizabeth's Walk, SW13 (8409 4400/ www.wetlandcentre.org.uk). Hammersmith tube then 283 bus/Barnes rail/33, 72 bus. **Open** *Mar-Oct* 9.30am-6pm daily (last entry 5pm). *Nov-Feb* 9.30am-5pm daily (last entry 4pm). Closed 25 Dec. *Tours* 11am, 2.30pm daily. *Feeding tours* free; noon, 3.30pm daily. **Admission** £6.75; £5.50 concessions; £4 4-16s; £17.50 family (2+2); free under-4s. *Tours* free. **Credit** MC, V.

This vast reserve provides habitats to replicate what was once common the length of the Thames Estuary, offering sanctuary and a breeding ground to native water birds and migrants from as far away as Siberia. Wild Life, to the west of the complex, has colonies of dragonflies and amphibians, while the World Wetlands zone takes visitors on a global safari through 14 naturalistic habitats from arctic north to tropical forest. The Waterlife zone offers you the chance to go pond-dipping or to discover how to create a wetland in your garden. Though you can wander at will through the zones, it's worth joining a guided tour for the wealth of information supplied by the enthusiastic staff. The Visitors' Centre offers a bird's-eye view of the complex from its huge observatory. *See also p156.*
Buggy access. Café. Nappy-changing facilities. Nearest picnic place: picnic area on grounds. Shop.

Wimbledon

Just as Kew is synonymous in most people's minds with its gardens, Wimbledon's identity is tightly bound up with the summer fortnight at the All England Lawn Tennis Club. Next door to the museum (*see p154*), **Wimbledon Park** has public tennis courts, a paddling pool, a sandpit and a large boating lake. Sporty local kids come here for a variety of facilities, including watersports and sports courses for the over-eights in the holidays (call 8947 4894 for more information).

There may not be any wombles on **Wimbledon Common**, but this huge, partially wooded expanse has cycle paths, five ponds, sites of special scientific interest and riding tracks. For riding lessons, try **Wimbledon Village Stables** (24A-B High Street, SW19, 8946 8579; *see also p256*) or **Ridgway Stables** (93 Ridgway, SW19, 8946 7400).

On a wide open space where the common joins Putney Heath is Britain's last hollow-post flour mill. This is where Baden-Powell began writing *Scouting for Boys* in 1908. Now the **Windmill Museum** (Windmill Road, 8947 2825; £1 adults, 50p children), it is open to visitors on weekends and bank holidays from April to October (school parties can go at other times by arrangement). The little café that adjoins it has tables outside with plenty of room for smaller children to run around, though beware of cars turning into the (free) car park alongside.

To follow the Windmill Nature Trail, buy a trail guide from the ranger's office (£1.50) – it has areas of special interest marked along the way. If you're visiting in winter, it's advisable to contact the ranger's office beforehand on 8788 7655 (9am-4pm). A short walk down the hill from the windmill and part of the nature trail, Queen's Mere is a pretty pond where you can watch coots, toads and herons go about their business.

To the west side of the common is **Cannizaro Park**, with an ornamental garden, rare trees and plants, a water feature and an open-air theatre that hosts a programme of shows in the summer (8543 2222). **Putney Vale Cemetery**, in the north-east corner of the common (accessible from Roehampton Vale), is one of the largest graveyards in London. Lillie Langtry was buried here in 1929. On the east side of the common, the disused **Bluegate Gravel Pit** forms an idyllic and peaceful lake, barely disturbed by the murmur of traffic on Parkside.

You need to cross the road and go down Calonne Road to discover Wimbledon's biggest surprise – set amid prime south London suburbia, the fully fledged **Buddhapadipa Temple**, a Thai Buddhist site, welcomes visitors at weekends (1-6pm Sat; 8.30-10.30am, 12.30-6pm Sun).

Wimbledon's cyclists are lucky to have an organisation that arranges Parks, Playgrounds and Pub rides (PPP; 8946 0912). This is a monthly programme of 10-15 mile (16-24 kilometre) cycle rides, along quiet or traffic-free routes with plenty of child-friendly stops. The trips are free, and start from Wimbledon station on the last Sunday of each month.

Wimbledon Broadway is home to two theatres: the extravagantly Edwardian **Wimbledon Theatre** (no.93, SW19, 8540 0362), which has regular children's shows and puts on a frenetic pantomime featuring minor celebs, and the **Polka Theatre** for kids (*see below*).

Deen City Farm

39 Windsor Avenue, SW19 (8543 5300/ www.deencityfarm.co.uk). Colliers Wood tube/ 200 bus. **Open** 9am-5pm Tue-Sun. **Admission** free; donations welcome.

This well-stocked little farm is home to cows, donkeys, sheep, goats, pigs and fowl, among other animals. It's also a breeding farm, where the animals are sponsored by individuals and school classes. If you're lucky, you may even get to see some newborns. There's a riding school for both able-bodied and disabled kids, and you can hire the party room for birthday parties. Deen City Farm's school holiday and half-term Young Farmer Days give eight- to 16-year-olds the chance to feed, muck out and generally look after the animals with the farm staff.

Buggy access. Café. Nappy-changing facilities. Nearest picnic place: Morden Hall Park. Shop.

Polka Theatre

240 The Broadway, SW19 (8543 4888/ www.polkatheatre.com). South Wimbledon tube/rail. **Open** *Box office* phoneline 9.30am-4.30pm Mon; 9am-6pm Tue-Fri; 10am-5pm Sat. *Personal callers* 9.30am-4.30pm Tue-Fri. **Tickets** £5-£12.50. **Credit** AmEx, MC, V.

South-west London's dedicated children's arts centre has frequent first-class new shows in two theatres, plus a whole load of workshops and after-school and holiday clubs. There's a playground just outside, lovely rocking horses inside and a jolly café serving own-made cakes, biscuits, fruit and hot lunch dishes. The toy stalls, which are outside the main auditorium, and the smaller Adventure Theatre (for under-fives), have show-related toys and pocket-money trinkets and stationery. It's easy to spend time here without even seeing a show, but the work receives consistently good reviews so you'd be mad not to.

Buggy access. Café. Nappy-changing facilities. Nearest picnic place: theatre garden. Shop.

Tiger's Eye

42 Station Road, SW19 (8543 1655). Colliers Wood or South Wimbledon tube. **Open** 10am-6.30pm daily. Closed 25, 26 Dec, 1 Jan. **Admission** *Mon-Fri* £3.50 2-10s; £2 under-2s. *Sat, Sun* £4.50 2-10s; £2.25 under-2s. **No credit cards.**

The Tiger's Eye is an indoor playcentre for children up to ten years old. It's a vast barn of a place, complete with towering soft play equipment to climb on, slide down and bounce off. In short, good fun.

Buggy access. Café. Nappy-changing facilities. Nearest picnic place: Merton Abbey Park/Merton Park.

Sightseeing

Wheel life on **Wimbledon Common**. *See p153.*

Wimbledon Lawn Tennis Museum

Centre Court, All England Lawn Tennis Club, Church Road, SW19 (8946 6131/www.wimbledon.org/museum). Southfields tube/39, 93, 200 bus. **Open** 10.30am-5pm daily. Closed 24-26 Dec, 1 Jan. Spectators only during championships. *Tours* Mar-Oct grounds only £12.50; £11.75 concessions; £11 under-16s. Phone for details. **Admission** £5; £4.25 concessions; £3.50 5-16s; free under-5s. **Credit** MC, V.

The Wimbledon Lawn Tennis Museum both casts some odd lights on the game – did you know that Victorian players called it 'sphairstike'? – and allows you to get as close as you're ever likely to to Wimbledon's famous trophies. From the sphairstike lawns of 19th-century England to the multi-million-pound sport of today, more than 150 years of social and sporting history are encapsulated in this well-designed space. Most interesting are the mock-up of an Edwardian tennis party and the section on tennis since 1968, with touch-screen commentaries on past and present stars and videos of past championships. The museum is full of unusual information of interest even to those who aren't big fans of the game, and for obsessives there's personal memorabilia aplenty, including some of Pat Cash's headbands and Boris Becker's autograph. During the championships, when the museum is open only to ticket holders, come in the first few days to avoid the crowds. Needless to say, the place does particularly brisk business when rain stops play and the covers are drawn over the hallowed lawns.

Buggy access. Café. Nappy-changing facilities. Nearest picnic place: benches outside museum/Wimbledon Park. Shop.

Eating & shopping

Next to Wimbledon Odeon is **Jim Thompson's Flaming Wok** (141 The Broadway, SW19, 8540 5540), a bar and restaurant serving rough approximations of Indonesian, Malaysian, Vietnamese, Thai and Burmese dishes. 'Junior Jim's' is a selection of kids' meals for £2.95, while on Sundays two kids eat for free for every two adults.

In the Centre Court shopping centre, **Footlights** (8944 9970) is a café, restaurant and bar offering Mexican, American and European food, plus a special under-12s menu (two courses plus a drink for £4.25). For all parents who adhere to the adage 'you can't go wrong with pasta', the imaginatively named **Café Pasta** (8 High Street, SW19, 8944 6893) is a lifesaver.

The **Hand in Hand** pub in Wimbledon Village (6 Crooked Billet, SW19, 8946 5720) has a no-smoking family room and a front courtyard. Children's meals are £2.95. Just off the common, the **Fox & Grapes** (Camp Road, SW19, 8946 5599) also welcomes children – though there's no kids' menu, the management is happy to serve smaller portions at reduced prices.

The main shopping area is **Wimbledon Centre Court** on Queen's Road, which has more than 60 shops, restaurants and bars under one roof, plus a shoppers' crèche and activities during school holidays for children. Further down Wimbledon Broadway are the usual variety of high-street outlets, including bike shop **Wheelie Serious** (124 The Broadway, SW19, 8543 5255). There's a small range of more unusual shops in Wimbledon Village, including many designer names. Kids are shod well in Start-rite and Jane Wood at **Footsies** (15 High Street, SW19, 8947 3677), while stylish celebrations come courtesy of **Party Party** (23 High Street, SW19, 8944 9495).

Preston & Butler (65 High Street, SW19, 8947 8884) sells a small variety of hand-painted clocks, aromatherapy oils and nightwear for both kids and adults. **Guitar City** (106 Wimbledon Broadway, SW19, 8241 2171) sells guitars and offers lessons for children in guitar, keyboard and drums.

Richmond

Richmond is less a London suburb than a town in its own right, with all the shops and facilities you'd expect, and more besides. Then there's **Richmond Park**, which, at eight miles (13 kilometres) across at its widest point, is the biggest city park in Europe and the nearest London gets to wild countryside. Most of it is rough and rolling grassland; on a sunny Sunday the open spaces fill with all-terrain buggies and ring with the sound of fractious toddlers. Herds of red and fallow deer roam freely, much to the fascination of kids, but remember that these are wild animals that can be fierce in autumn during the rutting season (signs warn you not to get too close to the deer).

The **Old Deer Park**, which you reach if you walk south from Kew Gardens, is home to all things sporty – there's the Royal Mid-Surrey Golf Club, the Richmond Athletic Ground, tennis courts, playgrounds and a wonderful outdoor swimming pool, part of Richmond's Pools on the Park complex (*see p265*). On sunny summer weekends, people come from miles to picnic on the grassy slopes around the pool (there are paddling pools for toddlers) and spend the day dipping in and out of the cool blue water. To learn more about the area's royal history, visit the **Museum of Richmond**.

Eating & shopping

The Richmond branch of **Wok Wok** (30 Hill Street, 8332 2646) has an excellent children's menu with oriental basics such as egg-fried rice, chicken satay and noodles any which way. There's also a justly successful Spanish tapas restaurant, **Don Fernando's** (27F The Quadrant, 8948 6447; *see p183*), where staff make a fuss of children as they tuck into snacky, colourful food. At **Café Flo** (149 Kew Road, 8332 2598) the children's menu includes sausage 'n' mash, chicken and chips, and pasta. If it has to be pizza there's a **Pizza Express** (20 Hill Street, 8940 8951).

Pocket money is all too easy to part with in this enclave of the well-heeled. **Waterstone's** (2-6 Hill Street, 8332 1600) has a well-stocked children's section, while the local outpost of **Tridias** toyshop (6 Lichfield Terrace, Sheen Road, 8948 3459; *see also p209*) is great for special presents – Father Christmas swears by its catalogue.

Museum of Richmond
Old Town Hall, Whittaker Avenue, Richmond, Surrey (8332 1141/www.museumofrichmond.com). Richmond tube/rail. **Open** *May-Sept* 11am-5pm Tue-Sat; 1-4pm Sun. *Nov-Apr* 11am-5pm Tue-Sat. Closed 25, 26 Dec, 1 Jan. **Admission** £2; £1 concessions; free under-16s. **No credit cards**.
The Museum of Richmond, as the name suggests, holds a comprehensive collection of information about this most royal of boroughs. Richmond was a seat of kings during the 12th century, when Henry I lived at Shene Palace on the south-west corner of what is now Richmond Green. Successive monarchs enjoyed its riverside location, until Henry VII redeveloped the entire site and renamed it Richmond after his Yorkshire earldom. Elizabeth I died here in 1603, but all that's left of the palace is the Tudor Gateway, the Old Palace Yard and Queen Elizabeth's Wardrobe – the aptly-named building that housed more than 2,000 of her spectacular gowns. The history lesson runs up to life in the town during World War II.
Buggy access. Lift. Nearest picnic place: Richmond Green. Shop.

Further south-west

Follow the river south (there are some stunning walks and bike rides in these south-western reaches) and you'll come to a clutch of fine country villas – **Marble Hill House** overlooking the Thames in Marble Hill Park is a perfect Palladian villa; neighbouring **Orleans House** (Riverside, Twickenham, 8892 0221; free; call for opening times) was built in 1710 for James Johnston, William III's secretary of state for Scotland, and was later home to the exiled Duke of Orléans, hence the name; and **Ham House** is a handsome, red-brick, riverside mansion with a beautiful garden. Carrying on along the river past Twickenham, you'll come to the **Museum of Rugby**.

From Twickers, the river passes the busy shopping centre of Kingston-upon-Thames then curves around to **Hampton Court Palace**. Once Cardinal Wolsey's country seat, this was taken over by Henry VIII, who spent much time and three honeymoons here.

Ham House
Ham Street, Richmond, Surrey (8940 1950/ www.nationaltrust.org.uk). Richmond tube/rail, then 371 bus. **Open** *House Apr-Oct* 1-5pm Mon-Wed, Sat, Sun. *Gardens* 11am-6pm/dusk Mon-Wed, Sat, Sun. Closed 25,

The amazing **Hampton Court Palace**. *See p156.*

Sightseeing

26 Dec, 1 Jan. *Tours* min 15 people; pre-booking essential Wed. **Prices** £7.50 non-members; £4 members. Phone for membership details, prices. **Admission** (NT) £6; £3 5-15s; £15 family (2+3); free under-5s. *Garden only* £2; £1 5-15s; free under-5s. **Credit** AmEx, MC, V.
This gracious house's uniqueness is down to the original 17th-century furniture, paintings and decor that still adorn its rooms. From the house, water meadows lead down to the Thames. The part of the grounds known as the wilderness is in fact a carefully planted, almost maze-like section divided into garden rooms. The gardens are currently being restored. *Café. Nappy-changing facilities. Nearest picnic place: Orangery Gardens. Shop.*

Hampton Court Palace

East Molesey, Surrey (8781 9500/www.hrp.org.uk). Hampton Court rail/riverboat from Westminster or Richmond to Hampton Court Pier (Apr-Oct). **Open** *Palace* Apr-Oct 10.15am-6pm Mon; 9.30am-6pm Tue-Sun. Nov-Mar 10.15am-4.30pm Mon; 9.30am-4.30pm Tue-Sun (last entry 45min before closing). **Park** dawn-dusk daily. **Admission** *Palace, courtyard, cloister & maze* £10.80; £7.20 5-15s; £8.30 concessions; £32.20 family (max 5 people); free under-5s. *Maze only* £2.50; £1.60 5-15s. **Credit** AmEx, MC, V.
The west face of this palace is Henry's Tudor extravaganza, the east face is Christopher Wren's 17th-century remodelling for William and Mary. Tour highlights include Henry VIII's hammer-beam-roofed Great Hall, the Renaissance Picture Gallery, and the huge Tudor Kitchens, where hundreds toiled to cater for the palace's average daily consumption of six oxen, 40 sheep and 1,000-plus larks, pheasants, pigeons and swans. Today, period-dressed minions make 16th-century dishes, turn meat on a spit and talk to visitors. Don't miss the Clock Court, which is overlooked by the magnificent Astronomical Clock that was specially made for Henry VIII by Nicholas Oursian in 1540, and the extensive gardens are an attraction in themselves – look out for the Great Vine, the world's oldest-known vine (it was probably planted by 'Capability' Brown around 1770 and still produces an annual crop of black grapes, which are sold to visitors).
At weekends, half-terms and holidays, children can do a Hampton Court trail. Outside, the famous Maze is a little scraggy, and so small that it looks impossible to get lost in.

Marble Hill House

Richmond Road, Twickenham, Middlesex (8892 5115/ www.english-heritage.org.uk). Richmond tube/rail/St Margarets rail/33, 90, 290, H22, R70 bus. **Open** *Apr-Sept* 10am-6pm daily. *Oct* 10am-5pm daily. *Nov-Mar* 10am-4pm Wed-Sun. Closed 24-26 Dec, 1-16 Jan. *Tours* by prior arrangement. **Admission** (EH) £3.30; £2.50 concessions; £1.70 5-15s; free under-5s. **Credit** MC, V.
Built for Henrietta Howard, the mistress of George II, and later occupied by Mrs Fitzherbert, George IV's secret wife, the house has been restored to its full Georgian splendour. There are concerts in the park on Sunday evenings in summer.
Café (in park). Nearest picnic place: Marble Hill Park. Shop.

Museum of Rugby/ Twickenham Stadium

Gate K, Twickenham Rugby Stadium, Rugby Road, Twickenham, Middlesex (8892 8877/www.rfu.com). Hounslow East tube then 281 bus/Twickenham rail. **Open** Museum 10am-5pm Tue-Sat; 2-5pm Sun (last entry 4.30pm). *Tours* 10.30am, noon, 1.30pm, 3pm Tue-Sat; 3pm Sun. **Admission** *Combined ticket* £6; £4 concessions; £19 family. **Credit** MC, V.
Rugby-loving tots enjoy the interactive exhibits, which include a real scrum machine, while old-timers can listen to early radio commentary and muse on the days when players still wore bow ties. The highlight is the excellent stadium tour: it's hard to be unimpressed by the stunning view from the top of the North Stand, and many a dad can't resist the chance to run through the players' tunnel on to the hallowed turf.
Buggy access. Nappy-changing facilities. Restaurant. Shop.

Meet the teacher

Justine Millard is the Education and Visitor Services Officer for wildlife conservation charity WWT Wetland Centre (*see p152*).

What do you do?
I run the formal education service (the schools programmes), and also provide a whole range of informal environmental education activities and events to visitors to the Wetland Centre.

What activities do children request most?
Children (and adults!) always enjoy going on our Great Pond Safaris at our interactive Pond Zone, where they can discover the hidden mini-beasts lurking beneath the water's edge. They also like coming nose-to-beak with our baby domestic geese and ducklings.

What other activities are there?
There are plenty of other fun activities that vary during weekends and holidays. You can go on a Dragon Hunt (dragonflies, that is!), a Big Batty walk, or try and search for Ratty (from *Wind in the Willows*). Follow our seasonal trails such as the Lost Duckling trail or join in Froggy Patrol and spot the noisy marsh frogs.

Do you wear a uniform?
The staff all wear green poloshirts, which have our logo on – two white swans in flight and 'WWT Saving Wetlands'.

What's the best part of your job?
What I like most is being involved in, and getting children involved in, conservation projects such as the recent release of 101 water voles into our Wildside area. I also enjoy organising special public events such as our 'Otterly Wild' weekend last August bank holiday.

Do you have a favourite bird or animal living on the reserve?
It's a difficult one to answer, as I like all the birds and wildlife that we get here. A particular favourite is the lapwing or peewit (so-called because of the noise it makes – 'pee-wit!'). This stunning bird has a black pointy crest on his head and in the sunlight the feathers on his back are shiny green and purple.

West London

Is West best? You decide.

The western run of this guide takes in some of the most elegant garden squares, pretty parks and mansion blocks to be found in London. If you stick close to the river, the elegance is sustained all the way to Twickenham, only there are more trees and huge swathes of parkland as the city gets left behind. The scruffier bits are still trendy, and, like as not, thanks to the sterling work of organisations like the London Wildlife Trust and the Kensington & Chelsea Environmental Education Working Group, they're becoming greener all the time. There are nature reserves under motorways, between railway lines and beside the once-filthy Grand Union Canal. The fact that huge roads leading to the M4 motorway tear through many of the most desirable areas matters not a jot to the fashionable westerners. Even the A40 flyover at Ladbroke Grove is cool.

Paddington & Bayswater

In days gone by the infamous Tyburn gallows near Marble Arch made the area around Paddington and Bayswater residentially unappealing. When the famous station, with its magnificent Isambard

Kingdom Brunel roof, was built in the 19th century, the area's gruesome past was swept aside in a population boom. The Grand Junction Canal and the railways brought workers and families to live here.

Nowadays, the area is mostly a prosperous, cosmopolitan one, made all the more exotic by its disreputable history and its remaining rough and ready pockets. Possibly because it has such a mix of communities, Paddington has in modern times become the focus of a long-running docu-soap 'Paddington Green', where everyone battles it out to survive in an entertainingly urban fashion.

The area's child-friendliness in terms of consumerism (the Whiteley's shopping centre, with its eight-screen cinema, is its hub) is undeniable, but it lacks the parks (though Kensington Gardens is only a short trike ride away; *see p68*) and family attractions to put it on the tourist map, unless the tourist happens to be into trains.

Paddington Station is the ideal venue for marmalade sandwich eating, especially since it received a total overhaul when the Heathrow Express opened a few years ago. The £63-million revamp created the elegant centrepiece of the station,

Child's play at **Chiswick House**. *See p167*.

A day at: Syon House

Syon House stands across the river from Kew Gardens and, like Kew, is worth visiting again and again, as the grounds and gardens change with the seasons.

If you come by public transport, there's a cheeky little back path off the A351 London Road adjacent to Brentlea Gate bus stop, where you can wander through to the main entrance area. If you have your own transport, you follow the walled gardens and go up the grand drive to the car park, which is generally overflowing with coaches of schoolchildren.

All the activities radiate out from the car park, and many people come here for just one activity. Although Syon House itself is a splendid medieval fairytale location, most kids will probably find other things more enjoyable. The **London Butterfly House** (8560 7272), for instance, is a memorable experience, where you wander around a tropical plant- and bird-filled conservatory that's home to thousands of multi-coloured butterflies. The only word of advice when visiting would be to be prepared for extreme butterfly bombardment, which some little people may find intimidating. They also have an interesting leaf-cutter ant exhibit, pools of fish and an insect house.

Next door is the **Aquatic Experience** (8847 4730), which is equally tropical and visitors step gingerly between pools of huge goldfish and tanks of crocodiles. At the back of this house is a pond dipping and identification area with nets for scooping. Both houses have gift shops selling plastic creepy crawlies and souvenir jewellery, and both have ample outside picnic space. Each house costs £5 for adults and £2.50 for children.

The next site that most children head for is **Snakes and Ladders** (8847 0946). This huge indoor adventure playground attracts parents from all over London as it can accommodate children of all ages. The playground is designed like a castle, with three tiers of play areas, which include slides, hanging ropes and masses of huge balls. They also have a good area for under-5s and a café where parents can chill out while viewing the whole scene. There's also an outside area with motorised bikes, which cost £1 a ride.

It would be advisable during the summer months to bring a picnic as the nicest locations to eat are outside. In the winter when indoor eating is the only real option, the **Patio Cafeteria** (8758 1175) has a selection of hot meals and a junior menu, which is dominated by fried fish and chicken with chips. On a recent visit, the peacocks that roam freely through the grounds wandered into the café, much to the delight of all the children eating.

If you do find the time and finances to visit the house and grounds too, you can easily spend a half day here. On the weekends, a wooden mini-steam railway is operated, which travels through the trees and around the flower-beds. The house itself is also quite an adventure as each room seems more impressive than the last, from the grand Roman hallway to the Red Drawing Room, with its crimson silk walls and Roman statues. The most memorable room is called the Ladies Room, which extends over 136 feet (41 metres) inspiring intense cart-wheeling urges.

Syon House

Syon Park, Brentford, Middlesex (8560 0883/ www.syonpark.co.uk). Gunnersbury tube/rail then 237, 267 bus. **Open** *House late Mar-early Nov 11am-5pm Wed, Thur, Sun, bank hol Mon. Last entry 4.15pm. Gardens closed 24, 25 Dec. Tours by arrangement.* **Admission** *House & gardens (including audio guide) £6.95; £6.50 concessions; £5.95 5-15s; £15 family (2+2); free under-5s. Gardens only £3.50; £2.50 concessions, 5-15s; £8 family (2+2); free under-5s. Tours free.* **Credit** *AmEx, MC, V. Café. Nappy-changing facilities. Nearest picnic place: Syon House Gardens/ Syon Park. Shop.*

called the Lawn. Here you'll find smart cafés and shops to while away the hours waiting for delayed trains. If your children are into spotting them, 10p will buy you a pass to admire all the platforms and watch the engines. Before you flee with your offspring to a different area it is worth mentioning the **Alexander Fleming Laboratory Museum**, which may be of interest to older children.

Alexander Fleming Laboratory Museum

St Mary's Hospital, Praed Street, W2 (7725 6528). Paddington tube/rail/7, 15, 27, 36 bus. **Open** 10am-1pm Mon-Thur. By appointment 2-5pm Mon-Thur; 10am-5pm Fri. Closed 24 Dec-1 Jan, bank hols. *Tours* included as part of visit. **Admission** £2; £1 concessions, children. **No credit cards**.
The whole museum focuses on recreating the environment in which Alexander Fleming discovered penicillin. It all started in 1928, when the scientist discovered a mouldy growth on a Petri dish of bacteria, which prompted him to start research of his own. The staff here are willing to answer any questions, and run special tours for family and school groups. The education programme caters to science classes, both in schools and in this historic lab. Visitors see a video about Fleming's life and the ways in which penicillin has changed global health care.
Shop.

Eating & shopping

Whiteley's is at the forefront of the Bayswater eating experience. Branches of **ASK** (7792 1977) and **Café Rouge** (7221 1509; *see also p184*) keep families happy, and fans of oriental cuisine appreciate the branch of **Poons** (7792 2884). The **Great American Bagel Factory** is a spacious, buggy-friendly environment serving a vast range of bagels with different fillings. Just outside Whiteley's is a branch of **TGI Friday's** (96-8 Bishop's Bridge Road, W2, 7229 8600; *see also p173*), where most children will find something appealing on the Sesame Street menu. Diagonally opposite is a new **Tiger Lil's** (7221 2622; *see also p180*), for fun stir-fries.

The area of Edgware Road running from Praed Street to Marble Arch has become known as 'Little Mecca', the hub of the Middle Eastern community in London. As a result, this little stretch is an ideal spot for a bit of other-worldly dining where most kids will be fascinated by the hubbly-bubbly rituals while enjoying simple falafels and juices at **Ranoush Juice** (no.43, 7723 5929). The ice-creams at **Regent Milk Bar** (no.362, 7723 8669; *see also p182*) are also worth the walk.

Queensway is the main shopping street, and Whiteley's is the jewel in its crown, home to any number of popular chain stores and trainer outlets. A newly opened outpost of **Gymboree** (*see p198*) on the first floor entertains pre-schoolers and their carers with 45-minute classes of play and music,

among other activities. The loos and mother and baby rooms are all gleaming and fragrant, after a recent refurb. Shopswise, **Gap Kids** (7313 9693), **Happy Toys and Gifts** (beanie baby heaven; 7221 7700) and **Comicstrip** (7221 7388) for computer games and accessories are the big draws for children. For music and Net connection, head to **Tower Records** (7229 4550). Outside, on Queensway, the **London Skate Centre** (no.35, 7727 4669) stocks ice skates, in-line skates and Roller blades to hire or buy, as well as fashionable skateboarding gear.

Maida Vale, Kilburn & Queen's Park

These areas lie north of the Westway, which thunders across Edgware Road. **Maida Vale** is characterised by wide avenues of mansion blocks, white stucco houses and the canal at **Little Venice**. Much of the activities here surround the Grand Union Canal, along which you can walk to London Zoo or Regent's Park in under an hour. Alternatively, you could get the Waterbus to Camden Lock (*see p93*), which takes 50 minutes and leaves on the hour between 10am and 5pm from Little Venice.

Just north of Maida Vale is an easily missed entrance to Paddington Recreation Ground. This is a huge play area dominated by masses of tennis courts and five-a-side football pitches. It also has a decent café and two excellent play enclosures for young children.

The next little pocket of serenity is **Queen's Park**, where parents and children flock at the first sign of spring.

Kilburn is not really famed for being a place you might go for a day out with your kids. The **Tricycle Theatre** (269 Kilburn High Road, NW6, 7328 1000; *see p216*) is the area's saving grace.

Queen's Park

Kingswood Avenue, NW6 (info 8969 5661). Queen's Park tube/rail. **Open** 7.30am-dusk. **Admission** free.
Children can enjoy the paddling pool, an animal enclosure with friendly goats and ducks, a big sand-pit play area and an action-packed playground. Added to this, the staff have a tempting collection of tractors that provides constant preoccupation for most little people. Older children can play pitch and putt or tennis on the beautifully maintained courts and lawns. During the summer holidays, children's magic, puppet and Punch & Judy shows are laid on at the bandstand (3-4pm Mon, Wed, Fri; call for details of next year's programme) and bouncy castles are inflated regularly (Tuesday and Thursday throughout the summer). The bandstand is also used by bands on Sundays. Dancing is encouraged. To round off a day out, there is an excellent café with a children's menu, with dishes from £2.50. Every year, one weekend in September, the park has its own day of celebration, with funfairs and stalls.
Buggy access. Café. Nappy-changing facilities.

Getting onto the swing of things at **Queen's Park**. *See p159.*

Eating & shopping

The best spots for child-friendly places to eat are found around Queen's Park. At the **Waterside Café** on Little Venice you can watch the barges float by while enjoying toasted sarnies and Italian ice-creams. The café in Queen's Park is possibly the nicest location to eat with children. Alternatives are found in Salusbury Road where **Baker & Spice** (no.75, 7604 3636) offers high-priced, high-quality goodies ranging from salads and quiches to decadent cakes, all cooked on the premises. Round the corner, the **Organic Café** (25 Lonsdale Road, NW6, 7372 1232) has a delightful, eclectic menu, beautiful fish dishes and imaginative, brunchy, snacky options for small appetites.

Salusbury Road, whose various boutiques for gifts and clothes prove popular with schoolgirls, is good for shopping generally. At no.81 is **Worldly, Wicked & Wise** (0800 216689), selling little wooden letter beads and other bits and bobs that are perfect for going-home presents. Nearby **Purple Heart** (13A College Parade, NW6, 7328 2830) has loads of pocket-money toys and an ample collection of tie-dye babywear.

Notting Hill

Is still very cool, a few years after the film of the same name made it almost terrifyingly trendy. If you're taking your children to Notting Hill Gate, make sure that you're looking good, unless you want to stick out like a sore thumb among the Stüssy-clad parents flapping along in their Birkenstocks pushing their leopard-print buggies.

Notting Hill's history is less than illustrious, however. Until the mid 1800s it was still yokel country, home to pigs and their pigmen. Once the Georgians built their lofty terraces here, the area's fortunes improved, until last century, when the area's working-class population rose up against the West Indian immigrants forced to live in their midst in 1958. Race riots ensued. The streets around were considered dodgy for years after that, until the yuppies came in the mid 1980s and Notting Hill was considered desirable again. It has never looked back. Every August, it hosts Europe's biggest street festival, the **Notting Hill Carnival** (*see p28*).

Notting Hill's main attraction is **Portobello Market**, the world's most famous antiques market. It started life as any other local street market, but it became increasingly fashionable over the decades, and now it's the hip place to stroll and pick up treasures, though bargains aren't really part of the equation round here.

Many Portobello parents find relaxation in nearby Holland Park (*see p162*), although Notting Hill does have a few little-known green spots. The first is **Avondale Park**, which has a small playground, a football pitch and a countryside atmosphere thanks to all the wild plants and flowers in the conservation area. Avondale Park is on Walmer Road, which is also the site of an unusual 200-year-old pottery kiln, a sign of times gone by when this was perhaps one of the poorest areas of London. Two other tiny open spaces can be found between Colville Gardens and Powis Square, just off Portobello Road. These two garden squares have decent play equipment and grassy areas for little legs to run around. The other garden squares that you often come across around Notting Hill are usually locked up for the exclusive use of their exclusive residents.

Further up Ladbroke Grove, before you reach Kensal Rise, is **The Making Place** (3 Exmoor Street, W10, 8964 2684; *see also p231*), where an adventurous programme of science and technology activities is run for children of an analytical frame of mind.

Over by the thundering Westway, or A40(M), due east from here, is London's best skate park, **Playstation**, where baggy-trousered surfers do impossible things on bits of maple wood with wheels underneath. Less frenetic and frankly scary than this teenage dirtbag heaven is the odd little wildlife garden, tucked under the Westway roundabout, as if to prove a point about urban wildlife. The **Westway Wildlife Garden** (1 Thorpe Close, W8) is tended by the North Kensington Amenity Trust, and gives locals the chance to sit and admire nature under a motorway: there are ponds, a marsh, wildflower meadow, trees and log piles for overwintering creepy crawlies.

For activities of a more indoorsy nature, little children rate **Bramley's Big Adventure** (36 Bramley Road, W11, 8960 1515; *see also p248*) extremely highly. Try it on a Sunday morning and join all the hungover ranks of parents with the papers while their offspring go wild in the playframe.

At the edge of Powis Square is the **Tabernacle** (7565 7890), a converted church where staff organise a range of streetwise activities including breakdance classes and DJ skills courses. They also run Tiny Tots dance classes, Mini Music classes and many more tumbling, bouncing and singing activities for toddlers. This is also the site of **Nectar**, an excellent café, where the eating is colourful: everything from fruit muesli breakfasts to salt fish and ackee dinners. The café has lots of outside seating in the former churchyard. *See also p183.*

Canalside Activity Centre

The Boat House, Canal Close, W10 (8968 4500). Ladbroke Grove tube or Kensal Rise rail. **Open** (for enquiries and bookings) 9am-6pm Mon-Fri; 10am-4pm Sat. Closed mid Dec-mid Jan, bank hols. *Classes & sessions* £5 members; £7 non-members; £4 non-members 9-18s; £2 members. **Membership** *per year* £50; £25 9-18s. **No credit cards.**
This unusual watersports centre, which is located near Sainsbury's, is open to children, families and carers and aims to promote health and education through much hilarious splashing about in the canal. Qualified instructors run courses and one-off sessions in kayaking, canoeing and general messing about in boats. Because most of the activities here are rather dependent on the weather, they take place between April and October. Ring for details of the courses run by the centre.
Buggy access. Nearest picnic place: canalside.

Emslie Horniman Pleasance Gardens Adventure Playground

Southern Row, W10 (8969 5740). Ladbroke Grove tube. **Open** *Termtime* 3-7pm Mon-Fri; 11am-5pm Sat. *School hols* 11am-6pm Mon-Fri. Closed 24 Dec-1 Jan. **Admission** free.
At this cumbersomely named park you will find a multi-coloured soft surfaced playground for infants, which is as close to Telly Tubby Land as you'll get around here. There is also an adventure playground and football pitch for older children. In the spring and summer staff open a small kiosk serving local Disotto's ice-cream, and there are good toilets and baby-changing facilities. The quiet garden has vine-covered walkways and water features. At the Golborne Road end, below the Trellick Tower, are the Meanwhile Gardens and a wildlife garden.
Buggy access. Nappy-changing facilities.

Playstation Skate Park

Bay 65-6, Acklam Road, W10 (8969 4669/Pro Shop 8968 8833/www.pssp.co.uk). Ladbroke Grove tube. **Open** noon-4pm, 5-9pm daily. Closed 24-26 Dec, 1 Jan. **Admission** £6 non-members; £4 members. **Membership** £10 per year.
One of the coolest places in London to break your wrist in – if you happen to be a Quiksilver-clad adolescent, that is – but this skate park, with its ramps and runways, is terrifying for any mum or dad. In 2001, Tony Hawk, the world's first $1m-a-year professional skateboarder, and master of the 'legendary' 900s, put on a display here. Many people who practise at Playstation look capable of following in his wheel tracks; if you think you're one of them, try the Pro Shop based at the park, which equips surfers with professional skateboards and in-lines.
Shop.

Sightseeing

Tony Hawk eat your heart out – **Playstation Skate Park.**

Eating & shopping

Child-friendly mainstays in the area include a branch of Café Rouge and a Pizza Express, but **Osteria Basilico** (29 Kensington Park Road, W11, 7727 9372) is rather more inviting and irritatingly popular, probably because of its divine pasta dishes, fresh focaccia and imaginative pizza choice. **Rotisserie Jules** (133A Notting Hill Gate, W11, 7221 3331) is a high-class sort of fastfood restaurant where the chicken is free range and the fries can be replaced with gratin dauphinois for the more discerning palate. High chairs are provided. **Dakota** (127 Ledbury Road, W11, 7792 9191; *see also p178*) is a perfect neighbourhood restaurant for families.

   Portobello Road is excellent for shopping and has a great atmosphere especially on a Friday and Saturday when the market's in full swing. It's not necessarily good for children's stuff but most teenagers will love it for the range of retro clothes and trendy fashion shops and stalls. You might find bargains on Golborne Road, near Ladbroke Grove tube station, where the antique sellers pick up their bargains to sell on in the posh bits of Notting Hill: it's also a good place to pick up second-hand designer children's togs. Children are well catered for close by, where **Sasti** (Unit 8, 281 Portobello Green Arcade, Portobello

Road, W11, 8960 1125) sells stripy kids' clothes, Mod8 shoes and lots of leopard-print numbers. Small collections of designer wear are also available at **Supra Girls** (212 Kensington Park Road, W11, 7229 4238) and the ultra-trendy **Cross** (141 Portland Road, W11, 7727 6760; *see also p198*), if you're looking for something particularly extravagant. Kensington Park Road is home to **Cheeky Monkeys** (no.202, 7792 9022; *see also p208*), which stocks nursery furniture, dressing-up costumes and lots of wooden toys.

Kensington & Holland Park

Holland Park is the most enchanting green space in London and the surrounding residential and shopping areas of Kensington are some of London's most exclusive.

   This is nanny territory, where children sucking silver spoons are pushed up and down the wide pram-friendly tree-lined avenues on their way to and from the park. This is the area's main outdoor resource and, due to its size and huge investment from the Royal Borough of Kensington and Chelsea, has plenty to offer everyone, of any age, whatever their financial status.

Holland Park
Holland Park Avenue, W8 (7602 2226/www.rbkc.gov.uk). Holland Park tube. **Open** 7.30am-10pm daily. **Map** p312 A8.
The park extends from residential Holland Park across to Kensington High Street. It's easy to get lost if you're a first-time visitor as it is pretty wild and forested in many parts. The main socialising area for children can be found at the exciting adventure playground, where peacocks strut and rabbits and squirrels caper, and children charge around tree walks and dangle from rope swings.

   Young children, who aren't up for dangling yet, prefer the well-to-do one o'clock club. The rest of the park should be explored as there are many lovely spots for toddling around or picnicking. There is a Zen garden, with waterfalls and little oriental stone bridges, a beautiful rose garden, a sandy play area for young diggers, and a well-signposted wildlife walk, which takes about an hour.

   The woods and formal garden surround Holland House, which was once owned by Sir Henry, Earl of Holland, and are now used by Youth Hostels Association members as one of its most delightful outposts. The ballroom of the house contains a very posh restaurant, Marco Pierre White's the Belvedere, where children are welcome to peruse the menu from the thoughtfully provided high chairs, but may not be able to afford much. The Holland Park Cafeteria (*see p163*) gives you the same beautiful location, for a fraction of the price.

   The Holland Park Open Air Theatre (June-Aug), beautiful though its setting is, is more of an adults' treat than a great night out for the family. The theatre is strong on opera, ballet and concert performances by the Royal Philharmonic Orchestra, great musical events for grown-ups but, with tickets at more than £20 a throw, best reserved for the keenest of musical children.
Buggy access. Café. Nappy-changing facilities. Restaurant.

Eating & shopping

The **Holland Park Cafeteria** is the obvious option for a relaxed meal with little ones. It's a typical canteen-style café whose menu lists simple lunches such as pizza slices and spaghetti bolognese. Although the interior is a bit stark, there is ample, picturesque outside seating.

Food is plentiful on Kensington High Street and the surrounding area and generally comes in the form of chain restaurants, such as **ASK** for pizzas (no.222, 7937 5540) and **Café Flo** (127 Kensington Church Street, W8; 7727 8142; *see also p184*), where children are well catered for with starter pasta portions. **Sticky Fingers** (1A Phillimore Gardens, W8, 7938 5338; *see also p186*) just off the high street is an American restaurant that has a rock 'n' roll theme, a kids' menu and a magician on Sundays. Holland Park Avenue is another popular place to eat as there are a number of posh pâtisseries with outside tables. But the best option has to be **Tootsies** (120 Holland Park Avenue, W11, 7229 8567; *see also p186*), which becomes a chaotic family venue every weekend with tables covered in balloons and colouring pads.

If you manage to drag yourself away from the park, **Kensington High Street** is a perfect place for a spot of shopping. If you exit the park on the high street, just to your left is the **Non-Stop Party Shop** (no.214-16, 7937 6500; *see also p245*), a huge fun filled shop with everything from personalised balloons to party equipment. Just opposite here is the excellent **Children's Book Centre** (no.237, 7937 7497; *see also p196*), which sells fun and educational learning tools from books to CD-Roms. The rest of the high street has all the major stores, including **French Connection**, with a pricey children's section with table football. Around the corner on Kensington Church Street is **What Katy Did** (no.49, 7937 6499; *see also p203*), a friendly shop full of kiddy couture.

Earl's Court & Fulham

From World War I onwards, the imposing houses built in the Earl's Court area for Victorian families were increasingly turned into flats for less wealthy residents. Eventually, the numerous flats and bedsits became homes for students and travellers passing

Walk: to Bunny Park

▶ Bunny Park is the locals' name for Brent Lodge Park: the prospect of bunnies at the end of a walk may be just what you need to keep a tiring toddler toddling.

▶ The walk starts at the bottom of **Green Lane**, off Lower Boston Road. The best way to get to the starting point is on the E8 bus from Boston Manor tube travelling in the direction of Hanwell. If you need an excuse for a sit-down already, the **Fox** on Green Lane (8567 3912) is a good child-friendly local pub.

▶ If you pass the Fox and walk to the end of the road you come to the **Grand Union Canal**, where it has just joined with the Brent River. Turn left here and go over the small bridge and you'll pass the **Hanwell Lock**, which is the largest set of locks in London, lowering boats through 53 feet (16 metres) over a third of a mile. Be warned that this process takes an incredibly long time. Rather than follow the canal towards central London, take a right turn on to the river walk. This part of the river can be a bit murky during the summer months, though if you're lucky you might spot some ducks, swans and fish. There is also a nice little picnic spot with a couple of tables just to your left. Follow the path along and you get a real country feeling, which is only broken when you cross under Uxbridge Road. The peace and tranquillity are regained as you walk through a beautiful meadow before reaching the magnificent **Wharncliff Viaduct**

built by Brunel. These arches are known as 'bat caverns' since conservationists turned the inner areas of the hollow brick piers into designated homes for bats.

▶ The path now works its way beneath the 70-foot (26-metre)-wide arches and into **Brent Lodge Park**, where you should take a left and follow the river along until the path bears round to the right. At this point leave the river behind and follow the path up the hill to the gate of the **Millennium Maze** on your left. The maze was obviously planted only a short time ago, but despite being only a foot high, it still manages to boggle at times. The benches surrounding the maze area are all covered in plaques bearing the millennial wishes of random people, which are worth reading for inspiration.

▶ Leaving the maze and heading up the hill takes you to the hub of the park's activities, where you will find a café for ice-cream and sandwiches, a playground and an animal centre. The centre (8758 5019) costs 25p for children and 50p for adults and houses a few squirrel monkeys, a pair of sleepy geckos and some scary spiders along with a few birds and the odd bunny. If you feel ambitious, you can walk back to the tube the same way, or else the nearest public transport is Hanwell overground station. This is about a ten-minute walk from the entrance to the park along countrified **Church Road**, where you'll pass a beautiful church and thatched cottage on the way.

through. At one time Earl's Court was known as Kangaroo Valley because of all the Australian travellers seeking temporary homes around here.

Its slightly scruffy streets and seedy image mean Earl's Court has never really established itself as a typical family location, so the resources for children are limited and most parents hang-out in neighbouring Hammersmith and Fulham. Earl's Court's main distinguishing feature is the vast **Exhibition Centre** (it hosts the Boat Show, the Ideal Home Exhibition and other big consumer events).

The **Brompton Cemetery** is the biggest green space in this built-up area. It's quite pleasant to walk in: look out for the grave of Emmeline Pankhurst, the suffragette who founded the Women's Social and Political Union in 1903. Nearby is the Oratory School, one of the best state secondary schools in London, favoured by Cherie and Tony Blair for their sons.

Moving south towards the river and Fulham's pleasant aspect, the outlook for children becomes brighter. **Bishop's Park** is the area's main park, located by a beautiful stretch of the Thames. Two other attractive green spaces are restricted to members only: the wonderful Hurlingham Sports Club and the Queen's (Tennis and Rackets) Club.

At the end of Bishop's Park is **Fulham Palace**, the official residence of the Bishops of London until 1973. Just off Fulham Palace Road is Fulham Road where locals shop, eat and socialise in the huge variety of posh boutiques and nice restaurants. Once you reach Fulham Broadway you enter **Stamford Bridge**, home to Chelsea Football Club. The Chelsea Village includes a huge Chelsea shop and restaurants to suit most fans.

Chelsea Football Club

Stamford Bridge, Fulham Road, SW6 (7386 7799/tours info 7915 2222/www.chelseafc.co.uk). Fulham Broadway tube. **Open** *Tours* 11am, 1pm, 3pm daily. Closed 25 Dec, 1 Jan, match days. *Shop* 10am-6pm Mon-Sat; 11am-4pm Sun. **Admission** *Tours* £8, £5 5-16s, concessions; free under-5s. **Credit** MC, V. **Map** p314 B13.
Many children are happy just to go to the rather mega megastore, where the stock is uniformly blue, but the bargain buckets yield excellent souvenirs, especially in sale times. Obsessive fans, meanwhile, may enjoy the tour, which lasts 75 minutes and takes in the pitch, the players' tunnel, showers and changing rooms, pressrooms and a video. Birthday parties can also be held here – call 7565 1408 for details. *Cafés. Restaurants. Shop.*

Fulham Palace

Bishop's Avenue, off Fulham Palace Road, SW6 (7736 3233). Putney Bridge tube/220, 74 bus. **Open** *Museum Mar-Oct* 2-5pm Wed-Sun. *Nov-Feb* 1-4pm Thur-Sun. Closed 24-31 Dec. *Tours* 2pm 2nd Sun of mth. **Admission** *Museum* £1; 50p concessions; free under-16s if accompanied by adult. *Tours* £3; free under-16s.
The main house dates from the 16th century while some of the surrounding buildings are even older. The museum, open to the public, traces the buildings' history and has some amus-

ing exhibits, not least the mummified rat. It doesn't cost anything to visit the lovely grounds, planted with many rare trees, which provide a sanctuary off the busy Fulham Palace Road. Next door, Bishop's Park is a fine place to entertain the children. In the park are two good play areas, a sand pit, a one o'clock club and lots of open spaces where people organise big team games throughout the summer. The small boating lake distinguishes itself as being the only one in London where you can take a pedalo out for free. As you head away from Hammersmith, the park tapers off into a riverside promenade, which leads all the way to Putney Bridge where you find lots of nice places to eat and drink. Within the park itself is a small but not very exciting café. Luckily, an ice-cream van is located at the entrance to the park on Stevanage Road serving high-quality home-made Italian ice-cream throughout the year. *Buggy access. Café. Nappy-changing facilities. Shop.*

Eating & shopping

Lou Pescadou (241 Old Brompton Road, SW5, 7370 1057), the lively fish restaurant, has a children's menu for £5.50, and tables outdoors. On a similar theme, **Fishnets** (Chelsea Village, Stamford Bridge, SW6, 7565 1430) welcomes youngsters for fish and chips and more fruits of the sea. Children who like chicken enjoy the friendly atmosphere at **Nando's** (204 Earl's Court Road, SW5, 7259 2544; *see also p184*). The well-known **Troubadour** (265 Old Brompton Road, SW5, 7370 1434) still has a laid-back vibe, much as it did in the 1960s, and a very good, homely coffee shop menu: hot daily specials are well priced and there's often entertainment (poetry reading, folk singing) laid on. On the Fulham Road, nearly every other doorway is an eating place, most of which seem to welcome children: there's a Café Rouge, a Ruby in the Dust, various pizza joints and any number of tapas bars, brasseries and cafés for snacks and light meals.

Shopping is more a Fulham thing than an Earl's Court attraction. **Patrick's Toys & Models** (107-11 Lillie Road, SW6, 7385 9864; *see also p210*) is a small shop packed to the rafters with toys. **Books for Children** (97 Wandsworth Bridge Road, 7384 1821; *see also p195*) has one of the best book selections around. Clothes shops (new and second-hand), sportswear and smart food shops are plentiful along both Fulham Road and Fulham High Street.

Shepherd's Bush & Hammersmith

When you think of these western outposts you immediately envisage roundabouts, which are not the greatest distinguishing feature for an area to be saddled with. **Shepherd's Bush Roundabout** has an interesting arty barometer at its centre, while Hammersmith roundabout houses a bus garage, shopping centre and the tube station. Luckily, beyond these traffic-congested road systems are some lovely residential areas, parks and riverside locations to hang out in. It is also a fun and buzzing place to live, with a diverse community, as the many journalists and columnists who have made their home here like to point out.

Just west of Shepherd's Bush is **Loftus Road**, to which dedicated QPR fans may need to make a pilgrimage. The grounds are also close to **Wood Lane**, that famous BBC address that most adults can remember writing on their letters to *Jim'll Fix It*. Most young kids will know it as the home of CBBC, and you are quite likely to spot the odd celebrity if you can be bothered to wait around outside. Even odder celebrities might pop up if you book yourself on a BBC backstage tour.

Alternatively, ambitious would-be TV stars could get involved in one of the numerous theatre projects running at Hammersmith's famous **Lyric Theatre** (King Street, W6, 8741 2311) or the **Riverside Studios** (Crisp Road, W6, 8237 1111).

Ravenscourt Park is the area's main green space and, as family-friendly parks go, it's one of the best. **Shepherd's Bush Common** is green, and a space, but that's about as much as you can say about it. It forms the centre of yet another roundabout (possibly the biggest in London). It does, however, provide a venue for fairs and circuses throughout the year and there are also some tennis courts here. If you're heading along Shepherd's Bush Road towards Hammersmith, you pass **Brook Green Park**, where there are tennis courts and a playground that has just undergone a major redevelopment, and now is even more choc-full of leaping children than before. Once you reach Hammersmith, you can walk along the river back to Fulham where the open spaces are undoubtedly prettier, and the walk is pleasurable in itself.

BBC Television Centre
Wood Lane, W12 (backstage tours 0870 603 0304/ www.bbc.co.uk/tours). White City tube. **Tours** *by appointment only*; regularly Mon-Sat; phone for details. Closed 25, 26 Dec. **Admission** *Tours* £7.95; £6.95 concessions; £5.95 concessions, 10-16s; £21.95 family (2+2 or 1+3). No under-10s. **Credit** MC, V.
BBC bods who run the tours promise to make them exciting: no two tours are the same, they say, because some studios may be in use by glittering Beeb stars, so they have to plan the tours around whatever's happening on the day. Children may be excited to come face to face with the all-too-familiar *Blue Peter* studio; newshounds enjoy the thrusting BBC news centre. Visitors also see the production galleries, editing suites and other hideouts of self-important telly people. If you fancy combining a tour with joining the audience for one of the BBC's shows, ring 8576 1227 for more on audience participation. Unfortunately, you don't get to sample the works canteen: there's a snack bar for refreshments in reception. The tours take 90 minutes and are really of most interest to media students.
Lifts. Nearest picnic place: Hammersmith Park/Shepherd's Bush Green.

Queen's Park Rangers Football Club
Loftus Road Stadium, South Africa Road, W12 (8743 0262/www.qpr.co.uk). White City tube. **Open** *Shop* 9am-5pm Mon-Fri; 9am-1pm Sat. *Tours* by appointment only. **Admission** *Tours* £4; £2 under-16s. **Credit** AmEx, MC, V.
West London's other football club, second-division QPR may not have the big bucks but it does have a loyal and vociferous fan base, and a good community programme for young fans. The match-day coaching package for children aged 5-16 gives them an exhausting morning of football training, followed by a welcome sit-down to see QPR play at home. The match-day birthday party includes a tour of the ground, two hours of outdoor football training, lunch from Nando's, a ticket to see the match and a goodie bag, all for £16 per head. For more information on QPR's football in the community programme phone 8740 2509.
Nappy-changing facilities. Nearest picnic place: Hammersmith Park. Shop.

Ravenscourt Park
Ravenscourt Road, W6 (7385 8963/www.lbhf.gov.uk). Ravenscourt Park tube. **Open** 7.30am-dusk daily. **Admission** free.
This chirpy park has plenty of fun places for kids to play. In the summer months the packed paddling pool is the most popular spot, which has the added entertainment of tube trains passing over the adjacent viaduct. The park is well landscaped and provides three play areas, including a challenging wooden adventure playground and a one o'clock club (8748 3180) for under-5s. There's also a big pond, a nature trail and an exotic scented garden designed for the visually impaired. Sporting activities come in the form of a large grass pitch area and a number of tennis courts. The café is a useful

Kew Bridge Steam Museum – hot stuff. See p167.

Walpole Park, home to **Pitshanger Manor & Gallery**.
See p168.

spot for lunch as there is a Kiddies Corner menu (£2.50), listing penne with tomato sauce or nuggets and chips. The outdoor eating area with a lawn and trees make it a popular place for local parents to park their pushchairs and enjoy a relaxed meal out: parents tend to go for the imaginative salads and the delicious home-made cakes. There's an annual flower show with children's fair on the weekend before August bank holidays. Regular fun days with bouncy castles and face-painting run throughout the summer hols.
Buggy access. Café. Nappy-changing facilities.

Eating & shopping

Shepherd's Bush Market has been running since 1918 and forms a central spot within the community. Its stalls are predominantly loaded with fruit, vegetables and fish with an Afro/Caribbean bias and there are a number of ethnic food stalls where you can grab a quick, and generally memorable, bite to eat.

Much of the shopping and eating around Hammersmith are concentrated on **King Street**, which has all the usual shopping chains. Also worth a mention is **Bushwacker Wholefoods** (no.132, 8748 2061) for organic baby food stuff and ecological household products. There is also the popular Polish deli **Polanka** (no. 258, 8741 8268), where traditional Polish dishes are served in an informal, child-friendly eating area. **Shepherd's Bush Road** has a fair selection of eateries, too, including a branch of **Café Rouge** (no.98-100, 7602 7732; *see also p184*) which has become a popular weekend lunch spot for families, as has the branch of **Jim Thompson** (243 Goldhawk Road, W12, 8748 0229), where the menu

lists the most innocuous oriental staples: fishcakes, satay, stir fries. There's a party atmosphere at **Patio** (5 Goldhawk Road, W12, 8743 5194), where family groups are made welcome and children enjoy reduced-price portions of East European delicacies, such as blinis and smoked salmon, plus sausage and roast potatoes.

Chiswick

Elegant Chiswick oozes quality of life. The area's buildings include some of the most beautiful townhouses from the 17th to 19th centuries. It is no surprise that **Chiswick House** is also one of the most magnificent 18th-century houses in London, based on the design of villas found in the suburbs of ancient Rome. This suburb of modern London has inevitably become a popular spot for wealthy families to settle in and as a result the activities available for children are of a particularly high standard.

Duke's Meadows, on the riverfront, is a substantial green space with tennis courts, recreation grounds, boathouses and sports facilities, some belonging to the adjacent Grove Park. You can take a pleasant riverside walk along the length of the Mall to the old parish church of St Nicholas, which was mainly rebuilt in 1882-4 but still retains its 15th-century ragstone tower. **Chiswick Common** and **Turnham Green** are more spaces to let off steam than parks with amenities, but make a pleasant enough diversion from the busy Chiswick High Road, and cricket is still played on the green in the summer. **Gunnersbury Park**, on Popes Lane, has plenty of play equipment, a boating lake, mini-golf, fishing pond, tennis courts, café and putting greens. The **Gunnersbury Triangle** was one of the London Wildlife Trust's first nature reserves, saved from the developers' chainsaws by local people in the 1980s.

If poor weather puts an end to frolicking in the park, indoor play opportunities are easy to find. The **Fountain Leisure Centre** (658 Chiswick High Road, W4, 8994 9596) at the Brentford end of Chiswick High Road is home to the Little Tikes activity area, where under-11s can play in a three-storey adventure castle. The centre also has a big pool with a wave machine and a few slides, as well as numerous clubs and classes from karate to badminton. **Art 4 Fun** (444 Chiswick High Road, W4, 8994 4100; *see also p230 and p233*) is a popular spot for children's parties. Alternatively, head out to **Snakes and Ladders**, an incredible indoor play world based at Syon House (*see p158*).

The **Kew Bridge Steam Museum** is located in a restored 19th-century pumping station, whose towering chimney is a distinguishing local landmark. Just down the road is the **Musical**

Museum, whose selective opening hours ensure it will stay one of London's more obscure treasures. If you're not musically or mechanically minded, the **Gunnersbury Museum** (Gunnersbury Park, Popes Lane, W3, 8992 1612; open from 1pm only) is less action packed, but offers visitors an insight into life in the Victorian era. The work of local painter William Hogarth, whose portraits and engravings constituted sharp social commentary on the state of the nation in the 18th century, are displayed in what was once his country retreat. Hogarth's House (Hogarth Lane, Great West Road, W4; 8994 6757), fully restored to its 18th-century condition, is free to get in, but closed in the mornings and on Mondays.

Chiswick House
Burlington Lane, W4 (8995 0508/www.english-heritage.org.uk). Turnham Green tube then E3 bus to Edensor Road/Chiswick rail or Hammersmith tube/rail then 190 bus. **Open** *Apr-Sept* 10am-6pm daily. *Oct* 10am-5pm daily. *Nov-Mar* 10am-4pm Wed-Sun. Last entry 30min before closing. Closed 24-26 Dec, 1-16 Jan. *Tours* by arrangement. **Admission** (EH) *includes audio guide* £3.30; £2.50 concessions; £1.70 5-16s; free under-5s. **Credit** MC, V.
The house is set in picturesque gardens, where you may come across obelisks hidden among the trees, a classical temple, a lake and a cascading waterfall. Lots of families come here on summer days and plonk down for a picnic, have lunch at the café (*see below*) or organise a game of cricket on the well-maintained grounds. In true Chiswick style, a game of afternoon cricket should be followed by a jaunt along the river, which is only a stone's throw away. The Burlington Café, in the grounds, is a splendid place for lunch. English Heritage, which runs the site, sometimes stages family activity days and re-enactments at Chiswick House: see the website for details. *Café. Nearest picnic place: Chiswick Park. Shop.*

Gunnersbury Triangle Nature Reserve
Bollo Lane, W4 (8747 3881/www.wildlondon.org.uk). Chiswick Park tube. **Open** *Reserve* open access daily. **Admission** free.
This area of land found itself enclosed by railway tracks and unfit for human habitation in the late 19th century. As the woodland grew up and the wildlife took over, it became one of the most important sites for urban wildlife in this part of the city. Following the trail, visitors can admire the pond and meadowland and try to spot the 19 species of butterfly that have been recorded as fluttering by here. You can visit here and have a walk and a picnic any time, but if you want to join in with activities, visit when the information cabin is open. The warden, based here full time in the summer, dreams up a wonderful programme of activities (craft workshops, minibeast safaris) for young visitors. They're free and run on a drop-in basis. The Reserve's open day is usually held in June: to find out more, call the warden and ask for a programme. There's a small information cabin, where you can ask the staff questions of urban ecology, pick up trail leaflets, find out about guided tours (summer only) or hire a net to go pond dipping. You never know what you might find. *Buggy access.*

Kew Bridge Steam Museum
Green Dragon Lane, Brentford, Middlesex (8568 4757/www.kbsm.org.uk). Gunnersbury tube/Kew Bridge rail/65, 237, 267, 391 bus. **Open** 11am-5pm daily. Closed 25 Dec,

Good Friday. *Tours* by arrangement. **Admission** *Mon-Fri* £3; £1 5-15s; £2 concessions; £7 family (2+3); free under-5s. *Sat, Sun* £4; £2 5-15s; £3 concessions; £10.50 family (2+3); free under-5s. **Credit** MC, V.
This Victorian riverside pumping station is an entertaining and educational place to visit, especially on weekends, when they have live steam shows, courtesy of the Cornish beam engine, which is fired up at 3pm. The Water for Life exhibition gives the lowdown on the history of London's water use and includes a walk-through sewer, which is not as unpleasant as it sounds. Many of the workers here are volunteers, whose interest in the subject and lively humour make this museum a fascinating place to spend an afternoon. Children's activities, both educational and fun, are run by the Education department. *See also p168* **Meet the teacher**. *Nearest picnic place: Kew Green. Shop.*

Musical Museum
368 High Street, Brentford, Middlesex (8560 8108). **Open** *Apr-Oct* 2-5pm Sat, Sun; *summer hols also* 2-4pm Wed. **Admission** £3.20; £2.50 concessions; free under-3s. **No credit cards**.
This converted church is full of miraculous self-playing instruments of all shapes and sizes, using various mechanical devices. There's even a self-playing violin among the collection of predominantly keyboard instruments. The 90-minute tour tells you about the origins of this intriguing collection. Run on a voluntary basis, the museum can only open from April to October, but there are plans to expand the facilities in a new, purpose-built premises in the near future. *Buggy access. Nearest picnic place: river bank across road.*

Eating & shopping

The **Burlington Café** (Chiswick House) is good for a light lunch (jacket potatoes, sandwiches and salads) indoors or outside in the lavish gardens. Chiswick High Street has the lion's share of places to eat including child-friendly chains like the **Yellow River Café** (no.12, 8987 9791; *see also p185*), which boasts a children's menu featuring a free toy bribe for each child. The **High Road** has such wide pavements that during the summer months virtually all the restaurants have tables outside, making them an embarrassment-free option for family meals. The ice-creams at **Foubert's** (nos.162-70, 8994 5202) come in a huge variety of flavours.

Hit the right key at the **Musical Museum**.

Chiswick High Road is adjacent to the villagey atmosphere of Turnham Green. Here you will find everything you would expect from a typical high street, including big branches of **Baby Gap** and a **Benetton** for euro-perky children's gear. **As Nature Intended** (no.201, 8742 8838) is a wholesome organic supermarket peddling the sort of glossy good health you see in Chiswick all the time. There are also a number of little boutiques worth exploring along Turnham Green Terrace, including **Tots in the Terrace** (no.39, 8995 0520) for continental clothing and accessories and **Snap Dragon** (no.56, 8995 6618; *see also p211*), which specialises in traditional wood toys and dressing-up clothes. Those looking for adventures on two wheels can visit **Action Bikes** (176 Chiswick High Road, W4, 8994 1485; *see also p207*), or on a board (snow or surf) can try **Boardwise London** (146 Chiswick High Road, W4, 8994 6769).

Further west

To the north of Syon Park, and the horrible M40, is appealing **Ealing**. It is no surprise that the logo for Ealing Borough Council is a tree. Ask any local person where the good parks are and they will reel off a list the length of your arm. You are never more than a stone's throw away from one, making it the ideal borough for squirrels and children.

Further west, the imposing **Osterley House**, set in its own parkland, is an excellent choice for a budget day out west (you get quite a lot of house for your admission price and walks and picnics in the park are free).

Go to Southall, Middlesex, for the Market, the closest there is to a proper Indian market outside the country itself. It is an amazing spectacle throughout the week. On Tuesdays live poultry are sold in cages, on Wednesday it's horses. It may be wise to take a vet with you if you're thinking of buying the children a pony. On Saturdays, it's a rainbow of colour, when saris and salwar kameez, dressmaking materials and trinkets, bangles and sandals are sold.

To the north, there's Wembley, best known for its stadium. Owned by the Football Association, the stadium is down for demolition. The arena and conference centre still host big-buck pop concerts and sporting events, but as to whether the twin towers of Wembley Stadium will always be a landmark in the north-western outpost of the city, no one seems to know.

Osterley House

Osterley Park, off Jersey Road, Isleworth, Middlesex (8232 5050/recorded info 01494 755566/ www.nationaltrust.org.uk). Osterley tube. **Open** *Park* 9am-dusk daily. *House* end Mar-early Nov 1-4.30pm Wed-Sun (closed Good Friday). *Tours*

by arrangement; min 15 people. **Admission** (NT) *House* £4.30; £2.15 5-15s; £10.50 family (2+2); free under-5s.

Osterley House was built for Sir Thomas Gresham (founder of the Royal Exchange) in 1576 but transformed by Robert Adam in 1761. Adam's revamp is dominated by the imposing colonnade of white pillars before the courtyard of the house's red-brick body. The splendour of the state rooms alone makes the house worth the visit, but the still-used Tudor stables, the vast parkland walks and the ghost said to be lurking in the basement add to Osterley's allure. The kitchens are vast and atmospheric. Children can pick up a house trail from the office to help them explore these delightful surroundings.

During August children's activities and workshops, such as art and craft workshops and insect safaris, take place every Wednesday. These must be booked ahead (01494 755572). *Café. Nappy-changing facilities. Nearest picnic place: front lawn/picnic benches in grounds. Shop.*

Pitshanger Manor & Gallery

Walpole Park, Mattock Lane, Ealing, W5 (8567 1227/ www.ealing.gov.uk/pitshanger). Ealing Broadway tube/rail. **Open** 10am-5pm Tue-Sat. Closed Good Friday, 25, 26 Dec, 1 Jan, bank hols. *Tours* by arrangement. **Admission** free.

A beautiful Regency villa situated in the idyllic surroundings of Walpole Park. Sir John Soane, architect of the Bank of England, rebuilt most of the house in 1801-3 using highly individual ideas in design and decoration. Among the exhibits worth seeing is the Hull Grundy Martinware collection of pottery. There is an art gallery adjacent to the museum (8567 1227) where contemporary exhibitions are held, plus a lecture and workshop programme for all ages.

In summer there events are held here, including the Walpole Park Jazz Festival and Space Camp for under-14s. Although the park isn't huge, it has a playground (under construction), a water garden, ornamental pond and an animal enclosure. *Buggy access. Lift. Nearest picnic place: Walpole Park.*

Meet the teacher

Derek Gooding is Education Officer at the Kew Bridge Steam Museum (*see p167*).

What do you do?
My job is to enlighten visitors about water supply history, pollution and our very large steam-driven pumps. That means I have to know a lot about river water – how it's pumped and cleaned.

What activities do children request most?
Kids seem to like the Grand Junction 90-inch (cylinder) beam engine, the waterwheel, the main hall engines and the hands-on sewer experience.

What's the best part of your job?
Watching children learn fast... and the real enthusiasm they show about the subject.

Do you wear a uniform?
Not usually. But I might have a makeover soon, to become Charles Dickens – who visited this museum twice – and wrote about his visits here in his *Household Words* publication.

Junior
Consumers

Eating

Tuck in!

The notion of child-friendliness means different things to different restaurateurs. Generally, you can assume a restaurant is welcoming towards children if special provision is made for young diners. Yet, in our experience, there are places that run the full chicken-nugget, high chair, crayons and balloon gamut, but whose boot-faced staff and offhand service lend a chill to the primary-coloured surroundings. We've left them out, naturally. Alternatively, some places look a sight too sophisticated to open their doors to toddling gourmets, yet their relaxed attitude to babies and children has been a revelation. They're included below.

We've listed our favourite child-friendly restaurants by area, in the belief that location is as important as cuisine when dining out en famille. Naturally, all top tot dishes are present and correct: noodles, pasta, pizza, burgers, and, yes, nuggets. Pubs that make a special effort to keep children occupied and well fed while their parents down a pint are also listed. If you're after a bargain, there are some places where children eat for free – worth bearing in mind if your children have eyes bigger than their stomachs: an anatomical aberration all too common in the under-tens. We also mention addresses for other branches of restaurants that we list, but note that all branches will not necessarily have the same facilities.

Southwark & Bankside

Butlers Wharf Chop House

Butlers Wharf Building, 36E Shad Thames, SE1 (7403 3403/www.conran.com). Tower Hill tube/London Bridge tube/rail/Tower Gateway DLR/47, 78, 142, 188 bus. Bar **Open** noon-3pm, 6-11pm Mon-Sat; noon-3pm Sun. **Brunch served** noon-3pm Sat, Sun. **Main courses** £6.75-£22. **Set brunch** (Sat, Sun) £13.95 two courses, £16.95 three courses, incl drink. **Set meal** (noon-3pm, 6-11pm Mon-Fri; 6-11pm Sat) £8 two courses, £10 three courses. *Restaurant* **Lunch served** noon-3pm Mon-Fri, Sun. **Dinner served** 6-11pm Mon-Sat. **Main courses** £12-£23. **Set lunch** £19.75 two courses, £23.75 three courses. **Credit** AmEx, DC, MC, V. **Map** p321 R8.
The treat at the Chop House (a Conran enterprise) is to be seated on the terrace by the Thames, with St Paul's framed by Tower Bridge to the west, and Canary Wharf to the east. The

Get your laughing gear round the food at **Giraffe**. *See p178.*

menu is enticing, with the likes of warm gammon, leek and montgomery cheddar tart, or char-grilled pork chop and bacon. For families, the fantastic Sunday lunches are probably the best bet.
Buggy access. High chairs. Tables outdoors (12, terrace).

The People's Palace

Level 3, Royal Festival Hall, South Bank Centre, SE1 (7928 9999/www.peoplespalace.co.uk). Embankment tube/Charing Cross or Waterloo tube/rail. **Lunch served** noon-3pm, **dinner served** 5.30-11pm daily. **Main courses** £12.50-£17. **Set lunch** £12.50 two courses, £17.50 three courses. **Set dinner** (5.30-7pm Mon-Sat, all day Sun) £16.50 two courses, £21.50 three courses. **Credit** AmEx, DC, MC, V. **Map** p319 M8.
A fine (if expensive) dining option in the Royal Festival Hall, with great riverside views. The Modern European food is consistently high in quality, and children have a menu of their own: pappardelle with tomato sauce and parmesan, sauté salmon, and a dessert of chocolate mousse with raspberry sauce, plus cheddar cheese, grapes and sesame crackers (£4). Very posh, but not at all intimidating.
Buggy access. Children's menu (£4). High chairs. No-smoking tables.

The City

Fish Central

149-51 Central Street, EC1 (7253 4970). Angel or Barbican tube/Old Street tube/rail/55 bus. **Lunch served** 11.30am-2.30pm, **dinner served** 5-10.30pm Mon-Sat. **Main courses** £5-£10. **Credit** MC, V.
Expect great hospitality at this long-established fish and chip restaurant. Food is simple and delicious, portions are large: the fish and chips here are sublime and puddings include hearty chocolate brownies or a berry basket. A great piece of hidden and affordable London. Booking advisable.
Buggy access. High chairs. Reduced-price children's portions. Tables outdoors (10, patio).

Bloomsbury & Holborn

Al's Bar Café

11-13 Exmouth Market, EC1 (7837 4821). Angel tube/ 19, 38, 55, 341 bus. **Open** 8am-2am Mon-Sat; 9.30am-11pm Sun. **Meals served** 8am-11pm Mon-Sat; 10am-11pm Sun. **Main courses** £5.80-£9. **Set lunch** (noon-6pm Mon-Sat) £6. **Credit** AmEx, MC, V. **Map** p317 M4.
The outdoor tables and simple, child-friendly menu (great breakfasts, burgers, chips and the odd flourish such as chicken and mash, all in big helpings) are the attraction here. The atmosphere is laid-back, too.
Buggy access. Tables outdoors (14, pavement).

Bank Aldwych

1 Kingsway, WC2 (7379 9797). Holborn tube. **Breakfast served** 7.30-11.30am Mon-Fri. **Brunch served** 11.30am-3.30pm Sat, Sun. **Lunch served** noon-3pm Mon-Fri. **Dinner served** 5-11.30pm Mon-Sat; 5.30-10pm Sun. **Main courses** £8.95-£19.50. **Set meal** (lunch, 5-7pm, from 10pm) £13.50 two courses, £15.50 three courses. **Credit** AmEx, DC, MC, V. **Map** p317 M6.
A big, bank-like space with pricey but excellent food (a typical meal might be cauliflower soup with rosemary oil,

Butlers Wharf Chop House. *See p170.*

followed by seared scallops, then summer pudding with clotted cream). During brunch the little nippers can enjoy a choice of chipolatas and mash, barbecue chicken and chips or rigatoni and tomato sauce, with sticky toffee pudding for dessert – all for £6.95.
Children's brunch menu (£6.95). High chairs. Nappy-changing facilities.

Covent Garden & St Giles's

Belgo Centraal

50 Earlham Street, WC2 (7813 2233/ www.belgorestaurants.co.uk). Covent Garden tube. **Meals served** noon-10.30pm Mon; noon-11.30pm Tue-Sat; noon-10.30pm Sun. **Main courses** £8.95-£18.95. **Set lunch** (noon-5pm) £5. **Credit** AmEx, DC, MC, V. **Map** p317 L6.
These trendy Belgian restaurants feature a colour-in 'mini Belgo' menu for under-12s, and the good news is that children eat free at any time (max two kids per adult). They can choose from either fish fingers or chicken nuggets served with a salad and fries or mash, followed by ice-cream, plus a fizzy drink or juice. The great value beat-the-clock and lunchtime deals and, of course, the excellent beer will keep parents equally happy.
Buggy access. Children's menu (free). High chairs.
Branches: Belgo Noord 72 Chalk Farm Road, NW1 (7267 0718); **Belgo Zuid** 124 Ladbroke Grove, W10 (8982 8400).

Café Pacifico

5 Langley Street, WC2 (7379 7728/ www.cafepacifico-laperla.com). Covent Garden, Leicester Square or Tottenham Court Road tube. **Meals served** noon-11.45pm Mon-Sat; noon-10.45pm Sun. **Main courses** £3-£5.10 (lunch), £7-£14 (dinner). **Credit** AmEx, MC, V. **Map** p317 L6.
Tex Mex food, massive portions, and plenty to distract kids, including a menu they can colour in and play games on while enjoying chicken nuggets or quesadillas with rice, with a drink and ice-cream sundae, for just £2.75. The large, airy premises are pretty kid-proof.
Buggy access. Children's menu (£2.75). Crayons. High chairs.

Global eating at **World Food Café**. *See p173.*

A stalwart of the veggie scene, and ever faithful to the original spirit of Neal's Yard. Great-looking organic loaves are sold at the ground-floor counter, with filled rolls, burgers, cakes and pastries all jostling for attention. There's a daily soup, too, and pretty much everything on offer is good value for this part of town. The tearoom is on the first floor; takeaway on the ground floor.
No smoking.

Neal's Yard Salad Bar
2 Neal's Yard, WC2 (7836 3233). Covent Garden or Leicester Square tube. **Meals served** *Summer* 11.30am-8pm Mon-Sat; 11.30am-7.30pm Sun. *Winter* 11.30am-7pm Mon-Sat. **Main courses** £5.50-£6.50. **No credit cards.** **Map** p317 L6.
Enjoy innovative vegetarian food alfresco in the pedestrian-only zone of Neal's Yard. Sandwiches, soup, pizzas and, of course, salads make up the majority of the action. Vegans are also well served, particularly with the desserts. But prices are high.
Buggy access. Tables outdoors (9, courtyard). Vegan dishes.

Rock & Sole Plaice
47 Endell Street, WC2 (7836 3785). Covent Garden or Leicester Square tube. **Meals served** 11.30am-10pm Mon-Sat; noon-9pm Sun. **Main courses** £7-£13. **Credit** MC, V. **Map** p317 L6.
A classy central chippie with lots of outdoor tables, offering a great break from a shopping trip in Covent Garden. Fabulous fresh fish and fine chips – even the mushy peas are good. Perfect.
Buggy access. High chairs. Tables outdoors (20, pavement).

Smollensky's on the Strand
105 Strand, WC2 (7497 2101/www.smollenskys.co.uk). Covent Garden or Embankment tube/Charing Cross tube/rail. **Bar** **Open** noon-11pm Mon-Wed; noon-midnight Thur-Sat; noon-10.30pm Sun. *Restaurant* **Meals served** noon-midnight Mon-Wed; noon-12.30am Thur-Sat. **Lunch served** noon-5.30pm, **dinner served** 6.30-10.30pm Sun. **Main courses** £8.85-£19.95. **Set lunch/pre-theatre menu** £14 two courses, £16 three courses. **Credit** AmEx, DC, MC, V. **Map** p319 L7.

Alternative London lives on at **Neal's Yard Bakery & Tearoom.**

Maxwell's
8-9 James Street, WC2 (7836 0303/www.maxwells.co.uk). Covent Garden tube. **Bar** **Open** noon-11pm Mon-Sat; noon-10.30pm Sun. *Restaurant* **Meals served** noon-midnight daily. **Main courses** £8.95-£16.95. **Minimum** £7 when busy. **Credit** AmEx, DC, MC, V. **Map** p317 L6.
Staff take their seasons seriously at this American theme restaurant, donning appropriate costumes at Christmas, Hallowe'en and Thanksgiving. Children get a special set menu, with staples such as burgers, spaghetti and hot dogs, and there are quizzes and colouring to keep them happy.
Buggy access. Children's menu (£4.50). High chairs. Nappy-changing facilities. No-smoking tables. Tables outdoors (6, pavement). Toys.
Branch: 76 Heath Street, NW3 (7794 5450).

Navajo Joe
34 King Street, WC2 (7240 4008). Covent Garden tube. **Bar** **Open** noon-11pm daily. *Restaurant* **Meals served** noon-midnight Mon-Sat; noon-11.30pm Sun. **Main courses** £9.95-£14.95. **Set lunch** £8.95 two courses. **Pre-theatre menu** (5.30-7.30pm Mon-Fri) £8.95 two courses. **Credit** AmEx, DC, MC, V. **Map** p319 L7.
Thundering club music, screaming customers, harried staff: this American theme restaurant has it all. But the food's not too bad. Portions are large and the food is fresh. And kids get to choose from usual staples such as ribs and chips, chicken and chips, pasta, quesadillas, with ice-cream and soft drink.
Children's menu (£4.95). Book dinner.

Neal's Yard Bakery & Tearoom
6 Neal's Yard, WC2 (7836 5199). Covent Garden tube. **Meals served** 10.30am-4.30pm Mon-Sat. **Main courses** £2-£3.60. **Minimum** (noon-2pm Mon-Fri; 10.30am-4.30pm Sat) £2.50. **No credit cards.** **Map** p317 L6.

Combining American cuisine, art deco style and a pianist playing jazz, Smollensky's is sophisticated enough for parents looking for the big chill and sufficiently accessible for kids, too. While parents might enjoy a succulent steak or slab of yellowfin tuna, kids can have staples such as pasta, fried chicken, and fish fingers from the 'mini me' menu. Phone for details of the weekend family entertainment.
Booking advisable. Buggy access. Children's menu. Entertainment (noon-4pm Sat, Sun). High chairs. No-smoking tables. Toys.
Branches: Smollensky's 02 Centre, 255 Finchley Road, NW3 (7431 5007); **Smollensky's Bar & Grill** Bradmore House, Queen Caroline Street, W6 (8741 8124).

TGI Friday's
6 Bedford Street, WC2 (7379 0585). Covent Garden or Embankment tube/Charing Cross tube/rail. **Bar Open** noon-11pm Mon-Fri; 11am-11pm Sat; 11am-10.30pm Sun. *Restaurant* **Meals served** noon-11.30pm Mon-Sat; 11am-11pm Sun. **Main courses** £7.75-£12.95. **Credit** AmEx, MC, V. **Map** p319 L7.
The atmosphere is silly, but the American-style food here is big, greasy and wonderful (and includes some spectacular desserts). The 'Sesame Street' kids' menu (pizza, fish and chips and chicken nuggets) is big enough to suit most tastes and there's free Organix baby food for the littlest mouths. Entertainment runs from cocktail demonstrations at the bar to face-painting at weekends.
Balloons. Buggy access. Children's menu (dinner). Face-painting (noon-4pm Sat, Sun). High chairs. No-smoking tables. Toys.
Branches: 702-4 Purley Way, Croydon (8681 1313); Watford Way, NW7 (8203 9779); 96-8 Bishop's Bridge Road, W2 (7229 8600); 25-9 Coventry Street, W1 (7379 0585).

World Food Café
Neal's Yard Dining Room, First floor, 14 Neal's Yard, WC2 (7379 0298). Covent Garden or Leicester Square tube. **Meals served** 11.30am-4.30pm Mon-Fri; 11.30am-5pm Sat. **Main courses** £4.55-£7.95. **Minimum** (noon-2pm Mon-Fri; 11.30am-5pm Sat) £5. **Credit** MC, V. **Map** p317 L6.
One of the best places to eat vegetarian food in London. The first-floor dining room, and the view from it, are lovely, and the food is innovative and tasty, picking up on influences from across the globe.
High chairs. No smoking.

Kensington & Chelsea

Benihana
77 King's Road, SW3 (7376 7799/www.benihana.co.uk). Sloane Square tube. **Lunch served** noon-2.30pm daily. **Dinner served** 6-10.30pm Mon-Fri, Sun; 6-11pm Sat. **Set meals** £14-£60 six courses. **Credit** AmEx, DC, MC, V. **Map** p315 F11.
Benihana puts the fun back into food. Families dine around tables with a hotplate in the centre. Food is then chopped, seasoned and set to cook right before your eyes. Kids' set Sunday lunches include a prawn appetiser, courgettes and carrots, and a choice of chicken and prawn pasta, teriyaki steak or hibachi chicken, with an ice-cream to follow. At the Swiss Cottage branch, there's a children's entertainer (1-3pm Sunday) who constructs balloon animals at your table and performs impromptu post-luncheon magic tricks. There are barbecues in summer.

Italian made easy – and stylish – at **Carluccio's Caffè**. *See p175.*

Children's menu (lunch Sun, £4.75, £5.25 and £5.50). High chairs. Vegetarian menu.
Branches: 100 Avenue Road, NW3 (7586 1303); 37 Sackville Street, W1 (7494 2525).

Big Easy
332-4 King's Road, SW3 (7352 4071). Sloane Square tube then 11, 19, 22 bus. **Bar Open** noon-11pm Mon-Sat; noon-10.30pm Sun. **Main courses** £3.95-£14.95. *Restaurant* **Meals served** noon-11.15pm Sun-Thur; noon-12.15am Fri, Sat. **Main courses** £7.95-£15.50. **Set lunch** (noon-4pm Mon-Fri) £7.95 two courses. **Credit** AmEx, MC, V. **Map** p315 E12.
Short of having Bruce Springsteen flipping burgers in the kitchen, Big Easy couldn't be more American. And the food is some of the best down-home cooking in town. The emphasis here is on barbecue, but there's a little bit of everything on the menu. Under-tens accompanied by adults eat free.
Children's menu (£4.95, dessert £3.95); under-10s accompanied by adults eat free. Crayons. Entertainment: country, blues and jazz music from 8pm daily. High chairs. Nappy-changing facilities. No-smoking tables.

Bluebird
350 King's Road, SW3 (7559 1000/www.conran.co.uk). Sloane Square tube then 11, 19, 22 bus. **Bar Open** noon-10pm daily. *Restaurant* **Brunch served** 11am-3.30pm Sat, Sun. **Lunch served** noon-3pm Mon-Fri. **Dinner served** 6-11pm Mon-Sat; 6-10pm Sun. **Main courses** £10.95-£19.50. **Set lunch** (Mon-Fri) £12.50 two courses, £16.50 three courses. **Credit** AmEx, DC, MC, V. **Map** p315 D12.
Along with the chic shop, florist's and food hall, this Conran complex has a buzzing, skylit restaurant. Game and crustacea are a speciality, and other dishes arrive via the wood-fired oven, rôtisserie and grill. At weekends the brunch menu has fish and chips, sausage and mash or tomato linguini for children; small-portion dishes can be prepared during the week.
Buggy access. Children's menu (weekends; £4-£5.50). High chairs.

Junior Consumers

Chutney Mary

535 King's Road, SW10 (7351 3113/
www.realindianfood.com). Bus 11, 22. **Lunch served**
12.30-2.30pm Mon-Sat; 12.30-3pm Sun. **Dinner served**
6.30-11.30pm Mon-Sat; 6.30-10.30pm Sun. **Main courses**
£9.25-£19. **Set meals** (lunch, 6.30-7.15pm, 10-11.30pm)
£11 two courses, £14 three courses. **Cover** £1.50. **Credit**
AmEx, DC, MC, V. **Map** p314 C13.
An elegant Indian restaurant, with food from various regions
of the subcontinent. The ever-evolving à la carte menu might
include goat's cheese salad, a vegetarian 'kebab' of fresh baby
corn and spiced mash, Bengali braised lamb or lobster malai.
Chefs will prepare half-price portions for children, without
spices, on request.
Buggy access. Entertainment: jazz band lunch Sun.
High chairs. No-smoking tables.

West End

Carluccio's Caffè

8 Market Place, W1 (7636 2228). Oxford Circus tube.
Meals served 8am-11pm Mon-Fri; 11am-11pm Sat;
11am-10pm Sun. **Main courses** £4.85-£9.95. **Credit**
AmEx, DC, MC, V. **Map** p316 J6.
Decor is simple and modern, and staff are good with children
(most dishes can be served in small portions or you can share
a selection of antipasti – mixed or vegetarian). Every branch
has a deli counter, so the good times can continue at home.
Buggy access. Reduced-price children's portions. Tables
outdoors (pavement).
Branches: St Christopher's Place, W1 (7935 5927);
Fenwick, New Bond Street, W1 (7629 0699).

Cheers

72 Regent Street, W1 (7494 3322). Piccadilly Circus
tube. Bar **Open** noon-3am Mon-Sat; noon-1.30am Sun.
Restaurant **Meals served** noon-10pm daily. **Main**
courses £6.95-£12.90. **Minimum** £6. **Set lunch** £5.95
noon-7pm. **Credit** AmEx, DC, MC, V. **Map** p318 J7.
Why not try 'Sam's spaghetti carbonara', take a trip through
'Woody's garden', or enjoy 'Frasier's feast'? The food here is
pretty good, and reasonably priced. And there's plenty put
on for kids, including a menu of burgers and fries, mini-
pizzas or pasta, all served with a drink. However, children are
only allowed in the restaurant until 6pm.
Buggy access. Children's menu (£4.95). Crayons. High
chairs. No-smoking tables. Toys.

China House

160 Piccadilly, W1 (7499 6996/www.chinahouse.co.uk).
Green Park tube. **Meals served** noon-11.30pm Mon-Sat.
Afternoon tea 3-6pm Mon-Sat. **Main courses** £7.75-
£9.95. **Credit** AmEx, MC, V. **Map** p318 J7.
Great Chinese food in one of London's most stunning restaurant locations. Check out the afternoon tea (3-6pm), with a
selection of Chinese teas (green, jasmine and oolong) and
sweet and savoury snacks. Children's portions are available
and there's kids' entertainment at weekends.
Buggy access. Children's portions (£4.50). Entertainment:
clowns and face-painting (weekends). High chairs.
No-smoking tables. Tables outdoors (2, patio).

Down Mexico Way

25 Swallow Street, W1 (7437 9895). Piccadilly Circus tube.
Bar **Open** 5pm-3am Mon-Sat. *Restaurant* **Meals served**
noon-midnight Mon-Sat; noon-10.30pm Sun. **Main courses**
£9-£13.50. **Credit** AmEx, DC, MC, V. **Map** p318 J7.

Ed's Easy Diner – decent fast food.

This place may be smart-looking, but things can get pretty
wild in the evenings. The best place for families is the first-
floor brasserie restaurant where the Down Mexico Way's
infamous dancers – who twirl across the floor between the
tables – gives the place a very lively atmosphere. The Latin
American food is OK, service is pretty good and kids will
enjoy choosing from the tapas menu (£2 per dish).
Entertainment: Mexican music and dancers (7pm, 10pm
Wed-Sat). High chairs.

Ed's Easy Diner

Old Compton Street, W1 (7287 1951). Leicester Square
or Tottenham Court Road tube. **Meals served** 11am-
midnight Mon-Sat; 11am-11pm Sun. **Main courses**
£3.95-£5.50. **Minimum** (6pm-midnight Fri-Sun) £3.60.
Credit MC, V. **Map** p317 K6.
The menu may be limited to hamburgers, hot dogs, chips and
milkshakes, but that's just the point. The American cheeseburger is everything it should be. The chips are crisp and
served in easily handled portions, the onion rings are greasy
and fresh, and the malted milkshakes are so sweet they make
your teeth hurt. And there are little versions of the burgers
for little people (£3.95; mini-milkshake £1.65). Children will
love the American diner look of the place, too.
Buggy access. Children's menu (£3.95). Crayons.
Branches: Brent Cross Shopping Centre, NW4 (8202
0999); 362 King's Road, SW3 (7352 1956); Trocadero,
Shaftesbury Avenue, W1 (7287 1951); 02 Centre, 255
Finchley Road, NW3 (7431 1958); 12 Moor Street, W1
(7434 4439).

Hard Rock Café

150 Old Park Lane, W1 (7629 0382/www.hardrock.com).
Hyde Park Corner tube. **Meals served** 11.30am-12.30am
Mon-Thur, Sun; 11.30am-1am Fri, Sat. **Main courses**
£7.95-£14.95. **Minimum** main course when busy. **Credit**
AmEx, MC, V. **Map** p318 H8.
Many people love to hate the Hard Rock Café, but the food
here is really rather good. The salads are enormous and come
stacked with fresh produce, chicken wings are juicy and
spicy and the burgers are not only meaty but are served with
every imaginable trimming. The 'lil' rock' menu offers diners a main course (cheeseburger, macaroni with cheese, pizza,
and so on) with french fries, apple sauce or baked beans and
a beverage for £4.25.
Buggy access. Children's menu (£4.25). High chairs.
No-smoking tables. Tables outdoors (10, pavement). Toys.

Junior Consumers

Masala Zone

*9 Marshall Street, W1 (7287 9966/
www.realindianfood.com). Oxford Circus tube.* **Lunch
served** noon-3pm daily. **Dinner served** 5.30-11pm Mon-
Sat; 6-10.30pm Sun. **Main courses** £5-£9.50. **Credit** MC,
V. **Map** p316 J6.

Top: Fish & chips

Faulkner's
See p180.

fish!
See p184.

Fish Central
See p171.

Geales
See p183.

Olley's
See p181.

Rock & Sole Plaice
See p172.

Seafresh
See p177.

Sea Shell
See p177.

Rock & Sole Plaice. *See p172.*

Masala Zone is a bit of an Indian Wagamama, with its no-
booking and no-smoking policy. Many dishes are based on
the tangy street food of Bombay, the sweet vegetarian
savouries of Gujarat and the meaty snack food of the north.
There are loads of mildly spiced options for kids, and even a
children's thali (£3), which can be made on request. And
there's enough room for pushchairs on the upper level.
*Buggy access. High chairs. No bookings accepted. No
smoking. Vegetarian menu.*

New World

1 Gerrard Place, W1 (7734 0396). Leicester Square tube.
Meals served 11am-11.45pm Mon-Sat; 11am-11pm Sun.
Dim sum 11am-6pm daily. **Main courses** £4.35-£8.80,
£1.70-£3.50 dim sum. **Credit** AmEx, DC, MC, V. **Map**
p319 K7.
This vast Chinese restaurant comes alive at weekend
lunchtimes, when it fills up with Chinese families guzzling
dim sum. Kids will enjoy choosing their dumplings from the
circulating trollies, and the whole family is bound to have a
lazy, delightful time at no great expense.
Buggy access. High chairs. No-smoking tables.

Planet Hollywood

*Trocadero, 13 Coventry Street, W1 (7287 1000/
www.planethollywood.com). Piccadilly Circus tube.*
Meals served noon-1am Mon-Sat; noon-11.30pm Sun.
Main courses £9.95-£16.95. **Credit** AmEx, DC, MC, V.
Map p319 K7.
Television screens lean perilously over the seating area here.
A shopping menu (T-shirts, posters and whatnot) is served
along with the food menu, on which you'll find nachos, Caesar
salad, steak roll and the like. Kids are offered the usual sta-
ples (hamburger, pasta, chicken and chips, dessert and drink).
But the atmosphere is fun and there are balloons and crayons.
*Balloons. Buggy access. Children's menu (£7.95). Crayons.
High chairs. Nappy-changing facilities. No-smoking tables.*

Rainforest Café

*20 Shaftesbury Avenue, W1 (7434 3111/
www.rainforest.co.uk). Piccadilly Circus tube.* **Meals
served** noon-10pm Mon-Fri; noon-8pm Sat; 11.30am-
10pm Sun. **Credit** AmEx, MC, V. **Map** p319 K7.
Take a trip into the rainforest – cascading waterfalls, thun-
der, lightning, the sounds of wild animals… and a set children's menu for a somewhat pricey £8.95. Popular kids'
choices include pizza, a hot dog, chicken and a burger, served
with carrot salad, and desserts of jelly, ice-cream, and banana
with custard and smarties. Party bags, cakes and face-
painters are thrown in. Some adults find the place a bit much,
but kids love the whole Rainforest experience.
*Children's menu (£8.95). Crayons and colouring-in sheets.
Face-painting. High chairs. Nappy-changing facilities.*

Stanleys

*6 Little Portland Street, W1 (7462 0099). Oxford Circus
tube.* **Meals served** noon-11pm Mon-Sat. **Main courses**
£8.50-£10.95. **Credit** AmEx, MC, V. **Map** p316 J5.
Eat diner-style at this informal British restaurant that specialises in slap-up sausage and mash dinners. The plush red
banquette seating and unlimited ketchup are a hit with kids,
as are the half-portions (sausage, mash and gravy, £5).
*Buggy access. High chairs. Nappy-changing facilities.
Reduced-price children's portions.*

Veeraswamy

*Mezzanine floor, Victory House, 99-101 Regent Street,
W1 (7734 1401/www.realindianfood.com). Piccadilly
Circus tube.* **Lunch served** noon-2.30pm Mon-Fri;

12.30-3pm Sat, Sun. **Dinner served** 5.30-11.30pm Mon-Sat; 5.30-10.30pm Sun. **Main courses** £9.75-£18. **Set lunch** (Mon-Sat) £11.75 two courses, £14.75 three courses; (Sun) £15 three courses, £7.50 under-8s, eat as much as you like. **Set dinner** (5.30-6.30pm, 10-11.30pm) £11.75 two courses, £14.75 three courses. **Credit** AmEx, DC, MC, V. **Map** p318 J7.

London's oldest Indian restaurant (established 1926) has an exciting and innovative menu. You might find fresh oysters stir-fried with Keralan spices, mulligatawny chicken and lentil soup or fish tikka kebabs. If kids don't fancy anything from the main menu, they can have egg and chips or chicken nuggets, and ice-cream for £7. Prices are high, but the setting and service are spectacular.

Buggy access. Children's menu (Sun; £7).

Westminster

Seafresh
80-81 Wilton Road, SW1 (7828 0747). Victoria tube/rail/ 24 bus. **Meals served** noon-10.30pm Mon-Sat. **Main courses** £5.55-£15.95. **Credit** AmEx, DC, MC, V. **Map** p318 J10.

An old-school fish and chip restaurant, decorated with all manner of seaside bits and bobs that will give younger members of the party something to gawp at. Fish is pretty good and portions are huge. Handy for both Victoria stations.

Buggy access. High chairs.

Texas Embassy Cantina
1 Cockspur Street, SW1 (7925 0077). Embankment tube/Charing Cross tube/rail. **Meals served** noon-11pm Mon-Wed; noon-midnight Thur-Sat; noon-10.30pm Sun. **Main courses** £7.50-£16.95. **Credit** AmEx, DC, MC, V. **Map** p319 K7.

This place wears its theme-iness with pride, has excellent service, a relaxed atmosphere, a great range of beers and decent food (we particularly rate the great enchiladas and mammoth desserts). Kids can sample Tex Mex food in their very own menu. And there are puzzles and word searches to keep them happy.

Balloons. Children's menu (£4.50). Crayons. High chairs. Tables outdoors (8, pavement).

Marylebone

Purple Sage
90-92 Wigmore Street, W1 (7486 1912). Bond Street tube. **Lunch served** noon-3pm Mon-Fri. **Dinner served** 6-10.30pm Mon-Sat. **Main courses** £7.50-£14. **Credit** AmEx, MC, V. **Map** p316 G6.

The Purple Sage is a sister restaurant to Maida Vale's Red Pepper (*see p186*). It's handy for Oxford Street, and is a cut above your average pizza and pasta chain operation – a fact reflected in the monthly changing menu, which offers some interesting choices: goat's cheese and sun-dried tomato tortellini, perhaps, or even guinea fowl ravioli. Desserts are heavenly, too. Note that pizzas are only available in the evenings.

Buggy access. High chairs.

Sea Shell
49-51 Lisson Grove, NW1 (7224 9000). Marylebone tube/ rail. **Lunch served** noon-2.30pm, **dinner served** 5-10.30pm Mon-Fri. **Meals served** noon-10.30pm Sat. **Main courses** £6.75-£16. **Credit** AmEx, MC, V. **Map** p313 F4.

Sante Fe: funky, friendly and affordable. *See p178.*

A very popular, spick-and-span fish and chip restaurant. Snow-white haddock, enclosed by groundnut oil batter and accompanied by fat chips, is a favourite. Further options include large salads and sticky puds.

Buggy access. Children's menu. High chairs. No-smoking tables.

Wagamama
101A Wigmore Street, W1 (7409 0111/ www.wagamama.com). Bond Street or Marble Arch tube. **Meals served** noon-11pm Mon-Sat; 12.30-10.30pm Sun. **Main courses** £4.80-£7.35. **Set meals** £8.50-£9.95. **Credit** AmEx, DC, MC, V. **Map** p316 G6.

Fairly priced, well-portioned, nourishing oriental food is what you'll get at Wagamama. There are loads of tasty little snacks (including great dumplings in various guises) and oodles of noodle/broth combos, plus rice dishes and salads. The food is vaguely virtuous, too, making it a favourite choice with those who have too little time to go elsewhere but enough sense to avoid KFC.

High chairs. Nappy-changing facilities. No smoking. **Branches**: 11 Jamestown Road, NW1 (7428 0800); 26-40 Kensington High Street, W8 (7376 1717); 10A Lexington Street, W1 (7292 0990); Lower ground floor, Harvey Nichols, SW1 (7201 8000); 4A Streatham Street, WC1 (7736 2333).

North London

Banners
21 Park Road, N8 (8348 2930). Finsbury Park tube/rail then W7 bus. **Open** 9am-11.30pm Mon-Fri; 10am-midnight Sat; 10am-11pm Sun. **Meals served**

9am-11.30pm Mon-Thur; 9am-midnight Fri; 10am-midnight Sat; 10am-11pm Sun. **Main courses** £7.95-£10.50. **Credit** AmEx, MC, V.

The spiritual home of the average left-leaning, Dylan-loving Crouch Ender, food here is of the greasy spoon, Jamaican, American and Mexican variety. Kids can tuck into chicken, chips and barbecue sauce, vegetarian sausage, or simple beans on toast. There's even a meal for babies (over six months old) of mashed potato, cheese and beans (£1.50). *Buggy access. Children's menu (until 7pm, £1.95-£3.25). Crayons. High chairs. Toys.*

Blue Legume

101 Stoke Newington Church Street, N16 (7923 1303). Stoke Newington rail/73 bus. **Open** 9.30am-6.30pm daily. **No credit cards.**

A Stoke Newington stalwart that has been serving laid-back breakfasts, mid-morning lattes and lunch specials for nearly a decade. Portions are generous, and prices are reasonable (home-cured gravadlax with scrambled eggs, salad and lots of brown toast costs £6.95). A popular place for local families, although there's not much room for more than about two buggies at once.
Buggy access. High chairs. Tables outdoors (4, pavement).

Café Mozart

17 Swains Lane, N6 (8348 1384). Highgate tube/ Gospel Oak rail/214, C2, C11, C12 bus. **Meals served** 9am-10pm daily. **Credit** MC, V.

Plenty of pavement tables make this the perfect place for a summer lunch after a stroll on the heath. Fabulous cakes are

Arkansas Café is carnivore heaven. *See p180.*

a real draw, but there's also a breakfast menu, and a list of hot daily specials. Service is friendly and efficient.
Buggy access. High chairs. No smoking. Tables outdoors (9, courtyard).

Giraffe

46 Rosslyn Hill, NW3 (7435 0343). Hampstead tube. **Brunch served** 8am-4pm Mon-Fri; 9am-4pm Sat, Sun. **Lunch served** noon-4pm Mon-Fri; noon-5pm Sat, Sun. **Dinner served** 5-11pm Mon-Fri; 6-11pm Sat, Sun. **Main courses** £7-£10. **Credit** AmEx, MC, V.

Food is eclectic and bursting with freshness at this bright and funky-looking brasserie. Food runs the gamut from innovative dishes such as firecracker chicken with noodles to a meze plate or comforting brunch. Kids can choose meat or veggie options from their own menu. The laid-back atmosphere and the accommodating staff make this a deserving winner of the 2001 *Kids Out* Best Family Restaurant Award.
Buggy access. Children's menu. Crayons. High chairs. No-smoking tables. Tables outdoors (3, pavement).
Branches: 29-31 Essex Road, N1 (7359 5999); 6-8 Blandford Street, W1 (7935 2333).

Idaho

13 North Hill, N6 (8341 6633/www.idahofood.co.uk). Highgate tube. Bar **Open** 6.30pm-midnight Mon-Sat; 6.30-11pm Sun. *Restaurant* **Brunch served** 11.30am-4pm Sat, Sun. **Dinner served** 6.30pm-11 daily. **Main courses** £12-£16. **Credit** AmEx, MC, V.

The postmodern cousin of the Dakota-Montana-Canyon clan. The atmosphere may be stark, but the staff are as nice as can be, and the food is excellent. At weekend brunch kids have their own menu, offering sausage and chips, burger and chips and chicken nuggets for £5 (including a juice or soft drink). Own-made ice-cream costs an extra £2. For sister restaurant **Canyon**, *see p182.*
Buggy access. Children's menu (weekends; £5). High chairs. Tables outdoors (70, terrace).
Branches: **Montana** 125 Dawes, SW6 (7385 9500); **Dakota** 127 Ledbury Road, W11 (7792 9191); **Utah** 18 High Street, SW19 (8944 1909).

Santa Fe

75 Upper Street, N1 (7288 2288). Angel tube. Bar **Open** noon-11pm Mon-Sat; noon-10.30pm Sun. *Restaurant* **Meals served** noon-10.30pm Mon-Sat; noon-10pm Sun. **Main courses** £6.95-£12.95. **Credit** AmEx, MC, V.

A funky South-western American atmosphere, friendly, laid-back staff and an eclectic, affordable menu are the draws at Santa Fe. Parents can enjoy dishes such as tasty flautas, enchiladas and corn pudding, while kids can tuck into tortilla pizza (chicken, roasted veg or sweetcorn and sausage) or spaghetti Santa Fe.
Buggy access. Children's menu (£3.95). High chairs. Nappy-changing facilities. No-smoking tables. Tables outdoors (12, pavement). Toys.

Shish

2-6 Station Parade, Willesden Green, NW2 (8208 9290). Willesden Green tube/260, 266 bus. **Meals served** 11.30am-11.30pm daily. **Main courses** £4.95-£8.95. **Set lunch** £4.99. **Credit** MC, V.

Shish has a pleasantly refreshing and aromatic array of dishes with Middle Eastern and Mediterranean accents. Meat is served off the stick with rice, couscous or, if you really must, French fries. The layout of the restaurant is very child-friendly, with counter seats arranged around a central food work station; there are also a few booths downstairs.
No smoking (downstairs).

Tiger Lil's

270 Upper Street, N1 (7226 1118/www.tigerlils.com).
Highbury & Islington tube/rail/4, 19 bus. **Lunch served**
noon-3pm Mon-Fri. **Dinner served** 6-11.30pm Mon-
Thur; 6pm-midnight Fri. **Meals served** noon-midnight
Sat; noon-11pm Sun. **Unlimited stir-fry** £12.50; £5.50
under-10s; free under-5s. **Credit** AmEx, MC, V.
This north London branch of the stir-fry chain is big and
airy, and the new menu simple and effective. There are
appetite-whetting snacks such as chicken dumplings, prawn
crackers and tiger prawns for starters, but the star of the
show is the unlimited stir-fry. You choose the ingredients
and cooks wok them before your eyes, adding your choice
of seasoned oils and sauces (including teriyaki, satay and
curried coconut).
Buggy access. Crayons. High chairs. Nappy-changing
facilities. Reduced-price children's portions. Toys.
Branches: 75 Bishop's Bridge Road, W2 (7221 2622);
16A Clapham Common South Side, SW4 (7720 5433); 500
King's Road, SW10 (7376 5003).

East London

Arkansas Café

Unit 12, Old Spitalfields Market, E1 (7377 6999). Liverpool
Street tube/rail. **Lunch served** noon-2.30pm Mon-Fri;
noon-4pm Sun. **Dinner served** by arrangement. **Main**
courses £4.50-£13.50. **Credit** DC, MC, V. **Map** p321 R5.
The motto of this basic but brilliant barbecue joint is 'we
don't serve fries', and it's true, it doesn't. But who needs
chips when you've got French corn-fed chicken, wild boar and
apple sausages, and char-grilled Barbary duck breast?
There's no children's menu but staff will cut a hamburger in
half for two to share, and the high pews are an interesting
alternative to high chairs.
Buggy access. No-smoking tables. Tables outdoors
(30, terrace inside market).

Top: Posh nosh

Bank Aldwych
See p171.

Bluebird
See p173.

Butlers Wharf Chop House
See p170.

Canyon
See p182.

Chutney Mary
See p175.

Idaho
See p178.

The People's Palace
See p171.

Veeraswamy
See p176.

Babe Ruth's

172-6 The Highway, E1 (7481 8181/www.baberuths.com).
Shadwell DLR/100, D1 bus. **Meals served** noon-11pm
Mon-Thur; noon-midnight Fri, Sat; noon-10.30pm Sun.
Credit AmEx, MC, V.
Great for boisterous kids, Babe Ruth's has an in-house one-
on-one basketball court, numerous interactive games and
constant satellite coverage of the world's major sporting
events. Parents will get time to enjoy the American diner staples and, if they can get the kids to sit down for long enough,
there's a kids' menu with cheese and ham pizza, fish strips,
barbecue ribs and so on.
Buggy access. Booster seats. Children's menu (£7.99).
Crayons. High chairs. Nappy-changing facilities.

Baradero

Turnberry Quay, off Pepper Street, E14 (7537 1666).
Crossharbour DLR. **Meals served** 11am-11pm Mon-Fri;
6-11pm Sat. **Main courses** £10.25-£16.50. **Credit** AmEx,
DC, MC, V.
An exuberant tapas bar and restaurant in a lovely setting,
overlooking a Thames basin quay. Staff are exceptionally
good-natured and efficient, and there's a big choice of tapas
to get stuck into.
High chairs. No-smoking tables. Tables outdoors
(21, terrace).

Elche

567-9 Leytonstone High Road, E11 (8558 0008).
Leytonstone tube. **Lunch served** 12.30-2.30pm Tue-Sat.
Dinner served 6.30-11pm Mon-Thur; 6.30pm-midnight
Fri, Sat. **Meals served** 12.30-10pm Sun. **Main courses**
£8.50-£15. **Tapas** £2.50-£5. **Set tapas** £10. **Set buffet**
(12.30-4pm Sun) £10 eat as much as you like, incl two
glasses of wine or sangria. **Credit** MC, V.
The fantastic, family-oriented Elche has been delivering some
of London's most imaginative Spanish food for more than a
decade now. The all-you-can-eat Sunday buffet is a great bet
for the whole family. Children eat half price and get plenty of
fuss from the staff. A great local.
Buggy access. Reduced-price Sunday buffet. High chairs.
Tables outdoors (3, pavement).

Elephant Royale

Locke's Wharf, Westferry Road, E14 (7987 7999). Island
Gardens DLR. **Meals served** noon-10pm Mon-Thur;
noon-10.30pm Fri, Sat; noon-10pm Sun. **Main courses**
£4.80-£19.50. **Set buffet** £14.50; £7.25 children (Sun).
Credit AmEx, JCB, MC, V.
A swish new Docklands Thai, with a fabulous site overlooking the *Cutty Sark* across the river. During the week business
people in suits rule the roost, but the Sunday buffet is made
for families. The friendly staff, a big ground-level fish tank
full of carp and an outdoor terrace where children can let off
steam are further pluses.
High chairs. Tables outdoors (16, terrace).

Faulkner's

424-6 Kingsland Road, E8 (7254 6152). Dalston
Kingsland rail/67, 76, 149, 242, 243 bus. **Lunch served**
noon-2pm Mon-Fri. **Dinner served** 5-10pm Mon-Thur;
4.15-10pm Fri. **Meals served** 11.30am-10pm Sat; noon-
9.30pm Sun. **Main courses** £7.50-£13. **Minimum** £4.
Credit MC, V.
You may feel as if you've been transported back to the East
End of the 1950s, but the fish and chips here are pretty good.
After that, try the trifle, apple pie or ice-cream for dessert.
Booking is advisable.
Buggy access. Children's menu. High chairs.

Hadley House
*27 High Street, E11 (8989 8855). Snaresbrook or
Wanstead tube.* **Lunch served** 11.30am-2.30pm Mon-Sat;
noon-9pm Sun. **Dinner served** 7-10.30pm Mon-Sat.
Main courses £8.50-£15.95. **Set dinner** (Mon) £16.50
three courses. **Credit** MC, V.
Hadley House offers imaginative, affordable food in generous
portions in an attractive and comfortable setting. Meat and
fish are always top quality, and desserts, such as raspberry
crème brûlée and warm tarte tatin with excellent cinnamon
ice-cream, are divine. This is a popular place for families, and
chefs will prepare reduce-priced portions for children.
*Buggy access. High chairs. Reduced-price children's
portions. Tables outdoors (6, patio).*

Jones Dairy Café
23 Ezra Street, E2 (7739 5372). Bus 26, 48, 55. **Open**
9am-3pm Thur-Sat; 8am-2pm Sun. **No credit cards**.
Jones is busiest on Sunday mornings when visitors to nearby Columbia Road flower market can pop in for bagels,
platzels, organic buns or cakes. On other days, diners sit down
to brunch-style food (omelettes, scrambled egg and smoked
salmon, tomatoes on toast) served at a leisurely pace. A pleasantly old-fashioned place.
Buggy access. High chairs. No smoking.

Viet Hoa
*70-72 Kingsland Road, E2 (7729 8293). Bus 26, 48, 55,
67, 149, 242, 243.* **Lunch served** noon-3.30pm, **dinner
served** 5.30-11pm daily. **Main courses** £2.15-£6.90.
Credit MC, V.
This popular café continues to pack in a huge influx of non-
Vietnamese hipsters alongside a smattering of Vietnamese
families. Upstairs, checked tablecloths and spacious canteen
seating contribute to an atmosphere that's as mellow as the
bossa nova background music. Downstairs, waiters in bow-
ties and waistcoats add a touch of formality. Prices are reasonable and the Vietnamese food made for sharing.
Buggy access. No-smoking tables.

South-east London

Joanna's
56 Westow Hill, SE19 (8670 4052). Crystal Palace rail.
Meals served 10am-11pm Mon-Sat; 10am-10.15pm Sun.
Main courses £7.95-£15.50. **Credit** AmEx, DC, MC, V.
The smiley staff are perfectly behaved towards young diners
in this local brasserie, where the antique fittings lend a snug,
reliable atmosphere. The children's menu is available every
day, and the burgers it lists are own-made and juicy. We trust
the chicken, pasta and sausage options are as delicious. A
bowl of ice-cream is included in the price. Adult options are
freshly prepared and generously proportioned.
*Buggy access. Children's menu (£3.75). Crayons.
No-smoking tables. Tables outdoors (5, pavement).*

Olley's
*67-9 Norwood Road, SE24 (8671 8259). Herne Hill rail/
3, 68 bus.* **Meals served** noon-10.30pm Tue-Sat.
Dinner served 5-10.30pm Mon, Sun. **Main courses**
£7.65-£18.25. **Credit** AmEx, MC, V.
Dreamy fish and chips, with grilled and steamed options for
the more health-conscious. Add to this a great wine list, great
coffees, complimentary crudités with dips and a genuinely
welcoming atmosphere, and the idea of a great meal out at
the chippie no longer seems so far-fetched.
Buggy access. Children's menu. High chairs.

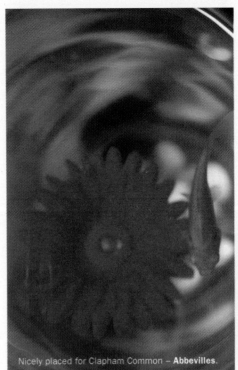

Nicely placed for Clapham Common – **Abbevilles**.

Pizzeria Castello
*20 Walworth Road, SE1 (7703 2556). Elephant & Castle
tube/rail.* **Meals served** noon-11pm Mon-Thur; noon-
11.30pm Fri; 5-11.30pm Sat. **Main courses** £4.30-£9.80.
Credit AmEx, MC, V.
You'll get a warm welcome at Pizzeria Castello, whose gar-
licky cuisine scents the Elephant & Castle every evening. The
menu displays a fairly standard selection of pizza, pasta and
basic Italian meat and fish dishes, but the service is very
friendly and it's popular with locals. Booking is advisable.
Buggy access. High chairs.

South-west London

Abbevilles
*88 Clapham Park Road, SW4 (7498 2185). Clapham
Common tube/35, 37 bus.* **Meals served** 9.30am-3.30pm
Mon-Fri. **Main courses** £5. **No credit cards**.
Set up as a charitable trust to give work experience to people
with learning difficulties, Abbevilles produces beautifully
presented dishes in simple, well-designed surroundings – all
at a budget price. A set menu includes barbecue ribs and roast
vegetable pasta; children's portions are always available.
Buggy access. High chairs. Tables outdoors (6, garden).

Boiled Egg & Soldiers
*63 Northcote Road, SW11 (7223 4894). Clapham
Junction rail.* **Open** 9am-6pm Mon, Tue; 9am-6pm,
7-11pm Wed-Sat; 10am-5pm Sun. **No credit cards**.

Ice-cream dreams

Arte Gelato

Golders Hill Refreshment House, off North End Way, NW3 (8455 8010). Golders Green or Hampstead tube. **Open** *10am-sunset daily.* **No credit cards**.

Mr Pazienti not only makes all his own ice-cream, but he grows the ingredients for the fruity ones, too. Visit in summer and you'll taste his black-berries, strawberries and raspberries in your cornet. All his ice-creams (22 flavours in summer, 15 in winter) are preservative-free, and some come in exotic flavours (marron glacé, for example). It's only £1 a scoop, so it's worth having two. Vegetarian meals are served, too. *Buggy access. High chairs.*

The Fountain

Ground floor, Fortnum & Mason, 181 Piccadilly, W1 (7734 8040). Piccadilly Circus tube. **Open** *8am-6pm Mon-Sat.* **Ice-creams served** *8-11.30am; 3-6pm Mon-Sat.* **Credit** AmEx, MC, V. **Map** p318 J7.

This ornate summer room has decor that suggests the store's days-of-empire beginnings. Its menu lists the most decadent of ice-cream options (from £4.75), all presented beautifully. These are big treats: the Piccadilly Poppet is a confection of coffee ice-cream with chocolate sauce and meringues; Lazy Sundaes Afternoon is an ice-cream, strawberries, cream and scone ensemble. The children's lunch menu lists wholesome fare: Welsh rarebit, sausage and mash, haddock and chips, or chicken goujons. *Children's menu (£4.25). Crayons. Nappy-changing facilities.*

Häagen-Dazs on the Square

14 Leicester Square, WC2 (7287 9577). Leicester Square tube. **Open** *Winter 10am-midnight Mon-Wed, Sun; 9am-2am Thur-Sat. Summer 9am-1am Mon-Wed Sun; 9am-2am Thur-Sat.* **Credit** AmEx, MC, V. **Map** p319 K7.

A myriad of chocolatey, nutty and fruity flavours, plus toppings galore (Belgian chocolate sauce, nut crunch, maple syrup, strawberry coulis – to name but a few). Two scoops plus two toppings are £4.20; four scoops with two toppings £5.90. There are sundaes, too (Cookie Crunch is cookies and cream ice-cream with chunks of cookie, hot chocolate fudge sauce, whipped cream and chocolate vermicelli). Pure indulgence. *High chairs. Nappy-changing facilities. No smoking.* **Branches**: 75 Hampstead High Street, NW3 (7431 1430); 83 Gloucester Road, SW7 (7373 9988); 88 Queensway, W2 (7229 0668); Unit 6, Covent Garden Piazza, WC2 (7240 0436).

Marine Ices

8 Haverstock Hill, NW3 (7482 9003). Chalk Farm tube. **Open** *10.30am-11pm Mon-Sat; 11am-10pm Sun.* **Credit** MC, V.

Light, creamy, Italian-style ice-cream served in a kaleidoscope of flavours, all at £1.30 a scoop. There is also a range of sundaes, plus milkshakes (£2.15). We like the ice-cream and love the old-fashioned Italian atmosphere. Lunches are available, too. A *Time Out* favourite. *Buggy access. High chairs.*

Regent Milk Bar

362 Edgware Road, W2 (7723 8669). Edgware Road tube. **Open** *7.30am-5pm Mon-Sat.* **No credit cards**. **Map** p313 E4.

This is the ice-cream parlour to visit if you're a fan of retro furnishings. The ice-creams are a bargain, too, at only 80p a scoop. There are traditional sundaes as well, including knickerbocker glory and banana split, and a selection of milkshakes (£1.50). *Buggy access.*

For Idaho, see p178.

A popular hangout for local families (it's sometimes very noisy), with gentrified caff food the order of the day. The children's menu is a scaled-down version of the adults' version, including boiled egg and soldiers (of course), or just soldiers with, say, baked beans, cheese or marmite. There are also salads and baked potatoes with numerous fillings. *Buggy access. Children's menu. High chairs. Tables outdoors (3, pavement; 8, garden).*

Canyon

Riverside, near Richmond Bridge, Richmond, Surrey (8948 2944/www.canyonfood.co.uk). Richmond tube/rail. **Brunch served** *11am-4pm Sat, Sun.* **Lunch served** *noon-4pm Mon-Fri.* **Dinner served** *6-11pm daily.* **Main courses** £9-£16. **Credit** AmEx, MC, V.

One of the best spots in London for alfresco dining, Canyon is like a chunk of California transplanted on to the Thames: the heated terrace makes it equally pleasant in winter and summer. Part of the Montana/Dakota family, it's a smart affair but very welcoming to children, with balloons, crayons and pictures to colour in. And everyone will enjoy the contemporary American food. For **Idaho**, see *p178*.

Balloons. Buggy access. Children's menu (£4, desserts £2). Crayons. High chairs. Tables outdoors (18, courtyard; 18, terrace). **Branches**: **Montana** 125 Dawes, SW6 (7385 9500); **Dakota** 127 Ledbury Road, W11 (7792 9191); **Utah** 18 High Street, SW19 (8944 1909).

Deli-Organic

60 Northcote Road, SW11 (7585 0344). Clapham Junction rail. **Meals served** *8am-7pm Mon-Fri; 9am-6pm Sat.* **Credit** MC, V.

A very pleasant, exceptionally friendly café and deli on the family-friendly Northcote Road, close to **Boiled Egg & Soldiers** (*see p181*). Food is strictly organic and sourced each day, so what's on the Mediterranean-slanted menu depends on what's available. The place is very child-friendly, and often has the usual coterie of Nappy Valley families tucking into cheese or egg on toast. There are also defrosted food cubes for the tots and a nice line in sculpted platters for the older ones. *Buggy access. Children's menus. Nappy-changing facilities. No smoking. Tables outdoors (2, pavement).*

The Depot

Tideway Yard, Mortlake High Street, SW14 (8878 9462).
Mortlake rail/209 bus. **Open** 10am-11pm Mon-Sat; 10am-
10.30pm Sun. **Lunch served** noon-3pm, **dinner served**
6-11pm Mon-Sat. **Meals served** noon-10.30pm Sun.
Main courses £9.95-£13.50. **Set meal** (Mon-Sat lunch,
all day Sun) £9.95 two courses. **Credit** AmEx, DC, MC, V.
The Depot has a great view of the Thames, and a varied seasonal menu, but it does get pretty busy with braying Barnes
locals. Kids can choose from the usual pasta, chicken and
chips and sausage and mash, and ice-cream for dessert.
Buggy access. Children's menu (£3.50, desserts £1.90).
Crayons and books. High chairs. No-smoking tables.
Tables outdoors (6, patio).

Don Fernando's

27F The Quadrant, Richmond, Surrey (8948 6447/
www.donfernandos.co.uk). Richmond tube/rail. **Meals**
served noon-3pm, 6-11pm Mon, Tue; noon-11pm Wed-Sat;
noon-10pm Sun. **Main courses** £8-£13. **Tapas** £3-£5.
Set meals £14-£18 two courses. **Credit** AmEx, MC, V.
Andalusian food is the forte of this family-run enterprise,
served in a long room with terracotta floor, Spanish wall
tiles and pottery. There's a 48-dish tapas menu, so even the
fussiest of eaters will find something to their fancy.
Buggy access. High chairs. No-smoking tables.

Grrrrreat stir-fries at **Tiger Lil's**. *See p180.*

West London

Coyote Café

2 Fauconberg Road, W4 (8742 8545). Chiswick Park
tube/Gunnersbury tube/rail. **Brunch served** 11am-4pm
Sat, Sun. **Lunch served** 11am-4pm Fri-Sun. **Dinner**
served 5-11pm Mon-Sat; 5-10.30pm Sun. **Main courses**
£3.95-£12.75. **Credit** AmEx, MC, V.
Louder than a pack of howling coyotes, this charming
bar/restaurant serves excellent Tex Mex food – but the
acoustics, and a boisterous crowd, mean the place gets very
noisy. The salads are big and beautiful, and the nachos fabulous, as are the meat dishes. Kids get to choose from nachos,
a mini-burger, chicken fingers and fish and chips (£2.95-
£4.95), and are welcome until 8pm.
Buggy access. Children's menu.

Geales

2 Farmer Street, W8 (7727 7528). Notting Hill Gate
tube. **Lunch served** noon-3pm Mon-Sat. **Dinner served**
6-11pm Mon-Sat; 6-10.30pm Sun. **Main courses** £7.25-
£11.50. **Credit** AmEx, MC, V. **Map** p312 A7.
Not a budget place but, for quality fish and chips, you'd be
hard pressed to find better: the batter is light as a feather, the
fish is fresh and delicious, chips are nice and crispy, and portions are massive. Puddings, such as treacle tart and apple
crumble, are excellent, too. A smart, but great, chippie.
Buggy access. High chairs. Tables outdoors (4, pavement).

Isfahan

3-4 Bouverie Place, W2 (7460 1030). Edgware Road tube/
Paddington tube/rail. **Meals served** noon-midnight daily.
Main courses £4.95-£7.90. **Set lunch** (noon-5pm) £9.95
two courses incl a drink. **Credit** MC, V. **Map** p313 E6.
This Persian restaurant has a great all-you-can-eat lunchtime
buffet – excellent value at just £5.95, and perfect for growing
kids. And if you visit in the evening, you can enjoy your food
over musical entertainment.
Buggy access. High chairs. Reduced-price children's
portions. Tables outdoors (10, pavement).

Julie's

135-7 Portland Road, W11 (7229 8331/
www.juliesrestaurant.com). Holland Park tube.
Wine bar **Open** 9am-11pm Mon-Sat; 9am-10pm Sun.
Lunch served 12.30-2.45pm Mon-Sat; 12.30-3.30pm
Sun. **Afternoon tea** served 3-7.30pm daily. **Dinner**
served 7.30-11pm Mon-Sat; 7.30-10pm Sun. **Main**
courses £8.50-£13. *Restaurant* **Lunch served**
12.30-2.45pm Mon-Fri; 12.30-3pm Sun. **Dinner served**
7-11.30pm Mon-Sat; 7-10.30pm Sun. **Main courses** £13-
£21. *Both* **House wine** £15 bottle, £4 glass. **Credit**
AmEx, MC, V.
A bohemian-looking, many-roomed restaurant and wine bar
that deserves a mention for its sanity-saving Sunday
lunchtime crèche. If your children eat from the kids' menu
(£9.50, including main course, sorbet or ice-cream and drink)
in the wine bar or restaurant, then the crèche is free; otherwise there is a nominal charge. Parents can enjoy organic food
that includes the likes of chilled gazpacho with flaked roast
almonds, sausages with mash and kidney bean tagine, and
chicken, celeriac and leek pie.
Buggy access. Children's set meal (Sun; £9.50). Crèche
(noon-3.30pm Sun). High chairs. Tables outdoors
(12, pavement).

Nectar

Tabernacle Arts Centre, Powis Square, W11 (7565 7808).
Ladbroke Grove, Notting Hill Gate or Westbourne Park
tube. **Meals served** 8.30am-11pm Mon-Sat; 10am-5pm
Sun. **Credit** AmEx, MC, V. **Map** p312 A6.
This chilled out, modern café is a popular hangout for trendy
young families. The menu provides a suitably eclectic choice
of great-value, tasty dishes, served in huge portions. Kids
can have special own-made burgers, cottage pie and meat or
vegetarian rotis (£2); anything from the main menu can be
prepared in small portions for half the price. To find Nectar
(it's tucked away), go through the wrought iron gates of the
Tabernacle Arts Centre.
Buggy access. Children's menu. High chairs. Tables
outdoors (5, pavement).

The chain gang

The restaurant chains listed below are well known, both for family-friendliness and the popularity of their menus with the young set. We've listed our favourite central London branch of each, but you'll find the food identical at all the branches, although decor and facilities may vary.

Bierodrome

173-4 Upper Street, N1 (7226 5835/ www.belgorestaurants.co.uk). Angel tube/ Highbury & Islington tube/rail. **Open** noon-midnight daily. **Lunch served** noon-3pm, dinner served 6-11pm Mon-Fri. **Meals served** noon-11pm Sat; noon-10.30pm Sun. **Main courses** £7.95-£10.95. **Credit** AmEx, DC, MC, V.

A huge range of beers and heavy fish- or meat-based food will keep parents happy, not to mention the fact that under-12s can eat for free from the carte (provided there's one adult for every two little ones). *Children's menu; under-12s eat free. Colouring books. High chairs. Tables outdoors (4, pavement).*

Café Flo

11-12 Haymarket, SW1 (7976 1313). Piccadilly Circus tube. **Open** 10am-11pm daily. **Breakfast served** 10am-noon daily. **Meals served** noon-11pm daily. **Main courses** £7.50-£15. **Set meal** £9.90 two courses. **Credit** AmEx, MC, V. **Map** p319 K7.

Kids at Café Flo have the choice of spaghetti in tomato sauce, sausage and mash or chicken and chips – served with a drink and dessert. *Buggy access. Children's menu (£5.95). No-smoking tables.*

Café Pasta

184 Shaftesbury Avenue, WC2 (7379 0198). Covent Garden tube. **Meals served** noon-11.30pm Mon-Sat; noon-11pm Sun. **Main courses** £4.95-£11.95. **Credit** AmEx, DC, MC, V. **Map** p317 K6.

Pretty much everything you'd expect from the pasta arm of Pizza Express. The same laid-back

Strada. *See p185.*

atmosphere attracts a nice mix of punters, from boozy suits to canny families, and the food is generally reliable and reasonably priced. *Buggy access. High chairs.*

Café Rouge

Hays Galleria, 3 Tooley Street, SE1 (7378 0097). London Bridge tube/rail. **Meals served** 10am-10pm Mon-Fri; noon-6pm Sat, Sun. **Main courses** £5.95-£10.25. **Credit** AmEx, DC, MC, V. **Map** p321 Q8.

Café Rouge is a safe bet for dining with kids. Staff are usually friendly, and the food on the children's menu is really quite good (chicken goujons, for example, appear to be made from whole pieces of chicken with real herbs). *Buggy access. Children's menu (£3.95). High chairs. No-smoking tables. Tables outdoors (150, terrace).*

fish!

3B Belvedere Road, SE1 (7234 3333/ www.fishdiner.co.uk). Waterloo tube/rail. **Meals served** 11.30am-10.30pm Mon-Sat; noon-10pm Sun. **Main courses** £8.50-£16.95. **Set meal** £9.95 two courses. **Credit** AmEx, DC, MC, V. **Map** p319 M8.

While parents can choose from a list of fresh fish, have it steamed or grilled, and match it with a choice of sauces, kids can enjoy spaghetti tuna bolognese, fish and chips and so on, with ice-cream or fruit salad, plus games and colouring pens. *Buggy access. Children's menu (£7.95). High chairs. Tables outdoors (9, pavement).*

ITS

60 Wigmore Street, W1 (7224 3484). Bond Street tube. **Meals served** noon-midnight daily. **Main courses** £4.60-£9.30. **Credit** AmEx, DC, MC, V. **Map** p316 G6.

A large outlet of the small and popular pizza and pasta chain. Pizzas are particularly good. A useful escape route from the Oxford Street hordes. *Buggy access. High chairs. No-smoking tables. Tables outdoors (4, pavement).*

Nando's

324 Upper Street, N1 (7288 0254/ www.nandos.co.uk). Angel tube/Highbury & Islington tube/rail. **Meals served** noon-11.30pm Mon-Thur, Sun; noon-midnight Fri, Sat. **Main courses** £4.90-£6.95. **Credit** DC, MC.

Terracotta walls, clay-tiled floors and wooden furniture create a homely atmosphere in this branch of the cod-Portuguese chain. Barbecued chicken is the thing here – adults can have it cooked in four different sauces, with a variety of accompaniments. Children have a choice of three meals: burger, chicken wings or chicken strips. Each includes chips and frozen yoghurt for dessert. *Buggy access. Children's menu (£3.95). High chairs. No-smoking tables.*

Pizza Express.

Pizza Express

9-12 Bow Street, WC2 (7240 3443). Covent Garden or Holborn tube. **Meals served** 11.30am-midnight daily. **Main courses** £4.95-£7.80. **Credit** AmEx, DC, MC, V. **Map** p317 L6.
With accusations that the pizzas are smaller (or have we got bigger?) and with increased competition, the crown does not sit so easily on the king's head these days, but Pizza Express remains a very popular spot for families. There are no special meals for children, but the vibe remains kid-friendly.
Buggy access. High chairs. No-smoking tables.

Strada

8-10 Exmouth Market, EC1 (7278 0800). Farringdon tube/rail. **Meals served** noon-11pm Mon-Sat; noon-10.30pm Sun. **Main courses** £4.95-£12.95. **Credit** AmEx, MC, V. **Map** p317 M4.
An invention of the mussel-bound Belgo Group, Strada is great for quality, yet affordable, pizza cooked in wood-fired ovens, plus a range of decent risottos and pasta dishes. Although there's no special menu for children, the famous Italian hospitality and comfy banquette seats make for an unhurried and family-friendly dining experience.
Buggy access. Tables outdoors (5, patio).

Wok Wok

7 Kensington High Street, W8 (7938 1221). High Street Kensington tube. **Meals served** noon-11pm Mon-Wed; noon-midnight Thur-Sat. **Dinner served** 5.30-10.30pm Sun. **Main courses** £5.95-£11.95. **Set lunch** (Mon-Fri) £6.95 two courses. **Set meals** £14.50-£19.20 per person (minimum six). **Credit** AmEx, DC, MC, V. **Map** p314 B9.
A western take on oriental food, with offerings from Malaysia, Thailand and Vietnam. It's a great place to take the family for a cheap bite: kids have a wider-than-usual choice, including chicken satay and spring rolls, served with fries, a soft drink and ice-cream.
Buggy access. Children's menu (£3.95). High chairs.

Yellow River Café

206 Upper Street, N1 (7354 8833). Angel tube/Highbury & Islington tube/rail/4, 19, 30, 43 bus. **Lunch served** noon-3pm Mon-Sat. **Dinner served** 5.30-11pm Mon-Wed; 5.30-

11.30pm Thur-Sat. **Meals served** noon-10.30pm Sun. **Main courses** £5.50-£9.50. Bento box £11.80. **Credit** AmEx, DC, MC, V.
The big restaurant upstairs and elegantly sweeping bar below guarantee enough space to swing a toddler or two. Bento boxes allow parents a choice of starter, main and soup for £11.80, while meals for kids include wun tuns and oriental meatballs. Good value, fresh ingredients and child-sized chopsticks ensure lasting appeal.
Buggy access. Children's menu (£5.45). High chairs. No-smoking tables. Toys.

Yo! Sushi

52 Poland Street, W1 (7287 0443/ www.yosushi.co.uk). Leicester Square, Oxford Circus or Piccadilly Circus tube. **Meals served** noon-midnight daily. **Credit** AmEx, DC, MC, V. **Map** p316 J6.
Colourful dishes, a robotic drinks trolley and a conveyor belt for the food make this a culinary adventure playground for kids. Special easy-to-use chopsticks and clip-on baby seats make it family-friendly, and the kids' menu includes fish fingers, vegetable noodles and chicken teriyaki. Children can also have a small version of anything off the conveyor belt for just £1.
Balloons and stickers. Booster seats. Reduced-price children's portions.

Yo! Sushi

Top: Fast food

Ed's Easy Diner
See p175.

Hard Rock Café
See p175.

Maxwell's
See p172.

Planet Hollywood
See p176.

TGI Friday's
See p173.

Red Pepper
8 Formosa Street, W9 (7266 2708). Warwick Avenue tube. **Lunch served** 12.30-2.30pm Sat; 12.30-3.30pm Sun. **Dinner served** 6.30-10.45pm Mon-Sat; 6.30-10.30pm Sun. **Main courses** £12.50-£15. **Credit** MC, V.
A popular restaurant with aspirations to be more than just a pizza parlour (daily specials include seared swordfish and tuna steak). A good weekend family lunch spot. Part of the same group as **Purple Sage** (*see p177*).
Booking advisable. Tables outdoors (5, pavement).

Rodizio Rico
111 Westbourne Grove, W2 (7792 4035). Bayswater or Notting Hill Gate tube. **Lunch served** 12.30-4.30pm Sat. **Dinner served** 6.30-11.30pm Mon-Sat. **Meals served** 1-11.30pm Sun. **Set buffet meal** £11.50 (vegetarian), £17.70. **Credit** MC, V. **Map** p312 B6.
Forget the weather and tuck into gutsy grills at this hacienda-style Brazilian joint. In the absence of a menu, you load up

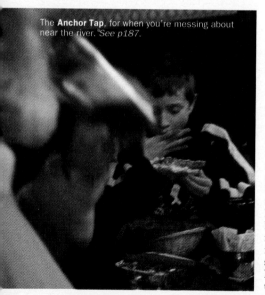

The **Anchor Tap**, for when you're messing about near the river. *See p187.*

at the buffet, choosing between 'meat' or 'vegetarian' options. Throughout the meal, waiters patrol with metre-long skewers, pausing to ply you with tender chunks of chicken, beef, pork ribs, ham and blood-rare Brazilian rump steak. Booking is essential for dinner.
Buggy access. High chairs. Tables outdoors (6, pavement).

Sausage & Mash Café
268 Portobello Road, W10 (8968 8898). Ladbroke Grove tube. **Meals served** 11am-10pm Tue-Sun. **Main courses** £2.50-£7. **Credit** MC, V.
For some excellent comfort food, take the family to this trendy little west London dive. It's cheap, it's cheerful and the creamy spuds and char-grilled bangers, doused in a thick brown gravy flavoured with plenty of wine and onion, are dreamy. For kids there's a set meal of chipolatas, mash, gravy and baked beans. Desserts are a little disappointing: stick to the sausages.
Buggy access. High chairs. Children's set meal (£3.50).

Sticky Fingers
1A Phillimore Gardens, W8 (7938 5338/ www.stickyfingers.co.uk). High Street Kensington tube. *Bar* **Open** noon-8pm Mon-Sat. *Restaurant* **Meals served** noon-11pm daily. **Main courses** £8.45-£15.95. **Credit** AmEx, DC, MC, V. **Map** p314 A9.
Bill Wyman is part owner of this place, a sort of Hard Rock Café for those who consider themselves slightly too cool for that sort of thing. The menu is nouveau burger bar; food is adequate. For kids there are the usual burgers, pasta and chicken nuggets. And if mum or dad is feeling generous, kids might get a logo T-shirt (£7.95) or baseball cap (£8.95).
Buggy access. Children's menu (£6.45). Entertainment (magician or face-painting 1-3pm Sun). High chairs.

Tootsies
120 Holland Park Avenue, W11 (7229 8567). Holland Park tube. **Meals served** 9am-11pm Mon-Thur, Sun; 9am-11pm Fri-Sat. **Main courses** £5.50-£9.50. **Credit** AmEx, MC, V.
Tootsies is an elegant version of casual American dining. And its ('famous, award-winning') burger actually lives up to the hype. Children can have mini (3oz) cheeseburger, sausage and mash and a salmon fish cake among other staples (all around £3.75), and ice-cream or banana split (from £1.50) for dessert. Or why not opt for the hand-blended, fresh banana milkshake. Heavenly.
Buggy access. Children's menu. Crayons. High chairs. No-smoking tables. Tables outdoors (4, pavement).

Pubs

Child-friendly pubs are big business these days. In the same way that restaurants are finding they must cater for children's needs to attract weekend customers, more and more pubs are introducing kids' menus, high chairs and nappy-changing facilities. Groups such as Charlie Chalk, Brewers Fare, Wacky Warehouse, Big Steak and Fullers have fairly generic pubs that serve up chicken nuggets for the children along with the pints. But if you're looking for something different, gastropubs such as the **Engineer**, **Lansdowne** and **Prince Bonaparte** (for all, *see pp187-189*) offer more upmarket food *and* a warm welcome for kids.

And the **Bierodrome** bar/restaurants (*see p184*), owned by the same people behind Belgo, offer an unbeatable selection of beers along with good food and facilities for children.

No matter how warm the welcome, families will still have to contend with Britain's archaic licensing laws, of course. Unless a pub has a children's licence (and the majority don't), you'll usually be restricted to certain parts of the pub, such as a family room or restaurant area.

Southwark & Bankside

Fire Station
150 Waterloo Road, SE1 (7620 2226). Waterloo tube/ rail. **Open** *11am-11pm Mon-Sat; noon-10.30pm Sun.* **Food served** *noon-11pm Mon-Sat; noon-9.30pm Sun.* **Credit** AmEx, DC, MC, V. **Map** p320 N8.
This isn't a good place for children during the week, when it's busy with after-work drinkers, but there's a kids' menu on Sunday, when the pace slows and atmosphere mellows.
Buggy access. Children's menu (Sun lunch; £4.95). High chairs.

The City

Anchor Tap
20A Horsleydown Lane, SE1 (7403 4637). Tower Hill tube/London Bridge tube/rail/Tower Gateway DLR. **Open** *11am-11pm Mon-Sat; noon-10.30pm Sun.* **Food served** *noon-9pm Mon-Sat; noon-5pm Sun.* **Credit** MC, V. **Map** p321 R8.
Warren-like old pub within the shadow of Tower Bridge. Children are allowed in the pub until 9pm – they can stay even later in the beer garden.
Buggy access. Children's main courses (£3.50). Garden. High chairs. No-smoking room in restaurant.

Dickens Inn
St Katherine's Way, E1 (7488 2208). Tower Hill tube/ Tower Gateway DLR. **Open** *11am-11pm Mon-Sat; noon-10.30pm Sun.* **Food served** *noon-4pm Mon-Fri noon-6pm Sat, Sun.* **Credit** AmEx, DC, MC, V. **Map** p321 S8.
A large old waterside pub with a pizzeria and traditional British restaurant attached (where children are welcome at any time). Kids' meals are around £3.
Buggy access. High chairs. Nappy-changing facilities. Reduced-price children's portions.

Covent Garden & St Giles's

Marquis of Granby
51 Chandos Place, WC2 (7836 7657). Covent Garden, Embankment or Leicester Square tube/Charing Cross tube/rail. **Open** *noon-11pm Mon-Sat; noon-10.30pm Sun.* **Food served** *noon-5pm daily.* **Credit** MC, V. **Map** p319 L7.
Kids are welcome until 7pm at this traditional, good-looking Victorian pub. On Sundays there's even the attraction of a roast at lunchtime.
Buggy access. Reduced-price children's portions (from £3).

The **Old Dairy** – part pub, part brasserie. *See p188.*

Junior Consumers

Kensington & Chelsea

Cadogan Arms
298 King's Road, SW3 (7352 1645). Sloane Square tube then 11, 19, 22 bus. **Open/food served** *11am-11pm Mon-Sat; noon-10.30pm Sun.* **Credit** AmEx, MC, V. **Map** p315 E12.
A traditional London pub with oak beams and log fires, and plenty of little nooks and crannies to hide away in. Children are welcome until 8pm. The menu lists burgers, chicken kiev and sausages and chips.
Buggy access. Reduced-price children's portions (from £2).

North London

Engineer
65 Gloucester Avenue, NW1 (7722 0950). Camden Town or Chalk Farm tube/C2 bus. **Open** *9am-11pm Mon-Sat; 9am-10.30pm Sun.* **Food served** *9-11.30am, 12.30-3pm, 7-10.30pm Mon-Sat; 9-11.30am, 12.30-3.30pm, 7-10pm Sun.* **Credit** MC, V.
No chicken nuggets here: the lucky kids at this gastropub get the likes of penne with plum tomatoes, cod tempura or organic sausages – and they're welcome in the evening as well as at lunchtime. Unsurprisingly, the place gets very busy, so booking is essential.
Buggy access. Children's menu (noon-3pm daily). Colouring books and crayons. Garden. High chairs. Nappy-changing facilities.

Best: Kids eat free

Belgo Centraal
Under-12s eat free at the mussel maestro.
See p171.

Bierodrome
Two children (under 12), one adult – and only the grown-up pays to eat à la carte. *See p184.*

Big Easy
USA-style generosity, as under-tens have free range of the menu. *See p173.*

TGI Fridays
Organix baby food is the freebie at TGI's.
See p173.

Tiger Lil's
As much stir-fry as an under-five can manage.
See p180.

Freemason's Arms
32 Downshire Hill, NW3 (7433 6811). Belsize Park or Hampstead tube/Hampstead Heath rail. **Open** noon-11pm Mon-Sat; noon-10.30pm Sun. **Food served** noon-10pm Mon-Sat; noon-9pm Sun. **Credit** MC, V.
This 1930s pub has a family area with a no-smoking section as well as a beer garden, plus half-portions of pasta, scampi, and so on. Children are welcome until 9pm. The garden is big, so there's plenty of room to run around in.
Buggy access. Family area. Garden. Nappy-changing facilities. Reduced-price children's portions (£3).

Lansdowne
90 Gloucester Avenue, NW1 (7483 0409). Chalk Farm tube/31, 168 bus. **Open** 7-11pm Mon; noon-11pm Tue-Sat; noon-4pm, 7-10.30pm Sun. **Food served** 7-10pm Mon-Sat; 1-2.30pm, 7-10pm Sun. **Credit** MC, V.
Another Primrose Hill gastropub that welcomes kids. Half-portions are available from a menu including home-made burgers, pasta dishes and soup. No restriction on hours.
Buggy access. High chairs. Nappy-changing facilities. Reduced-price children's portions.

Old Dairy
1-3 Crouch Hill, N4 (7263 3337). Finsbury Park tube/rail/Crouch Hill rail. **Open** 11am-11pm Mon-Sat; noon-10.30pm Sun. **Food served** 11am-9pm daily. **Credit** AmEx, MC, V.
A life-sized model of a cow and a farmer will help keep the kids amused. Children admitted until 6pm.
Buggy access. Children's menu (Sun; £2.50-£4.50). High chairs. Reduced-price children's portions.

Shillibeers
Carpenter Mews, North Road, N7 (7700 1858). Caledonian Road tube. **Open** noon-midnight Mon-Thur; noon-2am Fri; 6pm-2am Sat. **Food served** noon-3pm, 6-10pm Mon-Sat. **Credit** AmEx, MC, V.
In the same complex as the Unicorn Children's Theatre (*see p227*). Children's menus feature potato wedges, soup, nuggets and so on. Kids welcome until 10pm.
Buggy access. Children's menu (£3.50). High chairs.

The Woodman
128 Bourne Hill, N13 (8882 0294). Southgate tube/W9 bus. **Open** 11am-11pm Mon-Sat; noon-10.30pm Sun. **Food served** noon-3pm, 6-9pm Mon-Sat; noon-3pm Sun. **Credit** AmEx, MC, V.
The pub has a climbing frame, but the neighbouring park is the main draw for families. Half-portions of Sunday roast are available. The witching hour for kids is 9pm.
Buggy access. Garden. High chairs. Reduced-price children's portions (£4).

South-east London

Ashburnham Arms
25 Ashburnham Grove, SE10 (8692 2007). Greenwich rail/DLR. **Open** noon-3.30pm, 6-11pm Mon-Sat; noon-3.30pm, 7-10.30pm Sun. **Food served** noon-2.30pm, 6-8.30pm Tue-Fri; noon-2.30pm Sat, Sun. **Credit** (food only) MC, V.
The Ashburnham Arms boasts a garden with a slide and play equipment, with a conservatory for chillier weather. Part of the pub is open to children until closing time.
Buggy access. Garden. Reduced-price children's portions.

Crown & Greyhound
73 Dulwich Village, SE21 (8693 2466). North Dulwich rail. **Open** 11am-11pm Mon-Sat; noon-10.30pm Sun. **Food served** noon-2.30pm, 5.30-10pm Mon-Sat; noon-3pm Sun. **Credit** MC, V.
Large garden with a sandpit and play equipment. There is also a no-smoking section in the restaurant, with crayons and colouring books.

The **Hope & Anchor** – a beer garden in the heart of Brixton. *See p189.*

*Buggy access. Children's menu (from 6pm, £3.25).
Crayons. Garden. High chairs. Nappy-changing facilities.
Play area.*

Cutty Sark
*Ballast Quay, off Lassell Street, SE10 (8858 3146).
Greenwich rail/DLR/Maze Hill rail.* **Open** 11am-11pm
Mon-Sat; noon-10.30pm Sun. **Food served** noon-9pm
Mon-Sat; noon-7pm Sun. **Credit** MC, V.
There's a small riverside terrace at the Cutty Sark, and the
upstairs restaurant offers great views. Children are allowed
to stay until 9pm.
*Children's menu (£2.75). Reduced-price
children's portions.*

South-west London

Bread & Roses
*68 Clapham Manor Street, SW4 (7498 1779). Clapham
Common or Clapham North tube.* **Open** 11am-11pm
Mon-Sat; noon-10.30pm Sun. **Food served** noon-3pm,
7-9.30pm Mon-Fri; noon-4pm (African buffet only),
6-9.30pm Sat, Sun. **Credit** MC, V.
Possibly the most child-friendly pub in London. Mother and
baby groups are held regularly on the premises, along with
a music workshop (1-5pm Sun). Children are allowed in the
back room until 9.30pm. Board games and the likes of Jenga
are available, too.
*Buggy access. Children's menu (£2.95). Family room.
High chairs. Nappy-changing facilities. Toys.*

The Castle
*115 Battersea High Street, SW11 (7228 8181/
www.thecastlebattersea.co.uk). Clapham Junction rail/
239, 344, 345 bus.* **Open** 11am-11pm Mon-Sat; noon-
10.30pm Sun. **Food served** noon-3pm Mon-Sat.
No credit cards.
Better looking on the inside than the outside, but friendly
nonetheless. There are children's portions of organic roasts
and pasta dishes on Sundays. Children are welcome until
7.30pm, and there's a large garden.
*Buggy access. Children's menu Sun (£2.75, ice-cream
£1.50). Tables outdoors (courtyard, garden).*

Hand in Hand
*6 Crooked Billet, SW19 (8946 5720). Wimbledon
tube/rail.* **Open** 11am-11pm Mon-Sat; noon-10.30pm Sun.
Food served noon-2.30pm, 7-10pm Mon-Sat; noon-
2.30pm, 7-9pm Sun. **Credit** MC, V.
Right on Wimbledon Common. Children under 14 aren't
allowed in the bar, but there is a family room where staff
request that people don't smoke (open until closing time). The
menu is unimaginative, but safe bets include ploughman's
lunches and jacket potatoes.
Buggy access. Children's menu (£2.95). Family room.

Hope & Anchor
*123 Acre Lane, SW2 (7274 1787). Clapham North
tube/Brixton tube/rail.* **Open** 11am-11pm Mon-Sat;
noon-10.30pm Sun. **Food served** noon-2.30pm, 6-9pm
Mon-Fri; noon-4pm Sat, Sun. **Credit** MC, V.
There's a large beer garden incorporating a kids' play area
with slides, tyres and climbing frames, so this is a popular
place in summer. Sunday brings half-price roasts. Children
are allowed to stay until 8pm.
*Buggy access. Play area (in garden). Reduced-price
children's portions.*

Leather Bottle
538 Garratt Lane, SW17 (8946 2309). Earlsfield rail.
Open 11am-11pm Mon-Sat; noon-10.30pm Sun. **Food
served** noon-3pm daily. **Credit** MC, V.
The Leather Bottle's attractions include a large garden with
a purpose-built play area, plus a family room where children
are welcome until 7pm.
Buggy access. Play area (in garden).

The Point
*6-18 Ritherdon Road, SW17 (8767 2660). Tooting Bec
tube/Balham tube/rail.* **Open** 10am-11pm Mon-Sat;
10am-10.30pm Sun. **Food served** 10am-10pm daily.
Credit MC, V.
More of a café-bar than a pub, with plenty of space for
kids to run around. There's a children's menu in the restaurant, where there are no time restrictions; children can stay
in the bar until 6pm.
Children's menu (£2.95). Crayons. High chairs.

West London

Drayton Court
2 The Avenue, W13 (8997 1019). West Ealing rail.
Open 11am-11pm Mon-Sat; noon-10.30pm Sun.
Food served noon-3pm, 5.30-9pm Mon-Fri; noon-
9pm Sat; noon-6pm Sun. **Credit** MC, V.
Come to Drayton Court for a huge garden with a 'jungle gym',
plus a play area with swings and climbing frames. There's
also a family room inside, with a children's menu. Children
welcome until 8pm.
*Buggy access. Children's menu (£2-£4). Play area (in
garden). Family room. Play area.*

Old Ship
25 Upper Mall, W6 (8748 2593). Hammersmith tube.
Open 10am-11pm Mon-Fri; 9am-10.30pm Sat, Sun.
Food served opening time-half an hour before closing.
Credit AmEx, MC, V.
This family-friendly riverside pub opens its doors at 9am
at weekends for all kinds of breakfast, from eggs benedict
to a full English fry-up. Food service carries on all day, with
a kids' lunch menu.
*Buggy access. Children's menu (£2.75). Garden. High
chairs. Nappy-changing facilities.*

Prince Bonaparte
*80 Chepstow Road, W2 (7313 9491). Notting Hill Gate or
Royal Oak tube/7, 28, 31, 70 bus.* **Open** noon-11pm Mon,
Wed-Sat; 5-11pm Tue; noon-10.30pm Sun. **Credit** MC, V.
Map p312 A5.
This spacious gastropub in trendy Notting Hill gets packed
out with Gap kids and their parents at weekends, but the food
is good enough to make it worth the crush. Children are wel-
come until 9pm.
Buggy access. Reduced-price children's portions.

Swan
*66 Bayswater Road, W2 (7262 5204). Lancaster Gate
tube.* **Open/food served** 10am-11pm Mon-Sat; 10am-
10.30pm Sun. **Credit** AmEx, MC, V. **Map** p313 E6.
This pub has a children's licence, which means that kids are
allowed anywhere in the pub at any time, including on the
heated terrace overlooking the park. The interior is pretty
unattractive, but it's so very handy for Hyde Park.
*Buggy access. Children's toilet. High chairs. Reduced-price
children's portions (£2.50).*

Paul Smith for Children (*& below*). See p200.

Biff (*& below*). See p196.

Shopping

Hey, little big spenders!

Life's a whirl at **Daisy & Tom**.

S mart boutiques and the more tasteful toyshops tend to be clustered around the posher parts of town. Central London, in particular the West End, is bulging with famous brands as well as lesser-known delights.

There's more to shopping for children than babygros and Start-rites, however, which is why we've also included our favourite toyshops, the kind of bike shops that can guide you through the traumatic process of buying a child's first wheels, bargain buggy and hardware shops and the city's best children's bookshops.

It goes without saying that all the places in this chapter are geared up for childish visitors. Many provide a play area for tots' retail therapy and some are so welcoming you can't drag the children away. Note, however, that not all branches of shops have the same opening hours or facilities so you might want to check before you make a special journey.

All-rounders

Daisy & Tom
181-3 King's Road, SW3 (7352 5000). Sloane Square tube then 11, 19, 22, 49 bus. **Open** 10am-6pm Mon, Tue, Thur-Sat; 10am-7pm Wed; noon-6pm Sun. **Credit** AmEx, MC, V. **Map** p315 E12.
A wide range of books is beautifully presented in a large balconied room, from which a central staircase leads up to the clothes and shoes, where the rails yield gorgeous and expensive designer labels such as Petit Bateau, Catimini and Daisy & Tom's own brand. A third room has dolls and a fourth toys, games and baby equipment. Young shoppers have plenty to occupy them, including rocking horses on the balcony, a colouring table under the big clock and a play train; when that gets too much for them they can settle down in front of a five-minute marionette show of 'Peter and the Wolf' (which runs every half hour). Downstairs, the brightly painted but music-free horse and duck carousel runs at 11am, 1pm, 3pm and 5pm. Staff are friendly. *See also p198.*
Buggy access. Mail order. Nappy-changing facilities. Play area.

Lilliput's puppets on a string.

Harrods

87-135 Brompton Road, SW1 (7730 1234/
www.harrods.com). Knightsbridge tube/14, 74 bus.
Open 10am-7pm Mon-Sat. **Credit** AmEx, DC, MC, V.
Map p315 F9.

The fourth floor is home to all matters juvenile. In the clothing departments, designer-label babywear and quality layette essentials cover the early months. A good, imaginative range of toddler playclothes and traditional wear for high days and holidays leads you into a less appealing selection for children up to teenage: there's a school-uniform section, too. In the nursery, the essentials (cot beds, chairs, prams) tend to be of the traditional and beautiful kind: don't come here looking for three-way buggies and changing mats. The best bit of the fourth floor is the toy department, which is spacious and generous with toys for young visitors to play with. All the big play names are here, from Barbie to Brio, and every price range is represented, from 50p for a plastic dinosaur to £40,000 for a toy Ferrari. The book department has regular signings and occasions of its own, which fit in with a frenetic programme of themed events for children: Barbie Breakfasts, for example, or party days. There's also a children's theatre, with a treehouse to climb about in. Ring for details of what's on, when, and how to book. Teenagers should check Way In for fashion and the fifth floor for sportswear. Just near the toy department is Planet Harrods, like a posh Mcdonald's.
Buggy access. Café. Delivery service. Mail order.
Nappy-changing facilities. Play area. Restaurants.

Lilliput

255-9 Queenstown Road, SW8 (7720 5554/0800 783
0886/www.lilliput.com). Queenstown Road rail. **Open**
9.30am-5.30pm Mon, Tue, Thur, Fri; 9.30am-7pm Wed;
9am-6pm Sat. **Credit** MC, V.

Name a pram or high chair brand and we bet Lilliput will stock it (Mountain Buggy, £380; TrippTrapp high chair, £109). If your baby kicks off the blankets at night, a gingham Nursery Company sleepsuit might be worth a try. Equally useful (especially for holidays) are the clip-on high chairs and replacement car seat covers. If you're furnishing the bedroom or playroom, it'll be hard to resist the rocking crib, the open wooden dolls' house or the brightly coloured toy bench box, especially as the firm provides free delivery anywhere for large items. With such an extensive stock, two play tables of Brio and the newly opened warehouse containing toys, Lilliput is indeed a kingdom for little people.
Buggy access. Mail order. Nappy-changing facilities.
Play area.
Branches: 278 Upper Richmond Road, SW15 (8780 1682);
100 Haydons Road, SW19 (8542 3542).

Baby hardware & equipment

Baby Munchkins

186 Hoxton Street, N1 (7684 5994/
www.babymunchkins.com). Old Street tube/rail.
Open 10am-5pm Mon-Sat. **Credit** MC, V.

All-terrain pushchairs are a speciality at Baby Munchkins, with Mountain Terrain buggies costing £530 or Alu-Rax buggies at £139. Car seats, Tripp Trapp high chairs, contemporary rocking horses and Stokke cots are also available, along with lamb fleeces and Baby Bjorn carriers for cosy sleeping. While you're here, stock up on wooden toys, Jellycat and Miffy merchandise, organic food, and Sarah Barker shoes for active crawlers.
Buggy access. Delivery service. Mail order. Nappy-changing facilities.

Baby This 'N' Baby That
359 Forest Road, E17 (8527 4002). Blackhorse Road tube/rail. **Open** 10am-5pm Mon-Sat. **Credit** AmEx, MC, V. This friendly store with helpful service claims to stock everything but the baby. If you want traditional stuff, you can order Silver Cross prams for £400-£800; if you want a bargain, there's a three-wheeler for twins, complete with all the accessories, for £220; and if you want a brand name, you'll find Mamas and Papas, Bébécar, Maclaren and the rest.
Buggy access. Delivery service.

Dragons of Walton Street
23 Walton Street, SW3 (7589 3795/ www.dragonsltd.co.uk). Knightsbridge or South Kensington tube. **Open** 9.30am-5.30pm Mon-Fri; 10am-5pm Sat. **Credit** AmEx, MC, V. **Map** p315 E10.
An artfully cluttered furniture and wooden toyshop, for antiques and modern traditional objects. Children can try out Plan trains and wooden farmyards, teddy stools and old-fashioned high chairs. The prices are top whack: a child's four-poster for £5,000, a Georgian nursery chair for £500, and a rocking horse for £350.
Buggy access. Delivery service. Mail order.

Junior Consumers

E Gibbons
7-17 Amhurst Road, E8 (8985 3129). Hackney Central rail. **Open** 9am-6pm Mon-Sat. **Credit** MC, V.
This 19th-century department store retains its old-fashioned ways. You won't find any electronic games, but instead there are traditional toys including hula hoops, Raleigh bikes and tricycles from £29.95. There's also a selection of cots, beds and cupboards by Silent Night and Homeworthy among others.
Buggy access. Delivery service.

Family Care
90-94 Kingsland High Street, E8 (7254 8720). Dalston Kingsland rail. **Open** 10am-6pm Mon-Fri. **Credit** MC, V.
Basic designer clothes, toys and nursery items come cheap at this store. Three-piece baby outfits cost from £7, and there's a bargain Chicco Duo pram complete with car seat for £199. Among the usual toys by Fisher-Price and Mamas and Papas are fantastic motorised two-seater cars and jeeps for three- to seven-year-olds complete with safety belts (£210). The radio-controlled range is reputedly the biggest in town; prices range from £1.99 for a car to £225 for an aeroplane.
Buggy access. Delivery service. Mail order. Nappy-changing facilities. Play area.

Green Baby
345 Upper Street, N1 (7359 7037/www.greenbabyco.com). Angel tube. **Open** 10am-5pm Mon-Sat. **Credit** AmEx, MC, V.
Delights at this friendly purple-painted outlet include washable nappies by Tushies, Efie cuddly toys made from chemical-free natural cotton, Green Baby's own brand of creams, organic cradle cap oil, mandarin toothpaste and a goat hair brush so soft it can be used for baby massage. For stepping out there are strollers, Baby Trekkers and Huggababys. Mums can stock up on toiletries and Bravado nursing bras.
Buggy access. Delivery service.

Humla Children's Shop
13 Flask Walk, NW3 (7794 7877). Hampstead tube. **Open** 10.30am-6pm Tue-Sat; noon-6pm Sun. **Credit** AmEx, MC, V.

Shops by area

Southwark & Bankside
FW Evans (Toys, *p208*); Tate Modern (Museum shops, *p204*).

Bloomsbury & Holborn
Bikefix (Toys, *p207*).

Covent Garden & St Giles's
Action Bikes (Toys, *p207*); Benjamin Pollock's Toyshop (Toys, *p208*); O'Neill (Skate & surf, *p204*); Paul Smith for Children (Clothes, *p200*); Peter Rabbit & Friends (Toys, *p209*); Quiksilver (Skate & surf, *p206*); Skate of Mind (Skate & surf, *p206*); Slam City Skates (Skate & surf, *p206*).

Kensington & Chelsea
Brora (Clothes, *p196*); Butterscotch (Clothes, *p196*); Caramel (Clothes, *p196*); Daisy & Tom (All-rounders p191); Dragons of Walton Street (Baby hardware & equipment, *p193*); Early Learning Centre (The chain gang, *p201*); Harrods (All-rounders, *p192*); MikiHouse (Clothes, *p199*); Nursery Window (Baby hardware & equipment, *p195*); Oilily (Clothes, *p199*); Patrizia Wigan (Clothes, *p200*); Science Museum (Museum shops, p204); Traditional Toys (Toys, *p209*); Tridias (Toys, *p209*); Trotters (Clothes, *p201*); What Katy Did (Clothes, *p203*).

West End
Benetton (Up west, *p206*); Buckle My Shoe (Shoes, *p204 & p206*); Catimini (Clothes, *p196*); Disney Store (Toys, *p208*); Esprit (Up West, *p206*); Gap Kids (Up west, *p206*); Gymboree (Clothes, *p198*); Hamleys (Toys, *p204 & p208*); H&M (Up west, *p206*) Humla (Clothes, *p199*); JD Sport (Sportswear & trainers, *p206*); JJB Sports (Sportswear & trainers, *p207*); John Lewis (Up west, *p206*); Lillywhite's (Sportswear & trainers, *p207*); Minors (Clothes, *p199*); Mothercare (The chain gang, *p201*); Next (Up west, *p206*); Niketown (Sportswear & trainers, *p207*); Soccerscene (Sportswear & trainers, *p207*); Tartine et Chocolat (Clothes, *p201*).

Westminster
National Gallery (Museum shops, p204); Rachel Riley (Clothes, *p200*); Semmalina (Clothes, *p200*).

North London
Baby Munchkins (Baby hardware & equipment, *p192*); Bookworm (Toys, *p196*); Chamberlaine & Son (Toys, *p207*); Children's Bookshop (Toys, *p196*); Early Clothing (Clothes, *p198*); Encore (Second-hand, *p203*); Fagin's Toys (Toys, *p209*); Frederick Beck (Toys, *p210*); Gotham Angels (Clothes, *p198*); Green Baby (Baby hardware & equipment, *p193*); Happy Returns (Toys, *p210*);

Hobby Horse Riders (Clothes, *p199*); Humla Children's Shop (Baby hardware & equipment, *p193*); Infantasia (Baby hardware & equipment, *p195*); Instep (Shoes, *p204*); Kristen Baybars (Toys, *p209*); Mini Kin (Hair today, *p198*); Never Never Land (Toys, *p209*); Notsobig (Clothes, *p199*); Pom d'Api (Shoes, *p204*); Rainbow (Second-hand, *p203*; Toys, *p209*); Route 73 Kids (Toys, *p211*); Rub-a-Dub-Dub (Second-hand, *p203*); Soup Dragon (Toys, *p209*); Toe Tho (Clothes, *p201*); Toy City (Toys, *p211*); Toy Wonderland (Toys, *p211*); Trendys (Clothes, *p201*); Word Play (Toys, *p211*).

East London
Baby This 'N' Baby That (Baby hardware & equipment, *p193*); The Bike Shed (Toys, *p207*); Chocolate Crocodile (Second-hand, *p203*); E Gibbons (Baby hardware & equipment, *p193*); Family Care (Baby hardware & equipment, *p193*); M&G Junior Fashions (Clothes, *p199*); Merry-Go-Round (Second-hand, *p203*); Super Sport Shoe Warehouse (Sportswear & trainers, *p207*); Toy House (Toys, *p211*).

South-east London
Biff (Clothes, *p196*); Bookseller Crow on the Hill (Toys, *p196*); Decathlon (Sportswear & trainers, *p206*); Edwardes (Toys, *p207*); E sharp minor (Clothes, *p198*); Little Nippers (Hair today, *p198*); Toys 'R' Us (The chain gang, *p201*).

South-west London
Apex Cycles (Toys, *p207*); Barney's (Clothes, *p196*); Books for Children (Books, *p195*); Bunnies (Second-hand, *p203*); The Farmyard (Toys, *p208*); Fun Learning (Toys, *p208*); Havana's Toy Box (Toys, *p211*); The Toy Station (Toys, *p211*); Lilliput (All-rounders, *p192*); Little Bridge (Baby hardware & equipment, *p195*); Little Willie's (Clothes, *p199*); Membery's (Clothes, *p199*); Patrick's Toys & Models (Toys, *p211*); Piccolo Bella (Clothes, *p200*); The Shoe Station (Shoes, *p204*); Smartees (Clothes, *p201*); Stock House (Clothes, *p201*); Swallows & Amazons (Second-hand, *p204*); Tiny Set Toys (Toys, *p211*).

West London
Boomerang (Second-hand, *p203*); Cheeky Monkeys (Toys, *p208*); Children's Book Centre (Books, *p196*); The Children's Book Company (Books, *p196*); Clementine (Clothes, *p198*); Cookie (Clothes, *p198*); The Cross (Clothes, *p198*); First Sport (Sportswear & trainers, *p206*); Harlequin House (Toys, *p208*); Jigsaw Junior (Clothes, *p199*); The Little Trading Company (Second-hand, *p203*); Pixies (Second-hand, *p203*); Snap Dragon (Toys, *p211*); Stepping Out (Shoes, *p204*); Tots in the Terrace (Clothes, *p201*).

Junior Consumers

Early Clothing for junior fashion victims. *See p198.*

Much of Humla's furniture is modish and functional: chests and wardrobes painted by Heather Spencer and dinky child-sized chairs. There are also attractive biplane bookshelves and toy boxes; tractor bookends and circus bookshelves. But the most amazing items are the Scandinavian bunk beds, which not only have a spare bed in the bottom drawer but also double up as puppet theatres or feature a slide down to the floor (£300). The large traditional wooden toys include some amusing sit 'n' rides. Head several doors along to 9 Flask Walk (or to St Christopher's Place off Oxford Street) for Humla's selection of designer clothes and own-brand knits (*see p199*).
Buggy access. Delivery service. Play area.
Branches: 9 Flask Walk, NW3 (7794 8449); 23 St Christopher's Place, W1 (7224 1773).

Infantasia
Unit 103, Wood Green Shopping Centre, N22 (8889 1494/www.infantasia.co.uk). Wood Green tube. **Open** 9.30am-6pm Mon-Fri; 9am-6pm Sat; 11am-5pm Sun. **Credit** AmEx, MC, V.
An excellent nursery emporium with friendly service and friendlier prices. There are 50 different types of pram brands; 20 car seat types; 16 makes of cot and cot bed. You can take your damaged buggy in for a service and buy a new set of wheels for £15.
Buggy access. Delivery service. Mail order. Nappy-changing facilities.

Little Bridge
56 Battersea Bridge Road, SW11 (7978 5522/ www.littlebridge.force9.co.uk). Clapham Junction rail/49, 319, 345 bus. **Open** 9.30am-5.30pm Mon-Fri; 10am-5pm Sat. **Credit** AmEx, MC, V.

Made-to-measure painted furniture for the nursery sold here is not cheap: a set of table and chairs painted with a farmyard scene will set you back at least £475, but the quality is high and the designs are very attractive.
Buggy access. Delivery service.

Nursery Window
83 Walton Street, SW3 (7581 3358/ www.nurserywindow.co.uk). South Kensington tube. **Open** 10am-6pm Mon-Sat. **Credit** AmEx, MC, V. **Map** p315 E10.
Guarantee your child has sweet dreams with co-ordinated bedroom furnishings from Nursery Window. Toddlers love the rocking sheep (£125.95); babies can be pampered in a new range of cashmere and lambswool blankets.
Buggy access. Delivery service. Mail order.

Books

Books for Children
97 Wandsworth Bridge Road, SW6 (7384 1821). Fulham Broadway tube. **Open** 10am-6pm Mon; 9.30am-6pm Tue-Fri; 9.30am-5.30pm Sat. **Credit** MC, V.
This place is as good as a library, allowing your kid to settle down with a book without any pressure to buy – although you'll inevitably want to. Among the goodies are pop-up books, myths and legends and a board book selection for under-twos. Downstairs is a comprehensive non-fiction section, including school books for both teachers and pupils. The small video stock is growing, and the audio tape collection is one of the biggest in London.
Buggy access. Delivery service.

Bookseller Crow on the Hill

50 Westow Street, SE19 (8771 8831/
www.booksellercrow.com). Gypsy Hill rail. **Open**
9am-7.30pm Mon-Fri; 9am-6.30pm Sat; 11am-5pm Sun.
Credit AmEx MC, V.
A general bookshop with a terrific children's section, right at
the front. Local parents come in for a nose, while their children play with toys and read books at tables and chairs provided. Check the website to find out about forthcoming events
and author signings.
Buggy access. Mail order. Play area.

Bookworm

1177 Finchley Road, NW11 (8201 9811). Golders Green
tube. **Open** 9.30am-5.30pm Mon-Sat; 10am-1.30pm Sun.
Credit MC, V.
A warm and friendly children's bookshop, where two- to six-
year-olds can enjoy story time at 2pm every Tuesday and
Thursday. There's a table full of toys and colouring stuff if
the books alone aren't enough to entertain them while their
parents browse. Regular events involving favourite authors
are listed in the newsletter of the Bookworm Book Club: ring
the shop to be put on the mailing list.
Buggy access. Delivery service. Mail order.
Nappy-changing facilities.

Children's Book Centre

237 Kensington High Street, W8 (7937 7497/
www.childrensbookcentre.co.uk). High Street Kensington
tube. **Open** 9.30am-6.30pm Mon, Wed, Fri, Sat; 9.30am-
6pm Tue; 9.30am-7pm Thur; noon-6pm Sun. **Credit**
AmEx, MC, V. **Map** p314 A9.
This book and toy empire now sells chocolates and jewellery,
too. The huge selection of books is already accompanied by
CD-Roms, games, puzzles, Beanie Babies, Pokémon toys and
videos, all of which can be bought through the website.
Buggy access. Mail order.

The Children's Book Company

11 The Green, W5 (8567 4324/
www.childrensbookcompany.com). Ealing Broadway tube.
Open 9.30am-5.30pm Mon-Sat. **Credit** MC, V.
A huge asset to the local community, this bookshop, whose
stock covers the reading needs of all children, from birth to
14 years, is a pleasure to visit. In addition to books there are
book and tape spin-offs as well as character toys. Kids can
take books to the sofa to read; very young children play on
the rocking sheep. The staff run a storytelling session every
Thursday at 3.45pm and an author drops in every month.
Customers who sign up to the loyalty scheme receive a
newsletter, which programmes all forthcoming events. Check
the website for what's coming up and for more information
on the parents' courses.
Buggy access. Delivery service. Mail order. Play area.

Children's Bookshop

29 Fortis Green Road, N10 (8444 5500). Highgate tube
then 43, 134 bus. **Open** 9.15am-5.45pm Mon-Sat; 11am-
4pm Sun. **Credit** AmEx, MC, V.
The staff here demonstrate an impressive knowledge of children's books and will help kids find their way round the various sections, including a selection of audio tapes. Fiction is
displayed by age group: there are board books for babies,
early readers for five- to eight-year-olds and Harry Potter et
al for 8- to 12-year-olds. For author events, book signings and
the learned atmosphere attract many teachers and their pupils
to this jam-packed store. For solitary bookworms there are
display books and a reading chair in the corner.
Buggy access. Mail order. Play area.

Fashion

Clothes

Barney's

6 Church Road, SW19 (8944 2915). Wimbledon tube/rail.
Open 10am-6pm Mon-Sat; noon-5pm Sun. **Credit** MC, V.
French and Italian labels for newborns and children up to 14
years pack the rails. There's Jean Bourget, Les Robes, Petit
Bateau, Gasolio and Portofino as well as O'Neill, Paper Moon,
Kookai and Oxbow. Stocks of Orchard toys, teddies and other
soft animals increase around Christmas, but there's always a
good range of christening and new baby gifts, as well as hair
accessories for older girls.
Buggy access. Nappy-changing facilities. Play area.

Biff

43 Dulwich Village, SE21 (8299 0911). North Dulwich
rail. **Open** 9.30am-5.30pm Mon-Fri; 10am-6pm Sat;
11am-4pm Sun. **Credit** AmEx, MC, V.
Small children head straight for the toy table here, giving parents time to examine the extensive and eclectic range of clothing, shoes and swimwear. Petit Bateau is a popular line, and
the raw silk christening outfits are exquisite. There's a range
of fancy dress suits for ages four to six.
Buggy access. Delivery service. Mail order.
Nappy-changing facilities. Play area.

Brora

344 King's Road, SW3 (7352 3697/www.brora.co.uk).
Sloane Square tube then 11, 19, 22 bus. **Open** 10am-6pm
Mon-Sat. **Credit** AmEx, MC, V. **Map** p315 E12.
Brora has cashmere treats for the whole family for winter and
summer. Adorable soft babygros, lilac cashmere leggings,
booties and Inca design bonnets can all be wrapped and deliv-
ered through Brora Baby Direct as a luxurious new born gift.
Buggy access. Delivery service.
Branches: 81 Marylebone High Street, W1 (7224 5040).

Butterscotch

172 Walton Street, SW3 (7581 8551). South Kensington
tube. **Open** 10am-5.30pm Mon-Sat. **Credit** AmEx, MC, V.
Map p315 E10.
Behind the damask quilts and grandad pyjamas there's a cool
range of casual clothing. Poivre Blanc fleeces and O'Neill surf-
style skiwear pull in kids up to 14, while Giraffe clobber
(smart jumpers and leggings) and the Miniman range cater
for younger dudes.
Buggy access. Delivery service.

Caramel

291 Brompton Road, SW3 (7589 7001). South
Kensington tube. **Open** 10am-6.30pm Mon-Sat;
noon-5pm Sun. **Credit** MC, V. **Map** p315 E10.
A hip designer boutique for women, babies and children.
Highlights of the collection are the pashmina kimonos by
Channe de Biolly and the Marni range, exclusive in London
to Caramel. Brooklyn handknits, Quincy leather jerkins and
Caramel's own stunning collection show why Madonna is
apparently a fan.
Delivery service. Mail order.

Catimini

52 South Molton Street, W1 (7629 8099/
www.catimini.com). Bond Street tube. **Open** 10am-6pm
Mon-Wed, Fri, Sat; 10am-7pm Thur. **Credit** AmEx, MC,
V. **Map** p316 H6.

Animal motifs dominate these original and inventive clothes made in France. Zebra chairs beckon toddlers to the little colouring table, while a wooden rocking hen peeps out of the changing room. For older dressers (up to 12 years), the clothes are as chic as the baby stuff.
Buggy access. Delivery service. Mail order. Nappy-changing facilities. Play area.

Clementine
73 Ledbury Road, W11 (7243 6331). Notting Hill Gate tube. **Open** 10am-6.30pm Mon-Sat. **Credit** AmEx, MC, V. **Map** p312 A6.
This charming children's clothes and furniture shop occupies a light and airy corner on voguish Ledbury Road. The simple cotton look of Petit Bateau dominates the ground floor where goods for the newly born up to the teenager are found. Downstairs there are prams (including the sturdy Swedish Emmaljunga range), simple customised beds (from £300) made of pine and pretty bed linen and clothing from Damask.
Buggy access. Delivery service. Mail order. Nappy-changing facilities.

Cookie
66 Ledbury Road, W11 (7727 1133). Notting Hill Gate tube. **Open** 10am-6pm Mon-Fri; 11am-6pm Sat. **Credit** MC, V. **Map** 312 A6.
In the basement of Lulu Guinness's hat and handbag shop you'll find Denise Hurst's glamorous and shiny clothes and room decor. All stock can be made to order and you can have a design consultation to change your child's room by spending lots of dosh on fripperies like multicoloured sheepskin rugs and zany beanbags for £120.
Buggy access. Delivery service. Nappy-changing facilities. Play area.

The Cross
141 Portland Road, W11 (7727 6760). Holland Park or Notting Hill Gate tube. **Open** 10.30am-6pm Mon-Sat. **Credit** AmEx, MC, V.
Exclusive labels can now be bagged by mothers and babies at this cool shop. Childrenswear from birth to six years includes tiny street fashions from Little Punk and Quincy, babywear from Albetta Creation and tough toddling gear from OshKosh. The gifts and accessories are covetable, and wee girls enjoy selecting bits and bobs from the hair and make-up stash. There's a room for toys, of the quirky wooden variety, and all visiting children are encouraged to play with them.
Buggy access.

Early Clothing
79-85 Fortis Green Road, N10 (8444 9309). Highgate tube. **Open** 9.30am-5.30pm Mon-Sat. **Credit** AmEx, MC, V.
Your child can try on Start-rite, Buckle My Shoe or O'Neill shoes in a special enclave on a wooden church pew. Or pop into the changing rooms to check out any number of upmarket casual labels: OshKosh, Quiksilver, Catimini, Oilily, IKKS, Kenzo Jungle, DKNY.
Buggy access. Delivery service. Play area.

E sharp minor
6 Earlswood Street, SE10 (8858 6648/ www.esharpminor.co.uk). North Greenwich tube. **Open** 10am-4pm Tue-Sat. **Credit** MC, V.
Ella Sharp's wacky tailored knitwear is beautiful and original, for children between three months and ten years.
Buggy access. Delivery service. Nappy-changing facilities. Play area.

Gotham Angels
23 Islington Green, N1 (7359 8090). Angel tube. **Open** 10.30am-7pm Mon-Wed, Fri; 10.30am-8pm Thur; 10am-6pm Sun.
Children's (and women's) clothes with an eclectic edge. Witty childrenswear includes babygros printed with dog's faces and frills and sparkles galore. Prices tend to be on the high side.
Buggy access.
Branch: 141 Crouch Hill, N8 (8340 4080).

Gymboree
198 Regent Street, W1 (7494 1110/www.gymboree.com). Oxford Circus tube. **Open** 10am-7pm Mon-Wed, Fri, Sat; 10am-8pm Thur; 11.30am-5.30pm Sun. **Credit** AmEx, MC, V. **Map** p316 J6.
You can always find a bargain at Gymboree, especially since old stock is sold off at cut prices at the back of the shop every month or so. Cheery designs include pink cotton check trousers, tugboat T-shirts, animal babygros, dungarees, dresses, shirts and leggings.
Buggy access. Delivery service. Play area.

Hair today

There's a mini-salon lurking in the back of an increasing number of the clothes and shoe shops listed in this chapter. **Little Willie's** (*see p199*) offers the most complete experience in town – here, Vidal Sassoon-trained hairdressers cut littl'uns' hair for £10 as they pull faces in the mirror from their orange leather barber stools (fitted with baby seats). If your offspring are fidgety types, videos are on hand at **Trotters** (£9.50 and £10.50 for a cut; *see p203*), **Daisy & Tom** (*see p191* – £12; £6 for a fringe trim) on the King's Road, and **Swallows & Amazons** (£6.50 for a baby, £7 for a child over four; *see p204*) in Clapham. If price is a factor, your best bet is **Stock House** (*see p201*), where a leisurely, friendly cut costs £5.50 for babies and £7.50 for a child. Shoe shop **Pom d'Api** (*see p204*) in Hampstead charges £12.50 for children up to three years and £15 thereafter for haircutting. Though its rates might not be the cheapest, at least your kids can watch DVDs while being shorn. Children can also have a haircut on the fourth floor of **Harrods** (*see p192*); a first snip – with a diploma, no less, and a lock of hair – costs a hair-raising £23.

If you want a bit of beauty thrown in, the deft-fingered staff at **Little Nippers** in Greenwich (133 Vanbrugh Hill, SE10, 8293 4444) do the hair (from £6) and makeovers for junior glamour-pusses. First haircuts with lock, certificate and photo costs £10.50. At **Mini Kin** (79 Fortis Green Road, N10, 8444 1717) a dry style costs £12.50; a wash, cut and blow dry £18.50 and Baby's First Haircut £19.95 (to include certificate, ribboned lock and keepsake). If you're really looking to part with some cash, your daughter can have the 'Princess Treatment' and walk away with a new hairdo, a light makeover, peel-off nail polish and a squirt of perfume for £24.95.

Hobby Horse Riders

50-52 Crouch End Hill, N8 (8348 9782). Finsbury Park tube then W7 bus. **Open** 10.30am-5.30pm Mon-Fri; 10am-6pm Sat. **Credit** AmEx, MC, V.
This local clothes store, for newborns to eight-year-olds, arranges its stock, including designs by Marèse, Miniman and Petit Bateau, by colour, so entering the shop is like walking into a retail rainbow. Check out the colourful Buckle My Shoe wellies (and shoes) and Daisy Roots footwear for babes. All ages will enjoy a romp on the Jellycat jungle animal fur rugs (£40-£50).
Buggy access. Play area.

Humla

23 St Christopher's Place, W1 (7224 1773). Bond Street tube. **Open** 10.30am-6.30pm Mon-Sat. **Credit** AmEx, MC, V. **Map** p316 H6.
Humla began life as a children's knitwear market stall in Camden but now has three specialised outlets in London. The West End branch is the most upmarket with labels like OshKosh, Petit Boy and Petit Bateau giving it a designer feel. The own-brand jumpers are still what it does best, though.
Buggy access. Delivery service. Mail order. Play area.
Branches: 9 Flask Walk, NW3 (7794 8449); 13 Flask Walk, NW3 (7794 7877).

Jigsaw Junior

190 Westbourne Grove, W11 (7229 8654/www.jigsaw-junior.com). Notting Hill Gate tube. **Open** 10.30am-6.30pm Mon; 10am-6.30pm Tue, Wed, Sat; 10am-7pm Thur, Fri; noon-6pm Sun. **Credit** AmEx, MC, V. **Map** p312 A6.
Jigsaw's children's store fits in plenty of pinks and purples and fluffy jumpers for rock chicks aged up to 13. Babies can keep warm in beautiful woollen cardigans embroidered with flowers, while sports lovers might choose silver skiwear or turquoise and navy swimwear. There's no ramp down the short flight of stairs to the children's section; instead, there's a silver slide with cushions.
Buggy access. Mail order. Play area.
Branches throughout town. Check the phone book for your nearest.

Little Willie's

16 The Pavement, SW4 (7498 7899). Clapham Common tube. **Open** 11am-5pm Tue, Wed; 10am-5pm Thur-Sat. **Credit** AmEx, DC, MC, V.
Offspring of Willie Smart's salon at no.11, Little Willie's is a hairdressing parlour for children, with a few clothes and

accessories for sale. Freshly clipped youngsters can scribble on the blackboard door or try on beautiful shoes by Pom d'Api, Latrino, Babybotte and Daisy Roots. Lynnat bug T-shirts, felt dresses and jumpers, fleece shoulder bags (£16) and Country Kids tights (£9.95) complete the funky quality items for sale. *See also p198.*
Buggy access. Nappy-changing facilities. Play area.

M&G Junior Fashions

73 Kingsland High Street, E8 (7249 9728). Dalston Kingsland rail. **Open** 9.30am-6pm Mon-Sat. **Credit** MC, V.
With the most expensive babygro costing £3.99 and the most costly item in the shop £13.99 (a cot bumper and quilt), this East End store certainly offers value for money. Casual clothes for children up to ten and soft shoes for babies are set out on rails and hooks around the room. If you're dressing a tot on a tight budget, look no further.
Buggy access.

Membery's

1 Church Road, SW13 (8876 2910). Barnes Bridge rail. **Open** 10am-5pm Mon-Sat. **Credit** AmEx, MC, V.
This pretty little shop sells Petit Bateau stripes, OshKosh dungarees, Lapin Bleu flowers and its own Sally Membery label for newborns to eight-year-olds. Silk bridesmaid outfits can be made to measure here; prices start at a hefty £200.
Buggy access. Delivery service.

MikiHouse

107 Walton Street, SW3 (7838 0006/ www.Mikihouse.co.uk). Knightsbridge tube. **Open** 10am-6pm Mon-Sat. **Credit** AmEx, MC, V. **Map** p315 E10.
It's a relief to find clothes and shoes for children from six months to eight years that are well made as well as colourful and playful. All the items, from swimwear in the summer to skiwear in the winter, have the Japanese MikiHouse teddy bear label. Toys are also good quality and the accessories are stylish: you can buy a see-through plastic bag with bright flowers for the beach or a lunch set, complete with chopsticks.
Buggy access. Delivery service.

Minors

11 New Cavendish Street, W1 (7486 8299). Baker Street tube. **Open** 10am-6.30pm Mon-Sat. **Credit** AmEx, DC, MC, V. **Map** p316 H5.
Look no further for top-rank Italian and French designs for the under-16s: Buddy Guy, Petit Escargot, Marinus, Marc Brown, Catimini and a cute Mini-Catimini range for babies.
Buggy access. Delivery service. Play area.

Notsobig

31A Highgate High Street, N6 (8340 4455). Archway or Highgate tube. **Open** 9.30am-6pm Mon-Fri; 10am-6pm Sat; 11am-5pm Sun. **Credit** DC, MC, V.
Modish Highgate children are dragging their parents into this colourful and stylish clothes store, where babywear by Wo Wo and Cacharel makes a splash and achingly trendy children swear by Bengh and Maharishi stands out a mile. The look from LA and NY for children is vintage, and the designer clothes cut down from old cashmere originals are stunning. There are a few toys around, more at Christmas time, but all small children long for the repro American pedalcars and fire engines: they're adorable and cost from a prohibitive £380.
Buggy access. Delivery service.

Oilily

9 Sloane Street, SW1 (7823 2505). Knightsbridge tube. **Open** 10am-6pm Mon, Tue, Thur-Sat; 10am-7pm Wed. **Credit** AmEx, DC, MC, V. **Map** p315 F9.

Junior Consumers

Jigsaw Junior:
girl heaven.

The chain gang

Adams' fashions for 0-7-year-olds might be undistinguished, but at least they're bright and reasonably priced. The shop is great for both plain and logo-decked underwear, brightly coloured woolly tights in winter, a rainbow of jelly sandals in summer, and a cheeky selection of hats and accessories all year round. The bargain bins yield last season's lines. Many branches have coin-operated play vehicles, Lego tables and, horrors, sweetie dispensers.

At the **Early Learning Centre**, it's always playtime, and learning through play is the ELC's maxim. All pre-schoolers love these bright, cheery toyshops, but their popularity wanes as children become corrupted by playground fashions and clamour for the latest must-have toy. There are no guns or other weapons, no Barbies or Action Men, no Nintendos or Playstations at the ELC. Bob the Builder and Thomas the Tank engine have managed to make it in, though. Many of the bigger branches, including the Chelsea one, have play sessions for small children on a Tuesday morning.

Mothercare is like a supermarket for sprogs. Everything you might need for the nursery, and quite a lot you don't, is sold in its stolidly reliable range. Most parents agree that this stalwart is good for basics: wet wipes, potties, cots and bedding, children's underwear and toddlers' strollers. There are toys, tapes, CDs, books and videos to suit most children from babyhood up to five. Plans to go upmarket and stock Oilily, Petit Bateau and OshKosh are coming to fruition in the flagship London branches, such as Marble Arch. Most branches have lavatories and baby-feeding and changing rooms. Check out the comprehensive website, where you can order the catalogue.

Toys 'R' Us has zillions of toys, video games, outdoor playthings, bikes and home entertainment – and that's before you've even started on the Babies 'R' Us stock. All the latest toy fads are here. For tots you can find car seats and pushchairs, items for the nursery and kids' room, feeding and safety stuff and baby toys. If you can't face the supermarket aisles, try the website, where products are listed by age, category, price or brand.

Pricey Dutch label Oilily is as bright and loud as ever. This spacious white room is flooded by ceiling lights like stars that illuminate the pink alcoves and snaking tile design on the stone floor, and spotlight the bright colours on sale. Children can flop on the red sofa or play bead games at the round table, while their parents go shopping mad.
Buggy access. Delivery service. Mail order. Play area.

Patrizia Wigan

19 Walton Street, SW3 (7823 7080). South Kensington tube. **Open** 10am-6pm Mon-Fri; 10am-5.30pm Sat. **Credit** AmEx, MC, V. **Map** p315 E10.
Wigan's classic designs encompass beautiful velvet dresses and moleskin dungarees, a wedding collection for page boys, and Thai silk robes from £175 for bridesmaids. Look on the first floor for outfits for under-threes and on the ground floor for bigger clothes (up to 12).
Buggy access. Delivery service. Mail order. Nappy-changing facilities. Play area.
Branch: 19 Barnes High Street, SW13 (8876 4540).

Paul Smith for Children

40-44 Floral Street, WC2 (7379 7133/ www.paulsmith.co.uk). Covent Garden tube. **Open** 10.30am-6.30pm Mon-Wed, Fri; 10.30am-7pm Thur; 10am-6.30pm Sat; 1-5pm Sun. **Credit** AmEx, MC, V. **Map** p317 L6.
The limited but exclusive childrenswear at Paul Smith includes stunning print trousers, swimsuits and shirts. The bright colours are popular with girls. There are embroidered sandals, toddlers, trainers in pink and blue, and socks packed in an egg box. A small selection of toys rounds things off.
Delivery service. Mail order.
Branch: Westbourne House, 122 Kensington Park Road, W11 (7727 3553).

Piccolo Bella

6 Eton Street, Richmond, Surrey (8948 8601). Richmond tube/rail. **Open** 10am-5.30pm Mon-Sat. **Credit** MC, V.

Two sisters-in-law with five children between them opened Piccolo Bella to cater for distinctly upmarket under-tens. Behind the large glass front you find Baby Pex, Ambitoys and Daisy Roots shoes. There are special things, too: cuddly toys, pyjamas, gifts and a few pieces of baby hardware.
Buggy access. Delivery service.

Rachel Riley

14 Pont Street, SW1 (7259 5969/www.rachelriley.com). Sloane Square tube. **Open** 10am-6pm Mon-Sat. **Credit** AmEx, MC, V. **Map** p315 F10.
This old-fashioned boutique has glass counters displaying Rachel Riley's delicate designs. Soft leather slippers come in pinks and pale blues to match floral Liberty dresses, blue gingham pyjamas and unisex cotton poplin anoraks. Bibs, newborn robes and cotton cardigans are complemented by Petit Bateau baby underwear and babygros.
Buggy access. Delivery service. Mail order. Play area.
Branch: 82 Marylebone High Street, W1 (7935 7007).

Semmalina

225 Ebury Street, SW1 (7730 9333). Sloane Square tube. **Open** 9.30am-5.30pm Mon-Sat. **Credit** MC, V. **Map** p318 G11.
This shop is a small fairytale kingdom where children can play on a drawbridge with plastic frogs and snakes. Clothes include Cookie T-shirts, stripy knit jumpers from Cinnamon, shiny skirts from Gotham Angels, and other labels such as Kind Hearts and Gerson di Scafor, plus Semmalina's own. A boudoir chamber of the castle stocks second-hand annuals and hardbacks, Victory puzzles and upholstered kiddie armchairs. Suede baby bootees (£25) can be gift-wrapped in sequins and tissue and there are christening dresses and nighties, dolls' houses, marble bags, glass bug brooches and Tarina Tarantino jewels. There's even stuff for those on a pocket money budget.
Buggy access. Delivery service. Mail order. Nappy-changing facilities. Play area.

Adams
*Unit 11, Surrey Quays Centre, Redriff Road, SE16
(7252 3208/www.adams.co.uk). Surrey Quays tube.*
Open 9.30am-5.30pm Mon-Thur, Sat; 9am-8pm Fri.
Credit AmEx, MC, V.

Early Learning Centre
*36 King's Road, SW3 (7581 5764/www.elc.co.uk).
Sloane Square tube.* **Open** 9am-6pm Mon, Tue, Thur-
Sat; 9am-7pm Wed; 11am-5pm Sun. **Credit** AmEx,
MC, V. **Map** p315 F11.

Mothercare
*461 Oxford Street, W1 (7629 6621/
www.mothercare.com). Marble Arch tube.* **Open**
10am-7pm Mon-Wed, Sat; 10am-8pm Thur, Fri; noon-
6pm Sun. **Credit** AmEx, MC, V. **Map** p316 J6.

Toys 'R' Us
*730 Old Kent Road, SE15 (7732 7322/
www.toysrus.co.uk). Elephant & Castle tube/rail then
21, 53, 172, P13 bus.* **Open** 9am-8pm Mon-Fri; 9am-
7pm Sat; 11am-5pm Sun. **Credit** AmEx, MC, V.

So many toys, so little time,
at **Cheeky Monkeys**. *See p208.*

Smartees
*5 Bellevue Parade, Wiseton Road, SW17 (8672 3392/
www.smartees.co.uk). Wandsworth Common rail.*
Open 9.30am-5pm Mon-Fri; 9.30am-5.30pm Sat.
Credit AmEx, MC, V.
Child-friendly designer shopping for the under-eights, with
OshKosh (dungarees, £20), Petit Bateau, Hummelsheim and
Petit Boy among the labels. There are soft toys, wooden toys,
puzzles and Galt products to buy, plus a rocking horse and a
toy basket to keep young shoppers amused.
Buggy access. Play area.

Stock House
*155 Lavender Hill, SW11 (7738 0293). Clapham Junction
rail.* **Open** 9am-6pm Mon-Sat. **Credit** MC, V.
There's plenty of room for buggies in this light, spacious shop,
which specialises in European clothes and ballet wear. Prices
range from £5 to £40, with hair accessories, gaily painted
skipping ropes and colourful tights at the cheap end of the
scale, and beautiful hand-painted Buladresses from South
Africa and bright fleeces by Elizabeth Herron at the expensive end. *See also p198.*
Buggy access. Play area.

Tartine et Chocolat
*66 South Molton Street, W1 (7629 7233). Bond Street
tube.* **Open** 10am-6pm Mon-Sat. **Credit** AmEx, MC, V.
Map p316 H6.
Boys will be boys and girls will be girls in these sugar-sweet
Parisian designs. Bath stuffs, embroidered bibs, and pink and
white striped knickers and vests greet the baby girl; a white
cotton dress with smocking is available when she is older.
Mail order. Nappy-changing facilities.

Toe Tho
*55 Fortis Green Road, N10 (8442 0419). East Finchley
or Highgate tube.* **Open** 9.30am-6pm Mon-Sat.
Credit MC, V.

Pronounced 'tow-tow', the name Toe Tho is Swahili for 'kids'.
Clothing for girls in hot colours comes from Germany, France
and Italy. There are Mini Claire organza dresses, Stentaler
and Sarah Barker fabric shoes for pre-walkers, and you'll
find clothes by Alphabet, Abella and Whoopi for children
aged up to nine years.
Buggy access.

Tots in the Terrace
*39 Turnham Green Terrace, W4 (8995 0520). Turnham
Green tube.* **Open** 10am-6pm Mon-Sat. **Credit** AmEx,
MC, V.
Everything you need for children under 14, including
sweaters and socks, sunglasses and swimwear by Oilily,
Catimini, Miniman, Timberland, Kookai, Marèse and Kenzo.
Children of all ages enjoy trying out the children's chairs and
emptying out the toy basket.
*Buggy access. Delivery service. Mail order. Nappy-changing
facilities. Play area.*

Trendys
72 Chapel Market, N1 (7837 9070). Angel tube.
Open 9.30am-5.30pm Mon-Sat; 9.30am-3pm Sun.
Credit AmEx, MC, V.
This boutique has the best of Diesel, Replay, French
Connection, Cakewalk and Elle. There is a small selection of
equally covetable shoes by Moschino, Buckle My Shoe,
Kickers and Elle.
Buggy access.

Trotters
*34 King's Road, SW3 (7259 9620/www.trotters.co.uk).
Sloane Square tube.* **Open** 9am-6.30pm Mon, Tue, Thur-
Sat; 9am-7pm Wed; 10am-6pm Sun. **Credit** AmEx, MC, V.
Map p315 F11.
At Trotters, the clothes for under-11s are upmarket: you'll
find the likes of Diesel jeans, Oilily dresses and funky swim-
suits. Children can climb aboard the yellow Trotters Express

train to have their shoes fitted (the selection includes Start-rite, Mini Chukka, Dr Martens and pretty gingham sandals). *See also p198.*
Buggy access. Delivery service. Nappy-changing facilities. Play area.
Branch: 127 Kensington High Street, W8 (7937 9373).

What Katy Did
49 Kensington Church Street, W8 (7229 2201).
High Street Kensington or Notting Hill Gate tube.
Open 10.30am-6pm Mon-Fri; 10am-6.30pm Sat.
Credit AmEx, MC, V. **Map** p312 B8.
This small boutique of 'kiddy couture' stocks an eclectic, stylish selection including Bengh Per Principesse, Bunny London, La Princesse Au Petit Pois, Quincy and Belgian label Tree. What Katy Did's pale blue wooden panelled walls and whitewashed floors give a seasidey feel, enhanced by the rocking dolphin seat.
Buggy access. Mail order. Nappy-changing facilities.

Second-hand

Boomerang
69 Blythe Road, W14 (7610 5232). Olympia tube.
Open 10am-6pm Mon-Sat. **No credit cards**.
Boomerang sells new and nearly new clothes, as well as toys, nursery equipment, maternity wear, and kiddie and buggy boards.
Buggy access.

Bunnies
201 Replingham Road, SW15 (8875 1228). Southfields tube. **Open** 10am-5pm Tue. **No credit cards**.
People travel to this clothing agency to pick up a bargain. Prams and buggies spill on to the pavement and there's also plenty of nursery equipment inside. Clothes for eight year-olds and under range from cheap Mothercare and Ladybird rejects to OshKosh and Gap. You can also bring in old toys, books, puzzles, games, clothes and hardware on a sale-or-return basis.
Buggy access.

Chocolate Crocodile
39 Morpeth Road, E9 (8985 3330). Mile End tube then 277 bus. **Open** 11am-5pm Mon-Sat. **Credit** MC, V.
Chocolate Crocodile benefits from a great location next to Victoria Park. Many a mum delves among the second-hand clothes, new and old toys, books and equipment. New wooden toys by Dutch company Woodware and Charles Toys include ABC puzzles, xylophones and train sets. A play area keeps littl'uns busy while you browse.
Buggy access. Play area.

Encore
53 Stoke Newington Church Street, N16 (7254 5329). Bus 73. **Open** 10am-5.30pm Tue-Sat. **Credit** AmEx, MC, V.
Good second-hand clothes are available in the front room (from £2 for baby clothes; £8 for girls' and boys' garb), and the spacious backroom has a great selection of shoes. Kids' feet are properly measured and they're encouraged to run around to ensure their well-made Start-rites or Bundegaards are a perfect fit. You'll also find colourful wellies and new OshKosh clothes on sale. Encore also has a low shelf with toys to keep the tots entertained, a useful noticeboard and nappies on hand for emergencies.
Buggy access. Mail order. Nappy-changing facilities. Play area.

The Little Trading Company
7 Bedford Corner, The Avenue, W4 (8742 3152).
Turnham Green tube. **Open** 9am-5pm Mon-Fri; 9am-4.30pm Sat. **No credit cards**.
One child's rubbish is another's treasure in this small shop, where there are some great bargains to be had: on our visit we spotted a single buggy for just £9 and a Mamas and Papas beech changing table for £60. You'll also find Brio, Lego, Fisher-Price and Early Learning Centre toys, plus books and videos, party shoes and second-hand Roller blades; all items are taken on a profit-share, sale-or-return basis. Haircutting on Wednesday and Friday afternoons costs £8.50.
Buggy access. Delivery service. Play area.

Merry-Go-Round
12 Clarence Road, E5 (8985 6308/www.merrygr.net).
Hackney Central rail. **Open** 10am-5.30pm Mon-Sat.
Credit AmEx, DC, MC, V.
A wide variety of good quality clothes for babies, children and young adults, includes labels ranging from Gap, Next and M&S to OshKosh, Oilily and Bon Bleu. It also stocks casual and maternity wear for women, but the under-threes get the lion's share of the stock, with videos, toys, books and equipment. Buggies, cots and high chairs can be bought at a fraction of the new cost. With nappy-changing facilities and a play area, Merry-Go-Round is fun for all the family.
Buggy access. Nappy-changing facilities. Play area.

Pixies
14 Fauconberg Road, W4 (8995 1568/ www.pixiesonline.co.uk). Chiswick Park or Turnham Green tube. **Open** 10am-4.30pm Tue-Fri; 10am-3pm Sat.
Credit MC, V.
You can find wellies and car seats, board games and tricycles in this well-organised shop. The stock is set out on rails and shelves round the side, and storage boxes and a playpen full of toys take up the central area. There are designer cast-offs for the under-12s, but the swimwear and excellent Tripp Trapp high chairs are new.
Buggy access. Mail order. Play area.

Rainbow
249 Archway Road, N6 (8340 8003). Highgate tube.
Open 10.30am-5.30pm Mon-Sat. **Credit** MC, V.
Anoraks, swimwear, coats and other good-quality second-hand clothes have labels ranging from M&S to French Connection, Oilily and Moschino. Socks are priced at 50p, clothing starts at £2.95 and shoes sell well, especially trainers for babies. Any unsold clothes go to children's charities. There is a play table for trying out the second-hand toys and books, but if you want new ones, pop two doors down to the sister shop (*see p209*).
Buggy access.

Rub-a-Dub-Dub
198 Stroud Green Road, N4 (7263 5577). Finsbury Park tube/rail. **Open** 10am-5pm Mon-Fri; 9.30am-5.30pm Sat.
No credit cards.
New and second-hand clothes for the under-fives (including some designer labels) are the treats in this knowledge-ably run little store, but you'll also find some second-hand toys and baby hardware. Everything from a Maclaren pushchair to a Baby Bjorn carrier is tested before sale. Maxi-cosi car seats are popular: littl'uns up to 13 months can sleep in the smaller baby carrier and there's also a model for tots aged nine months to four years (£99). If you want to sell any goods yourself, bring them along and you can fix a price on the spot.
Buggy access. Delivery service. Play area.

Junior Consumers

Top: Museum shops

Only the most disciplined of museum visitors can ignore the shop on the way out. For many children, spending their pocket money is the best bit of the trip. These are the most fun.

National Gallery
Housed in the Sainsbury Wing of the National Gallery, the shop displays attractive arty merchandise that includes a Van Gogh *Sunflowers* mousemat and a cardboard Rousseau jungle print storage box. For the pre-school artist there are Galt paints, thick brushes in a plastic pot and a first painting set. Stationery is excellent, and a small selection of art books for young ones, including the likes of *Looking at Pictures* by Joy Richardson and *Miffy Goes to an Art Gallery*, is perfect for budding Picassos. *See p87.*

Science Museum
The shop's catalogue and its website arrange its educational but funky wares by age, category or department. But whatever the age of your child, the stuff here will inspire them to study the stars through a telescope, build their own canal system or launch a Saturn V Rocket that explodes into eight parts. *See p72.*

Tate Modern
There are display copies for kids to browse through among the large selection of art introduction books for three months to 16 years. Littl'uns can learn their ABC with Roy Lichtenstein or about paintings with *Miffy at the Gallery*. Secondary school kids can discover the life and works of Paul Klee, Monet and Edward Hopper in a very attractive series (£8.99 each). There are foam books at £4.99, Jigsaw Art colours and shapes for £1.99, Eric Carle's *The Very Busy Spider* at £5.99, William Weyman's pup photographs for £4.99 and a book on the colours of India. The luminous stationery is pretty tempting, too. *See p41.*

Swallows & Amazons
91 Nightingale Lane, SW12 (8673 0275). Clapham South tube. **Open** 10am-5.30pm Mon-Sat. **No credit cards.**
Rails of second-hand designer and chainstore clothes for young children (average £10) are upstairs; clothes for older boys and girls are on display on the ground floor. Second-hand hardware is also sold here. *See also p198.*
Buggy access. Play area.

Shoes

Buckle My Shoe
19 St Christopher's Place, W1 (7935 5589). Bond Street tube. **Open** 10am-6pm Mon-Wed, Fri, Sat; 10am-7pm Thur. **Credit** AmEx, MC, V. **Map** p316 H6.

The HQ of this mini-chain is an upbeat black and white shop with a wall of Jellycats and rails of Calvin Klein, Paul Smith, O'Neill and Gasolio.
Buggy access. Delivery service. Mail order.
Branches: Harvey Nichols, 109-25 Knightsbridge, SW1 (7235 5000); Brent Cross Shopping Centre, NW4 (8202 4423); Bentalls, Kingston-upon-Thames, Surrey (8546 1001).

Instep
45 St John's Wood High Street, NW8 (7722 7634). St John's Wood tube. **Open** 9.30am-5.30pm Mon-Sat; 11am-5pm Sun. **Credit** AmEx, MC, V.
Instep's own-brand of school, holiday and party shoes and boots are made in Italy. Trained fitters will fit mock croc boots, canvas sandals and patent pink shoes on to little or adult feet up to size seven. For babies there are pre-walkers by Timberland and first walking shoes by Start-rite and Babybotte, while older children can choose from a wide range of Ricosta and Start-rite shoes, Dunlop wellies, socks and tights by Ergee and Faulke, and school bags. There are toys on hand to keep small shoppers amused seven days a week.
Buggy access.
Branches throughout town. Check the phone book for your nearest.

Pom d'Api
32 Rosslyn Hill, NW3 (7431 9532). Hampstead tube. **Open** 10am-5.30pm Tue-Sat; noon-5pm Sun. **Credit** MC, V.
Classy French footwear sold here is currently causing a stir in the pre-schools. Newborns can kick in jester boots (£31), which come gift-wrapped in a tin covered with apples and hearts. Older fry can try patent leather white sandals (from £40) or trainers covered in 3-D leopard spots (from £55). Feet are measured on the cute brown leather child-sized sofa and matching yellow armchair.
Mail order. Play area.

The Shoe Station
3 Station Approach, Kew, Surrey (8940 9905/ www.theshoestation.co.uk). Kew Gardens tube. **Open** 9.30am-5.30pm Mon-Sat. **Credit** MC, V.
The Shoe Station prides itself on protecting small feet with accurate measuring by trained fitters. Shoes are hardwearing and practical: Babybotte, Start-rite, Elefanten and Buckle My Shoe cowboy boots. Outside is a shoe recycling bin for cast-offs.
Buggy access. Delivery service. Play area.

Stepping Out
106 Pitshanger Lane, W5 (8810 6141). **Open** 10am-5.30pm Mon-Fri; 9am-5.30pm Sat. **Credit** AmEx, DC, MC, V.
Staff aim to find the perfect shoe for every customer. There are tiny leather pre-walkers, beautifully embroidered booties and trendy backless trainers. Usual and more exotic shoes by Trotty, Mod 8, Naturino and Ricosta average at £30 and some models reach the £50 mark.
Buggy access. Delivery service. Mail order. Play area.

Skate & surf

O'Neill
9-15 Neal Street, WC2 (7836 7686/ www.oneilleurope.com). Covent Garden or Leicester Square tube. **Open** 10am-7pm Mon-Wed, Fri, Sat; 10am-8pm Thur; noon-6pm Sun. **Credit** AmEx, MC, V. **Map** p317 L6.

Pick a pocket-money toy or two at **Fagin's Toys**. *See p209*.

Up west

The best selection of children's boutiques, and the biggest branches of the chain stores, are to be found on Oxford and Regent Streets. If you're one of those people for whom even the thought of setting foot in the area brings you out in a hot flush, avoid the crowds (or at least the worst of them) by going on a weekday.

Regent Street is calmer than Oxford Street and there you'll find the joy of **Gymboree** (see p198). **Esprit** (178-82 Regent Street, W1, 7025 7700) has a gorgeous range, such as simple T-shirts with striking designs and funky pedal-pushers, while **Benetton** (255-9 Regent Street, W1, 7647 4249) is bright with lime, turquoise and pink items including some tie-dye, denims and the classic Airtexes. Of course, Regent Street is best known as home to toy mecca **Hamleys** (see p208). Delightfully cheap, imaginative baby and kidswear can be found on the first floor of **H&M** (174-6 Oxford Street, W1, 7612 1820). Its Chilboogi range comprises fun clothes inspired by city and street culture.

Trendier clothes – for double the price – are to be found at the various West End branches of **Next** (203/325/327 Oxford Street, W1, 7434 0477/7659 9730/7409 2746; 160 Regent Street, W1, 7434 2515). Among the khaki shorts and white denims at **Gap Kids** is the colourful, tough new sporty Gap Athletic range. There are several Gaps the length of Oxford Street but the store at 376-88 Oxford Street (7408 2400) is huge and has a feeding room that is not a toilet. It's also handily equipped with pagers and controlled cubicles from where you can call for assistance or moderate the muzak at the push of a button. Sportaholics could try the cavernous kingdom of **Niketown** on Oxford Circus (see p207). Shopaphobes, on the other hand, should head straight for **John Lewis** (278-306 Oxford Street, 7629 7711), where you can buy everything you need – and feed and change your baby in peace and quiet or visit the kiddie-friendly café – on one floor. There are sleepsuits, Elle stripy shirts, pyjamas, baby goods, school uniforms, sensible and silk shoes and advisers on hand to help.

But if the crowds get too much for you, take heart in the pedestrianised oasis of **St Christopher's Place** off Oxford Street, where you'll find not only Pizza Express, Cranks and Bean Juice opposite **Humla** (see p199), but also decent public loos. If you're looking for original, expensive shoes, **Buckle My Shoe** (see p204) is a delight.

The Californian beach-bum look for pint-sized street surfers can be accessed upstairs. Those all-important wallets, T-shirts and droopy trousers are expensive but adored by near-teens.
Buggy access.
Branch: 7 Carnaby Street, W1 (7734 3778).

Quiksilver

Units 1 & 23, Thomas Neal Centre, Earlham Street, WC2 (7836 5371/www.quiksilver.com). Covent Garden tube. **Open** 10am-7pm Mon-Sat; noon-6pm Sun. **Credit** AmEx, MC, V. **Map** p317 L6.
For many adolescent boys, this is the label to crave. This Australian surfwear shop has sporty clothes (for girls and boys aged two to adult) that are casual looking but hard-wearing. If the trousers (from about £40) and T-shirts (from about £15) seem too expensive for the relaxed look, check out the accessories – wallets from £9, and rucksacks from £18.
Buggy access.
Branch: Unit 7, North Piazza, Covent Garden, WC2 (7240 5886).

Skate of Mind

Unit 26, Thomas Neal Centre, Earlham Street, WC2 (7836 9060). Covent Garden tube. **Open** 10am-7pm Mon-Sat; noon-6pm Sun. **Credit** DC, MC, V. **Map** p317 L6.
Young teens come here for the decks as well as the essential look to ride them with. Baggy T-shirts and low-slung trousers for the skateboard set are all present and correct.
Branch: 4 Marlborough Court, W1 (7434 0295).

Slam City Skates

16 Neal's Yard, WC2 (7240 0928/www.slamcity.com). Covent Garden tube. **Open** 10am-6.30pm Mon-Sat; 1-5pm Sun. **Credit** AmEx, MC, V. **Map** p317 L6.
A mecca for skateboarding adolescents, who flock here for their decks and accessories, and all-important labels by Stüssy, Silas and Droors.

Sportswear & trainers

Decathlon

Canada Water Retail Park, Surrey Quays Road, SE16 (7394 2000/www.decathlon.co.uk). Canada Water tube. **Open** 10am-7.30pm Mon-Thur; 10am-8pm Fri; 9am-7pm Sat; 11am-5pm Sun. **Credit** MC, V.
A French megastore with efficient staff, where 60 types of sport are represented. Children's shoes and equipment are stocked – the store's own brand plus Adidas, Nike and so on.
Buggy access. Delivery service. Play area.

First Sport

Whiteley's Shopping Centre, Queensway, W2 (7792 1139/www.firstsport.co.uk). Queensway tube. **Open** 10am-9pm Mon-Sat; noon-6pm Sun. **Credit** AmEx, DC, MC, V. **Map** p312 C6.
This is the biggest London branch of a large chain of sportswear retailers. The trainer selection is impressive, with sizes for children from age four in Adidas, Reebok and Nike.
Buggy access.
Branches throughout town. Check the phone book for your nearest.

JD Sport

267 Oxford Street, W1 (7491 7677/www.jdsports.co.uk). Oxford Circus tube. **Open** 9am-8pm Mon, Tue, Sat; 9am-9pm Wed-Fri; noon-6pm Sun. **Credit** AmEx, MC, V. **Map** p316 H6.
This sportswear chain is renowned for its range of footwear, including teeny tiny trainers for little ones. All the big trainer names are represented, but chaotic service means it may be a while before you get the size you want.
Branches throughout town. Check the phone book for your nearest.

JJB Sports

*301-9 Oxford Street, W1 (7409 2619/www.jjb.co.uk).
Oxford Circus tube.* **Open** 10am-7pm Mon-Wed, Fri, Sat;
10am-8pm Thur; noon-6pm Sun. **Credit** AmEx, MC, V.
Map p316 H6.

There's a massive range of trainers (Adidas, Nike, Lotto), a
good line in reduced-price sportswear, replica kit and end-of-
lines and an army of callow youth in JJB T-shirts spending
an age discovering whether they have your child's size in the
bargain Nikes he's pinned his hopes on. Don't visit at the
weekend and expect to come away sane.
Buggy access.
Branches throughout town. Check the phone book for
your nearest.

Lillywhite's

*24-36 Lower Regent Street, SW1 (7409 2619). Piccadilly
Circus tube.* **Open** 10am-7pm Mon-Wed, Fri, Sat; 10am-
8pm Thur; noon-6pm Sun. **Credit** AmEx, DC, MC, V.
Map p319 K7.

The only shop in London where all sports are adequately represented, Lillywhite's is noted for its cricketwear and equipment in season, as well as all-year-round footie kit, swimwear
and skiwear. Its trainer selection for young feet is disappointing; you'll find more labels in funkier trainer places.
Buggy access.

Niketown

*236 Oxford Street, W1 (7612 0800/www.nike.com).
Oxford Circus tube.* **Open** 10am-7pm Mon-Wed; 10am-
8pm Thur-Sat; noon-6pm Sun. **Credit** AmEx, MC, V.
Map p316 J6.

Though this much-hyped sportswear store has no dedicated
children's section, small-size Nikes and leisurewear are on display on the top floor, with their hefty prices only too evident.
*Buggy access. Delivery service. Mail order. Nappy-changing
facilities.*

Soccerscene

*56-7 Carnaby Street, W1 (7439 0778/
www.soccerscene.co.uk). Oxford Circus tube.*
Open 9.30am-7pm Mon-Sat. **Credit** AmEx, MC, V.
Map p316 J6.

Premier League replica kits, football boots and trainers can
all be found in small sizes in this useful central London shop.
Mail order.

Super Sport Shoe Warehouse

*102-5 Whitechapel High Street, E1 (7247 5111). Aldgate
East tube.* **Open** 9.30am-6pm Mon-Fri; 10am-5.30pm Sat;
9am-5pm Sun. **Credit** DC, MC, V.

An uncool place full of cool names (Adidas, Nike, Reebok) at
astonishingly low prices. You can buy Nikes for children from
as young as four months old.
Branches throughout town. Check the phone book for
your nearest.

Toys

Bikes

Chains worth visiting for well-priced children's bikes
include **Daycocks** and **Halfords** (check the phone
directory for branches). We've found Daycocks has the
edge when it comes to knowledgeable service, but
Halford's has a spectacular range of children's models.

Action Bikes

*23-6 Embankment Place, Northumberland Avenue,
WC2 (7930 2525). Embankment tube/Charing Cross or
Victoria tube/rail.* **Open** 9am-6pm Mon-Wed, Fri; 9am-
7pm Thur; 9.30am-5.30pm Sat. **Credit** AmEx, MC, V.
Map p319 L8.

A well-stocked shop with helpful staff, under the arches at
Embankment. Most children's bikes stocked are of the 20- and
24-inch wheel variety, but there are a few smaller ones. Main
makes include Raleigh and Universal.
Buggy access. Delivery service. Mail order.
Branches: 19 Dacre Street, SW1 (7799 2233); 3 St Bride
Street, EC4 (7583 7373).

Apex Cycles

*40 Clapham High Street, SW4 (7622 1334/
apexcycles.com). Clapham North tube.* **Open**
9.30am-5.30pm Tue-Sat. **Credit** AmEx, MC, V.

Friendly staff sell Raleighs to new cyclists, Specialized and
Trek to the more experienced. Quality seconds are also sold,
and decent bikes may be accepted in part exchange.
Buggy access.

The Bike Shed

68 George Lane, E18 (8530 7436). South Woodford tube.
Open 9am-5.30pm Mon-Wed, Fri; 9am-5pm Sat; 9am-1pm
Sun. **Credit** AmEx, MC, V.

The shed has cheery staff and a good stock of children's bikes,
with a useful Raleigh part-exchange system: when your offspring has grown out of a bike, you can trade it for the next
size up.
Buggy access. Delivery service.

Bikefix

*48 Lamb's Conduit Street, WC1 (7405 4639/
www.bikefix.co.uk). Holborn tube.* **Open** 8.30am-7pm
Mon-Fri; 11am-5pm Sat. **Credit** DC, MC, V. **Map**
p317 M5.

This small, well-established shop specialises in two-wheeled
people carriers. If you're after a waterproof pull-along buggy
(replete with tall red flag) or a low-slung recumbent bike ,this
is the place to go.
Buggy access. Delivery service. Mail order.

Chamberlaine & Son

*75-7 Kentish Town Road, NW1 (7485 4488/
www.chamberlainecycles.co.uk). Camden Town tube.*
Open 8.30am-6pm Mon-Sat. **Credit** AmEx, DC MC, V.

Possibly the best children's bike shop north of the river.
Chamberlaine stocks a comprehensive range of two-wheel-
ers from GT, Raleigh and Peugeot and imports an amazingly colourful brand called Cool! Loekie. All bikes are well set
up before leaving the shop. An ideal starting point for the
novice junior.
Buggy access. Delivery service. Mail order.

Edwardes

*221 Camberwell Road, SE5 (7703 3676/5720).
Elephant & Castle tube/rail then P3, 12, 68, 171,
176 bus.* **Open** 8.30am-6pm Mon-Sat. **Credit** AmEx,
MC, V.

South-east London's busiest, always full of earnest-looking
adults in full Gore-tex regalia and expensive lids, waiting
for their smart bikes to be repaired. There's an excellent
range of shiny children's bikes by Peugeot, Bronx, Raleigh,
BMX and mountain bikes, and trailers and seats for little
ones. Repairs are executed quickly, thoroughly and reasonably cheaply.
Buggy access. Delivery service. Mail order.

Junior Consumers

FW Evans

111-15 Waterloo Road, SE1 (7928 2208/
www.evanscycles.com). Waterloo tube/rail. **Open**
9am-8pm Mon-Fri; 9am-6pm Sat; 11am-4pm Sun.
Credit AmEx, MC, V. **Map** p320 N8.
Those in the vicinity of Waterloo should find everything they
need in this large, well-stocked emporium. Nothing in the way
of toddler bikes, but it does have the entire Trek range, and
that's about as good as kids' cycling gets.
Buggy access. Delivery service. Mail order.
Branches: 51-52 Rathbone Place, W1 (7580 4107); 77-9
The Cut, SE1 (7928 4785); 127 Wandsworth High Street,
SW18 (8877 1878).

Fun & games

Cheeky Monkeys

202 Kensington Park Road, W11 (7792 9022).
Notting Hill Gate tube. **Open** 9.30am-5.30pm Mon-Fri;
10am-5.30pm Sat. **Credit** MC, V. **Map** p312 A6.
London's five Cheeky Monkeys may vary in size but all have
the same, regularly updated stock of gifts for children. There
are some beautiful wooden toys: a blue-shuttered dolls' house
and a wooden London bus with removable passengers are
among the favourites. Dressing-up treats include a mermaid
outfit, fairy wings, dinosaur suits and ladybird raincoats.
Buggy access.
Branches throughout town. Check the phone book for
your nearest.

Disney Store

140-144 Regent Street, W1 (7287 6558). Piccadilly
Circus tube. **Open** 10am-8pm Mon-Sat; noon-6pm Sun.
Credit AmEx, MC, V. **Map** p316 J6.
Disney merchandise, toys and clothes, including *102
Dalmatians* nightwear, Tigger and Pooh babygros and shiny
Tinkerbell and Buzz Lightyear playsuits; you can even dress
your baby as one of the seven dwarves. Videos and DVDs of
current releases are also on sale.
Buggy access. Delivery service. Mail order.
Branches throughout town. Check the phone book for
your nearest.

Fun Learning

Bentall's Centre, Clarence Street, Kingston-upon-Thames,
Surrey (8974 8900). Kingston rail. **Open** 9am-6pm
Mon-Wed, Fri, Sat; 9am-8pm Thur; 11am-5pm Sun.
Credit MC, V.
Fun Learning has toys for everyone from 5- to 15-year-olds,
including some brainteasers and puzzles that will even flum-
mox adults. Eager learners try out the educational software
at the computer table in the centre, while others head straight
to the toys and books arranged around the edges, encompassing themes such as the night sky and the animal kingdom. There's outdoor equipment, including skipping ropes
and hula hoops, too, and a large craft area, where kids can
make pipe-cleaner figures, tissue flowers or use Hama Beads
to make coasters and placemats.
Delivery service. Mail order. Nappy-changing facilities.
Play area.

Hamleys

188-96 Regent Street, W1 (7494 2000/www.hamleys.com).
Oxford Circus tube. **Open** 10am-8pm Mon-Fri; 9.30am-8pm
Sat; noon-6pm Sun. **Credit** AmEx, MC, V. **Map** p316 J6.
'The world's most famous toyshop' is a dream – or a nightmare – depending on which way you look at it. On entering
you are bombarded with battery-operated Hoppy Bunnies,
magic displays and circling paper gliders in the chaotic
demonstration area. Round the corner three Steiff bears take
off in a rocket before you enter a jungle full of soft wild animals. The basement is more peaceful with puzzles and
games. Send your child up the Ghost Stair to the giant talking book on the second floor where you'll find everything
you need for pre-school and nursery-aged kids. The third
floor is stuffed with dolls and a great range of dressing-up
clothes, while floor four houses radio-controlled trains, planes
and cars, Action Man and Scalextric. At the top, the Lego
Café is an oasis of kiddy portions, high chairs and nappy-
changing facilities, watched over by a larger-than-life talking Lego Darth Vadar (£499.99) and circled by an outsize
train running round the balcony. To avoid the worst of the
crowds, go on a weekday.
Buggy access. Delivery service. Mail order.
Branch: 3 The Piazza, WC2 (7210 4646).

Traditional toys

Benjamin Pollock's Toyshop

44 The Market, Covent Garden, WC2 (7379 7866/
www.pollocks-coventgarden.co.uk). Covent Garden tube.
Open 10.30am-6pm Mon-Sat; noon-5pm Sun.
Credit AmEx, MC, V. **Map** p319 L7.
This first-floor shop is famous for its cardboard Victorian theatres. Other toys include British lead soldiers and Beefeaters,
Russian dolls, a wooden Noah's Ark, tin toys and cut-out
models. Appealing books include traditional pop-up classics
such as Struwelpeter and Max and Moritz; postcards include
commedia dell'arte. There are also Punch & Judy puppets
(from £100) and others from the Czech Republic and Bavaria.
A colourful alphabet caterpillar with finger puppets costs
£35, but there is a shelf of cheaper items for smaller earners.
Mail order.

The Farmyard

63 Barnes High Street, SW13 (8878 7338). Barnes Bridge
rail. **Open** 9.30am-5.30pm Mon-Sat. **Credit** AmEx, MC, V.
Despite the name, it's not just beasts you'll find here. The
Farmyard is perfect for gifts: one wall is filled with bright
wooden toys – a double decker bus, a lorry of building blocks
and a Noah's Ark. Opposite are smaller knick-knacks such as
glow-in-the-dark stars, games and puzzles, Madeline dolls and
pop-up puppets. Kids can dress up as a fairy or a princess for
a party, and there's a gift-wrapping service, too.
Buggy access. Mail order. Play area.
Branch: 54 Friar's Stile Road, Richmond, Surrey (8332
0038).

Harlequin House

3 Kensington Mall, W8 (7221 8629). High Street
Kensington tube. **Open** 11am-5.30pm Tue, Fri, Sat.
No credit cards. Map p314 B9.
The longer you look, the more you'll find in this quirky, hig-
gledy-piggledy puppet and mask kingdom. A magnificent
Punch & Judy totem pole marks the centre of the store and is
surrounded on all sides by intriguing goodies. To the left are
glove and finger puppets, from felt dragons to finger mice
and pigs in a box. Masks adorn the back wall: Venetian, papier-mâché, *commedia dell'arte*, party, neutral and cardboard
cut-outs. Wooden puppet theatres start at £25 but you can
get a nifty material one to hang in a doorway for £35. Even
if you don't buy, the gruesome four-foot latex witch and the
American ventriloquist dolls are worth a peek anyway.
Mail order.

Kristen Baybars

7 Mansfield Road, NW3 (7267 0934). Belsize Park tube/Gospel Oak rail/C2, C12 bus. **Open** 11am-6pm Tue-Sat. **No credit cards.**
Craftswoman Kristen Baybars works in the back room painting period dolls' houses to order. One of her specialities is a jigsaw puzzle the size of a thumbnail. You can appreciate the blunt sign 'any unaccompanied children will be sold into slavery' as you slide open the doors of Baybars' exquisitely furnished dolls' houses. Children just can't be boisterous in this shop.
Buggy access.

Never Never Land

3 Midhurst Parade, N10 (8883 3997). East Finchley tube. **Open** 10am-5pm Tue, Wed, Fri, Sat. **Credit** MC, V.
You can just squeeze a buggy into this tiny shop specialising in dolls' houses and furniture. Kits of cottages and Georgian townhouses start from £75 and ready-made models begin at £130.
Buggy access. Mail order.

Peter Rabbit & Friends

42 The Market, Covent Garden, WC2 (7497 1777). Embankment or Covent Garden tube/Charing Cross tube/rail. **Open** 10am-8pm Mon-Sat; 10am-6pm Sun. **Credit** AmEx, MC, V. **Map** p319 L7.
Somehow Winnie the Pooh and the Wombles have found their way into Beatrix Potter land. The stock downstairs is largely tacky. Upstairs has the (more covetable) book sets, videos, nightwear, duvet covers, soaps, spoons, a four-foot Peter Rabbit and postcards.
Buggy access. Delivery service. Mail order.

Rainbow

253 Archway Road, N6 (8340 8003). Highgate tube. **Open** 10.30am-5.30pm Mon-Sat. **Credit** MC, V.
Speciality wooden toys in this quirky shop include farms, fun dolls' houses (£70-£180), pull-along wooden crocodiles and ducks and a push-along terrier. There are also dressing-up clothes and puppet theatres. With the sister shop at No.249 full of second-hand clothing (*see p203*), you'll have lots to load into the car in the parking bay outside.
Buggy access.

Soup Dragon

27 Topsfield Parade, Tottenham Lane, N8 (8348 0224/ www.soup-dragon.co.uk). Finsbury Park tube/rail then W7 bus. **Open** 9.30am-6pm Mon-Sat. **Credit** MC, V.
Soup Dragon has fun clothes and toys for small children under ten, to suit every pocket. Bell trees for babies start from £6.90, and beautiful hand-crafted sit-and-ride toys for toddlers cost from £27.50. There are forts, farms, castles, airports, garages and all sorts of dolls' houses. Imaginative English-made knitwear sits alongside cool Dracula outfits (from £15.90).
Buggy access. Play area.
Branch: 106 Lordship Lane, SE22 (8693 5575).

Traditional Toys

53 Godfrey Street, SW3 (7352 1718). Sloane Square tube then 11, 19, 22 bus/49 bus. **Open** 10am-5.30pm Mon-Fri; 10am-6pm Sat; 11am-4.30pm Sun. **Credit** AmEx, MC, V. **Map** p315 E11.
This menagerie of toys includes dressable American Muffy VanderBear with his friend Hoppy the Rabbit, bear and cow wooden tricycles (£49.99) and entrancing Julip horses. Traditional toys indeed.
Buggy access. Delivery service. Mail order.

Tridias

25 Bute Street, SW7 (7584 2330/www.tridias.co.uk). South Kensington tube/14, 74 bus. **Open** 9.30am-6pm Mon-Fri; 10am-6pm Sat. **Credit** MC, V. **Map** p315 D10.
Children are allowed to play with the traditional toys stocked here, which include Georgian Plan dolls' houses and tasteful dolls, plus prams and double buggies for same. In addition, there's a well-stocked art section and some imaginative dressing-up clothes; we particularly liked a striking space suit (£19.99).
Buggy access. Delivery service. Mail order. Play area.
Branch: 6 Lichfield Terrace, Sheen Road, Richmond, Surrey (8948 3459).

Local toyshops

Fagin's Toys

84 Fortis Green Road, N10 (8444 0282). East Finchley tube. **Open** 9am-5.30pm Mon-Sat; 10am-3pm Sun. **Credit** AmEx, MC, V.
Traditional and educational toys aimed firmly at the local clientele. Smart frames, baby walkers and tiny trikes are sold for toddlers, and there are Orchard and Living and Learning games for older kids. The outdoor department shows off the smallest of the TP aluminium climbing frames, while the cheapo section boasts bangles, plastic frogs and whoopee cushions for less than a pound. Pretty much a must for Muswell Hillbillies.
Buggy access. Play area.

First stop for toys in N16: **Route 73 Kids**. *See p211.*

Get outta town

The shrink-wrapped 'retail and leisure experience' offered by the out-of-town shopping centre may not be to everybody's taste, but shopaholics with young children to consider adore them. The one with the biggest fan club is the smoke-free **Bluewater**, the 'day-out destination' shopping centre, in Kent, easily accessible from London Bridge Station.

There are a mind-boggling 320 shops at Bluewater. Exploring them without knee-high accomplices can be arranged in advance if you book your child into the Academy crèche (£5 per hour for children from six months). The crèche is split into two sections, the first, for children up to four, has 50 places. Academy 2, for children up to 12, has 150 places. Children are watched over by staff with NNEBs as they play with educational toys, arts and crafts materials or computers or take part in various sporty activities. It's enough to make toddlers disown their parents when they come to collect them. The centre has a number of Welcome Halls, where the parent-and-child loos, feeding rooms and nappy-changing facilities can be visited before the fun starts. The Kids Concierge desk has a stash of pushchairs and toddler reins for hire. A glass and steel atrium houses the Wintergarden, where all the usual fast food suspects are lined up for family lunch experiences; otherwise there are vast numbers of theme restaurants (TGI Fridays, Ed's Easy Diner etc) that make a meal out of catering for children. Cafés and pâtisseries, ice-cream shops and sweet counters lie in wait along the mall to induce that unforgettable tantrum experience (another reason for using that crèche).

Once shopping, eating and ablutions are taken care of, exploring the great outdoors is encouraged, especially during the summer. Bluewater has its own fishing lake (bring your own equipment and licence, and pay £6 to a Park Ranger). There are three miles of cycle paths (bikes, tandems and quads for hire from £3 for 30 mins). The boating lake can be rowed upon in the summer, at a cost of £6 per 30 minutes or £9 per hour. In the Wintergarden, young children may well clamour for £1 to visit the hideously named Critter Country, where an animatronic menagerie lies in wait to give them a thrill: Bert the Frog, Sydney the Swan and the imaginatively named Foxie the fox can all be spied in the undergrowth. Young children are given sweets and a badge to mark their visit.

No other shopping centre within reach of the capital can quite live up to Bluewater, but there are several more that have the parking, the crèche, the toilets and the range of shops to make retail therapy all the more therapeutic. **Brent Cross Shopping Centre** has the advantage of being in London, on the tube line, and having a playcare and activity centre, called Nipperboat. **Lakeside Thurrock**, more Bluewater-like in outlook, but without all the outdoor stuff, has a Stay 'n' Play Crèche for two- to seven-year-olds and children's films shown in the Warner Village cinema at 10.30am every Saturday. Wimbledon's **Centre Court Shopping Centre** has a Kids Club shoppers' crèche and a tram link to Croydon.

Bluewater
Greenhithe, Kent (08456 021021/ www.bluewater.co.uk). Greenhithe rail/A206 off M25 or A2. **Open** *10am-9pm Mon-Fri; 9am-8pm Sat; 11am-5pm Sun.*

Brent Cross Shopping Centre
Brent Cross, NW4 (8202 8095/ www.brentcross-london.com). Brent Cross or Hendon Central tube/North Circular Road (A406). **Open** *9am-8pm Mon-Fri; 9am-7pm Sat; 11am-5pm Sun.*

Centre Court Shopping Centre
4 Queen's Road, Wimbledon, SW19 (8944 8323). Wimbledon tube/rail. **Open** *9.30am-7pm Mon-Wed, Fri; 9.30am-8pm Thur; 9am-7pm Sat; 11am-5pm Sun.*

Lakeside Thurrock
West Thurrock, Essex (01708 869933). Lakeside rail/Junction 30/31 off M25. **Open** *10am-10pm Mon-Fri; 9am-7.30pm Sat; 11am-5pm Sun.*

Junior Consumers

Frederick Beck
22-6 Camden Passage, N1 (7226 3403). Angel tube. **Open** 9.30am-5.30pm Mon, Tue, Thur, Fri; 9am-5.30pm Wed, Sat. **Credit** AmEx, MC, V.

The staff in this odd mix of electrical shop and toy emporium pretend not to like kids, but the presence of a Hornby railway set, plus Brio and bead tables suggests they're not as stern as all that. Papo figures (Joan of Arc, pirates, knights and Romans) are all the rage, but there are other exciting goodies in this creaky, wooden-floored space, including marbles, Schleich animals, cap guns, make-up and Le Toy Van dolls' houses. In fact, it's hard to imagine that you'll leave empty-handed, especially given the choice of pocket-money priced goodies.
Buggy access. Delivery service. Play area.

Happy Returns
36 Rosslyn Hill, NW3 (7435 2431). Hampstead tube. **Open** 9.30am-5.30pm Mon-Fri; 10am-6pm Sat; noon-5.30pm Sun. **Credit** MC, V.

You'll return to this toy and party shop again and again to stock up on Christmas and birthday presents. On the top floor are balloons, cards, wrapping paper, Brio trains, Barbie outfits, stickers, finger paints and Miffy boogie bags (£12.99); below you'll find kites and drums, cricket bats and Airfix, Bob the Builder and Cluedo. There's no snobbery about mixing quality with commercial brands here, so you're likely to come across a Tweenies scooter next to Ambi soft toys for newborns, plastic armour, Playmobil, Sylvanian Families, Duplo, Noddy, Plan, Action Man and Tomy.
Buggy access.

Havana's Toy Box
Putney Exchange Shopping Centre, Putney High Street, SW15 (8780 3722). Putney Bridge tube/Putney rail. **Open** 9am-6pm Mon-Sat; 11am-5pm Sun. **Credit** AmEx, MC, V.
Wooden toys, soft toys, dressing-up clothes and night stuff are all squeezed into this tiny boutique for under-sixes. Goodies on show include farms, trucks, push-along animals, Beanies, fairy dresses, Sarah Barker baby shoes, kiddie sleeping bags and night lights with jungle design lampshades. You should find something in that lot.
Mail order.

Patrick's Toys & Models
107-11 Lillie Road, SW6 (7385 9864/ www.patrickstoys.co.uk). Fulham Broadway tube. **Open** 9.15am-5.45pm Mon-Sat. **Credit** MC, V.
This family-run business has been selling toys and models for over 50 years. Patrick's maintains a balance between traditional favourites and latest crazes in the toy department, and stocks models galore upstairs: rockets, planes, cars, military and science fiction figures. Straw bonnets, rubber masks and sheriff's badges will please the small-budget shopper, while old classics like Hornby, Scalextric, toy guns and go-karts will excite active kids. Even the ceiling is covered in tricycles.
Buggy access. Delivery service. Mail order.

Route 73 Kids
88 Stoke Newington Church Street, N16 (7923 7873/ www.route73kids.com). Bus 73. **Open** 10am-5.30pm Tue-Sat; noon-5pm Sun. **Credit** AmEx, MC, V.
The exciting window display at Route 73 Kids is enough to make you hop off the 73 bus as you're going past. This toy trove is small and cramped, but it's well set out with a central circular table of pocket money-priced delights and a ceiling bedecked with wooden and material mobiles, Jellycat animal rugs and a wooden rocking dolphin. The comprehensive baby range includes Ambi, Lamaze and a wobbly-backed Kouvalia snail. An art section sells liquid paint, protective Miffy aprons and marbling, weaving and sponging kits for £8. Performers can try fairy wings and skirt, while puppeteers have a go with the Manhattan Finger Puppet Theatre and Darwin the Wizard marionette.
Buggy access. Delivery service. Mail order. Nappy-changing facilities. Play area.

Snap Dragon
56 Turnham Green Terrace, W4 (8995 6618). Turnham Green tube. **Open** 9.30am-6pm Mon-Fri; 10am-5.30pm Sat. **Credit** AmEx, MC, V.
Colourful, original toys for under-11s occupy this tiny purple outlet. You can excavate dinosaur bones from clay with a Dino Dig or hatch eggs in water to produce shrimp-like 'pets' called Sea-Monkeys (from £5.99). Trad wooden toys – babywalkers, shape sorters, puzzles, rocking horses – are also well represented.
Buggy access. Delivery service.

Tiny Set Toys
54 Lower Richmond Road, SW15 (8788 0392). Putney Bridge tube/22 bus. **Open** 9.30am-5.30pm Mon-Sat; 10am-2pm Sun. **Credit** MC, V.
Britain's major stockist for TP aluminium climbing frames will also help fit them for £25. Swings, slides and paddling pools are piled up at the back of the three-level shop. Sports equipment can be found downstairs, opposite the Barbies, buggies and other dolls. You can snaffle pocket-money bargains such as bubble-blowing kits for 50p and Matchbox cars

for 75p on the first floor; here you'll also see traditional wooden sit-and-ride toys, teddy bears and rocking horses. On the top floor at Tiny Set Toys are piles of Lego, jigsaws, games and so on.
Buggy access. Delivery service. Mail order.

Toy City
Unit 62, Wood Green Shopping City, N22 (8881 0770). Wood Green tube. **Open** 9am-6pm Mon-Sat; 11am-5pm Sun. **Credit** AmEx, MC, V.
Everything modern and branded is crammed into this much-needed small local store, with budget tricycles and rocking horses suspended from the ceiling. You can hop into a Batman, Spiderman or Superman outfit or kit Barbie out with a new wardrobe. For imaginative play there are plastic soldiers and animals, and for creativity Galt paints, plus plenty of Lego, Brio and Duplo. If you're planning a kids' party, the cards, wrapping paper and helium balloons will do the trick.
Buggy access.

Toy House
67-9 Queens Market, E13 (8552 5420). Upton Park tube. **Open** 9am-6pm Mon-Sat. **No credit cards.**
This house is choc-a-bloc with hordes of branded toys and cheapies, much of which costs under £1. You can buy sports and swimming equipment all year round, get a cuddly bear gift-wrapped for Valentine's Day, or buy fibre-optic trees at Christmas. Greeting cards, balloons, silk flowers and 30 party bags for £1.25 will make your bash go with a bang.
Buggy access. Delivery service.

The Toy Station
10 Eton Street, Richmond, Surrey (8940 4896). Richmond tube/rail. **Open** 10am-5.30pm Mon-Fri; 10am-6pm Sat; noon-5pm Sun. **No credit cards.**
This small shop crams its action goods on to two floors; even the stairwell is jam-packed. You can pick up a robotic puppy or a bow and arrow on your way down to the plastic creatures (red-kneed tarantula) and radio-controlled raptor lurking among the games and Airfix kits. The top floor is well stocked with the usual suspects (Lego, Brio, Meccano) and has Baby Born, Scalextric and lots of Beanies.
Buggy access.

Toy Wonderland
10-11 Northways Parade, Finchley Road, NW3 (7722 9821/www.toywonderland.co.uk). Swiss Cottage tube. **Open** 10am-6pm Mon-Sat; 11am-3pm Sun. **Credit** AmEx, MC, V.
The plastic wonders you'll find in this chaotic venue are the likes of life-size machine guns, magnifying glasses, boomerangs and Polly Pocket knick-knacks. You can dress a two-year-old up as Winnie the Pooh or turn an eight-year-old into Spiderman. Other favourites are electronic guitars, Hornby trains and Warhammer, and you shouldn't miss the glittery stickers.
Buggy access. Delivery service. Mail order.

Word Play
1 Broadway Parade, N8 (8347 6700). Finsbury Park tube/rail then W7 bus. **Open** 9am-5.30pm Mon-Sat; 11am-5pm Sun. **Credit** AmEx, MC, V.
Tasteful books and musical instruments pull in Crouch End's parents in droves at weekends. Fancy maracas, cymbals, bells and xylophones provide a somewhat noisy accompaniment to the likes of glass painting and shell craft in the art section. You'll have to buy a sleepover kit (£9.99) to find out exactly what's in it.
Buggy access.

Junior Consumers

Activities & Fun

Everyone loves
the **Tate Modern**.
Honest. *See p218*

Arts & Entertainment

For fledgling culture vultures.

Young theatre-goers will have to wait a few more years until they see a central London arts centre that's dedicated just to them (see p224). Meanwhile, kids don't do too badly with a chirpy purpose-built theatre in south London, a pint-sized purpose-built marionette theatre in north London, and a floating purpose-built theatre on the canal. What's more, there are any number of theatre, art, dance and film clubs, in venues across the capital, all longing to entertain them. Check *Time Out* magazine's children's pages every week for forthcoming family arts events and previews of theatre performances.

Big-name circuses that visit London annually include Zippo's and the Chinese State Circus, both of whom spend a week or so in each venue (Blackheath, Peckham Rye, Alexandra Park and Highbury Fields are popular big-top pitching places). Again, check *Time Out* magazine for listings.

Many of the performance spaces, clubs and workshops we list below cater for children with disabilities and special needs; ask about facilities when you book. Bear in mind, too, that arts workshops and classes change termly, so always ring to check your chosen activity is still taking place.

Arts centres

Barbican Centre

Silk Street, EC2 (7638 8891/cinema hotline 7382 7000/ textphone 7382 7297/arts education programme 7382 2333/www.barbican.org.uk). Barbican tube/ Moorgate tube/rail. **Open** *Box office* 10am-8pm Mon-Sat; noon-8pm Sun. **Film Club** *Membership* £5; films £3 non-members; £2.50 members. **Gallery** 10am-6pm Mon, Tue, Thur-Sat; 10am-8pm Wed; noon-6pm Sun, bank hols. **Admission** *Library* free. *Exhibitions, films, shows, workshops* phone for details. **Membership** (BarbicanCard) £10. **Credit** AmEx, MC, V. **Map** p320 P5.
Arts lovers of all ages are served well by the Barbican, with its cinemas, concert halls, theatre and library. Free events for kids aged from three take place regularly in the children's library: storytellers, poets and magicians pop in to prove that libraries can be lively places. The library activities are hugely popular and numbers have to be limited; always phone to check there's space for your child before turning up. Family Film Club (Saturday mornings) is aimed at 5- to 11-year-olds, and combines screenings of films from around the world with workshops and activities. Children must be accompanied. The last Saturday of each month sees demonstrations in storytelling, make-up, animation, puppetry and/or dance. Family festivals, which are scheduled for school holidays and bank holiday weekends, are devised to complement productions and musical events in the theatres and concert halls and include workshops, puppet-making events and storytelling sessions. These are either free foyer events or ticket-only shows and workshops, which must be booked ahead. Joining the BarbicanCard scheme entitles you to monthly programmes and notices of special family events.

South Bank Centre

Belvedere Road, South Bank, SE1 (7960 4242/ www.sbc.org.uk). Waterloo tube/rail. **Open** *Box office* 9am-9pm daily. *Front desk* 10am-9pm daily. *Stilgoe Saturday Concerts* 3.30pm Sat; tickets £4.50-£12. **Tickets** prices vary; phone for details. **Credit** AmEx, MC, V. **Map** p319 M8.
Encompassing three spaces – the Royal Festival Hall, the Queen Elizabeth Hall and the Purcell Room – the South Bank does its bit to see children get rhythm. Regular concerts aimed at children cover a wide spectrum of styles, from classical and world, to new music and pop. Individual musicians, small ensembles and major orchestras form part of the programme, which caters for children as young as one. Frequent projects and workshops allow children to make some noise alongside professional musicians, and free walk-in activities take place in the centre's foyers.

One to look out for is the quarterly Stilgoe Saturday Concerts at the RFH, hosted by former broadcaster and lyricist Richard Stilgoe in conjunction with musicians from the nation's leading music colleges and the National Children's Orchestra (all aged under 14). Aimed at families, the concerts introduce audiences to classical favourites performed by the orchestra and treble choirs from primary and prep schools. Another favourite at the Festival Hall is the Gong Club, an unusual opportunity for children (aged seven and over) to learn to play the instruments that make up the Indonesian Gamelan, while learning about Java and its customs. Instruments include drums and gongs, and all music is taught by ear. Phone for details.

Both the resident symphony orchestras – the Philharmonia and the London Philharmonic – perform regular youth concerts, usually on Saturday mornings, at the Royal Festival Hall. Other children's music events are listed in the Centre's monthly brochures. The school holidays witness frequent free foyer workshops, and during the summer the Centre has daily all-day children's activities. The Hayward Gallery (see p217) is also part of the South Bank Centre.

Stratford Circus

Theatre Square, E15 (8279 1001/ www.stratford-circus.org.uk). Stratford tube/rail/DLR. **Open** *Box office* 11am-6pm or 30min after show starts Mon-Sat. **Tickets** £10; £3-£5 concessions, under-16s. *Go-card* £24 (6 shows). *Courses* prices vary; phone for details. **Credit** MC, V.
East London's Centre for the performing arts opened its doors in June 2001. Its directors have developed a quite frenetic programme of dance, theatre, comedy and music events, as well as a strong commitment to youthful participation in all

> ► Some of the places listed in this chapter also put on children's parties; see chapter **Parties**.

Activities & Fun

Getting creative in the garden of **Dulwich Picture Gallery**. *See p217.*

activities. Courses in DJ-ing, dance, drama, writing, music, choreography and other skills take place in the five studios and performance spaces housed in the building (titled Circus 1 to Circus 5). Stratford Circus was developed, thanks to lottery money, to build a centre for the performing arts, and to refurbish Theatre Royal Stratford East, next door. Dance and drama groups for older children (14 plus) start at just £1 a session; for further details and information on courses and performances, call for this season's programme of events.

Tricycle Theatre
269 Kilburn High Road, NW6 (7328 1000). Kilburn tube/Brondesbury rail. **Open** *Box office* 10am-9pm Mon-Sat; 2-9pm Sun. Children's shows 11.30am, 2pm Sat. Children's films 1pm Sat. **Tickets** *Sat theatre* £4.50; £4 advance bookings; *Sat films* £4; £3 under-16s. *Mailing list membership* £6. **Workshops** £20 per 10wk term; prices vary for half-term courses; phone for details. **Credit** MC, V.
This jewel in Kilburn's careworn high street aims to reflect the area's ethnic diversity in the work it showcases. Although this applies more to its adult programme, the Tricycle does a surprisingly good job of bringing international pieces and ideas to its children's stage. The theatre shows may be a magic show, performing puppets, or an adaptation of a classic requiring audience participation. Saturday lunchtime family films take place in the smart 300-seater cinema. Be prepared for lots of noise – the Tricycle vibe is intimate and informal, and children can run around until the film begins.

The dance and drama workshop programme, after-school and during school holidays, includes Music Playhouse and Dance Playhouse for three- to five-year-olds, and Jumping Jacks for toddlers (from 18 months) and parents, is a daytime class of gentle movement, nursery rhymes and song. Classes are always over-subscribed, so make sure you book

early. The Paint Box Studio for arts and crafts has a range of workshops for all ages during the holidays. The buffs at the cinema are currently establishing a film-making facility for young people aged over 15 (phone 7372 6611 for information). The arts staff also run an outreach programme for disadvantaged and special needs children, particularly from the local area.

Art galleries

Courtauld Institute Gallery
Somerset House, Strand, WC2 (7848 2549/ education 7848 2922/www.courtauld.ac.uk). *Covent Garden or Holborn tube.* **Open** 10am-6pm daily (last entry 5.15pm); *31 Dec* 10am-4pm; *1 Jan* noon-6pm. Closed 24-26 Dec. *Tours* phone for details. **Admission** £4; £3 concessions; free under-18s, students. Free to all 10am-2pm Mon (not bank hols). *Annual ticket* £10. **Credit** MC, V. **Map** p319 M7.
The Courtauld, home to some of the world's most famous paintings, is also popular for its free Saturday drop-ins (11am-12.30pm). On the first Saturday of each month, children (aged 6 to 12) and their parents can enjoy a 30-minute talk in front of a painting, followed by a practical activity in the gallery such as painting with egg tempera (a binding powder colour) and learning to draw reflections in water. Holidays are equally hands-on, when kids (aged 5 to 16) can indulge in the likes of print-making and mosaics for around £10-£15. Students on GCSE, GNVQ and A-level courses can attend full-day sessions. Gallery trails are always on offer, and free sign-interpreted events are becoming a regular feature (book in advance). *See also p58*

Dulwich Picture Gallery

Gallery Road, SE21 (8693 5254/
www.dulwichpicturegallery.org.uk). North Dulwich or
West Dulwich rail/3, 37, 176, P4 bus. **Open** 10am-
5pm Tue-Fri; 11am-5pm Sat, Sun, bank hol Mon.
Closed Good Fri, 24-26 Dec, 1 Jan. *Tours (incl entry*
fee) 3pm Sat, Sun. **Admission** £4; £3 concessions;
free under-16s. Free to all Fri. **Credit** MC, V.
The Dulwich Picture Gallery, one of the loveliest galleries
in London, provides children with a hands-on approach to
art. An after-school club on Friday gives 9- to 12-year-olds
the chance to nurture their talent through arts and crafts
activities, whether creating a collage or improving their
drawing. The Saturday morning art school offers 10- to 14-
year-olds a number of short courses that explore different
artistic techniques, from portraiture to silk painting (around
£40 per four-week course). Half-term craft-based activities
supplement the summer drop-ins and week-long courses, all
of which are inspired by temporary exhibitions. Call for further details.

Hayward Gallery

Belvedere Road, South Bank Centre, SE1 (box office
7960 4242/www.hayward-gallery.org.uk). Embankment
tube/Waterloo tube/rail. **Open** *During exhibitions*
10am-6pm Mon, Thur-Sun; 10am-8pm Tue, Wed.
Admission varies; phone for details. **Credit** AmEx,
DC, MC, V. **Map** p319 M8.
The Hayward holds children's events throughout the year
in conjunction with its temporary exhibitions, focusing
predominantly on 20th-century work. Free with the entrance
ticket, the artist-led workshops feature a wide variety of
practical activities, including model-making, painting, drawing, sculpting and photography. In an attempt to encourage
children to visit the gallery on their own during the
school holidays, the Hayward offers under-16s free entry.
Although there is no art trolley, the gallery's permanent
education space is used for everything from reading to dressing up. *See also p37.*

London International Gallery of Children's Art

O2 Centre, 255 Finchley Road, NW3 (7435 0903/
www.ligca.org). Finchley Road tube. **Open** *Gallery* 4-6pm
Tue-Thur; noon-6pm Fri-Sun. **Admission** *Gallery* free;
donations requested. **Workshops** *Half-term, school hols*
£8 per session. *Classes* £50-£55 (6 classes).
No credit cards.
This is the only gallery in London devoted to works of art
by children from around the world. A registered charity,
the LIGCA celebrates the creativity of young people and
aims to promote international understanding through cultural
exchange. One-off workshops exploring the visual arts are
programmed throughout the year (phone for details); in
the past these have included the chance to make mad hats
or pinhole cameras, origami, or sculpture (out of discarded
objects). The six-week painting and drawing courses for
5- to 12-year-olds, which are taught by specialised artists,
are designed to let children explore a variety of techniques
and ideas and express themselves with confidence, through
art. Phone for details.

National Gallery

Trafalgar Square, WC2 (7747 2885/
www.nationalgallery.co.uk). Embankment/Leicester
Square tube/Charing Cross tube/rail. **Open** 10am-6pm
Mon, Tue, Thur-Sun; 10am-9pm Wed. **Admission** free.
Exhibitions £7; £5 concessions; £3 students; £14 family
(2+4). **Map** p319 K7.

London's pride and joy, the National Gallery, boasts a forward-
looking and highly dedicated Education Department. Free sessions on Saturdays (11.30am-12.30pm) provide lively and
interactive talks (for children aged 5 to 11) that cover a diverse
range of paintings by way of a different theme each week.
Aiming to engender a club-like feel, there are always trails and
quizzes available. An exciting new addition are the free
'Second Saturday' and 'Second Sunday' slots (11.30am and
2.30pm on the second Saturday and Sunday of every month),
where young and up-coming artists lead children (aged 4 to
11) in drawing sessions. The under-fives aren't forgotten
either: 'Storytelling on the Magic Carpet' is conducted during
most school holidays (call for details). And the holidays
herald extra events that range from boisterous workshops to
performances by actors from the Young Vic. *See also p87.*

National Portrait Gallery

2 St Martin's Place, WC2 (7306 0055/www.npg.org.uk).
Leicester Square tube/Charing Cross tube/rail.
Open 10am-6pm Mon-Sat; noon-6pm Sun.
Admission free. **Map** p319 K7.
A fascinating chance to put faces to historical names. Anybody
who borrows a free activity rucksack from the information
desk (subject to availability) will be amused for hours by the
intriguing and imaginative things it contains. There's fuzzy
felt, so you can make your own version of a painting, for example, and even a beard and whiskers so you can disguise yourself as one of the Victorian men on display. Free activities are
staged for families with children aged seven upwards during
the major holidays; you have to ring to request inclusion on the
gallery mailing list to receive details of these events. The new
interactive IT gallery, complete with 11 terminals and assist-
ing staff, will keep all screen-savvy children enthralled with
highly visual and word-free activities. *See also p87.*

Tate Britain has one of London's
best art trolleys. *See p218.*

Activities & Fun

form music suggested by any of the gallery's paintings, thereby encouraging participants to express their reactions to artworks in a musical way. The prices listed above are approximate, so ring for details of workshops, which change with each new exhibition. *See also p76.*

Tate Britain

Millbank, SW1 (7887 8000). Pimlico tube/88, 77A, C10 bus. **Open** 10am-5.50pm daily. **Admission** free. *Special exhibitions* prices vary; phone for details. **Credit** MC, V. **Map** p319 L11.

Placing the emphasis firmly on family learning, Tate Britain offers a stimulating selection of child- and adult-friendly activities. The main educational resource is the art trolley, which rolls between noon and 5pm every Sunday; children aged under 11 select materials from a passing wheeled receptacle to then create their own artworks with the help of two gallery educators. Children have to bring their own overalls. For less messy games try Art Space (1-5pm) and its jigsaws and other puzzling entertainments.

Workshops are available during major school holidays, offering everything from mask moulding to print making (phone for prices). And a number of Tate Trails will lead young enthusiasts through the galleries where they will learn to employ observational exercises to help them learn about particular works. Look out for the new Studio – self-guided activities from 2-5pm on Sunday afternoons (suitable for kids aged 5 to 12) which are being launched in conjunction with Tate Britain's centenary development. *See also p88.*

Tate Modern

25 Sumner Street, SE1 (7887 8000). Southwark tube. **Open** 10am-6pm Mon-Thur, Sun; 10am-10pm Fri, Sat. **Admission** free. **Map** p320 O7.

Tate Modern's family programme is energetically committed to turning children on to modern art. Young artists aged from seven have their own guides, in the shape of the Education Department's 'Viewpoints' and 'Time Capsule' games (both family Explorer trails, available free at the box office). Viewpoints takes in the Landscape/Matter/Environment space, where works by Monet, Beuys and Rothko await to inspire. Time Capsule is dedicated to the exploration of the History Suite, and the art of Mondrian, Warhol and Henry Moore. The children's audio tour (£1), with narration by Michael Rosen, also starts with landscape, before moving on to the Still Life Trail, which takes in works by Bill Woodrow and Marcel Duchamp (and his urinal) among others. Families visiting at the weekend can join in with Artmixx (Saturday morning) – workshops run by the Tate's resident team of artists. Sunday's activity is called Start, for which children are given a map, bag and puzzle kit and sent on a madcap exploration of the galleries. These activities are free, suitable for ages five and upwards (accompanied by an adult) and don't require booking. The Education Department also organises activities, workshops, trails and performances for family fun every half-term and school holiday.

The monthly Tate Tales introduces a poet or storyteller who leads role-play and improvised performance based around an artwork. Other activities are organised around individual exhibitions, and a comprehensive schools' workshop programme runs throughout the year. *See also p41.*

Wallace Collection

Hertford House, Manchester Square, W1 (7563 9500/ /www.wallace-collection.com. Education department 7563 9551). Bond Street tube. **Open** 10am-5pm Mon-Sat; noon-5pm Sun. **Admission** free; under-8s must be accompanied; older children must have an accompanying adult in the building. **Map** p316 G5.

Orleans House Gallery

Riverside, Twickenham, Middlesex (8892 0221/ www.richmond.gov.uk/depts/opps/leisure/arts/orleanshouse). St Margaret's or Twickenham rail/33, 90, 290, H22, R68, R70 bus. **Open** *Apr-Sept* 1-5.30pm Tue-Sat; 2-5.30pm Sun. *Oct-Mar* 1-4.30pm Tue-Sat; 1-4.20pm Sun. **Admission** *Gallery* free. **No credit cards**.

Visiting sculptors and artists head the line-up for children at the Orleans House Gallery, home to a fine collection of 18th-, 19th- and 20th-century art. Leading the after-school clubs (3.45-5pm) on Wednesday and Thursday, as well as holiday and half-term workshops, the Orleans experts also run more unusual activities such as plaster work and photography. Clubs cost £5 per session and school-holiday workshops £6 per session. Activities are usually themed to tie in with current exhibitions, so children may make artworks and create sculptures, according to what they have seen in the gallery.

Royal Academy

Burlington House, Piccadilly, W1 (7300 8000/ www.royalacademy.org.uk). Green Park or Piccadilly Circus tube. **Open** 10am-6pm Mon-Thur, Sat, Sun, 10am-10pm Fri. **Admission** varies with exhibition; phone for details. **Credit** AmEx, MC, V. **Map** p318 J7.

During half-term holidays, family workshops run daily from 10.15am until 1pm. An introductory slide-show is followed by a tour of the galleries and a practical activity relating to one of the art techniques – painting, pastels, collage and so on – that may have caught the imagination. In the summer holidays and the renowned annual Summer Exhibition, one of the family workshops (free with entrance ticket) is run by musicians from the London Philharmonic Orchestra, who per-

Home to the Wallace family's magnificent art collection, an ice-cream cooler that belonged to Catherine the Great and the largest collection of armour in London, the Wallace Collection holds morning and afternoon activity sessions during half-term and holidays for children aged five to ten. Whether it be art-, drama- or armour-oriented, every workshop costs £5 per child and is led by an artist or actor. If you simply want to explore the collection, try one of the illustrated family quizzes. Phone the collection for a brochure of events planned for families: all sessions must be booked in advance. *See also p96.*

Whitechapel Art Gallery
80-2 Whitechapel High Street, E1 (7522 7888/recorded info 7522 7878/www.whitechapel.org).Aldgate East tube. **Open** 11am-5pm Tue, Thur, Fri; 11am-8pm Wed; 11am-6pm Sat, Sun. **Admission** free. **Map** p321 S6.
Canon Samuel Barnett and his wife Henrietta, the Christian Socialists who founded this gallery a century ago, believed that art should be accessible to everyone. As well as being free to see, all the art displayed here inspires a whole education programme for students from primary and secondary schools. Education for all is such a towering priority here that this relatively small gallery employs three full-time education staff. There are free workshops, talks and after-school activities, puzzles and trails devised for all exhibitions. Events and exhibitions change regularly, so for the latest news on what's happening at this all-inclusive gallery, call for a programme. *See also p114.*

Cinemas

For the ultimate big screen big-sound experience, head for the **Empire** (08700 102030/www.uci-cinemas.co.uk), **Warner Village** West End (7437 4347/www.warnervillage.co.uk) or the **Odeon** (0870 505 0007/www.odeon.co.uk) in Leicester Square. These West End giants make action movies a memorable event, but their prices (£10 adults, £5 children) won't be forgotten in a hurry. Add the price of popcorn and fizzy drinks and a family trip to the cinema seems a costly business.

Help is at hand from Saturday morning Kids' Clubs, which run in most multiplexes and one-off local cinemas (unfortunately not available in

Best: Film clubs

For serious buffs
Movie Magic at the **NFT**. *See p221.*

For stargazers
Everyman Kids at **Everyman Cinema**. *See p221.*

For big fun
Clapham Picture House Kids' Club. *See p220.*

For great value
Saturday mornings at the **Ritzy Cinema**. *See p222.*

For comfort and joy
Cinema at the **Tricycle Theatre**. *See p216.*

London's starring roles

London gives us her 'brooding', 'scary', 'carefree' and 'romantic' in a selection of the city's most memorable film roles:
- Shadowy cobbled streets and looming warehouses in Shad Thames (Bermondsey, SE1), spell certain menace in *Oliver!* (1967) and *The Elephant Man* (1980).
- Bond, James Bond, messes about on the river (Docklands, E14) and makes the Dome look impressive in *The World Is Not Enough* (1999).
- Portobello Road (W11) looks rather homely and unassuming, unlike the luminous Julia Roberts in *Notting Hill* (1999; pictured).
- The Peace Pagoda, the pond and the tennis courts of Battersea Park, SW11, all feature in the meeting of the spotty dogs in *101 Dalmatians* (1996).
- More cobblestones, this time in the old Covent Garden Market, WC2, ring beneath Eliza Dolittle's step in *My Fair Lady* (1964).
- Spielberg's version of *Peter Pan, Hook*, winds up in Kensington Gardens, W8, with Robin Williams grovelling at the statue of Pan.

Leicester Square). The Clubs screen children's favourites (not always very recent) for low admission prices. UCI cinemas offer a 'Film Feast' for children, which includes a drink and popcorn at some of its locations (ring 08700 102030/www.uci-cinemas.co.uk for details). Warner cinemas have a cinemaniacs club, which encompasses Saturday morning films and movie gossip magazines, (more information from www.warnervillage.co.uk).

For more on the IMAX, *see p37 and p246*. For the **Barbican**'s film clubs, *see p215*; for the **Tricycle Theatre**'s, *see p216*.

Clapham Picture House
76 Venn Street, SW4 (7498 3323/ www.picturehouse-cinemas.co.uk). Clapham Common tube. **Film Club** *Activities* 11.15am, *Screening* 11.45am Sat. **Tickets** £3; members £2. *Membership* £3; £2 children. Under-5s must be accompanied by an adult. **Credit** MC, V.
The Clapham Picture House wins the prize for imagination when it comes to children's activities. An alliance with Battersea Dogs' Home means that six times a year the cinema selects a hound-related film and Battersea handlers bring in a pooch for the children to cuddle. Clapham's Kids' Club runs every Saturday, hosting a crafts workshop before the children's screening: kids can make spaceships before *Star Wars*, a magic shield before *The Magic Sword* or sculpt plasticine figures before Morph animations. The audience is given three questions to answer after the film, with prizes at stake for correct responses. Birthday boys and girls would do well to choose this cinema for their celebrations, as they not only get to meet the projectionist but start the film rolling, too. Members of staff are employed to babysit during the show.

Electric Cinema

191 Portobello Road, W11 (recorded info 7727 9958/ 7229 8688/www.the-electric.co.uk). Ladbroke Grove or Notting Hill Gate tube. **Open** *Box office varies depending on programme.* **Film Club** 1pm Sat. **Tickets** £3 members; £4 non-members, accompanying adults. *Membership* £3. **Credit** MC, V. **Map** p312 A7.

Children (aged 4 to 12) join the Kids' Club to enjoy activities and games before the 1.30pm screening of the latest family smash hit, or a less recent popular classic. Older children (over-fives) can be left to watch without grown-ups fidgeting beside them all the time. Perks for members include the thrill of starting the film yourself on the week of your birthday, having your photo taken and receiving a certificate. Pre-film activities are usually tied in with the screening, and can be anything from making your own wand (*Cinderella*) to taking part in a dance competition (*Bugsy Malone*).

Everyman Cinema

5 Holly Bush Vale, NW3 (7435 1600/info line 74311777/ www.everymancinema.com). Hampstead tube. **Open** *Box office 6-10pm Mon-Fri; 10.30am-10pm Sat; 2-10pm Sun.* **Film Club** 10.45am Sat. **Tickets** *(incl 45min workshop after film screening)* £5 adults, children. **Credit** MC, V.

Everyman Kids is a starry new initiative for 8- to 12-year-olds, spearheaded by Eve McGregor, in association with Film Education and Natural Nylon, a production company formed by Ewan McGregor, Jude Law and Sadie Frost. The club runs in seasons of six weeks, with educational workshops held fortnightly. Designed to appeal to film-loving children, such as they once were, the workshops are occasionally conducted by luminaries of the silver screen, such as the entertaining Mr McGregor himself or the highly acclaimed director of *Truly, Madly, Deeply* and *The English Patient,* Anthony Minghella. Children can write to mail@everymancinema.com to receive information on future films and special offers. Workshop activities might involve film discussion, artwork or storyboard building. No membership fee.

Movie Magic at the NFT

National Film Theatre 2, BFI on the South Bank, SE1 (7928 3232/www.bfi.org.uk/moviemagic). Waterloo tube/rail. **Open** *Box office phone bookings 11.30am-8.30pm daily. Personal callers 5-8.30pm Mon-Thur; 11.30am-8.30pm Fri-Sun.* **Film Club** *Workshops times vary, Sat.* **Tickets** £3.50 film, workshop (children only). Advance booking essential. **Credit** MC, V. **Map** p319 M8.

The National Film Theatre's reputation for diverse and comprehensive film programming is upheld even in its children's repertoire. We're not just talking your run-of-the-mill Hollywood releases – NFT juniors can also enjoy a cross-section of old favourites, foreign language films, black and white classic comedies and even foreign animations. Parents can drop their kids off before the screening and leave them to it. Shown on Saturday afternoons, the children's film is preceded by a related workshop suitable for 6 to 12-year-olds with activities that range from model-making to meeting film industry figures. Screenings without the workshop also take place on Sundays and in the holidays. Phone for the NFT's programme of special events and festivals, which lists family performances of British Film Institute educational touring projects and interactive screening events. No membership fee.

Phoenix Cinema

52 High Road, N2 (box office 8444 6789/info 8883 2233). East Finchley tube. **Open** *Box office opens 15min before first daily screening; times vary; phone for details.* **Film Club** *Activities 11am; film screening noon Sat.* **Tickets** £3 adults, under-16s; £1.50 Freddies members. **Membership** £15 1st child, £9 subsequent children. **Credit** MC, V.

The Saturday children's club is called 'Phoenix Freddies'. No goodies, just a membership card and pamphlet every three months about forthcoming screenings, which include an hour's film-related activities, such as drawing, making flipbook animations and monster building, before the film at noon. The club is for 6- to 12-year-olds, you can't book and there are only 20 places, so it's strictly first come, first served.

Activities & Fun

Best: Classes

For bouncing babies
Jumping Jacks at the **Tricycle Theatre**. *See p216.*

For dying swans
Dance Attic's ballet. *See p228.*

For head bangers
Drumhead. *See p231.*

For arty types
Art 4 Fun. *See p230.*

For drama queens
Sylvia Young Theatre School. *See p229.*

For mad professors
The Making Place. *See p231.*

Rio
103-7 Kingsland High Street, E8 (7241 9410/www.riocinema.co.uk). Dalston Kingsland rail. **Open** *Box office* opening times vary depending on programme. **Film Club** 4-15pm Tue (term time only) 11am Sat. **Tickets** £3; £2 under-16s. **Credit** MC, V.
The Rio is well loved for its friendliness and community roots. Children take over the venue for the regular Saturday Morning Picture Club, which shows recent Hollywood children's films. Membership is free, and children receive a special card that is stamped every time they visit the cinema. Once they have collected ten stamps they are rewarded with one free entry, and 25 stamps warrants a poster.

Ritzy Cinema
Brixton Oval, Coldharbour Lane, SW2 (7733 2229/www.ritzycinema.com). Brixton tube/rail. **Open** *Box office* times vary depending on performances. **Film Club** 10.30am Sat. **Tickets** £2; £1 under-16s. **Credit** MC, V.
Turn up early for these Saturday screenings, or you'll end up in a crush of popcorn and fizz and pint-sized movie buffs. There are two films every Saturday, for under-sevens and over-sevens respectively. Children aged over five may be left to watch with their friends while parents enjoy free coffee, tea and newspapers in the café. Phone for details of film-related fun, games and activities after the film, or pick up a programme on your next visit.

Music venues

See also p215 **South Bank Centre.**

Coliseum
St Martin's Lane, WC2 (box office 7632 8300/fax credit card bookings 7379 1264/textphone 7836 7666/ www.eno.org). Leicester Square tube/Charing Cross tube/rail. **Open** *Box office* 10am-8pm Mon-Sat. **Tickets** prices vary with show; phone for details. **Credit** AmEx, MC, V. **Map** p319 L7.
While listening to opera might not be the most obvious activity for a child, the Coliseum's educational programme certainly makes it an option. Choosing shorter and more accessible pieces, a team of experts runs regular workshops before the performances to help introduce the work to

the young audience. Children aged seven and over can attend with an accompanying adult, and they will be talked through the plot, led in improvisational work and sung to by a member of the cast.

London Arena
Limeharbour, Isle of Dogs, E14 (7538 1212/ www.londonarena.co.uk). Crossharbour & London Arena DLR. **Open** *Box office* 9am-7pm Mon-Fri; 9am-7pm Sat. **Tickets** prices vary with show; phone for details. **Credit** MC, V.
Children's pin-ups Bob the Builder, the Tweenies and Woody and friends from *Toy Story* are all gigging in this huge aircraft hangar of a place in the next year. The ice shows for children take place during every October half-term. The Arena is also home to London Knights, the capital's only super-league ice hockey team.

Royal Albert Hall
Kensington Gore, SW7 (7589 8212/ www.royalalberthall.com). South Kensington tube. **Open** *Box office* 9am-9pm daily. **Tickets** (BBC Prom) from £10; £5 under-16s. **Credit** AmEx, MC, V. **Map** p315 D9.
Probably the biggest musical event for children in the RAH calendar is the annual *Blue Peter* prom, which features a programme of popular classical music geared towards children and presented by a *Blue Peter* celebrity *(see also p28).* Once the hall's major overhaul is finished (due in 2003), there'll be more events for youngsters, including children's tours and a proper education programme.

Royal College of Music
Prince Consort Road, SW7 (7589 3643/ www.rcm.ac.uk). South Kensington tube. Chamber concerts term time only 1.05pm Mon-Fri. **Admission** free. **Auditions** Sat morning (times vary; phone for details). **Map** p315 D9.
London's top music college stages free chamber concerts for anyone who wants to hear them. Children who yearn to study music may enjoy listening to the students here, and can also turn up on a Saturday to audition for prestigious music classes (for children aged eight and over; phone the Junior Department for more information).

Royal Opera House
Bow Street, WC2 (7304 4000/www.royaloperahouse.org). Covent Garden tube. **Open** *Box office* 10am-8pm Mon-Sat; *backstage tours* 10.30am, 12.30pm, 2.30pm Mon-Sat. **Tickets** Shows prices vary; phone for details. *Backstage tours* £7; £6 under-19s. **Credit** AmEx, MC, V. **Map** p319 L6.
Since its renovation, this gorgeous building is open to everyone. But despite having an active schools programme, the ROH doesn't do much to encourage children through its portals except welcome them to matinée performances of opera and ballet and put on the occasional family day. Children who are big fans of these art forms may like to pop in for a programme of productions, or join the mailing list (£8.50 per year; ring 7212 9123 to join).

Wigmore Hall
36 Wigmore Street, W1 (7935 2141, education dept 7258 8240/www.wigmore-hall.org.uk). Bond Street tube. **Open** *Box office* 10am-7pm Mon-Sat; 10.30am-6.30pm Sun. **Credit** AmEx, DC, MC, V. **Tickets** *Family concerts* £6; £3 children. **Map** p316 H5.
Having just celebrated its centenary, this marbled chamber music venue holds family classical concerts throughout the

year. For those craving wider musical variety the Wigmore also hosts jazz and classical 'creative music days' where participants aged over five try out instruments and finish the day with a performance. Holiday 'Young People's Days' (£10) are on offer for children over 11, while the regular 'Chamber Tots' caters for the under-fives.

Theatres

Some of the places listed below are dedicated children's theatres, but most are grown-up houses with a strong commitment to family shows. Always ring to find out the age-suitability of a show before you book. Most of the show times we list are for during the term; ring for details of extra dates during school holidays.

BAC (Battersea Arts Centre)

Lavender Hill, SW11 (7223 2223/www.bac.org.uk). Clapham Junction rail/77, 77A, 345 bus. **Open** *Box office* 10.30am-6pm Mon; 10.30am-9pm Tue-Sat; 4-7pm Sun. *Puppet Centre* 2-6pm Mon, Wed, Sat. *Shows* 2.30pm Sat. Tickets Saturday shows £5.75; £4.50 children, concessions; £3.50 young BAC club members. **Membership** £10.75 children; £16.50 family. **Credit** AmEx, MC, V.
Living up to its self-appointed status as the 'National Theatre of Fringe', the BAC's children's programme books in a wide range of children's theatre and puppet theatre companies for its Saturday afternoon slot. The shows are usually aimed at the four to seven age range.

Upstairs, the Puppet Centre (7228 5335) is a resource centre for anyone interested in the ancient art of puppetry. The staff here can tell you all you need to know about the puppets on display, and the companies performing around the UK. On Saturday afternoons children are welcome upstairs after the show to workshops where they can make their own puppet (£4; adult carers free). Arts Factory courses in drama, performance and storytelling cater for young people aged 3 to 15. The courses cost from £45.75 per term; (£39.50 concessions; £34.50 Young BAC members). Phone for a brochure to join the Young BAC club and book yourself on a course.

Broadway Theatre, Catford

Rushey Green, Catford, SE6 (8690 0002/ www.broadwaytheatre.org.uk). Catford rail. **Open** *Box office* 10am-6pm Mon-Sat. **Tickets** £3.50-£20. **Credit** AmEx, DC, V.
Having undergone a £2.2-million refurbishment, this theatre has been restored to its original 1930s appearance. Part of the new image is a name change – the theatre, formerly known as Lewisham (which was confusing, since it's in Catford), is now called the Broadway Theatre, Catford. At the glitzy end of children's theatre, many pre-school special productions, including Playbus, Bananas in Pyjamas and other crowd-pleasers stop off here, and its Christmas panto is a big-time affair. Lewisham is well known for its black theatre, and the venue holds a yearly black pantomime just before Christmas, which draws in the crowds. Most poptastic 11-year-olds will love the 'Dream Concert' series held throughout the year, when look-alike bands and singers – most recently *faux* Geri Halliwell and Steps – perform on the main stage. The theatre's secondary studio space is used for community-based productions, including performances by local dance schools and theatre groups.

Staging *The Sorcerer's Apprentice* at **The Bull**. See p224.

See p224.

Activities & Fun

The Bull
68 High Street, Barnet,
Herts (8449 0048/tours
82755375/www.thebull.org.uk).
High Barnet tube. **Tickets**
Children's shows £3.95 in advance,
£4.25 on the door. *Courses* from £40
per term; £80 for summer school.
Credit MC, V.
Hosting around 200 performances a year,
the Bull always has something on offer for children. Its two theatre spaces are used for everything
from musical comedies to heavier-weight plays, and under-
fives are offered free pre-show theatre tours and a chance to
meet the performers every Sunday. Ring for details of the
Bull's 12 different drama and movement courses that run
every term, as well as the special half-term projects and a two-
week professional summer school. All courses work towards
a final production. Booking is essential.

Chicken Shed Theatre
Chase Side, Southgate, N14 (8292 9222/
www.chickenshed.org.uk). Cockfosters/Oakwood tube.
Open *Box office* 10am-5pm Mon-Fri; Sat varies depending
on production times. **Tickets** £2-£13.75. **Credit** MC, V.
The enormous Chicken Shed Theatre has four performance
spaces – a main auditorium, a studio, an amphitheatre and a
bar performing area. The theatre company boasts 800 members, and most of its work is original material. Children can
enjoy anything from Shakespeare to musicals to contemporary dance shows, as well as the odd major commercial production. The large-scale Christmas show is always a
favourite, and signed and visually described performances
are a regular feature. The theatre's ethos is one of inclusive-
ness: all children with disabilities and learning problems can
join the workshops and classes. 'Tales from the Shed' (for
under-fives) is a popular workshop series that invites youngsters and their parents or carers to experiment with puppetry,
mime, dance and song. Older children can join in the weekly
after-school workshops, which combine music, dance and
drama in a lead-up to a public performance. Week-long summer schemes are also on offer. The Chicken Shed has a long
waiting list for places on these courses.

Colour House Theatre
Merton Abbey Mills, Watermill Way, SW19 (8542 6644/
www.wheelhouse.org.uk). Colliers Wood tube. **Open** *Box*
office 10am-5pm Mon-Fri; 1hr before the start of show.
Children's shows 2pm, 4pm Sat, Sun. **Tickets** £5. **Courses**
(ages 5-16) £100 per 14wk term. **No credit cards**.
A small and intimate venue, surrounded by the bustle of
Merton Abbey Mills craft market. In-house children's shows
(for age three and over) are original adaptations or musicals,
and you can buy CDs of the performances on the way out.
Jumping on the stage-school band wagon, the Colour House's
new 'performance musical theatre courses' are aimed at children determined to make it to the West End stage. Classes
(every Saturday or Sunday and Monday evenings) help kids
prepare songs and dance from contemporary hits and musicals, culminating in an end-of-term show.

Edward Alleyn Theatre
Dulwich College, SE21 (8299 9232). West Dulwich rail/
Brixton tube then 3 P4, P13, 115 bus. **Children's shows**
10.30am Sat. **Tickets** £5; £3 concessions. **Courses**
from £13 a session, £60 a week. **No credit cards**.
This 180-seater theatre brings in a different children's company about ten times a year, and caters for children aged 3to
11. Performances by Dulwich College students are often suit-

able for older children and families,
and include musicals, popular shows
and classic theatre. Edward Alleyn
is a good bet for two- to three-week
holiday courses in drama and music.
Seven- to 11-year-olds benefit from a
relaxed teaching format where they
can turn up when they want to, rather
than attend the full course. Activities
are based around games, improvisation
and role-play. The senior courses (ages 12-16)
are aimed at those with a more serious attitude
towards theatre, and tend to be structured around a particular practitioner or text.

Half Moon Young People's Theatre
43 White Horse Road, E1 (7709 8900/
www.halfmoon.org.uk). Limehouse rail/DLR/
Stepney Green tube. **Open** *Box office* 10am-5pm
Mon-Fri. **Children's shows** 2pm Sat. **Tickets** £4.50;
£3.25 children, concessions. **Courses** Ages 5-18. *Price*
members £1.50 per wk. **Credit** MC, V.
A main staple of London's theatre for children, the Half Moon,
consisting of a single large black room, is an unpretentious
affair. The performances, however, are of a consistently high
standard. The Saturday show (for five- to ten-year-olds) provides a mix of storytelling and physical theatre. Touring productions provide the majority of the entertainment, although
the theatre produces its own shows twice yearly: expect anything from puppetry and traditional shows to interactive
installation pieces. The Half Moon runs weekly Youth
Theatres during term time, which teach children and young
people how to develop their theatrical, performance and
technical skills. Less formal than most theatre schools, the
classes allow children to experiment in a multicultural setting. The Youth Theatre performs regularly at the Half Moon,
and is recognised nationally for its high standards. A disability Youth Theatre for 14- to 18-year-olds also runs once a
week. Membership is free.

Jackson's Lane Community Centre
269A Archway Road, N6 (8341 4421/
www.jacksonslane.org.uk). Highgate tube. **Children's**
shows 11am, 2pm Sat. **Tickets** £4. **Courses** £3.50-£8.50
per session. **Credit** AmEx, MC, V.
A welcoming venue that hosts small children's productions
incorporating storytelling and puppetry. The theatre based
here runs musical drama classes both after school and at
weekends. The Kaos! Organisation and Debbie Campbell both
use the space for their drama sessions, which focus on team-
work and may include performance projects.

Lauderdale House
Highgate Hill, Waterlow Park, N6 (8348 8716/
www.lauderdale.org.uk). Archway tube. **Open**
Box office 30min before performance; bookings
not accepted. **Tickets** £3.50; £2.50 concessions.
Courses vary; phone for details. **No credit cards**.
A 16th-century Tudor merchant's house backing on to
Waterlow Park is home to this beautiful arts space. A different show each week, ranging from puppetry to music and
magicians, is performed by various visiting companies. To
ensure your child's seat on the floor, it's advisable to turn up
30 minutes before the performance. Phone for details of dance,
drama and art courses for children aged 18 months to 14
years. The termly classes take place both during and after
school, with an emphasis on fun learning. There are also
seasonally themed Family Days, which are usually free – call
the venue for more information.

The unicorn Theatre for
Children has been given £4.5
million of lottery money
to create a permanent,
child-centred, purpose-
designed theatre

The
future's
bright

Activities & Fun

Lyric Theatre Hammersmith

King Street, W6 (8741 2311/www.lyric.co.uk).
Hammersmith tube. **Open** *Box office* 10am-7pm Mon-
Sat. **Children's shows** 11am, 1pm Sat. **Tickets** £5.50;
£4 concessions. **Credit** AmEx, MC.
Hosting regular Saturday morning and school-holiday children's shows in its smaller studio auditorium, the Lyric is generally a receiving venue for both small and large theatre
companies. However, it does also commission new work, particularly at Christmas when shows are innovative and challenging while maintaining appeal for children of all ages.

The Netz

West Norwood Library, 1 Norwood High Street, SE27
(7926 8070/www.lambeth.gov.uk). West Norwood rail.
Open *Box office* 9am-4pm Mon-Fri. **Children's shows**
2pm 1st Sat every mth. **Tickets** £3. **Credit** MC, V
(only in advance).
Attached to a library, this 200-seater theatre is surprisingly
well equipped. Visiting companies put on children's performances once a month, with additional shows during the holidays. The Netz will soon have a series of regular workshops
up and running; call for details.

Polka Theatre

240 The Broadway, SW19 (8543 4888/
www.polkatheatre.com). Wimbledon or Wimbledon South
tube. **Open** *Box office* 9.30am-4.30pm Mon; 9am-6pm Tue-
Fri; 10am-5pm Sat. **Children's shows** daily, times vary;
phone for details. **Tickets** £5-£10. **Courses** times &
prices vary; phone for details. **Credit** AmEx, MC, V.
The Polka must be the most child-centred place this side of
Mothercare. This dedicated children's theatre, now 21 years
old, stages five major productions for children a year, the
majority of which are home-grown, although touring produc-

Come to child-centred shows at the **Polka Theatre**.

tions are also received. And entertainment is not limited to the
stage: once kids have seen the show and played the games and
quizzes in the programme, past production exhibitions can be
admired in the foyer. Then there's the outdoor playground,
rocking horses and ride-on toys indoors for the little ones. And
don't forget the production-related stalls, where children can
spend their pocket money. Note that babies and children under
four aren't allowed in the main theatre, they have their own
Adventure Theatre, where parents and carers have proper
seating, though in practice they often choose to hunker
down with their toddlers to see puppet productions and two-
handers, perhaps based on fairy tales.

Clubs and courses (for 3- to 11-year-olds) every holiday and
half-term form the basis of the Polka's education programme.
Exploring theatre techniques, voice and characterisation, the
participants are often given the opportunity to perform on one

Got your umbrella?

As summertime approaches, many children's
theatre companies send up a prayer for dry
weather and head outside. London's long-
established **Open Air Theatre** in Regent's Park
(7486 2431/www.open-air-theatre.org.uk) hosts
a children's show every August, performed by its
own New Shakespeare Company. Family tickets are
also available for Shakespeare's *A Midsummer
Night's Dream*, staged every year, and the annual
musical, which starts its run in June. Take your
own picnic and watch the performance from the
lawn, or buy a burger from the theatre barbecue.

The **London Bubble Theatre Company** (7237
4434/www.londonbubble.org.uk) is another
company to look outside for. Touring the city's
parks and woods for around six weeks every
summer, its pioneering 'promenade' style is an
experience in itself. There is no fixed seating –
the audience follows the actors through the park
carrying rugs, stopping to watch each scene in a
different location. Often featuring puppetry and
pyrotechnic effects, the performances enthral
children aged from six.

A guaranteed child-pleaser when it comes
to fresh air frolics is the **Flying Chesticoffs**,
an anarchic clown duo who tour local parks

and festivals care of children's theatre
company Kazzum (7223 0703). Their act
combines acrobatics, clowning routines and
audience participation.

Those who are ready to embark upon some Bard
work should head for **Shakespeare's Globe** (7401
9919/www.shakespeares-globe.org; *see also p40
and p226*). This reconstructed Elizabethan theatre
was painstakingly recreated to offer audiences an
experience as close as possible to a 16th-century
performance. The venue provides a truly defining
example of open-air theatre in the round, with its
tiered seating and circular thatched roof open to
the sky. That's an excellent way for secondary
school pupils to brush up their Shakespeare.

For free, sometimes chaotic, outdoor
entertainment, try the Bandstand in the **Horniman
Museum Gardens** (8699 1872; *see also p139*),
where puppet shows and magicians provide the
fun on summer holiday afternoons. Also, check
out the Royal National Theatre's Watch This Space
season. This is the National's annual free summer
fiesta of outdoor theatre, which takes place in
Theatre Square, on the South Bank. It runs from
June-August every year (info line 7452 3327/
www.nationaltheatre.org.uk/summertime).

Activities & Fun

Puppet wizardry at **Little Angel Theatre**. *See p228.*

of the Polka's stages at the end of the course. Other workshops exploring activities as varied as prop making, origami and puppetry are also available. Children up to the age of 16 can attend similar after-school clubs during term time. Particularly popular are the theatre's 'Polka Days', which combine a morning workshop with an afternoon performance.

Royal National Theatre
South Bank, SE1 (box office 7452 3000/ www.nationaltheatre.org.uk). Waterloo tube/rail. **Open** *Box office* 10am-8pm Mon-Sat. **Children's shows** half-terms & school holidays; phone for details. **Tickets** prices vary; phone for details. **Credit** AmEx, DC, MC, V. **Map** p319 M8.

The 'dream made concrete' recently celebrated 25 years as the controversial home to the three great stages: Olivier, Lyttleton and Cottesloe. The first is a wide, open platform for the big shows, the second has a more traditional proscenium arch space for middle-size productions, while the Cottesloe's flexible studio space is best suited to the avant-garde stuff. Children and their families are treated to a range of free foyer entertainments throughout the year, but mostly during the school holidays. Half-terms usually see a cuddly sort of show from a well-established children's theatre company. The Christmas holidays are marked by the NT's big family show, which in the past has included exemplary interpretations of *Peter Pan* and *The Ugly Duckling*. In the summer, the fun moves outside to the newly completed Theatre Square. *See p225.*

Sadler's Wells
Rosebery Avenue, EC1 (7863 8000/ www.sadlers-wells.com). Angel tube. **Open** *Box office* 10am-8.30pm Mon-Sat. **Children's shows** phone for details. **Tickets** £10-£35. **Credit** AmEx, MC, V. **Map** p317 N4.

An institution in the London dance world, Sadler's Wells has an increasingly reliable programme for children. Concentrating on its younger audience at Christmas, Easter and in the summer, the large-scale productions are highly polished and imaginative, coming courtesy of such well respected companies as the RSC and the Birmingham Rep. While the main shows are aimed at kids aged five and over, the venue also adapts its adult productions to be suitable for slightly older children (aged seven upwards), staging a family matinée on Saturday. Free family workshops, featuring activities such as drama, mask making and circus skills, are on offer before some performances (ring for details). Sadler's Wells is also retaining its second home, the more centrally located Peacock Theatre in Holborn, for younger companies and longer runs of more populist children's fare.

Shakespeare's Globe
New Globe Walk, Bankside, SE1 (7401 9919/ www.shakespeares-globe.org). Mansion House/ London Bridge tube/rail. **Open** *Box office* (Oct-Apr) 10am-6pm Mon-Sat; 10am-5pm Sun. **Tickets** £5 (standing)-£27; £10 per child performance workshop. *Tours* 10.30am-5pm daily Oct-Apr. **Tickets** £7.50; £6 Students, OAPs, £5, 5-15 year olds; free under 5's. **Credit** AmEx, MC, V. **Map** p320 O7.

This reconstruction of Shakespeare's own theatre is built only a hundred yards from where the original stood. Productions of William's repertoire are staged here from April to September. The weather precludes winter acting just as it did in Shakespeare's day. Phone for details of the Globe's 'Childsplay' Saturdays, when children (7-11) can accompany their parents to this beautiful playhouse overlooking the Thames, then go off to enjoy a lively storytelling, drama and art workshop with Globe educators while their parents watch a very authentic, naturally lit, heckling-encouraged performance. The children are invited to join the grown-ups for the last act of the show. Older children may feel they can handle the whole performance, especially if it's on their GCSE reading list. Students from Key Stage 2 up to postgraduate level can join a huge variety of workshops and study days devised by the busy Education Department (7902 1433). Prices are liable to change in 2002, so call to check first.

Theatre Museum

Tavistock Street (entrance Russell Street),
WC2 (7943 4700/group bookings 7943 4806/
www.theatremuseum.org). Covent Garden tube. **Open**
10am-6pm Tue-Sun. Last entry 5.30pm. Closed 24-26 Dec,
1 Jan, bank hol Mon. *Tours* 11am, 2pm, 4pm Tue-Sun.
Admission £4.50; £2.50 concessions; free under-16s, over-
60s. *Tours* free. **Credit** AmEx, MC, V. **Map** p319 L6.
Families enjoy the Thursday and Saturday workshops, which
involve trail sheets that pose questions about the costumes,
and prop and costume design sessions led by resting actors.
Study sessions and workshops, some for school groups, look
at theatrical techniques and theories. Some of the sessions are
on a drop-by basis, but phone first to check.

Unicorn Theatre for Children

Unicorn at the Pleasance Theatre, Carpenters
Mews, North Road, Islington, N7 (7700 7208/
www.unicorntheatre.com). Caledonian Road tube. **Open**
Box office 10am-6pm Mon-Fri. **Children's shows** times
vary with production; phone for details. **Tickets** £5-£10.
Credit AmEx, MC, V.
'Rising to the challenge of a child's imagination', the
Unicorn is one of the leading producers of children's theatre in the country. The theatre was established in 1947 in
the belief that 'the best of theatre for children should be
judged on the same high standards of writing, directing,
acting and design as the best of adult theatre', and that
belief has guided its productions for children aged 4-12,
their families and teachers, over the decades. For many
years Unicorn was based in the Arts Theatre, in the West
End. The theatre is currently housed temporarily in the
Pleasance, but with its productions being staged in venues
across London including the Open Air Theatre in Regent's
Park, the Pleasance and the Royal Opera House. Unicorn's
roving days will soon be over, thanks to the dedication of
the company and a sizeable lottery grant, allocated by the
Arts Council of England (*see p224*).

Warehouse Theatre

Dingwall Road, Croydon (8680 4060). East Croydon rail.
Open *Box office* 10am-5pm Mon; 10am-8.30pm Tue;
10am-10pm Wed-Sat; 3-7pm Sun. **Children's shows**
11am Sat. **Tickets** £4; £3 children. **Credit** AmEx, MC, V.
Two- to nine-year-olds enjoy the culturally rich offerings of
this small and intimate fringe theatre. Visiting companies
take centre stage every Saturday morning, supplemented by
an ever-growing holiday programme.

Wimbledon Theatre

The Broadway, SW19 (8540 0362/
www.wimbledontheatre.co.uk). Wimbledon tube/rail.
Open *Box office* 10am-8pm. **Children's shows** times
vary with production; phone for details. **Tickets** from £9;
£7 children. **Credit** MC, V.
Children's productions are staged at least once a month, not
forgetting the bonanza panto at Christmas. An enormous
venue holding 1,650, the Wimbledon often plays host to teeny-
bopper tribute bands. Despite its size, the theatre manages to
retain an intimate atmosphere, occasionally staging drama,
dance and music workshops in its smaller studio space.

West End shows

The long-runners and musicals listed below are
suitable for under-16s. They're all pretty lengthy,
however, so children younger than around seven
may find them somewhat hard going.

Blood Brothers

Phoenix Theatre, Charing Cross Road, WC2 (7369 1733).
Leicester Square tube. **Time** 7.45pm Mon-Sat; matinée
3pm Thur, 4pm Sat. **Tickets** £12-£35. **Credit** AmEx,
MC, V. **Map** p317 K6.
Willy Russell's grand, ambitious melodrama has a social con-
science as well as good songs. The story concerns twin brothers, separated at birth and brought up in radically different
economic environments, whose fates are tragically linked.

Cats

New London Theatre, Drury Lane, WC2 (7405 0072).
Covent Garden or Holborn tube. **Time** 7.45pm Mon-
Sat; matinée 3pm Tue, Sat. **Tickets** £12.50-£32.50.
Credit AmEx, MC, V. **Map** p317 L6.
An exciting and easily accessible show, *Cats* prowls through
TS Eliot's *Old Possum's Book of Practical Cats.* Those sitting
in the front row will find themselves on a revolving stage, and
the entire auditorium has been decorated as a scrapyard. Kids'
Club, a three-hour workshop, including backstage tour, drama
and improvisation, allows children to experience the world of
Cats first hand. It takes place the first and third Saturday of
every month, so ring for details.

The Complete Works of William Shakespeare (Abridged)

Criterion Theatre, Piccadilly Circus, WC2 (7413 1437).
Piccadilly Circus tube. **Time** 8pm Wed-Sat; matinée
3pm Thur, 5pm Sat, 4pm Sun. **Tickets** £8-£29.50.
Credit AmEx, MC, V. **Map** p319 K7.
Light relief for schoolchildren trying to get their heads
round the Bard. High-energy and hilarious, 37 plays are
condensed into 1 hour 55 minutes. If Shakespeare leaves
you cold, or you fancy a history, rather than an English
Literature lesson, try the Complete History of America
(Abridged) on Tuesdays at 8pm.

The King & I

London Palladium, Argyll Street, W1 (7494 5020). Oxford
Circus tube. **Time** 7.30pm; matinée 2.30pm Wed, Sat.
Tickets £15-£37.50. **Credit** AmEx, MC, V. **Map** p316 J6.
An endearing, if slightly soppy story, a ginormous dress, an
amazingly sumptuous set, a piping chorus of cute children
and some memorable songs make this an attractive proposition for young musical lovers.

Bravo!

Kids Week is a hugely successful venture run
by the Society of London Theatres. Running for
the last week of the summer holidays (end of
August), it gives children aged 5-16 a chance to
see a West End show free, when accompanying
a paying adult. As well as the performance,
children can take part in a range of show-related
activities: backstage tours, meet the cast,
singalongs and workshops, depending on which
show they choose. Kids Week was devised to
get bottoms on seats during the quiet holiday
period, but proved so popular last year, it
packed the theatres. To find out more about
Kids Week, and to receive information about
August 2002 and other workshop programmes
planned for children, call the information line
(0870 444 6066) or visit www.kidsweek.co.uk.

Top **Cats**. *See p227.*

The Lion King

Lyceum Theatre, Wellington Street, WC2 (0870 243 9000). Covent Garden or Holborn tube. **Time** 7.30pm Mon-Sat; matinée 2.30pm Wed, Sat. **Tickets** £15-£35. **Credit** AmEx, MC, V. **Map** p319 L7.

This innovative production uses puppets and live actors and stays close to the Disney movie's storyline, so children can wonder at the performance without losing the plot.

Les Misérables

Palace Theatre, Shaftesbury Avenue, W1 (7434 0909). Leicester Square tube. **Time** 7.30pm Mon-Sat; matinée 2.30pm Thur, Sat. **Tickets** £7-£32.50. **Credit** AmEx, MC, V. **Map** p317 K6.

A glossy take on the Victor Hugo novel, the show has a fairly complicated plot that might throw some children off the scent. Nevertheless, the staging is dramatic and effective, as reflected by its international success.

Mamma Mia!

Prince Edward Theatre, Old Compton Street, W1 (7447 5400). Piccadilly Circus or Leicester Square tube. **Time** 7.30pm; matinée 3pm Thur, Sat. **Tickets** £15-£35; £18-£40 Fri, Sat. **Credit** AmEx, MC, V. **Map** p317 K6.

Plot isn't *Mamma Mia!*'s strongpoint, so children of all ages enjoy this all-singing, all-dancing Abba extravaganza.

My Fair Lady

Drury Lane Theatre Royal, Catherine Street, WC2 (7494 5000). Covent Garden tube. **Time** 7.30pm; matinée 2.30pm Wed, Sat. Tickets £7.50-£37.50. **Credit** AmEx, MC, V. **Map** p317 L6.

Cockney sparrow Martine McCutcheon and Jonathan Pryce star as Eliza Dolittle and Professor Higgins until April 2002. It might not be the most profound of productions, but it's a luvverly night out all right.

Puppet theatre

Little Angel Theatre

14 Dagmar Passage, off Cross Street, N1 (7226 1787/ www.littleangeltheatre.com). Angel tube/Highbury & Islington tube/rail. **Open** *Box office* 9.30am-5.30pm daily. Closed 24-25 Dec, 1 Jan. **Children's shows** 11am, 3pm Sat, Sun; extra shows in school holidays. **Tickets** £6.50-£7.50; £5.50-£6.50 under-18s, concessions. **Credit** AmEx, MC, V.

This 100-seater was founded in 1961 and is London's only permanent puppet theatre. Expect all kinds of artistry, from the beautiful marionettes to glove, rod and shadow puppets. There are regular weekend shows by the resident company and visiting puppeteers, plus performances on weekdays during school holidays. The Little Angel Theatre Company has staged some notable children's shows based on well-known stories, including beautiful adaptations of fairy tales by Hans Andersen and The Brothers Grimm. The minimum age is three: there's a strictly no babies policy. Call ahead to check age suitability for a particular show, and for details of the forthcoming workshop programme.

Puppet Theatre Barge

Blomfield Road, Little Venice, W9 (7249 6876/ www.puppetbarge.com). Warwick Avenue tube. **Open** *Box office* 10am-8pm daily. Closed 25 Dec, 1 Jan. **Children's shows** times vary, phone to check. **Tickets** £6.50; £6 under-16s, concessions. **Credit** MC, V.

A visit to the Puppet Theatre Barge is an experience even before the curtain goes up. Moored at Little Venice in central London from October to June, and travelling to different locations in Henley, Marlow and Richmond the rest of the year, this unique floating marionette theatre stages regular family shows. It's a tiny venue, so book ahead. There are activities and workshops, but only if arranged by schools. Shows, which take place on a small stage and require a degree of concentration, are unsuitable for children aged under two.

Performance workshops

Centrestage

office: 33 Margaret Street, W1 (7328 0788/ www.centrestage.co.uk). **Age** 3-16. **Classes** Sat mornings. **Fees** £200+VAT per 12-wk term. **Holiday workshops** £120+VAT per wk.

It may be on the brink of establishing an agency for putting daughters (and sons) on the stage, but Centrestage's main premise is to get children hooked on the arts in a fun and non-pressurised environment. The three-hour Saturday sessions are divided into an hour of dance, drama and singing, and occasional masterclasses incorporate extra activities such as circus skills and puppetry.

Club Dramatika!

King Alfred School, North End Road, NW11 (8883 1554). Golders Green tube. **Classes** 10-11am Sat; 4-5pm Wed. **Fees** £6 per session.

Run by Vicky Levy, former head of drama at King Alfred, Club Dramatika! offers weekly sessions that provide children aged four to ten with the chance to explore improvisation and performance skills, as well as the opportunity to release creative energy.

Dance Attic

368 North End Road, SW6 (7610 2055). Fulham Broadway tube. **Classes** from £48 for 11wk term; phone for details of individual class prices.

A professional dance and rehearsal studio, Dance Attic's Saturday- and Sunday-morning ballet classes for children come highly recommended. Children can work toward their RAD exams, or just aim for fun and flexibility. A wide range of less classical dance classes, including jazz and hip hop, are also available.

Drama Club

12 Hardy Close, Timber Pond Road, Surrey Quays, SE16 (7231 6083). **Classes** times vary; phone for details. **Fees** from £50 for 12wk term.

Split between two venues, the Drama Club holds classes for 5 to 12-year-olds at the Time and Talents Centre in Rotherhithe, and for 5 to 11-year-olds at the Open Door Community Centre in Wimbledon. These one-hour drama- and movement-based sessions aim to develop self-confidence in the participants, incorporate improvisation, text apprecia- tion and team-building exercises. Public performances are staged at least once or twice a year, and children over 12 can move on to join the South West Youth Theatre, also held in Wimbledon. Samantha Giblin, the artistic director, also runs a children's party service.

Havil Hall

New Peckham Varieties at Magiceye Theatre, Havil Street, SE5 (venue 7703 5838/ office 7708 5401 office). Peckham Rye rail/Oval or Elephant & Castle tube/12, 36, 171, 345, 45A, P3 bus. **Classes** times vary; phone for details. **Fees** £1.50-£3. **Membership** £15 per yr; £6 per term.

An introduction to drama, dance, music and theatre for the very young (from four years), teaching communication skills, mime, improvisation and group work. Older attendees work on improvised and scripted work developing speech and per- formance skills. There's also a one-term project for new mem- bers and classes for over-16s.

Helen O'Grady's Children's Drama Academy

Headquarters based in Guernsey (01481 254419). **Classes** times vary; phone for details. **Fees** £5 per lesson.

Now in its third year, Helen O'Grady's Drama Academy is running classes for children aged 5 to 17 all over London. Firmly excluding itself from the talent school camp, the academy focuses on building up self-esteem and life skills, welcoming hyperactive, shy, disabled and special needs children. Three terms a year parents can watch an open lesson, as well as a public performance in the summer. Children with a more serious interest in drama can use the classes to prepare for stage school.

Hoxton Hall

130 Hoxton Street, N1 (7739 5431/ www.hoxtonhall.co.uk). Old Street tube. **Classes** times vary. **Fees** £1 per session.

Hoxton Hall has a refreshingly organic approach to performance art. Not only do the children learn a variety of dramatic techniques and perform twice a year to family and friends – they actually devise the plays themselves. Through a process of improvisation, children as young as eight help to create a storyline that is then performed using techniques as wide-ranging as digital performance and mime. Hoxton also holds a weekly craft club for 5- to 11-year-olds, in which they often make costumes and musical instruments to be used in the theatre perfor- mances themselves.

As well as its comprehensive programme of theatre work- shops, Hoxton Hall runs an innovative ten-week music course for 11- to 15-year-olds. Acting as a band, participants choose their favourite songs from the radio and learn how to play them, aided by professional musicians. The children devise choreography to accompany the songs, which are then performed for an audience. The Christmas children's shows are especially popular.

Laban Centre

Laurie Grove, SE14 (8692 4070/www.laban.co.uk). New Cross tube/rail. **Classes** Sat. **Fees** from £28 for 11wk term.

This higher education college is home to Saturday children's dance classes. A relaxed, improvisation-based class is held for toddlers, who work with sound, rhythm and movement. Sessions for older children are more structured and technique- based, while those aged 13 to 18 can go on to join Laban's new Youth Dance Company.

Millfield Theatre School

Silver Street, Edmonton, N18 (8807 6680). Silver Street rail/34, 102, 144, 217, 231, 444 bus. **Classes** Sun; phone for details of times & session prices.

Classes including dance, acting and singing as well as the more technical side of theatre practice – costume, lighting and sound – are designed for 9 to 16-year-olds. Members of the school can even make their own pop videos and record new soundtracks to their favourite films.

Perform

263 Hampstead Road, NW1 (7209 3805/ www.perform.org.uk). **Classes** times vary. **Fees** £103 for weekday 10-wk term; £154.50 weekend 10-wk term. **Credit** MC, V.

The only school in London specialising in children aged four to seven, Perform offers a free-trial workshop to all children attending for the first time. Perform has developed a programme of formulated games and exercises to help children increase their four Cs: confidence, concentration, co-ordination and communication. Perform has 17 centres around London.

Pineapple Performing Arts School

7 Langley Street, WC2 (7836 4004/ www.pineapple.uk.com). Covent Garden tube. **Classes** children from 4.15pm Mon-Fri; noon-3pm Sun. **Fees** from £2 per session. **Membership** £50. **Map** p317 L6.

There is a diverse range of workshops and classes here, from musical theatre and street theatre technique through to stage make-up and auditioning skills. Courses are tailored to suit children aged from five.

Stagecoach

head office: The Courthouse, Elm Grove, Walton-on- Thames, Surrey (01932 254333/www.stagecoach.co.uk). **Classes** times & venues vary; phone for details. **Fees** from £125 for 13wk term.

Britain's largest part-time theatre school, Stagecoach hogs the stage when it comes to weekend classes in dance, drama and singing tuition. There are over 50 workshop centres in London for children aged from four, call Stagecoach Head Office for details of your nearest one.

Sylvia Young Theatre School

Rossmore Road, NW1 (7402 0673/ www.sylviayoung.freeuk.com). Marylebone tube. **Classes** times vary; phone for details. **Fees** from £4.50 per class. **No credit cards.**

The fact that so many of Sylvia's pupils reach the heady heights of the RSC and national theatres is proof that this stage school is one of the best London has to offer. Whereas the full-time academic school is aimed at children aged 9 to 16 with a serious vocational interest in drama and dance, Sylvia also runs a Saturday school for those after a bit of fun. Children aged from four can choose from a range of classes, including street dance. One-week summer schools led by teachers from the school are conducted, when a wider range of activities, such as circus skills, is on the menu.

Workshops

Art

Art 4 Fun
Various venues (Head office 8994 4800/ www.art4fun.com). **Workshops** *Sat, Sun, after school.* **Fees** *half-day* £20; *full-day courses* £30. **Credit** MC, V.
Arts activities of all descriptions are on the agenda: children of all ages can experiment with ceramics, wood, glass, silk, clay and all kinds of other media that parents would rather not have cluttering up their kitchens. Workshops take place on Saturday, and there is a Sunday club as well as after-school sessions. An extra bonus is the 'Little Artists' club, which allows one- to four-year-olds the chance to play with clay, salt dough and papier mâché with the help of their parents. Full- and half-day courses are put on during the summer, often incorporating more unusual activities such as chocolate making and weaving. Art 4 Fun has studios in Notting Hill (7792 4567), Muswell Hill (8444 4333), West Hampstead (7794 0800), Mill Hill (8906 3333) and Chiswick (8994 4100).

Bravura Creative Art Studios
612 Fulham Road, SW6 (7731 7633/www.bravura.co.uk). Parsons Green tube. **Open** *May-Aug* 10.30am-5pm Mon-Wed, Sun; 10.30am-9pm Thur; 10.30am-6pm Fri, Sat. *Sept-Apr* 10.30am-5pm Tue, Wed, Sun; 10.30am-9pm Thur; 10.30am-6pm Fri, Sat. **Workshops** *school holidays* 10.30am-12.30pm, 2-4pm daily; *term time* 7-9pm Thur. **Fees** *from* £16 per session; phone for details. **Credit** AmEx, DC, MC, V.
Bravura holds a secret, in the form of its 'Silver Alchemy', a special clay that turns silver when fired in an oven. Children aged seven and up can spend hours creating jewellery, pots and sculptures, which will then be turned into a semi precious metal by the lick of a flame. Magic! Bravura also holds 'Splat' during half-term and holidays, a creative club where children can make everything from door plaques to candle holders. Children can be left unaccompanied and all materials are included in the fees. Ring for details of themed workshops; the Harry Potter ones always go down well.

Ceramics Café
215 King Street, W6 (8741 4140/ www.ceramicscafe.com)). Ravenscourt Park tube. **Open** 10am-10pm Tue-Thur; 10am-6pm Fri, Sat; noon-7pm Sun. **Fees** *Studio fee* £2; *materials* £3-£12. **Credit** MC, V.
Functional crocks can be personalised with your own designs here in the capacious kiln. Children of all ages enjoy decorating their own tableware, and consuming snacks and drinks from the café to get the creative juices flowing. This branch is a good choice for parties, too: the party package (for children aged from five) costs £10 per child, for a minimum of ten children. The huge party room can accommodate 30 comfortably. Note that under-14s must be accompanied by an adult.
Branch: 1A Mortlake Terrace, Kew Green, Richmond, Surrey (8332 6661).

Colour Me Mine
168-70 Randolph Avenue, W9 (7328 5533/ www.colourmemine.com). Maida Vale tube. **Open** 9am-9pm Mon-Thur; 9am-7pm Fri, Sat; 10am-7pm Sun. *After-school club* 4-6pm Tue, Thur. **Fees** *Studio fee per person* £6.60; £5.50 concessions; £4.40 under-12s. *Materials* £3-£45. *After-school club* £15; materials included. **Credit** AmEx, MC, V.
Anybody can pop into the CMM studios at any time and create mosaics, paint ceramics and daub on glass. If the children feel they want something a bit more structured, CMM's after-school club is suitable for kids aged six and up. Mosaic and bead workshops are also available at this time for the same price. Parents can bring toddlers to create special footprint plates (£39-£70). Just turn up.
The staff cater for parties and also organise holiday workshops where busy parents can drop their children off for a few hours to paint pots, make mosaics or design jewellery.
Branch: 452 Muswell Hill Broadway, N10 (8444 6886).

Pottery Café
735 Fulham Road, SW6 (7736 2157/ bridgewater-pottery.co.uk). Parsons Green or Putney Bridge tube. **Open** 10am-6pm daily; workshops during holidays. **Fees** *holiday workshops* £17. **Credit** AmEx, DC, MC, V.
Two-hour summer holiday workshops for 5- to 11-year-olds prove popular on rainy days. Parents receive free coffee on 'Baby Day' every Wednesday, if they turn up with their toddlers for a spot of pottery painting. Phone for prices.

Food

Le Cordon Bleu
114 Marylebone Lane, W1 (7935 3503/ www.cordonbleu.net). Bond Street tube. **Children's classes** 10am-noon Sat. **Fees** £100 2 classes; £410 per 8 wk term. **Credit** MC, V. **Map** p316 G5.
Le Petit Cordon Bleu is a children's club for mini-chefs aged from 7 to 11 years. You can sign up for seasonal cookery courses or short cooking weekends. Call for a brochure.

The Kids' Cookery School
107 Gunnersbury Lane, W3 (8992 8882/ www.kidscookery.org). Acton Town tube. **Open** *office* 9am-5.30pm Mon-Fri. **Courses** phone for dates and times. **Fees** *from* £15 per hour. **No credit cards.**
A registered charity offering children aged 3 to 14 the chance to take part in classes in food preparation, cooking and food therapy. The school welcomes children with eating disorders, physical disabilities and behavioural problems. Fees include the ingredients and a recipe card. A maximum of eight children per class is accepted.

Music

If you're looking for a suitably qualified music teacher, contact Incorporated Society of Musicans (10 Stratford Place, W1C 1AA, 7629 4413/www.ism.org), a professional association for musicians and music teachers, for advice and fee information.

Bush Hall Music House for Children
310 Uxbridge Road, W12 (8932 2652/ www.musichouseuk.com). Shepherd's Bush tube. **Open** 9.30am-6pm daily. **Classes** times vary; phone for details.

Courses prices vary. **Children's performances** 6pm, where listed. **Registration fee for drop-in classes** usually £2. **Tickets** prices vary. **Credit** MC, V.

With over 150 qualified tutors, Bush Hall should have a class and an instrument to suit your child. If you prefer to keep things in-house, Bush Hall teachers will come to your home for individual lessons. Otherwise, regular music and performance arts workshops are held in Shepherd's Bush, Kensington and Notting Hill, as well as masterclasses, group tuition in woodwind, strings, keyboard and voice, plus music and movement classes for the under-fives. Concerts are staged for families and friends at the end of every term. New to the curriculum is a music appreciation class for deaf children. *See also p247.*

Camberwell Choir School

81 Camberwell Church Street. SE5, St Giles Church Hall, 161 Benhill Road, SE5 (venue) (7701 2464). Bus 12, 36, 171, 345. **Fees** £1. **No credit cards.**

Now music is considered something of a luxury in the general scheme of children's education, places like this are a boon to impoverished but cultured parents. The Choir School is a community arts project providing high-quality music and arts tuition for local children, aged eight to fourteen. A registered charity, the school aims to provide access to the arts at affordable prices. Phone for details.

Drumhead

For locations, times & prices contact Pauline Madden (7733 5578/07790 857126) or Sandra Dyer (7394 6109/07790 405826).

Percussion and drumming workshops for children and adults together. All drums and instruments are provided and the programme includes a range of physical and rhythmic warm-ups, games, songs and group pieces.

The London Suzuki Group

Various venues (7386 8006/www.suzukimusic.net). **Prices** vary; phone for details.

Children aged from three to their mid-teens can benefit from the Suzuki Method, which aims to draw out inherent musical ability through learning by listening. Lessons involve group activities, parental participation and step-by-step tuition. Founded in 1972, this group now has 16 teachers working in Bayswater and Highgate, and holds residential and non residential holiday courses as well as the regular weekly classes. Programmes exist for violin, viola, cello and piano players.

Music Workshops

The Whippersnapper workshop room, Brockwell Lido, Dulwich Road, SE24 (7738 6633/www.thelido.co.uk). Herne Hill rail/Brixton tube/rail/3, 37, 196 bus. **Classes** times vary; phone for details. Fees from £3.50. **No credit cards.**

A must for fun-loving young musicians, the Whippersnapper holds musical and theatrical workshops on a termly and drop-in basis, aimed at babies, toddlers and the under-fives. Art and acrobatics workshops are also held here for children aged from 7 to 11.

Mwalimu Express

Bread & Roses pub, 68 Clapham Manor Street, SW4 (7498 1779). Clapham Common tube. **Workshops** 1-5pm, Sun. **Fees** free.

Mwalimu Express is a weekly chance for the whole family to go down the pub to investigate the music and cuisine of a particular region of Africa. The musicians invite the young members of the audience to take part in relaxed free workshops, including percussion, singing and storytelling. There is also a monthly film club showing African children's films.

The Ocean

270 Mare Street, E8 (8986 5336/www.ocean.org.uk). Hackney Central or Hackney Downs rail. **Open** Box office 10am-6pm daily. **Classes** phone for details. **Fees** vary; phone for details.

This new £23-million music project in Hackney includes Rising Tide, a training centre for children and adults. After-school and evening courses cover singing, keyboard, drumming – even music production classes – for kids aged seven and over. There is also a Saturday school for 11- to 16-year-olds. All classes are taken by professional musicians, working on performance, communication and presentation.

Science & environment

Camley Street Natural Park

12 Camley Street, NW1 (7833 2311/www.wildlondon.org.uk). King's Cross tube. **Open** Summer 9am-5pm Mon-Thur; 11am-5pm Sat, Sun. Winter 9am-5pm Mon-Thur; 10am-4pm Sat, Sun. **Admission** free. **Map** p317 L2.

Just around the corner from King's Cross Station, this nature reserve is open to the public as a park. Children can indulge in a spot of pond dipping at any point – just ask at the office for a net. More dedicated environmentalists might like to join the Wildlife Watch Club (free), for 8- to 14-year-olds, which meets once a month for some outdoor adventure. Each session will be based around a different theme, such as spiders, bats or even mini-beast hunts. Throughout the year, Camley Street also holds special free activity days, which often involve boat trips, barbecues and stalls. In the summer holidays, an environmental drop-in play-scheme means children can turn up and enjoy various craft activities, including clay modelling, tipi-making, trails and quizzes.

The Making Place

3 Exmoor Street, W10 (8964 2684/www.the-making-place.co.uk). Ladbroke Grove tube. **Open** 10am-3pm daily. **Workshops** 10am-3pm half-terms (phone to check). **Fees** £10 per child. **No credit cards.**

Adventures in science and technology are the order of the day at this place, housed in a purpose-built technology centre, in the grounds of Barlby School. During term time, the staff here run workshops for teachers and pupils, but during half-term the fun starts. Children aged 5-12 can come along for the day bringing a packed lunch, and use all the centre's facilities, computers, machinery and tools, under the watchful eye of their teachers. They also have a go at making things: from small explosions, to tooth casts to motorised vehicles. Children must be accompanied by an adult, but adults get in free.

Roots & Shoots

The Vauxhall Centre, Walnut Tree Walk, SE11 (7582 1800). Lambeth North tube. **Open** July-Apr 9.30am-5.30pm Mon-Fri. May, June 9.30am-5.30pm Mon-Fri; 10am-2pm Sat. Please phone before visiting. **Admission** free; donations welcome.

This one-acre site contains a pond, a summer meadow, a new paradise corner and beehives, not to mention a huge population of 800 workers. David, the Wildlife Outreach Officer, runs wildlife study days for school groups, and seasonal family days for everyone, when they can learn more about the flora and fauna here, and take part in honey extraction from the hives (in season), pond dipping and other activities. Ring for details of the next family day, or to ask David's advice about wildlife gardening. Ask to be put on the mailing list for details of all open days and activities.

Activities & Fun

Parties

And they'll cry if they want to.

If you've got the money, the party people and places listed below have the technology to make a child's birthday the social event of the term. The only trouble is, if you make your child's party too memorable and magical, they'll always want one. They'll never get to the stage when a trip to the cinema and a burger is enough, and will be asking for *piñatas*, exotic locations, paintballing or the hire of their own cinema even when they're 18. But if you do decide to indulge, the kids' party scene is quite an industry, so there are plenty of good places to choose from. Many of the restaurants in **Eating** (*pp170-189*) are happy to accommodate parties, too.

Lots of the people and organisations listed below operate from home, which is why only phone numbers, for enquiries only, have been listed. Most of the venues have facilities for disabled visitors, and many of the party people can tailor their package for children with special needs.

Activities

Arts & crafts

Art 4 Fun
172 West End Lane, NW6 (8959 7373/ www.art4fun.com). West Hampstead tube/rail.
Open 10am-7pm daily; by appointment until 10pm.
Credit AmEx, DC, MC, V.
Art 4 Fun gives children the chance to do what they do best: make a mess. Tie-dyeing, sculpting, painting ceramics, marbling and cartooning are just some of the activities on offer at this safe, well-supervised creative café. More importantly, children can enjoy all this for a bargain price of £3.95 each

> ▶ For more **football** parties, *see p255*; for more **pony** parties, *see p256*; for more **theatre** venues, *see pp223-30*; for more **cinemas**, *see pp220-22*; and for **restaurant** venues, *see p170-86*.

Acting up at a **Tiddleywinks** party. *See p235.*

Magical Makeovers. *See p235.*

for an entire day (plus the cost of the items they're decorating, from £1). For details of other branches, call or visit the website. *See also p230.*

Colour Me Mine
168-70 Randolph Avenue, W9 (7328 5577/ www.colourmemine.com). Maida Vale tube. **Open** 9am-9pm Mon-Thur; 9am-7pm Fri, Sat; 10am-7pm Sun. **Credit** AmEx, MC, V.
Creating and chomping seems to be the winning combination at England's first paint-your-own ceramics café. Children are given two hours to decorate ceramic models and hence produce their own masterpieces – fairies and dinosaurs are popular choices – while they feast on mouthwatering morsels of youth-approved snack foods. Such festivities are of course supervised by staff, who glaze and fire the ceramics (and post them out after the event), serve food and even clear up afterwards. Packages start at £12 per head, for a minimum of 12.

Nellie's Art Parties
7428 7600. **No credit cards**.
'High energy, visually stimulating and very messy' is how Fenella Shepherd (aka Nellie) describes her children's art parties. Held in two studios in Camden and Notting Hill (call for details), the two-hour parties are a spin-off from her highly popular art classes, and are tailor-made to a theme chosen by the birthday boy or girl. Children spend the first hour painting, glittering and collaging a giant mural, followed by a craft making session (so all participants go home with a finished product), tea (provided by Nellie's mum) and games. Catering for 3- to 13-year-olds, at £16 per head it's comparable in cost to the ceramic studios. Parties are held either at the clients' own venue or in Camden or Notting Hill.

Cookery

Cookie Crumbles
0845 601 4173/07966 530784.
Children as young as five can have fun making bread, jammy tarts and crocodile sandwiches in home cooking parties supervised by Cordon Bleu chefs – who clean up afterwards, too. Parties run for two hours, for a minimum of six

children (a maximum of 25). Prices start at £145 per two hours for a party of six including all ingredients. The Crumbles team can provide party bags and aprons for an extra charge. Ring this number to find out about kids' cookery workshops all over London.

Fix a Feast
Call Gayle (8675 9657) or Lucy (7350 2536).
Two hours of quality interactive entertainment, a tea party, a spotless cooker and home-made goody bags are all part of these food-fuelled parties. Once you have called the Fix a Feast team, either Lucy Booth or Gayle Wilde will arrange to pay you a visit, look over the preparation space and discuss which items, from an extensive list, your child would like to make. On the day the feast team arrive with all their equipment, and all you need supply is a birthday cake, a few party games and your choice of drink. Fix a Feast costs £130 for a two-hour party including food for up to eight children (extra kids £7.50 a head, maximum 12 children). Children aged six to eight make three dishes, those aged eight to 12 make four.

Drama

Fat Story Shop
7690 8064.
Actors Simon Thomson and Peter Eastland – former presenters on CBBC One's *Tellyquest* – run this lively outfit, which specialises in interactive storytelling sessions. Their parties, aimed primarily at five- to nine-year-olds, are all about imagination and creativity. Other activities such as mask-making and music can be involved, too, with everything run by experienced staff. Prices start at £140 for 90 minutes.

Lydie Children's Parties
7622 2540.
Lydie charms children aged four to nine (and adults) with her enchanting French accent and lively themed parties. She'll turn your living room into a fantasy grotto complete with decoration and balloons in which the children become the characters in stories of Peter Pan, Beauty and the Beast, Aladdin, Batman and so on. There are tales, activities and her own games. A two-hour party for up to 26 children including decorations and goody bags costs £250 at home, £280 elsewhere.

Marvellous Productions
8679 0917/www.marvellous-productions.com.
Fancy a trip on a magic carpet? Then call Mrs Marvel, aka actress Roya Hamid. Parties for the under-eights kick off with a magic carpet ride to Storyland with one of the Mrs Marvel clowns; over-eights prefer the drama workshops run by a clown in civvies. The 'destination' is dictated by the child's interest. This story or drama session can be followed by mask-making or prop-making workshops, where busy little hands will endeavour to create a prop from the story. Prices start at £80 for face-painting up to £400 for a mask-making workshop; the magic carpet costs from £125 for one hour.

Miss Sparkle
8986 4841/0958 653115.
The repertoire of former drama tutor Rain Harris includes performances for under-fives, incorporating her visually exciting handmade puppetry. With lots of audience participation, she builds a story around a theme, which could be Beauty and the Beast, heroes or an enchanted garden. The parties also involve low-key clown-style magic with the birthday child as helper; balloon modelling and non-competitive games. Art and crafts – making crowns or tiaras, for example – are also a possibility. Older children up to the ages of

13 or 14 are offered drama parties – a recent event being a Grease party – with costumes and dance, culminating in the production of a video or a performance in front of an audience of parents. Prices start at £65 for an hour, or £90 for a whole two-hour party, and every child gets a prize.

Splodge
7350 1477.
A relatively new company, Splodge has quickly made its mark on the kids' party scene. It organises creative parties and workshops for children aged two to ten, using art, music, movement and drama. The aim is to create an interactive event with a theme tailor-made for the individual: ring the hotline and you'll be asked about your child's favourite stories, songs, films and so on – Harry Potter is unsurprisingly popular – in order to make sure everything is perfect. Prices range from £150 to £300 per party, lasting two to three hours.

Tiddleywinks
8964 5490.
Kate Gielgud's drama parties for four- to seven-year-olds involve dressing up and acting out a story. Murder mystery parties for 8- to 13-year-olds have different themes, from horsey happenings to James Bond exploits. Dressing-up clothes and props are provided. From £165 for two hours.

Face-paints & make-up

Face painting
7267 2308.
Claudia Hunt is a professional make-up artist, so she can complete quite elaborate faces quickly and efficiently. She charges a minimum of £50 for ten kids, and £1 per extra child. No design is too difficult for Claudia, and she's also prepared to create special effects, like cuts and bruises.

Magical Makeovers
01932 244347/07957 681824.
This company offers a party service for girls aged from six to 15. A team of make-up artists and hairdressers will come to your house and give all the party-goers a 'makeover', with manicure, hair-styling (using accessories that are theirs to keep) and make-up. Prices run from £150 for eight children.

Mini Makeovers
8398 0107/www.minimakeovers.com.
Girls just wanna have fun, and, according to Mini Makeovers, lots of glitter, make-up and hair accessories to boot. For girls only, aged five to 12, this popular party firm will in two hours transform members of a party into princesses, fairies, or, for 8- to 12-year-olds, mini-Steps or S Club 7 stars (bar the costumes). The standard rate is from £130 for the minimum of eight; then £13.50 a head. This includes their hair accessories and a little gift in a silver bag to take home.

Sport

The Elms Soccer School Parties
8954 8787/theelms@virgin.net.
The Elms Soccer School promises that it has the answer for anyone who lives, sleeps and talks football. Children are taught by an FA-qualified coach at a venue of their (or their parents') choice, and are also provided with football-themed party invitations, balloons and goody bags to take home. Parties are up to one and a half hours long, and prices range from £95 to £120.

Kick it
7737 5987.
Have a football party in the park or in your garden. One coach will take a maximum of 16 boys and girls from three to 12 years (£80 for 90 minutes). Owner Joseph DeGraft is also an expert at teaching football to under-fives.

Mile End Climbing Wall
Haverfield Road, E3 (8980 0289). Mile End tube. **Open** noon-9.30pm Mon-Thur; noon-9pm Fri; 10am-6pm Sat, Sun. **Credit** AmEx, MC, V.
Located in a converted pipe-bending factory, the Mile End climbing wall provides strenuous activity for parties of children aged from eight. You provide the party trimmings, the company provides the instructors (one per eight children), who teach climbing and abseiling techniques. The cost is £28 per instructor for an hour (they'll be exhausted after that long), plus £1.50 for each child. The party room is available free of charge.

Pro-Active Leisure
*32 Ashurst Road, North Finchley, N12 (8446 3132/ 3166).***Open** 10am-5pm; 24hr answerphone.
An extensive range of exciting theme-based parties including Gladiators, Circus Skills, Crystal Ball Maze and Mini Olympics is offered by Pro-Active Leisure. New departures include makeover parties, discos and karaoke. The company also has a range of entertainers, from clowns and puppeteers to storytellers. Pro-Active's people can set up outside if you have a big garden, but as the activities are so dependent on good weather, they recommend you hire a hall for the celebration. Their database can point you in the direction of a suitable hall for hire in your area. Prices vary according to venue and the number of children that need entertaining. Ring for details.

That's the way the **Cookie Crumbles**. *See p234.*

Swashbuckling parties on board the
Golden Hinde. *See p237* and *p246*.

Westway Sports Centre

1 Crowthorne Road, W10 (8969 0992). Latimer Road tube. **Open** noon-9pm Mon, Tue, Thur-Sun; noon-11pm Wed. **Credit** AmEx, MC, V.

Energetic children can choose an activity from football, tennis, netball, basketball, hockey and, particularly popular, climbing. The Westway Sports Centre provides coaches, venue, all equipment, decorations and invitations; catering is also available. Prices start from £65 for ten children (up to a maximum of 25).

Young guns

Allied Command

0800 917 0821/www.paintballgames.co.uk. **Credit** MC, V.

Allied Command offers children's parties for under-18s at its Effingham (Surrey) and Tring (Herts) locations. at a cost of £17.50 a child for a full day, including 150 paintballs, and a barbecue lunch. Minimum age 11, and booking is essential (give at least two week's notice).

Campaign Paintball

Old Lane, Cobham, Surrey, KT11 (01932 865999/ www.campaignpaintball.com). Effingham Junction rail. **Credit** MC, V.

Paintballing takes place in 180 acres of forest near Cobham. Birthday parties are for children aged 11 to 17; Tony Blair's son Euan raved about a birthday party spent here. Prices are £17.50 per child for the day, including equipment, barbecue lunch 100 paintballs, and an end of day presentation. They also run half days and evening games. Reserve at least a week in advance.

Holmbush Paintball

Holmbush Farm, Faygate, West Sussex (0500 454555/ www.holmbushpaintball.co.uk). Horsham rail then short taxi ride. **Credit** MC, V.

Twelve combat arenas set in 250 acres of forest near Gatwick Airport. A full day is £15 per person, including 100 paintballs. Catering costs £1.50 to £2.50. There's also a special junior event on the last Sunday of every month. Minimum age 12.

Nellie's Art Parties. *See p234.*

Quasar

13 Junction Road, N19 (7281 5001). Archway tube. **Credit** MC, V.

Shooting 'em up with laser guns is the object here, in team games that adapt themselves easily to children's parties. A party package, complete with meal (burgers, chips and so on), costs £9.95 a child. Over-sevens only, in parties of up to 20.

Ship ahoy!

A love for the sea and the great outdoors is as good a reason as any for taking up as a pirate in Inner London. And that's exactly why Jacqueline Pink started doing kids' parties on the 16th-century reconstructed *Golden Hinde*. Birthday parties for children aged four to 11 include two pirate escorts, stories, treasure hunts, hoisting the anchor and party food in 'The Pirate's Den'. Once in pirate guise, Jacqueline becomes a derring-do swashbuckler, taking part in the entertainment of groups of ten to 30 people. Activities take place throughout most parts of the ship, with children visiting the deck, the captain's cabin on the half deck and also the armoury.

The job of a *Golden Hinde* pirate is definitely an active one, which is why it's usually done on a part-time basis. According to Jacqueline: 'It's quite physical work with loads of stairs to climb. We always get the children to go down the stairs backwards for safety. The parties are really like a tour of the ship, so I usually start at the bottom and then work my way to the top.'

Despite all the messing about, parties on board the *Golden Hinde* are as much about education as they are about offering a fun-packed hour and a half to children. There's the chance to learn about the food that pirates ate, which may well have consisted of hard tack biscuits, maggoty meat and often rancid drinking water. Thankfully, the menu has changed since then. For the last half hour of the parties, kids take to the Den, a small café opposite the ship where they can wind down with snacks of sandwiches, crisps, sausage rolls, biscuits, cake and juice.

Jacqueline explains: 'There's a basic script behind the pirate parties, but it's really up to you to add your own character, see what works for a particular group, and basically make it as entertaining as possible for the kids. I've had some children who take it so seriously they've even wondered if I'm really going to chop their hands off when I've been describing some of the punishments that were doled out to rebellious members of the ship's crew!' *See also p246.*

Cakes

For those who want to make their own party cakes, there are a couple of step-by-step guides to choose from: Carol Deacon's *No-Time Party Cakes* (£14.99 from bookshops) includes a fairy-tale castle and shows how to model figures and animals quickly and easily, and *New Children's Party Cakes* by Anna Farrell (£9.99 from bookshops) includes 35 cakes aimed at complete novices, both available for £3.99 from the Book People (01942 723333).

Ready-made themed birthday cakes can be bought at most supermarkets: football, fairies, cartoon characters and treasure troves are typical themes. They cost from about £7.

Chorak
122 High Road, East Finchley (8365 3330). East Finchley tube. **Open** 8.30am-6pm daily. **Credit** MC, V.
Cakes for all occasions are made on the premises with themed and very ornate party cakes made to order.

Jane Asher Party Cakes
22-4 Cale Street, SW3 (7584 6177/www.janeasher.co.uk). South Kensington tube. **Credit** AmEx, MC, V.
Come to Ms Asher's cake kingdom in Kensington to look at the catalogue and have a cake decorated to order. There are 3,000 designs to choose from. Prices start at about £55, and you need to give ten days' notice. If you like making your own, this is a sugarcraft and baking equipment shop, too.

Purple Planet
318-20 Portobello Road, W10 (8969 4119/ www.purpleplanet.co.uk). Ladbroke Grove tube. **Open** 10am-5pm Mon-Sat; 10am-4pm Sun. **Credit** AmEx, MC, V. **Map** p312 A6.
This party supply shop also has a sugarcraft and cake-baking section for people who want to decorate their own cakes. You can buy gold, silver and glittery edible paints. The range of party candles is an inexpensive way of impressing small children: try the fountain ones (£2.50). In terms of general party wares, there are streamers, balloons, tableware and banners. For dressing up, there are masks, theatrical make-up and bad-taste jokes.

Costumes

See also p17 of the **Good Toy Guide**.

Mail order

Hill Toy Company
0870 607 1248/www.hilltoy.co.uk.
The good old reliable Hill Toy Company has an appealing range of affordable dressing-up clothes. Try its Dalmatian suits (£19.95-£22.95) for size (ages one to nine), or make like the Sundance Kid in this supercool cowboy kit, complete with 'cowhide' waistcoat and scarf (£29.95), and hat (£6.95). The pretty fairy tutus are a snip at £12.95, while the full-on pink fairy dress, complete with wings and wand is a pretty reasonable £22.95.

The birthday cake of your child's dreams, from **Jane Asher Party Cakes**.

Activities & Fun

Hopscotch
8674 9853.

A huge range of outfits to get boys and girls in the party mood, from the ever-popular angel fairies and the new disco queen costumes to futuristic astronauts for the post millennium. Prices range from £11.95 to £29.95. All have been tested for ease of use and comfort by Hopscotch's team of mini-testers. There's also a selection of animal hats, from cats and pigs to zebras and even a dragon, which make quick dressing-up solutions for £11.95. Accessories include sequinned bags, necklaces, wands, halos, hats and wigs.

J&M Toys
01274 599314.

Based in Bradford, J&M Toys can supply an extensive range of fancy dress costumes, running from the astronaut kit (£15.95-£16.95) to a fisherman, a firefighter and all manner of adorable furry animals. There's a fabulous complete knight outfit (suitable for three- to eight-year-olds) that includes sword, shield, tabard and hat (and costs £15 plus £3.50 p&p). The company's multicultural hats (around £3) are worth a look. There's a great range of inexpensive accessories, too.

Small people, big imaginations, with clothes from the **Hill Toy Company**. *See p239.*

Make Believe

01483 203437/www.make-believe.co.uk.
Calling all you would-be witches and wizards out there. Here's your chance to hit Hallowe'en in real style, not just draped in your mum's old sheets and dripping with tomato ketchup. Mail order company Make Believe, founded by former *The Price is Right* hostess Carol Myson, has 32 imaginative and well-made outfits to suit every party-goer, and will ensure that no one cries at your party. The outfits may be on the pricy side, running from £19.99 for a Howling Ghost to £45.99 for Pretty Witch, but they are very pretty, 100% polyester and machine washable. Animals and Star Wars characters, too.

Shops

Escapade

150 Camden High Street, NW1 (7485 7384). Camden Town tube. **Open** 10am-7pm Mon-Fri; 10am-6pm Sat; noon-5pm Sun. **Credit** AmEx, MC, V.
There are 2,000 costumes for hire here, a small proportion of which fit children. To hire a bear costume, or full Buzz Lightyear regalia, you pay £18 for three days (deposit £30).

Harlequin

254 Lee High Road, SE13 (8852 0193). Hither Green rail/Lewisham rail/DLR. **Open** 10am-5.30pm Mon, Tue, Thur, Sat; 10am-1pm Wed; 10am-6pm Fri. **Credit** MC, V.
A colourful little dressing-up shop with a selection of children's costumes to hire, from Indian braves to hopping frogs. Expect to pay from £9.95 for the simplest costume, with accessories and kits from £3.50.

Deals on wheels

The Party Bus

01753 548822/0836 605032.
This converted bus will park in your drive (or nearby) and holds up to 24 children at a time. Each party is pitched according to the age group: games, magic and puppets for small children; a disco or a penny arcade for older ones. Prices are from £275 to £300 and include all catering except a cake. Party bags cost an extra £1.50 per child. For ages four to nine.

The Wonderbus

8968 3798/www.wonderbus.co.uk.
Although the parties organised on this bright blue bus are stationary events, this team will travel anywhere within the Greater London area. Coming complete with a friendly uniformed driver (José), Jessica Christie-Miller's funky double-decker allows up to 25 children at a time to run riot on the two imaginatively designed floors, which are decked out with soft flooring for dancing and playing, chill-out sections for reading and snacking, a ball pond for letting off steam, and music ranging from poptastic treats to jazz. The starting price is £285, which includes a party member and helper, food, pass the parcel and other prizes. Ages are from two to seven years, with sessions organised for set age groups.

The Wonder Years

07000 123455.
Children with a taste for stardom can don their dark glasses and film star clothes and cruise London in a limo. Book a tour or take trips to and from, say, Planet Hollywood. Soft drinks are supplied. Car hire costs from £160 for the first three hours. Cars seat from six to eight.

Zap the living daylights out of the over-sevens at **Quasar**. *See p237.*

Entertainers

See also p244.

Ali Do Lali

01494 774300.
This popular magician and illusionist will saw mums in half, breathe fire and pull rabbits from hats. He will entertain any number of children – having performed for up to 3,000 guests at a time. Ali also does shows and discos for older kids and traditional parties for ages two and up. Party bags, tables and chairs can also be supplied.

Ali Pali

01306 713330.
Ian Ray transforms into a genie to entertain any number of children during his visual and imaginative two-hour shows, aimed at five different age groups. Performances, which incorporate magic and humour, are based on an Arabian Nights theme with touches of Aladdin and Sinbad, and a flying carpet ride for the party child at the end. Ray can take over the organisation of an entire party, including venue and catering. A two-hour show costs £190.

Blueberry Playsong Parties

8677 6871.
Songs with action, games and dancing for children aged one to seven. Puppet Bobo makes an appearance, too, and he's very popular. Margo and her gang will travel to your venue and usually do a 45-minute slot within a party (£75) for up to 20 children.

Carolyn & Cindy's Parties
8940 8407.

Carolyn and Cindy put on puppet shows from nursery rhymes and stories including Sleeping Beauty and George and the Dragon for ages five and upwards. Girls can act out fairy tales like Cinderella and there's Camelot for boys. There's lots of audience participation and dressing up, too. They also do disco parties and maypole dancing. Balloons, prizes, pass the parcel and a present for the birthday child are provided. They can cater for anything from ten to 300 children, depending on the venue; prices from £170.

Chris Howell
7376 1083.

Magician Chris Howell, who came to the UK from Michigan five years ago to study theatre arts, delights young audiences with his magic tricks and ambitious balloon animals: 'I love that look of fascination in children's eyes when the magic actually happens in front of them', he says. He entertains older guests as well. An hour of magic and balloons costs £75.

Christopher the Chameleon
01932 254333.

Currently popular with west London party people, the 'Christopher the Chameleon' musical puppet show is a spin-off of the Stagecoach theatre company (*see p229*). Puppet Christopher is the main party impresario: he takes children on a magical journey where they meet other characters, learn song and dance routines and play games of make-believe in a magical atmosphere designed to stimulate creativity and imagination. Performances, which can take place in virtually any space (as long as there's a power supply), last for one hour and are currently based around themes of fairies and wizards, pirates and circuses. Prices are around £120.

Diane's Puppets
7820 9466.

Diane Goldie's large repertoire of puppet shows provides entertainment for all children from one to around seven, including those with special needs. All the puppets are devised and handmade by Goldie, who is also an experienced storyteller and scenic artist. The shows on offer include the Bobby Bunny Show for two- to five-year-olds, the Great Pirate Caper featuring the Bottle O'Rum Rap, and Frog Prince Fashion, an update of the old-fashioned fairy-tale genre. Prices are £100 for one-hour sessions, while the £150 two-hour sessions include face-painting.

Juggling John
8672 8468.

One of London's top children's entertainers, Juggling John invites youngsters to meet his friends Reggie the Racoon and Ronnie the Robot. If you're looking to see some fire-eating, sword juggling and other circus-inspired acts to liven up a run-of-the-mill children's party, then Juggling John is the right man to contact, boasting such past clients as Children's ITV and the Disney Channel.

Lee Warren
8670 2729.

Magician Lee's show lasts about an hour and is ideal for four- to eight-year-olds. The classic shows are full of colour and fun and involve plenty of joining in – children come up and help, often dressing up as a pirate or princess, and earn a certificate. His young audiences find it especially hilarious when tricks appear to be going wrong. Lee can deal with from eight to 600 children and charges from £85.

Little Blisters
8948 3874.

This six-year-old company is run by two parents who have worked in theatre, TV and film. All their entertainers are trained actors and shows are original and dramatic. Their present show uses magic and music, along with characters like Pearl the Mermaid, Lucy the Chimp and Galaxy Warrior. Face-painting, circus skills and balloon modelling are all included, tailored to small or older children (maximum group 35). Parties cost from £100 to £170.

Marmaduke the Magical Clown
01992 446211.

For younger children, there's a magic and animal act with barn owls, chinchillas and lizards. Over-eights will love Animal Encounters – an animal act with rare and endangered animals including fruit bats, snakes and armadillos – or a combination of games, competitions, magic, animals and a disco. Marmaduke and his cuddly creatures are willing to travel around the South-east. Prices (in London) are £160 for an hour, £210 for one and a half hours.

Merlin Entertainments
tel/fax 8866 6327.

This children's entertainment service has more than 40 entertainers on its books, from jugglers, stilt-walkers, magicians and clowns to junior discos and fire-eaters for children aged from three upwards. A one-hour magic show costs from £80.

Peter McKenna
7703 2254/0956 200572.

Magic Circle member Peter McKenna appears as Bimbo the Clown, Mezmo the Wizard or Peter the Balloon Man to entertain children of all ages for one- or two-hour shows including magic, balloon modelling and a mini-disco. Prices start at £80 for one hour, £115 for two.

Smartie Artie Party
01582 461588.

A one-man travelling circus, who will travel to the location of your choice and provide partiers with raucous acts of entertainment ranging from comedy magic and ventriloquism to balloon modelling and puppet shows. Phone for price details.

ZoZo the Clown
Contact Le Club Tricolore 7924 4649.

ZoZo the bilingual clown, the original creation of Teresa Scibor, holds parties either bilingually or entirely in French, during which children not only enjoy themselves immensely but also learn to associate language with communication, rather than with education. ZoZo is a loveable character with bright orange hair, who travels from his home in Bon-Bon by hot air balloon and carries a magic banana bag. He uses songs, games, stories and magic, together with an inimitable clowning style, to entertain large or small groups of children and encourage them to speak French without them even realising. Prizes and rewards are distributed to all party children. ZoZo's parties start at £80 for up to 15 children for one hour, £95 for over 15 children (when he is joined by his helper Fifinette). Le Club Tricolore, where ZoZo the Clown hangs out when he's not being zany, runs French language classes for children.

Equipment hire

Disco

Jukebox Junction
12 Toneborough, Abbey Road, NW8 (7328 6206).
St John's Wood tube. **Open** by appointment 9am-5pm
Mon-Fri. **No credit cards**.
Hire one of two Seeburg 1970s jukeboxes and up to 50 singles from a choice of 3,500 at Jukebox Junction. £175 a night,
plus £50 deposit.

Young's Disco Centre
20 Malden Road, NW5 (0800 980 2321/7485 1115/
www.disco999.co.uk). Belsize Park or Chalk Farm tube.
Credit MC, V.

Sound systems and DJs for children's parties cost from £100
for a two-hour weekday party, and from £130 at weekends,
depending on venue and type. Hire a karaoke machine for
around £200; plus another £80 for a disco. Popcorn and
candyfloss machines are also available.

Marquees

Minimarkees
20 Bradmore Park Road, W6 (8741 2777).
Keep the chaos out of the house with a Minimarkee – available in all shapes and sizes for all occasions. Frame tents start
at £80 and go up to £250; multi-pavilions cost from £130 for
a three-by-three footer; for a real treat hire a big top ten (from
£325). Trestle tables, dancefloors, heating, matting and lights
are all available.

Clowning around

You know that moment. You've been introduced to
a new group at a party, everyone's commented on
the state of the weather, English football and their
drinks requirements, and the question 'what do
you do?' comes up. At which point you hope no
one has a desperately embarrassing job – and
then the apparently sanely named Sean Hampson
reveals that for work purposes he is in fact called
Boo Boo. And he's a clown.

The next question's always a poser, but the ruder
among us would simply ask what drives a grown
man to become – well – a figure of fun. And the
answer would be that after an evening class in
juggling led to Sean doing a one-off appearance at
his godson's birthday party, a career change was
born. Training with popular magic man Papalarny
and a two-year stint of working with an Essex party
agency brought him to where he is now, a fully
fledged professional with four years of entertaining
under his belt.

Though he plays it for laughs, Boo Boo is
nonetheless a bit of a postmodern clown,
eschewing the traditional trappings: 'I like to
create a theatre experience with a bit of magic,
and to offer traditional games with music', he
explains. 'I do clown around a lot during a birthday
party but all the stage make-up and specific clown
paraphernalia don't really work for me'.

Sean performs mainly in Fulham, Wandsworth
and Hammersmith, but can be called out to most
London addresses. Weekends are busiest for
bookings but he also does weekday nursery or
school-leaving parties. Party pieces for younger
children include juggling, games and the conga;
over-nines get to meet Boo Boo's slightly cooler
alter ego Sean the DJ, who has them dancing to all
the latest hits from Britney, Steps, Westlife et al.

Sean's a one-man band, but he shares ideas and
experiences with a network of other entertainers.
Most surreally, he's even done paintballing as a
kind of 'bonding' exercise with his competitors.
They didn't wear clown outfits – but they did get
spattered. Boom boom.

Sean Hampson
7727 3817/www.mr-booboo.co.uk.

Going for broke

Although it seems a sin to smash to pieces an item that has been so lovingly put together, tradition dictates that this is exactly what you do when presented with a Mexican *piñata*. No doubt a great way for children (of all ages) to let off steam, the colourfully decorated papier mâché containers come in the shape of ships, stars, flowers, fish, birds, animals and extravagant shapes, all modelled out of paper and cardboard and filled with small gifts.

The *piñata* is hung from the ceiling (or a tree, or whatever), the children are blindfolded, spun around, and then one by one, stick in hand, they get a chance to smash the *piñata* (if they can) to smithereens and claim the spoils – usually sweets, fruit, nuts and small toys. Not as simple as it sounds. The *piñata* can be lowered and raised just to add to the sense of fun and excitement, and quite often a competitive dad might feel the need to join in.

You can make a *piñata* yourself, or, in London, buy one from Mexicolore, which sells them either pre-filled or for you to put your own goodies in. Prices from £14.95.

Mexicolore
28 Warriner Gardens, SW11 (7622 9577/ www.mexicolore.co.uk/www.pinata.co.uk). Battersea Park or Queenstown Road rail. **Open** by appointment. **No credit cards.**

Organisers

Action Station
7263 8468/www.theactionstation.co.uk.
Action Station has something for everyone, from drama, storytelling and theme parties to mini-sports days. Four-to six-year-olds will love the Magical Storytelling parties (£100 for one hour). There are also puppet, magic, balloon modelling and fairy parties (from £80). Boys might prefer pirate adventure parties (aged five and upwards), junior gladiators (six and upwards), mini-Olympics or a trampoline party. Other ideas include discos, film parties (from £100), circus skills (from £130) and puppet-making workshops. Even toddlers aren't left out – they can have a mural painted in their room.

Adam Ant's
8959 1045.
One-man entertainment powerhouse Adam Ant supplies the kit and the performers for magic shows, puppet theatre, balloon modelling and other fun and games for the under-eights. Hireable equipment runs from tables and chairs to ball ponds and bouncy castles. Rates are reasonable – from £70 an hour depending on location. Ring for a catalogue.

Happy Times
8207 3737.
Barbara Rolnick's company can organise anything from traditional clowns, magicians and puppets to a Martian bouncy castle. If you're brave, you'll go for the jungle parties, where kids can meet and even touch creatures from barn owls, bird-eating spiders and talking frogs to fruit bats and a 15ft (4.5m) Indian python. Parties start at £90. Catering, decorations, spectacular cakes and party bags can also be provided. For the Christmas season book Santoe – 'younger and better looking' than his uncle Santa Claus – who performs a 45-minute Christmas magic show for all ages.

Laurence Temple, the Party Wizard
8840 5293.
Laurence Temple is a brilliant all-rounder, who comes highly recommended by 17 years' worth of fans. Workshops and storytelling using magic, mime, songs and percussion – either privately or collaboratively with organisations such as Lauderdale House – are his forte, but he can also organise the likes of theme parties, bouncy castles and mini-discos. Call him for a quote.

Puddleduck Parties
8788 7240.
This company claims to provide 'stress-free' themed parties for children of all ages, and can package everything from entertainers, tableware and goody bags to home-made food and cake. Themes include Batman, Teddy Bear's Picnic, Pirate, Fairy Princess, Circus or your own choice. Also available are drama parties, art and craft, sport and discos.

Twizzle Entertainment
8780 5234.
A slick party service, Twizzle can book entertainers, magicians, clowns, character visits ('Barbie', for example) and theme parties such as Star Wars, Action Man or Cinderella. On a more mundane level, tables and chairs, party bags, food, bouncy castles, ball ponds and other props are also available.

Paraphernalia

Mail order

abigsmile.com
A one-stop online party shop, www.abigsmile.com offers a range of party possibilities. Give the little ones a Tinky Winky, Pokémon or Dan the Digger party, with all the trimmings. Pre-teens can have a 'glamorous girls' party with glamour tableware, loot bags and banners (£13.99 for eight of each), and there is also a range of accessories, from party poppers to glittery masks and silly string.

Baker Ross
8808 6948/www.bakerross.co.uk.
Baker Ross, the school arts suppliers, is a good bet for mail order party bag toys, although you do have to buy a few of the items in bulk (you might have to ask yourself what you're going to do with the 140 unused transfer tattoos). Some things are sold in smaller quantities, however, and still work out cheaply: 12 Mr Clown Gift Bags cost 2p each, and can be filled with a selection of toys from as little as 5p each. All mail orders worth £35 or more come with a free gift.

Party Angels
01908 282552/www.partyangels.co.uk.
Party Angels will deliver themed packs of partyware direct to your door – just add kids and food. The packs are designed for eight children and contain place settings for each child plus extras such as hats, blowers, goody bags, novelty treats and candles with holders. Mermaids, ballerinas and unicorns are on offer as well as themes like football, pirates and aliens. There are also traditional options such as Winnie the Pooh and clowns. Packs cost £29.99 plus £2.99 p&p. Additional place settings are available.

Party Directory
01276 850501.
This new mail order catalogue has 27 styles of themed tableware, including Toy Story 2, Noddy, Star Wars, the Little Mermaid and Batman. There are also accessories and presents. Prices start at £1.99 for a packet of eight plates.

Party Pieces
01635 201844.
This catalogue has some pretty cool novelties – witness the pink cardboard Cadillac that holds your drink and sandwiches, the loot bags to be secured with pirate stickers and the tiny black and white football candles with matching gift bags, napkins and tablecover. Personalised invitations, inexpensive toys and dressing-up accessories are also available.

Partyworks
0870 240 2103/www.partybypost.co.uk.
Co-ordinated tableware, presents and games for themed parties, dressing-up clothes and accessories, an essential directory of party activities, cake making, balloons and decorations, plus presents and party bags (£2.50 for a handsome pre-filled range), from respected toyshop **Tridias** (see p209).

Smiffy's
0800 590599/www.smiffys.com.
Founded as far back as 1894, Smiffy's is said to be the oldest and largest joke, novelty and wig factory in Europe. It supplies dressing-up kits for children and adults plus accessories, masks, hats, costumes, face paints, make-up and party poppers. Balloons come in foil or latex and you can even order a flamboyant carnival headdress.

Shops

Balloon and Kite Company
613 Garratt Lane, SW18 (8946 5962/ www.balloonandkite.com). Tooting Broadway tube/ Earlsfield rail. **Open** 9am-5.30pm Mon-Sat. **Credit** AmEx, MC, V.
London's widest variety of balloons, from foil cartoon character shapes to balloon canopies. Helium gas hire is available, or balloons can be helium-filled in the shop. Filled latex balloons are £1 each; foil balloons £2.99. Delivery and decoration service available.

Balloonland
12 Hale Lane, NW7 (8906 3302/www.balloonland.co.uk). Edgware tube/Mill Hill Broadway rail. **Open** 9.30am-5.30pm Mon-Fri; 10am-5.30pm Sat. **Credit** MC, V.
Balloon and party specialists offering a seven-day delivery service. Helium party packs, helium gas rental, balloon clusters and balloons attached to soft toys or chocolates are overall guaranteed to make any party go with a swing.

Circus Circus
176 Wandsworth Bridge Road, SW6 (7731 4128). Fulham Broadway tube. **Open** 10am-6pm Mon-Sat. **Credit** AmEx, V.
Party tableware, cards, costumes (from £9), toys, novelties for party bags, decorations, inflatable hire, cakes and catering. Can also organise entertainers.

Just Balloons
127 Wilton Road, SW1 (7434 3039). Victoria tube/rail. **Open** 9am-6pm Mon-Sat. **Credit** MC, V.
Every kind of balloon you could possibly want, especially novelty ones, from inflatable giraffes to bananas and globes.

The Non-Stop Party Shop
214-16 Kensington High Street, W8 (7937 7200). High Street Kensington tube. **Open** 9.30am-6pm Mon-Sat. **Credit** AmEx, MC, V. **Map** p314 A9.
This shop is all about having a good time; this is evident in its displays of year-round fireworks, wrapping paper, cards, helium balloons, party hats, wigs, false noses, masks, streamers and more.

Oscar's Den
127-9 Abbey Road, NW6 (7328 6683/ www.oscarsden.com). St John's Wood or Swiss Cottage tube. **Open** 9.30am-5.30pm Mon-Sat; 10am-2pm Sun. **Credit** AmEx, MC, V.
Mick Jagger, the Duchess of York and Phil Collins are some of the celebrities who have treated their offspring to the spoils available at Oscar's. Everything you could ever need for a party is here, from entertainers, all year-round fireworks, soft play areas, inflatables and ball ponds (from £40 plus VAT). Bouncy castles cost from £35 plus VAT and entertainers start at £95 for one hour, £125 for two. Worth a visit for ideas alone – but you're bound to make a purchase.

Party Party
11 Southampton Road, NW5 (7267 9084/ www.partyparty.uk.com). Chalk Farm tube/Gospel Oak rail. **Open** 9.30am-5.30pm Mon-Sat. **Credit** MC, V.
As the name suggests, Party Party is packed with bright ideas for children's and teenage parties. There are party bags, novelty cakes and helium-filled balloons, paper plates, cake tins and party poppers. Fancy-dress costumes cost from £7.99 to £22.99 to buy.

Oscar's Den – all your party needs, from the clown down. *See p245.*

stormy seas – with a costumed crew and then sit down to eat maggoty hard tack – OK, crisps and sausage rolls – at the captain's table. Mermaid parties are also available. For £165, the *Golden Hinde* can cater for 15 kids aged four to 11 for 90 minutes provide entertainers and party bags. *See also p237.*

HMS Belfast

Morgan's Lane, Tooley Street, SE1 (7940 6328/ www.iwm.org.uk). London Bridge tube/rail. **Open** *Mar-Oct* 10am-6pm daily. *Nov-Feb* 10am-5pm daily. Last entry 45min before closing. **Admission** £5.40; £4 concessions; free under-16s (must be accompanied by an adult). **Credit** MC, V. **Map** p321 R8.
Entrance to the ship is free for children up to 16, so you could organise a trip as part of your own party, but for £8 per child you can have the use of a room for the day, goody bags, free quiz sheets, an HMS *Belfast* poster and baseball cap and a birthday card. For every five children one adult goes free. Catering is £5 extra per child, a ship-shape cake costs £70 and for £150 you get the services of party organiser Captain Corky for two hours – kids can climb in hammocks and dress up in costume. Available for up to 26 children. Phone to make a booking.

London Waterbus Company

58 Camden Lock Place (7482 2550). Camden Town tube. **Credit** MC, V.
Have your child's party on a canal boat going down the river from Camden Lock or Little Venice (Warwick Avenue tube). You can hire the boat during the day (£155 for the two-hour minimum); bring your own refreshments, games, balloons, entertainer or whatever you like. The maximum number of children is around 20. Alternatively, you could just take the regular tour (50 min), with one-way tickets costing £2.80 (children) and £4.20 (adults), and combination tickets with London Zoo also available. Note: services only run at weekends during winter. *See p93.*

Cinemas

BFI London IMAX Cinema

1 Charlie Chaplin Walk, South Bank, Waterloo, SE1 (7902 1234/group bookings 7960 3120/café 7960 3118). Waterloo tube/rail. **Credit** AmEx, MC, V. **Map** p320 M8.
The Film Café at Waterloo's IMAX cinema offers party packages for children aged five to ten. For £5.95 each child can tuck into sausage rolls, mini-pizzas, fruit trifle, crisps, a platter of assorted sandwiches and a carton of juice. The IMAX cinema offers a discount for groups of ten or more.

Kids Club

Clapham Picture House, 76 Venn Street, SW4 (7627 7555). Clapham Common tube. **Credit** MC, V.
Kids Club parties take place in a specially decorated upstairs room at the Clapham Picture House. For £8 each, children get entry to the film at 11.45am, a mini-popcorn and a drink plus a goody bag. The birthday child also gets to visit the projection box and start the film. If you're after a special birthday treat, book at least two months in advance for a themed party with a specific film that the cinema will do its best to provide (no Disney). For more information call Maya Nakamura on the above number. There's no catering but parents are welcome to arrange their own. Adults pay £2 to see the film.

Screen West

The New Boat House,136-42 Bramley Road, W10 (7565 3030/7565 3321/bookings 7437 6292/ www.screenwest.co.uk). Latimer Road tube. **Credit** MC, V.

Party Superstore

268 Lavender Hill, SW11 (7924 3210/www.party superstore.co.uk). **Open** 9am-6pm Mon-Wed, Fri, Sat; 9am-7pm Thur; 10.30am-4.30pm Sun. **Credit** AmEx, MC, V.
The biggest party shop in London, with a floor devoted to children's jollies, which includes a huge range of decorated paper plates, cups and tablecloths. Costumes (for sale only, no hire) and fireworks are also available.

Venues

All aboard

Golden Hinde

St Mary Overie Dock, Cathedral Street, SE1 (08700 118700/www.goldenhinde.co.uk). London Bridge tube/rail. **No credit cards. Map** p321 P8.
Enduringly popular pirate parties on a grand 16th-century ship complete with 22 cannons and pirates' den. Kids enjoy merry capers – like a treasure hunt, games and stories of

A state-of-the-art preview cinema that offers an hour in an air-conditioned 74-seat screening room followed by an hour in an adjoining function room (from £200). Staff will try and source favourite films, or you can take along a video of your choice. The function room is big enough for plenty of running around on a child-friendly wooden floor. Four large sofas, five tables, 20 chairs and a CD player are available and you can take in your own food and snacks.

Meet the animals

Battersea Park Children's Zoo
Battersea Park, SW11 (zoo 7924 5826/Splodge 7350 1477). Sloane Square tube then 19, 137 bus/Battersea Park or Queenstown Road rail. **No credit cards.**
This little zoo is home to some of the smallest monkeys in the world (marmosets), the loveable pot-bellied pig Tum Tum, otters, reptiles and meerkats. Parties, run by Splodge (*see p235*), are held daily from March to October (Saturdays and Sundays only in winter), in any two-hour slot between 10am and 5pm. There's lots of touchy-feely animal stuff along with art activities, treasure hunts and puppet shows, in tailored packages (from £150). The capacity is ten to 30 children. *See also p147.*

London Aquarium
County Hall, Riverside Building, Westminster Bridge Road, SE1 (7967 8000/children's tour enquiries 7967 8007/www.londonaquarium.co.uk). Westminster tube/Waterloo tube/rail. **Open** 10am-6pm daily. Last entry 5pm. Phone for opening times during hols. **Credit** MC, V. **Map** p319 M9.
Go wallow in waterworld at the Aquarium if you have between ten and 20 over-sixes to entertain. The entrance fee is £5.25 a child (£8.75 for accompanying adults) and after an hour-long kids' tour they actually get to the fish – a privilege denied the average visitor. There are currently no catering facilities, but plans are afoot to develop children's parties here. *See also p38.*

London Zoo
aka Rampage at London Zoo, Regent's Park, NW1 (7722 3333/www.londonzoo.co.uk). Baker Street or Camden Town tube then 274, C2 bus. **No credit cards.** **Map** p316 G2.
There are more than 600 species, including invertebrates, reptiles, fish, birds, gorillas, tigers and bears, in this landmark zoo. A fab day out in itself if your offspring are intent on bonding with wildlife. However, the affiliated aka Rampage, a company that offers various children's activities here, can make a birthday visit extra special. It runs two parties, both of which supplement zoo tours, food and general party paraphernalia with extra activities: for £17 a head, the Doctor Squiggles puppet party for younger children, which features a safari with 'the crazy cartoonist explorer and his puppet friends', and for £19, an art activity party. There's a 25-head maximum and a 15 minimum (ten during the week). *See also p94.*

Westway Stables
20 Stable Way, W10 (8964 2140). Ladbroke Grove or Latimer Road tube. **No credit cards.**
Westway Stables offers riding adventures, plus games and food. Depending on their riding ability, children can go to the park and do a horseback treasure hunt or play gymkhana games, then brush the ponies and plait their manes. Prices are £25 a head for a maximum of about 20, including food (there are several menus to choose from).

Museums

Bethnal Green Museum of Childhood
Cambridge Heath Road, E2 (8983 5200/recorded info 8980 2415/www.museumofchildhood.org.uk). Bethnal Green tube/rail. **Open** 10am-5.50pm Mon-Thur, Sat, Sun. Closed 24-26 Dec, 1 Jan, Good Friday. **Admission** free; donations welcome. Under-8s must be accompanied by an adult.
Parties for groups of around ten children are held in a downstairs room, and there's also a soft toy play area. The café provides a lunch box. A good idea is to tie a party in with the museum's workshops, which take place on Saturdays. Parties cost £3.50; £5 with workshop. For over-threes.

Science Museum
Exhibition Road, SW7 (7942 4747/www.nmsi.ac.uk). South Kensington tube. **Credit** AmEx, MC, V. **Map** p315 D9.
There are no specific party facilities at the Science Museum, but the thrilling prospect of staying up late and dossing down within the hallowed portals of the museum makes the monthly science sleepovers a favourite birthday treat for children aged eight to 11. Booking early is essential (three months ahead is usual): ask for an application form on the number above.

Face the music

Bush Hall on the Shepherd's Bush Road opened in May 2001 and operates not just as a characterful members' club, but also as an excellent place for children (and adults) to fine-tune their musical skills, or at least lend their ears to the range of music that's on offer through workshops and specially organised gigs or ensembles.

An outreach programme offers birthday party packages for under-fives. Parents simply have to relay to the staff any favourite stories, food, animals and songs for a personalised musical treat whereby a special theme is written with the birthday child as the central character. Staff then come to your house or chosen venue and work their magic.

Parties can also be held at Bush Hall and include musical games – musical statues and the more rough-and-tumble bumps are popular faves – rhythm and movement, singing and playing musical instruments, all accompanied by the piano. It's a great way of taking any strain out of keeping handfuls of youngsters entertained. As part of the treat the lucky birthday child gets to have his or her mates serenading them with 'Happy Birthday', and face-painting, clowns and a disco dancing fest are all thrown in for good measure.

Prices start at £75. *See also p231.*

Bush Hall Music House for Children
310 Uxbridge Road, W12 (8932 2652/ www.musichouseuk.com). Shepherd's Bush tube. **No credit cards.**

Playgrounds & games

Bramley's Big Adventure
*136 Bramley Road, W10 (8960 1515/
www.bramleysbig.co.uk). Ladbroke Grove tube.* **Open**
10am-6.30pm daily. Closed 25 Dec, 1 Jan, Aug bank hol.
Credit AmEx, MC, V.
An indoor adventure playground complete with slides, inflatable balls, monkey swings and much more, where 75 minutes
of play, a party meal, goody bags and balloons cost from £7
per child for ages 0-11 (weekends £9). Up to 40 children can
be seated in the party room; larger parties can hire the whole
playground. There are extras available: Bramley the
Brontosaur will visit for 20 minutes (£10). There are separate
play areas for babies and under-fives and a café for parents.

Clown Town
222 Green Lanes, N13 (8886 7520). Southgate tube.
Open 10am-7pm Mon, Tue, Thur-Sun. **No credit cards.**
This jungle playcentre has a monkey tree house, tarzan ropes,
net climbs and ball ponds. Supervised parties cost £7.50 at
weekends, £6.75 weekdays. Included are invites, an hour of
play, an hour of food and drinks and a party bag for each child.
Age range is three to 12, height limit 4ft 11in (130cm), with a
minimum of eight children in the week, 12 at weekends.

Coram's Fields
93 Guilford Place, WC1 (7837 6138). Russell Square tube.
Open *Apr-Sept* 9am-7pm daily. *Oct-Mar* 9am-6pm daily.
Admission free (adults admitted only if accompanied by
child under 16). **No credit cards. Map** p317 L4.
This shady playground has a paddling pool, play
equipment, sports area and a small pets' corner with
sheep, goats, a pig and rabbits. You can hire out a party
room for £18.50 – the smaller room seats up to 60 – and
there are kitchen facilities, so take your own food.

Discovery Planet
*Surrey Quays Shopping Centre, Redriff Road, SE16
(7237 2388). Surrey Quays tube.* **Open** 10am-6pm
Mon-Sat; 11am-5pm Sun. **Credit** MC, V.
This indoor adventure playground has them all hot and sticky
before cooling them off with ice-creams and fizz. Choose from
bronze, silver or gold parties for a minimum of eight children
(£5.99-£9.99 per head), which include your own party room
and host. Gold and silver parties include Burger King food,
soft drinks and ice-cream, plus goody bags. If you opt for the
gold, extras, such as a giant balloon for the birthday child,
birthday cake and extra large goody bags, are included.

Kidzmania
28 Powell Road, E5 (8533 5556). Clapton rail. **Open**
10am-6.30pm daily. **Admission** £3.50 for 90min.
No credit cards.
An indoor adventure playground with ball ponds, chutes,
slides, ropes, bouncy things and climbing things. For £7.50
a child (in a group of ten to 40) you get an hour and a half of
play followed by 40 minutes of scoff, with a host. For one- to
12-year-olds.

Namco
*County Hall (riverfront entrance), Westminster Bridge
Road, SE1 (7967 1066/www.namcostation.co.uk).
Westminster tube/Waterloo tube/rail.* **Open** 10am-
midnight daily. Closed 25 Dec. **Admission** free.
Map p319 M9.
A potentially bank-breaking but enduringly popular option
for a kids' party, this vast arena of sound and light is home

to more than 200 video games and simulators, the fastest
dodgems in Europe and a high-tech mini-bowling alley. Prices
vary from 30p to £2 a game.

Pippa Pop-ins
*430 Fulham Road, SW6 (7385 2458). Parsons Green
tube.* **Credit** MC, V.
This beautifully appointed nursery is the ultimate child-
friendly venue. All kinds of parties can be organised for a
maximum of 30 children aged two to 12, from traditional tea
parties to barbecues and even miniature dinner parties.
Entertainers can be hired if required. Prices vary according
to type of party and numbers.

The Playhouse
*The Old Gymnasium, Highbury Grove School, corner
of Highbury Grove & Highbury New Park (7704 9424).
Highbury & Islington tube/rail/4, 19, 236 bus.* **Open**
10am-6pm Mon-Thur; 10am-7pm Fri-Sun.
No credit cards.
Another indoor adventure playground, and a cheap, energetic
party option at £2.20 per child for two hours of play, plus
£25 for the room. You can provide food yourself or get the
catered option (an extra £4.75 a head). The age range is 6 to
11, and capacity seven to 22.

Snakes and Ladders
*Syon Park, Brentford, Middlesex (8847 0946/
www.syonpark.co.uk). Gunnersbury tube then 237, 267
bus.* **Open** 10am-6pm daily; last admission 5.15pm.
Credit MC, V.
Syon Park offers a party room with a host, an hour and a
half on a play frame, party bags, cake, invitations and
T-shirts. Prices per head are £9.65 with a hot meal, £8.65 for
cold. *See also p158.*

Take in a show

Jackson's Lane
269A Archway Road, N6 (8340 5226). Highgate tube.
Credit AmEx, MC, V.
There are three rooms for children's parties, available at
weekends at a rate of £50 for up to four hours. You don't have
to see one of the lovely kids' shows here (11am and 2pm
Saturday, for three- to eight-year-olds), but if you do you get
a pound off the tickets, bringing them to £3. Catering – of the
pizza, chips and ice-cream variety – is done by the in-house
café, Veggie House (8348 7666), for about £3.50 a head.

Lyric Theatre Hammersmith
*King Street, W6 (8741 2311/www.lyric.co.uk).
Hammersmith tube.* **Open** *Box office* by phone 10am-7pm
Mon-Sat. **Tickets** £5.50; £4 concessions. **Credit** AmEx,
DC, MC, V.
There are children's shows aimed at three- to seven-year-
olds here at 11am and 1am on Saturdays (tickets £4; £5.50
adults): young theatre-goers can make use of a dedicated
no-smoking area and terrace next to the café to eat a hot or
cold meal (£5.50/£4.50).

Puppet Theatre Barge
*Blomfield Road, Little Venice, W9 (07836 202745).
Warwick Avenue tube.* **Credit** MC, V. **Map** p312 C4.
Magical waterborne puppet shows at weekends and daily
during school holidays, usually at 3pm, for £6.50 for adults
and £6 for children. There's a private space available for
hire when the curtain comes down – you provide the food,
drink and merriment.

Sport & Leisure

From athletics to yoga, London is fit for sports lovers of all ages.

The capital is extremely well served with child-friendly facilities and high-quality instructors – along with superb professional sport from football to ice hockey, basketball to rugby union.

Some activities are more aesthetic than athletic, while others can be enjoyed without the need for ten team-mates, expensive gear and a referee.

Note that exact details of classes and opening times are given where possible, but it's still always best to phone to check such details first. For many classes and most courses you need to book in advance. Larger establishments accept at least Visa and MasterCard as methods of payment.

Participation Sports

Athletics

Success at the Sydney Olympics and the high profile enjoyed by athletes like Denise Lewis and Jonathan Edwards have pushed British athletics into the spotlight. Track and field is a vibrant sport at grass-roots level, too, with most clubs running a junior section for children aged nine and over.

There are 18 different disciplines in athletics, and most children, no matter their physical dimensions, will find at least one they're good at.

South of England Athletics Association *Suite 1, 23 Mitcham Lane, SW1 (8664 7244/ www.seaa.org.uk).*
The SEAA has details of local clubs. There's also a comprehensive national directory at www.british-athletics.co.uk.
Belgrave Harriers *Contact Paul or Kim Collier (8946 6859/www.belgraveharriers.com).*
Ealing, Southall & Middlesex *Perivale Park Track, Stockdove Way, Greenford, Middlesex. South Greenford rail. Contact Alan Keeler (www.esm.org.uk).*
Herne Hill Harriers *Tooting Bec Track, Tooting Bec Road, SW17. Tooting Bec tube. Contact Steve Bosley (8687 0386/www.hernehillharriers.co.uk).*
Thames Valley Harriers *Linford Christie Stadium, Du Cane Road, W12. White City tube. Contact Kathy Davidson (01895 676513/www.thamesvalleyharriers.com).*
Victoria Park Harriers *Victoria Park Track, St Mark's Gate, off Cadogan Terrace, E9. Hackney Wick rail. Contact Richard Newbold (7254 4546/www.vph.org.uk).*
Woodford Green & Essex Ladies *Ashton Track, Chigwell Road, Woodford Bridge. Woodford tube. Contact Keith Hopson (8524 1959).*

Wanna touch base? The **London Baseball Association** can help you out. *See p250.*

Badminton & squash

Both sports have excellent junior development programmes and most clubs welcome children on court. To find your nearest, contact the **Badminton Association of England** (01908 268400/www.baofe.co.uk) or the **Squash Rackets Association** (8746 1616/www.squash.uk.com). The following all have junior squash classes; phone for prices and times.

Dulwich Sports Club *Burbage Road, SE21 (7274 1242). Herne Hill rail.*
New Grampian Squash Club *Shepherd's Bush Road, W6 (7603 4255). Hammersmith tube.*
Wimbledon Squash & Badminton Club *Cranbrook Road, SW19 (8947 5806). Wimbledon tube/rail.*

Baseball & softball

The two sports have joined forces to create a single agency, **BaseballSoftballUK** (7453 7000/www.baseballsoftballuk.com). With the weight of America's Major League Baseball behind it, the organisation has put together impressive packages to teach the basics to children aged six upwards.

Windsor is already an established centre for junior baseball. Based at Windsor Boys School, the Little League run by the Windsor Bears club attracts some 500 players. Six- to nine-year-olds are known as 'PeeWees'; they then move on to the 'Bronco' class until they're 12. Under-16s then play in 'Pony' competitions. This progression has taken players right to the top: two of the current GB squad began playing with the Bears as 12-year-olds.

To find a club with junior teams, contact Geoff Ellingham (*see below*) or one of the following:

Baseball

Essex Darts *Phil Chesterton (01376 551254).*
London Baseball Association *Mark Crandall (7298 2204/www.londonsports.com).*
South London Ravens *Robin Webb (8251 7050).*
Windsor Baseball & Softball *John Boyd (07769 655496).*
London Meteorites Baseball & Softball *Geoff Ellingham (7582 2325).*

Softball

Thames Valley Softball Club *John Middlemist (0118 962 8469/www.tvsoftball.com).*
Wandsworth Softball Club *Mark Kostura (8947 9565/MEKinsiders@aol.com).*

Basketball

Hoops has a cool image to play as well as watch (*see p263*), and London is a great place to learn how to dribble, slam and dunk. There are clubs all over the capital playing in local leagues, and the sport is extremely well organised at junior level with competitions right up to national standard. To find your nearest, call the **English Basketball Association** (0113 236 1166/www.basketballengland.org.uk).

Climbing

Most of the world's best climbers first discovered the delights of getting high when they were in their early teens, and London's indoor centres all cater for children aged around eight-plus with safe, structured sessions that are run by qualified instructors. Few sports are more instantly addictive: in addition to the challenge of conquering a fear of heights, there's the satisfaction of reaching the top of the wall, along with the unique combination of physical and mental agility that's needed to deal with seemingly intractable obstacles.

Slam dunk! Follow in the footsteps of the **London Towers**. *See p263*.

Run, jump, throw

Over the last decade, thousands of youngsters have enjoyed an introduction to athletics in the company of Maureen Jones. A UK athletics senior coach, Jones organises regular holiday courses at tracks around the capital. Her aim is to give an insight into all the different events for children aged eight to 15, while the most intrepid can even have a go at Jones's speciality, the pole vault.

Courses take place during the Easter and summer holidays from 10am until 3pm and cost £11 per day. Venues include Tooting Bec Track, the Spectrum Centre in Guildford, the Millennium Arena in Battersea Park, Teddington School and the Harriers Centre in Epsom. You can phone Maureen on 8224 7579 or email her at rjt@maureenjones.fsnet.co.uk.

For general information on climbing, contact the **British Mountaineering Council** (0161 445 4747/ www.thebmc.co.uk). To have a go, try one of the climbing centres below.

Castle Climbing Centre
Green Lanes, N4 (8211 7000/www.castle-climbing.co.uk). Manor House tube. **Open** 2-10pm Mon-Fri; 10am-7pm Sat, Sun. **Admission** *Registration* £7.50; £4 children. *Classes* £8; £3.50 children.
This Grade II-listed Victorian pumping station was originally designed to look like Stirling Castle. But the folly could have been designed with its future use in mind, since it offers a 120ft drop ideal for aspiring spiderboys and girls. The centre has its own children's club on Friday evenings and Saturday and Sunday mornings, and on midweek afternoons during school holidays, at a cost of £16 per session including climbing, instruction and equipment. Minimum age eight and all children must be accompanied by an experienced adult climber. Equipment can be hired for a small fee. Booking is essential.

Mile End Climbing Wall
Haverfield Road, E3 (8980 0289/ www.mileendwall.org.uk). Mile End tube. **Open** noon-9.30pm Mon-Thur; noon-9pm Fri; 10am-6pm Sat, Sun. **Admission** *Registration* £4, then £5.50 per session. *Children's introduction* £6 Fri; £5 Sat, Sun.
Located in a converted pipe-bending factory, the centre runs children's sessions every Friday evening and Saturday morning, as well as birthday parties and a summer holiday programme. Booking essential.

Westway Climbing Complex
Westway Sports Centre, 1 Crowthorne Road, W10 (8969 0992). Latimer Road tube.
New climbing facilities (indoor and out) plus more tennis courts and football pitches have just been unveiled at this sports centre under the Westway. Phone for details of sessions and prices.

Cricket

There may be a decline in cricket in state schools, but clubs all around the capital have stepped in to develop the game for boys and girls aged seven and up. Many run junior sections, with 11-year-olds and under playing an adapted form of the game called 'Terrier Cricket', in which everyone gets an equal chance to bat, bowl and field. Safety is to the fore, with all under-16s required to wear a helmet when batting, wicket-keeping or fielding close to the wicket against a hard ball. Most clubs will provide this, along with the other essential protective equipment, until a youngster decides whether they want to play regularly.

Surrey County Cricket Club, based at the AMP Oval (*see p263*), has an enthusiastic programme designed to tempt under-16s into the sport. Outreach projects take coaching into schools.

Activities & Fun

School teams are invited to train at the Oval; Kwik Cricket tournaments run throughout the summer and under-16s can watch all Surrey Championship games for free. There are hundreds of clubs around London. To find your nearest, contact the relevant County Board office:

Essex *Tony Debenham (01245 252420)*.
Hertfordshire *Derek Dredge (01707 658377)*.
Kent *Paul Millman (01227 456886)*.
Middlesex *David Holland (7266 1650)*.
Surrey *Mike Edwards (7820 5735)*.

London Community Cricket Association

PO Box 17, Wallington, Surrey (8669 2177/ londoncricket@hotmail.com).
More than 400,000 people live in Islington, Hackney and Tower Hamlets, yet these boroughs have just two grass cricket pitches between them. The LCCA was founded in 1984 and helps to promote the game in some of the most recreationally disadvantaged parts of the capital, as well as developing cricket projects with inner-city schools and youth organisations.

Cycling

In Denmark, 60 per cent of children cycle to school. In the UK, a mere two per cent do. This feeble statistic, when combined with the fact that a UK cyclist is 12 times more likely to be killed or injured than a Danish one, raises fundamental questions about our attitude to both green transport policies and safety on the road.

In response, Safe Routes to Schools supports projects throughout the country that encourage children to cycle and walk to school by improving street design, calming traffic and linking with the 5,000-mile National Cycle Network, which opened in June 2000. For more information, see the *Official Guide to the National Cycle Network* by Nick Cotton and John Grimshaw (Sustrans, £9.99). **Sustrans** is the pressure group working to create a safer environment for cycling: check it out at www.sustrans.org.uk or see www.ridethenet.org.uk. The **London Cycling Campaign** (7928 7220/ www.lcc.org.uk) acts as an umbrella for local groups while working to create a cycle-friendly city.

By far the best guide to family rides around the capital is the *London Cycle Guide* (Haynes, £8.99), published in association with the London Cycling Campaign. The book contains 25 outings of varying difficulty, with maps and route planners.

Cycle Training

32 Carden Road, SE15 (7564 5990/www.tao.org.uk/ cycle-training). Nunhead rail. **Admission** £25 per hr (first hour); £20 per hr thereafter.
Established in 1998 to promote cycling and emphasise the freedom it gives to riders of all ages, Cycle Training offers tuition for everyone aged from five. Older children, who have mastered riding the bike, are given lessons in road safety and assertive cycling.

Cycle sport

There are three main cycling venues in London, all offering a range of activities for all ages. **Herne Hill Stadium** is the capital's only purpose-built velodrome for racing. **Hillingdon** is a tarmac track for racing and tuition. **Lee Valley Cycle Circuit** has a tarmac track, a mountain bike/BMX circuit and a Saturday morning club for children aged 4 to 16. All have kids clubs; phone for details of times and prices.

Herne Hill Stadium *Burbage Road, SE24 (7737 4647). Herne Hill rail.*
Hillingdon Cycle Circuit *Springfield Road, Hillingdon (Stewart Benstead 85703230). Hayes & Harlington rail.*
Lee Valley Cycle Circuit *Quarter Mile Lane, E15 (8534 6085/www.leevalleypark.com). Leyton tube.*

This little dribbler might need help from a football coach. *See p254.*

Dance

The **Central Council for Physical Recreation's Movement and Dance** incorporates 17 organisations offering a wide range of dance-related activities. For a free leaflet giving contacts for all these groups, send an SAE to: Portland Green, National Promotions Officer for Movement and Dance, CCPR, Francis House, Francis Street, SW1P 1DE (7854 8518).

A useful resource is the **London Dance Network** (www.london-dance.net), which comprises some 50 artists, venues, producers and agencies whose brief is to promote awareness of the strength and diversity of dance in London.

The following centres around town offer a range of dance classes for children; phone for details. For details of dance workshops, *see p229*.

Chisenhale Dance Space *64-84 Chisenhale Road, E3 (8981 6617/www.chisenhaledancespace.co.uk). Mile End tube.*
Danceworks *16 Balderton Street, W1 (7652 5756). Bond Street tube.* **Map** p316 G6.
Drill Hall *16 Chenies Street, WC1 (7637 8270). Goodge Street tube.* **Map** p317 K5.
Greenwich Dance Agency *Borough Hall, Royal Hill, SE10 (8293 9741). Greenwich rail.*
The Place *16 Flaxman Terrace, WC1 (7887 7669/ www.theplace.org.uk). Euston tube or King's Cross tube/rail.* **Map** p317 K3.
Ravenscourt Theatre School *30-40 Dalling Road, W6 (8741 0707). Hammersmith tube.*
Rona Hart School of Dance *Rosslyn Hall, Willoughby Road, NW3 (7435 7073). Hampstead tube.*
Tricycle Theatre *269 Kilburn High Road, NW6 (7328 1000). Kilburn tube.*

Some children love the formality and rigidity of ballet, but many more prefer the freedom of the following, more unusual, techniques:

Biodanza The facets of biodanza emphasised in children's classes (for six-year-olds upwards) are vitality, creativity and 'affectivity' (the capacity to care for and relate to each other). Call Marita Sanguinetti (7485 2369) for details on the classes in Camden, Hampstead and Covent Garden.
Capoeira The dynamic leaps, cartwheels and handstands of this exciting Brazilian martial art-cum-dance show agility, flexibility, self-expression and freedom. Youngsters from the age of eight can take part in classes. Classes are held on Saturdays at the Place, 17 Dukes Road, WC1 (7281 2020); and for 8- to 12-year-olds at 4.30pm on Fridays at the Art of Health & Yoga Centre (*see p263*).
Chantraine Chantraine was created in France more than 40 years ago, and no formal training is needed to take part and its free-spirited approach is ideal for children. There are three centres in the London area; classes are for children aged from four. Classes are held daily in central London (ring Patricia Woodall, 7435 4247) and Wanstead (Kate Byrne, 8989 8604).
Medau The technique devised by Heinrich Medau is all about rhythm, spatial awareness and natural movement. For more information, call the Medau Society on 01372 729056.

Disability sport

A number of organisations have responsibilities in this area, which, as the success of the Paralympic movement and personalities like Tanni Grey-Thompson have shown, is finally being given the recognition and funding it deserves.

An interesting new development is between Wimbledon Football Club, the Limbless Association and the One2One Ability Counts programme operated by the English Federation of Disability Sport. The partnership provides regular training sessions with qualified coaches, opportunities to play in tournaments, plus free kit and match tickets. Training takes place every week at the **Furzedown Recreation Centre**, Ramsdale Road, SW17, and the junior squad welcomes players aged 7 to 14. For more details, phone 8767 6542.

In addition to the organisations listed below, the following offer sports programmes: **British Blind Sport** (01926 424247/www.britishblindsport.org.uk); **British Deaf Sports Council** (01943 850214); **English Sports Association for People with Learning Disabilities** (01924 267555/www.esapld.co.uk); **Limbless Association** (8788 1777/www.limbless-association.org).

British Wheelchair Sports Foundation
(01296 395995/www.britishwheelchairsports.org).
This is the umbrella body for 17 wheelchair sports, from archery to rugby. It organises a number of major events each year at Stoke Mandeville in Buckinghamshire, provides a comprehensive information service and is currently developing regional sports camps for disabled children aged six-plus.

English Federation of Disability Sport
(0161 247 5294/www.efds.co.uk).
This is the umbrella organisation for disability sport. Its local office is the London Sports Forum for Disabled People (7354 8666/minicom 7354 9554www.londonsportsforum.org.uk).

Fencing

When it comes to sheer verve and excitement, few sports have more cut and thrust than fencing. It's physically demanding, very skilful and a cool alternative for children who don't enjoy team games. Most sessions comprise warm-up activities to develop co-ordination, flexibility and balance, formal work towards the nine fencing grades, followed by the bit that everyone enjoys best: free fighting. The sport has a strong safety ethic, and no one is allowed to participate without full protective clothing, a mask and the supervision of a qualified instructor.

For details of clubs and regional organisers around London, contact the **British Fencing Association** (8742 3032/www.BritishFencing.com).

Don't try this at home. **North-East London Gymnastics Club**. *See p258.*

Activities & Fun

Finchley Foil Fencing Club *Christ's College, East End Road, N2 (Clare Halsted, 7485 1498). East Finchley tube.*
Haverstock Fencing Club *Haverstock School, Haverstock Hill, NW1 (8374 5740). Belsize Park tube.*
Kingston Fencing Club *Beverley School, College Gardens, Blakes Lane, New Malden, Surrey (Joseph Shackell, 8393 4255/www.cgal.demon.co.uk). Motspur Park rail.*
RLS Fencing Club *Chase Community School, Churchbury Lane, Enfield, Middlesex (8379 3766). Enfield Town rail.*
Streatham Fencing Club *Dunraven Lower School, Mount Nod Road, SW16 (8677 6207). Streatham Hill rail.*

Football

Football dominates the sporting scene in this country – and with good reason. At the top level, it's a billion-pound industry, with 13 professional clubs in London. Lower down the pyramid, over 45,000 clubs cater for all standards and ages, and both sexes.

Finding a club

Most local newspapers have a column of classified ads placed by clubs looking for players. When helping your child to find a team to play for, make sure that he or she is of the appropriate standard.

Also ask about:
● Whether the club coaches hold FA qualifications. If possible, watch a session to see how well organised it is.
● The number of children in each age group. Some clubs have large memberships, which may mean only the best get to play regularly.
● The atmosphere and ethos: is it a club where winning is all that matters, or is 'sport for all' the priority? Are parents and supporters encouraged to lend a hand, and is their contribution valued?
To find a girls' team, contact the **Football Association** (01707 651840) or Ann Mason, secretary of the **Greater London Women's League** (8977 3658). Fulham, which is the country's first professional women's team, runs an extensive girls' development programme: 0details from Natalia Lodge (8336 7481).

Coaching

All the professional clubs in London run 'Football in the Community' coaching courses, fun days and skills clinics. These are suitable for boys and girls of all standards from the age of around six upwards. They usually take place within the club's immediate locality and are staffed by FA-qualified coaches. Phone for details and dates (for addresses, *see p266*):

Arsenal (7704 4000); **Charlton Athletic** (8850 2866); **Brentford** (8758 9430); **Chelsea** (7385 5545); **Crystal Palace** (8771 8841); **Fulham** (7384 4759); **Leyton Orient** (8556 5973); **Millwall** (7231 0379); **Queens Park Rangers** (8740 2509); **Tottenham Hotspur** (8365 5000); **Watford** (01923 440449); **West Ham United** (8548 2707); **Wimbledon** (8771 1772).

Similar schemes operate through the County FAs. Call the following offices for details: Essex (01245 357727); Hertfordshire (01462 677622); Kent (01634 843824); London (8690 9626); Middlesex (8424 8524); Surrey (01372 373543/www.surreyfa.co.uk).

Finally, there are plenty of commercial football clinics to choose from, some of which dangle the promise of visits from Premiership stars. A **Fila Soccer Camp** (0151 707 9300/www.soccercamps.co.uk), for example, costs £60 for five days (10am-3.45pm) and caters for children aged eight to 15, who all receive a goody bag.

Golf

Too many golfers still want their clubhouses to be a refuge from children (and, in some cases, women) for the sport to offer a uniformly warm welcome to would-be juvenile thwackers. But youngsters should take heart because the **English Golf Union** (01526 354500/www.englishgolfunion.org) has developed 'Tri-Golf' for 6- to 12-year-olds and is aiming to introduce the game to 3,000 primary schools by the end of 2002.

The Golf School
Regent's Park, NW1 (7724 0643). Baker Street tube. **Open** 8am-9pm daily. **Map** p316 G2.
Staff welcome children who are 'old enough to take instruction' (the coaches have taught golf-mad children as young as five). Membership for juniors is £30; the Saturday afternoon clinic for young golfers costs £5 per hour (book in advance). Club hire is £1.

Gymnastics & trampolining

Although still dominated at elite level by eastern Europe, British competitive gymnastics is steadily improving. It's a lovely sport both to watch and take part in, which helps to explain why the governing body, **British Gymnastics** (01952 820330/www.baga.co.uk), has around 100,000 members.

Through its clubs and schools, sessions for four-year-olds and under are based around soft-play equipment and simple games. After that, there's a series of proficiency awards. As well as a general scheme for boys and girls, there are separate awards for rhythmic gymnastics and sports acrobatics. The **British Trampoline Federation** (01952 820330/www.thebtf.co.uk) offers a similar structure.

In response to the issue of how and when to teach small children using adult equipment, Bill Cosgrove, a former national gymnastics coach, created **TumbleTots** and, later, Gymbabes and

Have an ice time at **Lee Valley Ice Centre**. *See p258.*

Hoof dreams

The riding schools below all welcome children. Some run 'Own a Pony' days and weeks, which involve some lucky rider's parents paying about £40 (for a day) or over £100 (for a week) for the privilege of looking after their favourite pony in the school: mucking out, grooming, feeding and watering, exercising and schooling. Children participating in this usually receive two or more hours' riding as part of the deal.

Many places run birthday party packages, based around a ride and a party tea with equine friends looking on. Many also have facilities for disabled riders. Riding lessons and hacks must all be booked in advance: ask the management whether they run 'taster' sessions for new young riders. Most rates below are the children's rate and per hour.

Riders, whatever their age, should always wear a hard hat (establishments can usually lend one if you don't have your own, sometimes for a small fee) and boots with a small heel, not trainers or gumboots. Your bottom will thank you for wearing sturdy jeans or jodhpurs.

Aldersbrook Riding School

Empress Avenue, E12 (8530 4648). Manor Park rail/Wanstead tube. **Lessons** *from £14.*
Aldersbrook is a small, friendly riding school with a countryside feel to it. There are eight ponies and four horses working here. Lessons take place in an outdoor manège; hacking on Wanstead Flats.

Ealing Riding School

Gunnersbury Avenue, W5 (8992 3808). Ealing Common tube. **Lessons** *£17.*
This riding school has a benevolent attitude towards children. Riders aged from five can take part in many activities, including the occasional gymkhana. Lessons take place in an outdoor manège.

Hyde Park & Kensington Stables Ltd

63 Bathurst Mews, W2 (7723 2813/ www.hydeparkstables.com). Lancaster Gate tube. **Lessons** *Individual £32; Course of ten from £260.* **Map** *p313 D6.*
Children aged from five can enjoy hour-long instruction of patient, streetwise ponies in the glamorous surroundings of Hyde Park. All rides must be booked in advance.
Branch: Kensington Stables, 11 Elvaston Mews, SW7 (7589 2299).

Lee Valley Riding Centre

Lee Valley Regional Park Authority, Lea Bridge Road, Leyton, E10 (8556 2629). Clapton rail/ 48, 55, 56 bus. **Lessons** *£15.*
Local children love to help at this well-appointed riding school, where 28 extremely placid horses and ponies enjoy the breezy open spaces of Walthamstow Marshes. During hot weather some hacking out is available to regulars.

London Equestrian Centre

Lullington Garth, Finchley, N12 (8349 1345). Mill Hill East tube. **Lessons** *from £15.*
This busy yard in comfortable North Finchley has 30 assorted horses and ponies; some are delightfully placid and deservedly popular with local children. There's a junior members club for regular young customers, who may be able to take part in occasional informal gymkhanas. Children aged from four can come here to ride. Restaurant on site.

Richmond Park Stables

293 Park Road, Kingston-upon-Thames, Surrey (8546 8437). Hampton Wick rail/371 bus. **Lessons** *£22.50.*
It's almost like riding in the countryside, taking lessons at Richmond Park. The staff here are willing to let children as young as two and a half take up the reins. Older riders can badger their parents to pay for pony camp days in the holidays, and participation in the membership scheme.

Ross Nye's

8 Bathurst Mews, W2 (7262 3791/ www.ridingschools.co.uk). Lancaster Gate tube. **Lessons** *£30; £25 Pony Club members.* **Pony Club Membership** *£30 per year.* **Map** *p313 D6.*
If your children are serious about ponies, it makes sense to join Ross Nye's pony club, as membership gives many pony privileges. Children aged from six can learn to ride here (instructional rides take place in Hyde Park). Club members can join in on very good value Pony Club Days in the Christmas holidays (£30 per day) and take part in exciting, week-long pony camps in the stables' Surrey farm.

Suzanne's Riding School

Brookshill Drive, Harrow Weald, Middlesex (8954 3618). Harrow & Wealdstone rail. **Lessons** *from £15.*
Suzanne's has 200 acres of rolling Harrow Weald for its horses to canter over. The school is an important local social centre, with a weekend café and a separate junior riding school.

Willowtree Riding Establishment

The Stables, Ronver Road, SE12 (8857 6438). Grove Park or Lee rail. **Lessons** *from £7.50 30min.*
Captain the one-eyed Shetland is great for small children to learn to ride on at this friendly local riding school (*pictured*). This is the only riding school we know of that has enchanting pure bred Arab ponies in its riding school stock.

Wimbledon Village Stables

24A/B High Street, SW19 (8946 8579/ www.wvstables.com). Wimbledon tube/rail. **Lessons** *from £25.*
Wimbledon's riding club (phone for membership details) allows children all sorts of perks to feed their pony habit: gymkhanas, newsletters, special events. Riding takes place on Wimbledon Common.

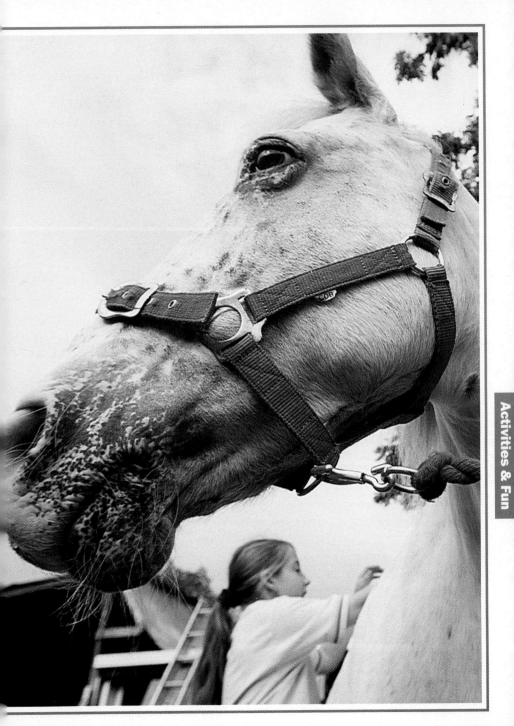

Could this be a future Schumacher? **Daytona Raceway** at Milton Keynes. *See p259.*

Gymbobs. For details of the 500-plus TumbleTots centres around the country, call 0121 585 7003 or see www.tumbletots.com.

The following clubs offer a range of age-appropriate activities, most offering trampolining as well. Both sports are available at many public sports centres.

Avondale Gymnastics Club *Hollyfield Road, Surbiton, Surrey (8399 3386). Surbiton rail.*
Enfield Girls Gymnastics Club *Aylward School, Silver Street, N18 (8807 4736). Silver Street rail.*
Plumstead Leisure Centre, *Speranza Street, SE18 (8855 8289). Plumstead rail.*
Hillingdon School of Gymnastics *Victoria Road, South Ruislip, Middlesex (8841 6666). South Ruislip tube.*
Islington Gym Club, Arts & Media School *Turle Road, N4 (8983 6799). Finsbury Park tube/rail.*
North-East London Gymnastics Club *Carpenters & Dockland Centre, 98 Gibbins Road, E15 (8534 4151). Stratford tube/rail/DLR.*
Redbridge School of Gymnastics *Pulteney Road, E18 (8530 3810). South Woodford tube.*
Richmond Gymnasium Centre *Townmead Road, Kew, Surrey (8878 8682). Kew Gardens rail.*

Ice skating

London's ice rinks offer an ideal combination of free skating, formal instruction and discos, where children can strut their stuff and show off the skills they've learned in classes. Session times vary from day to day as the ice needs regular refreezing and sweeping, but venues are generally open from 10am until 10pm. The prices listed below include skate hire.

For more information about the sport, contact the **National Ice Skating Association** (0115 853 3100/www.iceskating.org.uk).

Alexandra Palace Ice Rink
Alexandra Palace Way, N22 (8365 4386). Wood Green tube. **Open** 11am-1.30pm, 2-5pm Mon-Thur; 11am-1.30pm, 2-5pm, 8.30-11pm Fri; 10.30am-12.30pm, 2-4.30pm, 8.30-11pm Sat, Sun. **Admission** *Mon-Fri* £3.90; £3.30 children; *Sat, Sun* £5.20 adults, £4.20 children. *Fri, Sat evening* £5.50 per person.
A six-week course of lessons at this international-size rink costs from £39. All prices include skate hire.

Broadgate Ice Rink
Broadgate Circle, Eldon Street, EC2 (7505 4068). Liverpool Street tube/rail. **Open** late Oct-Apr. **Admission** £7; £4 children. **Map** p321 Q5.
This tiny outdoor rink is a wonderful discovery amid the high-tech offices of the City. *See also p46.*

Lee Valley Ice Centre
Lea Bridge Road, E10 (8533 3154). Walthamstow Central tube, then 158 bus. **Open** noon-4pm; 8.30-11pm daily. **Admission** £5.90; £4.90 children.
The disco nights are popular at this large, well-maintained rink, but because it's hard to get here by public transport, it's never too busy. Rink management say Lee Valley has high-quality ice (it certainly feels hard enough when you land on it) and the warmest skating environment in the UK.

Leisurebox
First Bowl, 17 Queensway, W2 (7229 0172). Bayswater tube. **Open** 10am-1.45pm, 2-4.45pm, 5-6.45pm, 8-10.45pm Mon-Thur; 10am-1.45pm, 2-4.45pm, 5-6.45pm, 7.30-10.45pm Fri, Sat; 10am-1.45pm, 2-4.45pm, 5-6.45pm, 8-10pm Sun. **Admission** £6 incl skate hire; £6.50 from 7.30pm Fri, Sat. **Map** p312 C7.
Once known as Queens, this is the most famous rink in London, where countless top skaters have learned their moves before becoming famous. The disco nights with live DJs on Fridays and Saturdays are legendary, but beginners and families are also well looked after.

Michael Sobell Leisure Centre
Hornsey Road, N7 (7609 2166/www.aquaterra.org). Finsbury Park tube/rail. **Open** 10.30am-2pm Sat; 2.30-4pm Sun. **Classes** *Beginners* 6.45-8pm Mon. *After school* term time 4-5.30pm Wed, Fri. *Parent & Toddlers* term time

1-2pm Mon. *Beat on Ice* 7.30-10pm Wed, Fri; 7.30-9.30pm Sun. **Admission** £3 per person incl skate hire; £2.70 parent and toddler session.
Children from four upwards are welcome at this small rink, which runs popular after-school sessions on Wednesdays and Fridays, 4-5.30pm. A six-week course of lessons costs £29.

Streatham Ice Rink
386 Streatham High Road, SW16 (8769 7771/ www.streathamicearena.co.uk). Streatham rail.
Open 10am-4pm, 4.15-7pm, 7.30-10pm Mon-Fri; 10.30am-5pm, 5.30-7.30pm, 8-11pm Sat; 10.30am-5pm Sun. **Admission** £6; £5.50 under-12s; £2.50 under-4s.
Another of London's best-known rinks, where a six-week course of lessons costs £39 for adults, £30 for children and £23 for 'toddlers' aged up to four. Prices include skate hire.

Karting

Many of the world's top Formula One racers got their taste for speed as children on a kart circuit. It's thrilling stuff for children of eight and over as the little buggies zip around at speeds exceeding 30mph. Safety is always uppermost, however. Drivers receive a full briefing before they begin and anyone disobeying the marshals is removed from the track. The venues listed below welcome children and can be booked for exciting, if expensive, parties; some of the others are more geared towards the corporate market.

Daytona Raceway
Atlas Road, NW10 (8961 3616/www.daytona.co.uk). North Acton tube. **Open** 9am-10pm daily.
Children aged 8 to 13 can enjoy ten-minute trials for £15 on Sunday mornings. Over-13s are eligible to race with adults: £20 for a 15-minute practice session, while the standard entry fee for a meeting starts at £40. Booking is essential for the Junior Club on the first and third Sunday of the month. Parties can also be held here. This track is indoors; the branch at Milton Keynes (01908 695694) is outdoors.

Docklands F1 City
Gate 119, Connaught Bridge, Royal Victoria Dock, E16 (7476 5678). Royal Albert DLR. **Open** 10am-6pm daily. **Admission** from £10 per person.
This go-kart track is the widest in London (beginners will be pleased to hear) and 800m in length. Children (only those who meet the height requirement of 5ft 2in) are given their own track times during which to play. The Cadet Club is the place to learn how to kart safely, with the assistance of the crack F1 City racing team. Phone for details of sessions.

Playscape Pro Racing
390 Streatham High Road, SW16 (8677 8677/ www.playscape.co.uk). Streatham rail. **Open** 10am-10pm daily. *Children's practice* 10am-5pm Mon-Fri. **Admission** £42.50 for 2hrs adults. *Test sessions* from £20 per 30min session per person; parties £195 plus VAT per 10 drivers. *Cadets* £25 per child.
The raceway can be booked for children's parties (aged eight-plus), or for half-hour taster sessions. Those who become addicted can find out about the Playscape Cadet School, a founder member of the RAC's Association of Racing Kart Schools. The School operates on the first and third Saturday of each month (9.30am-noon) and students are put through their paces before gaining an RAC racing licence.

Martial arts

Most local sports centres will be home to at least one martial arts club; while others are based in church halls and community centres. Look for evidence of a lively but disciplined atmosphere, with well-organised and age-appropriate teaching. Ask the instructor about his/her qualifications – the grading systems used in judo and karate, for example, help to ensure that teachers are of a suitable standard. Also ask for proof of insurance cover: martial arts usually involve physical contact and accidents can happen. However, few community facilities extend their insurance to the instructors who rent them.

For more information, contact the **Amateur Martial Association** (07973 507716/www.amauk.co.uk). The association can give details of your nearest classes. The **National College of Martial Arts** (7278 5608) offers various classes for children, with the emphasis on self-discipline rather than combat.

Call the following for information on classes.

Academy Health & Fitness Centre
West Hill House, 62 West Hill, Dartford, Kent (7729 5789 daily/01322 229124 Mon-Thur/ www.bobbreen.co.uk).
Kung fu is an ancient art which the Chinese regard as part of the historical tapestry of their lives. This excellent centre offers Saturday morning classes for children aged seven upwards. Booking is advisable.

The Budokwai
4 Gilston Road, SW10 (7370 1000). Gloucester Road tube. **Map** p314 C12.
This is one of Britain's premier martial arts clubs, offering judo tuition for children aged 6 to 12.

Hwarang Academy
The Place, 17 Duke's Road, WC1 (7722 8102). Euston tube. **Map** p317 K3.
The Korean martial art of tae kwondo is now an Olympic sport, and youngsters aged eight to 18 can learn its spectacular kicks on Sunday afternoons and Tuesday evenings.

School of Japanese Karate (Shotokan International)
8368 6249.
Karate is the most popular Japanese martial art in this country. There are no holds or grappling, just strikes and kicks. David and Lilian Alleyn, who run this well established and highly respected school, teach children aged five upwards. Call the above number to find out about venues.

Netball

Most girls learn how to play netball at school. For those who enjoy its combination of speed, skill and sleight of hand, London is a strong netball area with plenty of clubs around the capital – most running junior sections for girls aged 11 and older. To find your nearest, contact the **All-England Netball Association** (01462 442344/www.aena.co.uk).

Activities & Fun

Orienteering

For adults, orienteering is like tackling the *Times* crossword while out on a run. The aim is to navigate around a course, which can vary in length from two to 12km (1¼-7½ miles), moving from one control point to the next using a specially drawn map. For children, though, orienteering is all about woodland, hidden targets and adventure. Few sports are more family-friendly, and orienteering is a great way to make country walks fun. Some of the permanent courses are suitable for buggies, while many events include a special route for very young children with or without mum and dad, where a line of string takes them round a set of controls marked by the likes of Postman Pat or Rupert Bear.

London's permanent courses offer an excellent introduction to the sport. There are 45 around the city, some in remarkably urban locations. You buy a map and information pack from a sales point, then tackle the course at a time convenient to you. A leaflet giving a complete list of courses is available from the **British Orienteering Federation**, 'Riversdale', Dale Road North, Darley Dale, Matlock, Derbyshire, DE4 2HX (01629 734042/ www.britishorienteering.org.uk).

For details of local events, which are held regularly around London, contact the **South Eastern Orienteering Association** (8948 6056/ www.post2me.freeserve.co.uk/orienteering).

Rugby union

Most rugby union clubs have a junior section, playing 'mini-rugby' on Sunday mornings in front of hordes of screaming parents. In the younger age groups – some clubs take children as young as six – the aim is to encourage handling, passing and running, with tackling outlawed. Female rugby has made rapid progress in recent years, and there are more than 100 girls' teams in this country, feeding in to a well-established network of women's clubs.

The governing bodies, **Rugby Football Union** (8892 2000/www.rfu.com) and **Rugby Football Union for Women** (01635 42333/www.rfu-women.co.uk), can direct you towards a club offering junior rugby, although you only need turn to the sports pages of a local newspaper to find out what's available. The RFU for Women website also has interesting material on future plans.

Skateboarding

Although the names of stunts like hot-dogging, double deckers and hanging tens may not mean much to most parents, there's no denying skateboarding's popularity with the kids. On the one hand, the sport has retained its cool and radical edge, with children still skating for free at traditional haunts like the South Bank, Shell Centre and beneath the Westway. On the other, there's **Playstation Park** (*see p161*), which runs classes for beginners and is reckoned to be one of the best skateparks in Europe, with superb ramps, vert and street course.

Skateboard UK, an unofficial website at www.sk8uk.co.uk, is an excellent source of news, events and information on places to skate.

Skiing & snowboarding

There's nothing quite like the feel of proper snow, but a few practice turns on a dry slope make excellent preparation for the real thing. Gloves,

Bowl 'em over at the **Hollywood Bowl Finchley**. See p262.

long sleeves and trousers are compulsory as the surface can deliver a nasty burn should you fall. Also note that if you're thinking of taking a mixed-ability group out for an open recreational session, perhaps as a birthday party activity, the minimum requirement is to be able to perform a controlled snowplough turn and use the ski lift.

Note that the feel of real snow can be yours from winter 2002 at the former Beckton Alpine Centre, whose old slope and mogul field is currently being converted into a snow dome (with the real cold stuff).

For more information, both about Beckton, and skiing in general, contact the **Ski Club of Great Britain** (8410 2000/www.ski-club.co.uk).

Bromley Ski Centre
Sandy Lane, St Paul's Cray, Orpington, Kent (01689 876812). St Mary Cray rail. **Open** noon-10pm Mon-Thur; 10am-10pm Fri; 9am-6pm Sat; 10am-6pm Sun. **Admission** £13; £9.50 children for two hours; *Ski taster* 4-6s £8.50 for 1hr; *Beginners* 7-15s (2 2hr lessons).
Three lifts serve the 120-metre slope with mogul field and nursery slope. Skiing and snowboarding taster sessions cost £12 and £13 respectively. Booking essential.

Sandown Sports Club
More Lane, Esher, Surrey (01372 467132/ www.sandownsports.co.uk). Esher rail. **Open** 10am-10pm Mon-Fri, Sun, 1-8pm Sat. **Admission** £14; £11 children for 2hrs.
The 120-metre main slope, 80-metre nursery area and 90-metre snowboarding slope are closed during horse racing meetings. Tuition is available for seven-year-olds upwards, although special half-hour lessons can be arranged for children as young as four. Call for times and prices of the Junior Ski Club. Advance booking essential.

Swimming

Most local authority pools run lessons for children aged from around three upwards, plus parent and baby sessions to develop water confidence from as young as three months. However, these can be over-subscribed and have long waiting lists. Ask at your local pool for a timetable and booking details.

When children are past the lesson stage, joining a club is the best way to improve, meet like-minded friends and, perhaps, swim competitively. Again, look on the noticeboards, ask at your local pool or contact the **Amateur Swimming Association** (01509 618700). An example is the **Camden Swiss Cottage Swimming Club** (7483 1771), based at Swiss Cottage and Kentish Town Pools, where a £10 junior membership and £16 monthly subscription gives access to a number of sessions each week. *See also p264.*

Dolphin Swimming Club
University of London Pool, Malet Street, WC1 (8349 1844). **Classes** 9.15am-2.45pm Sat. **Admission** £209 for 11 individual 30min lessons; £67.10 for 11 30min small-group sessions (max 5 per group).

There are some children whose fear of the water needs more specialised help than even a caring parent can provide. The Dolphin Swimming Club teaches aquaphobic children (and adults) to overcome their fear. Ring for details.

Water polo

'Aquagoal' is a version of this fast and furious game with amended rules for ten-year-olds upwards. Like handball, the aim is to score goals in your opponent's net – but without touching the side or bottom of the pool. It's a great challenge, then, for good swimmers. Contact the **Amateur Swimming Association** (01509 618700) for general info about the sport or see www.swimming.org. The National League website (www.nwpl.co.uk) has useful club contacts.

Tennis

Public courts offer easy access at cheap prices, but may be of poor quality and lack a coaching programme. Private clubs, on the other hand, require the commitment of an annual fee, which can be anything from £10 to £500-plus per person. But for families who plan to play the game together or want access to qualified instruction for a young beginner, they represent good value. Look for a club that values children rather than sees them as an inconvenience: are times set aside for children to play casually? Is equipment available for first-timers? If not, search elsewhere.

Most London boroughs run Easter and summer holiday courses: contact your local sports development team or public library for details.
Lawn Tennis Association *7381 7000.*
The LTA's Information Department publishes free, comprehensive county guides giving contacts for hundreds of private clubs and public courts listed by borough, and the name and address of the County Development Officer. Details of tennis holidays are also available.
David Lloyd Leisure *0870 888 3015.*
Phone for your nearest venue.
Islington Tennis Centre *Market Road, N7 (7700 1370/www.aquaterra.org). Caledonian Road tube.*
Redbridge Sports Centre *Forest Road, Barkingside (8498 1026). Fairlop tube.*
Regent's Park Tennis Centre *York Bridge Road, NW1 (7486 4216/www.rptc.co.uk).*
Individual coaching can be arranged through contacting one of the centre's coaches; prices from £7.50 per session.
Westway Tennis Centre *1 Crowthorne Road, W10 (8969 0992/www.westwaysportscentre.com). Latimer Road tube.*

Tenpin bowling

'Bowling is for everyone, from the age of 4 to 84,' says the British Tenpin Bowling Association. A trip to the local centre makes for a great birthday party or family day out – indeed, the BBC's *Watchdog* programme rated a bowling party better value for money than a comparable event at TGI Friday's, Pizza Hut or Wacky Warehouse. Computerised scoring has made the game less complicated – but for youngsters keen to progress towards the magical 'perfect score' of 300, there's a network of regional and national youth tournaments and leagues. Contact the **British Tenpin Bowling Association** (8478 1745).

All the centres listed are open seven days a week, typically 10am-11pm. Admission prices vary according to the time of day, but average around £3 per game, and the hire of soft-soled bowling shoes £1 extra. Phone for details of children's parties.

Acton Super Bowl *Royale Leisure Park, Western Avenue, W3 (8896 0707). Park Royal tube.*
Airport Bowl *Bath Road, Harlington, Middlesex (8759 1396). Hatton Cross tube.*
GX Superbowl *15-17 Alpine Way, E6 (7511 4440). Beckton DLR.*
Harrow Super Bowl *Pinner Road, North Harrow, Middlesex (8863 3491). North Harrow tube.*
Hollywood Bowl Finchley *Leisure Way, High Road, N12 (8446 6667). Woodside Park tube.*
Leisurebox *First Bowl, 17 Queensway, W2 (7229 0172). Bayswater tube.* Map p312 C7.
Lewisham Bowl *11-29 Belmont Hill, SE13 (8318 9691). Lewisham rail/DLR.*
Rowans Bowl *10 Stroud Green Road, N4 (8800 1950). Finsbury Park tube/rail.*
Streatham Megabowl *142 Streatham Hill, SW2 (8678 6007/www.megabowl.co.uk). Streatham Hill rail.*

Volleyball

Though a minor sport in this country, volleyball is great fun to play for children aged nine upwards. Many clubs around the capital run junior teams, with 9- to 14-year-old beginners playing three-a-side 'mini-volley' on a badminton-sized court with a lower net. To find your nearest club, contact **London Volleyball Association** development officer Gary Beckford (8539 5276) or see www.whiteeaglesvc.org.uk/london, a website in association with the White Eagles Volleyball Club.

Watersports

It's a myth that you need to plan a long drive out of the capital if your children want to mess about on the water. With more than 430 acres of briny in Docklands, plus numerous reservoirs and the vast natural resource of the Thames, London actually boasts some of the best watersports venues in Europe. Most are very family-friendly (most cater for children aged from eight) – indeed, watersports are ideal activities for parents and children to enjoy

together – and keen to dispel the notion that sailing is only for the rich. Phone for details of courses and sessions at the following clubs.

The **Royal Yachting Association** (023 8062 7400/www.rya.org.uk) operates a Young Sailors' scheme, while the website lists numerous training courses. **Capital Sailing** (07050 223817) has details of RYA courses and marine activities around London. There's a vast online resource at www.uksail.com.
Broadwater Sailing Club *Moorhall Road, Harefield, Middlesex (Membership secretary 01494 436314). Denham rail.*
A very family-friendly club based at Broadwater Lake, close to the Grand Union Canal. Casual sailing is available seven days a week, and there's an annual 'junior fun week'. Phone for details of prices.
Capital Rowing Centre *Kingston Rowing Club, Lower Ham Road, Kingston-upon-Thames, Surrey (07973 314199/capitalrowing@tesco.net). Kingston rail.*
This is a rowing school, where adults and children can receive expert tuition before going off and joining a club. Groups and school parties are also catered for.
Docklands Sailing & Watersports Centre *Millwall Dock, 235A Westferry Road, E14 (7537 2626/ www.docklandswatersports.co.uk). Crossharbour DLR.*
Children (aged from eight) and adults can choose from canoeing to dragonboat racing, windsurfing and dingy saling. All levels are catered for, although children are required to be confident in the water before they have a go at anything: give the centre a call before you visit. The Dock has a restaurant and bar if all that exercise leaves you in need of refreshment, as well as facilities and sailing courses for the disabled.
Lea Rowing Club *Spring Hill, E5 (8806 3097). Stamford Hill or South Tottenham rail.*
Rowing and sculling for all young people aged from 10 who can swim at least 50 metres. The Lea also runs intensive school holiday rowing courses.
Lee Valley Watersports Centre *Banbury Reservoir, Harbet Road, E4 (8531 1129). Angel Road rail.*
Sailing courses, plus canoeing and waterskiing, on 94 acres of water for eight-year-olds upwards. Phone for details of courses and prices.
London Corinthian Sailing Club *Linen House, Upper Mall, W6 (8748 3280/www.lcsc.org.uk). Hammersmith tube.*
Dinghy sailing courses for beginners.
Royal Victoria Dock Watersports Centre *Gate 5, Tidal Basin Road, off Silvertown Way, E16 (7511 2326). Royal Victoria DLR.*
Low-cost summer sailing, canoeing and rowing for eight-year-olds upwards.
Shadwell Basin Project *Glamis Road, E1 (7481 4210). Shadwell DLR.*
Downriver from Tower Bridge and run on a voluntary basis, this multi-activity centre offers affordable summer sailing, canoeing and dragon-boat racing for children aged nine years upwards.
Surrey Docks Watersports Centre *Greenland Dock, Rope Street, SE16 (7237 4009). Surrey Quays tube.*
Sailing, windsurfing and canoeing for eight-year-olds upwards takes place in the sheltered dock throughout the school holidays and half terms. Children take part in the structured RYA's sailing courses, which take three days to complete. Once they have their certificates the young sailors qualify to take part in Thursday and Friday 'Splashdown' events.

Westminster Boating Base *136 Grosvenor Road, SW1 (7821 7389). Pimlico tube.*
Right in the heart of London, this charitable training centre offers low-cost sailing and canoeing on the tidal Thames for ten-year-olds upwards. Booking is advisable.

Yoga

Just as yoga is booming among adults, so imaginative teachers are exploring its potential for children. Though often characterised as an inward-looking pursuit, it's actually an expressive art that uses the whole body.

This approach evolved at the **Art of Health & Yoga Centre**, where Fenella Lindsell and Jade Anderson created 'Yoga Bugs'. There are now more than 30 trained 'Yoga Bugs' teachers and classes are being introduced into schools. The therapeutic aspect of yoga is being developed at the **Yoga Therapy Centre**, which runs weekly classes for children with asthma.

Art of Health & Yoga Centre *280 Balham High Road, SW17 (8682 1800/www.artofhealth.co.uk). Tooting Bec tube.*

Holistic Health *64 Broadway Market, E8 (7275 8434/ www.holistic-health-hackney.co.uk). Cambridge Heath rail.*
Has a Yoga Babes (age 3-6) on a Thursday 4-4.30pm.

Iyengar Institute *223A Randolph Avenue, W9 (7624 3080/www.iyi.org.uk). Maida Vale tube.*
Ring for an information pack on classes and courses.

Sivananda Yoga Vedanta Centre *51 Felsham Road, SW12 (8780 0160/www.sivanandayoga.org/london). Putney rail.*
Children's classes are held noon-1.30pm Sunday. Admission is by donation only.

Triyoga *6 Erskine Road, NW3 (7483 3344/www.triyoga.co.uk). Primrose Hill rail.*
Europe's largest dedicated yoga centre runs children's clubs for six- to ten-year-olds and 11-plus, costing £5. Children's classes from 4pm Mon, Wed; ring for details.

Yoga Therapy Centre *60 Great Ormond Street, WC1 (7419 7195/www.fyogatherapy.org). Holborn tube.* **Map** p317 L5.
Toddler yoga classes are held on a Wednesday, and baby yoga and massage on Thursdays.

Spectator Sports

Football continues to be the sport children most want to watch. However, almost all Premiership matches are now off-limits to the casual spectator – it's club members and season-ticket holders only. Other sports are far more accessible and just as exciting, especially if you go as a group for a party treat.

Basketball

London Towers
Crystal Palace National Sports Centre, Ledrington Road, SE19 (8776 7755/www.london-towers.co.uk). Crystal Palace rail. **Admission** £8 adults; £6 children.

The Towers are not only the best team in Britain, they're among the leading clubs in the whole of the Northern Hemisphere and reached the final stages of the Euroleague last season just to prove it. There's a game most weeks from October to April and the atmosphere is loud, street-cool and very family-friendly.

Cricket

Both these grounds stage at least one Test Match each summer. Tickets for these matches require advance booking (unlike county matches, where you can pay on the gate) and information is usually released during the preceding winter. Call or check the websites for details.

Middlesex
St John's Wood Road, NW8 (7289 1300/ www.middlesexccc.com). St John's Wood tube. **Admission** £9-£10 adults, £4.50-£5 children.
Middlesex are in the Second Division of both the County Championship and National League, and going through difficult times. That said, Lord's is a magnificent venue to watch a game and any child interested in cricket will be thrilled to attend. The season runs from mid-April to mid-September.

Surrey
AMP Oval, SE11 (7582 7764/www.surreyccc.co.uk). Oval tube. **Admission** £7-£10 adults, £3-£5 children.
The Oval is an excellent ground with fewer airs and graces than Lord's. What's more, Surrey are the best in the country in the County Championship and a force in Division One of the National League, too. Their team is crammed with internationals, although the likes of Alec Stewart and Graham Thorpe turn out for their county only rarely.

Football

Any mad-keen young football fan will enjoy being given 'membership' of the team they support. But if that team plays in the Premiership, it certainly doesn't mean a steady supply of match tickets. A top club may have three or four times as many members as the capacity of their ground, while the likes of Arsenal even have a waiting list for season tickets. In the Nationwide League, it's far easier to get in to games. Indeed, lower-division clubs positively encourage youngsters and families with cheap tickets and special deals: at Leyton Orient, a children's season ticket costs just £30, little more than £1 a match.

Ticket prices and membership packages are too numerous to list for each club: call for details or check out the website. As a rule, a seat at a Premiership match will cost £25-£30 for an adult, half that for children, with a discount for club members. Nationwide League prices are around £15-£25, again with reductions for children and club members. The season runs from August to May.

Taking the plunge

Most swimming pools are 25 metre-long rectangles. For differing reasons, the pools listed below are a little bit special. Please note that opening times and admission prices change seasonally, particularly in the case of the lidos. Do ring to check times and prices before you visit:

In

Barnet Copthall Pools
Great North Way, NW4 (8457 9900). Mill Hill East tube. **Open** 6.45am-8am, 9am-9.30pm Mon-Fri; 9am-4.30pm Sat, Sun. **Admission** £2.70; £1.50 children.
Three pools and a diving area, with coaching and clubs.

Crystal Palace National Sports Centre
Ledrington Road, SE19 (8778 0131/diving courses 8659 4561). Crystal Palace rail. **Open** 8am-5pm Mon-Wed, Fri; noon-7pm Thur; 10am-7.45pm Sat; 10am-1pm, 2-5.45pm Sun. **Admission** £2.35; £1.25 children.
One of London's two 50-metre Olympic-size pools, plus fabulous diving facilities.

Gurnell Leisure Centre
Ruislip Road East, W13 (8998 3241). Perivale tube. **Open** 7am-7pm Mon, Fri, 7am-9pm Tue-Thur, 8am-4.45pm Sat, Sun. **Admission** £2.60; £1.45 children; free under-5s.
The capital's other 50-metre Olympic-size pool.

Ironmonger Row Baths
Ironmonger Row, EC1 (7253 4011). Old Street tube/rail. **Open** 6.30am-9pm Mon, 6.30am-8pm Tue-Thur, 6.30am-7pm Fri; noon-6pm Sat; noon-5pm Sun. **Admission** £2.80; £1.20 children; £7.50 family.
Take a trip back in time at this 1930s 30-metre pool and Turkish baths (one of only three remaining in London).

Latchmere Leisure Centre
Burns Road, SW11 (7207 8004). Clapham Junction rail. **Open** 7am-9.30pm Mon, Wed, Sat, Sun; 7am-7pm Tue; 7am-7.30pm Thur, 7am-8pm Fri. **Admission** £2.70; £1.90 children.
Lane swimming main pool, teaching pool and a beach area with palm trees. The main pool shelves on a shallow slope, and there's a wave machine on the hour.

Queen Mother Sports Centre
223 Vauxhall Bridge Road, SW1 (7630 5522). Victoria tube/rail. **Open** 6.30am-8pm Mon; 9.30am-8pm Tue; 7.30am-8pm Wed, Fri; 8am-5.30pm Sat, Sun. **Admission** £2.40; £1 children. **Map** p318 J10.

Main pool, teaching pool and separate diving area in this refurbished centre that's always packed with schoolchildren.

Swiss Cottage Sports Centre
Winchester Road, NW3 (7974 6490). Swiss Cottage tube. **Open** 7am-9pm Mon-Fri; 9.30am-5.30pm Sat, Sun. **Admission** £2.70; £1 children. Choose from a 33-metre pool for lane swimming and a 22-metre one for lessons and children's clubs.

York Hall Leisure Centre
Old Ford Road, E2 (8980 2243). Bethnal Green tube/rail. **Open** 7.15am-8.30pm Mon, Sat; 7.15am-9.30pm Tue, Thur; 7.15am-5.30pm Wed, Fri; 7.15am-3.45pm Sun. **Admission** £2.35; £1 children.
Built as a bath house in the 1920s and still housing Turkish and Russian Baths, the 33-metre main pool and separate children's pool here provide real East End character.

Out

Charlton Lido
Hornfair Park, Shooters Hill Road (corner of Charlton Park Lane), SE18 (8856 7180). Charlton or Kidbrooke rail. **Open** May-Sept 10.30am-6pm daily. **Admission** £2.50; £1.60 children; £5.70 family.
South-east London's other lido is not as glamorous as the Evian one, but is still a godsend on a hot day. Its two-foot-deep children's pool is wonderful for very young kids.

Evian Lido
Dulwich Road, SE24 (7274 3088/ www.thelido.co.uk). Herne Hill rail. **Open** May-Sept 6.45am-7pm Mon-Fri; 11am-7pm Sat, Sun. **Admission** 6.45-10am £2; £1.50 under-16s. 10am-7pm £4; £2.50 children.
A new sponsor (you can't miss the logo on the bottom of the pool) should help this wonderful 1930s lido stay open. As well as the swimming pool, there are paddling pools and sunbathing terraces, though these have an uncomfortable lack of shade. Phone for details of classes and children's activities.

Finchley Lido
High Road, N12 (8343 9830). West Finchley tube. **Open** May-Sept 9am-9.30pm Mon-Fri; 9am-4.30pm Sat, Sun. **Admission** £2.70; £1.50 children.
There are two indoor pools here (*pictured*), but the outdoor pool and terrace are popular in summer.

Hampstead Heath Swimming Ponds
(7485 5757). Men & women's ponds, Millfield Lane, N6. Gospel Oak rail. Mixed pond, East Heath Road, NW3. Hampstead Heath rail. **Open** 7am-dusk daily, all year round. **Admission** free.

Children need to be aged eight-plus, able to swim at least 25 metres and accompanied by an adult in the water. Note that the authorities close the pool in times of ice and algal bloom, so call first.

Oasis Sports Centre
32 Endell Street, WC2 (7831 1804). Covent Garden tube. **Open** *7.30am-8.30pm Mon-Wed; 7.30am-8pm Thur; 9.30am-5pm Sat, Sun.*
The 28-metre outdoor pool is open all year round and great for a bracing dip. But if it's too cold, head for the indoor pool. Phone for admission prices.

Park Road Pools
Park Road, N8 (8341 3567). Hornsey rail/ Alexandra Palace rail then bus W7. **Open** *Lido* May-Sept 11am-6pm daily; indoor pools 7.15am-6pm Mon; 7.15am-9.30pm Tue-Thur; 7.15am-7.30pm Fri, Sat; 7.15am-6.30pm Sun. **Admission** *lido* £4 adults; £1.90 concessions. *Indoor pools* £2.95 adults; £1.90 concessions.
Outdoors, on sunny days, it's difficult to find a patch of grass to put your towel down. The water in the outdoor pool is heated, which means swimming in the rain is an option.

Parliament Hill Lido
Gordon House Road, NW3 (7485 3873). Gospel Oak rail. **Open** *Sept-Feb* 7am-10.30am daily. *May-Sept* 7-9am, 10am-6pm daily. Closed for maintenance early spring (ring for details). **Admission** £3.50; £1.50 children.
A lovely 1930s lido, teeming on hot days.

Richmond Pools on the Park
Old Deer Park, Twickenham Road, Richmond, Surrey (8940 0561). Richmond tube/rail. **Open** *Mar-Sept* 7am-10pm Mon-Fri; 8am-6pm Sat, Sun. **Admission** £3.50; £2.50 children.
A 33-metre indoor pool and the same size outside, plus a sunbathing area.

Tooting Bec Lido
Tooting Bec Road, SW17 (8871 7198). Tooting Bec tube/Streatham rail. **Open** *June-Sept* 10am-8pm daily. *Oct-May* closed except for club members.

Admission £2.60-£3.10; £2.10-£2.25 children. **Membership** £15; £80 season ticket for members. At 94 metres by 25 metres, this is the second largest open-air pool in Europe. Popular in summer.

Splash it all about

Brentford Fountain Leisure Centre
658 Chiswick High Road, Brentford, Middlesex (8994 6901). Gunnersbury tube. **Open** 9am-7pm Mon; 10am-9.45pm Tue; noon-6pm Wed; 10am-8pm Thur; noon-9pm Fri; 9am-5.30pm Sat, Sun. **Admission** £3.10; £1.25 children.
Leisure pool with 40-metre aquaslide, underwater lighting and wave machine alongside a conventional teaching pool.

Goresbrook Leisure Centre
Ripple Road, Becontree, Essex (8593 3570). Becontree tube. **Open** 12.15-10pm Mon; 9am-6.30pm Tue; 9am-12.15pm, 1.15-10pm Wed; 10am-10pm Fri; 10am-4pm Sat; 9am-6.30pm Sun. **Admission** £3.20; £1.65.
Fountains, cascades and a 60-metre flume.

Leyton Leisure Lagoon
763 High Road, E10 (8558 4860). Walthamstow Central tube. **Open** 7am-10pm Mon-Fri; 8am-6pm Sat, Sun. **Admission** *peak times* £3.40, £1.50 children. *Off peak* £2.20; 70p children.
Flume, slides, fountains, rapids and cascades in a tropical island setting.

Northolt Swimarama
Eastcote Lane North, Northolt, Middlesex (8422 1176). Northolt tube. **Open** 7am-7pm Mon, Fri; 7am-10pm Tue; 9am-10pm Wed; 7am-7.30pm Thur; 8am-4pm Sat, Sun. **Admission** £2.50; £1.35 children.
Three pools, a 60-metre slide and diving boards.

Pavilion Leisure Centre
Kentish Way, Bromley, Kent (8313 9911). Bromley South rail. **Open** 11am-2pm, 4-7pm Mon-Thur; 10am-7pm Fri; 8am-9pm Sat, Sun. **Admission** *Peak* £3.25; £2.05 children. *Off peak* £2.75; £1.80 children.
Large leisure pool with gentle shallows, flumes and a wave machine at weekends (plus lane swimming and a separate toddlers' pool).

Waterfront Leisure Centre
High Street, SE18 (8317 5000). Woolwich Arsenal rail. **Open** 3-8pm Mon-Thur; 3-6pm Fri; 9am-5pm Sat, Sun. **Admission** £4.25; £3.10 children.
Three pools, a 65-metre 'anaconda' slide, five-lane multi-slide, waves, jets and a water 'volcano'.

Wavelength Leisure Centre
Griffin Street, SE8 (8694 1134). Deptford rail. **Open** session times change regularly, ring for details. **Admission** £2.80; £1.45 children.
Flumes, waves, wild water and cannons.

FA Carling Premiership

Arsenal *Arsenal Stadium, Avenell Road, N5 (7413 3366/www.arsenal.co.uk). Arsenal tube.*
Charlton Athletic *The Valley, Floyd Road, SE7 (8333 4010/www.cafc.co.uk). Charlton rail.*
Chelsea *Stamford Bridge, Fulham Road, SW6 (7386 7799/www.chelseafc.co.uk). Fulham Broadway tube.* Map p314 B13.
Fulham *Craven Cottage, Stevenage Road, SW6 (7893 8383/www.fulhamfc.co.uk). Putney Bridge tube.*
Tottenham Hotspur *White Hart Lane, High Road, N17 (08700 112222/www.spurs.co.uk). White Hart Lane rail.*
West Ham United *Boleyn Ground, Green Street, E13 (8548 2700/www.westhamunited.co.uk). Upton Park tube.*

Nationwide League

Brentford *Griffin Park, Braemar Road, Brentford, Middlesex (8847 2511/www.brentfordfc.co.uk). Brentford rail.* Division 2.
Crystal Palace *Selhurst Park, Park Road, SE25 (8771 8841/www.cpfc.co.uk). Selhurst rail.* Division 1.
Leyton Orient *Matchroom Stadium, Brisbane Road, E10 (8926 1111/www.leytonorient.com). Leyton tube.* Division 3.
Millwall *The Den, Zampa Road, SE16 (7231 9999/www.millwallfc.co.uk). South Bermondsey rail.* Division 1.
Queens Park Rangers *Rangers Stadium, South Africa Road, W12 (8740 2575/www.qpr.co.uk). White City tube.* Division 2.
Watford *Vicarage Road, Watford, Herts (01923 496010/www.watfordfc.com). Watford High Street rail.* Division 1.
Wimbledon *Selhurst Park, Park Road, SE25 (7413 3388/www.wimbledon-fc.co.uk). Selhurst rail.* Division 1.
'The Dons' currently share Crystal Palace's ground.

Best: Sporting treats

Getting to grips with the Mile End Climbing Wall
If the children have been driving you up the wall, here's your chance for revenge. *See p251.*

Ice skating at Leisurebox
Take a twirl – and a tumble – at this well-known rink. *See p258.*

Karting at Daytona Raceway
Not a cheap party option, but thrill-a-minute stuff for boy and girl racers (and their parents...). *See p259.*

Riding at Wimbledon Village Stables
Saddle up and trot on. *See p256.*

Scoring a strike at Rowans Bowl
A great time for alley cats of all ages. *See p262.*

Horse racing

Although the image of exotic headgear perpetrated by Royal Ascot might suggest that a day at the races is an entirely adult activity, in fact all 59 courses around the UK offer a warm welcome to children. Admission for under-16s is free at the majority of meetings, and most racecourses stage special 'family days'. Children love the hubbub of the parade ring where the magnificent thoroughbreds can be seen at close quarters, and there are plenty of places to eat and drink – or you could take a picnic.

The Racecourse Association publishes an excellent free guide, *Come Racing*, available by calling 01344 625912. The RCA website at www.comeracing.co.uk has details of (and links to) all the British courses, a full calendar and previews of major meetings.

Admission prices stated below are for adults attending regular meetings; children go free.
Ascot *High Street, Ascot, Berks (01344 622211/www.ascot.co.uk). Ascot rail.* **Admission** £5-£15.
Epsom Downs *Racecourse Paddock, Epsom, Surrey (01372 726311/www.epsomderby.co.uk). Epsom Downs rail.* **Admission** £5-£16.
Kempton Park *Staines Road East, Sunbury-on-Thames, Surrey (01932 782292/www.kempton.co.uk). Kempton Park rail.* **Admission** £6-£17.
Lingfield Park *Racecourse Road, Lingfield, Sussex (01342 834800/www.lingfield-racecourse.co.uk). Lingfield rail.* **Admission** £12-£15.
Sandown Park *Esher Station Road, Esher, Surrey (01372 463072/www.sandown.co.uk). Esher rail.* **Admission** £5-£17.
Windsor *Maidenhead Road, Windsor, Berks (01753 865234/www.windsorracing.co.uk). Windsor & Eton Riverside rail.* **Admission** £5-£16.

Ice hockey

London Knights
London Arena, Limeharbour, E14 (7538 1212/www.knightice.co.uk). Crossharbour DLR. **Admission** £12-£18 adults, £7 children.
British ice hockey has enjoyed a resurgence in recent years, and the Knights have certainly played their part. Match night at London Arena is an upbeat, family-oriented affair, with plenty of rough, tough action to relish. Children love it. The season runs from September to April.

Rugby league

London Broncos
The Valley, Floyd Road, SE7 (8853 8815/www.londonbroncos.co.uk). Charlton rail. **Admission** £10-£15 adults, £3-£5 children.
The Broncos are still determined to prove that rugby league can succeed outside its northern heartland, although it's a tough task to win over the southerners. Still, the club tries hard and there's always a host of family-oriented entertainment to enjoy if the action in the Tetley's Bitter Super League fails to inspire. The season runs from March to October.

Rugby union

While England continue to dominate the international oval-ball scene in this part of the world, the club game struggles to make ends meet. The move to professionalism has brought numerous teething troubles, mostly financial, as exemplified by the half-empty grounds for matches. Nevertheless, the three top London clubs all have a slew of internationals in their line-ups, and a trip to a match is an absolute bargain compared to football. The season runs from September to May and admission is about £10-£25 for adults, £2-£10 for children.

Harlequins *Stoop Memorial Ground, Langhorn Drive, Twickenham, Middlesex (0870 887 0230/ www.quins.co.uk). Twickenham rail.*
London Wasps *Rangers Stadium, South Africa Road, W12 (8740 2545/www.wasps.co.uk). White City tube.*
Saracens *Vicarage Road, Watford, Herts (01923 475222/www.saracens.com). Watford High Street rail.*

Twickenham Stadium

Rugby Road, Twickenham, Middlesex (8892 2000/ www.rfu.com). Twickenham rail.
This superb ground plays host to England international matches and a full programme of club, county and representative matches. While tickets for the Six Nations Championship are almost impossible to obtain unless you're a member of a rugby club, the other games are more accessible and cheaper.

Stock car & banger racing

Wimbledon Stadium

Plough Lane, SW17 (8946 8000). Wimbledon Park tube. **Admission** £10; £5 children.
Sunday-night meetings at Wimbledon Stadium are terrific entertainment for all ages. 'Racing' is not the most important thing for the drivers of stock cars and bangers – nor for the spectators, either. What really matters are the crashes…

Family Fitness

A growing number of private fitness clubs are now targeting the family market – although in some cases their motives are as much to do with profit as the health of the nation. But there are exceptions.

The David Lloyd Leisure Group has always taken a family-friendly approach, while the growing Esporta chain states that 'children are an integral part of the clubs, with activities for all ages'. Both run regular children's programmes, and provide family restaurants, bars and socialising areas.

Holmes Place (Crouch End, Ealing, Putney and Wimbledon), Pinnacles (Bromley, Surbiton, Windsor and Woking) and Dragons (Croydon, Ewell, Guildford, Muswell Hill, Northolt) are among the chains providing classes organised by FitClub International. These range from 'Tearless and Fearless' for the under-fives, through to 'Giggle and Wiggle' workouts for teenagers.

The Park Club in Acton has taken the concept a stage further, claiming to 'recognise that there are times when you need to be together as a family – and times when you need space for yourself'. There's a vast array of activities for children aged four upwards, plus a family pool, two acres of secure woodland, an outdoor activity zone, video surveillance and security tagging.

All very nice – but at a cost that many will find out of reach. The public sector, in contrast, has yet to move much beyond 'family swim' sessions, with the **Kingfisher Leisure Centre** in Kingston a notable exception. Here, there's an impressive children's activity programme, holiday courses, family membership packages (or 'pay as you go') and even a 'healthy options' menu in the restaurant.

Meanwhile, most YMCAs around the capital cater for fives and overs. At Central YMCA, for example, the 'Y Active' scheme runs ten-week courses in swimming, basketball and gymnastics at £15 for children of members, £20 for non-members, and Saturday term-time sessions for just £1.60 plus £10 annual membership.

Cannons *The Porchester Centre, Queensway, W2 (7792 2919). Queensway tube.* **Family membership** from £59.85 per yr, plus £1.95, 50p children per session. Ring for full details of membership.
Central YMCA *112 Great Russell Street, WC1 (7343 1700). Tottenham Court Road tube.* **Map** p317 K5. Phone for full details.
Crystal Palace National Sports Centre *Ledrington Road, SE19 (8778 0131). Crystal Palace rail.* **Membership** from £210/yr plus 'pay as you go' session fees.
David Lloyd Leisure *(0870 888 3015).* Eleven clubs in Greater London, all offering family membership. **Membership** *Typical package* (including tennis) might be £122 per mth plus £475 joining fee, plus £21 per mth per child over 6 (under-6s free).
Dragons *331 Imperial Way, Purley Way, Croydon, Surrey (8686 8811).* **Membership** from £20 per mth per adult, £45 family, plus £50 joining fee.
Esporta *(0118 912 3500).* Esporta has eight clubs located in Greater London. **Membership** £50-£70 per mth per adult, plus a £150-£200 joining fee; children £10-£25 per mth (there's no joining fee).
Holmes Place *(7795 4100).*
This is the head office of the vast Holmes Place empire; there are more than 30 branches in Greater London; ring the number above to find a family-friendly one near you.
Kingfisher Leisure Centre *Fairfield Road, Kingston-upon-Thames, Surrey (8546 1042). Kingston rail.* Membership £810/yr family, plus £50 joining fee.
The Park Club *East Acton Lane, W3 (8743 4321/ www.theparkclub.co.uk). Acton Central rail.* **Membership** £550 joining fee, plus from £125 per mth adults; under-11s free if parent joins.
This is one of the smartest, as is evident from the fees.

Activities & Fun

Days Out

Days Out

Family fun outside the capital.

When you've done with all the sights and attractions that London has to offer, escape the city and head out for a day. Most children jump at the chance to get in the car or catch a train to an out-of-town sight, especially if a picnic is thrown into the bargain.

And those of you who are bewildered at the thought of theme parks, take note – though we've included our favourite ones in this chapter, there are plenty of other family-friendly options, from activities to zoos.

Tickets & information

For main entries below we include full details of opening times and admission prices, but be aware that these can change without notice. If you're planning a trip around one particular sight, always phone first to check that it's open. We've noted if you should reserve a place or ticket in advance but do double check before making a special trip.

Though we've given basic directions for sights, it's always best to check on a detailed map first. Likewise, check train times and details for national rail enquiries, call 08457 484950.

Activities

We've listed some very wholesome places where children can take the air (and possibly a mouthful of lake water) and get active. **Bewl Water** is paradise for people of all ages who love to mess about in boats, catch their own supper, or just walk and admire the scenery. At **Painshill Park**, kids can get involved in making their own den in the woods, then sing songs around a camp fire and help make their own dinner.

Bodiam Castle – what a stunner. *See p273.*

Days Out

Most physically demanding, a spot of water-skiing tuition in Chertsey, Surrey, is an extreme sport for all water babies and speed freaks to enjoy. Infinitely more relaxing, an hour's balloon trip is an expensive, but enchanting way to admire the countryside.

Extreme survival (for an hour or so)

Painshill Park

Painshill Park Trust, Portsmouth Road, Cobham, Surrey (01932 864674/Summer Camp Hamilton 01932 866743/www.painshill.co.uk). By train Cobham or Weybridge rail. By car M25 (Junction 10) and A3, exit at junction with A245 towards Cobham, entrance in Between Streets (A245), 200m east of A245/A307 roundabout, Cobham. **Open** *Apr-Oct* 10.30am-6pm Tue-Sun, bank hols (last entry 4.30pm). *Nov-Mar* 11am-4pm Tue-Thur, Sat, Sun, bank hols (last entry 3pm). Closed 25, 26 Dec. *Tours* groups of 10 or more only, by arrangement. **Admission** £4.50; £4 concessions; £2 5-16s; free under-5s. **Credit** MC, V.

The outward bounders at Painshill run day camps for children aged 7 to 11 on three school holidays. You can choose between Easter Camp Hamilton, Summer Camp Hamilton or Christmas Camp Hamilton, which last for two weeks, four days and three weeks respectively.

The activities are similar each year, with three main structures: an outdoor trail, an indoor activity and a creative one, where children make something to take home with them. The most popular activity is the woodland quest, where the children go to a pre-selected part of the woods and create a camp from scratch, before being treated to a barbecue cooked by the staff. The materials, strategically left around, are poles – semi-fastened to make it easier to put together – rope, string and bracken. The end product looks like a basic house and they later play inside, sometimes making chairs – again with custom made twigs and branches.

The camps start at 9.30am, finish at 3.30pm and cost £20 per day. Packed lunches are recommended if you don't want a barbecue, and you're advised to bring outdoor water-proofed clothing. The camps take 30 kids a day and there are six adults looking after them.

With a little planning, you can make your child's activities coincide with some cultural ones of your own. Painshill holds study days for adults throughout the year. The programme varies annually, but popular topics include lectures on art and history, with many discussions on botany. You can attend the lectures and occasional guided tours; expect to pay about £20 for the lecture and tour, or around £15 just for the lecture.

The Painshill Park gardens are also splendid enough to keep parents busy while their children get the pioneering spirit. They were lavishly landscaped in the 18th century, but subsequently allowed to run wild; now they have been spectacularly restored (although it's very much a work in progress). Highlights of a hike round the grounds include a series of follies (a Turkish tent, a Gothic temple, a grotto and a huge water wheel) as well as some lovely lakes and views.

If a slap-up meal seems more inviting to you, the Hamilton restaurant offers meals and snacks in a family-friendly environment, with nappy-changing facilities, high chairs and ample pushchair space. It's open during the summer from 10.30am to 5pm.

Buggy access. Nappy-changing facilities. Nearest picnic place: picnic meadow on site. Restaurant. Shop.

Factfile: fishing

Bewl Valley Sailing Club, Bewl Water, Lamberhurst, Kent TN3 8JH (01892 890930/ www.bvscbewl.demon.co.uk). **Open** 9am-5pm Mon-Fri; 9am-6pm Sat, Sun. **Credit** MC, V.

● **Boat/bank fishing**: You can either fish from a boat or from the bank. Hiring a boat will cost £20 for the day and seats three people. Buoyancy aids are free.

● **Fishing times**: Bank fishing takes place from sunrise to one hour after sunset. Boat fishing starts at 9am and ends at 10pm or one hour after sunset, whichever is earlier. The Fishing Lodge (open from 8.30am to 6pm) has daily times displayed inside.

● **Courses for children**: for kids aged 8-15 yrs there is a 'junior course' in summer. It aims to teach them how to cast a fly safely, although no fish are caught during the sessions.

● **Courses for adults**: Beginners' courses are offered, which teach the basics of fly fishing (call Bewl Bridge Fly Fishers Club, 01304 611301). These take place about three times a month in summer, usually on Saturdays or Wednesdays.

Phone for exact details of courses as dates vary from year to year. For both you need to book at least a week in advance, as you'll receive course notes which explain what you should expect from the course.

Gone fishing

Bewl Water

Bewl Water, Lamberhurst, Tunbridge Wells, Kent (01892 890661/www.bewl.co.uk). By train Wadhurst rail, then taxi, or Tunbridge Wells rail, then Heritage Hopper bus. By car M25, then A21. **Open** 9am-dusk daily. Closed 25 Dec; Concert Day (13 July 2002). **Admission** *per vehicle* Apr-Oct £3.50 Mon-Fri; £4.50 Sat, Sun. Nov-Mar £2.50 daily. *Concert tickets* prices released Mar 2002; phone for details.

As long as you make sure you get to Bewl by car – thereby avoiding the train and hefty taxi fare journey, which will kill any enthusiasm in your party – it cannot fail to appeal to even the most reluctant of children. Or parents, for that matter.

Once there, you have 450 acres of ample green fields in which to stretch your legs. You can catch up on some R&R on one of the undulating hills overlooking the reservoir, or try a number of watersports ranging from canoeing to wind-surfing. It's a picnic-lover's paradise: clean family-sized benches rest under shady trees and the grounds are ideal for excitable children to run around on. The Enid Blyton-ness of it is further enhanced by the groups of inquisitive ducks that will attempt a friendly chat with you before waddling off.

The lake has 15 miles of shoreline and is 29.5 metres at its deepest, which as there are no lifeguards, prohibits swimming. Fly-fishing, however, is available and very popular as

Best: Destinations

For white knuckles
Thorpe Park. *See p290.*

For fishy goings-on
Brighton Sea Life Centre. *See p282.*

For savage beasts
Woburn Safari Park. *See p280.*

For creepy crawlies
Chessington World of Adventures. *See p289.*

For rock 'n' roll
Margate. *See p284.*

For making secret dens
Painshill Park. *See p271.*

the many little fishing boats strewn along the lake demonstrate. The largest trout caught so far weighed a whopping 7.5kgs and whatever you catch is yours to take home and eat. In fact, any fish you catch you are obliged to kill and take home. The fish are all trout, and on average weigh about 1kg.

In order to fish you need an 'environment agency licence', which Bewl sometimes has, or you can buy it from any post office. You need a fishing permit for the day, which you can buy when you get here. This costs £15 for adults for eight fish and £9.50 for two fish (£4 for under-15s). The staff at Bewl suggest that children under eight years don't fish as they're probably not strong enough to cast the line; but they're happy for parents who know how to fly fish to teach their kids on the premises.

In summer, you can hire bikes and ride, or hike, around the reservoir on the recommended 20km walk. This is not for the faint-hearted as it takes about six hours to complete. If you can't face that much exercise, jump on the ferry boat that leaves every hour from 11am to 4pm (£3 for adults, £2 kids) and either cruise around the lake or stop off half way round to go the rest of the way on foot. Several picnic spots and shelters are dotted along the way, allowing the less athletic to gaze at the views while surreptitiously catching their breath.

The appropriately named Lookout Restaurant serves staple English food, from sandwiches to three course meals and includes an old-fashioned cream tea and cakes. It's very family-friendly, with lots of pushchair space and a baby and nappy changer in the toilet for disabled people. If the weather permits, however, sit outside, as the restaurant has a pleasant terrace with a stunning view of the reservoir. The Mediterranean-style decor – huge green parasols and a herb and flower rockery garden – will make you think you're somewhere on the continent on a sunny day.

Fully trained RYA (Royal Yachting Association) instructors will teach any keen windsurfers over eight to windsurf within the two-hour lesson. The £25 fee includes the board, rig, wetsuit, spray-top (which acts as a wind shield in chilly weather), buoyancy aid and safety cover. Alternatively, there's rowing or powerboat instruction available nearby.

Younger children will love the outdoor playground – gamely set in the trees – which is suitable for those aged from 5 to 11 and includes all the usual favourites such as rope bridges, swings and slides.

Note that the tackle shop sells flies but you must bring your own fishing rod and appropriate clothing.

For Bewl Water Outdoor Centre (canoeing, sailing, climbing, rowing, powerboat instruction, etc) call 01892 890716. *Nappy-changing facilities. Restaurant. Shop.*

Splashdown

JB Waterski
Thorpe Road, Chertsey, Surrey (0870 606 1270/ www.jbwaterski.com). By train Virginia Water rail, then taxi. By car M25 (Junction 11 or 13). **Open** *June-Aug* sunrise-sunset daily. *Apr, May, Sept, Oct* 11am-7pm Wed-Sun. *Nov-Mar* 11am-5pm/dusk Wed, Sat, Sun. Closed 25 Dec, 1 Jan. **Admission** £14 1hr; £17 2 hrs; £20 4hr pass Mon-Fri; £25 day pass Mon-Fri. **Rental** £1 lifejacket; £2 wetsuit. **Credit** MC, V.

Water-skiing used to be the preserve of the rich and glamorous, but nowadays it's open to anyone with enthusiasm and, preferably, a good sense of balance. Cable skiing is a cheaper and easier way of water-skiing. The difference is that instead of being pulled by a boat, you are towed around a lake by an overhead cable. This eliminates the difficulty of dealing with the boat's wake and its varying speeds. But it certainly doesn't look glamorous.

The minimum age for kids is 12, and if either you or your children are novices, take the beginner's package. This will include a half hour lesson, the skis and an hour on the cable. The hardest part of learning to cable-ski – apart from standing upright – is negotiating the bends, but apparently even the most clueless can learn this skill during the lesson. In fact, within an hour of skiing, you'll find yourself whizzing by with the best of them.

If you'd rather watch, bring your own picnic and lounge on the grass or the man-made beach nearby. The Outdoor Café serves the usual café food, burgers and fries.

Expect to feel exhausted after two hours of cable skiing. Most people do three or four laps and then take a short break before jumping back on.
Buggy access. Café. Nearest picnic place: (note that food must be bought on site) tables and benches on site. Shop.

Up, up & away

Adventure Balloons
Winchfield Park, London Road, Hartley Wintney, Hants (01252 844222/www.adventureballoons.co.uk). Phone for details of transport. **Open** *Apr-Oct* daily; phone to book. **Price** £135 per person. No child reductions. **Credit** MC, V.

Adventure Balloons specialises in passenger balloon rides around London and the Home Counties. Balloons fly from several towns in Berkshire, North Hampshire, South Hampshire, Hertfordshire, and Surrey. You can expect to travel between two and 20 miles at a dizzying altitude of about 3,000 feet, although the direction you actually fly in is at the mercy of the unpredictable winds.

Children need to be over seven years old and stand at least 4ft tall (that's enough to be able to look over the basket). You don't need to have a set number of people in your party, as you can join other balloonists in the basket, which holds 14 to 16 passengers. The flight itself lasts approximately an hour and on landing you will receive both champagne or fruit juice and a personalised flight certificate signed by your pilot. At £135 per person, it's a pricey outing but, assuming you're not terrified of heights, should make for an invigorating and unforgettable experience.

Castles

Tales of dragons, dungeons and princesses in distress are thrilling for children of all ages, which is why castles are given such positive press as great family days out. Even a child with the keenest imagination, however, glazes over remarkably quickly when led through room after room of priceless antiques. Parents with young kids in tow are advised to tailor castle visiting to the needs of their small companions. We chose three castles to visit: **Windsor** (London's 'local' castle), **Leeds** (good old-fashioned fairytale style) and **Bodiam** (mysterious ruin).

Many children barely glance at the fantastic art collection at Windsor assembled over four centuries by English sovereigns, but are enchanted by the real-life pageantry. They wander happily through the maze and grotto at Leeds for hours. Bodiam – the furthest afield of the three – is paradise for the young: on sunny days it's a gigantic playground, with hundreds of kids of all ages happily cavorting in the ruins.

Bodiam Castle

Near Robertsbridge, East Sussex (01580 830436/ www.nationaltrust.org.uk). By train Robertsbridge rail, then taxi. By car M25 (Junction 5), then A21. **Open** *mid Feb-Oct* 10am-6pm/dusk daily. *Nov-mid Feb* 10am to 4pm/dusk Sat, Sun (last entry 1hr before closing). Closed 25 Dec, 1 Jan. *Tours* groups of 10 or more people only, by arrangement. **Admission** (NT) £3.70; £1.85 5-16s; £9.25 family (2+ up to 3); free under-5s. **Credit** AmEx, MC, V.

Bodiam, a National Trust property, is not exactly a stone's throw from central London. But once you're off the motorway it's a pleasant journey, with enticing signs beckoning down country lanes to antique shops and farm shops selling fresh produce.

It's strange that Bodiam should be so inspiring, since there's nothing much left but a 14th-century husk of stone and mortar and vestigal traces of the interior rooms. But the layout of the castle is very straightforward and easy to grasp. You stroll from the parking area past ancient oaks and hollies across the wooden bridge spanning the moat and through the Great Gatehouse. With its grassed courtyard lying inside four fortified outer walls, the concept of fortification couldn't be made clearer.

Painshill Park may look serene, but don't think you'll get away with doing nothing here. *See p271.*

Days Out

Flying high over **Windsor Castle**. *See p275.*

Without the priceless accumulated clutter of kings and queens displayed in glass cases, visitors instead get the opportunity to focus on the evocative reminders of what castle life was once like. The guard rooms still have stone benches from which to gaze out through slits in the castle walls at approaching enemies.

Another reminder of castle life are the 28 fireplaces suspended in the walls. The staircases leading up to the two towers are perilously steep (and obviously unsuitable for buggies, although if you're lucky you can borrow the single backpack the castle lends to visitors). But the climb is well worth it. Views of the surrounding countryside are breathtaking, as is the sheer drop down into the moat. They weren't great on child-proofing in the Middle Ages, though, so Bodiam would be more of a challenge for parents with tiny tots.

But the real beauty of Bodiam is that children rule the roost here. They scamper over the walls, peer around corners, and explore every nook and cranny. As the guidebook unabashedly boasts: 'Bodiam is everyone's fairytale castle.'

Two years ago, Bodiam initiated a new summer programme of weekends in August to bring the castle to life for families with a selection of characters wandering the ruins in period costume. There are representatives of the kinds of people who would have lived at the castle in its heyday, from the so-called gong farmer who cleaned up sewage, to the leather worker and his wife, and the various lords and ladies. The castle has a National Trust café in renovated quarters. And Bodiam now has a children's guidebook available for £1.95 at the recently revamped gift shop.

The castle offers school visits (prebooking required) special access to the corner towers, where there is a room containing armour, chain mail, longbows and crossbows and another room with medieval-style games and costumes and musical instruments. Schools also have sole access to a picnic area that is covered. Indeed, Bodiam can be bleak in the rain, though the castle has enough rooms intact for visitors to duck into during a downpour. An alternative to the National Trust café is The Castle Inn (Main Street, 01580 830330) just opposite the car park.

Car park. Nearest picnic place: castle grounds. Restaurant. Shop.

Leeds Castle

Maidstone, Kent (01622 765400/www.leeds-castle.co.uk). By train Bearsted rail, then connecting coach service. By car M20 (Junction 8). **Open** *Castle Mar-Oct* 11am-6pm daily (last entry 5pm). *Nov-Feb* 10am-4pm daily (last entry 3pm). Gardens *Nov-Feb* 10am-3pm daily. *Mar-Oct* 10am-5pm daily. Closed 25 Dec, open-air concert days in June, July. *Tours* pre-booked groups only. **Admission** Castle, gardens, attractions *Mar-Oct* £11; £6-£9.50 concessions; £7.50 4-15s; £32 family (2+ up to 3); free under-4s. *Nov-Feb* £9.50; £5.50-£8 concessions; £6 4-15s; £27 family (2 + up to 3); free under-4s. **Credit** MC, V.

They say Leeds Castle was a day's horse ride from London. For most visitors today, it's a more tedious motorway journey. But maybe the most important thing to remember when visiting Leeds Castle is that, confusingly, it is nowhere near the northern city of the same name.

The castle is set in lovely Kentish parkland and rises dreamily out of a lake. What's more, its beauty is unspoiled by the encroachment of car parks and fast food joints. On the walk to the castle (there's a shuttle, too) you can watch the mallards and mandarin ducks on the lake, together with the rare black, as well as the more ordinary white, swans. The grounds are a crazy quilt of colours and textures. Weather permitting, you can bring a picnic for the benches either inside the castle grounds or before you enter the castle gates. There is also a good range of eateries catering to children; the most striking of these is the 17th-century Fairfax Hall.

In summer months, ring for an events leaflet to find out about children's classical concerts (now in their third year) and open-air theatre events at Leeds. The castle hosts other special year-round events, too, including an annual Easter Egg hunt and an annual hot air-balloon festival, which sends a colourful bevy of balloons wafting over the Kentish countryside. Note that pushchairs can be used on the ground floor of the castle only with special permission from the duty guard.

The first room in the castle itself, the Heraldry Room, is empty save for the rows of portraits of the royal owners of Leeds Castle. You admire coats of arms while listening to a simplified explanation of heraldry. For nearly three centuries Leeds was residence to medieval kings and queens, so the royal cast of characters is ample. The figure of Henry VIII – who made many changes at Leeds – looms large here as does Eleanor of Castile, wife of Edward III. (Leeds was once known as the Queen's Castle because so many kings gave it to their wives.) On a darker note, two women, a duchess and Queen Joan of Navarre, were imprisoned at Leeds long ago for witchcraft.

The royal bathroom in the Queen's quarters is intriguing. The fire blazes in the stone fireplace. Alongside are buckets for the hot water that was brought up from the kitchen. It's worth going upstairs to the modernised quarters largely for the view over the lake, in which you can see reflected the twisted shapes of the Judas trees. As you're leaving the main island just before going through the gate tower you come to the quirky Dog Collar Museum, with its collection of dog ornamentation spanning four centuries.

But it's the outdoor attractions that really captivate children. Head for the gardens. However, before you do that remember there is a nappy-changing facility in the toilet block near the restaurants and shops; the other one is near the main entrance. There's a delightful Culpeper cottage garden, but children are usually eager to get to the maze. Built with some 2,400 yews only a decade ago, it has a profusion of pathways. When eventually you reach the centre, you come to a spooky grotto, decorated with mythical beasts fashioned with stone and shell mosaics. In a lively illustrated children's book called

Leeds Castle and the Magic Key (£9.95), this grotto provides the opening scene with a cast of characters including a black swan, other local water fowl and Henry VIII. The castle is also planning to launch an interactive website with a quiz area for children.

In contrast to Windsor, which receives funds both from the Crown and the government, Leeds is maintained purely by the private Leeds Castle Foundation. Given the entrance prices, consider taking up the excellent combined travel and entrance fee deal offered – train travel from Victoria or Charing Cross, plus a shuttle bus from Bearsted station, plus an entrance ticket costs £10.30 for children, £20.50 for adults (call Connex on 0870 603 0405 for more details).

Nearby, only about five miles up the road on the M20, is the **Museum of Kent Life** (Lock Lane, Sandling, Maidstone, 01622 763936/www.museum-kentlife.co.uk). Here, children can stroke farm animals in the courtyard (foot and mouth permitting), admire the birds in the aviary and learn about various aspects of farming life through their hands-on exhibits. The farmhouse is furnished in the Victorian period. *Cafés. Nappy-changing facilities. Nearest picnic place: benches in grounds. Restaurants. Shop.*

Windsor Castle

Windsor, Berks (01753 831118/info 01753 869898/ www.royalresidences.com). By train Windsor and Eton Riverside rail. By car M4 (Junction 6). **Open** *Mar-Oct* 9.45am-5.15pm daily (last entry 4pm). *Nov-Feb* 9.45am-4.15pm daily (last entry 3pm). Closed 25, 26 Dec. **Admission** *includes Queen Mary's Dolls' House, The Gallery, Albert Memorial Chapel, St George's Hall, State Apartments* £11; £9 concessions; £5.50 5-16s; £27.50 family (2+2); free under-5s. *Audio guide* £2.95. **Changing of the guard** *Apr-July* outside the Guardroom in the Lower Ward 11am Mon-Sat; on alternate days for the remainder of the year. The sentries are changed throughout the day. **Credit** AmEx, MC, V.
Windsor, the most accessible castle from central London, is more crowded than ever these days, as many families opt for the whole Berkshire experience by combining a trip to the castle with a jaunt to nearby Legoland (*see p289*). There's a convenient shuttle service connecting the two attractions.

The first view of the castle's crenellations and towers set against the sky is dramatic, but the effect is somewhat tainted by the string of fast-food joints along the way to the entrance. If you have the time, pack a picnic to enjoy along the nearby riverbanks afterwards: when children are carrying their sandwiches and crisps in their rucksacks they are more easily distracted from Burger King. The castle has a banded system that allows you to re-enter the grounds if you need to make a food foray. However, don't forget to notify the personnel when exiting at the Henry VIII gate. There is a new covered admissions centre, under which you can shelter during a shower; children's audio cassettes are available at the guidebook shop opposite for £2.95.

The North Terrace affords a dramatic view of the surrounding countryside below and the grounds of the Royal Windsor Horse Show. This takes place one week a year, usually in May. The entrance to the state apartments and Queen Mary's Dolls' House are here, as is a depot for parking prams. (Toilets are also conveniently at hand.)

There are often 20-30 minute queues at the dolls' house, but it's a wondrous thing. Pity it can't be touched or at least shown to better advantage for younger children. The engineering equipment – lights and plumbing – were made to work when it was given to Queen Mary in 1924. And the miniature kegs actually contain vintage wines. Still, you can ask younger children to hunt for the miniature pram or

wheelbarrow in the landscaped garden or the grand piano and the throne. See who can get the right number of place settings at the dining table set impeccably for 14. Children are keen on the car collection stored in the garages and the crown jewels locked up behind tiny bars. In the adjoining hallway are the twin French dolls named Marianne and France, sumptuously dressed in tiny leather gloves, a garden party gown with matching shoes and hat and an ermine evening cloak.

Tear yourself away from this miniature world and head straight up the Grand Staircase, flanked by two knights mounted on horses. The highlight of the rest of the apartments is the fabulous Windsor collection of medieval weaponry. This is contained in the Grand Vestibule, the Queen's Guard Chamber and the newly restored St George's Hall.

An amazing array of trophy swords, pairs of pistols and even a 19th-century Inca and Ethiopian crown can be found in the Grand Vestibule. You can also gaze at Napoleon's scarlet cloak that was captured at Waterloo or the bullet that killed Lord Nelson at Trafalgar in 1805. The sequel to the Grand Vestibule is the Queen's Guard Chamber: floor to ceiling weapons here again. Carved eagles and lions adorn the ivory Indian throne.

St George's Hall in the State Apartments, now fully restored following the 1992 fire, smells as new as a show home. When you leave the state apartments you can also check for the line-up of royal Range Rovers parked in the Quandrangle just outside. When at Windsor, the royals live just across the manicured lawn.
Nappy-changing facilities. Nearest picnic place: benches in grounds. Shop.

Other castles

Hever Castle

near Edenbridge, Kent (01732 865224/ www.hevercastle.co.uk). By train Edenbridge Town rail, then taxi or Hever rail, then 1-mile walk. By car M25 (Junction 5), then B2042 and B269 or M25 (Junction 6) then A22, A25 and B269. **Open** *Castle & Gardens* Apr-Oct 11am-5pm daily (last entry 4pm). Mar, Nov 11am-4pm daily (last entry 3pm). *Tours* groups (min. 20 people) by prior arrangement. **Admission** *Castle & Gardens* £8.20; £7 concessions; £4.50 5-14s; £20.90 family (2+2); free under-5s. *Gardens only* £6.50; £5.60 concessions; £4.30 5-14s; £17.30 family (2+2); free under-5s. **Credit** MC, V.
Hever was the childhood home of Anne Boleyn, and it became the setting for her courtship by Henry VIII. The castle was lavishly restored in the early 20th century by the American millionaire Waldorf Astor and filled with treasures. It now features impressive collections of paintings and furniture as well as two rare historic Books of Hours, beautifully illuminated manuscripts inscribed by Anne Boleyn. The well-tended gardens contain an elaborate yew maze, along with an adventure playground and a water maze set on Sixteen Acre Island.

Hever is known for its re-enactments of Tudor revelry and regularly stages jousting tournaments and medieval archery among its special events at half-terms and holidays. In May there is the Merrie England weekend, involving foot soldier combat, medieval music and crafts. At Easter there is a traditional Easter egg trail. There is also a summer festival of music and plays staged by the lake.
Adventure playground. Buggy access (grounds only). Café. Nappy-changing facilities. Nearest picnic place: benches in grounds. Restaurant. Shop.

Tonbridge Castle

Castle Street, Tonbridge, Kent (01732 770929).
By train Tonbridge rail, then short walk. By car
M25 (Junction 5), then A21. **Open** 9am-4pm Mon-
Sat; 10.30am-4pm Sun, bank hols (last entry 1hr
before closing). Closed 25, 26 Dec, 1 Jan. *Tours* for
groups only, by arrangement. **Admission** *Castle*
& grounds £3.80; £1.90 5-16s, concessions; £9 family
(2+2); free under-5s. *Grounds* free. **Credit** MC, V.
This is a good example of a motte and bailey castle with
a 13th-century gatehouse. The admission price includes
an audio tour with a six-minute film about the history of
the castle, which children enjoy. There are also panoramic
views from the battlements.
Nearest picnic place: Bailey Lawn on castle grounds.
Shop.

Now wash your hands

Foot and mouth, BSE, E. coli – each new 'farming
crisis' has seen plummeting confidence in
the standards of hygiene on British farms.
But though some sites may be guilty as
charged, no farmyard in the world is an antiseptic
paradise and it's necessary to distinguish
between problems endemic to the industry and
the micro-organisms commonly carried by farm
animals. Even healthy herds can harbour a range
of germs capable of causing disease in humans,
including salmonella, E.coli and such other
delights as campylobacter and cryptosporidia.
If you contract any of these diseases you will
be at best in for a bad bout of sickness and at
worst – as in the case of the four-year-old boy
who picked up E. coli during a school visit to
a farm – serious and permanent damage. But it's
important to keep the risks in perspective. Of the
45 million visitors to open farms between 1994
and 1999, only 44 contracted E. coli – that's
less than one in a million. And with proper
precautions the risk of picking up any of the
germs that animals commonly carry is small.

   To avoid risking your own or your children's
health around animals on a farm or petting zoo,
observe these simple rules:

● Ensure that children – and grown-ups – wash
their hands with soap and clean water after any
contact with the animals. All farms should have
clearly signposted washing facilities with hot
water and soap.

● Don't let habitual thumb-suckers pet the
animals or touch their pens.

● Wash your hands (and your children's)
before eating or drinking.

● Eat only in approved 'clean' areas and
never eat food that has fallen on the floor.

● Do not touch any newborn animals or
their mothers.

● Cover cuts or grazes with a waterproof plaster.

● Pregnant women should avoid lambing ewes.

Farms & Zoos

Animal attractions

There is a persistent myth that city children can't
tell one end of a cow from another. Not true, as
anyone who has ever spent any time around
Reception-age children can surely testify. One of
the great highlights for the Reception year is the
summer trip to a farm, and there aren't many
London children who don't have fond memories
of a school day out at one.

   In fact, there are dozens of venues within a two-
hour drive of London where you can get up close
and personal with the animal kingdom. We've
chosen our favourites below.

Down on the farm

Bocketts Farm Park

Young Street, Fetcham, near Leatherhead, Surrey (01372
363764/www.bockettsfarm.co.uk). By train Leatherhead
rail, then taxi. By car M26 then A246. **Open** 10am-6pm
daily. Closed 25, 26 Dec, 1 Jan. **Admission** £3.95; £3.50
3-17s; £2 2s; free under-2s. **Credit** MC, V.
Think of an idyllic English farm with a red-brick farmhouse
and a big old barn, an orchard, acres of wheat, chickens and
ducks, a carthorse and little woolly sheep bleating on the hill-
sides, the whole thing tucked snugly into a fold of the North
Downs. Well, you have successfully imagined Bocketts Farm.
Bocketts has been farmed continuously since the 18th century, and now that truly mixed farms are the exception rather
than the rule, it is a relic of a bygone age as well as a great
day out for the family.
   The first thing you'll see at the farm is the large covered
area where some of the friendlier animals are kept. On any
given day you may see goats here with their kids, Haggis the
Aberdeen Angus and his round-horned pals, Ernie the barn
owl obligingly staying up during the day to let visitors stroke
his soft back, and a menagerie of rabbits and other rodents
in the contact areas. You might even like to try your hand at
milking a (wooden) cow. The covered barn also ensures a
good time on wet winter days. Beyond the barn past the stables you'll find the race track. Yes, really – one of the highlights of a day at Bocketts Farm is the pig race, which takes
place twice a day and involves seven piglets racing hell for
leather up a hill to reach the pig nuts provided for them at the
top. Choose your colours and roar your chosen piglet on. Race
times vary, so phone for details.
   Three large and well-equipped play areas allow children to
run off steam and there are indoor and outdoor bale moun-
tains to climb on and jump off. A pedal-tractor circuit provides amusement for younger kids and there are some
endearingly old-fashioned games such as Bowling for a Pig
(not a live one…) and a giant wooden jigsaw to complete.
Tractor and trailer rides allow small children to reach more
of the farm before their legs give out and pony rides are perennially popular.
   The Old Barn tea rooms sell hot and cold food and a small
selection of baby foods, along with ice-creams, teas and coffees. There are plenty of high chairs and a wall of bead mazes
and puzzles at the back. The well-stocked shop back in the

covered animal enclosure sells some of the large outdoor play equipment in use on the farm as well as clothing, toys, games and knick-knacks, all with an agricultural theme.
Buggy access. Café. Nearest picnic area: on site. Shop.

Other farms

Binghams Park Farm
Potten End Hill, Water End, Hemel Hempstead, Herts (01442 232373/shop 01442 243300/ www.binghams.co.uk). By train Berkhamstead rail. By car M25 (Junction 20), A41, then A4146 to Potten End, or M1 (Junction 8), then A4146) to Potten End. **Open** 9am-5.30pm/dusk daily. Closed 25-27 Dec, 1 Jan. **Admission** £3; £2.50 concessions, 2-16s; free under-2s. **Credit** MC, V.
A traditional farm open throughout the year with special activities – such as treasure hunts and nature quizzes – for children at weekends and during school holidays. Take home a scarecrow or a corn dolly, or a bird box for your own garden. Or come in winter for a nature ramble along frosty woodland trails. If you hold your children's party here, the kids will be introduced to and can feed the animals, make a birthday scarecrow to take home, have a tractor ride, as well as enjoy a picnic supplied by yourself. During October there is an Apple Weekend, British Cheese Week, Half Term Pumpkin Workshops and a Pumpkin Festival with haunted tractor rides; there are Autumn Nature Rambles in November, while in December you can visit 'Farmer Christmas' in the woods. Note that the 'Pick Your Own' season starts in June (British Strawberry Week).
Buggy access. Café. Car park. Nappy-changing facilities. Nearest picnic place: picnic area on grounds. Shop.

Godstone Farm
Tilburstow Hill Road, Godstone, Surrey (01883 742546/ www.godstonefarm.co.uk). By train Caterham rail, then 409, 410, 411 bus. By car M25 (Junction 6). **Open** Mar-Oct 10am-6pm daily. Nov-Feb 10am-5pm daily. Closed 25 Dec. **Admission** £3.95 2-16s, including one adult; free under-2s. **Credit** AmEx, MC, V.
This forty- acre Surrey farm has been tramped by millions of small feet since it opened to the public in 1980. It has become a favourite day-out location for the schools and preschools, and wandering its spacious animal enclosures and play areas, it's easy to see why. The cows, goats, sheep, hens, ducks, geese and small animals of Godstone are an obvious draw. For some of them, namely the sheep and poultry, their role in the rural education of pre-school urban-ites goes beyond merely ambling about in pastures and pens: the sheeps are used in shearing displays in spring, while the fowl provide eggs for the incubators, where the hatching process is carried out in the public gaze.

When the animals have been duly admired and petted, small children make an undignified rush for the huge covered barn, where a fantastic assortment of rides on tractors, trucks, bikes and trolleys can be trundled about at speed, with fond parents and teachers looking on from benches. If the weather's fair, the adventure playground, on the top field, is terrific, with its wooden walkways, ropes, tyres, tunnels, slides and a set of ropes on pulleys, which children love to do their best Tarzan impersonations on, and which inevitably become the focus for some heated arguments when one group of children is accused by another, of hogging them. Cool them down with ice-creams from the shop, lunch from the café, or a serene bunny-cuddling session.
Café. Car-park. Nappy-changing facilities. Shop.

Close encounters of the woolly kind.
Ashdown Llama Farm. *See p280.*

Odds Farm Park
Wooburn Common, High Wycombe, Bucks (01628 520188/www.oddsfarm.co.uk). By train Beaconsfield rail. By car M40 (Junction 2), or M4 (Junction 7). **Open** Oct-Dec 10am-4pm Thur-Sun (last entry 3.30pm). Jan-Mar 10am-4pm (last entry 3.30pm) daily. 10am-5pm (last entry 4.30pm) daily. **Admission** £4.25; £3.75 concessions; £3.25 2-16s; free under-2s. **Credit** MC, V.
Feed rabbits and from babies' bottles, or collect eggs from the chickens at this friendly hands-on farm. Tractor and trailer rides take place daily through the summer (weather permitting). You can even hold your child's birthday party here – there are two private rooms to choose from: 'Bunnies Burrow' or 'Piggies Playpen', which can be hired from 10.30am to 12.30pm or 1.30 to 3.30pm (half an hour later in the summer) at a cost of £8.95 per child over 2 years (under-2s £5.20), which includes entrance to the farm park, a bag of special animal food for each child, free admission for 4 adults, party food and goodie bags. Note that admission prices are due to rise in March 2002.
Buggy access. Car park. Nappy-changing facilities. Shop.

Days Out

Two sides of **Drusillas Park**.
A visitor

South of England Rare Breeds Centre

Highlands Farm, Woodchurch, Ashford, Kent (01233 861493/www.rarebreeds.org.uk). By train Ashford rail. By car M20 (Junction 10), then A2070, B2067. **Open** *May-Sep* 10.30am-5.30pm daily. *Oct-Apr* 10.30am-4.30pm Tue-Sun. Closed 25, 26 Dec. **Admission** £3.50; £3 concessions; £2.50 3-15s; free under-3s. **Credit** AmEx, MC, V.

The South of England Rare Breeds Centre gives visitors the chance to see British breeds that were once common, such as cows with handlebar horns, sheep with long, curly fleece and spotty pigs, ginger pigs, tall ducks, as well as the now-famous 'Tamworth Two'. Children can get hands on with the animals, enjoy beautiful woodland walks and trailer rides and get the coolbox out and tuck into its contents in the picnic areas. Throughout the year there's a host of special events for both kids and their parents, such as Hallowe'en and Christmas activities, craft and gift markets, and Easter Bunny hunts.

Buggy access. Café. Nappy-changing facilities. Nearest picnic place: picnic area in playpark. Shop.

The call of the wild

Drusillas Park

Alfriston, East Sussex (01323 874100/ www.drusillas.co.uk). By train Polegate rail. By car M23 or A23, then A27. **Open** *Summer* 10am-6pm daily. *Winter* 10am-5pm daily. Last entry 1hr before closing. Closed 24-26 Dec. **Admission** £7.99; £5.99 concessions; £6.99 3-13s; free under-3s. **Credit** MC, V.

If Howletts (*see p279*) is a walk on the wild side, Drusillas Park is a far more manageable proposition for smaller children. Residents include monkeys, penguins, rats, meerkats, mongooses, porcupines, beavers, otters, owls, ring-tailed lemurs, ruffed lemurs, cervals, llamas, maras (which look like a cross between a hare and guinea pig), snakes, spiders, crocodiles, iguanas, fish, mice, birds, pigs, wallabies, emus, cows, sheep, goats, Shetland ponies – all of them small, most of them friendly, and with imaginatively designed enclosures to allow maximum interaction with their small visitors. The viewing bubbles in the meerkats' enclosure, for example, allow visitors to get very close to the perennially curious meerkats.

Drusillas is an easy day out with children. The park isn't huge so it's kind to shorter legs and there's nowhere you can't get to with a buggy. One of the three picnic areas is under cover, and the restaurant is a friendly-looking jungle-themed place that serves all the usual child favourites plus a small selection of baby jars. Drusillas also recognises that children need to let off steam and they have set aside well-equipped areas for the purpose. The acre-square playground incorporates swings, slides, ropes and climbing frames and there's an indoor play barn for wet weather. Other attractions include panning for gold, the new jungle adventure golf course and a train ride through the llama paddock. Toddlers are specially catered for in their own play zone where they can enjoy the ball pit and the ride-on toys away from the flying feet of their older siblings. End the day with a trip to the wacky workshop, where you can get involved in mask-making and other arty activities with an animal theme.

Buggy access. Cafés. Nappy-changing facilities. Nearest picnic place: picnic areas on grounds. Restaurant. Shops.

... and a native.

Howletts

Bekesbourne, near Canterbury, Kent (01227 721286/ www.howletts.net). By train Bekesbourne rail. By car A2 towards Dover from Canterbury, turn off at Bekesbourne turning, follow signs. **Open** *Nov-Mar* 10am-dusk daily (last entry 2.30pm). *Apr-Oct* 10am-6pm daily (last entry 4.30pm). Closed 25 Dec. **Admission** £9.80; £7.80 concessions, 4-14s (£7.80/£6.20 if booked in advance on website); £28 family (2+2), £32 (2+3); free under-4s. **Credit** MC, V.

Howletts Wild Animal Park is an achievable day trip from London. It's a two-hour drive, or an hour and forty minutes by train. Incongruously close to the edge of the Cathedral City, Howletts is home to elephants, tigers, Atlas lions, gorillas, antelopes and many more beautiful and dangerous creatures besides, housed in conditions as close to their natural habitat as possible. Founded by the late and eccentric John Aspinall in 1958, it's an extraordinary place that has had major successes in breeding animals back from the edge of extinction. Now it's home to the largest family group of gorillas in captivity, and a 16-strong breeding herd of African elephants. Aspinall attributed the breeding programme's success to the close bonding fostered between the animals and their keepers but acknowledged the risks attached to his controversial practice.

Bring a picnic to one of the designated areas or eat at the Conservatory Restaurant. The gift shop sells soft toys, pocket money toys and T-shirts among other animal-themed merchandise. The whole park is buggy-friendly.

See below for Port Lympne, also set up by John Aspinall. *Buggy access. Nappy-changing facilities. Nearest picnic place: picnic area on park. Restaurant. Shop.*

Port Lympne Wild Animal Park

Lympne, nr Hythe (01303 264647/www.howletts.net). By train Ashford rail, then link bus. By car M20 (Junction 11), then follow signs. **Open** *Oct-Mar* 10am-2.30pm (last entry), closes dusk. *Apr-Sept* 10am-4pm (last entry) closes 6pm. Closed 25 Dec. **Admission** £9.80, £7.80 children; £28 family (2+2), £31 family (2+3). **Credit** AmEx, DC, MC, V.

The sister wild animal park to Howletts near Canterbury (*see above*), both set up by John Aspinall. This one is more like a safari park: the grounds are vast, set on a hilltop with gorgeous views overlooking Romney Marsh and the beasts have plenty of room in which to roam. In fact, parents of toddlers should think twice before setting off on the full circuit: many of the more thrilling animals (tigers, wolves, gorillas) are close to the main house, while the herd animals are to be seen grazing further away. The house (which is open to the public) was built for Sir Philip Sassoon and has a fine muralled room by Rex Whistler.

Buggy access. Café. Car park. Nappy-changing facilities. Picnic area. Shop.

More wild animals

Marwell Zoological Park

Colden Common, Winchester, Hants (01962 777407/ www.marwell.org.uk). By train Eastleigh rail, then bus. By car M3 (Junction 11), then B2177 or M27 (Junction 10 westbound/Junction 5 eastbound). **Open** *Summer* 10am-6pm daily (last entry at 4.30pm). *Winter* 10am-4pm (last

entry at 2.30pm). **Admission** £9, £8 concessions; £6.50 3-14s; free under-3s; £29.50 family (2+2). **Credit** MC, V. Leopards and zebras, red pandas and golden lion tamarins, as well as birds, reptiles, amphibians and fish – there's plenty to see at Marwell. Take the train round the park and see how many of the park's 200 species you can spot. Penguin World is an award-winning enclosure with Humboldt penguins, where the birds can be seen underwater through three large viewing windows. World of Lemurs is a pretty walled garden setting for rare primates from Madagascar. The warm atmosphere of Tropical World is a rainforest in microcosm with exotic plants, frogs, butterflies, chameleon and the tiny mouse deer. The park is fully accessible for disabled visitors and has facilities for a complete day out, including a family restaurant, picnic areas and children's amusements.
Buggy access. Café. Nappy-changing facilities. Nearest picnic place: picnic areas on grounds. Restaurant. Shop.

Whipsnade Wild Animal Park
Whipsnade, Dunstable, Beds (01582 872171/ www.whipsnade.co.uk). By train Luton or Hemel Hempstead rail, then taxi or bus (both about 10 miles away from the Park). By car M25 (Junction 21) or M1 (Junction 9 and Junction 12), then follow signs. **Open** *Mid Feb-mid Mar* 10am-5pm daily. *Mid Mar-early Oct* 10am-6pm daily. *7-27 Oct* 10am-5pm daily. *End Oct-mid Feb* 10am-4pm daily. Last entry 1hr before closing. Opening times for 2002 may change, phone to check. **Admission** £10.70; £8 concessions; 3-15s; free under-3s. £2 car park opposite the main gate. *Tours* free tour bus around the park; phone for times. Car entry into the Park £8.50 (£4.25 for members). **Credit** AmEx, MC, V.

Whipsnade Wild Animal Park is one of Europe's largest wildlife conservation parks and is set in 600 acres of beautiful parkland on the Chiltern Hills. Home to more than 2,500 animals, many of which are endangered in the wild, there is a whole host of family favourites to enjoy: elephants, giraffes, bears, tigers, rhinos, hippos and many more. Children will especially love the Runwild Play Area, Children's Farm, the Great Whipsnade Railway (as will frayed parents) and the penguin feeding, but the Birds of the World demonstrations, Squirrel Monkey Island and Tiger Falls are also hugely popular. Get there early during peak times if you want to make the most of the place.
Buggy access. Café. Car park. Nappy-changing facilities. Nearest picnic place: picnic area on grounds. Restaurant. Shop.

Woburn Safari Park
Woburn Park, Beds (01525 290407/ www.woburnsafari.co.uk). By train Leighton Buzzard, then taxi, or Flitwick, then taxi. By car M1 (Junction 13). **Open** *Mar-Oct* 10am-5pm daily. *Nov-Feb* 10am-3pm Sat, Sun. Closed 25 Dec. **Admission** *early Mar-late July, early Sept-late Oct* £12.50; £9.50 concessions; £9 3-15s; free under-3s. *Late July-early Sept* £13; £10 concessions; £9.50 3-15s; free under-3s. *Family tickets* 2 adults and 2 or more paying children: £2 off second and subsequent children. 1 adult and more than 2 paying children: £2 off third and subsequent children. **Credit** MC, V.
The Duke of Bedford's vast grounds have been turned over to a grand safari park, home to lions, Siberian tigers, bears, wolves, monkeys, elephants, rhinos, and so on. The idea is to drive your car (as many times as you like in a day; it takes about an hour) around the grounds, getting up close to the various beasts who'll either ignore you or maybe nibble at your car aerial. After that full-on experience, you can take a swan boat on to the lake, or repair on foot to see squirrel mon-

keys, penguins, lorikeets and, from 2002, sealions in their new pool. There are plenty of play areas for children (of varying degrees of difficulty) and a railway line that chunters around the safer parts of the park. Once finished with the animals, adults may like to visit the spectacular Woburn Abbey with its stunning Tudor portraits, but their children probably won't let them.
Buggy access. Café. Nappy-changing facilities. Nearest picnic place: on site. Restaurant. Shop.

Special interest

Ashdown Llama Farm
Wych Cross, Forest Row, East Grinstead, West Sussex (01825 712040/www.llamafarm.co.uk). By train East Grinstead rail, then taxi. By car M25 (Junction 6), then A22. **Open** 10am-5pm daily. Closed 25, 26 Dec. **Admission** £3; £2.75 concessions; £2.50 3-16s; free under-3s. **Credit** MC, V.
Get eyeball to eyeball with the elegant supermodels of the animal kingdom at Ashdown Llama Farm. Forget what you've heard about llamas' unappealing personal habits – they only spit when they're upset and the llamas at Ashdown Farm have nothing to be unhappy about. This is the largest herd of breeding llamas in the country and depending on the time of year visitors may get to see exceptionally cute and adorable baby llamas wobbling along behind their mothers on spindly legs. One of the farm barns houses a fibre exhibition, if you want to find out more about knitting a llama suit. There are picnic areas and a large and spacious play area for children when the llamas have had enough of their attentions. The gift shop sells a beautiful range of alpaca knitwear, and llamabilia such as traditional South American hats made from llama wool. Friendly staff will tell you all you could ever need to know about rearing llamas, alpacas and mohair goats for their wool. And in fact it all begins to sound rather appealing.
Buggy access. Café. Nappy-changing facilities. Nearest picnic place: picnic area on grounds. Shop.

Birdworld
Holt Pound, Farnham, Surrey (01420 22140/ www.birdworld.co.uk). By train Aldershot, Bentley or Farnham rail, then taxi. By car A3, then A31. **Open** *mid Feb-Oct* 9.30am-6pm daily. *Nov-mid Feb* 9.30am-4.30pm daily. Closed 25, 26 Dec. **Admission** £9.25; £7.25 concessions; £6.25 3-14s; £27.95 family (2+2); free under-3s. **Credit** MC, V.
The 26-acre park outside Farnham in Surrey is home to dozens of species of bird from England's native wren to the rather more exotic vulture. A daily highlight is watching the penguins cluster round their keeper to be fed – book in advance and you can even feed them yourself. Penguin Island is the park's most popular attraction; you can see them diving and playing underwater from the viewing enclosure. Bird enclosures and aviaries are organised according to habitat, so the seabirds all hang out on a route called the Seashore Walk, and native birds can be seen in the woodland part. The place for exotics and parrots is hot and sticky. The park is good buggy terrain with plenty of wide, smooth paths. The restaurant overlooks the wildfowl pond, but on a fine day the picnic areas allow for a pleasant lunch to the sound of birdsong. Little children enjoy Jenny Wren Farm and the playgrounds, bigger ones are entranced by the birds of prey and their daily diet of dead chicks.
Buggy access. Café. Nappy-changing facilities. Nearest picnic place: picnic area on grounds. Restaurant. Shop.

Gardens

Bedgebury, The National Pinetum

*Goudhurst, Cranbrook, Kent (01580 211044/
www.forestry.gov.uk). By train Etchingham or Tunbridge
Wells rail (Heritage Hopper bus service runs between
May-Sept on Sat, Sun, bank hols). By car A21 SE of
Tunbridge Wells, then B2079.* **Open** 10am-7pm/dusk
daily (last entry 2hrs before dusk). **Admission** £3, £2.50
concessions; £1.20 5-16s; free under-5s. **Credit** MC, V.
Bedgebury Pinetum is the National Conifer Collection, and
boasts the finest collection of conifers in the world. Originally
planted by Viscount Marshall Beresford of Bedgebury, an
officer of Wellington at Waterloo, the pinetum was founded
as a joint venture between the Forestry Commission and the
Royal Botanic Gardens at Kew, with the first plants (having
been raised at Kew) being planted in Bedgebury in 1925. The
pinetum is an all year round attraction, from spring, when the
wildflowers, rhododendrons and azaleas are ablaze with
colour, to winter when many of the conifers are at their best.
Above all, it's a fabulous place for a picnic (and hide and seek),
whether by the lake or spread out among the trees. There are
a number of activities hosted during the summer, such as tree-
planting, and special events (such as 'Fungi – friend or foe')
feature throughout the year, many of which are organised by
the Education Department. Disabled access is limited and a
fit helper is essential. Note that the café is closed on a Monday.
*Buggy access. Car park. Nearest picnic place: picnic areas
throughout the Pinetum. Shop.*

RHS Gardens, Wisley

*Wisley, Woking, Surrey (01483 224234/www.rhs.org.uk).
By train West Byfleet or Woking rail, then taxi or bus.
Wisley Bus runs from Woking to Wisley May-Sept (call
01483 224234 for times). By car M25 (Junction 10), then
follow signs.* **Open** *Mar-Oct* 9am-6pm Mon-Sat. *Nov-Feb*
10am-4.30pm Mon-Sat (last entry 30min before closing).
Sundays garden open to members and their guests only.
Closed 25 Dec. *Tours* by arrangement only. **Admission**
£5; £2 6-16s; free under-6s. **Credit** MC, V.
Wisley is the flagship garden of the Royal Horticultural
Society, so this is really one for grown-ups, though there's
plenty to impress the young ones, too. Highlights include the
magnificent Rock Garden, rock pools and Alpine Houses, a
splendid array of Glasshouses and a delightful woodland garden, which erupts with colour during spring. During the year
the education department hosts a number of demonstrations,
workshops and exhibitions relating to anything remotely horticultural – phone for further details and prices.
*Buggy access. Car park. Nappy-changing facilities. Nearest
picnic place: on grounds. Restaurant. Shop.*

Seaside

London's more 'local' seasides, at least the ones
accessible by train, are of the resort variety. Wild
and rocky coastlines and empty sandy beaches may
be the stuff of idyllic family holidays, but a day-
return train ticket from the smoke buys you an
altogether more bumptious sort of seaside. If you're
up for a whiff of ozone, a stick of rock, pleasure
beaches, piers and playgrounds, try trendy
Brighton, saucy **Southend** or brassy **Margate**.
They're all within 90 minutes of the capital.

Brighton

It's always an exciting moment, walking down the
hill from Brighton railway station and catching
your first sight of the sea. Since Regency times,
Londoners have been making this seaside
pilgrimage, which combines not only a blast of
English Channel air, but also hedonistic city fun
in abundance. Children will have absolutely no
reason to whine that they are bored as there's
stacks here to keep them amused. Just don't
come here expecting a tranquil day on the
pebbled beach (which, incidentally, provides
parents of younger children with the ideal excuse
for owning an all terrain pushchair). Brighton
is phenomenally busy, and its eight million annual
visitors all seem to descend on the place during
hot summer weekends. People come here to enjoy
the buzz, and for families that means a trip to
glittering, tacky **Brighton Pier**, where
archetypal seaside fun awaits.

Many millions have recently been spent on
redeveloping the seafront, and the new meandering
Promenade running between the piers provides
constant entertainment. The beach has been
decorated with large sculptures, some of which make
great climbing frames for the little ones. They also
enjoy stopping off to watch the action on the beach
basketball court and neighbouring volleyball court
(which also makes a fantastic sandpit). In season
you'll often find free music, theatre and dance events
at the Ellipse performance area. And if that fails
to thrill, there are always flocks of exotic street
performers, and also fairground rides, the most
splendid of which is an 1888 carousel. If the family
is feeling active, you can hire roller blades, scooters
and bikes, including tandems and quadricycles.
This may be an especially good option if you have
a teenager in tow.

The newly arrived £1 million children's free play
area by the **West Pier** has proved a boon to visiting
parents. Colourfully themed on pirates and tropical

Brighton breezy

Brighton has the most to offer a day-tripping
family. This is what we like to do beside
this particular seaside:

● Hanging out at the **Promenade** between
the two piers. *See above.*

● Cooling off at the new seafront **playground
and paddling pool** by the West Pier. *See p282.*

● Making friends with the fish at the **Brighton
Sea Life Centre**. *See p282.*

● Whiling away an afternoon shopping in
the **Lanes**. *See p282.*

Days Out

seas, it boasts three interlocking play areas, including a paddling pool, sandpits and dry play equipment. The latter is especially useful as it provides something to do all year round. There are also children's showers and toilets, disguised as beach huts.

If things are getting too frenetic and you have lost sight of your brood in the crowd one time too many, head either east of the Pier, where the beach is more expansive and quieter, but also rather run down and drab. The **Volks Electric Railway** is near here. There's a section of naturist beach along here, frequented mostly by gay men.

Alternatively, walk on from the West Pier to **Hove**. The promenade is wider, quieter and the adjacent lawns make a good place for a picnic. Go into **Brunswick Square** to feast if you need some shade (which is in short supply on the seafront). It's dog free here, so you can safely kick a ball about, unlike the gardens in nearby Adelaide Crescent and Palmeira Square, which are plagued by poo. Kite fliers on the Hove stretch make a colourful spectacle on breezy days.

On bad weather days you can happily spend a few hours at the **Sea Life Centre**, a large underground aquarium. There's a ball pond facility attached to the café, which you can use without paying admission if you are eating there. Or for a bit of culture, take the kids to the **Royal Pavilion**, where they can learn all about this most exotic royal palace commissioned by the Prince Regent in 1811. Or you could wander around the **Lanes** and **North Laine**, a maze of little shops to rival Covent Garden. Children especially enjoy the **Animal House** (12 Bond Street, 01273 206836), stocked floor to ceiling with cuddly animals from all around the world.

Try your luck in **Brighton**'s seaside amusements.

Attractions

Brighton Pier
(01273 609361/www.brightonpier.co.uk). **Open** *Winter* 10am-11.30pm daily. *Summer* 9am-11.30pm daily. **Admission** free.
The Palace of Fun is a noisy state-of-the-art amusement arcade screaming with aggressive simulators and flashing slot machines. The end of the pier has the fun fair rides, including a collection of smaller rides for children, and two roller coasters. In theory, the funfair rides are meant to be working while the pier is open, but in practice they are often shut at the beginning and end of the day, and when trade is quiet.
Bars. Buggy access. Café. Nearest picnic place: benches on pier. Restaurants. Shops.

Brighton Sea Life Centre
Marine Parade, Brighton (01273 604234/ www.sealife.co.uk). **Open** *mid Feb-Oct* 10am-6pm daily. *Nov-mid Feb* 10am-4pm daily. Last entry 1hr before closing. Closed 25 Dec. **Admission** £6.50, £4.25 4-14s; £18.25 family (2+1); £22.25 (2+2); £26.25 (3+2); £29.75 (2+4); free under-4s. **Credit** AmEx, MC, V.
As an island nation we are of course surrounded by the creatures of the deep and the 130-year-old Brighton Aquarium is a fine place to get to know them. Meet the locals – flounder and mackerel and whiting and bass. Then get to grips with the big guys – the sharks in Brighton's extraordinary underwater tunnel, the gliding rays who seem to love coming out of the touch pool to have their tummies stroked. Children usually love the seahorses, bobbing placidly along like little aliens. Most of the centre is accessible to buggies, all except the viewing platform above the sharks, but you can get quite close enough to these beasts inside the glass tunnel. When you've had enough of watching the fish, you can scoff a plateful of their cousins (with chips) in the Sea Life café.
Buggy access. Café. Nappy-changing facilities. Nearest picnic place: beach, benches on seafront. Shop.

The Royal Pavilion
Old Steine, Brighton (01273 290900/ www.royalpavilion.brighton.co.uk). **Open** *June-Sept* 10am-6pm daily. *Oct-May* 10am-5pm daily. Closed 25, 26 Dec. *Tours* 11.30am, 2.30pm daily. **Admission** £5.20; £3.20 5-16s; £13.60 family (2+up to 4); £8.40 family (1+up to 4); free under-5s. *Tours* £1.25 per person (no child reductions). **Credit** AmEx, MC, V.
When George IV asked the country's finest craftsmen to build him a jolly beach house, he was rewarded with one of the most fanciful, opulent and at times downright camp buildings in the country. With its onion domes and rooms full of showy furniture, it would look at home next to the Taj Mahal. Parents of babies be warned: it isn't pushchair friendly, unless you are strong enough to negotiate steep stairs, and there's nowhere to leave your buggy folded up.
Café. Nappy-changing facilities. Nearest picnic place: Pavilion gardens. Shop.

Volks Electric Railway
285 Madeira Drive, Brighton (01273 292718). **Open** *Easter-mid Sept* 11.15am-5pm Mon-Fri; 11.15am-6pm Sat, Sun. **Tickets** £1.30 single, £2.30 return; 70p, £1.20 return 5-14s; £3.10, £5.70 return family (2+up to 3); free under-5s. **No credit cards.**
This is the oldest electric passenger carrying train in the world: most of its carriages are over 100 years old. It takes you on a ride along the beach from the Palace Pier to

Or simply stroll along the beach.

Blackwater. The one-way journey drops you about three minutes from Brighton Marina, which is fun to stroll round and play a game of 'which boat would you choose for your cruise?' Peter Pan's playground is also along here, which has fairground rides, mostly for small children, and is a quieter alternative to the pier.

Nearest picnic place: beach, benches on seafront. Shop.

Eating & drinking

The seafront is awash with chic bars and restaurants, most with ample outdoor space to accommodate families, although high chairs and nappy-changing facilities are in short supply. The fish and chip outlets are an easy and cheap option. You can buy a children's fish and chip meal for just 99p (one per full paying adult) on the pier. Cross Kings Road for the **Regency** (no.131, 01273 325014), a tourist favourite, frying up what some rate as the best fish and chips in town, with a big family welcome. Or for a more sophisticated seafront restaurant experience go to **Alfresco** (Milk Maid Pavilion, Kings Road Arches, 01273 206523) for good Italian food and splendid views (main courses from £6). Even though there is no specific children's menu, the place welcomes youngsters, which is just

as well, as it now finds itself next door to the newly arrived £1 million children's free play area (by the West Pier). The place we like best, however, is the **Dorset Street Bar** (corner of Gardener Street and North Lanes, 01273 605423), where the children's menu runs to quite sophisticated meals of moules marinière and smoked salmon bagels, as well as nugget/sausage/egg and chips combos. The milkshakes are very good and colouring-in facilities are provided.

Tourist information

10 Bartholomew Square, Brighton, BN1 1JS (0906 7112255/www.visitbrighton.com (premium rate 50p per minute).
Information centres are located at Bartholomew Square and Hove Town Hall.

Getting there

By car: Journey time from central London is about two hours on the M23/A23. Be aware that parking is expensive and prices go up seasonally. Follow the signs to car parks in the city centre, but be prepared

Days Out

to queue at weekends. Many central car parks are short-term only with the daytime hourly rate rising after four or six hours. There are cheaper car parks at Trafalgar Street, London Road, Carlton Hill, Brighton Station and east of the Palace Pier on Madeira Drive (pay and display). You need parking vouchers for the streets (from shops and garages), or pay and display.

Parking on the streets in Hove is less competitive than Brighton, although in both areas much that is centrally located is residents only.

By train: Victoria has a speedy 49-minute connection (for information, call National Rail enquiries on 08457 484950/www.connex.co.uk). Journeys are a little longer from King's Cross and London Bridge (timetables are available on www.thameslink.co.uk).

Margate

The flashiest resort on the Isle of Thanet (Kent's most easterly tip), Margate is downmarket, but winsome. Like many 'kiss me quick' style seaside resorts, its attractions seem outdated, yet the more innocent charms of this historic old town make it unbeatable for a nostalgia trip, and the sandy beach is a delight.

One of Margate's best points is its practically beach-side station. You can struggle off the Victoria train, laden with buckets and spades, cross the main road via a typically marigold-heavy ornamental roundabout, past the reasonably well-kept loos (bear those in mind when visiting with small children), down some steps and you're ankle deep in golden sand.

Unless you're down on a particularly hot bank holiday weekend, you can usually find a patch of sand to call your own on Margate's main beach. It doesn't have a blue flag (the nearest blue flag beach to Margate is pretty Birchington, a few stops up the railway line), but it has won awards for its clean and tidy beach.

When the tide is out, rock pools reveal themselves, much to the delight of crab-obsessed young children, who dabble in them with nets and crab lines. When the tide is in, you still seem to have to wade quite far before the water comes up to your waist. The tameness of the millpond-flat sea, and its warmth in summer, make it comfortable for lolling about with small children, beach-ball throwing and floating lazily on your back. Margate is the only seaside we've seen where young women go for a bathe with their bags still on their shoulders.

It's easy to spend the whole day on the beach, especially if you hire a windbreak and parasol from the many beach-furniture providers operating from huts on the sands. Deckchair hire costs £1, plus 50p

deposit. Rubber rings, cheap buckets and spades, beach balls, ice-creams, drinks and snacks are sold from beach stalls, so there's no need to further investigate the gift shops on Marine Parade, but of course, you have to.

There's a special pedalo pool and lido fenced off from the sea with floating buoys. Pedalo hire costs £5, which seems a bit steep, seeing as you only get to sail your vessel around quite a restricted circuit. You only have to part with £1 to ride on one of the beach's four donkeys, which amble up and down the sands doing their best, mournful Eeyore impressions and enduring passionate hugs from their diminutive jockeys. The donkeys start out from the beach playground, which is a rather sweet mini funfair for small children, where all the 'rides' (bouncy castles, swingboats, Thomas the Tank Engine roundabouts) cost 50p and prove irresistible to the under-fives.

Those 50ps soon fly out of your purse, however, and worse is to come if older children and teenagers discover **Dreamland Fun Park**, Margate's answer to Chessington (actually, it makes Chessington look like Disneyworld).

If you can wrest the children away from Margate's number one visitor attraction, there are other, much more quirky places to explore. Combine a trip to Margate Caves with a peek at the strange Shell Grotto, but call both places first; the Grotto, in particular, has erratic opening hours.

Attractions

Drapers Windmill
St Peter's Footpath, Margate (01843 226227). **Open** *May-Sept* 2-5pm Sun. *July, Aug* 6.30-8pm Thur; 2-5pm Sun. **Admission** £1; 20p under-16s; £2 family (2+2). **No credit cards.**
This Kentish Smock mill was restored by the Drapers Windmill Trust and contains a small museum. The sails go round when there's wind enough and there's someone competent enough to operate the mill. Make this landmark a picturesque point for a picnic after walking along St Peter's Footpath from Margate's historic old church of St John, off Margate High Street. Always phone before visiting as the place is staffed by volunteers.
Nearest picnic place: field behind windmill. Shop.

Dreamland Fun Park
Belgrave House, Belgrave Road, Margate (01843 227011). **Open** High season *Easter, July, Aug, 1st week Sept, Oct half-term* 11am-10pm daily. Low season 11am-5.30pm daily. **Admission** free; rides priced individually; day pass wristbands (allowing free access to rides) £11.99; £7.99 children (under 1.35metres in height). **Credit** MC, V.
Dreamland is 'the largest seaside leisure complex in southern England', according to Margate's brochure. It is extensive, but some of the rides may seem tame to theme park aficionados. The rickety Scenic Railway rollercoaster is a must, if only for historical reasons (it was built in 1863). Other, newer, tummy-flipping rides include the Frisbee, like a pendulum that turns 360 degrees with you in it, the Looping Star, which also turns you upside down and the Log Drop, which makes your stom-

ach drop. Go for a reviving walk on the beach before sampling candy floss, hot dogs, popcorn and other goodies, which may come back to haunt you on the Wild Mouse rollercoaster. *Buggy access. Cafés. Nappy-changing facilities. Nearest picnic place: beach. Shops.*

Margate Caves
1 Northdown Road, Margate (01843 220139).
Open *Easter-Oct* 10am-4pm daily. *July, Aug, bank hols* 10am-5pm daily. *Tours* free, for pre-booked groups of 15 or more people. **Admission** £2; £1 5-16s; £5 family (2+2); free under-4s. **No credit cards**.
These man-made caverns, hewn from Margate rock, are about a ten-minute walk from the beach (Tourist Information will provide you with a map to find them). They were once used by smugglers and have also been a prison, and a church during periods of religious persecution. They're currently used as an effective means of silencing small children fizzing with E numbers after an overdose of candy floss and the other type of Margate rock. Ring before visiting, as this is a one-man show. *Nearest picnic place: benches outside caves. Shop.*

Shell Grotto
Grotto Hill, Margate (01843 220008). **Open** *Easter-Oct* 10am-5pm Mon-Fri; 10am-4pm Sat, Sun. Hours can vary; phone first to check. **Admission** £2; £1 under-16s; £5 family (2+2). **Credit** MC, V.
Victorian schoolboys, digging in a field, discovered this extraordinary curio: a series of underground tunnels lined with 2,000 square feet of shell mosaics. Opinion is still divided as to who created them. Are they pagan (as HG Wells thought), or are they a more recent folly? Whatever, they're amazing and worth seeking out. The grotto is a short walk from Margate Caves (*see above*), so people usually take in both landmarks on their Margate tour.
Café. Nearest picnic place: Dane Park. Shop.

Eating & drinking

Margate has no shortage of fish and chip, burger and pizza shops, all very cheap and none very good. It is more rightly famous for its dearth of decent places to eat. For prime location and a varied menu, you can't beat the Marine Sands café, right on the beach, and run by a very efficient, smiley woman, who serves up hot roasts to the pensioners, nuggets and chips to the children and scampi and salad to bikini-topped teenagers. The **Spread Eagle** (25 Victoria Road, 01843 293396) is worth leaving the beach for. Its ale is real, its grub hearty and its children's menu hits the spot. The new Wetherspoons pub, the **Mechanical Elephant** (28-30 Marine Terrace, 01843 234100) has a pleasant designated family area, where children must stay, and choose between turkey dinosaurs, fishy whales, sausages and other delights on the menu.

Tourist information

11-13 The Parade, Margate, Kent CT9 1EY (01843 220241/www.tourism.thanet.gov.uk). **Open** *Oct-Easter* 9.15am-4.45pm Tue-Sat. *Easter-Sept* 9.15am-4.45pm Mon-Sat; 10am-4pm Sun.

Getting there

By train: Margate and Birchington are only 1 hour and 30 minutes from Victoria station (trains depart every 30 minutes). Margate station is a few minutes from the beach.
By car: M2 from London, then A28 to Margate.

Southend

Don't say 'Sarfend', the locals get narky, but this, the closest seaside resort to London, really is chirpy Cockney country. The brevity of the train ride here, and the variety of attractions that have built up around the seven miles of gentle estuary coastline make it a Big Treat option for children of all ages.

Southend is the largest town in Essex and one of the main providers of that great tooth-rotting seaside essential: rock. Southend's rock factory provides the sweeties for Brighton and many other southern resorts, and its ice-cream plant keeps holiday makers across the country refreshed. The only thing that Southend lacks is decent sand, but the powers-that-be have sorted that little problem: they ship it in, tons of the stuff, to provide the sort of golden sand that everyone demands for their castles. Estuary mud does not feel right between the toes.

Bucket-and-spade shops, ice-cream and sweet sellers, purveyors of shell boxes, pictures and windchimes and of course 'Kiss me Quick' hats line the prom. When you're duly equipped with beach essentials – beachballs, windbreaks, rubber rings and sun block – descend to the strand and set up camp. If the tide's out, there's a long walk to a decent swim, although each of Southend's beaches has outdoor paddling pools (as well as showers and loos) to keep mini bathing beauties happy till the tide comes in.

The beaches have Tidy Britain Group Seaside Award Flags and the favourite with children is **Three Shells**, because it's next to the pier. Leigh, five minutes down the line from Southend Central, offers a quieter vibe, a lovely beach and an excellent seafood restaurant.

Southend's pier is rightly famous. Jutting 1.33 miles out to sea, it's the main attraction for day trippers, especially those whose children aren't clamouring for **Adventure Island**, the resort's surprisingly large theme park.

If the weather's dodgy, holiday makers make a beeline for the newly refurbished **Sea Life Adventure**, not far from the pier, where a Little Tikes Play Centre is an added attraction when the fish pall.

Attractions

Adventure Island

Marine Parade & Western Esplanade, Southend (01702 468023/www.adventureisland.co.uk). **Open** *Easter-mid Sept* 11am-8pm or 11pm daily, depending on weather. *Oct-Mar* 11am-6pm or 8pm Sat, Sun, bank hols. **Admission** free but rides extra. **Credit** MC, V.

They say they have more rides than Chessington or Thorpe, here. A bold and perhaps misleading statement, but there's no denying that Adventure Island is good value for money. Fans of rides with names like the Dragon's Claw, the Vortex, Green Scream (after too much pistachio ice-cream perhaps?) and Raging Flume may find their wristband day pass gives them all the thrills they can handle, if the queues aren't too long. Small children enjoy the roundabouts and Viking Boat rides and love jolly Mr Smee's Adventure, the new Jungle Safari. There are places to eat, or enjoy a picnic and all the ice-cream, popcorn and candy floss you can handle.

Buggy access. Cafés. Nappy-changing facilities. Nearest picnic place: Adventure Island gardens. Restaurant. Shops.

Sea Life Adventure

Eastern Esplanade, Southend (01702 601834/ www.sealifeadventure.co.uk). **Open** 10am-7pm daily. Closed 25 Dec. **Admission** *Aquarium only* £4.95; £3.50 concessions; £3.50 4-16s; free under-4s. *Combined ticket for Aquarium & Play Centre* £5.50. *Play Centre only* £2 under-4s; £3 4-16s. **Credit** MC, V.

After a ten-month refurbishment programme, the new owners have reopened the centre which now includes a Little Tikes adventure play area, a cafeteria and a whole new load of British and exotic sea life. There's a rule against touching rays, but you can still watch them gliding about in an open pool; the sharks still eye you from an overhead tunnel, lobsters and crabs lurk in rockpools, sticklebacks remind parents of their childhoods and jellyfish and piranhas give everyone the heeby jeebies. Phone for details of school-holiday events: one of the most popular is the 'rockpool talk', when children are allowed to get hands-on with the inhabitants of the centre's rocky enclosures.

Buggy access. Nappy-changing facilities. Nearest picnic place: beach, picnic area in Sea Life Adventure gardens. Restaurant. Shop.

Southend Pier

Western Esplanade, Southend (01702 215622). **Open** *Summer* 8am-9pm Mon-Fri; 8am-10pm Sat, Sun. *Winter* 8am-dusk daily.

You can walk along it, or take the train (Southend is the only resort to have a pier train). Children enjoy the end-of-the-pier fun: there are rides, ice-creams and arcades. On the way, you can watch the fishermen reeling in dinner. Boat trips round the Southend coast start from the pier head, where the Pavilion hosts end-of-the-pier entertainments throughout the season. Admission to **Southend Pier Museum** (at the shore end of the pier; 01702 611214/614553) is 50p and accompanied children under 12 go free. Opening times are 11am-5pm Tue, Wed, Sat, Sun from the second week in May to late October. The museum explores the history of the pier since its beginnings, with an old pier train and interesting temporary exhibitions.

Eating & drinking

The best eating options are a bit of a walk from the seafront, but **Fisherman's Wharf** (Western Esplanade, SS1, 01702 346773) is a good catch for seafood lovers of all ages. It has a children's menu and a good line in shellfish, as well as fresh fish and chips. On the High Street, **Tommassi's** (no.9, 01702 435000) has a tempting Italian children's menu; many go for macaroni madness or chunky chicken dippers, then eye up the various ice-cream options. A walk away from the West Pavilion and Westcliff is **Piccolo's** (1-4 Shorefield Road, 01702 390370) for pizza, pasta and more varied Italian dishes. In pretty **Leigh-on-Sea**, five minutes down the Fenchurch Street line, is the highly thought of **Boatyard Restaurant** (8-13 High Street, 01702 477392), with its sun terrace and estuary views. The food is smart modern European, and small portions are served to children.

Tourist information

19 High Street, Southend-on-Sea, Essex SS2 6ER (01702 215120/www.southend.gov.uk). **Open** *Jan-July, Sept-Dec* 9.30am-5pm Mon-Sat. *Aug* 9.30am-5pm Mon-Sat; 11am-4pm Sun.

Getting there

By train: About seven trains an hour run from London's Fenchurch Street station to Southend Central (journey time 50 minutes). (National Rail Enquiries 08457 484950/www.c2c-online.co.uk). The same number run from Liverpool Street to Southend Victoria (same journey time). (National Rail Enquiries 08457 484950/www.ger.co.uk). **By bus**: National Express Coaches run from London Victoria (0990 808080/www.gobycoach.com). **By car**: M25, Dartford Tunnel, then A127 or A13 to Southend.

Other resorts

Broadstairs seems like Margate's more sensible older sister, and has a charming, staid atmosphere and more innocent amusements for the children. It also has the Charles Dickens connection: **Bleak House**, his holiday home, looks out over the sea. Ring (01843 583334) or log on to www.tourism.thanet.gov.uk for tourist information and brochures.

Clacton's sunshine coast in Essex has sandy beaches, amusements, a pier and watersports activities. More information from Clacton Tourist Information Centre (01255 423400/www.essex-sunshine-coast.org.uk).

Sandy beaches, a river estuary wall that offers excellent crabbing opportunities, a miniature railway and gentle fairground rides make **Littlehampton** a fabulous day out by the seaside. There are also boat trips to nearby

Arundel Castle. Call the Tourist Information Centre on 01903 713480 or go online to www.sussex-by-the-sea.co.uk.

Whitstable is one of Kent's most quirky beaches. It's shingle, but the water's warm and the famous seafront **Oyster Fishery Company** (booking essential, on 01227 276856/www.oysterfishery.co.uk) is one of the best restaurants in the south east for a family lunch. Ring the local tourist board on 01227 275482 or log on to www.canterbury.co.uk.

Rye is no longer by the sea, but just to the east is the vast and windswept **Camber Sands**, while to the west is ancient **Winchelsea** with its shingle and sand beach.

Steam Trains

Note that steam train timetables change month to month, but most lines run special trains to accommodate the half-term hordes. Ticket prices given are for round trips only; most prices are due to rise in January 2002.

Bluebell Railway

Sheffield Park Station, on A275 between Lewes & East Grinstead (01825 723777/talking timetable 01825 722370/www.bluebell-railway.co.uk). By train East Grinstead rail, then 473 bus. By car M23 (Junction 10), then A275. **Open** *Easter-Sept* daily. *Oct-Apr* Sat, Sun, school hols, bank hols. **Admission** £8; £4 3-15s; £21.50 family (2+3); £6.40 concessions; free under-3s. **Credit** MC, V.

The Bluebell Line was the UK's first preserved standard gauge passenger railway, re-opening part of the Lewes to East Grinstead line of the old London Brighton & South Coast Railway in 1960. Since then it has developed into one of the largest tourist attractions in Sussex. There are special events, such as the 'Stepney Specials' – as part of their two-train service over the half-term, you can travel behind *Stepney* as he pulls his special train between Sheffield Park and Kingscote. Also, from October until Christmas Eve, there are a series of *Santa Specials*, which run from Sheffield Park to Kingscote, a nine-mile journey through the Sussex country-side, and through the atmospheric Sharpthorne tunnel, on the way to Kingscote. The ticket price includes a meeting with Santa as you board the train, a gift for your child, mince pies for the adults (a glass of wine is extra), children's entertainer and a free ride on the children's roundabout. The Santa Special tickets start at £3 for children (rising to £9 in the observation car) and £10 for adults; all children under the age of one go free. If all of this is bringing out the trainspotter in you, why not sign up for a one-day course (8am to 4.30pm) on driving a steam engine (there are eight people on each course and after one hour's briefing you can use the controls, driving under instruction. There is also a five-day course, during which you'll get to fire the engine too. Call for details on 01273 731873.

Buggy access. Café. Car park. Nappy-changing facilities. Nearest picnic place: at all stations. Shop.

Legoland's learner drivers. *See p289.*

Be prepared

Theme parks often have their own microclimates – there may be blazing sunshine all the way there but that doesn't mean the day will be fine from start to finish. Here are a few essentials for a great day out.

- A light mac or cagoule
- Layers of clothes – cardigan or sweatshirt, T-shirt
- Waterproof trousers or shorts (skirts tend to get soaked in log flumes and cling to your legs)
- Trainers or comfortable shoes
- A rucksack with cartons of drinks, fruit, biscuits and sandwiches
- Wet wipes
- Books, tapes and games for the journey.

Didcot Railway Centre

Didcot, Oxon (01235 817200/ www.didcotrailwaycentre.org.uk). By train Didcot Parkway rail. By car M4 (Junction 13), then A34, or M40/A40 then follow signs. **Open** 10 days in Feb, early Apr-Sept, 1wk in Oct, 27 Dec-1 Jan daily, 10am-4pm or 5pm. Last entry 30min before closing. *Tours* bank hols (times depend on events; phone for details). **Admission** *incl tour* £6.50; £4.50 3-16s; £5.50 concessions; £19 family (2+2); free under-3s. **Credit** MC, V.
Isambard Kingdom Brunel designed his Great Western Railway to be the finest in the world. Today you can visit the Railway Centre and enjoy the smell, sound and smoke of the steam engines, and see the activities of a steam locomotive depot, including engines being coaled, watered and turned on the turntable. The admission price includes unlimited travel on the trains during your visit. Thomas the Tank Engine is a big draw here – there are rides behind 'Thomas' as well as lots of children's activities.
Buggy access. Café. Car park. Nappy-changing facilities. Nearest picnic place: picnic grounds at centre. Shop.

Kent & East Sussex Railway

Tenterden, Northiam & Bodiam stations (01580 765155/ www.kesr.org.uk). By train Headcorn rail, then link bus to Tenterden. By car A28 off M20. **Open** *May-Sept* trains run 10.30am-4.40pm daily; weekends only at other times of year; ring for details. **Tickets** £7.50; £3.75 3-15s; £20 family. **Credit** MC, V.
The main base is at the thriving market town of Tenterden, but you can also join this fabulous old steam railway line at Northiam or Bodiam. Trains, carriages and line have been scavenged and rebuilt by a motley band of galloping enthusiasts, who dress up in period costumes and drive their steam and diesel engines through 10-odd miles of exquisite English countryside. If you stop at Bodiam you can visit the medieval castle (*see p273*), otherwise the round trip takes about two hours. There's a reduced service in winter, but the trains run all year: at Christmas you can board the Santa Express for mince pies and mulled wine; Thomas the Tank Engine is a predictable year-round visitor. For details of 2002 train times, or to receive a timetable and dates of special

events, ring the above number. Note that the facilities for disabled visitors are particularly good on this line.
Buggy access. Café (Tenterden and Northiam stations). Car park. Nearest picnic place: facilities at all three stations. Shop.

Romney, Hythe & Dymchurch Railway

New Romney Station, Kent (01797 362353/ www.rhdr.demon.co.uk). By train Folkestone Central rail, then 711 bus to Hythe. By car M20 (Junction 11), then follow signs. **Open** *Mar-Oct* weekends only. *Easter-Sept* daily; ring for train timetable info as times change monthly. **Admission** £9.50, £4.25 children. **Credit** MC, V.
A miniature railway barrels merrily from the Nuclear Power Station in Dungeness (a weird, wild promontory that's also home to an RSPB Nature Reserve/01797 320588 and a desolate pebble beach) all the way to Hythe in the East. Along the way it stops at New Romney and the coastal village of Dymchurch, the self-proclaimed 'Children's Paradise' which boasts an amusement park and a fine sandy beach. It also passes some beautiful, flat scenery and seems to sweep through any number of back gardens. The railway was built by the millionaire racing driver Captain Howey in 1927 and everything (track, engines, the sweetest carriages) is one third actual size. It's a real treat – on a warm day.
Buggy access. Cafés (2). Nappy-changing facilities. Nearest picnic places: all stations. Shops.

The Watercress Line

The Station, Alresford Hampshire (01962 733810/talking timetable 01962 734866/ www.watercressline.co.uk). By train Alton rail. By car A3, A31 to Alton. **Open** changes monthly; ring for details. Closed Jan. **Tickets** £9; £2 3-16s; £20 family. **Credit** MC, V.
The little Hampshire town of Alresford is famed for its watercress beds; the dark green leaves that grow here are eaten all over the country. Now it's the dark-green steam engines, however, that bring the tourists to this neck of the woods. The line is run by keen volunteers, who finally fulfilled their dream of resurrecting the old trains in 1977. The trains run throughout the year, and their route takes in rolling Home Counties countryside at its most alluring.
Although the mid-Hants Watercress Line is based in Alresford, it's easier to catch one of its puffing stars from the prosperous market town of Alton, which has a direct rail link with London's Waterloo. The ten-mile, two-hour round trip to Alresford can be broken up by stopping at the smart village stations of Ropley, or Medstead & Four Marks between the two main stations. Both places provide some pretty picnic places: Ropley has a children's play area and souvenir shop, as well as the engine shed and yard to look over; Medstead and Four Marks Station is quiet and countrified, with some wonderful woodland walks about half a mile away. It's worth noting that Alton has a very high concentration of picturesque pubs for relaxed family lunches. Alresford, slightly less busy, is a touch more upmarket, and has some beautiful places to walk, smart shops to visit, and friendly inns to lunch in. The Information Office here can furnish you with leaflets and friendly advice about what to do in and around the town. On certain days during the school holidays the blue train dresses up and makes like Thomas the Tank. Ring to request a timetable and to find out about the next TT day, in addition to other themed children's days, such as the teddy bears day or Santa specials at Christmas.
Buggy access (footbridge at Alton). Nearest picnic place: designated area at Ropley station. Shop.

Don't worry about the elephants at **Chessington World of Adventures** – they're not real.

Theme Parks

Chessington World of Adventures

Leatherhead Road, Chessington, Surrey (0870 444 7777/ www.chessington.com). By train Chessington South rail. By car M25 or A3 (Junction 9). **Open** *late Mar-end Nov times vary; phone for details.* **Height restrictions** *varies on rides.* **Admission** *on the day* £19.95, £12 concessions; £16 4-12s; £63 family (2+2 or 1+3), free under-4s. *Online advance bookings (undated)* £18; £14 4-12s; £59 family. *Online advance bookings (dated)* £17; £13 4-12s; £55 family. Allow minimum 2 days to process advance ticket purchases. *Unlimited entry pass* (includes all Tussaud's attractions) £219 family; £70 individual, valid for one year. **Credit** MC, V.

Is it a zoo or is it a theme park? Well, actually it's a bit of both. Genuine thrill seekers would be more at home at Thorpe Park or Alton Towers, the more grown-up attractions in the Tussaud's stable, but for a totally absorbing day out there's not much better than this. From the front gate you can choose to ride the Safari Skyride, a good bet because it helps you to get an overview of the park before you choose where to home in on and you get a bird's eye view of the seal enclosure into the bargain. The zoo aspect of the park has recently been enhanced by the Trail of the Kings enclosures in Animal Land where you can be a whisker away from some big cats or whoop it up with the gorillas. Visitors can learn more about animals like Persian leopards, Sumatran tigers, Asian lions and three generations of gorillas, including Shani's new baby Shanga born in March 2001 via African-style game lodges. There are many other species to encounter too spread out over the vast 65-acre park. Be sure not to miss feeding time for the seals and discover the habits of insects down in the Creepy Caves. Aside from your swinging safari there are more traditional rides to explore. Divided into zones The Mystic East, Forbidden Kingdom, and Mexicana. The big three are Samurai with its gyrating rotor arms, Rameses Revenge, and the big coaster Vampire (which is closed for 2001 but will return revamped for serious thrill seekers in 2002). Beanoland has a new addition in the Bash Street Bus ride but the whole area is a bit of a let-down as most of the attractions are old end-of-the-piet type coconut shy stalls which you have to pay extra to enjoy. The Action Man assault course by contrast is good hands (and knees) on fun. New for 2001 are Toadie's crazy cars and the pink knuckle delights of the Berry Bouncers in the gentle Toytown zone, and even the Flying Jumbos are experiencing a technicolour renaissance with their new lick of paint. For pit stops there's Pizza Hut, KFC, McDonalds. There's also a whole host of themed restaurants the best of which are the Mexican Diner and the Krazy Keg family inn.

Buggy access. Café. Car park. Nappy-changing facilities. Shops.

Legoland

Winkfield Road, Windsor, Berks (08705 040404/ www.legoland.co.uk). By train Windsor and Eton Riverside or Windsor Central rail. By car B3022 Windsor/Ascot Road. **Open** *mid Mar-early Nov* 10am-5pm or 6pm daily (until 7pm during school hols). **Admission** £19; £16 3-15s; £13 concessions. *Two-day peak pass* £26; £23 children. *Two-day off-peak pass* £36; £29 children. *Annual peak pass* £55; £46 children. *Annual off-peak annual pass* £36; £29. **Credit** AmEx, MC, V.

Putting the 'theme' back in theme park, Legoland's cute characters hold fort with their particular brand of construction-brick fun. Catering solely to the younger end of the market, there are no hair-raising adventures to be had here, but kids can pan for gold, float in balloons, drive their own boats, and thrash through the water on jet skis into the bargain. Queues inside the park can be horrific, so head off early and make a bee-line for the Driving School area before the

Expect showers at **Thorpe Park**.

throngs descend. The Dragon rollercoaster, Spinning Spider dodgems and Space Tower are among the most thrilling experiences here but there's nothing too frightening, and plenty for the very young in the Duplo Gardens. There's a bit more to do here than simply sit back and ride, with a range of self-powered vehicles to test your muscles, plus push button fountains to set off and plenty of interactive opportunities to enjoy in new Lego Creation Centre. This glass-fronted structure is where expert modellers will put the kids through their building paces and then there's a chance to design and road test your own computer-generated racing car. The walk-through model village only adds to the appeal of this gentle fun experience. Some of the attractions tie in with the latest Lego sets, all of which are available to buy on site, so you can continue the make-believe back at home, too. New for 2001 is Life on Mars, a 15-minute alien-filled show that's held at regular intervals in the theatre.

Pack some lunch and head to the picnic area at the rear of the park near the Wave Surfer jet skis or up by the mansion house, which is the safest bet for food as the on-site facilities are over-subscribed and very expensive for what you get. There are lovely walks to enjoy through tree lined avenues, a maze to discover and up at the castle you can buy rubber swords and have a go at your imaginary foes.

Buggy access. Cafés. Nappy-changing facilities. Nearest picnic place: picnic areas on site. Restaurants. Shops.

Thorpe Park

Staines Road, Chertsey, Surrey (0870 444 4466/ www.thorpepark.co.uk). By train Staines rail. By car M25 (Junction 11 or 13). **Open** *late Mar-early Nov* various times depending on season between 10am-5.15pm daily. **Height restrictions** varies, depending on rides. **Admission** *on the day* £19; £12-£14 concessions; £15 4-12s; £59 family (2+2 or 1+3); free under-4s. *Online advance bookings (open)* £17; £13 4-12s; £55 family. *Online advance bookings (dated)* £16; £12 4-12s; £51

family. *Advance phone bookings (open)* £18; £14 concessions, 4-12s; £57 family. *Advance phone bookings (dated)* £17; £14 concessions; £13 4-12s; £55 family. Allow minimum 2 days to process advance ticket purchases. **Credit** AmEx, MC, V.

Not the place to go if you're intending to stay high and dry. A visit to Thorpe Park is bound to include at least one close encounter with a large body of water, especially in Neptune's Kingdom, where chutes, flumes and slides abound. For starters there's the exhilarating but gut-clenching experience of hurtling through mid-air with nothing to hold on to but the handles of a plastic inflatable raft. After that, what could be better than swirling around and around in rapids with jets of water squirting at you from all sides? For those with nerves of steel, the aquatic adventure continues with Amity Coves' star attraction, the 85ft Tidal Wave log flume – is it fear or the G-force that's making you smile? And if that's not enough, how does a backwards rollercoaster ride in the pitch dark grab you? Big spills aside, there are milder forms of fun to enjoy.

A trip to Thorpe Farm is a ride in itself. Families can make the trip either by waterbus or via the railway to this enchanting turn-of-the-century working farm, complete with duck pond, rare breeds and children's petting area. Younger visitors might also like Ranger's County, with its jungle boats, attractive banana swingboats and the ranger's carousel, where kids can track down and tame their own big game. Newer attractions include Detonator, with its 100ft vertical drop, which slams a G-force of 5.5 into you; Vortex – a kind of sideways on ferris wheel 65ft in the air, which rotates at high speed 15 times per minute; and Zodiac, a Mexican hat-style ferris wheel rotating through 360 degrees. There's literally something for everyone, though for maximum fun it's best to visit in summer. Fuelling stops include Burger King, KFC and various themed diners.

Buggy access. Cafés. Nappy-changing facilities. Nearest picnic place: on site. Restaurants. Shops.

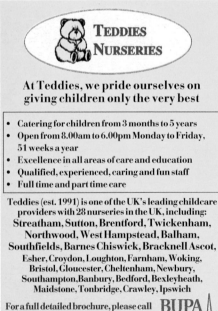

Directory

Directory

The following pages should come in useful when it comes to getting around, seeking help and learning more about the city. Where necessary, we've included full contact details.

Councils

Barnet, NW4
8359 2000/www.barnet.gov.uk.

Brent, HA9
8937 1234/www.brent.gov.uk.

Camden, NW1
7278 4444/www.camden.gov.uk.

Corporation of London
7606 3030/www.corpoflondon.gov.uk.

Ealing, W5
8579 2424/www.ealing.gov.uk.

Greenwich, SE18
8854 8888/www.greenwich.gov.uk.

Hackney, E8
8356 5000/www.hackney.gov.uk.

Hammersmith & Fulham, W6
8748 3020/www.lbhf.gov.uk.

Haringey, N22
8489 0000/www.haringey.gov.uk.

Hounslow, W4
8583 2000/www.hounslow.gov.uk.

Islington, N1
7527 2000/www.islington.gov.uk.

Kensington & Chelsea, W8
7937 5464/www.rbkc.gov.uk.

Lambeth, SW2
7926 1000/www.lambeth.gov.uk.

Lewisham, SE6
8314 6000/www.lewisham.gov.uk.

Merton, SW19/20
8543 2222/www.merton.gov.uk.

Newham, E6
8430 2000/www.newham.gov.uk.

Richmond-upon-Thames
8891 1411/www.richmond.gov.uk.

Southwark, SE5
7525 5000/www.southwark.gov.uk.

Tower Hamlets, E14
7364 5000/www.towerhamlets.gov.uk.

Waltham Forest, E17
8527 5544/www.walthamforest.gov.uk.

Wandsworth, SW18
8871 6000/www.wandsworth.gov.uk.

Westminster, SW1
7641 6000/www.westminster.gov.uk.

Education

Contact your local council for details of your local Early Years Partnership and Children's Information Service.

Advisory Centre on Education (ACE)
(0808 800 5793/Exclusion advice line 0808 800 0327/www.ace-ed.org.uk). **Open** *advice lines* 2-5pm Mon-Fri.
Ring for advice pertaining to your child's schooling.

Anti-Bullying Campaign
7378 1446.
If school bullies make your child's life a misery, contact the Anti-Bullying Campaign for practical advice.

British Association for Early Childhood Education
136 Cavell Street, E1 2JA (7539 5400/www.early-education.org.uk).
Ring the British Association for Early Childhood Education for information on education from birth to eight years. Send an SAE for extra information.

Gabbitas Educational Consultants
Carrington House, 126-130 Regent Street, W1B 5EE (7734 0161/www.gabbitas.co.uk).
Write to or ring Gabbitas, the independent schools consultants, for advice on choosing the right independent school for your child, and to receive a selection of suitable schools in your area. The *Gabbitas Guide to Independent Schools* costs £12.99 including p&p, and the *Gabbitas Guide to Special Needs* £16.99.

Home Education Advisory Service
01707 371854/www.heas.org.uk.
Call the service for information if you are thinking of educating your child at home, and to order information packs and leaflets. An introductory pack costs £2.50, and a year's subscription to the Home Education Advisory Service £11.

ISC Information Service
London & South East 7798 1560/www.iscis.uk.net.
The Independent Schools Information Service works to help parents find information about independent schools in their area.

National Association for Gifted Children
0870 770 3217/www.nagcbritain.org.uk.
Help and support for the parents of gifted children.

Parenting Education & Support Forum
8 Wakley Street, EC1V 7QE (7284 8389/www.parent-forum.org.uk). **Open** 10am-5pm Mon-Thur.
Information about parenting classes and support for parents.

Pre-School Learning Alliance
7833 0991/www.pre-school.org.uk.
Runs courses and workshops for parents of under-fives in pre-schools around the country. It also offers a pack for pre-school leaders wishing to run courses, called 'Looking at Learning Together'.

Fun & games

Indoor play

Crechendo
8772 8120/www.crechendo.com.
Crechendo runs active play classes throughout London. Children aged from four months to four years can take part in the programme. Ring the above number for details of your nearest class.

Gymboree Play & Music
0800 092 0911/www.gymboree.com.
A parent and child play organisation, based on music and movement, for children aged 16 months to 4 and a half years. New recruits receive a free trial session.

National Association of Toy & Leisure Libraries (NATLL)
7387 9592/www.natll.org.uk.
Provides information on the more than 1,000 toy libraries across Britain. Is also a good source of useful publications on related subjects.

Tumble Tots
0121 585 7003/www.tumbletots.com.
Tumble Tots is a parent-and-baby play class for children from six months up to school age. The children play on a range of equipment to help build co-ordination and

social skills. They also take part in music and singing sessions. Membership costs £14.50 per year; prices per session varies with the area. Ring this central number to find out about Tumble Tot play centres in your area.

One o'clock clubs

If a park has a one o'clock club, it's more likely to be geared up for children, and have well-maintained play equipment. These weekday clubs, which generally open around lunchtime (12.30-1.30pm) and go on until school's out, are a meeting place within a park for parents and carers of pre-school children. The best are in a pretty, tree shady part of the park, with outdoor play apparatus and ride-on toys, sand pit and sometimes a paddling pool in hot weather. In the indoor playroom are painting, Duplo, dressing-up and story-time options. Many have a noticeboard for advertising second-hand baby equipment, jumble sales, nanny shares and meetings. On sunny days parents bring picnics and lounge around chatting while minding immobile babies and keeping an eye on busy toddlers.

Below is a list of parks with one o'clock clubs. Most clubs stay open all year round (Monday to Friday, though some shut one day of the working week), closing only for bank holidays and those grey days between Christmas and New Year. Few charge admission, most merely ask for a contribution to the tea and coffee funds.

North London
Barnard Park *Copenhagen Street, N1 (7278 9494). Angel tube.*
Clissold Park *Stoke Newington Church Street, N16 (8809 6700). Bus 73.*
Finsbury Park *Young Children and Family Drop-in Community Centre, Jamboree Playhuts, Seven Sisters Road, N4 (8802 1301). Finsbury Park tube/rail.*
Highbury Fields *The Bandstand, Highbury Fields, N5 (7704 9337). Highbury & Islington tube/rail.*
Islands Club at the Grove *Alexandra Park, Muswell Hill, N22 (8883 7173). Bus 134, 144, 144A, W3, W7.*
Peggy Jay Centre *Parliament Hill Fields, NW5 (7485 6907). Gospel Oak rail.*

East London
Haggerston Park *Queensbridge Road, E2 (7729 6662). Bus 26, 48, 55.*

Millwall Park *Stebondale Street, E14 (7515 6807). Mudchute DLR.*
Springfield Park *Springfield Lane, E5 (8806 0970). Clapton rail/253 bus.* Just outside the park.
Victoria Park *Cadogan Terrace, E9 (8986 6150). Bus 277, S2.*
Wapping Park *opposite St Patrick's Church, off High Street, E1 (7481 9321). Wapping tube.*

South-east London
Crystal Palace Park *Crystal Palace Park Road, SE20 (8659 6554). Crystal Palace rail.*
Geraldine Mary Harmsworth Park *St George's Road, SE1 (7820 9724). Lambeth North tube.*
Kennington Park *Bolton Crescent, SE5 (7735 7186). Oval tube/36, 45, 131, 159 bus.*
Leyton Square *Peckham Park Road, SE15 (7639 1812). Bus 53, 78, 172, 381.*
Myatts Fields *Cormont Road, SE5 (7733 3609). Bus 45.*
Norwood Park *Salters Hill, SE19 (8761 1752). Gypsy Hill rail.*
Peckham Rye *Peckham Rye Road, SE15 (8693 0481). Bus 12, 63, 312.*
Ruskin Park *Denmark Hill, SE5 (7733 6659). Denmark Hill rail.*
Southwark Park *Hawkstone Road, SE16 (7231 3755). Canada Water tube/Surrey Quays DLR.*

South-west London
Agnes Riley Gardens *Corner of Clarence Avenue & Poynders Road, SW4 (8673 1277). Clapham South tube.*
Battersea Park *Prince of Wales Drive, SW11 (8871 7541). Bus 44, 319, 344, 345.*
Bishops Park *Rainbow Playroom, Stevenage Road, SW6 (7731 4572). Putney tube/14, 74, 220 bus.*
Brockwell Park *Arlingford Road, SW9 (8671 4883). Herne Hill rail.*
Clapham Common *Windmill Drive, SW4 (8673 5736). Clapham Common or Clapham South tube.*
Hillside Gardens *Hillside Road, SW2 (8678 0698). Bus 109, 250, 468, P13.*
Marble Hill Park *Richmond Road, Twickenham (8891 0641). Richmond tube/rail/Twickenham rail.*
Streatham Vale Park *Abercairn Road, SW16 (8764 3688). Streatham Common rail/60, 118 bus.*
Vauxhall Park *Fentiman Road, SW8 (7582 3209) Vauxhall tube/rail.*
Windmill Gardens *Blenheim Gardens, SW2 (8671 5587). Brixton tube/rail/ 3, 45, 109, 159 bus.*

West London
Acton Park *East Acton Lane, W3 (8743 6133). East Acton tube.*
Holland Park *Abbotsbury Road, W14 (7603 2838). Notting Hill Gate tube/31, 328 bus.*
Lammas Park *Playcentre, Elers Road, W13 (8810 0240). South Ealing tube.*
Meanwhile Gardens *Elkstone Road, W10 (8960 7894). Westbourne Park tube.*
Ravenscourt Park *Under-fives Centre, Ravenscourt Park, W6 (8748 3180). Ravenscourt Park tube.*

Health
Late-night chemists

Bliss Chemists
50-56 Willesden Lane, NW6 (7624 8000). Kilburn tube/98 bus. **Open** 9am-11pm daily; 9am-7pm Christmas Day & New Year's Eve. **Branch:** 5-6 Marble Arch, W1 (7723 6116). *Marble Arch tube.* **Open** 9am-midnight daily, 365 days a year.

Warman Freed Pharmacy
45 Golders Green Road, NW11 (8455 4351). Golders Green tube. **Open** 8.30am-midnight daily, 365 days a year.

Zafash Pharmacy
233-235 Old Brompton Road, SW5 (7373 3506). Earl's Court tube. **Open** 24 hrs daily, 365 days a year.

Support
Contact-A-Family
(7383 3555/helpline 0808 808 3555/ www.cafamily.org.uk). **Open** 10am-4pm Mon-Fri.
Ring the number to find out about local support groups for parents of children with disabilities.

National Asthma Campaign
(helpline 0845 701 0203/www.asthma.org.uk). **Open** 9am-7pm Mon-Fri.
Contact the campaign for advice and help if you, or your child, has asthma.

Serene (incorporating Cry-sis)
(7404 5011/www.our-space.co.uk/ serene.htm). **Open** 8am-11pm daily.
If a constantly crying baby has you in tears, contact Serene for advice and support.

Help for parents
Childcare

Academy Childcare
Family Zone, Victoria Station forecourt (7983 7219). **Open** 8am-6pm Mon-Fri; 10am-6pm Sat; 11am-5pm Sun.
Academy run crèches in lots of places; this one, in Victoria station, welcomes children aged three months to four years weekdays and 2-12 years weekends for up to four hours. There are all-day nursery places, too.

Bestbear
8675 3131/bestbear.co.uk. **Open** 24-hour answerphone.
Log on to the bestbear website for information about tried, tested and recommended childcare agencies and everything you need to know about hiring childminders, nannies, au pairs, or

Directory

Web wise

Many libraries have computer terminals with Net access. Ring your local council (*see* p294) to find one near you. Otherwise, visit one of the Internet cafés listed below, which admit babies and children. Food served tends to be of the sandwich, toastie and cake variety, accompanied by coffee, tea and soft drinks, although all of the following except easyEverything are licensed premises.

Café Internet
22-4 Buckingham Palace Road, SW1 (7233 5786). Victoria tube/rail. **Open** 9am-9pm Mon-Fri; 10am-8pm Sat; 10am-6pm Sun. **No credit cards. Map** p318 H10.
Internet access costs £1 per 15 minutes; £2 per hour.

Cyberia
39 Whitfield Street, W1 (7681 4200). Goodge Street tube. **Open** 9am-9pm Mon-Fri; 11am-7pm Sat; 11am-6pm Sun. **Credit** MC, V. **Map** p317 K5.
Internet access from 50p per 15 mins.

easyEverything
9-13 Wilton Road, SW1 (7233 8456/www.easyEverything. com). Victoria tube/rail. **Open** 24 hrs daily. **No credit cards. Map** p318 H10.
Internet access from £1 per hour. Branches around town.

Global Café
15 Golden Square, W1 (7287 2242/www.globalcafe.net). Piccadilly Circus tube. **Open** 9am-11pm Mon-Fri; 10am-11pm Sat. **Credit** MC, V. **Map** p318 J7.
Free Net access for members, annual membership £5.

Webshack
15 Dean Street, W1 (7439 8000/www.webshack-cafe.com). Tottenham Court Road tube. **Open** 10am-11pm Mon-Sat; 1-9pm Sun. **No credit cards. Map** p317 K6.
Net access from £1 for 40min.

becoming a child carer. Phone the information line if you have no access to a computer. Information packs cost £8 for parents and £4 for prospective carers.

Childcare Link
0800 096 0296/www.childcarelink.gov.uk. **Open** 9am-9pm Mon-Fri; 9am-noon Sat.
Parents can ring up, or log on, for information on childcare options open to them, and request leaflets on same.Where possible, callers will be given a list of childcare organisations in their area. The website also provides childcare contact details for parents.

Childminders
6 Nottingham Street, W1 (7935 3000/ www.childminders.co.uk). **Open** 8.45am-5.30pm Mon-Thur; 8.45am-5pm Fri; 9am-4.30pm Sat.
A long-established babysitting agency. Sitters on their books are locally based nurses, teachers and nannies across London.

Daycare Trust
21 St George's Road, SE1 6ES (7840 3350/ www.daycaretrust.org.uk). **Open** 9.30am-5.30pm Mon-Fri.
National childcare charity promoting high-quality and affordable childcare. Publishes useful booklets including *No More Nine to Five, childcare in a changing world* (£5).

Kids' Club Network
(7512 2100/www.kidsclubs.com). **Open** 9.30am-5.30pm Mon-Fri.
Information on after-school clubs.

Nannytax
PO Box 988, Brighton, East Sussex, BN2 1BY (01273 626256/www.nannytax.co.uk). **Credit** MC, V.
For £164.50 a year Nannytax will register your nanny with the Inland Revenue, issue his or her payslips and organise National Insurance payments. There's employment advice on the website for nannies, too.

National Family and Parenting Institute
430 Highgate Studios, 53-79 Highgate Road, NW5 1TL (7424 3460/ www.nfpi.org). Kentish Town tube/rail. **Open** 9.30am-5.30pm Mon-Fri/24 hour answerphone.
An excellent resource centre for all families, with factsheets and booklets on all aspects of parenting.

The Parent Company
6 Jacob's Well Mews, W1 (7935 0123/ www.theparentcompany.co.uk). **Open** 9am-5pm Mon-Fri.
Information and seminars on employing nannies.

Simply Childcare
16 Bushey Hill Road, SE5 (7701 6111/ www.simplychildcare.com). **Open** 9am-5.30pm Mon-Fri.
As the company has expanded so the name has changed, but the service of the organisation formerly known as the Register is the same. If you are seeking a nanny to work in or near London you can pay £22 for inclusion in three issues of this 32-page printed list (or £30 for five issues).

Entry on the list is free for prospective nannies looking for full or part-time work, or a nanny. There is also an information pack available for £9.95 including p&p.

Parent courses

Holy Trinity Brompton
7581 8255/www.htb.org.uk.
Run 'The Parenting Course' for parents with kids under the age of 12, and 'Parenting Teenagers', for parents of children aged 13-18. Both courses involve four two-hour sessions.

The Parent Company
7935 0123/www.theparentcompany.co.uk.
Runs seminars on weekday evenings on diverse subjects from time management to discipline. Seminars cost £45 per session per person, £60 for two people; ring for details.

Parent Network
(Parentline Plus 0808 800 2222/ www.parentlineplus.org.uk). **Open** 8am-10pm Mon-Fri; 9.30am-5pm Sat; 10am-3pm Sun.
Runs nationwide courses on how to cope with being a parent. For more details phone the free helpline, Parentline Plus.

Parent Support Group
(helpline 8469 0205/www.psg.org.uk). **Open** 24hrs.
As well as the helpline, staff run one-to-one support sessions and parenting skills courses to parents and carers of adolescents who are acting in an antisocial or criminal manner.

Parents for Inclusion
7735 7735/www.parentsforinclusion.org.
Organises a series of workshops for parents of disabled children. A helpline (7582 5008) operates 10am-noon, 1-3pm Tue-Thur.

Information

Literature

Families magazine
Families North PO Box 14965, NW3 5WA (7794 5690); **Families East** Enterprise House 113-115 George Lane, E18 1AB (8694 8694); **Families South East** PO Box 11591, SE26 6WB (8699 7240); **Families South West** PO Box 4302, SW16 1ZS (8696 1680); **Families West** PO Box 10820, W4 5GX (8930 4707); **Families North West** PO Box 357, HA1 1GF (8810 5388); **Families Upon Thames** PO Box Walton-on-Thames, KT12 5AG (01932 254584). www.familiesmagazine.co.uk.
All areas of London are covered by this informative freesheet, available in libraries, nurseries and selected children's shops, which lists places to visit, things to do, independent health practitioners and a wealth of information for anyone bringing up a child in London.

London Baby Directory
10 Grove Park Terrace, W4 3QG (www.babydirectory.com).
This is the ultimate listings book for parents. Priced £6.99, it is an A-Z of all the contacts

and services you'll ever need while bringing
up kids in London. There are now directories
for the Home Counties and the north-west.
Log on to the website for further info.

Time Out magazine
*Universal House, 251 Tottenham Court
Road, W1T 7AB (7813 3000).*
For up-to-the-minute information about
where to go and what to see in London, check
out the Around Town and Children sections.

Libraries

Every local borough has a string
of libraries to its name; we don't
have the space to list them all.
Below is a selection of large,
central London libraries with
good children's sections.

Barbican Library
*Barbican Centre, Silk Street, EC2 (7638
9447/www.barbican.org.uk). Barbican
tube/Moorgate tube/rail.* **Open** 9.30am-
5.30pm Mon-Fri; 9.30am-7.30pm Tue;
9.30am-12.30pm Sat. **Map** p320 P5.
The children's library here has comfortable,
raked seating and a big, well-organised
choice of titles. Occasional events are laid on
for the under-fives, but space is limited and
admission is on a first-come-first-served
basis. Ring the children's library to find out
what's on for kids in the next month or so.

Commonwealth
Resource Centre (CRC)
*The Commonwealth Institute, Kensington
High Street, W8 (7603 4535/
www.commonwealth.org.uk). High Street
Kensington tube.* **Open** 10am-4pm Mon-Sat.
The CRC is a comprehensive focal point for
material about Commonwealth countries. It
is ideally suited to students studying for
school projects, with more than 20,000
books, atlases, periodicals, travel guides,
plus a wealth of multimedia resources. The
Institute hosts temporary exhibitions by
contemporary artists throughout the year,
which focus on the Commonwealth and
related themes. Visit the website to find out
what's on; it may help with your homework.

Kensington & Chelsea
Central Library
*Phillimore Walk, W8 (7937 2542). High
Street Kensington tube.* **Open** 9.30am-8pm
Mon, Tue, Thur; 9.30am-5pm Wed, Fri, Sat.
Map p314 A9.
Under-fives are treated to a story session
10.30-11am every Tuesday. It's a popular
slot, and as numbers are limited to 30, it's
worth picking up your free ticket earlier in
the week. On Mon, Tue and Thur homework
club runs 3.30-6.30pm. The Children's
Library is a pleasant place to be, with little
chairs in the under-fives section and
window seats to sit and read in.

Marylebone Library
*109-117 Marylebone Road, NW1 (7641
1041/www.westminster.gov.uk/libraries).
Baker Street tube/Marylebone tube/rail.*

Open *Children's Library* 9.30am-5.30pm
Mon, Tue, Thur, Fri; 10am-5.30pm Wed;
9.30am-1pm, 2-5pm Sat. **Map** p313 F4.
This children's library has a huge selection
of books and educational resources for
young people of all ages. There are two
under-fives sessions every week: at 10.30-
11.30am on Tuesdays children enjoy a story
session and craft activities; at 2.15-3.15pm
on Thursdays the play is more toy-based.

Victoria Library
*160 Buckingham Palace Road, SW1 (7641
4289/www.westminster.gov.uk/libraries).
Victoria tube/rail.* **Open** 9.30am-7pm Mon,
Tue, Thur; 10am-7pm Wed; 9.30am-5pm
Sat. **Map** p318 H10.
The Children's Library has its under-fives
sessions, with toys and stories, every
Wednesday at 10-11.30am and a monthly
special event. The cheerful library staff also
organise events and activities for young
children up to eight throughout the year.
These mostly take place around the school
holidays, and are geared to seasonal
festivals, such as Hallowe'en and Christmas.
There are summer reading schemes, parties
and puppet shows also planned.

Travel

The prices we've listed for
transport and services were correct
at the time of going to press, but
bear in mind that some prices
(especially those of tube tickets) are
subject to a price hike each January.

Public transport
information

All the information below can
be accessed online at
www.transportforlondon.gov.uk
and www.thetube.com, or by
phoning 7222 1234. **Transport
for London**, or TfL (formerly
London Transport) also runs
Travel Information Centres, which
provide maps and information
about the tube, buses, Tramlink,
riverboat, Docklands Light
Railway (DLR) and National Rail
Services within the London area.
You can find them in the following
rail and tube stations: Brent Cross
Bus Station, Euston Station,
Hammersmith Bus Station,
Heathrow Airport Terminals,
King's Cross Station, Liverpool
Street Station, North Greenwich
Bus Station, Oxford Circus Station,
Paddington Station, Piccadilly
Circus Station, St James's Park

Station and Victoria Station, and
West Croydon Bus Station.
    To find out more about Mayor
Ken Livingstone's **Transport
Strategy for London**, log on to
the Greater London Authority
website www.london.gov.uk.

Transport for London's
Accessibility Unit
7491 4600.
Ring this number to find out which tube
stations are buggy friendly and which bus
routes have low-floor buses.

London Transport
Users' Committee
*Clements House, 14-18 Gresham Street,
EC2V 7PR (7505 9000).*
This is the official watchdog monitoring
customer satisfaction with transport in
London; it campaigns for a better deal for
London travellers.

Capital Transport
7388 2489.
Campaigns for accessible, affordable,
safe and reliable transport in London.

Fares & tickets

Adult fares
The single underground fare for adults
within Zone 1 is £1.50, or £1.90 for Zones
1 and 2, rising to £3.60 for an all-zones (1-6)
single fare. Single bus fares are 70p for a
journey outside Zone 1 and £1 for a
journey within Zone 1 or one which crosses the Zone
1 boundary.
    If you are staying in London for more
than a day, it's always better value to buy
a Travelcard (*see p298*).

Child fares
On all buses, tubes and local trains, under-
16s are classified as children; under-5s
travel free. Under-16s pay a child fare until
10pm; after 10pm (buses only) they pay an
adult fare. Fourteen- and 15-year-olds must
carry Child Photocards, available from any
post office: take a passport-size photo and
proof of age (passport or birth certificate)
with you. The single underground fare for
children in Zone 1 is 60p, or 80p covering
Zones 1 and 2; rising to £1.50 for an all-zone
(1-6) ticket. Single child bus fares cost 40p to
anywhere in London.

One-Day LT Cards
One-Day LT Cards will only be of interest if
you intend to travel during peak times (ie
before 9.30am on weekdays) and make
several journeys during the day. They are
valid on buses (including night buses),
underground services (except those running
to and from Bakerloo line stations north of
Queen's Park; this section of track is not run
by Transport for London) and Docklands
Light Railway (DLR) services, but not on
overland rail services or airbuses. The cards
cost £5.10 for Zones 1 and 2; £6.20 for Zones
1-4 and £7.70 for Zones 1-6 (child £2.50
Zones 1 and 2; £3 Zones 1-4; £3.30 Zones 1-6).

Travelcards

These can be used on the tube system, buses, rail services within London, Docklands Light Railway and some Green Line buses, and can be bought at all tube and rail stations as well as at appointed newsagents. Travelcards also entitle you to one-third off the cost of travel on scheduled riverboat services. The most convenient cards for short-term visitors are the One-Day or One-Week Travelcards, though monthly and yearly tickets are also available for longer stays.

One-Day Travelcards can be used after 9.30am on weekdays and all day at weekends. You can make unlimited journeys within the zones you select. They cost £4 for Zones 1 and 2, £4.30 for Zones 1-4 or £4.90 Zones 1-6 (£2 for a child all-zone ticket). One-Day Travelcards are now valid until 4.30am and can be used on N-prefixed night buses.

Family Travelcards are available for families and groups of one or two adults travelling with between one and four children. Like regular One-Day Travelcards, they are valid after 9.30am Monday to Friday and all day on weekends and public holidays, and can be used until 4.30am; they cost £2.60 for Zones 1 and 2, £2.80 Zones 1-4 or £3.20 Zones 1-6 (child 80p Zones 1-6).

If you'll be travelling on consecutive weekend days, it's probably worth getting a **Weekend Travelcard**, which allow travel on consecutive weekend days or public holidays, and are valid on N-prefixed night buses. They cost £6 for Zones 1 and 2, £6.40 Zones 1-4 and £7.30 Zones 1-6 (child £3 Zones 1-6).

One-Week Travelcards offer unlimited journeys throughout the selected zones for seven days, including use of N-prefixed night buses, and are valid around the clock. Weekly Travelcards cost £15.90 for Zone 1; £18.90 for Zones 1 and 2; £22.40 for Zones 1-3; £27.60 for Zones 1-4; £33.30 for Zones 1-5; £36.40 for all zones (child £6.60 Zone 1; £7.70 Zones 1 and 2; £10.30 Zones 1-3; £12.80 Zones 1-4; £14.10 Zones 1-5; £15.40 Zones 1-6).

Carnet

If you're planning on making a lot of short-hop tube journeys within Zone 1 over a period of several days, it makes sense to buy a carnet of ten tickets for £11.50 (£5 for children). This brings down the cost of each journey to £1.15 rather than the standard £1.50. Note that if you exit a station outside of Zone 1 and are caught with only a carnet ticket, you are liable to a £10 penalty fare.

'Saver' tickets

If you make a number of single journeys by bus, buy a book of six single bus tickets in advance of travel, to be used on all bus services, including night buses. A book of adult tickets costs £3.90, while the children's rate is £2.10.

Photocards

Photocards are required for all bus passes and Travelcards except the One-Day and Weekend versions. Child photocards are required for 5- to 15-year-olds using child Travelcards and bus passes. Fourteen and 15-year-olds need a child photocard in order to buy any ticket at the discounted rate.

London Underground

Timetable

Tube trains run daily, starting at around 5.30am every day except Sunday, when they start an hour to two hours later depending on the line. The only exception is Christmas Day, when there is no service. Generally you won't have to wait more than ten minutes for a train, and during peak times the service should (in theory) run every two or three minutes. Times of last trains vary, though they're usually around 11.30pm-1am every day except Sunday, when they finish 30 minutes to an hour earlier.

The only all-night public transport is by night bus (*see below*).

Docklands Light Railway (DLR)

7363 9700/www.dlr.co.uk.
The DLR is administered as part of the tube system. Its driverless trains run on a raised track from Bank (Central or Waterloo & City lines) or Tower Gateway, close to Tower Hill tube (Circle and District lines), to Stratford, Beckton and down the Isle of Dogs to Island Gardens, then under the Thames to Greenwich and on to Lewisham. Trains run from 5.30am to around 12.30am Monday to Friday, 6am-12.30am Saturday and 7.30am-11.30pm Sunday.

The DLR is keen to promote itself as much as a tourist attraction as a transport system. To this end it offers Rail and River Rover tickets, which combine unlimited travel on the DLR with a riverboat trip between Greenwich and Westminster Piers (boats departing from 10.30am to 6.30pm; *see p299*) plus discounts on selected museums and sights. Starting at Tower Gateway, special trains leave on the hour (from 10am) with a DLR guide giving passengers the low-down on the area as the train glides along. Tickets cost around £7.80 for adults, £3.90 for children; family ticket £20.50 (two adults and up to three children).

Buses

Travelling on London's extensive bus network is one of the most pleasurable ways of getting to know the city. However, allow plenty of time: progress through the invariably dreadful traffic can be very slow. Certain routes still use the venerable red Routemaster buses (the ones you can hop on and off at the back) but modern buses are taking over. The latter are cheaper to run as they are operated by a single driver/conductor, but this also makes them slower.

Night buses

Night buses are the only form of public transport that runs through the night. They operate from around 11pm to 6am, about once an hour on most routes (more frequently on Fridays and Saturdays). All pass through central London and the majority stop at Trafalgar Square, so head there if you're not sure which bus to get. All types of Travelcard are accepted on night buses. Pick up a free map and timetable from one of the LT Travel Information Centres.

Night bus fares from central London are the same as day-time fares, however there are no child fares.

For more information call the London Buses helpline on 7918 4300. For free local guides and bus timetables call 7371 0247.

Green Line buses

Green Line buses (0870 608 7261/www.greenline.co.uk) serve the suburbs and towns within a 40-mile (64km) radius of London. Their main departure point is Eccleston Bridge, SW1 (Colonnades Coach Station, behind Victoria).

Stationlink buses

The red and yellow Stationlink buses are convenient for the disabled, the elderly, people laden with luggage or those with small children. The service connects all the main London rail termini (except Charing Cross) on a circular trip. Buses run every hour from about 9am to 7pm (phone for details). The fare is £1 for adults, 50p for fives to 15s. For information call 7222 1234.

Rail services

National rail enquiries

0845 748 4950.
Ring this number to find out how the trains are running on your route, and timetable information.

Independently owned commuter services run out of all the city's main line rail stations. Travelcards are valid on these services within the relevant zones. **Silverlink** (01923 207258, www.silverlinktrains.co.uk) is a useful and underused overground service that carves a huge arc through the north of the city, running from Richmond (in the south-west) to North Woolwich (in the east), via London City Airport. The line connects with the tube network at several stations.

Families who frequently travel by rail together may consider investing in a **Family Railcard**, which for £20 gives two adults, two other adults, and up to four children discounted fares on most off peak journeys. Adults save a third of the ticket price; children 60%. The card usually lasts 12 months, but until May 2002 you can buy one that lasts 15.

Tramlink

Launched in May 2000 in the Croydon area, the tram service links you to the tube network at Wimbledon and national rail services at Mitcham Junction, East and West Croydon, Beckenham Junction, Elmers End and Birkbeck stations, and to the south London bus network. The single adult fare is 90p in one zone (zones 3 or 4) and £1.30 for travel in both. There is a flat fare of 40p for children. You can also buy a One Day bus and tram pass (£2.80 adult; £1.20 children). Weekly tram passes cost from £8 (£4 children).

Water transport

Often overlooked, the river makes a speedy way of getting about, and is less congested than other modes of transport. The times of services vary, but, as a rule, most operate every 20 minutes to one hour between about 10.30am and 5pm. Services may be more frequent and run later in summer. Call the individual operators below for details of schedules and fares. The names in bold below are the names of piers: the central ones are on the maps at the back of this Guide.

Westminster-Greenwich (50mins)
Westminster Passenger Services (7930 4097).
Westminster-Tower (30mins)
City Cruises (7930 0533).
Westminster-Festival (5mins)-**London Bridge City** (20mins)-**St Katharine's** (5mins)
Crown River Cruises (7936 2033).
Westminster-(Thames) Barrier Gardens (1hr 10mins)
Thames Cruises (7930 3373).
Westminster-Kew (1hr 30mins)-**Richmond** (30mins)-**Hampton Court** (1hr 30mins)
Westminster Passenger Service Association (7930 2062).
Embankment-Tower (30mins)-**St Katharine's** (5mins)-**Greenwich** (25mins)
Catamaran Cruises (7987 1185).
Greenland Dock-Canary Wharf (2mins)-**St Katharine's** (5mins)-**London Bridge City** (3mins)-**Blackfriars** (4mins)-**Savoy** (2mins)
Collins River Enterprises (7237 9538).
Savoy-Cadogan (18mins)-**Chelsea** (2mins)
Riverside Launches (0831 574774).
Waterloo/Westminster-Tower (30mins)
City Cruises (7030 9033).
Greenwich-(Thames) Barrier Gardens (25mins)
Campion Launches (8305 0300).

Taxis

Black cabs

Radio Taxis (7272 0272) and **Dial-a-Cab** (7253 5000) both run 24-hour services for black cabs (with a pick-up charge). Any enquiries or complaints about black cabs should be made to the Public Carriage Office (7230 1631, 9am-4pm Mon-Fri). Remember to note the badge number of the offending cab, which should be clearly displayed in the rear of the cab and also on its back bumper.

Minicabs

Minicabs (saloon cars) are generally cheaper than black cabs, especially at night and weekends. However, the drivers are usually unlicensed, often untrained, sometimes uninsured, frequently unreliable and, occasionally, dangerous. Having said that, there are plenty of trustworthy and licensed minicab firms; ask for a recommendation from friends and acquaintances. **Addison Lee** (7387 8888) is one of the bigger companies, and claims to do pick-ups from all areas. Women and children travelling alone may prefer to use **Lady Cabs** (7254 3501), which employs only women drivers. **London Taxis International** (www.london-taxis.co.uk) is notable in that it has have child seats available for younger passengers. Whoever you use, ask the price when you book and confirm it with the driver when the car arrives.

Driving

You'll go off the idea of bringing the car as soon as you try to find somewhere to park. If you park illegally, you'll probably get a £60-£80 parking ticket (which will be reduced by 50 per cent if you pay within 14 days). Worse still, you may find your car has been immobilised by a wheel clamp, or even towed away and impounded (if your car disappears from its illegal parking spot, it will have been towed, phone 7747 4700 to trace it).

Central London is scattered with parking meters. However, finding a meter that's free could take several hours. And even if you do locate one, it'll cost you up to £1 for every 15 minutes to park there, and you'll be limited to two hours on the meter. Parking on a single yellow line, a double yellow line or a red line (designating a red route) at any time during the day is illegal, and you're likely to end up being fined, clamped or towed.

However, in the evening (from 6pm or 7pm in much of central London) and at various times at weekends, parking on single yellow lines becomes both legal and free. If you find a clear spot on a single yellow line during the evening, check a nearby sign before you leave your car: this sign should tell you at which times parking is legal on this particular yellow line, as times vary from

council to council and even from street to street. It's a similar story with meters, which become free after a certain time in the evening and at various times on weekends: check before paying. Parking on double yellow lines and red routes is, by and large, illegal at all times.

NCP (7499 7050) has a number of phenomenally expensive 24-hour car parks in and around central London. Prices vary with location, but expect to pay £6-£10 for two hours up to £30-£50 for 24 hours. A word of warning, though. The vast majority of public car parks in central London are underground, and despite the best efforts of the owners, a few are frequented by drug users. In other words, take care when leaving and returning to your car, and take your valuables with you.

Tourist information

London Tourist Board & Convention Bureau
7932 2000 admin line/London Line 0906 866 3344/www.londontouristboard.com.
Call the LTB for information about where to stay and sights to see in the capital. Its London line (60p per minute) has information for families planning a trip to London. The website has a fun for kids section on the home page. You can ring or write to LTBCB at Glenn House, Stag Place, London, SW1 5LT to ask for a special London Information Pack before your visit.

Tourist information centres, listed below, can provide free maps of central London and advice on visitor attractions.
Heathrow Terminals 1, 2, 3
Tube station concourse, Heathrow Airport. **Open** 8am-6pm daily.
Liverpool Street Station *Tube Station concourse, EC2.* **Open** 8am-6pm Mon-Fri; 8.45am-5.30pm Sat, Sun.
Southwark Information Centre
London Bridge, corner of Tooley Street, SE1. **Open** 10am-4pm Mon-Sat; 11am-4pm Sun.
Victoria Station *Victoria Station forecourt, SW1.* **Open** 8am-7pm Mon-Sat; 8am-6pm Sun.
Waterloo International Terminal
Arrivals Hall, South Bank, SE1. **Open** 8.30am-10.30pm daily.

For information on travel in the rest of Britain, try the **Britain Visitor Centre** *1 Regent Street (south of Piccadilly Circus), SW1 (no phone/www.visitbritain.com).* Piccadilly Circus tube. **Open** *Jan-July, Oct-Dec* 9am-6.30pm Mon-Fri; 10am-4pm Sat, Sun. *Aug, Sept* 9am-6.30pm Mon-Fri; 9am-5pm Sat; 10am-4pm Sun. **Credit** AmEx, MC, V. Personal callers only.

Advertisers' Index

Please refer to the relevant pages for
addresses and telephone numbers.

Index

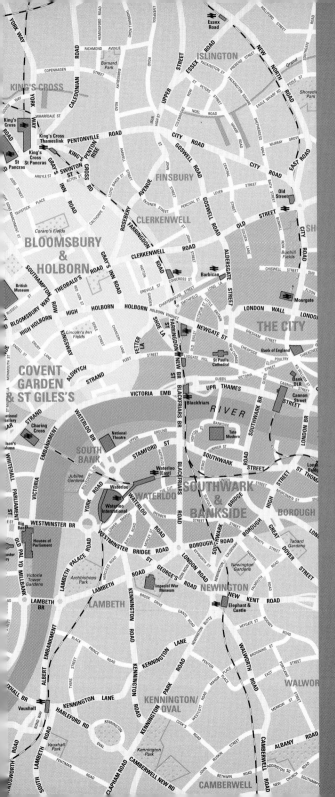

Legend

Places of interest or entertainment	▨
Rail stations	▨
Underground stations	⊖
Parks	▨
Hospitals	▨
Casualty units	✚
Churches	✚
Districts	**MAYFAIR**

Maps

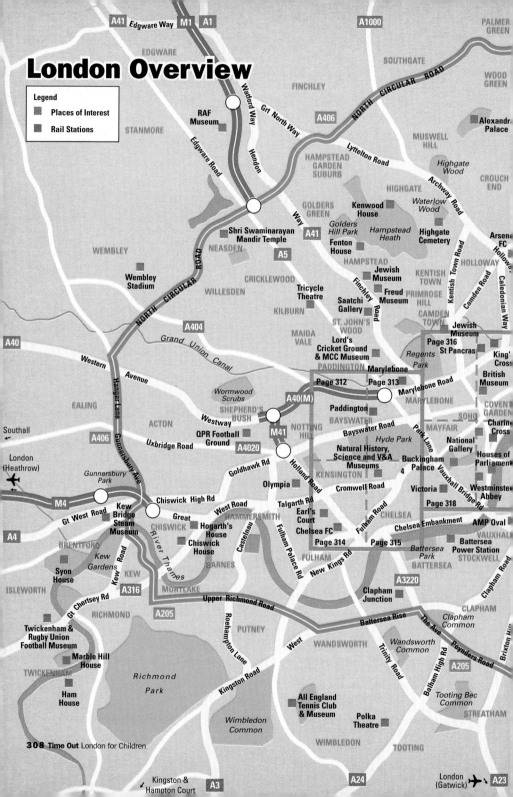

London Overview

Legend
- Places of Interest
- Rail Stations

A41 Edgware Way | M1 | A1 | A1000 | PALMER GREEN

EDGWARE

SOUTHGATE

FINCHLEY

NORTH CIRCULAR ROAD

WOOD GREEN

Watford Way

Grt North Way

A406

Alexandra Palace

MUSWELL HILL

RAF Museum

STANMORE

Edgware Road

Lyttelton Road

HAMPSTEAD GARDEN SUBURB

Hendon

Highgate Wood

CROUCH END

HIGHGATE

Archway Road

GOLDERS GREEN

Kenwood House

Waterlow Wood

Way

Shri Swaminarayan Mandir Temple

A41

Golders Hill Park

Hampstead Heath

Highgate Cemetery

Arsenal FC

NEASDEN

Fenton House

Kentish Town Road

Holloway

WEMBLEY

A5

HAMPSTEAD

Camden Road

CRICKLEWOOD

Jewish Museum

KENTISH TOWN

Caledonian Way

Wembley Stadium

WILLESDEN

Tricycle Theatre

Finchley Road

Freud Museum

PRIMROSE HILL

NORTH CIRCULAR ROAD

KILBURN

Saatchi Gallery

CAMDEN TOWN

A404

ST. JOHN'S WOOD

Jewish Museum

A40

Grand Union Canal

MAIDA VALE

Lord's Cricket Ground & MCC Museum

Regents Park

Page 316

St Pancras

King's Cross

Western Avenue

Hanger Lane

PADDINGTON

Marylebone

British Museum

EALING

Wormwood Scrubs

A40(M)

Page 312

Page 313

Marylebone Road

MARYLEBONE

COVENT GARDEN

Southall →

ACTON

Westway

SHEPHERD'S BUSH

Paddington

MAYFAIR

Charing Cross

London (Heathrow) ✈

A406

Gunnersbury Ave

QPR Football Ground

M41

NOTTING HILL

BAYSWATER

Bayswater Road

Park Lane

National Gallery

Uxbridge Road

A4020

Goldhawk Rd

Hyde Park

Natural History, Science and V&A Museums

Buckingham Palace

Houses of Parliament

Gunnersbury Park

Olympia

Holland Road

KENSINGTON

Victoria

Vauxhall Bridge Rd

Westminster Abbey

M4

Chiswick High Rd

West Road

Talgarth Rd

Cromwell Road

Page 318

Gt West Road

Kew Bridge Steam Museum

Great Hogarth's House

HAMMERSMITH

Earl's Court

Fulham Road

Chelsea Embankment

AMP Oval

A4

CHISWICK

Chiswick House

Castelnau

Chelsea FC

CHELSEA

VAUXHALL

BRENTFORD

Kew Road

River Thames

BARNES

Fulham Palace Rd

Page 314

Page 315

Battersea Park

Battersea Power Station

STOCKWELL

Syon House

Kew Gardens

KEW

FULHAM

New Kings Rd

BATTERSEA

ISLEWORTH

A316

MORTLAKE

Upper Richmond Road

A3220

Clapham Junction

Clapham Road

Twickenham & Rugby Union Football Museum

Gt Chertsey Rd

RICHMOND

A205

Roehampton Lane

PUTNEY

West

Battersea Rise

Clapham Common

CLAPHAM

The Ave

Poynders Road

Marble Hill House

Richmond Park

Kingston Road

WANDSWORTH

Wandsworth Common

Trinity Road

A205

TWICKENHAM

Ham House

Wimbledon Common

All England Tennis Club & Museum

Polka Theatre

Tooting Bec Common

Balham High Rd

Brixton Road

STREATHAM

WIMBLEDON

TOOTING

Kingston & Hampton Court

A3

A24

London (Gatwick) ✈

A23

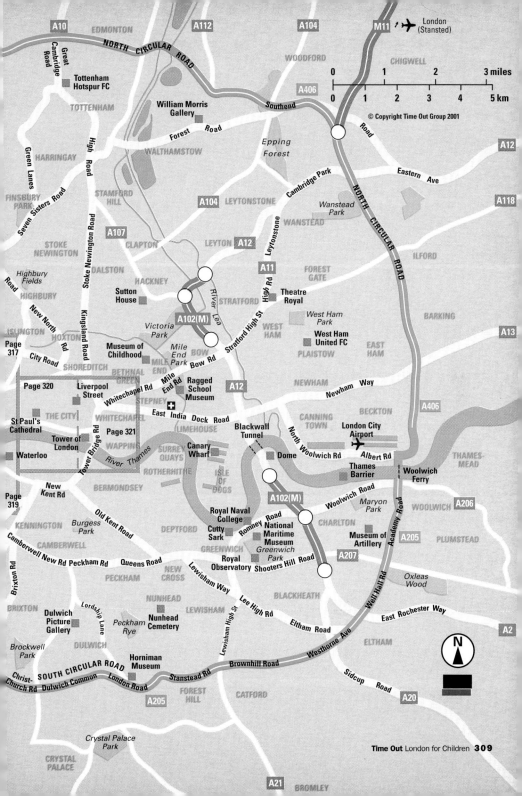

Central London
by Area

Kilburn High Road

GREENCROFT GDNS
HILLGROVE
ADELAIDE ROAD
KING HENRY'S ROAD
PRIMROSE HILL
PRIMROSE HILL
REGENT'S PARK ROAD
PRINCE ALBERT ROAD
London Zoo
REGENT'S PARK
CAMDEN
CAMDEN ROAD
ROYAL COLLEGE
CAMDEN HIGH STREET
DELANCEY ST
PANCRAS
SOMERS TOWN
EVERSHOLT STREET
Euston

MAIDA VALE
ST JOHN'S WOOD
MAIDA VALE
ST JOHN'S WOOD ROAD
PARK ROAD
Queen Mary's Gardens
OUTER CIRCLE
ALBANY STREET
EUSTON ROAD
GOWER ST

Grand Union Canal
EDGWARE ROAD
MARYLEBONE ROAD
Marylebone
MARYLEBONE ROAD
MARYLEBONE
PORTLAND PLACE
FITZROVIA
TOTTENHAM COURT ROAD

HARROW ROAD
WESTWAY
A40(M)
PADDINGTON
PRAED STREET
SUSSEX GARDENS
EDGWARE ROAD
BAKER STREET
WIGMORE STREET
OXFORD STREET
REGENT STREET
SOHO
WEST END
CHINA-TOWN

Eastbourne
BISHOP'S BRIDGE ROAD
WESTBOURNE GROVE
BAYSWATER
BAYSWATER ROAD
Marble Arch
OXFORD STREET
MAYFAIR
PICCADILLY
HAYMARKET
PALL MALL

KENSINGTON GARDENS
The Round Pond
HYDE PARK
The Serpentine
PICCADILLY
GREEN PARK
ST JAMES'S
ST JAMES'S PARK

KENSINGTON ROAD
KENSINGTON ROAD
KNIGHTSBRIDGE
CARRIAGE DRIVE
CONSTITUTION HILL
BUCKINGHAM PALACE GARDENS
WESTMINSTER

KNIGHTSBRIDGE
Science Museum
Victoria & Albert Museum
Harrods
SLOANE STREET
BELGRAVE
GROSVENOR PLACE
BUCKINGHAM GATE
VICTORIA

CROMWELL ROAD
Natural History Museum
BROMPTON
BELGRAVIA
ECCLESTON
Victoria
ECCLESTON BR
VAUXHALL BRIDGE ROAD

EARL'S COURT
SOUTH KENSINGTON
KENSINGTON & CHELSEA
FULHAM ROAD
SYDNEY STREET
KING'S ROAD
PIMLICO ROAD
CHELSEA BRIDGE ROAD
PIMLICO

WEST BROMPTON
Brompton Cemetery
FULHAM ROAD
KING'S ROAD
ROYAL HOSPITAL ROAD
Chelsea Physic Garden
CHELSEA EMBANKMENT
GROSVENOR ROAD
GROSVENOR ROAD

FULHAM
CHEYNE WALK
ALBERT BR
BATTERSEA
RIVER THAMES
NINE ELMS LANE
NINE ELMS

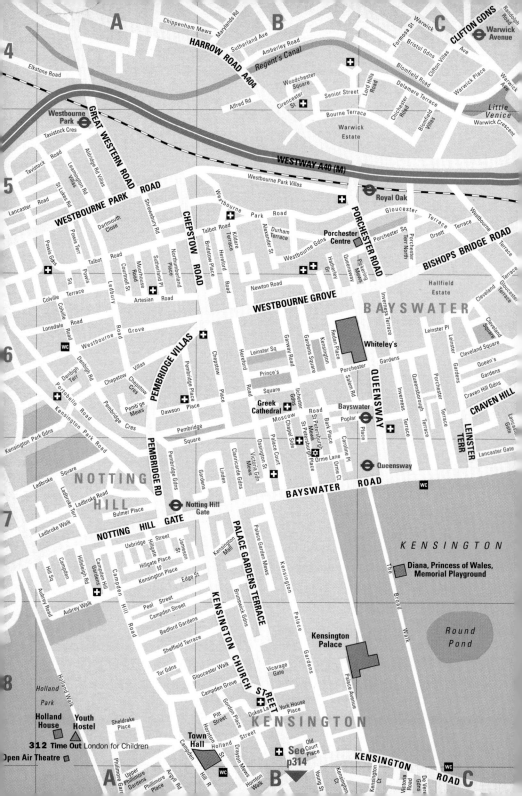

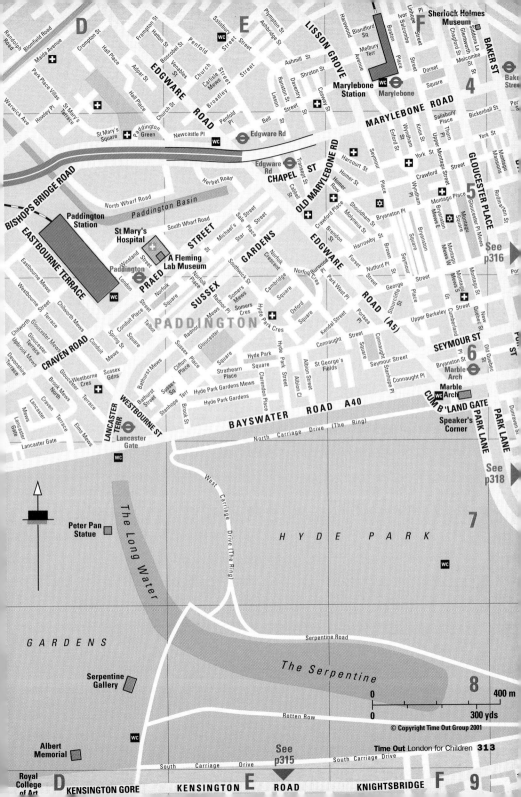

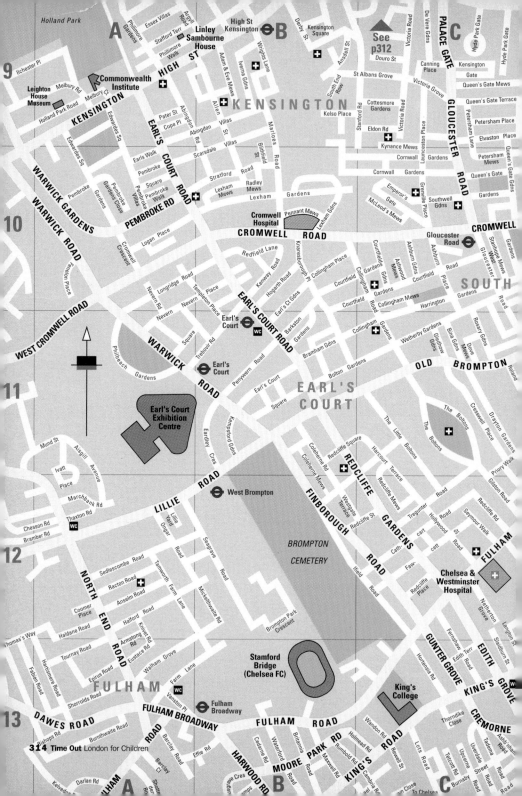

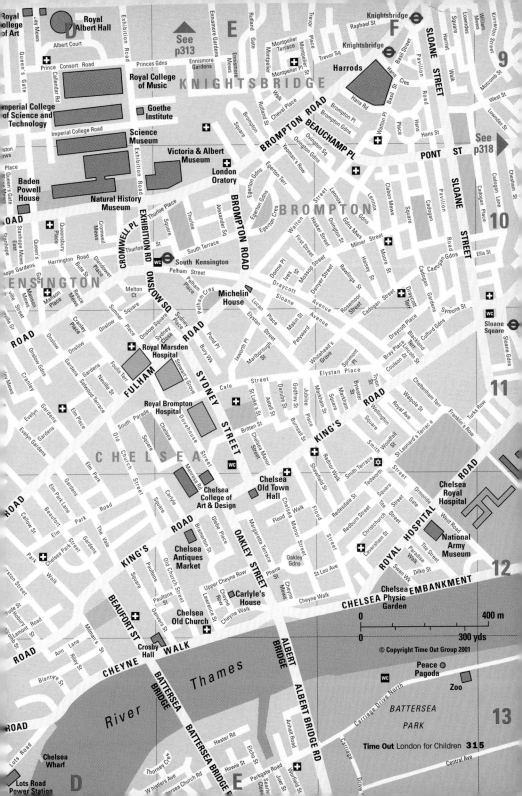

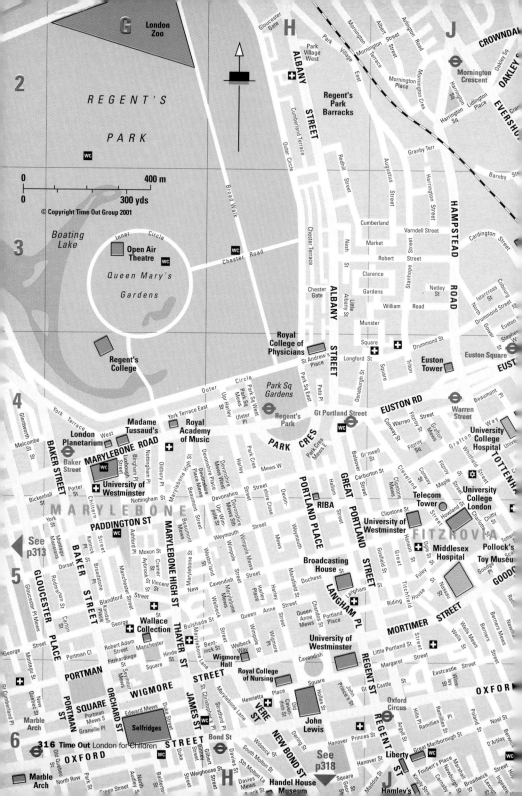

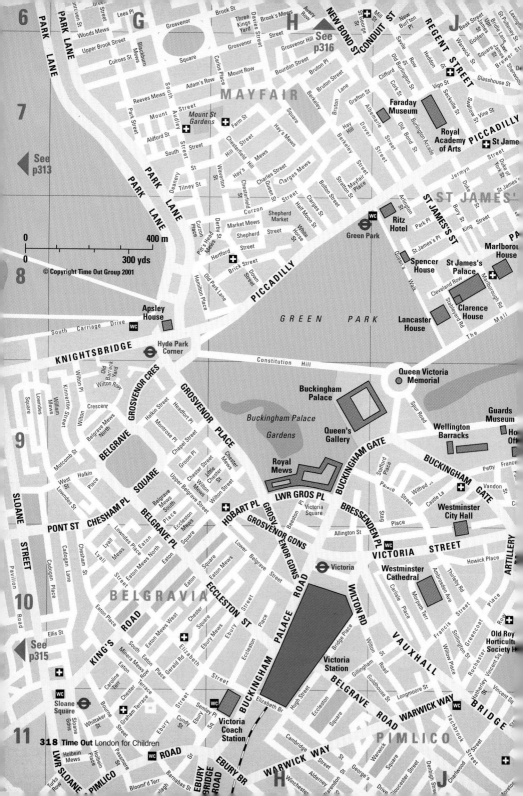

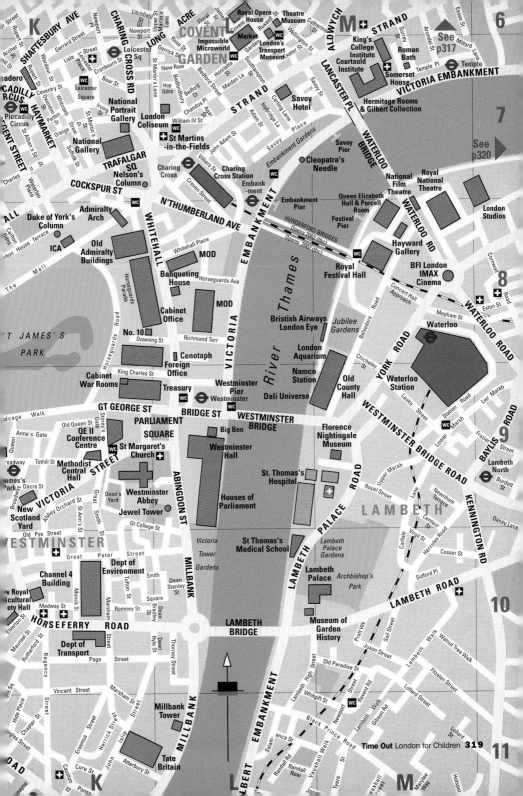

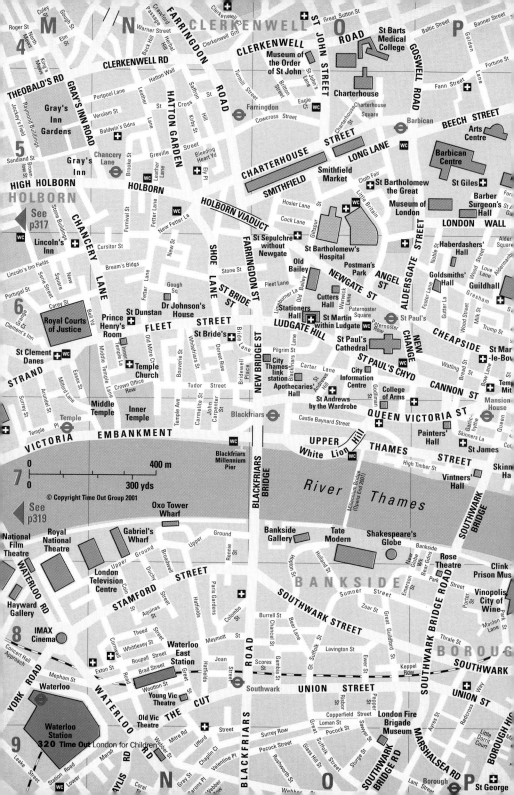

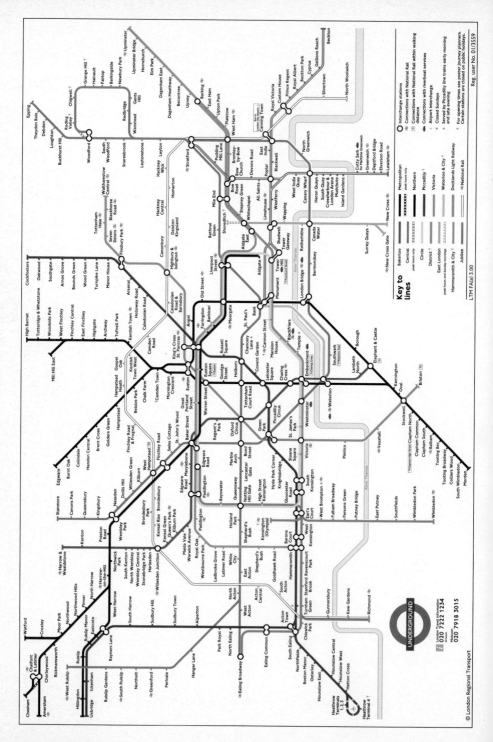

Time Out

KidsOut
Good Toy
Guide

National Association of
Toy & Leisure Libraries

200 top toy ideas

plus all the latest gadgets and games

In association with the National Association of Toy & Leisure Libraries

More Magic from Upstarts!

See what we've pulled out of the hat! . . . more TV branded magic, more from the award-winning 'Who Wants To Be A Millionaire?, more top-selling puzzles and more exciting unique branded games.

In fact, the Upstarts product range continues to expand, building on our excellent relationships with key brands and bringing them to life with great ideas, great game play and great characters.

Upstarts®!

From the publishers of

**Published by
Time Out Guides Ltd**
Universal House
251 Tottenham Court Road
London W1T 7AB
www.timeout.com

Telephone	(020) 7813 3000
Fax	(020) 7813 6001
Advertising Tel	(020) 7813 6020

Editor Melanie Dakin
Writer Tanya Burton
Associate Editor/Project Manager
Carole Burton

Cover Ben de Lotz, Dan Conway

| NATLL Tel | (020) 7387 9592 |
| NATLL Fax | (020) 7383 2714 |

**The NATLL Toy Appraisal Panel 2001
Claire Hodgeson**, Childcare
Co-ordinator, Riverside Community
Health Project, Newcastle upon Tyne;
Lola Honeyman, Retired Special Needs
Teacher, Dorset; **Susan Knowles**,
Paediatric Audiologist, Service for
Hearing-Impaired Children, Kingston-
upon-Thames, Surrey; **Jenny Kosky**,
Neighbourhood Nursery Teacher,
London Borough of Enfield; **Rosalie
Millar**, Nursery Manager, Cherry Tree
Nursery, Ayr; **Karen Morris**, Senior
Nursery Officer, Hillfields Centre of
Excellence, Coventry; **Wendy Moss**,
Play Development Worker, Play Radnor,
Powys; **Gaynor Stubbs**, Head Teacher,
Wensley Fold Church of England
School, Blackburn; **Ruth Bristow** and
Mandy McKay, Lincoln Toy Library,
Lincoln; **Angela Knott**, Canford Heath
Toy Library, Poole; **Caroline King**, Infant
School Teacher, The Borrowers Toy
Library, Ripon; **Debbie Wrist**, Daventry
Toy Library, Daventry

NATLL: the National Association
of Toy & Leisure Libraries,
68 Churchway, London NW1 1LT.
Registered Charity No. 270291
A Company Limited by Guarantee,
Registered in England Number
1221864. Every effort has been made
to ensure that details (advertising and
toy appraisal material) are both
comprehensive and correct. NATLL
cannot, however, be held responsible
for any loss or damage, howsoever
caused, arising from any errors or
omissions contained in such material,
which is reproduced in good faith.

Repro Icon Reproduction, Crowne House
56-58 Southwark Street, London SE1 1UN.

Printing Southernprint, Factory Road, Upton
Industrial Estate, Poole, Dorset BH16 5SN.

ISSN 1356-8272

Introduction

From birth, children are learning.
Through play and observation
they discover the tools that will
help them to make their way
in the world. Children need
toys that are absorbing and
challenging but most of all
they need toys that are fun.
Parents want their children
to play with toys that are safe,
strong and educational. Our
team of researchers has taken
all these factors into acount.
Selected by the National
Association of Toy & Leisure
Libraries, this year's line-up
of toy testers includes parents,
teachers, child psychologists
and, most importantly, children
themselves. Each toy has been
intensively tested in a variety of
settings, over a number of
months, and every product
has gone to at least six family
homes and has been used in
many group situations.

The point of the tests is to
find out how the toys perform
according to criteria like play
value, safety, value for money,
durability, appeal, design and
learning potential.

The Good Toy Guide includes
only the very best of what's
on offer. We've done our
homework in order to give you
a guide you can trust, whether
you're looking for presents for
Christmas, searching for the
ideal birthday gift or just
planning a special treat.
Melanie Dakin, Editor

Good Toy Guide

Contents

How to use

Toys appearing in the Guide have been divided into 14 sections. Toys that perform particularly well across all the criteria in each category are given the status of Gold Award Winner or Silver Award Winner. Two Overall Winners are chosen in the Birth-12 months and 3 years+ categories. If a toy does not meet the criteria, it is not in the Guide. This year sees the introduction of an 'Inclusion' category. Essentially this is a criterion that rates a toy for its suitability for children with special needs; it is applied throughout each category, and a Gold Inclusion Award and Silver

Inclusion Awards (*see below*) are given to those that stand out as examples of excellence.

Bear in mind that toys can be classified in different ways – for example, our Numbers & words section contains some games, puzzles and electronic toys – so it's worth checking all relevant sections. If you can't find a certain toy in your local stores, refer to manufacturers list on page 32 of this guide. All these companies will be happy to help you find your nearest stockist; some also offer mail order.

We have supplied our own age recommendations, which sometimes differ from those

on the toy's packaging. Many toys will be attractive to children of a different age, but be sure to follow any safety guidelines (especially for children under three). Recommended retail prices are also given.

Toy libraries are free for everyone to use and stock some of these products (budgets permitting). There are over 1,000 toy libraries in Britain, with more being set up all the time. For details, contact the National Association of Toy & Leisure Libraries on (020) 7387 9592 or at www.natll.org.uk.

Time Out
KidsOut
Good Toy Guide
National Association of Toy & Leisure Libraries

Gold Inclusion Award

Tocki Range

(Willis Wheel Mirror, Dice with 6 Tubes, Mini Dumbells, Holographic Shaker/Rattle, Dumbell Clicker, Dorchester Dinki, Small Rotating Frame and Lighthouse Roller)

Available from Tocki, price £5-£80 approx. 2 years+

Essentially, the Tocki range is based on particles of glitter that are suspended in liquid and housed in perspex tubes. The glitter makes visual effects when the tube is moved, not unlike a snowscene toy. The sheer variety of this sturdy range is outstanding, and the items tested particularly well among children with special needs. Tactile, with breathtaking visual effects and chunky wooden housings, these toys encourage imagination, concentration, relaxation and dexterity, and stimulate communication.

▶ **Kindergarten Tunnel**

※ **Silver Inclusion Award** ※

Available from TP Activity Toys, price £40. 12 months-6 years
Suitable for everyday use, this durable pop-out tunnel is three metres long and has clear sides so that children can feel confident while they play. Easy to transport and store, it's a real bargain, too.

▶ **Knee High Ocean Table**

※ **Silver Inclusion Award** ※

Available from Krucial Kids, price £99.95. 18 months+
Made from solid wood, this bead table has an abstract marine theme. Thread the fish-shaped along the wires that weave among treasure chests and a shipwreck. A highly robust toy that helps to develop visual tracking and dexterity.

Good Toy Guide

Birth-12 months

Light + Sound Buggy Driver

※ Highly Recommended ※

Available from Early Learning Centre, price £20. 6 months+
Children can't resist taking to the road with this buggy-bound play centre. Complete with steering wheel, gear stick, indicators and realistic sounds, it has bags of play value. Battery operated, strong and well made, it really is very good value for money.

Farmyard Friends Car Mobile

※ Highly Recommended ※

Available from Mothercare, price £9.99. Birth+
Secured to the window by suction pads, this fabric toy features various affixed 3D rattling animals. An absorbing and tactile toy for babies on the move.

Hungry Horse Musical Pull

Available from Mothercare, price £9.99. Birth+
Pull the horse from the stable to hear the music. Made from fabric and attached by a velcro link-loop, this will hang virtually anywhere.

Hungry Horse Activity Toy

Available from Mothercare, price £9.99. Birth+
Another hungry horse, this time with a chirping chick on its back. A mirror and chewable hard stirrups add play value and sensory appeal.

Ocean Friends Travel Gym

Available from The Ninja Corporation, price £24.99-£30.99. Birth-12 months
Four soft fabric marine animals, a carry bag and changing mat accompany this attractive pop-up gym. It encourages dexterity and concentration and is a doddle to assemble and put away.

Light & Sound Crib Toys

Available from Tesco Stores, price £7.99. Birth+
This range of shimmering fabric toys includes a star, moon and sun all operated by a string pull, which activates over two minutes of music and twinkling lights.

Activity Toby Tortoise

Available from Mothercare, price £7.99. Birth+
Featuring a clear plastic shell exposing small, coloured, rattling balls, a mirrored tummy and teething ring feet, this tactile toy is a multi-sensory treat.

Mothercare My First Doll

Available from Mothercare, price £6.99. Birth+
A squeaky tummy adds interest to this soft, cuddly, velour doll. A toy with plenty of imaginative play value that also helps develop nurturing skills.

Gold Award Winner

The Hungry Pelican

Available from K's Kids (ABC Nursery Distribution Ltd), price £17.99-£18.99. Birth-2 years
A fabulously colourful and tactile bird. Its beak leads down to a stomach, which is visible through the hole in its middle, and the accompanying small soft friends – a crab, a fish, a shrimp and an octopus – double as hearty snacks. Audio elements include rattling feet, squeaky cheeks and scrunchy wings, and each of the smaller animals makes similar sounds. Apart from having great novelty value, it hones dexterity, co-ordination and concentration. Well made and washable, this can easily be attached to a cot or playpen.

Stroll & Go Hippo by Lamaze

Available from Flair Leisure Products Plc, price £16.99-£17.99. Birth-2 years
This happy hippo consists of a mirror, crinkly ball rattle and a string tail. A stimulating attachment for the cot or pram.

Inchworm

Available from K's Kids (ABC Nursery Distribution Ltd), price £9.99-£12.99. Birth-18 months
This cheerful velour worm features a mirror, bells and a rattle. Not only is it a multi-activity toy that kids can snuggle up with, it also helps to develop dexterity, co-ordination and concentration.

Good Toy Guide

Sparkling Symphony Gym

Available from Fisher-Price Toys, price £35 approx. Birth-3 years
This superb piece of kit plays classical tunes and nursery rhymes as lights twinkle. Babies can activate the sounds and lights via the dangling star, sun and moon, and for toddlers, it converts into a mini-keyboard.

Pop-Up Baby Gym

Available from Worlds Apart, price £19.99. 3-12 months
A squeaky ball, star rattle and mirrored cube dangle from this portable gym. It's machine washable and easy to store, too.

Grip and Grab Rattle by Lamaze

Available from Flair Leisure Products Plc, price £6.99-£7.99.
3 months-2 years
Beautifully designed, these triangular plastic tubes house small coloured balls, which are visible through the clear spheres at each corner. Rather like a rain stick, it makes wonderful sounds and is chewable, too. Older kids can use it as a maze game.

Flip Flop Activity Blocks by Lamaze

Available from Flair Leisure Products Plc, price £14.99-£15.99.
3 months-2 years
Four tactile, multi-textured cubes are joined by velcro, and each features a different sound and 3D activity.

◄ Busy Bunny Teether

Available from Mothercare, price £5.99. Birth+
Just the right size for little hands, this fabric and plastic teether boasts a mirror and rattle, crackly feet and an absorbing fluffy tail. A stimulating toy, this rabbit's hard, textured ears proved to be soothingly chewable.

Lights 'N' Sounds

Available from Tomy, price £7.99-£9.99. 6 months+
Baby-sized electronic geegaws for the executive youngster. The Lights 'N' Sounds phone has a voice-activated interactive handset, and the Lights 'N' Sounds Ball features dial, roller and push button pads.

Baby Wheels

Available from Tolo Toys Europe Ltd, price £3.50 each. 6 months+
This range of chubby plastic vehicles includes a police car, aeroplane, fire engine and a sports car. Refreshingly simplistic, and of very high quality, they are perfect for imaginative play.

Shape Sorter Play Bench

Available from Tolo Toys Europe Ltd, price £9-£11. 9 months+
Knocking the shapes through the holes is not as easy as it looks. Grooves around the holes' edges mean that children have to give each shape a bit of a bashing on the way through.

Pull Along Pony

Available from Tolo Toys Europe Ltd, price £9-£11. 12 months+
The galloping action and clip-clop sound of this pony and cart are an absolute delight. A versatile toy, the reigns detach to separate the cart and pony, giving plenty of added play value.

◄ First Mirror by Lamaze

Available from Flair Leisure Products Plc, price £14.99-£15.99
Birth-4 years
This soft fabric wedge holds a velcro-fastened, detachable, non-breakable plastic mirror. The shape can be used as an ingenious body prop under the chest when a child lies on the floor, making it ideal for some children with special needs. It's all fully washable and the mirror and vivid print are great for helping children to focus and concentrate.

12-36 months

KidsOut Good Toy Guide

Gold Award Winner

Jungle Water Slide

Available from **Tolo Toys Europe Ltd**, price **£11-£13. 6 months+**
This superb, multicoloured water toy is crammed with activities and detail. An animal sits on each of the shaped cups, which have corresponding covers and double as pourers. A lever activates the animals' launch down chutes into your tub. Other Tolo Toys share the Gold Award: the Highchair Activity Centre (£9-£11); the Rolling Shape Sorter (£9-£11), suitable from 6 months; and the Musical Surprise Bear (£8-£10), suitable from 3 months.

Soft Sorter by Lamaze

※ Highly Recommended ※

Available from Flair Leisure Products Plc, price £14.99-£15.99. 6 months-2 years
Each of the stuffed shapes that come with this shape sorter makes a different sound. Brightly coloured and immediately appealing, little fingers will not be able to resist exploring the various holes.

Family of Ducks by Lamaze

※ Highly Recommended ※

Available from Flair Leisure Products Plc, price £12.99-£13.99. 12-36 months
Three eggs are tucked inside the mother duck. When turned inside out, all but one turn into delightful little ducklings, the other, is a swan, and all can be used as finger puppets.

Take Along Playhouse by Lamaze

※ Highly Recommended ※

Available from Flair Leisure Products Plc, price £19.99-£20.99. 12-36 months
This detailed, padded cloth playhouse features a kitchen, bathroom and bedroom. The fabric boy and girl can sit in the bath, go to bed or wash up at the sink, while their pet dog eats its dinner.

Tesco Mystical Friends Bean

※ Highly Recommended ※

Available from Tesco Stores, price £4.99. 2 years+
The novelty value of this range of bean-filled characters is astonishing. The attention to detail is superb; kids can boggle at the golden wart on the witch's face, or gasp at the fairy's ribboned slippers and metallic hair. An inspiration for developing minds.

Click Clack Track

※ Highly Recommended ※

Available from Early Learning Centre, price £15. 2 years+
Well made from solid wood, this is simplicity itself. As the cars roll down each section of track, they weigh it down and move on to the level below. Magic.

First Rhymes

※ Highly Recommended ※

Available from Living and Learning, price £9.99. 2 years+
Featuring either frogs, bears or monsters, these kits include an audio cassette, five finger puppets and a booklet containing lyrics and tips. A fantastic introduction to elementary counting and recall.

Wobbly Wheels Fire Engine and Police Car

Available from VTech Electronics (UK) Plc, price £9 approx. 6 months+
Push the vehicle along to hear it talk and play music. Its oval wheels add a pleasantly lop-sided gait.

Tiny Love Peek-A-Boo

Available from East Coast, price £12.50 approx. 6 months+
Available as a mouse or a bird, this toy-on-a-stick can be made to retract into a cone and then pop out.

Good Toy Guide

Wiggly Giggly Plush

Available from Imperial Games Ltd, price £12.99. 6 months+
Made from egg-yolk yellow velour and as round as a ball, this bird-like creature has a squeaky beak and makes cute sounds when rolled.

Tesco Party Animals Assortment

Available from Tesco Stores, price £8.99. 12 months+
These large, very soft and multi-textural toys feature a variety of sounds from crunching noises to tinkling bells. Available as either a hippo or an elephant party animal.

Yoho Ahoy Figures

Available from Cassidy Brothers Plc, price £5.99. 12 months+
These brightly coloured plastic figurines greet with a cheery 'Yoho Ahoy!' when a button is pressed. Great fun for landlubbers.

Weebles – Shape Sorter Express

Available from Flair Leisure Products Plc, price £10.99. 12 months+
Comprising an engine with two attachable trucks and passengers, this well-made and detailed shape sorter has bags of novelty value.

Tesco Musical Moving Giraffe

Available from Tesco Stores, price £7.99. 12 months+
This musical cuddly toy giraffe has bendy limbs, which can be used to attach it on to a child's cot or pushchair, and it bobs its head in time to the music.

▶ Interactive Talking Thomas + Friends

✳ Silver Award Winner ✳

Available from Golden Bear Products, price £12.99-£14.99 each. 6 months-7 years
Old faves Thomas, Lady, Harold and James make realistic engine sounds when moved, speak at the touch of a button and interact when placed close to one another.

I'm a really useful engine

Snail Rocker

Available from Pin Toys by John Crane Ltd, price £50 approx. 12 months+
The relatively small size of this rocker makes it a perfect first activity toy. Suitable for independent play, this is beautifully made from solid rubberwood.

Chad Valley Light Up Musical CD Player

Available from Woolworths, price £9.99. 18 months+
This soft, pretend CD player plays tunes, accompanied by twinkling lights. Visually appealing and great for co-ordination, it also features instrument and animal sounds.

Talk 'n' Learn Muck

Available from IQ Builders, price £19.99 approx. 18 months+
This electronic push-along truck, which is based on the popular Bob The Builder TV series, helps children to identify colours, numbers and the names of tools.

Sevi Zookids

Available from DKL Marketing Ltd, price £12.99. 12-24 months
Consisting of a sheep, an elephant, a pig and a lion, these beautifully crafted smooth, wooden animals have removable velour coats and are all on wheels. They're a joy to handle and great fun to dress up.

My First Drum Set

Available from Boots the Chemist, price £10. 12-24 months
A wonderful toy to strengthen co-ordination skills, this kit includes a cymbal, triangle and sticks. An instant hit that will bring out the percussionist in any child.

Fizz's Tickle Time

Available from Tiger Electronics UK Ltd, price £9.99. 12-36 months
Parts of the body are the theme of this hand-held game, which is based on the 'Tweenies' character Fizz.

Baby Butterfly

Available from Smoby, price £8.25. 12-36 months
This butterfly-shaped piano features six musical buttons, three instrument sounds, and lights that flash in time to the music.

Baby Buddies

Available from Mothercare, price £3.99. 24 months+
Extremely realistic, these dolls are great for imaginative life play. Made from soft plastic, they are cuddly and a good size for smaller hands.

Farmyard Playground

Available from Tigerprint for Marks & Spencer, price £15. 24 months-4 years
Fold the plastic together to create a play barn complete with tractor, trailer, farmer and livestock. Then match the sounds to the animals.

◀ Fill and Spill by Lamaze

✳ Silver Award Winner ✳

Available from Flair Leisure Products Plc, price £9.99-£10.99. 6 months-2 years
Each of the clear balls in this wonderfully absorbing and visually stunning toy contains a spinning plastic disc, depicting an insect on one side and a monochrome geometric pattern on the other. The balls are housed in a sturdy tube with openings at each end allowing kids to explore the principles of cause and effect.

Arts & crafts

Tattoo Blopens

Highly Recommended

Available from P&M Products Colour Workshop, price £5.99. 5 years+
Removable, reusable body art. The kit contains four pens, 14 designs and comprehensive instructions. An immensely popular and fun activity, and one that's great value, too.

Smoby 2 in 1 Desk and Easel

Available from Smoby, price £34.99. 2-5 years
Ergonomic and made from bright, chunky plastic, this comfy sloping desk has pencil holders and secret storage, or can be used as an upright easel with a dry wipe board. Stool included.

Crazy Colours Palette

Available from Flair Leisure Products Plc, price £6.99. 2-8 years
Ten tubs of wonderfully coloured Play-Doh. A good value set with bags of play potential.

Hama Maxi

Available from DKL Marketing Ltd, price £5.99. 3-5 years
Create interesting bead sculptures with these plastic craft kits. The range includes a teddy bear, an elephant, a dog and a duck.

Magna Doodle

Available from Fisher-Price Toys, price £15 approx. 3 years+
An old favourite and still going strong, this laptop drawing board has a carry handle and magnetic stencils. Well worth the price.

Chad Valley Greeting Card Designer

Available from Woolworths, price £3.99. 4 years+
Design your own occasion cards with this kit, comprising stencils, cards, envelopes and crayons.

Crazy Frog Scribbler

Available from Tigerprint for Marks & Spencer, price £12. 4 years+

This frog-faced reusable drawing unit features moving eyes and a sliding tongue that deletes work from the screen. Great fun.

Blopens Fashion Kit

Available from P&M Products Colour Workshop, price £8.99. 5 years+
Customise clothes with this collection of fabric pens, sequins, gems and stencils. *Très chic.*

Large Jewellery Set

Available from Early Learning Centre, price £10. 6 years+
This large box of bits and bobs contains all you'll need to create some pretty spectacular jewellery. The beads come in a variety of colours and have lots of sparkle.

Crayola Mega Art Case

Available from Binney + Smith, price £9.99. 4-12 years
Everything the junior artist could desire. A great value set that will keep the kids occupied for hours either indoors or out.

Gold Award Winner

Magnet Crafts Fridge Magnets

Available from Dowling Magnets Europe Ltd, price £10.99-£13.99. 9-12 years
This fabulous fridge magnet kit offers hours of fun and creativity. Along with brightly coloured magnetic shapes, some of which have raised bumps for 3D effects, the box includes foam shapes, jewels, glitter glue and eyes, providing infinite decorative potential. Perfectly suited to all abilities, this high-quality, value-for-money kit is sure to draw a crowd.

▼ Crayola Shark's Fin Gel Case

Available from Binney + Smith, price £14.99. 6 years+
This fin-shaped case holds eight Crayola PRO Liners Drawing Pens, four Crayola PRO Brush Tips colouring pens, three Crayola PRO Superfine Writing Pens, 12 Crayola PRO Sketch and Colour Pencils, three Crayola PRO Gel Pens, a pencil sharpener and a rubber. The colours are vibrant, and the gel pen set includes fluorescents and metallics. Removable pen trays make the case a useful and ultra cool accessory.

▲ Crayola Ultimate Art Case

Available from Binney + Smith, price £14.99. 4-8 years
A treasure trove of art materials, this impressive set includes six Crayola Washable Colouring pens, two Crayola Mini Stampers, eight Crayola Coloured Pencils, six Crayola SuperTips colouring pens, eight Crayola Crayons, a Crayola Colour Writer pen, stencils, a pencil, a pencil sharpener, a rubber, glue and scissors. The carry case, which doubles as a work surface, incorporates two detachable pods for storing pencils and pens. Great for holidays and to take along on days out this set is very good value and has bags of play potential.

Creative Range

Available from Imperial Games Ltd, price £3.99-£10.99. 6-14 years
These all-inclusive craft kits make interesting gifts. The range includes, Wake-Up Clock, Chocofun, Build a Camera and Love You Too.

Blitzer Air Art

Available from P&M Products Colour Workshop, price £4.99. 7 years+
A fabulous airbrush set comprising an air pump, stencils and brush tip pens. Best of all it can be used with other pens, making it a real bargain.

Blopens Carnaeval Masks

Available from P&M Colour Workshop, price £7.99. 7 years+
Feathers, glitter and stickers are just some of the decorations accompanying the Blopens in this kit. It contains all you need to make amazing party masks.

Chad Valley Craft Club Potters Wheel

Available from Woolworths, price £14.99. 8 years+
A very hands-on activity, complete with clay, paint, beads and stencils.

▶ Vivid Velvet

Available from P&M Products Colour Workshop, price £3.49-£9.99. 5 years+
Pre-printed designs are outlined with felt, ready to be coloured in with the felt tips provided. A popular activity that involves little preparation, creates hardly any mess and gives instant results, the range includes a Bedroom Kit, Desk Kit, Postcard Kit and Wildlife Kit. Each completed piece makes a useful object such as a desk tidy or waste paper basket.

Good Toy Guide

Construction

Gold Award Winner

Geomag

Available from
Treasure Trove
Toys and Gifts,
price £14.99-£65.
3 years+
Magnetic metal rods and
spheres are the only
components included here
but they are more than enough
to create fabulous structures and
shapes. Essentially scientific, this
kit demonstrates the
principles of magnetism
using high-quality
materials. The
pieces feel
durable enough to
be passed from
child to child
over the
years, so
buying
additional
sets is a
viable option.
Instantly appealing,
absorbing and educational,
Geomag helps to hone dexterity,
co-ordination, observation and
aid concentration.

▲ Mega Bloks Wagon

✸ Silver Award Winner ✸

Available from Mega Bloks,
price £19.99. 12 months-5 years
Robust and colourful, this brick-filled
truck will delight even the most
recalcitrant child. The truck is as
much a feature as the blocks, and
can be used as a base for structures
or for storage. With enough bricks to
share, this set can provide long
sessions of absorbed play. It also
helps to hone dexterity and develop
maths and counting skills.

▼ K'nex Classix F1 Racer, K'nex Classix Rescue Flyers and C20 Models

✸ Silver Award Winner ✸

Available from Hasbro UK, price
£4.99, £6.99, £19.99. 6-12 years
The first two of these kits are great
introductions to the K'nex
construction system, containing
enough pieces to make three
separate vehicles. The K'nex C20
Models is a bumper 259-piece set
allowing kids to make over 20
structures, from cars to fairground
rides. All the sets have colour coded
components and come with clear
instructions to create sturdy models
with moving parts. Great for sole or
group play, they promote strategy,
an understanding of elementary
mechanics and creativity.

My Dolls' House and Noah's Ark Toy Kits

✸ Highly Recommended ✸

Available from Toykits, price
£12.99-£15.99. 3-6 years
These quaint cardboard kits are
wonderfully old-fashioned and can
be used to create 3D models. The
dolls' house comes with furniture
and a family, while Noah comes with
a selection of animals and his
brood. A good project for small
groups, each set can encourage
imaginative play and storytelling.

Abrick Farm

Available from Ecoiffier, price
£14.99. 18 months-5 years
Comprising bricks, a barn, animals
and accessories, this really is a
pretty comprehensive collection.
Close attention to detail and
lots of exciting pieces make it
a great gift.

Abrick Chicken Farm Set

Available from Ecoiffier, price
£4.99. 18 months-5 years
Housed in a chicken-shaped
container, this small set includes
blocks, animals, vehicles and
accessories. A great starter set, or
useful addition to the above, which
has lots of play potential.

Discover Car

Available from Quercetti, price
£19.95. 4-12 years
Putting this see-through car
together helps children grasp
some of the mechanical functions
of a real motor vehicle. Robust,
ingenious and fabulous value
for money.

Gearbotics Sonic T-Rex

Available from Learning Resources,
price £22.95. 5 years+
A motor, gears, connectors and
body pieces are all included in this
set, which uses scientific and
mathematical principles to make a
walking model of a T-Rex.

Lego Technic Bionicle – Gali and Tabu

Available from Lego UK Ltd,
price £4.99 each. 7 years+
Robot models with moving parts.
Good colours, great value, and a
must for the Lego collector.

Electronics & multimedia

Muttzart's Symphony Sounds

Available from VTech Electronics (UK) Plc, price £15 approx.
Birth-2 years
This electronic musical puppy barks and plays peek-a-boo. Touch the bone on its foot to activate a night light and soothing music.

Busy Bertie's Workbench

Available from VTech Electronics (UK) Plc, price £20 approx. 12 months+
Bob enthusiasts can have fun hammering away on this workbench. Kids can even learn cause and effect, number skills, letters and shapes into the bargain.

Smoby Baby Nature Discovery Table

Available from Smoby, price £24.99. 12-36 months
Plastic and fabric textures, flashing lights and familiar sounds make this an attractive bet for active toddlers. A visual and aural treat, it's also robust and well designed.

Puff-A-Long Play Train

Highly Recommended

Available from IQ Builders, price £14.99 approx. 1-3 years
This pull-along train with carriage incorporates an animal theme shape-sorter, plays music and makes farmyard sounds.

Bob The Builder – Fix It Fun!

Highly Recommended

Available from BBC Multimedia, price £24.99. 3-6 years
Based on the hit TV show starring Bob and his friends, this Game Boy Colour title encourages kids to do their chores before going on a picnic. Each task is achieved by playing a game and when nine games out of ten are completed, lunchtime can commence.

Bob The Builder's Computer

Highly Recommended

Available from IQ Builders, price £34.99 approx. 3-8 years
This compact computer has more Bob activities than you can shake a stick at. There are 15 tasks and five different levels to explore, covering reading, maths and logic. Special features include a chunky gear stick to help smaller children navigate, a good sized keyboard and a welcome English-accented voice.

My Laptop

Highly Recommended

Available from VTech Electronics (UK) Plc, price £20 approx.
4-9 years
There are 20 activities to choose from including letters, numbers, music and games, and with three levels and a two-player mode, there's lots of scope for interactive fun. The controls are quick to respond and its simplicity and logic will encourage prolonged use.

Slimline MPE-342

Highly Recommended

Available from VTech Electronics (UK) Plc, price £130 approx. 9-12 years
This nearly grown-up laptop features a full range of IT functions, 65

Tweenies – Ready To Play

Available from BBC Multimedia, price £19.99. 3-6 years
Based on the ever-popular television series, this CD-Rom is jam-packed with 13 activities and games. There are various sections or themes, which include story time, news time, play time, and mail time, where personalised mail is delivered to the user to encourage them to try their hand at elementary emailing. Instructions and the explanation of commands is very clear, and verbal directions are repeated if the user hesitates for a time. Activities include arts and crafts, maths, music and reading.

activities including languages and maths, extra cartridges for typing and additional languages, and can be upgraded to include email and a digital camera.

Bob The Builder – Can We Fix It?

Available from BBC Multimedia, price £19.99. 3-6 years
In this educational CD-Rom, Bob and his gang have to fix a number of problems. The 13 activities available include matching, finding, designing and animation.

Noddy's Magic Adventure

Available from BBC Multimedia, price £19.99. 3-6 years
Great for co-ordination and dexterity, this PlayStation game involves Noddy having to find and return a wand that some goblins are using to cast wicked spells.

Reader Rabbit

Available from The Learning Company, price £19.99. 3-8 years
This range of educational CD-Roms covers pre-school to lower Key Stage 2 abilities and includes nursery, junior and Year 2 tasks, plus maths skills for 6-8-year-olds. Each subject involves simple games and activities and has a checking facility to monitor progress.

Interactive Poo-Chi

Available from Tiger Electronics UK Ltd, price £24.99. 4 years+
The original and best, Poo-Chi will interact with humans and other Poo-

Chis and the whole gamut of bird/cat/mouse spin-offs to boot. It can sit, bark, sing and snore, and it won't make a mess on your carpet.

Mouseland Laptop

Available from IQ Builders, price £44.99 approx. 4-8 years
Rodent-shaped, and featuring 30 activities and a two-player mode, this is a very attractive introduction to IT with clear vocal commands and a useful teaching mouse.

Interactive ET

Available from Tiger Electronics UK Ltd, price £34.99. 6 years+
There are 400 words and 1,000 phrases in this endearing toy's vocabulary. Just like in the film, ET's finger and heart glow, he has moving eyes, neck, arms and mouth. He can also interact with Furbies, Shelbies, Yoda *et al.*

Butterfly Secrets

Available from IQ Builders, price £29.99 approx. 6 years+
This attractive butterfly-shaped laptop features 22 educational games, an organiser, address book, fortune teller game, secret diary and a personalised password. Great fun.

Accelerator PC Trainer

Available from Oregon Scientific, price £59.99. 6-10 years
A very attractive and authentic-looking laptop with 50 activities covering a broad range of IT skills. It can be expanded and enhanced with additional smartcards.

◀ Bontempi Hit Organ

※ **Silver Award Winner** ※

Available from Comus UK Ltd (Bontempi), price £80. 4-8 years
A musical box of delights, covering three octaves, 24 sounds, 24 styles and sporting full-sized keys. It comes complete with a three-stage programme of music reading and keyboard skills, and is designed to function as a first instrument as well as a toy. The pre-set tunes and recording facilities provide instant entertainment, too.

▲ Geosafari Laptop

※ **Silver Award Winner** ※

Available from Educational Insights, price £34.99. 8 years+
Essentially a games console, this laptop comes with 63 double-sided cards that contain over 2,000 questions, covering subjects from geography and science to trivia and history. Educational and fun, it can be played at many levels with numerous players, and is ideal for family groups or parties.

Accelerator Eclipse

Available from Oregon Scientific, price £79.99. 6-10 years
Loaded with 60 activities including maths, language and logic, this desktop has good potential. Offering a wide range of real IT skills, its capabilities can be extended with additional smartcards.

Scooby-Doo Phantom of the Knight

Available from The Learning Company, price £24.99. 7-12 years
Players have to use logic and analyse situations to guide Scooby and friends through a spooky castle and find the kidnapped princess. This CD-Rom has very good graphics and sound effects, and is suitable for a wide range of abilities.

Digital Recording Studio

Available from Toybrokers Ltd, price £24.99-£29.99. 11-16 years
This scientific and musical studio teaches the basics in sound recording and electronic sound manipulation. Well designed and with clear instructions, it's easy to use and gives good results.

Games

On the Farm

Available from Living and Learning, price £5.99. 3 years+
Inside the box is a printed farm scene, along with animal cards and dice. Players count and match the animals and put them in their correct homes.

In the Jungle

Available from Living and Learning, price £5.99. 3 years+
Match, count and sort the jungle dwellers in this adventurous boxed game that offers loads of scope.

Out in Space

Available from Living and Learning, price £5.99. 3 years+
Guide the astronauts to their craft by collecting and matching the aliens. Cosmic.

Domino Plus

Available from Rede Educational Ltd, price £28. 3 years+
These beautifully made giant wooden dominoes are fabulous for little hands and are good for use in the garden.

Chad Valley Wooden Snakes 'n' Ladders and Ludo

※ Highly Recommended ※

Available from Woolworths, price £6.99. 3 years+
Featuring firm favourites and beautifully produced, this compendium features a double-sided wooden board and easy-to-handle counters.

Hide & Seek Sound On The Farm

※ Highly Recommended ※

Available from Educational Insights, price £10. 3 years+
Match the sounds to the pictures to score points with this portable game, which features several skill levels and very funny graphics.

In The Ocean

※ Highly Recommended ※

Available from Living and Learning, price £5.99. 3 years+
It's time to go under the sea for an exciting 3D marine adventure. Discover what lies beneath with this

exceptionally visual game that will test your memory, matching and counting skills. Quick to play, it's a good introduction to aquatic species and their underwater environs.

My First Scrabble

Available from Mattel Toys, price £14 approx. 3-6 years
An infant version of the old chestnut, this uses colour-coded word tiles and word cards to introduce children to spelling and word construction over four levels. Great stuff.

Spotty Dog Game

※ Highly Recommended ※

Available from Orchard Toys, price £5–£6. 3-6 years
Spin the arrow to a number, find the corresponding picture of the dog, then turn over the card to see how many bones you've won in the dog's basket. A charmingly simple counting and matching game.

Colour Match Express

※ Highly Recommended ※

Available from Orchard Toys, price £6.50. 3-6 years

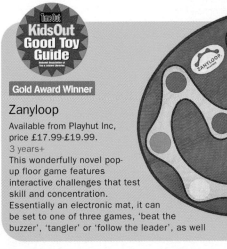

Time Out KidsOut Good Toy Guide

Gold Award Winner

Zanyloop

Available from Playhut Inc, price £17.99-£19.99.
3 years+
This wonderfully novel pop-up floor game features interactive challenges that test skill and concentration. Essentially an electronic mat, it can be set to one of three games, 'beat the buzzer', 'tangler' or 'follow the leader', as well as a free-play mode. Great for co-ordination, developing motor skills and concentration, it also works well as a wall-mounted activity. An enormously fun and portable device that is easy to store, wipe clean, and somewhat addictive, too.

The aim of the game is to fill a coloured train with a collection of corresponding animals. This is a great dice-driven matching game that is quick, easy to learn and suitable for quite young children.

Match & Count

Available from Orchard Toys, price £5. 3-6 years
Match the pictures to the numbers. Easy to play and with vivid drawings, it's very good value for money.

Giant Shape Snap

Available from Orchard Toys, price £3.50. 3-6 years
These large shaped cards feature the name of the shape and bright pictures. Also useful for colour recognition and counting skills.

Chad Valley Build a Beetle

Available from Woolworths, price £4.99. 4 years+
Bug the life out of the losers by being the first player to complete their beetle and win the game.

Wiggly Worms

❋ Highly Recommended ❋

Available from Mattel Toys, price £10 approx. 4 years+
Twenty worms wriggle around inside a bright red apple. Players must find worms that match the colour of the card they hold in this fast and furious memory game.

Electronic Spin the Beetle Game

❋ Highly Recommended ❋

Available from Character Games Ltd, price £14.99. 4-8 years
Cross 'Simon Says' with 'Spin the Bottle', add a bug and a battery, and this is what you get. Tasks range from standing up to pretending to be a pop star. A good activity for all the family.

Hoppers

❋ Highly Recommended ❋

Available from Ravensburger, price £8. 6 years+
Based on peg solitaire, this appealing and compact game

▲ Finders Keepers

❋ Silver Award Winner ❋

Available from Benjamin Toys Ltd, price £8. 3-7 years
Uncomplicated, fast-moving and adaptable, this game is based on matching pictures and speed of recognition. Each player chooses three squares from a container, and then has to cover each of the corresponding pictures on the circular board as quickly as possible. Brightly coloured, with good illustrations, this is visually appealing, and hones concentration and observation skills.

consists of cards, lily pads and frogs and has 40 challenges for differing abilities.

Rapi-Ding

Available from The London Game Company Ltd, price £7.99. 6 years+
Fast moving against-the-clock board game for all the family.

Operation Space Chase Place Value Game

Available from Learning Resources, price £11.95. 6 years+
Pilot the spaceships to their destination by solving mathematical problems. Immense fun, this can be played on different levels, and really does speed up mental arithmetic.

Boku

❋ Highly Recommended ❋

Available from The London Game Company Ltd, price £11.99. 6 years+
A two-player game played on a hexagonal board with 36 marbles each. A test of strategy and wit, Boku is played worldwide by all ages of children.

Rush Hour Junior

❋ Highly Recommended ❋

Available from Ravensburger, price £10-£12. 5-8 years
Designed for solo play, this involves challenge cards, a travel board, 16 vehicles and clearing a path for that all-important ice-cream van. Great for novice road ragers and their fuming parents.

Sound FX Mania

❋ Highly Recommended ❋

Available from Educational Insights, price £12.99. 5-10 years
Compulsive and challenging fun, this hand-held electronic game is easy to grasp and extremely hard to put down. Small and ideal for travel, it relies on sound and light sequences, which develop concentration, observation and memory skills.

Who Wants to be a Millionaire? Junior

❋ Highly Recommended ❋

Available from Upstarts, price £24.99. 8-12 years

Based on the enduring money-spinning TV programme, this general knowledge board and quiz card game features questions pitched at the younger player, and is is great for enhancing confidence and know how.

Uno Extreme

Available from Mattel, price £14.99 approx. 7 years+
A fabulous fast-action version of the popular word game for 2-10 players with an exciting motorised playing card 'launcher'.

Rapidough

Available from The London Game Company Ltd, price £24.99. 8 years+
Think Pictionary but with dough. Kids can unleash all of their spontaneous creativity by making models of the pictures shown on the cards. It's all against the clock, but will anybody know what on earth they are?

▶ Safari

✷ Silver Award Winner ✷

Available from The London Game Company, price £14.99. 4 years+
A vivid board game featuring wooden animals, an explorer and foliage. The aim is to collect one of each animal before your opponents do, which makes for a simplistic or more strategic game depending on players and approach. The pieces can be played with separately and there are tips for simplifying or intensifying the game.

Flags of the World

Available from The London Game Company Ltd, price £7.99. 8 years +
A wonderful game that helps children to identifying the different national flags. A broad selection of countries are represented, making the game a fantastic resource tool for learning about capital cities and geography in general, too.

Who Wants to be a Millionaire?

Available from Tiger Electronics UK Ltd, price £34.99. 10 years+
Complete with Chris Tarrant's voice (uh-huh), sound effects, flashing lights and the theme tune, this game virtually recreates the TV show. Progress through the 15 levels to win the mint.

Imaginative play

Gold Award Winner

Woodkins

Available from Great Gizmos, price £12.
4-10 years
The cut-out doll comes of age. Now she is made of wood, you get to style her clothes and she might be black, white, Asian or South-east Asian. Ingeniously, this sectioned doll is cut from a flat piece of wood that she slots into, not unlike a puzzle. To dress her, swatches of fabric are stretched over a body section.

Her wardrobe can be extended by introducing other fabrics and materials, and to round off each look, there's a selection of facial expressions to choose from. A junior stylist's dream.

Fill and Spill Bird Puppet

✷ Highly Recommended ✷

Available from James Galt & Co Ltd, price £9.99. 12 months+
Younger children love filling the huge beak of this colourful velour bird with the accompanying crab, starfish and fish, just as much as they enjoy playing with it as a furry, squawking glove puppet.

Let's Pretend Elmo

Available from Fisher-Price Toys, price £30 approx. 12 months+
Red, furry and lots of fun, Elmo speaks, moves and plays let's pretend, depending on how he is positioned. Entertaining fun.

Ark & Figures

Available from Myriad (made by Ostheimer) £6.90-£215. 18 months+

These sets, sold separately, range from an ark, Noah and his wife, and pairs of animals two by two. All are hand-crafted from wood, hand-painted and look and feel beautiful.

All Ears Blue

Available from Fisher-Price Toys, price £30 approx. 2 years+
Linked to the TV programme Blue's Clues, this blue dog responds to touch, and comes with a trumpet, ice lolly and a drink. Instantly appealing, it inspires lots of imaginative games.

Bullyard – Farm Animals

Available from Euro Toys and Models Ltd, price £1.45-£2.50. 2 years+
Well-made, detailed and realistic, these solid plastic animals are seriously good value.

Old MacDonalds' Alphabet Tractor

Available from VTech Electronics (UK) Plc, price £20. 2-5 years
A push-along tractor with removable talking animals, plus alphabet hay bales, music and sound effects.

Tiger Tabbard

Available from Charlie Crow, price £9.99. 2-8 years
A fun furry tiger outfit featuring tunic and separate headgear. Animal magic.

Bob The Builder Tool Case

* Highly Recommended *

Available from Martin Yaffe Int Ltd, price £9.99 approx. 3 years+
This moulded tool case contains a plastic saw, screwdriver, hammer, spanner, wrench, nails, nuts and bolts – the full works for fix-it fans.

Bob The Builder Dress-Up Play Set

* Highly Recommended *

Available from Martin Yaffe Int Ltd, price £19.99 approx. 3-5 years
Instantly recognisable, this outfit comes complete with hard hat and belted tools. Enough pieces to share, though the tool belt is a highly covetable item.

Traditional Dolls' House

* Highly Recommended *

Available from Plan Toys by John Crane Ltd, price £110-£120. 3 years+
Complete with attic, veranda, and balcony, this four-roomed house is beautifully constructed from replenishable rubberwood. Immense attention to detail, intricate furnishings, realistic styling and impressive dimensions make this an infinitely charming playset.

Rainbow Tunnel

* Highly Recommended *

Available from Myriad (made by Speil & Holz Design), price £14.99-£16.49. 3 years+
Six arched wooden slices of ascending size, fit together to make a rainbow. The beautifully crafted, chubby pieces are a joy to handle.

Timmy's Train Set – 100 Pieces

* Highly Recommended *

Available from Red Robin Toys Ltd, price £65-£70. 3-10 years
Children can have hours of fun with this extensive wooden train set.

▶ Bob The Builder Friction Vehicles

* Silver Award Winner *

Available from Martin Yaffe Int Ltd, price £4.99-£6.99. 3 years+
'Where can I buy them?' 'Can I keep them?' 'Can I buy them from you?' And that was just the parents talking. These vehicles were so popular, we were lucky to get them back from our tests. Strong and tactile, with loads of detail and moving parts, these are easy to use, they roll along for ages and make a satisfying noise. Great for children of all abilities, they have years of go in them.

Complete with storage box, engine, carriages, bridge, points, junctions, crossovers, shed and station, and compatible with other sets, this is a real investment piece.

Nursery Rhymes

* Highly Recommended *

Available from Flair Leisure Products plc, price £19.99-£21.99. 3-7 years
Children can guide their own stories and rhymes with this imaginative and stimulating felt book, which comes with its own bag of stick-on shapes.

Race 'n' Repair Action Team

* Highly Recommended *

Available from Little Tikes, price £29.99-£34.99. 3-10 years
This racing car comes with its own carrier truck and tools. When it breaks down it tells you what is wrong and gives instructions on how to fix the problem. Complete with noises and vibrations, it's an ideal gift for boy or girl racers.

Girls Dressing Up Chest (5)/Boys Dressing Up Chest (5)

* Highly Recommended *

Available from Dekkertoys, price £24.99. 4-6 years

▲ Tesco 90 Piece Road & Rail Superset

❋ Silver Award Winner ❋

Available from Tesco Stores, price £29.99. 3 years+
A good old-fashioned wooden train set, comprising an engine, four carriages, three cars, animals, trees, buildings, road signs, a wooden track with bridges, a level crossing and a plastic road layout. Fantastic for freestyle play, parents testing the set felt it was good value for money and liked the fact that you could buy it in a supermarket along with your groceries.

The set for boys includes a cowboy, pirate, clown, policeman and a devil, and the one for girls has a princess, fairy, nurse, squaw and witch outfit. Try getting them back into their own clothes afterwards.

Betty's Bike

❋ Highly Recommended ❋

Available from Bandai, price £12.99 4-11 years
Part of the Betty Spaghetty range, this sees Betty on a bike, with her dog, Jake, in the basket. Fabulous value for money and great attention to detail with lots of bits to fiddle with, this toy will be almost constantly in use.

Candy Floss Machine

❋ Highly Recommended ❋

Available from General Creation, price £29.99. 8 years+
We thought that these things only existed in heaven. Made from durable plastic and with a safety cut-out system, this will turn regular sugar to floss in 30 seconds. An out of this world confectionery treat.

Space Pirates

Available from Tomy, price £49.99. 3 years+
This pirate ship is packed to the brim with interesting details. A magnetic crew and accessories for the high seas are all included.

Bob The Builder Playmat Construction Set

Available from Martin Yaffe Int Ltd, price £29.99-£34.99. 3 years+
Scoop, Muck and Dizzy... as the song goes, together with Bob and Pilchard are included with this plastic road mat, which can be used to create lots of building site scenarios. Each character has its own soundbox and individual sayings. Pilchard says 'miaow'.

Singing Kipper

Available from Martin Yaffe Int Ltd, price £17.99 approx. 3 years+
Not quite Billy The Bass, but this cuddly Kipper the Dog sings his TV theme tune and moves his head in time to the music.

Plan City

Available from Plan Toys by John Crane Ltd, price £20-£45. 3 years+
This wooden mini metropolis range includes a fire station, petrol station, multi-storey car park and repair and service centre. All come with vehicles. Additional sets of vehicles, road signs, street lights and foliage are available.

Thomas and Friends Wooden Railway System

Available from Flair Leisure Products plc, price £50. 3 years+
This mini train set comes with Thomas, two carriages, a bridge and a station master, and includes both Action Switch and Clickity Clack track.

Stacking House

Available from Myriad, (made by Spiel & Holz Design), price £14-£16.50. 3 years+
Wonderfully tactile, these chunky wooden stacking systems comprise five pieces in ascending size that make up a house. Available in nude or coloured wood.

Groovy Girls

Available from Manhattan Toy Europe Ltd, price £5.99-£11.99. 3 years+
New additions to this immensely popular range are Sarita, a black doll, Zizi, her pet cat, some cool dungarees and a plush armchair.

Izzy Wizard

Available from Charlie Crow, price £20-£25. 3-7 years
A deep purple and gold tunic, decorated with stars, and a huge hat make this most authentic attire for the wizard-in-training. Blistering broomsticks it's Potter time!

Girls Dressing Up Chest (3)/Boys Dressing Up Chest (3)

Available from Dekkertoys, price £19.99. 4-6 years
Both chests contain three complete outfits. For the girls, a princess, a nurse and a fairy, and for the boys, a cowboy, a pirate and a clown.

Popstars

Available from R&J Travis, price £19.99-£25.99. 6-11 years
Dressing-up outfits for the more stereotypical child, this range includes Pretty, Psychedelic, Combat, Scary, and Smart for girls and Combat only for boys.

Bendos

Available from Imperial Games Ltd, price £3.99-£16.99. 4-8 years
Some new sets for this popular range including, Construction Site, Waterpark, Jet Ski and Decker, complete with bendy figurines.

Good Toy Guide

Life play

Cookin' Sounds Gourmet Kitchen

⁂ Highly Recommended ⁂

Available from Little Tikes, price £59.99-£64.99.
2 years+
Well laid out, and featuring sink, microwave, hob, oven, accessories and work surface, this is a well-built playset. It has bags of novelty value, very realistic sound effects and, naturally, all mod cons.

Sizzlin' Kitchen

⁂ Highly Recommended ⁂

Available from Early Learning Centre, price £50. 2 years+
The pressure cooker whistles on the hob while the crockery washes in the dishwasher. Lots of emphasis on detailed activity.

Chicco Trekking Stroller

⁂ Highly Recommended ⁂

Available from MV Sports and Leisure Ltd, price £29.99. 2-8 years
Lifelike with great detail, this is a replica of a popular full-sized pushchair, complete with carry tray, plastic cover, clip-fastening harness and adjustable handles.

Delux Baby Stroller

⁂ Highly Recommended ⁂

Available from Benjamin Toys Ltd, price £40. 3 years+
A three-wheeler that has adjustable handles, a footrest, underseat tray and harness, plus great attention to detail and good design sense.

Plan Toy Musical Instruments

Available from Plan Toys by John Crane Ltd, price £12.
12 months+
Beautifully designed and crafted from wood, this range includes a drum and xylophone. Both come with beaters, and have a very high quality of timbre.

Discover Sounds Workshop

Available from Little Tikes, price £27.99-£29.99.
12 months+
Featuring some interesting functions, this electronic activity centre includes a ball chute, ball dispenser and shape sorter, with a great selection of chunky tools and accessories.

Play Family Garage

Available from Fisher-Price Toys, price £30 approx. 18 months-4 years
This three-storey garage with lift, petrol pump, telephone, car wash and four sound buttons is as popular as it is versatile.

Play Family House

Available from Fisher-Price Toys, price £30 approx. 18 months+
A wonderfully detailed plastic house

Time Out KidsOut Good Toy Guide — National Association of Toy & Leisure Libraries

Overall Award Winner

Good Toy Guide (sidebar)

Duplo Dolls

Available from Lego UK Ltd, price £7.99-£29.99. 2 years+
Lego goes from strength to strength, and its new Duplo Dolls range is an inspired addition. Each doll measures six inches, a good size for small hands, and comes with her own mini version of herself. We tested 'Anna', who came with a bedroom set, and 'Sarah', who came with a fully equipped kitchen. The themes tie in very well with children mimicking adults, which is mirrored by the dolls having their very own dolls. Play involved lots of dressing and undressing, cooking, putting to bed, cuddling, storytelling and conversation. Strong, easy to clean, with lorry-loads of play value, these are a sound investment.

with family and baby included. The cot with baby sounds and music is particularly endearing.

Ready – Step 'n' Go Roller Skates

Available from Little Tikes, price £12.99-£14.99. 2-5 years
These first rollerskates can extend to fit your child's growing feet, and feature three stability settings. Designed to fit shoe sizes 5-10.

Mamas & Papas Pliko Argento

Available from Halsall, price £35. 2-8 years
A replica of the full-size bestseller, this buggy sports a raincover, twist hand grips, reclining seat, safety bar, harness and basket.

Happy Street High Street

Available from Early Learning Centre, price £35. 2 years+
For use both indoors and out, this pop-up house can be a post office, tea room and a greengrocer's all in one. It comes with carry case, too.

Bob The Builder Remote Control TV

Available from Martin Yaffe Int Ltd, £15.99 approx. 2 years+
Kids can really keep up with the trends with this infra-red remote control television. Features include play, fast-forward and rewind functions, plus it has its very own theme tune as well.

Hotpoint Cooker

Available from Cassidy Brothers, price £24.99. 3 years+

Gold Award Winner

Fire Engine

Available from Playhut Inc, price £19.99. 3 years+
This pop-up fire engine sports an inflatable steering wheel and detachable door flap. Large enough for three or four small children to use together, it's exceptionally robust and can stand up to considerable amounts of wear and tear. Apart from the fire engine, it can be used as a house, a den, a shop or a castle, depending on the child's imagination. Its unique selling point, though, has to be the fact that it has no bottom, so children move it along using their feet, just like the Anthill Mob in Wacky Races.

Move over Jamie Oliver, tomorrow's master chefs will have great fun trying out this realistic electronic cooker with glowing hob, grill and sizzling sounds. Play food included.

Chad Valley Carrier/ Car Seat Set

Available from Woolworths, price £14.99. 3 years+
This lilac car seat has a removable hood and cover, transforms into a rocking bath and comes complete with doll.

Chad Valley Bathtub Baby

Available from Woolworths, price £6.99. 3 years+
Included with this set is a bath, bath toys, a towel, robe, bottle and a somewhat realistic baby.

◀ Kitchen Furniture

✳ Silver Award Winner ✳
Available from Pin Toys by John Crane Ltd, price £32-£72. 3 years+
Brightly coloured, beautifully crafted and finished in solid wood, this range of kitchen

US Patrol Set

Available from Tomy, price £29.99. 3-10 years
Both car and train are included with this set. Each runs on separate tracks, which are also included.

Pop Out High Street

Available from Worlds Apart, price £34.99. 3 years+
Four buildings in one, this toy street includes a bank, post office supermarket and shop. Ideal for group play, it's easy to assemble and fold away again afterwards.

Suburban House

Available from Playmobil, price £69.99-£79.99. 4 years+
This construction house and family furniture includes a microwave, washing machine, cooker and sink. The attention to detail is spot on, with knobs that turn, doors that open, and perspex in all the right places. Our testers were cooking, washing and laundering at the drop of a hat. Kitchen sink dramas may well ensue.

set comes with loads of exciting pieces and is packed with great detail. A perfect tool for role-play.

Rescue Heroes and Voice Tec Rescue Heroes

Available from Fisher-Price Toys, price £8-£13. 4-7 years
A range of poseable goodie action figures with extra large feet for stability. The Voice Tec figures say over 100 rescue phrases and come in a variety of hero guises, from firemen to lifeguards.

Family Life – Millie's Bathtime in Sylvania

Available from Flair Leisure Products Plc, price £8.99. 4 years+
A miniature playset featuring mummy and baby mouse, a high chair, a bath, potty, toys and crockery. Great quality and value for money.

Facesaver Helmet

Available from MV Sports and Leisure Ltd, price £19.99. 5 years+
Stay safe with this protective motorcycle-style helmet. Fully

◄ Flatbed Truck
❋ Silver Award Winner ❋

Available from Playmobil, price £27.99-£29.99. 4 years+
Another great piece of design, this stunning vehicle features a let-down ramp, a road warning sign and other accessories. Highly imaginative, the accompanying broom, spade and toolbox only add to the fun.

adjustable, and supplied with multi-fit pads, it is designed to minimise injury to the face, mouth and jaw area, as well as the head.

▼ Recycling Truck
❋ Silver Award Winner ❋

Available from Playmobil, price £24.99-£27.99. 4 years+
Dustbins and accessories are included with this self-assembly truck. Attention to detail is remarkable, and includes a roof lid, tipping truck and flashing lights. Fantastic quality, it stands up to lots of rough play, and really does offer good value for money.

Numbers & words

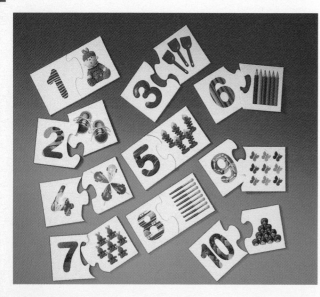

◄ Numbers Photo Puzzle
❋ Silver Award Winner ❋

Available from Living and Learning, price £4.99. 2-4 years
Chunky and great to handle, this puzzle is eye-catching, well designed and of very high quality. Kids can learn counting skills, number recognition and enjoy learning maths. A wonderfully simplistic toy that is outstanding value for money.

Watch 'n' Learn
❋ Highly Recommended ❋

Available from Oregon Scientific, price £14.99. 3-5 years
Wearing a watch is a grown up thing to do and shows independence, so children will be overjoyed with this one. Made from chunky moulded

Leap Pad/Leap Pad Books

Available from LeapFrog Toys (UK) Ltd, price £10-£12 and £49.99. 4 years+

Exciting and attractive, this educational talking book system incorporates excellent features. Easy to set up and use, it consists of an electronic holder with an attached easy-grip pen. Insert a book into the holder, switch on, and away you go. The child controls each activity in the book with the pen, following clear written and spoken directions, symbols, sounds and prompts. The books teach reading, phonics, general knowledge and spelling, and subjects covered include science, music and foreign languages. They're all high-quality publications, and feature popular Disney characters and Richard Scarry stories.

plastic, it teaches the alphabet and how to tell the time through visuals and sound and features both LCD and analogue displays.

Boots Cash Register

Highly Recommended

Available from Boots the Chemist, price £15. 3 years+
Complete with scanner, coins, credit card and quiz book, this will keep kids occupied for long periods as they get to grips with its range of functions and learn elementary money-handling skills.

Funny Phonics Puzzle Cards

Highly Recommended

Available from Learning Resources, price £4.95. 5 years+
Fabulous phonic fun. The range includes Long Vowels, Beginning Blends, 2 Letter Word Endings and 3 Letter Word Endings. Excellent self-checking teaching aids for home and school use.

Fast Track Learning Dominoes

Highly Recommended

Available from Learning Resources, price £7.95. 6 years+

Mathematical games for 1-4 players, the range includes addition, subtraction, division and multiplication. Suitable for all children, and with a marine theme throughout, these should appeal to even the most number-phobic kids.

Counting Crocodile + Alphabet Adder

Highly Recommended

Available from Early Learning Centre, price £10. 3-6 years
Thoroughly reptilian, these dual puzzles are an absolute delight. One features the numerals 1-10, and on the flip side it spells each number out. The other features each letter of the alphabet in upper case, while the flip side depicts them in lower case. Strong, durable and made from solid wood, they are well designed and eye-catching.

Pie in the Sky Fraction Game

Highly Recommended

Available from Learning Resources, price £9.95. 7-11 years
Who ate all the pies? This board game has a culinary theme and the winner is the first to complete three in a row. A game for 2-4 players, this is fun and quick to play.

Magnetic Time Teacher

Available from Learning Resources, price £14.95. 4-8 years
Telling the time never seemed so much fun. This full-sized clock-shaped magnetic board with movable hands comes complete with markers and magnetic pieces.

Spell-A-Puzzle

Available from Benjamin Toys, price £5.99. 4-7 years
Self-checking shaped puzzles featuring a picture and its name or title spelt in lower case letters.

20 French Words

Available from Tigerprint for Marks & Spencer, price £5. 4-7 years
Word puzzles featuring a picture and each word spelt in French. A great introduction to learning a new language.

Ring-A-Round Mix and Match Word Game

Available from Learning Resources, price £15.95. 6 years+
Turn the rings to match letters and pictures, match all three rings to spell a word. The other side of the game board features a harder phonics game.

Gold Award Winner

Bob The Builder – Read Along Bob

Available from Martin Yaffe Int Ltd, price £19.99-£22.
3 years+

Soft and cuddly, this Bob is a storyteller. The accompanying book pages correspond with the numbers on Bob. Press the number, and Bob reads that page. The story can be read from beginning to end or non-sequentially, and Bob can be cuddled as well. The book and the figure are of very high quality, and Bob's belt has lots of soft tools for added interest. A good product for listening and reading skills, and sustaining attention.

◀ Leapfrog Range: Count and Sing Express

✳ Silver Award Winner ✳

Available from LeapFrog Toys (UK) Ltd, price £19.99. 2 years+
Three passengers sit in this train with Leap the frog. An interactive toy, it features various activities in game, music, maths or learn mode, all of which reinforce number and word skills or shape recognition. There are enough features for it to remain useful for a few years, too.

◀ Leapfrog Range: Ship Ahoy Sorter

✳ Silver Award Winner ✳

Available from LeapFrog Toys (UK) Ltd, price £14.99. 12 months+
This electronic shape sorter teaches shape and colour recognition, matching, animal names and animal sounds. With three game modes, it is strong and easy to use, and is great for developing concentration and listening skills.

▼ Leapfrog Range: Twist + Shout Multiplication

✳ Silver Award Winner ✳

LeapFrog Toys (UK) Ltd, price £12.99. 7 years+
Teaching maths and times tables with music and humour, this set helps to develop logic, reasoning and problem solving skills, and is great fun in group situations. Play modes can be physical, loud and rather dramatic, making it a wonderful teaching tool.

▶ Leapfrog Range: Flying Friends

✳ Silver Award Winner ✳

Available from LeapFrog Toys (UK) Ltd, price £19.99. 2-5 years
Leap the frog and his friends sit in a bright yellow aeroplane. This toy has a learn and a game mode, and teaches colours, shapes and numbers, and about spatial relationships. The characters are removable for added play value.

Good Toy Guide

Outdoor play

Smoby Bumble Bee Coupe

✳ Highly Recommended ✳

Available from Smoby, price £39.99. 12 months-5 years
Complete with a push-along handle and foot plate for non-pedalling feet, this ride-in car is purpose-built to cater for riders and drivers. Sturdy, well made and attractive, this will see a child through from toddler to school-age.

Thomas Sit 'n' Ride

✳ Highly Recommended ✳

Available from Tomy, price £24.99. 1-3 years
A versatile toy that can be used either as a push-along or ride-on toy, depending on size and agility. Featuring the ever-popular Thomas, kids can press the beeper to hear his distinctive theme tune.

Feber Baby Activity Gym

✳ Highly Recommended ✳

Available from Feber International, SA, price £149-£179. 18 months-6 years
A large activity structure that includes, among other things, a slide, steps, climbing frame and rocker, steering wheel, gear stick and starter key.

Baby Activity Tree

Available from Feber International, SA, price £99-£119. 18 months+
This attractive, chunky plastic tree has tunnel access, a sound keyboard, plus a basket and a ball. Strong enough to climb on and in, the tree is suitable for all abilities.

Roar 'n' Rev Monster Truck

✳ Highly Recommended ✳

Available from Little Tikes, price £49.99-£54.99. 18 months-7 years
Monster, monster, monster! This jeep-style ride-on vehicle has realistic sound effects, a chunky build with authentically huge wheels, and it looks as good as it drives. A pleasant change from the cosy coupe.

Tweenies Tricycle

Available from Martin Yaffe Int Ltd, price £24.99-£27.99. 18 months-4 years
This three-wheeler has a useful rear bucket and parent pole, and is adorned with Tweenies motifs.

Bob The Builder Tri-Scooter

✳ Highly Recommended ✳

Available from MV Sports and Leisure Ltd, price £19.99. 2 years+
A large front wheel and two smaller wheels at the rear give this scooter the stability that young children need – and it looks very stylish.

Bob The Builder Wheelbarrow + Tools Set

✳ Highly Recommended ✳

Available from MV Sports and Leisure, price £14.99. 2 years+
Bob and Wendy are figureheads on the spade and fork handles of this handy gardening set, which comes complete with a sturdy wheelbarrow.

Bob The Builder Trike

Available from MV Sports and Leisure Ltd, price £29.99-£34.99. 2 years+
A sturdy Bob-themed trike with a plastic toolbox on the back.

Happy Air Tricycle

✳ Highly Recommended ✳

Available from Kettler, price £69.99. 2-5 years
Sturdy, robust and of superb quality,

Time Out KidsOut Good Toy Guide

Gold Award Winner

Big XXL-Traxx

Available from Big-Spielwarenfabrik, price £85-£90. 3 years+
Is it a tractor or a go-cart? Who cares? All we know is that this is some of the classiest outdoor gear that you are likely to get your hands on. The quality of this vehicle is second to none. Crafted from high specification plastic, it is sturdy enough to survive the hardest of knocks. Attention to detail is outstanding. It is pedal-powered, has a positionable seat, removable roof and optional trailer. Fabulous steering and suspension are the icing on the cake.

this trike has a detachable parent handle and a steering lock, making it safer for smaller children. Great for agility, confidence and co-ordination, it has an extendable frame and adjustable seat.

Mega Bounce Zone
⊛ Highly Recommended ⊛

Available from Worlds Apart, price £64.99. 3 years+
This inflatable play area features an integral wall and hoops to bounce through. Great for honing physical dexterity and co-ordination, it is beautifully made from quality materials, and, more importantly, inflates and deflates in seconds.

Pop-up Goal
⊛ Highly Recommended ⊛

Available from Worlds Apart, price £17.99. 3 years+
Relive those World Cup memories with this pop-up goal post. Suitable for instant shootouts and target practice either indoors or out, it's handy enough to use on holiday, has bags of play value and is great value for money.

The Animal Barn Puppet Theatre

Available from The Ninja Corporation, price £44.99-£54.99. 3 years+
This pop-up puppet theatre comes with two puppets and loads of scope for imaginary games and dramas. It's strong, easy to wipe clean and packs away neatly.

Wave Multiplay Centre

Available from Early Learning Centre, price £160. 3 years+
Kids can have plenty of fun in the sun with this sturdy and colourful outdoor play centre, complete with swing, slide and climbing frame. Perfect for all-terrain adventures.

Bruder Cement Mixer

Available from Euro Toys and Models Ltd, price £26.95. 3 years+
This large truck has great detailing and provides lots of scope for imaginative and life play.

Fuchs – Sit n' Ride

Available from Euro Toys and Models Ltd, price £97.95. 3 years+
An attractive tractor that is sturdy, durable and comes with its own front loader.

Big Traffic Trailer

Available from Big-Spielwarenfabrik, price £20-£30. 3-8 years
Three wheels on my wagon...
A sturdy trailer that fits on to some vehicles in the enduring Big range. The trailer contains bollards, a light, shovel, broom and some road signs.

Big XXL Offroad Traxx
⊛ Highly Recommended ⊛

Available from Big-Spielwarenfabrik, price £85-£90. 3-8 years
An extra large, chunky, offroad-style vehicle with big wheels, an adjustable seat position and enclosed chain drive. The stunning design, sturdy build and cool detailing make this a fabulous all-rounder that'll appeal to most kids.

Spin Dragon

Available from Halsall, price £30-£32. 3-12 years
Whether spinning on its nose or driving around obstacles, the simple hand controls on this ride-on toy make it a doddle to guide.

Big John Traffic
⊛ Highly Recommended ⊛

Available from Big-Spielwarenfabrik, price £60-£70 3-10 years
Eat your heart out, Bob the Builder.

▲ Imaginative Sounds Interactive Playhouse
⊛ Silver Award Winner ⊛

Available from Little Tikes, price £199. 18 months-6 years
A sensor triggers sounds when there is motion in this house, making it a real hoot for curious kids. Complete with window shutters, a slit door, a doorbell and telephone, there's scope for lots of imaginative play here. Popular across the board, it features voices and effects, and can be open on all sides.

This ride-on tractor has an adjustable seat, enclosed chain drive and front-wheel steering. The fabulous design and detailing on this durable vehicle only add to its appeal.

All Surface Swingball
⊛ Highly Recommended ⊛

Available from Mookie Toys, price £19.99. 6 years+
Ideal for holidays and days out, this swingball set has its own moveable base. Complete with bats, and housed in a nifty carry case, it's very compact and easy to store.

◀ Smoby Log Cabin
⊛ Silver Award Winner ⊛

Available from Smoby, price £149-£199.99. 1-4 years
This cosy wood-effect playhouse has shuttered windows, stairs, a slide and storage space. Large enough for small groups to play in together, it makes a great chill-out area for quiet times, too.

Puzzles

Marie

Available from Rede Educational Ltd, price £45. 3 years+
An extra large puzzle depicting a young African girl in national costume, plus a laminated picture of the same to copy and colour.

Mini Magnetic Puzzles

Available from Krucial Kids, price £4.99. 3 years+
A range of six magnetic puzzles, each with their own magnetic play boards, with themes ranging from bugs, shells, dinosaurs and frogs, to butterflies and fish. Great games to play while on the move.

Four Seasons

Available from Rede Educational Ltd, price £38. 3 years+
These brightly coloured tray puzzles depict the four seasons and make great teaching aids.

▶ Build a Farm Puzzle

✳ Silver Award Winner ✳

Available from Tigerprint for Marks & Spencer, price £5. 3-6 years
The animals in this 28-piece puzzle can be played with separately, extending its play value. A quality puzzle with good graphics and it's affordable too.

The Jigmap

✳ Highly Recommended ✳

Available from Gibsons, price £6.95. 8-12 years
An interesting and fun way to explore Britain and Ireland, this 150-piece shaped puzzle features all major towns and cities, plus some famous landmarks. Educational fun and great value.

Small Clowns

Available from Rede Educational Ltd, price £4.75 each-£45 per set. 3 years+
An assortment of small, well-designed and crafted tray puzzles bearing the numbers 0-9.

Shaped Puzzles – Fairytale Fun

Available from James Galt + Co Ltd, price £5.99. 3-5 years
Little hands will be kept busy solving these sturdy card puzzles, each featuring a fairytale theme.

The Magic Key – Story Building

✳ Highly Recommended ✳

Available from Tigerprint for Marks & Spencer, price £6. 4-7 years
Construct the jigsaw by following the story, though the pieces will not fit if used out of context. An educational aid that can be used to support the national curriculum's literacy programme.

Rocket Maths Puzzle

✳ Highly Recommended ✳

Available from Tigerprint for Marks and Spencer, price £5. 4-7 years
Each separate piece of this well-designed puzzle shows a sum that adds up to ten. Using a strong and popular space-related theme, this

Gold Award Winner

Harry Potter On-Reflection Jigsaw

Available from Character Games Ltd, price £4.99 and £7.99. 9 years+
Available as either a 200- or 500-piece activity set, these circular puzzles are really rather clever. When completed, they are distorted. However, when the reflective cylinder that they come in is placed in the middle of the circle, the reflection solves the mystery. Rewarding and with a twist in the tail, there's definitely an incentive to see these games through to the finish. Great value for money, and of particular interest to Harry Potter enthusiasts, they're sure to make cracking gifts.

puzzle supports the national curriculum Key Stages 1 & 2 and is great value for money.

Circle Iris Geometric Puzzle

※ Highly Recommended ※

Available from Myriad (made by Spiel & Holz Design), price £36.99-£39.99. 5 years+
Different patterns can be created using this colourful wooden circular puzzle, which comes in its own tray. There are 20 pieces and five different shapes to play with, which are all satisfyingly weighty and pleasantly tactile.

Taz Sculpture Puzzle

Available from Character Games Ltd, price £29.99. 13 years+
Involving and challenging fun for serious puzzle enthusiasts, this themed puzzle invites you to create a 3D sculpture jigsaw from the bottom up. A devil of a task that'll keep them busy for hours.

▲ L'ABC Français

※ Silver Award Winner ※

Available from Orchard Toys, price £7.50-£8. 3-7 years
Learn the alphabet in French with this 50-piece floor puzzle. A French/English translator and pronunciation guide is printed on the box, so puzzlers can dive straight in. The idea is to match the words around the edge with an object in the middle of the puzzle. *Formidable.*

Science & nature

▶ Duelling Dino Dig

※ Silver Award Winner ※

Available from Educational Insights, price £9.99. 7 years+
One for the budding archaeologist, this kit has all you need to excavate dinosaur remains from a block of sand, using all due care and attention. Kids can then follow the instructions to build a display skeleton of either a Tyrannosaurus Rex, Triceratops, Stegosaurus or Velociraptor depending on which kit you choose. A must for dino enthusiasts.

Bug Collectors' Kit

Available from Early Learning Centre, price £10. 4 years+
Complete with net and microscope, this kit encourages children to explore the insect world.

Ultimate Saturn V Rocket

Available from Benjamin Toys, price £35. 5 years+
An authentic-looking, self-assembly rocket that stands almost one metre high and features rocket sounds and launch vibrations.

Sea Monkeys on Mars

Available from Educational Insights, price £9.99. 6 years+
Another setting for these endearing and enduring organisms, the kit contains a tank, eggs, water purifier and food. This time around they are

learning how to conquer the inhospitable environs of Mars. The little critters are guaranteed to live for two years despite the terrain.

Kitchen Discoveries

Available from Living and Learning, price £7.99. 5-9 years
Conduct experiments using materials from this kit along with things from your kitchen cupboard.

Triop World

✴ Highly Recommended ✴

Available from Interplay UK Ltd, price £8 approx. 7 years+
A true life skills experience enabling kids to grow strange live creatures in water from earthbound eggs. They get quite big, shedding their skin as they go, and die in a short space of time, so are good lessons in lifespan, birth and death. The set includes enough eggs for two generations plus food.

Quantum Alphascope Microscope

Available from Learning Resources, price £29.95. 10 years+
A small, light and portable microscope, that is battery operated and comes with a range of fun accessories.

Mini Cable Car

Available from Myriad (made by Walter Kraul), price £3.99.
10 years+
A budget self-assembly cable car at a pocket-money price.

Big Cable Car Kit

Available from Myriad (made by Walter Kraul), price £14.50-£15.50.
10 years+
This kit contains everything you need to make a fully operational wooden cable car. Once assembled, it will stretch across a room and is strong enough to transport small objects. Great fun and with an unusual theme, it has the potential to become an integral part of both bedroom and garden adventures.

Tumbling Gnome and Slope

Available from Myriad (made by Walter Kraul), price £1.49-£4.49
3 years+ and 8 years+ for assembly
Available ready-made or as a craft kit, these gnomes are 'driven' by an internal ball bearing. The kit includes detailed instructions, pre-cut felt pieces, glue, a ball bearing and a small tube from which to fashion a body. Once made, they are durable and decorative in a nostalgic, lo-fi kind of way. The gnomes' tumbling antics are enticing to watch and are well worth the effort. A rewarding and dextrous exercise that's educational as well as fun.

▶ Spy Kit

✴ Silver Award Winner ✴

Available from Logiblocs Ltd, price £24.95-£27.95. 7-12 years
Using building blocks to create circuits, this set has all the necessary components to build a microphone, recorder, amplifier and a speaker. Fun, eye-catching and educational, this kit promotes scientific understanding and helps to develop strategic skills.

Skills & activities

Little Wonder Softwood Wonderland

※ Highly Recommended ※

Available from Treasure Trove Toys and Gifts, price £9.99. Birth+
Pieces of wood and fabric are laced together to make this unusual doll. Each limb offers a different tactile experience, and limbs extract and retract at the pull of a string.

Chad Valley Electronic Whack-A-Ball

※ Highly Recommended ※

Available from Woolworths, price £9.99. 18 months+
A fast and furious activity where kids can take turns to hammer the balls through the holes or play off against each other. It's simple and helps to develop agility and co-ordination.

Tigger Trampoline

※ Highly Recommended ※

Available from MV Sports and Leisure Ltd, price £34.99-£39.99. 3-7 years
This generous-sized trampoline with padded handrail is perfect for safe and dynamic physical fun. Strong and sturdy, it's a value for money play item that'll withstand ridiculous amounts of wear and tear.

Minky Makes Time To Create/Minky Makes Presents

※ Highly Recommended ※

Available from Formative Years, price £12.99. 3-8 years
Each video features an hour of instructions for various activities, broken down into manageable five- minute segments. A great way to learn how to make things such as papier maché, jewellery, balloon animals and juggling balls.

The Magic Key Fun Activity Wipe Clean Book

※ Highly Recommended ※

Available from Tigerprint for Marks & Spencer, price £6. 4-7 years
Packed with 14 activities, this hardback book is ideal for travelling and periods of bed rest. Characters are recognisable from the 'Oxford Learning Tree' series, which is used in schools to support the national curriculum literacy programme.

Lights Out

※ Highly Recommended ※

Available from Tiger Electronics UK Ltd, price £15.95. 9 years+
A hand-held strategy/logic game that is great fun, if rather addictive. Capable of a vast number of games and puzzles, and suitable for solo or competitive play, it can, and will be, enjoyed by all the family.

Floaties Range

Available from Styrox, price £4.99-£20.99. 3 months-7 years
Have fun and be safe in the water with this handy range of swimming aids that includes armbands, a swim seat and swim vest. Firm favourites with parents and professionals, all Floaties products come in age and weight sizes that should be strictly adhered to.

Time Out KidsOut Good Toy Guide

Gold Award Winner

Remote Control Roadster

Available from Tomy, price £29.99. 3 years+
Absolutely spectacular and great fun, this is as novel and simple to operate as a toy car gets. The control device is a cordless steering wheel, that responds to directional movement, while a set of easy to use buttons dictate forward and backward motion. The sound effects are convincing and the brake lights really flash. Stylish and racy, it represents fabulous value for money, and is sturdy enough to survive any number of hard knocks.

Winnie the Pooh Magic Doodle Board

Available from MV Sports and Leisure Ltd, price £17.99-£19.99. 2 years+
This popular themed plastic drawing unit has a honeycomb-effect casing, stencils and stamps.

Tons of Fun Activity Centre

Available from Krucial Kids, price £323 (this item is intended for use in nursery/playgroup settings) 2-4 years
A versatile and high-quality group activity centre that is ideal for group use. Features on this cube-shaped play structure include a mirror, bead frame, building blocks and an integral storage bag.

Two-Sided Board

Available from Plan Toys by John Crane, price £11. 2 years+
A satisfying problem-solving puzzle-board game that requires the use of logic. Its simple wooden shapes can be turned and placed together to create a whole host of new shapes.

Junior Colorino

Available from Ravensburger, price £9. 2 years+
Picture cards are slid into a transparent board in this colour recognition board game. Kids then build the picture on top of the image using the correct coloured pins.

Junior Scalextric

Available from Hornby Plc, price £29.99. 3 years+
A first set for smaller children that is instantly appealing, and of particular interest to older siblings!

▶ Twisted Form Board

※ Silver Award Winner ※

Available from Plan Toys by John Crane Ltd, price £12. 18 months -4 years
Simply pick up a wooden piece, twist it at the join, and a brand new shape will emerge. Brilliantly simplistic and beautifully crafted from wood, this is of superb quality and is well worth the money.

JCB Site Engineer Set

Available from Halsall, price £12-£15. 3-8 years
A compact tool set that is made from quality materials and is quite reasonably priced.

Marble Tower

Available from Pin Toys by John Crane Ltd, price £18-£20. 4 years+
A colourful and decorative wooden version of this highly popular and enduring toy.

Sooty Magic Pencil Case

Available from Flair Leisure Products Plc, price £2.99. 6-10 years
Ahh... the good old broken pencil trick still looks impressive.

◀ Mr Piano & Friends

※ Silver Award Winner ※

Available from Mega Bloks, price £24.99.
18 months-6 years
A piano with a difference, this has building block keys and information blocks for kids to use to join notes together and form a tune. Features include a voice prompt, demo, record/playback and horn and violin modes. Immediately appealing, this toy worked well with groups of children and encouraged social and creative interaction.

Gyromatic

Available from Benjamin Toys Ltd, price £13. 5 years+
An automatic, battery operated gyroscope complete with base tray marked with an indented path.

Design a Fashion Shop

Available from Tigerprint for Marks & Spencer, price £5. 6 years+
Build a 3D boutique using colour change pens, card and stickers. All fixtures and models are included.

Wow Magic

Available from Character Games Ltd, price £2.99. 6 years+
A range of three boxed magic sets that are affordable by present pocket money standards and produce rewarding results.

Climb@tron

Available from Benjamin Toys Ltd, price £6. 7 years+
Suction pads facilitate this robot's ability to walk up windows, walls and across ceilings.

Lego Steven Spielberg Moviemaker Set

Available from Lego UK Ltd, price £159.99. 11-15 years
Make Lego film sets, direct Lego actors, shoot on digital camera and edit, then apply your own sound and visual effects using PC software. Movie-making tips and a great deal of experience guaranteed. Lights, camera, action!

Manufacturers

**ABC Nursery
Distribution Ltd**
(K's Kids)
01582 503 503

Bandai
01489 790 944
www.bandaieurope.com

**BBC Worldwide
Multimedia**
0870 241 0623/
www.bbcmultimedia.
co.uk

Benjamin Toys Ltd
01438 726002

BIG
www.big.de

**Binney & Smith
(Europe) Ltd**
01234 217786
www.crayola.com

Boots the Chemist
08450 708090
www.welbeing.com

Cassidy Brothers Plc
01253 766 411
www.casdon.co.uk

Character Games Ltd
0161 633 9808

Charlie Crow
01782 417133
www.charliecrow.com

Comus UK Ltd
(Bontempi)
01282 606600
www.bontempi.com

Dekkertoys Ltd
01727 798 400
www.cesar-group.com

DKL Marketing Ltd
01604 678780
www.dkl.co.uk

Dowling Magnets
01200 445113

**Early Learning
Centre**
08705 352 352
www.elc.co.uk

**East Coast
Nursery Products**
01692 406 841

Ecoiffier
(see Smoby Ltd)

Educational Insights
01438 726 002

**Euro Toys
and Models**
01691 828004
www.euroetm.co.uk

Feber International
0808 100 1372
www.feber.es

Fisher-Price Toys
01628 500 302
www.mattel.com

**Flair Leisure
Products**
020 8652 9633
www.flairplc.co.uk

Formative Years
01342 826 555
www.formative-
years.co.uk

General Creation
01827 67888
www.generalcreation.
com

Gibsons Games
020 8685 1515
www.gibsonsgames.
co.uk

**Golden Bear
Products Ltd**
01952 608 308
www.goldenbeartoys.
com

Great Gizmos Ltd
01293 543 221
www.greatgizmos.co.uk

Hasbro UK Ltd
00800 224 27276
www.hasbro.co.uk
www.knex.co.uk

Halsall
01253 779 317
www.time4toys.com

Hornby Plc
01843 233525
www.scalextric.com

Imperial Games Ltd
01704 841 771

Interplay UK Ltd
01248 853 909

IQ Builders
01235 546 700
www.iqbuilders.co.uk

**James Galt +
Co Ltd**
0161 428 9111
www.galt.co.uk

John Crane Ltd
01604 678 790
www.john-crane.co.uk

Kettler (GB) Ltd
01527 591 901
www.kettler.net

Krucial Kids
01708 345 123

K's Kids
(see ABC Nursery
Distribution Ltd)

Leapfrog Toys
0800 169 5435
www.leapfrog.com

**The Learning
Company**
01664 481 563
www.learningco.co.uk

**Learning
Resources Ltd**
01553 762 276
www.learning-
resources.com

Lego UK Ltd
08457 080070
www.lego.com

Little Tikes
0800 521 558
www.littletikes.com

Living and Learning
01223 864 864
www.livingandlearning.
co.uk

Logiblocs
01727 763 700
www.logiblocs.com

**The London Game
Company Ltd**
020 7837 2666
www.londongame.com

**Manhattan Toy
Europe Ltd**
020 8944 3160
www.manhattantoy.com

Martin Yaffe Int. Ltd
01706 346 500

Mattel Toys
01628 500 306
www.mattel.com

Mega Bloks
01235 820 055
www.megabloks.com

Mookie Toys
01525 722 716
www.mookietoys.com

Mothercare Plc
01923 210 210
www.mothercare.com

**MV Sports and
Leisure Ltd**
0870 840 4255

Myriad (incorporating
Ostheimer, Walter
Kraul and Spiel + Holz)
01725 517 085

**The Ninja
Corporation**
0151 495 1677

Orchard Toys
01159 373 547
www.orchardtoys.com

Oregon Scientific
01628 580205
www.oregon
scientific.co.uk

**Pin Toys
and Plan Toys**
(see John Crane Ltd)

**Playhut –
Playaway UK**
01628 488 944
www.playhut.com

Playmobil UK Ltd
01268 490 184
www.playmobil.com

**P&M Products
Colour Workshop**
01737 230000
www.blopens.com

Quercetti
(see Treasure Trove
Toys + Gifts Ltd)

Ravensburger
01869 363 800

**Rede Educational
Ltd**
01342 717 538
www.redeplay.co.uk

**Red Robin Toys
Ltd**
01733 371170

R&J Travis Ltd
01442 865 303
www.travis.co.uk

Smoby UK Ltd
01291 636 900
www.smoby.co.uk

Styrox (UK) Ltd
01252 316 626
www.styrox.co.uk

Tesco Stores Ltd
0800 505555
www.tesco.com

Tiger Electronics
00800 224 27276
www.tigertoys.co.uk

**Tigerprint for
Marks & Spencer**
020 7387 8844
www.hallmark-uk.com

Tocki
01430 410 515
www.tocki.co.uk

Tolo Toys Europe Ltd
01799 542 601
www.tolotoys.com

Tomy
023 8066 2600
www.tomy.co.uk

Toybrokers Ltd
01480 414 361

Toykits
020 8399 6689
www.toykits.com

TP Activity Toys Ltd
01299 872 800
www.tptoys.com

**Treasure Trove Toys
+ Gifts Ltd**
01285 771 002
www.mailorder
express.co.uk/www.
educationaltoys.co.uk

Upstarts
01473 834 444
www.upstarts.co.uk

**VTech Electronics
(UK) Plc**
01235 546 810
www.vtechuk.com

Woolworths
01706 862 789
www.woolworths.co.uk

Worlds Apart
0800 389 8591
www.worldsapart.co.uk